CW01192534

Cardiff City

100 Years of Professional Football

Terry Grandin was born in Cardiff in 1941 and has been married to Rita for 46 years. They have two children Sarah and Jason, and five grandchildren Ella, Freya, Lauren, Tillie and Max. He made his first visit to Ninian Park in September 1949 and has been a keen follower of the Bluebirds ever since. Educated at Cardiff High School, he was a member of Newport County's youth team in the late 50s, before joining Cardiff Hibernian in the Cardiff Combination League where he played until reaching the age of 50.

In 1991 he joined Cardiff-based Westgate Sports Agency as a sports journalist and statistician and every season since then has reported on Cardiff City's home matches. In 1998 he wrote his first book *Red Dragons in Europe* and he followed that with three others entitled *Tappy: From Barry Town to Arsenal, Cardiff City and Beyond*, *Seasons in the Sun,* and *Fully Booked.*

Cardiff City
100 Years of Professional Football

Terry Grandin

VERTICAL EDITIONS

www.verticaleditions.com

First published in the United Kingdom in 2010 by Vertical Editions, Unit 4a, Snaygill Industrial Estate, Skipton, North Yorkshire BD23 2QR

www.verticaleditions.com

ISBN 978-1-904091-45-5

A CIP catalogue record for this book is available from the British Library

Cover design by HBA, York

Printed and bound by MPG Books, Bodmin

This book is dedicated to my grandchildren Ella, Freya, Lauren, Tillie and Max. And not forgetting Louis.

Contents

Acknowledgements

I would like to thank Karl Waddicor of Vertical Editions for the many hours of work he has put in to set out this book in such an expert manner. Also I must thank Wales News Pictures, Richard Shepherd and Derek Showers for use of their valued collection of photographs, as well as all the Cardiff City staff photographers who have made a pictorial record of matches for many years.

1
History

Early Years

The sound of ball hitting willow around the fields of Sophia Gardens in the warm summers of Victorian Cardiff was far removed from the helter-skelter of association football. Yet it was from those days of horse drawn carriages scuttling around the dimly lit streets of a rapidly growing town that the first notion of starting a local football club was born.

Prime mover in trying to keep the Riverside Cricket Club together during the long winter months was Bristol-born lithographic artist, Bartley Wilson. Though unable to walk without the aid of sticks, Wilson was a keen member and organiser of the cricket club, and he set up a meeting of all interested parties at his home in the shadow of Cardiff Castle during the autumn of 1899. He was disappointed with the lack of enthusiasm at that first meeting but persevered and following a second and better attended get-together, the result was the formation of Riverside FC with Wilson duly elected secretary of the new club.

Friendly matches with local teams were arranged during the first season with home games being played at their Sophia Gardens base, and they were accepted into the Cardiff & District League in readiness for the 1900-01 season. The first known colours of Riverside FC were somewhat unusual as the shirts were chocolate and amber quarters while the shorts, known at that time as knickers and later as knicks, were black. The club improved their Sophia Gardens home by installing gas and water in their changing rooms and the availability of better facilities led to an increase in membership.

BARTLEY WILSON

Bristol-born Bartley Wilson served Riverside/Cardiff City for over fifty years. A disabled lithographic-artist who had come to Cardiff in 1895 to work for the Imperial Printing Company, he was a keen cricketer and joined Riverside Cricket Club from which he formed Riverside F.C. in the late summer of 1899.

Bartley Wilson, the man responsible for forming the club in 1899

An amalgamation with Riverside Albion came in 1902 but it was a further three years before the first honour, the Bevan Shield, was won by the blossoming club. It was around this time that Cardiff was made a city, and the committee put in a request to change their name to Cardiff City. This was refused on the grounds that the club was not playing at a sufficiently high enough standard. Steps were immediately taken to join an upgraded South Wales Amateur League and in 1908 it paid dividends as the club were finally allowed to change their name to Cardiff City.

Interest in the football club was now growing faster than the facilities at Sophia Gardens would allow and the committee were forced to turn down an invitation to join the newly-formed Second Division of the Southern League. This was because of the lack of an enclosed pitch, turnstiles, or any adequate conditions for spectators. The hard-working committee, led as ever by Wilson, refused to be beaten and a friendly match was arranged against Crystal Palace of the Southern League in October 1909 to gauge the level of support. Such was the interest generated that the game was actually played at Cardiff Arms Park, the home of Cardiff RFC. The result was a 3-3 draw and the gate receipts amounted to the princely sum of £33.

Delighted with the response from the public, a second friendly match was agreed four weeks later against the mighty Bristol City, at that time an established Division One outfit. Gate receipts jumped to £50, but once Bristol's guarantee fee had been paid there was little left in the Cardiff coffers. To make matters worse they were soundly thrashed 7-1.

Wilson and his committee were now in determined mood and Middlesbrough, also of Division One, agreed to come and play in Cardiff. This time the game was played at the Harlequins Ground, Newport Road, nowadays home to St Peter's RFC but previously the sports ground of Cardiff High School. The visitors included England internationals Steve Bloomer and Alf Common, the first footballer to be transferred for a four-figure fee, but to home supporters delight, City won 2-1 and also ended up £39 in profit on the day.

Buoyant with the support from the general public, Wilson began talks with the Bute Estate, owners of much of Cardiff, with a view to finding land suitable for a growing football club. After a number of possible sites were turned down, an offer of waste ground between Sloper Road and the railway sidings in Leckwith was accepted, but only after Cardiff Corporation agreed to assist in the preparation of the land.

This important step by the club made the move to professionalism inevitable and they were admitted to the Second Division of the Southern League in 1910. A Board of Directors was elected with Sydney Herbert Nicholls, a former Wales rugby international and local businessman, becoming the first chairman while Wilson was the obvious choice as secretary.

The patch of land along Sloper Road was part waste tip and part allotment and the assistance of voluntary helpers as well as corporation workers was essential in the levelling and preparation of the site. Mounds of ash were deposited either side of the playing area to provide banking for spectators, and the whole site was enclosed by a white timber fence. The final touches were made with the provision of a small wooden stand with canvas roof and very basic changing rooms.

A serious problem then surfaced late in the day when one of the original guarantors dropped out, leaving a shortfall in the monies required. The Marquis of Bute's son, Lord Ninian Crichton-Stuart, agreed to make up the missing sum and in gratitude for his financial support the new ground was called Ninian Park instead of the originally suggested Sloper Park.

Did You Know...
Cardiff City's first captain was Davy McDougall who came to Ninian Park from Glasgow Rangers in 1910

With playing facilities taking a turn for the better, Wilson now came to the fore by taking full responsibility for improving the playing standards in readiness for Southern League football. His first professional signing was Jack Evans, an outside left hailing from North Wales but who was playing for Cwmparc where he worked as a printer. Evans received six shillings (30p) signing-on fee to cover his travelling expenses.

It was now becoming obvious that the quickly-growing club required a manager and so Wilson engaged the services of Davy McDougall as player-manager and captain. McDougall was a left half with Glasgow Rangers but he had also played for Bristol City and it is highly probable that Wilson's contacts at the Bristol club had alerted him to the availability of the Scottish player.

McDougall took over team recruitment and began looking for players known to him in the north-east and Scotland. Although bringing new blood to south Wales was an expensive business, he was fully aware that the club would make little progress without a marked improvement in playing standards. Among others, he signed up John Duffy, Billy Watts and

John Ramsey from Dundee, James McDonald from Aberdeen, and Bob Lawrie who had been with Third Lanark.

Ninian Park was opened on Thursday, 1 September 1910 with a friendly game against Division One champions, Aston Villa. Kick-off was scheduled for 5.00pm to allow supporters to get to the match after their day's work. The formal kick-off was made by bowler-hatted Lord Ninian Crichton-Stuart in front of a crowd totalling 7,000. Cardiff City had discarded their chocolate and amber shirts and were now wearing blue shirts, white shorts and blue socks.

Lord Ninian Crichton-Stuart 1883-1915

The myth of how the club became known as the Bluebirds was about to start. The suggestion that it was because of a play at the New Theatre called 'The Blue Bird' is a feasible reason and well worth considering. However, perhaps there is a more simple solution. Bartley Wilson was born in Bristol and had many friends there; Bristol City played in red and were known as the Robins, so Cardiff City in their new blue strip naturally became the Bluebirds. Whatever the reason, the Bluebirds nickname is unique to Cardiff City as no other club in the history of the Football League has ever had the same name.

The honour of scoring City's first goal at Ninian Park went to Welsh-speaker Evans but Villa proved too strong and ran out 2-1 winners.

Born in Bala, North Wales, Evans was a left winger who was virtually ever-present over a 15-year span bridging World War One. During his time with City he made 184 league appearances scoring six goals, won eight caps for Wales and played in the FA Cup final of 1925 before transferring to Bristol Rovers in 1926.

Playing for Villa that day was Arthur Layton who became a Bluebird and made a couple of league appearances for Cardiff City during the promotion season of 1920-21.

The club finished a creditable fourth in their first season in the Southern League but despite that successful debut, the Board felt that a stronger hand than McDougall's was needed at the helm if they were to make even more progress. They advertised for a full-time secretary-manager and were rewarded when 38-year-old Fred Stewart, the manager of Stockport County, declared an interest. He was quickly appointed on a three year contract at the princely sum of £4 per week, excluding expenses, and would be at the forefront of all things to do with Cardiff City for the next 22 years.

Stewart set about changing the playing staff in a bid to win promotion and his first signing was Billy Hardy from Hearts, a player he had known from his time at Stockport. It was said that Stewart was so desperate to sign Hardy that he paid the £25 fee out of his own pocket. Hardy would go on to give superb service to the club for many years. McDougall became surplus to requirements and joined Newport County as player-manager in 1912.

The following year, Stewart paid Spurs £1,000 for full back Charlie Brittan and a signing of that magnitude signalled a major step forward for the club. It took City two seasons to reach Division One of the Southern League and they remained there until the outbreak of World War One (1914-18).

Competitive football returned in 1919 and Cardiff City were luckier than most clubs as only one player, full back Tom Witts, failed to survive the conflict. Sadly, Lord Ninian Crichton-Stuart also fell in the Great War. As Lieutenant-Colonel of the Welsh Regiment, he was killed in action on 2 October, 1915 when leading his men into battle in a night attack on the Hohenzollern Redoubt. He was only 32 years old.

Stewart began looking for new players even though the directors had kept the club afloat during the War from their own pockets and money was still scarce. He was allowed to pay Bradford City £1,000 for inside forward Billy Grimshaw and EE 'Bert' Smith, an Irishman from Donegal, was signed after a trial. Smith would go on to win four caps while with the Bluebirds. Stewart kept up his search for players to push the club forward and Arthur Cashmore, a centre forward from Darlaston, but who had previously been with Manchester United and Oldham, joined the playing staff.

Had it not been for a six-match run without a victory, City could have won the Southern League Championship in 1920. As it was, they finished in fourth position in their first season post-war and earned enough profit to wipe out their substantial debts. They were also able to improve conditions at Ninian Park by building an all-seater Canton Stand complete with bench seats.

The City directors lodged an application to join an extended Football League and were delighted when informed on 31 May, 1920 that their application had been successful. Furthermore, instead of being part of a newly constructed Third Division, they were about to become members of the Second Division of the Football League along with Leeds United, just 21 years after Riverside FC came into being, and only ten years since becoming a professional club.

The Roaring Twenties and Miserable Thirties

Stewart once again set about improving the playing staff in readiness for elevation to Football League status by obtaining the signature of Jimmy Gill from The Wednesday, now known as Sheffield Wednesday, for a fee of £750. Gill would go on to repay that investment many times over by appearing in 184 league matches and scoring 82 goals during his six seasons at the club.

On 30 August 1920, Cardiff City played their first Football League match at Ninian Park when 25,000 fans watched Clapton Orient force a 0-0 draw. Home supporters did not have to wait too long for a victory as five days later they roared City to a 3-0 win over Stockport County, manager Stewart's former club. Cashmore scored the first Football League goal at Ninian Park, and a brace from Billy Grimshaw secured the victory and a quick double over the Cheshire side who had been beaten at Edgeley Park by City in the opening game of the season.

Did You Know...
Arthur Layton, who signed for the Bluebirds from Middlesbrough in the summer of 1914, had been in the Aston Villa side that opened Ninian Park in September, 1910

In November 1920, Stewart went back to The Wednesday and set a record fee for a full back when he paid a massive £3,500 for 32-year-old Jimmy Blair.

Stewart's side proved more than a match for most of the teams in the division and they won promotion to the top flight at the first attempt in front of average crowds of over 28,000. In fact, champions Birmingham City only pipped Cardiff to the title by virtue of a better goal average. The Bluebirds also had an excellent run in the FA Cup beating Sunderland, Brighton and Southampton away from home before meeting Division One's Chelsea in round four at Ninian Park. A crowd of no less than 50,000 saw Cashmore give City a 1-0 win to set up a semi-final tie with fellow Division Two side, Wolverhampton Wanderers.

The game played at Anfield ended in a scoreless draw but was notable because it was the first occasion that reigning monarchs, King George V and Queen Mary, had attended a football match. The replay took place at Old Trafford in front of 74,000 fans but a penalty from rising star Fred Keenor was not enough and City bowed out after a 2-1 defeat.

The Bluebirds now found themselves playing in Division One after just one season in the Football League. Stewart recruited more players, including Jimmy Nelson from Belfast Crusaders, but they had to wait until the seventh match before recording a victory. Middlesbrough were their first victims and it came at Ninian Park with Jimmy Gill netting twice and Harry Nash adding the third in a 3-1 success. Boro' were top of Division One at

January 1921. The Cardiff City team in their first season in the Football League. Note the Canton Stand under course of construction. L-R Jimmy Blair, Jimmy Gill, Billy Hardy, Bert Smith, Jack Evans, Ben Davies, Billy Grimshaw, Charlie Brittan (capt), Fred Keenor, George Sayles and George Beare

the time while the Bluebirds were bottom after suffering those six straight defeats.

On 21 January, 1922 Len Davies struck the first Football League hat-trick by a Cardiff City player in a 6-3 win over Bradford City, and that first season in Division One proved so successful that 19 victories from 42 matches left the Bluebirds in fourth position despite that poor start.

Manager Stewart was forced to use no less than 30 players during that season mainly as a result of first team members being away on international duty. That was clearly evident the following year when on 14 April,1923 no less than six Cardiff City players were absent representing their countries. Playing in the Wales v Ireland match at Wrexham were Fred Keenor, Len Davies and Jack Evans, while the Irish side included Tom Farquharson and Bert Smith. Jimmy Blair was at left back for Scotland against England at Hampden Park. Without all these first teamers, City took on Sheffield United at Ninian Park and beat them 1-0 thanks to a Joe Clennell strike.

Did You Know...

The first Cardiff City player to be ever-present in a season was Scottish international full back Jimmy Nelson who played all 42 Division One matches in 1923-24

Season 1923-24 proved to be the best ever league campaign for the City as they came to the final Saturday top of the table one point ahead of second-placed Huddersfield Town. The Yorkshiremen were 3-0 winners at home to Notts Forest in their last match leaving the Bluebirds requiring victory at Birmingham City to secure the Division One title.

With the score at 0-0, City were awarded a penalty when Jimmy Gill's header was punched out by a home defender, but the normally reliable Davies shot straight at the home keeper. The match ended scoreless and City lost the title by 0.024 of a goal. No other side would ever lose out by such a narrow margin.

On 16 February, 1924, Cardiff City became the first British club to provide both team captains in a full international match. In a game between Wales and Scotland at Ninian Park, Fred Keenor captained Wales while the Scots were skippered by Jimmy Blair.

The following year brought the club's first appearance at Wembley in only the third cup final to be staged at the new arena.

It took three games to dispose of Darlington in round one and Fulham were dispatched 1-0 in round two. The Bluebirds then travelled to Meadow Lane where they beat Notts County 2-0 before knocking out Leicester City in thrilling fashion. With the scores locked at 1-1, Willie Davies scored the winner direct from a corner with the last kick of the match.

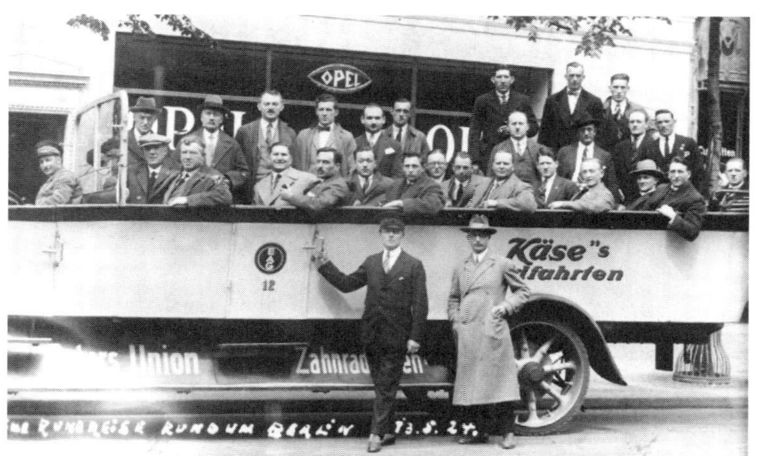

The Cardiff City squad and officials in Berlin on a close season tour just before playing Borussia

Blackburn Rovers were tough opponents in the semi-final played back at Meadow Lane but City raced into a three goal lead through Harry Beadles, Joe Nicholson and Jimmy Gill and though Rovers pulled one back, the Bluebirds were on their way to Wembley.

Sheffield United had already won the cup on four occasions, and they made it five when a tragic error by wing half Harry Wake let England international winger Fred Tunstall through for the only goal of the game. The Bluebirds were beaten but skipper Fred Keenor vowed that he would take his team back to Wembley Stadium as soon as possible.

Jimmy Nelson became the first Cardiff player to be dismissed in a league match when he was sent off during the 3-2 defeat in the opening game of the 1925-26 season against Manchester City at Maine Road.

In the first week of November, City shook the football world by making a double transfer swoop in Scotland. Motherwell received a club record fee of £5,000 for their centre forward Hughie Ferguson, and Clyde were paid £2,000 for their classy outside left, George McLachlan.

On New Year's Day, 1926 the Bluebirds suffered their worst ever league defeat when old rivals Sheffield United won 11-2 at Bramall Lane with both Ferguson and McLachlan in the side. Conditions that day were described as wretched with freezing rain turning the pitch into a quagmire. City went down to ten men when Jimmy Blair went off injured but by then they were already losing 7-1 thanks to an inspired display from Irish international Billy Gillespie.

Did You Know...

The Cardiff City v Arsenal FA Cup final of 1927 was the first to be broadcast on national radio by the BBC

But it was not all gloom as the Bluebirds now had a record number of 16 international players on the books. Nine had represented Wales, four appeared for Scotland, and three turned out for Ireland. Another player, Tom Watson, was capped by Ireland before the end of the season.

The following year was famous for the Wembley success but on the league scene there were many worrying aspects with the General Strike of 1926 being held mainly responsible for keeping attendances down to the 14,000 level. The Bluebirds ended 1926-27 in 14th place but they certainly turned on the style in the FA Cup.

Aston Villa were beaten 2-1 in round three at Ninian Park and a long trip north-east to Darlington was made worthwhile after a 2-0 victory.

Fred Keenor had suffered injuries and a loss of form earlier in the season but he was recalled for the round five tie at Bolton Wanderers and was inspirational in another 2-0 win.

Division Two promotion challengers Chelsea were next up for the Bluebirds and a crowd of 70,184 were at Stamford Bridge to see the sides draw 0-0. The midweek replay brought a further 47,853 through the turnstiles at Ninian Park for a match that would ultimately play a part in changing one of the laws of the game. City led 2-0 through Sam Irving and Len Davies when Chelsea were awarded a penalty. Andy Wilson stepped up to take the spot-kick and City's Tom Farquharson retreated into the back of his goal. As Wilson ran up to kick the ball, the keeper rushed out of goal and blocked the ball on the six-yard line. Several months later the law was subsequently changed to make sure the goalkeeper stayed on his line until the kick was taken. Chelsea eventually pulled level but Ferguson struck the winner from the spot to send the Bluebirds into the semi-final where they were drawn against Reading.

23 April 1927, Cardiff City 1 Arsenal 0. The goal that brought the FA Cup to Cardiff. Arsenal keeper Dan Lewis fumbles Hughie Ferguson's shot over the line with Len Davies close at hand

City's last-four tie was played at Molineux and they were never in danger of losing as goals from Ferguson (2) and Wake easily saw off any challenge from the Division Two side.

On St George's Day, 23 April 1927, the cup was taken out of England for the first and only time when the Bluebirds beat Arsenal 1-0 with that goal from Hughie Ferguson. On the wing for City was 19-year-old Ernie Curtis who at the time was the youngest player to appear in a Wembley final. Skipper Keenor received the trophy from King George V just seven seasons after the Bluebirds had entered the Football League. It was the first cup final to be publicly broadcast live by radio throughout the country.

That was not the end of their cup exploits for they also beat Rhyl 2-0 to win the Welsh Cup, thereby becoming the first club to win cup competitions in the same season in different countries.

City became treble-winners when they went on to win the Charity Shield by beating Corinthians 2-1 at Stamford Bridge.

The club invested much of the profits from the cup run into constructing a cover for 18,000 spectators over the Grangetown end.

The next league season gave no hint of what was to be in store as City finished the term in sixth place, but low crowds and lack of money had taken its toll and the following 1928-29 season, the Bluebirds went down in bottom place despite having the best defence in Division One with the least number of goals (59) scored against them. Sadly, they only managed to score 43 goals and finished up seven points from safety to be relegated along with Bury.

One of the reasons for their demise was the sale of quality players such as Sam Irving, Willie Davies and Ernie Curtis without bringing in adequate replacements.

City lasted two seasons in Division Two before dropping further down into Division Three South in 1931 with once again, a lack of goals and only eight victories being the prime cause of their demise.

In January 1931, Keenor severed his ties with Cardiff City after 19 years service as a player when he was allowed to join Crewe Alexandra. He remains synonymous with all things good about the Bluebirds having appeared in 371 league games, playing in two FA Cup finals, and winning 31 caps for Wales while at Ninian Park. He made a further 116 league appearances at Gresty Road for the Railwaymen before going into non-league football. When he finally retired, he came back to live in Cardiff and died in 1972 at the age of 78.

Did You Know...
Cardiff City missed out on the 1923-24 Division One title to Huddersfield Town by just 0.024 of a goal. If modern rules had been used the two sides would have been level on goal difference but City would have won the title having scored one more goal than their rivals

During their first year in Three South, City posted their highest ever league victory when they swamped Thames 9-2 in February, 1932 at Ninian Park. Walter Robbins struck five and there was one each for Jim McCambridge, Les Jones and Albert Keating while the ninth came from an own goal. Scorer of one of the goals for the visitors was none other than former City favourite Len Davies. Thames were in even worse financial trouble than City and when they realised that they had no change of strip for the match at Ninian Park, and no funds to purchase new kit, Davies came to the rescue and provided ten of his Wales international shirts for his team-mates to wear. After that season Thames resigned from the League before being disbanded.

Results continued to be poor during the next season and after the Bluebirds finished 1932-33 fourth from bottom of Division Three South, the inevitable happened and manager Fred Stewart's resignation was accepted. He had been in control for 22 years.

Bartley Wilson took over from Stewart for the following season. With results showing no improvement, he soon gave way to Ben Watts-Jones in March 1934 but City were forced to apply for re-election after finishing rock bottom of the division. In just seven short years, the Bluebirds had gone from a Wembley success to relying on their friends to keep them in the Football League.

Watts-Jones remained in charge for only three seasons until being replaced by Bill Jennings, a former Wales international who had been brought to the club as trainer.

To add to the club's woes, in January 1937 the centre stand at Ninian Park was destroyed by fire, yet there were small signs that the worst was over both on and off the field, and an improvement in results over the next two seasons brought the fans back to Ninian Park in increasing numbers.

The 1938-39 season saw the debut of resourceful wing half Billy Baker and he would become a prominent member of future City sides. But a final position of 13th in the division was not thought good enough for new chairman Herbert Merrett and he appointed Cyril Spiers as secretary-manager to replace Jennings for the 1939-40 season. Spiers immediately set about changing the personnel by bringing in a number of new faces including inside forward Trevor Morris from Ipswich, and amateur centre forward Wilf Wooller, a Wales rugby international, who would go on to captain Glamorgan at cricket.

Did You Know...
Cardiff City finished bottom of Division Three (South) in 1933-34 after suffering 27 defeats in the 46 league matches

All these events were overshadowed by the advent of World War Two and after just three matches of the 1939-40 season, the Football League was suspended in September 1939 and not re-started in full until the 1946-47 season.

Post-War Recovery

Football continued at Ninian Park throughout the War years and a number of prominent players of that era such as Bill Shankly, Johnny Carey, Raich Carter and Jimmy Murphy all turned out as 'guests' for the Bluebirds at various times.

It was on 14 April 1945 that the Bluebirds were involved in a two-legged cup tie that would enter the history books. A week earlier, the Bluebirds won the first leg 2-1 at Ashton Gate against Bristol City but the Robins were leading 2-1 at Ninian Park in the second leg at full time. Thirty minutes of extra time were played, then another thirty minutes as the match had to be played to a finish. It was reported that many fans went home for tea and then came back to watch the end of the game. After an incredible 202 minutes, Billy Rees scored to give the Bluebirds a 4-3 aggregate victory.

In November 1945, Cardiff City played the first Soviet club to tour the West when they met Moscow Dynamo at Ninian Park. The Russians were on a four game visit and drew 3-3 with Chelsea, trounced the Bluebirds 10-1, beat Arsenal 4-3 in a match played in thick fog, and then drew 2-2 with Rangers. As Dynamo wore blue, City turned out in red shirts for a match watched by a crowd of 31,000.

A resumption of organised football was made in 1945-46 but the first official season was not until a year later.

A shock awaited City fans when Cyril Spiers, who had stayed at the club during the duration of the War, abruptly resigned and left to join Norwich City. Club chairman Merrett wasted no time in going the short distance to Newport and engaging Billy McCandless who had been so successful with County in 1938-39 when the club were champions of Division Three South. Unfortunately for County the War years, added to the loss of McCandless, had a devastating effect on the club. They were unable to cope with the higher standard of football and dropped straight back to the lower division after just one season.

Did You Know...
The Bluebirds' best run in the league came in the 1946-47 season between September 1946 and March 1947 when they played 21 matches, winning 19 and drawing the other two

Jackie Pritchard, a promising goalkeeper, was the only Cardiff City player to perish during World War Two. Several others, including Billy James and Billy Baker, were prisoners of war and in James's case the privations suffered after being captured by the Japanese would lead to an early retirement from the game.

The Football League fixtures for 1946-47 were the same as those that had been issued for the abortive 1939-40 campaign. This meant that Cardiff began their season at Norwich City where Spiers was now manager. Of the Bluebirds team on duty that day in August, only goalkeeper George Poland had played league football before the War. Stan Richards scored for the Bluebirds but the Canaries won 2-1.

Once McCandless began his work he instilled consistency into the side and was well rewarded when his team of ten Welshmen and one Englishman won the Division Three South championship in 1946-47. Wing Colin Gibson, who was born in Normanby, was the odd man out.

Crowds were high everywhere, none more so than at Ninian Park where 51,626 were present on Easter Monday 1947 for the derby match with Bristol City which ended 1-1 after Stan Richards netted for the Bluebirds. Such was Cardiff's supremacy throughout that season that they finished nine points clear of second placed Queens Park Rangers. Locally-born centre forward Richards scored on his debut at Norwich, and by the end of the season had collected 30 league goals to create a record for the club that would stand for over 50 years.

The following season, McCandless ended his brief stay at Ninian Park by accepting an offer to manage Swansea Town where he made it a personal treble by leading the Swans to the Division Three South title in 1948-49.

In a surprise move, Spiers was brought back from Norwich City for a second spell as the Bluebirds prepared for life in Division Two. Alf Sherwood, Ken Hollyman and Billy Baker were all permanent fixtures in the team and there was also a place for Dougie Blair, son of former City stalwart Jimmy, who had joined the club from Blackpool.

Attendances at Ninian Park were averaging 36,000 with no less than 56,018 in the ground in October 1948 to watch Tottenham Hotspur win 1-0.

The 1950-51 season brought hope of what was to come when the Bluebirds narrowly missed out on promotion. Preston and Manchester City went up with Cardiff just two points behind in third place. Wilf Grant, who had joined the club from Southampton in 1950 in exchange for inside forward Ernie Stevenson, was switched from the wing to centre forward and his goals proved crucial to City's hopes of a return to the top flight.

8 September 1947, Cardiff City 5 Southampton 1.
L-R George Curtis (Southampton), Glyn Williams, George Lewis (Southampton), Fred Stansfield , and Arthur Lever

The Bluebirds fulfilled their promise by finishing the next season as runners-up to Sheffield Wednesday. It required a tremendous end to the campaign to secure second place after a number of indifferent performances had left them well adrift of the pace. Ken Chisholm had been signed from Coventry City to provide more firepower up front and he responded with a number of timely goals but City had to win their last three matches, all at Ninian Park, to take the final promotion place. Blackburn Rovers and Bury were beaten and it all came down to the final match of the season against top six side, Leeds United. An amazing 45,925 fans crammed into the ground despite the fact that Newcastle United were playing Arsenal in the FA Cup final at Wembley at the same time. Two goals from Grant, making it 26 in all competitions, and one from Chisholm gave City a 3-1 victory and promotion to Division One after an absence of 23 years.

The first season back at the top ended in a creditable 12th place and the fans showed their approval by averaging over 38,000 for home matches. City's record attendance for a league match at Ninian Park came on 22 April, 1953 when 57,893 watched league champions Arsenal hold out for a 0-0 draw.

In December of that year, the club paid their highest transfer fee to date when they signed Wales international centre forward Trevor Ford from Sunderland for £30,000. He immediately began repaying the fee by scoring the only goal of the match on his home debut against Middlesbrough.

Although the club improved their position to finish tenth in 1953-54, the unpredictable Spiers resigned at the end of the campaign for reasons never fully made public. Trevor Morris, who had come to the club as a player from Ipswich but whose career had been ended by injury, moved up from club secretary to take over the reigns. He reinforced his squad by going to Sunderland and agreeing a triple deal costing £9,000 by signing Johnny McSeveney, Harry Kirtley and Howard Sheppeard from the Roker Park club all at the same time. His most expensive signing was Ron Stockin, a goal-scoring inside forward who cost £12,000 from Wolves but the club still made a poor start by conceding 14 goals in their opening four matches. This included two defeats by Preston to the tune of 5-2 at Ninian Park and 7-1 at Deepdale.

Morris's first season in charge saw a dramatic fall in City's fortunes and only a 3-2 victory over second-placed Wolves on the last day of the 1954-55 season staved off relegation. Ford grabbed two of the goals and the other came from his new strike partner, Gerry Hitchens.

Wolves paid City back in full for that defeat when they returned to Ninian Park on 3 September the following season. They were ahead after only 15 seconds through Johnny Hancocks, were 5-0 up at half time, and ended up thrashing the Bluebirds 9-1 to equal the biggest ever away win in Division One. Even City's goal, scored when it was 9-0, came from former Wolves inside forward Stockin.

5 September, 1949, Cardiff City 2 Hull City 0
Hull keeper Billy Bly gathers from Ernie Stevenson

A sequel to this defeat came on New Year's Eve, later that year when the Bluebirds went to Molineux for the return match. They won 2-0 with goals from Ford and Hitchens to take the Midland club's ground record.

Desperate to ring the changes, Morris agreed a strange deal with Arsenal. The Gunners took right wingers Mike Tiddy and Gordon Nutt to Highbury in exchange for Brian Walsh, also a right wing, and £20,000. It was a deal that would serve the Bluebirds well.

City fans witnessed a remarkable debut on 10 December, 1955 when Charlton Athletic came to Ninian Park. Making his first start against Charlton was centre forward Neil O'Halloran and he netted a hat-trick in a 3-1 victory. Centre half and skipper Danny Malloy, who had been signed from Dundee for £17,000, also made his debut against Charlton and he would prove to be the mainstay of City's team over the next few seasons.

Sadly, the writing was already on the wall for the club and at the end of the 1955-56 season the Bluebirds were struggling down in 17th place although attendances were still averaging over 28,000 in the top flight.

During the close season, City said goodbye to veteran full back Alf Sherwood who moved on to Newport County. He had joined the club in 1941 and enjoyed 15 years of success at Ninian Park as the Bluebirds went from Division Three South to Division One. He made 354 league appearances for City and was capped 39 times, still a record for a player at the club.

Did You Know...

Three successive home games during December 1957 brought no less than 18 goals for the Bluebirds. They beat Barnsley 7-0, Stoke City 5-2 on Boxing Day, and then swamped Liverpool 6-1

Season 1956-57 showed no better form and the Bluebirds lost their place in the top division when they were relegated, along with Charlton, after managing only ten wins from 42 matches. The loss of Ford proved crucial in that relegation season despite the emergence of Hitchens. Ford was suspended by the Football League in November 1956 after extracts from his autobiography relating to illegal payments to players was published. His last game for the Bluebirds came in a 1-1 draw with Manchester City at Ninian Park on 3 November. He had his ban cut to three years on appeal but then signed for PSV Eindhoven in Holland before ending his career at Newport County.

The form of raw youngster Hitchens had attracted a number of the top clubs however, and in December 1957 he was transferred to Aston Villa. He would later go on to win seven caps for England and enjoy a lengthy spell in Italy where he played for Inter, Atalanta, Torino and Cagliari before returning to Wales. Tragically he died of a heart attack at the age of 48.

During this period, City had an amazing sequence of matches in the FA Cup. In 1955-56, 56-57, and 57-58 they were drawn away to Leeds United in the third round. As if that coincidence was not enough, the Bluebirds won all three games by the same 2-1 scoreline.

At the end of the 1957-58 campaign, with results not having picked up despite the drop to Division Two, manager Morris resigned to take the well-worn path to the Vetch Field as manager of Swansea Town. Once again, the club filled the post from within and coach Bill Jones took over the hot seat.

Did You Know...
On the morning of 28 December, 1957, Cardiff winger Colin Hudson was married at a Newport church. As soon as the ceremony was over he rushed to Ninian Park along with best man Alan Harrington where they both played in a 6-1 victory over Liverpool

The Bluebirds made a poor start to the next season but in a masterstroke, Jones signed Derek Tapscott from Arsenal for a fee of £10,000. It would prove to be one of the best bargains in City's history. Tapscott had been top scorer for three successive seasons at Highbury but had lost his place through injury. Tappy's confidence flowed throughout the side and results improved. With youngster Graham Moore also forcing his way into the first team, City began an upturn in fortune to end the season in ninth position.

It was all set for a promotion push and in 1959-60 the team responded and an epic 1-0 victory over promotion rivals Aston Villa on Easter Saturday ensured a return to Division One. The winner came from Moore in front of an ecstatic 52,364 crowd, but with the title in their grasp, a poor finish to the season saw them relinquish top spot to Villa.

Arsenal were the visitors to Ninian Park on 24 September, 1960 and a goal by Derek Tapscott gave the Bluebirds a 1-0 victory in front of almost 33,000 fans. The goal was hotly disputed by the Arsenal players and manager George Swindin, as they all thought that he had used his hand to score. After the game Tappy went into the Arsenal dressing room to see his old team-mates only to hear Swindin telling him to get out. When Tappy failed to move quickly enough, the Arsenal manager began taking his coat off ready to do battle with City's striker. Tappy was ushered out of the dressing room by fellow Welsh international Jack Kelsey while a couple of players held Swindin at bay. Little did Tapscott know that in a few years time that disagreement would come back to haunt him.

22 April 1959, Cardiff City 2 Sunderland 1. Brian Walsh beats John Goodchild before netting winner

Floodlighting came to Ninian Park in 1960. The club was one of the last to install the lights that were formally opened by Zurich Grasshoppers on 5 October, 1960, but the return to Division One would not be a long stay.

Mel Charles arrived from Arsenal for £28,000 but he failed to arrest the slide. Leaving the club was Derrick Sullivan who joined Exeter City after playing in nine different positions during his time at Ninian Park. He appeared in 275 league games and played for Wales at the 1958 World Cup finals along with Colin Baker and Ron Hewitt. Also leaving were Peter

Donnelly, a bustling forward who joined Swansea Town, and Brian Walsh who left for Newport County after making over 200 appearances for the Bluebirds.

Within two seasons the Bluebirds were back in Division Two, partly because they allowed Malloy to leave the club but also because they sold Moore to relegation-rivals Chelsea for £30,000 when they should have kept both men.

Up until this time, players were only allowed to be paid the maximum wage of £20. This wage capping was disputed in the courts and professional footballers were allowed to earn more, depending on whether the club could afford it. All City's players were offered £30 per week but Malloy asked for a little extra as he was the captain. The club refused to budge, so the popular skipper left to join Doncaster Rovers as player-manager.

Jones brightened the dark mood of the Welsh public when he went to Newcastle United and signed Ivor Allchurch for an £18,000 fee. However, the return of the golden boy of Welsh football couldn't save Jones and poor results at the start of the 1962-63 season led to his dismissal.

In November 1962, City appointed George Swindin, the former Arsenal keeper and manager, as their new boss. When he was introduced to the players both Derek Tapscott and Mel Charles were filled with dread. After all, Swindin was the man ready to fight Tappy after he had scored a winner against Arsenal, while Charles had never got on with Swindin after he was made to play a friendly for the Gunners a day before a Wales international match. Both players were true professionals however and never allowed that dislike to get in the way of their football.

Did You Know...

Cardiff City were beaten 8-3 by Everton on 28 April, 1962 despite including five Wales internationals in their side

Swindin excited home fans by signing the legendary John Charles from Roma in 1963 and on his home debut, Charles cracked a 75 yard goal beyond Norwich keeper Kevin Keelan to announce his arrival. Technically, it was an own goal as if the ball had not struck Keelan's shoulder, it would have been a goal kick.

Swindin had a poor relationship with his players and man-management was not one of his strong points. Two disappointing seasons followed and there was another change at the top when in June 1964, on the day City were appearing in a Welsh Cup final, he was forced to resign and the board appointed Jimmy Scoular in his place.

The Scoular Years

Jimmy Scoular's arrival corresponded with City's first steps in European competition and there were many notable matches at Ninian Park and abroad while the craggy Scot was in charge.

Scoular had skippered Newcastle United to their FA Cup victory in 1955 before becoming player-manager at Bradford where he had future Bluebirds Ian Gibson and Ronnie Bird under his wing. He retired from playing at the end of the 1963-64 season and joined City a few weeks later.

Entry to the Cup Winners Cup was open to the winners of the Welsh Cup and the Bluebirds almost made that trophy their own during Scoular's reign.

While their league form remained indifferent in 1964-65 when they finished in 13th place, the fans rallied when it came to the European matches.

Esjberg of Norway were their first opponents and after a 0-0 draw in the away leg, a Peter King header put City into the second round where they were drawn against the cup holders, Sporting Lisbon. The away leg came first and in an astonishing match, goals by winger Greg Farrell and Tapscott gave City a magnificent victory. The return leg was a dour bruising affair with Tappy in particular singled out for some rough treatment, but City held out for a 0-0 draw and a place in the quarter-final.

Once again a tough draw paired them with Real Zaragoza, the holders of the Inter-Cities Fairs Cup which was the forerunner of the UEFA Cup. Skipper Gareth Williams and King made it a 2-2 draw at La Romerada but a crowd of 38,458 at Ninian Park on 3 February, 1965 went home disappointed. A late goal from Canario, a former member of Di Stefano's awe-inspiring Real Madrid side, proved enough to put the Spanish club through.

Scoular had a big clear out of players in readiness for the following season but it had little effect as the Bluebirds slumped to just one place off relegation in Division Two. One notable event during the season however was the introduction of 16-year-old substitute John Toshack who scored on his debut against Leyton Orient in November, 1965.

There was another milestone when City's home league match with Coventry City was the first to be beamed back to the away side's ground. About 10,000 Sky Blue supporters were at Highfield Road to watch their side win 2-1 on giant screens.

6 May 1964. Cardiff City players leaving for close-season tour of Italy

The Football League Cup provided some light relief as the Bluebirds marched through to the semi-final. Crewe, Portsmouth, Reading and Ipswich all fell by the wayside as City reached the last four and a two-legged tie against a West Ham United side sporting such heroes as Bobby Moore, Martin Peters and Geoff Hurst. They would all gain fame by being part of England's World Cup winning side a few months later. Sadly, the gulf in class was all too evident to see and although George Andrews bagged a brace at Upton Park, the Hammers came to Ninian Park for the second leg 5-2 up on aggregate. Another five goals for the London side against a solitary score by Bernard Lewis ended City's hopes with a 10-3 aggregate defeat.

There was little improvement in Cardiff's league fortunes for the next few seasons despite Scoular making changes in personnel and another narrow squeak came with a 20th place finish at the end of the 1966-67 season.

Cup football, and in particular the European variety, provided a welcome change from the league struggles. After being knocked out of the Cup Winners Cup by the classy Belgian outfit, Standard Liege, City shocked the football world by reaching the semi-final in the 1967-68 season. Peter King began the good work by netting in a 1-1 draw against Shamrock Rovers in Dublin and Bobby Brown and Toshack made sure of progress by scoring in the return leg at Ninian Park.

Worcester-born King was at the club from 1960 to 1973 and became one of the most versatile players at Ninian Park. He appeared in 356 league games and scored 67 goals before retiring from the game.

Holland was the next destination and once again the under-rated King was on the mark as the Bluebirds held Dutch side NAC Breda to a 1-1 draw. Brown, Toshack, Barrie Jones and Malcolm Clarke fired the goals in a comfortable 4-1 home, second leg victory.

Scoular had evolved a clever plan of using an extra defensive player, usually Clarke, in the away legs and this system worked to perfection on a number of occasions.

The Bluebirds were now in the quarter-finals for the second time and determined to go one better even though the draw meant they had to beat Moscow Torpedo. A header by

Barrie Jones gave them a slight advantage to take to Tashkent, for that was where Torpedo's home leg was played, 2,000 miles away from their Moscow home.

Because the Russian capital was experiencing sub-zero temperatures, the switch meant that the tie took place close to the Chinese/Soviet border. It was the longest trip ever undertaken by a football club in European competition. City's star on the night was goalkeeper Bob Wilson who had been signed by Scoular from Aston Villa reserves in 1964. He made a number of superb saves and was only beaten by a single goal to take the tie to a play-off.

UEFA decided the third match would be played in Augsburg, West Germany, but City were in trouble as defensive lynch-pin Don Murray was unfit and reserve defender Richie Morgan, who had not appeared in a single league match, was drafted into the starting line-up. A brilliant performance by the Bluebirds aided by a goal from Norman Dean sent them through to the semi-final.

Did You Know...
Gary Bell conceded two penalties on his debut for the Bluebirds in a 7-1 defeat away to Wolverhampton Wanderers on 21 September, 1966

Don Murray was one of the finest players ever to wear a City shirt. He played for the club from 1962 to 1974 after making his debut as a 17-year-old against Middlesbrough in the 1962-63 season. He benefitted from playing with John Charles at the start of his career and then later Brian Harris, but was mostly influenced by Scoular himself.

SV Hamburg were City's opponents in the last four and they had a star-studded team full of internationals. Uwe Seeler and Willi Schulz had been in West Germany's World Cup Final side against England in 1966 to show just how tough a task it would be for City to make the final. Dean fired the Bluebirds in front at the Volksparkstadion only for the Germans to equalise midway through the second half. Wilson was again in magnificent form as the Bluebirds held out for a superb 1-1 draw. The second leg at Ninian Park on 1 May, 1968 drew 43,070 fans but although Dean netted his customary goal and Brian Harris weighed in with the only goal he ever scored for City, the match ended in heartbreaking fashion when Franz-Josef Hoenig scored the winner in the 90th minute after an error by Wilson.

Harris had come to the club from Everton in 1966, only a few months after starring for them in an FA Cup final victory over Sheffield Wednesday. He brought experience and stability to the City backline for a number of seasons although his first game in City colours ended in a 7-1 defeat at Plymouth Argyle.

Cardiff's cup form spilled over into the league and they showed an improvement in 1967-68 when they finished in 13th place, reaching fifth spot the following term when Toshack led the way with 22 league goals closely followed by fans favourite Brian Clark who added 17.

Did You Know...
Johnny Vincent was signed from Middlesbrough for £35,000 in October 1972 and two days later scored on his City debut–against Middlesbrough

Scoular then paid a club record fee of £35,000 to Coventry City for little inside forward Ian Gibson at the start of the 1970-71 season but it was an outgoing deal that angered many fans. The City Board accepted a bid of £110,000 from Liverpool for John Toshack in November, and though Alan Warboys was brought in somewhat belatedly on Christmas Eve to replace him, the Bluebirds would eventually miss out on promotion after finishing third behind Leicester City and Sheffield United.

Warboys cost £40,000 from Sheffield Wednesday and he became a firm favourite with the fans after scoring four goals at the Canton Stand end in the first half against Carlisle United before leaving the field with a thigh injury. After scoring his third goal, he raced to the dugout with hand outstretched for the bonus Scoular offered anyone who netted a hat-trick.

Four days later on 10 March, 1971 Real Madrid came to town in the quarter-final of the Cup Winners Cup. The Bluebirds had dispatched PO Larnaca of Cyprus 8-0 on aggregate before crushing FC Nantes 7-2 over both legs to set up a mouth-watering clash against the European giants.

Ninian Park was packed with 47,500 Bluebirds fans who will never forget Nigel Rees crossing for Clark to head past Real keeper, Borja.

The Spaniards proved to be a better side at the Bernabeu and after an ill-tempered game went through on aggregate with a 2-0 victory.

City's league form once again dipped dramatically and during the next few seasons the club hovered perilously close to the relegation zone. In 1973, when wings were added to the main Grandstand, a further run of poor league results brought an end to Scoular's nine year reign as manager when he was sacked by new club owner David Goldstone. The Scoular years will however go down in City folklore for containing some of the best moments in Bluebirds history.

Decline and Fall

Chairman Goldstone brought in the experienced former Leicester City and Manchester United manager Frank O'Farrell to replace Scoular. The new man went to Spurs for Jimmy Andrews who agreed to become the first team coach.

O'Farrell only stayed 158 days before accepting a lucrative appointment in the Middle East. Andrews took over the hot seat but City finished the 1973-74 season needing a point from their final game against Crystal Palace. An equaliser from Tony Villars left the Bluebirds safe but consigned Palace to Division Three.

The inevitable relegation was only delayed a year, partly because 36 goals scored in a season were never going to be enough.

A further sad sign of the times was the transfer of Leighton Phillips to Aston Villa. City were in the Cup Winners Cup once again and due to meet the crack Hungarian side, Ferencvaros. Yet terms were agreed with Villa and Phillips was withdrawn from the squad flying to the Hungarian capital, Budapest. Supporters were understandably upset and only 4,228 turned up at Ninian Park for the return leg which the Hungarians won 4-0.

24 September 1977, Cardiff City 3 Fulham 1. Bill Irwin and Keith Pontin keep Fulham at bay

Andrews signed the Spurs and former Wales captain Mike England on a free transfer and Doug Livermore came to the club from Norwich City for an £18,000 fee. In October 1975 Australian World Cup star Adrian Alston arrived from Luton Town and these three signings were influential in taking City into a promotion position.

A crowd of 35,501 packed into Ninian Park on 14 April, 1976 to see champions-elect Hereford United lose 2-0 to the Bluebirds thanks to goals from Livermore and Alan Campbell. The win gave City promotion back to Division Two but elation was tempered by the news that England had left the club after not being given the coaching job originally promised.

Kenton Utilities bought out Goldstone but there was very little money available to Andrews and two unproductive seasons followed. When Alston decided to go and play in America, Andrews was given permission to sign Robin Friday from Reading. After scoring twice on his debut against Fulham in January, 1977, Friday's form deserted him and he went missing on a number of occasions. After just 20 league appearances his contract was cancelled.

In September, 1977, City set an all-time low for an attendance at a home Cup Winners Cup tie when only 3,631 bothered to turn up to watch FK Austria Memphis draw 0-0 in a first round match. New chairman Bob Grogan decided that a change at the top was necessary and in November 1978, Andrews was dismissed and Richie Morgan installed as caretaker-manager. The 34-year-old had been at Ninian Park all his career and had joined the club's commercial staff when he ended his playing days.

The players responded well to the new regime and the Bluebirds finished the season in ninth spot, their best position for seven seasons.

Did You Know...

The youngest Cardiff City player to be sent off is Linden Jones who was four days short of his 18th birthday when dismissed in a 4-1 victory at Blackburn Rovers on 28 February, 1979

But average attendances had plummeted to 6,500 and in order to increase the use of the facilities and raise further income, the Board allowed Cardiff Blue Dragons RL to use Ninian Park. Grogan had by now appointed Ron Jones as general manager and it was his job to run the club with particular attention to the financial side of the business.

To add to their woes, City were not re-elected to the Football Combination and they withdrew their third team from the Welsh League, effectively losing all fixtures for reserve or youth players. Crowds dipped below 4,000 and in November 1981, Morgan was relieved of his duties as manager and former West Brom and Wales full back Graham Williams was appointed coach with full control over team affairs. Williams had been working at a leisure centre and was a surprise appointment but he only lasted 11 games, nine of which were defeats, before being dismissed along with Morgan. This was most unfair on Morgan who had no say whatsoever on the football side yet was still given his cards.

Len Ashurst, who had been manager at Newport County, took over in March 1982 but he was unable to stop the rot and City went back to Division Three after failing to beat champions Luton Town in their final match.

During the summer the former Sunderland full back recruited Jimmy Goodfellow, his assistant at County, as trainer-coach and then set about changing the playing staff. In came a number of free transfer players including Roger Gibbins from Cambridge United, Jeff Hemmerman from Portsmouth, and Paul Bodin from Newport County.

It was in September 1982 that City supposedly made their 'record' transfer deal when Godfrey Ingram was signed from San Jose Earthquakes for a reputed £180,000. As he departed back to the same club only nine weeks later for a similar fee it has often been suggested that no money ever changed hands.

City's small squad were tested to the limit but with Dave Bennett outstanding down the wing and Hemmerman regularly banging in the goals, they kept in the promotion hunt. Young keeper Andy Dibble suffered a serious injury against Bradford City leading to no less than five custodians being used throughout the season. The Bluebirds then struck a poor patch of form with only two victories from ten matches, one of those defeats coming at buoyant Somerton Park. John Aldridge struck the only goal of the game to take County to the top of Division Three and leave City hanging on to fourth spot.

In May 1983, however, 11,758 fans were in Ninian Park to watch the Bluebirds beat Orient 2-0 with goals from John Lewis and Bennett to send City up as runners-up behind Portsmouth. The Bluebirds had lost only one match at Ninian Park yet could only attract an average crowd of 7,500 which was not enough to maintain the momentum.

Fed up with the lack of money at his disposal, Ashurst left for Sunderland in March 1984 and Jones appointed Jimmy Goodfellow and club captain Jimmy Mullen in a dual role. With the club deep in debt and no money to bring in fresh faces the signs were ominous.

On a brighter note, long-serving Phil Dwyer passed Tom Farquharson's league appearance record of 445 matches. He also won ten caps for Wales during his 14-year stay at Cardiff City.

There was plenty of transfer activity at the club but it was all one way as Dibble, Gary Bennett and leading scorer Gordon Owen all departed. Coming in were Mike Ford, who made his debut at Leeds in December 1984, and also former England star Gerry Francis who played in seven of the early matches before leaving for Swansea City. The Bluebirds equalled their worst ever start to a season with eight defeats from their first nine games. Goodfellow didn't even last until September before being dismissed in favour of former City and Derby County inside forward, Alan Durban.

Durban could do nothing to stop the downward spiral and relegation to Division Three was followed by the drop into the basement in 1985-86 with crowds now down to an average of 3,000.

The club was put up for sale by Kenton Utilities and they released control to Tony Clemo. Durban was sacked in May 1986 and later that month Frank Burrows agreed to set about changing the fortunes of the stricken club. He brought in Alan Curtis from Southampton and Graham Moseley from Brighton on free transfers and also convinced Jimmy Goodfellow to come back to the club as physio.

City remained inconsistent, failing to win a home game for four months and Burrows was forced to constantly switch his small squad. Chris Pike came in on loan from Fulham and Kevin Bartlett was recruited from Fareham Town. There was also a debut for 16-year-old full back Jason Perry against Exeter City in March 1987, but only 1,510 fans watched the final home game of the season when Hartlepool were beaten 4-0 to leave the Bluebirds in 13th place in Division Four.

Jimmy Gilligan came to the club from Lincoln City in time for the 1987-88 season. Another newcomer was Phil Bater but he became the first City player to be sent off on his debut when he was dismissed at Wrexham.

The unfortunate Moseley broke his arm against Peterborough and after regaining fitness was involved in a car accident which was to lead to his retirement. Several keepers were brought in on loan to cover his absence including George Wood from Crystal Palace.

Did You Know...

The Bluebirds record transfer deal for many years was the £180,000 allegedly paid to San Jose Earthquakes for Godfrey Ingram in September 1982. As the player returned to the same club for a similar figure a few months later it was doubtful whether any money changed hands

The Bluebirds finished the season in fine style with five straight victories and promotion was gained in front of 9,852 fans as the Bluebirds beat Crewe 2-0. They made it a double celebration by defeating Wrexham by the same scoreline to win the Welsh Cup and a return to Europe after an absence of 11 years.

Burrows realised the hard work had only just begun when Oxford United offered £150,000 for utility player, Ford. The sum was readily accepted but the manager was told there would be no money available to strengthen the side, though he was allowed to take veteran keeper Wood on a permanent basis.

Gilligan struck a hat-trick as Derry City were dispatched 4-0 in the Cup Winners Cup but the Bluebirds were knocked out in the next round by Aarhus.

The Gilligan-Bartlett partnership was soon blossoming but in February 1989, the club sold Bartlett to West Brom for £125,000. The 1988-89 season closed with the Bluebirds in 16th place largely due to the fact that they only managed to score 14 league goals on their travels throughout the entire season.

Once again the next season began in the same old way with players being sold to balance the books. Terry Boyle, Nicky Platnauer, Paul Wimbleton and Ian Walsh all left the club while Pike finally made his move from Fulham a permanent one.

After defeats in the opening two league matches, Burrows accepted an offer to become John Gregory's assistant at Portsmouth. Chairman Clemo turned to Len Ashurst who came back for a second spell at Ninian Park. He brought in Cohen Griffith from Kettering and keeper Gavin Ward but he could do nothing when Portsmouth came in with a £215,000 bid for Gilligan which was immediately snapped up.

But 1990 was also the year when the Ayatollah was born. There were about 150 City fans on the terraces at Sincil Bank, home of Lincoln City, all of them fed up watching what turned out to be a boring 0-0 draw. Suddenly, while the match was in progress, riot police arrived complete with helmets, visors and a small camera crew. It was such a ridiculous situation that a City supporter known as Eric the Red started doing the Ayatollah. He began running around the terraces trying to get the rest of the fans to join in which some of them did. There were various routines being done at the time, mainly to stop the boredom of watching City during one of their more painful times, but it was the Ayatollah that caught on.

Did You Know...

Seven clubs have scored more than 100 league goals against the Bluebirds with the most by Preston who have netted 159 goals in 82 matches

Eric the Red's involvement came abruptly to an end in a Welsh Cup semi-final at the Vetch Field in 1994. After celebrating a City goal with the Ayatollah, he was arrested and charged with 'incitement to riot'. Fortunately for him, film evidence proved he was entirely innocent and he was later released.

The Ayatollah has now developed to such an extent that it can be seen on the rugby pitch, swimming pools, and in Olympic and Commonwealth Games.

A miserable year with eight home defeats eventually ended in relegation back to Division Four and Ashurst lasted one more season of basement football before tendering his resignation. It was at this time that Rick Wright was unveiled as the financial benefactor who had wiped out much of City's debts. With young Welsh players such as Jason Perry, Damon Searle and Nathan Blake making their way into the first team, the future began to look a little brighter.

Wright became financial controller the following season and immediately began giving Ninian Park a long overdue facelift. He also introduced a number of innovative schemes which were good for the club. One revolutionary idea was that the cost of a match ticket would be decided by the club's position in the league - the lower they were placed the less the fans had to pay.

Eddie May was installed as club coach in full control of team affairs and he was given the financial assistance to go out and buy a number of experienced players such as Carl Dale from Chester and Paul Ramsey from Leicester City. Ramsey was made club skipper and May set about the task of reviving City's fortunes.

Derek Brazil joined from Manchester United after a loan spell at Swansea, and although it was an average season in the league, the Bluebirds won the Welsh Cup with victory over Hednesford Town at the National Stadium in front of 10,300 fans.

Austrian side Admira Wacker came to Ninian Park for the first leg of the Cup Winners Cup in 1992-93. They were coached by Siggi Held who had played for West Germany in the 1966 World Cup final. The Austrians were technically superior and a 1-1 draw at home was followed by a 2-0 defeat in Vienna. Robbie James was unable to play in the first leg when it was discovered at a late stage that he was banned after receiving two cautions while playing for Swansea City against Panathinaikos in 1989.

The 1992-93 season would turn out to be one of the club's best seasons for many a year as they secured the Division Three championship. They also retained the Welsh Cup with a 5-0 victory over Rhyl thanks to a splendid hat-trick from fans favourite, Phil Stant.

Wright had agreed the signing of Kevin Ratcliffe and his experience proved invaluable as City at last moved out of the bottom division.

Instead of maintaining the improvement, all did not go well at Ninian Park for the start of life in Division Two. Players became restless and Ramsey and Ratcliffe were amongst those who left the club. No season tickets were put on sale as Wright claimed he did not want to stay at the helm. He also had a row with Stant over a bonus payment that was only resolved when fan power brought about the striker's return from a loan spell at Mansfield Town.

Standard Liege became City's last Cup Winners Cup opponents in 1993 and although Tony Bird put City ahead just after half time in the away leg, the Belgian giants stormed back to win 5-2. A Robbie James goal, City's last in Europe, was all the Bluebirds had to show at Ninian Park as Arie Haan's side won comfortably 8-3 on aggregate.

City's only light relief came in an FA Cup run that included a 1-0 defeat of Manchester City when Nathan Blake scored a superb goal to give the Bluebirds victory. Mark Grew also played a big part by saving a late penalty from Keith Curle.

True to form, however, Blake was sold to Sheffield United during the week that City played Luton Town in the next round. The Hatters included teenage striker John Hartson in their line-up but it was a disputed goal that gave the visitors a 2-1 success.

At the end of the 1994-95 season, City were relegated back to Division Three and while Wright was negotiating the sale of the club to a consortium led by Midlands businessman Jim Cadman, Eddie May was dismissed and Terry Yorath brought in by the prospective buyers to manage the Bluebirds.

29 January 1994, FA Cup Round Four. Cardiff City 1 Manchester City 0. Tony Coton is beaten by Nathan Blake's superb strike

When that bid finally floundered, May was brought back for a short period before Samesh Kumar agreed a deal with Wright and took over as chairman. He replaced May with Kenny Hibbitt but it was not long before the former Wolves player was moved to a post upstairs as director of football and Phil Neal came into the club as manager.

In Neal's first season of 1995-96, the Bluebirds managed only 11 victories and 41 goals in the basement division to finish third from bottom, with only Torquay United and Scarborough below them. Neal left Cardiff under a cloud to join Steve Coppell in an abortive attempt to change Manchester City's fortunes. Hibbitt returned as manager with Russell Osman, who had ended his career as a non-contract player at Ninian Park, as his assistant.

In November, 1996 Osman became manager with Hibbitt reverting to his original post of director of football. This lasted only five matches before Hibbitt resumed his managerial duties with Osman his assistant.

City suddenly found some lasting form and with veteran Steve White leading the line, new signing Jeff Eckhardt solid in defence, and young striker Simon Haworth beginning to show his ability, the Bluebirds made it to the 1997 Division Three play-offs. Northampton Town won the first leg 1-0 at Ninian Park in front of 11,369 fans, and with a 3-2 victory at the County Ground went through to the final at Wembley where they beat Swansea City.

Inconsistency was the name of the game for the Bluebirds and the following season Cardiff ended up fourth from bottom after drawing 23 of their 46 league matches. Kumar decided it was time for yet another change at the top and Hibbitt was moved back upstairs and Frank Burrows returned in February, 1998 to take over the vacant position.

Hibbitt was on such a long contract that he would stay at Ninian Park for almost another two years as the club were unable to agree a financial pay-off.

Burrows had left a coaching job with Premiership club West Ham to come back to the club he had left in 1989. He proved that he had lost none of his mastery of wheeling and dealing in the transfer market by bringing in new faces such as Richard Carpenter, Mark Bonner and Mark Delaney who had arrived from League of Wales club Carmarthen Town. They joined an experienced squad that included Jon Hallworth, Kevin Nugent and the highly promising Jason Fowler. Delaney was soon on the move to Aston Villa but Burrows improved his squad still further by signing Andy Legg and Jason Bowen from Reading, together with Danny Hill, a former loan player at Ninian Park when he was with Spurs.

After at one time looking like champions, City scraped the last automatic promotion place behind Brentford and Cambridge United in 1998-99 and finally moved out of the basement zone. Kumar resigned as chairman at the end of the season and long-time City fan and director Steve Borley took over his duties.

The new season started with a lot of optimism but only two victories, against Oxford United and Notts County, in the opening 16 league matches left the Bluebirds struggling in the lower reaches of the division.

Once again the lack of finance hampered any chances Burrows had of improving the squad and he left the club in the hands of his assistant Billy Ayre.

Richie Humphries joined on loan from Sheffield Wednesday but fans really became excited when the club moved into Europe to obtain the signature of a strapping central defender from Germany called Jorn Schwinkendorf. Sadly, he was not good enough and after just five first team appearances he made a swift return to the other side of the channel.

Jason Bowen top-scored during the season with 12 league goals but City showed little consistency. Although a single goal from Scott Young gave them victory in the final game of the season at home to Bristol Rovers, the change in leadership had little effect. The result was the Bluebirds were once more relegated to the basement in 21st position, one point short of safety.

New Dawn

There was a wind of change around Cardiff City during the summer of 2000. Lebanese businessman Sam Hammam paid £3m for the club and once again hopes were high that there was sufficient financial backing to get the side moving back up the divisions. Bobby Gould was installed as manager but that situation lasted only until October when Alan Cork took over and Gould moved to the role of director of football.

Danny Gabbidon joined initially on loan from West Brom and with Scott Young and Rhys Weston now in defence along with Andy Legg, the team gradually began moving up the table.

Hammam had stated on a number of occasions that he would not be spending any more of his own money, but it suddenly appeared that with Rob Earnshaw, Paul Brayson and newly-signed Leo Fortune-West, the club's most expensive player at £300,000 scoring regularly, the Bluebirds had now become a reasonable side. A 6-1 thrashing of Exeter City on New Year's Day in front of 9,038 fans pushed City up to third spot but the top attendance came against promotion rivals Chesterfield on 16 April, 2001 when 13,602 watched a 3-3 draw. Paul Brayson netted twice for the Bluebirds, including a penalty, and the other goal came in the final minute from young midfielder, Kevin Evans.

A hat-trick from Fortune-West at York towards the end of the season in another 3-3 draw just about guaranteed promotion and the Bluebirds moved up to second place by defeating Shrewsbury Town 3-1 in the final home match.

City were back in Division Two, formerly Division Three, but it wasn't enough for the ambitious chairman. He wanted top flight football for Cardiff and decided to bring in the players that he thought would get the club there in double-quick time. In quick succession the City transfer record was smashed as first Graham Kavanagh arrived from Stoke in a deal reckoned to be worth £1m, only to be followed a few days later by Spencer Prior from Manchester City. City fans couldn't believe it when Peter Thorne was added to the list when he was signed from Stoke for an incredible £1.7m. With the arrival of goalkeeper Neil Alexander from Livingston, the Bluebirds were now a match for most other teams in Division Two.

Unfortunately, a poor start put paid to any hopes of running away with the league title. Three victories from the opening ten matches kept the club rooted in mid-table.

At the turn of the year they had improved to tenth spot and after disposing of Tiverton Town and Port Vale in the opening rounds of the FA Cup, they were now ready to take on Premier Division leaders Leeds United in the third round.

On a never-to-be-forgotten night, Mark Viduka gave Leeds the lead only for Kavanagh to fire a free kick into the top corner of the net to level the score. Alan Smith was dismissed after tangling with Andy Legg but it was not until the closing minutes that Scott Young lashed in a Fortune-West knock-down to give City a shock win. It turned out to be the beginning of the end for Leeds as they slumped dramatically down the divisions to League One.

A few weeks later, Lennie Lawrence was installed as manager with Cork demoted to assistant.

League form remained inconsistent but in an inspired run-in to the end of the season, City won ten and drew three of the last 13 matches to finish a point short of Reading who were in the final automatic promotion place.

Did You Know...

Peterborough's Simon Rea became the second fastest sending-off from the kick-off in League history when he was red carded 15 seconds after the start against the Bluebirds at Ninian Park on 2 November, 2002

Stoke City were the opponents in the play-offs and as the Bluebirds had taken four points off the Potters during the league season, hopes were high that a visit to the Millennium Stadium was on the agenda. After all, Stoke had been beaten in the 1999-00 and 2000-01 play-offs, and we had taken their two best players from them in Kavanagh and Thorne.

The first leg at the Britannia Stadium went to plan with Earnshaw and Fortune-West giving City the lead, only for former loan signing, Deon Burton to crucially pull one back in the 84th minute. The second leg at Ninian Park was watched by 19,367 fans but it proved to be a dark day for Bluebirds supporters. In the final minute, James O'Connor scored for the visitors to take the game into extra time. Worse was to follow as substitute Souleymane Oulare gave Stoke a 3-2 aggregate win in the 115th minute.

Not being promoted was a hammer-blow for Hammam as he had gambled on spending big to reap the benefits. The extra season in Division Two paying high salaries would prove to be the start of his downfall and the club's financial problems.

Lennie Lawrence brought in the experienced Gary Croft at full back for the 2002-03 season as the Bluebirds looked to put their play-off disaster well and truly behind them. Defender Chris Barker also arrived at the club and with Peter Thorne fit enough to play in every league match, there was optimism that the automatic promotion place demanded by Hammam would be reached.

Rob Earnshaw won his spot back up front from Andy Campbell after netting a hat-trick against Boston United in the Worthington Cup, and he would go on to break the record of 30 league goals in a season set by Stan Richards back in 1946-47.

Lawrence made use of the loan market and Alan Mahon and Chinese international Fan Zhiyi turned out for the Bluebirds as they kept up the race for promotion. However, despite being in the top four since the ninth match of the season, they tailed off badly with no victories and only one goal from their last five matches. This left them struggling to even make the play-offs but they edged into sixth place just one point ahead of Tranmere Rovers.

In the final game of the season, Earnie scored in a 1-1 draw at Crewe to create two new records, 31 league goals in a season and 35 in all competitions.

Old foes Bristol City were the opponents in the play-off semi-final and as the Robins had done the double over the Bluebirds in the regular season there were many that doubted Cardiff could make it to the Millennium Stadium. A superb match at Ninian Park saw Peter Thorne head the only goal of the game, and then came the save of the season at Ashton Gate. Neil Alexander turned a Brian Tinnion header round the post to help City to a 0-0 draw and a final against Queen's Park Rangers.

The stadium was a mass of blue as an evenly-fought final went into extra time. Lawrence pulled off leading scorer Earnshaw for Andy Campbell and the rest is history as Campbell brilliantly lobbed Rangers keeper Chris Day to win City promotion with just four minutes remaining. Alexander created his own record by becoming the first keeper to play all three games in the play-offs without conceding a goal.

Lawrence knew that the squad would need improving for life in Division One and he went for experience with Australian international Tony Vidmar and Wales cap John Robinson arriving at Ninian Park for the start of the season. They were joined by Richard Langley and Alan Lee and the Bluebirds looked well prepared for the higher grade. But with only four victories from the opening 12 matches they were locked in mid-table and once again a poor finish with only one victory from their last seven games left them in a disappointing 13th place. Attendances however, were on the increase and 19,202 watched a 0-0 draw with West Ham in October, 2003.

The emergence of youth products Joe Ledley, James Collins and Cameron Jerome lit up the following season but there were already signs that all was not right with the club finances. Lawrence signed Tony Warner to replace the popular Alexander but the Scot regained his rightful place between the goals by the end of the season. Robert Page found it difficult to hold down a first team spot with the silky skills of Gabbidon and Collins barring the way and soon left for pastures new, while Gary O'Neil enjoyed one of the best loan spells of any player at Ninian Park but Junichi Inamoto was largely disappointing despite bringing a big following of Japanese supporters to every game.

Did You Know...
Rob Earnshaw is the only player to have scored hat-tricks in the Premiership, Divisions 1, 2 and 3, the FA Cup, the League Cup, and in an international

As the cash crisis dug deep, Earnshaw was sold in a quick sale to West Brom and when the meltdown continued, club skipper Graham Kavanagh joined Wigan.

Eight points from the last four games saved face for the Bluebirds who ended the season in 16th position, just four points above the drop.

There was a great deal of activity during the summer of 2005 as Hammam desperately tried to keep hold of a club with debts spiralling out of control. Lawrence was dismissed and Dave Jones brought in to provide some stability although he had little or no money to use in the transfer market and was forced to start the season with a number of free-transfer signings. The loss of Gabbidon and Collins who were sold to West Ham on the cheap, and to a lesser extent, Jobi McAnuff, could not be covered by free transfers or loan signings although Darren Purse did provide a solid base in central defence along with Dutchman Glenn Loovens.

One loan signing that did excite the fans was Jason Koumas who struck 12 goals during the season and made many more with some brilliant play from midfield. However, when it came to the crunch to make the deal permanent, Koumas was left in the lurch as Hammam never had the funds to secure his signature from West Brom.

Under the circumstances, Jones did well to steer the club through some difficult times both on and off the field. He lifted the Bluebirds back into the top half of the table but few supporters would have guessed the turnaround in the club's fortunes during the following season. Hammam had brought in Peter Ridsdale to oversee the building of the new stadium and sort out the finances, but it was soon evident that neither could be achieved while Hammam stayed at the club.

With the former owner finally agreeing to step down, the new stadium plans began to make progress and Jones was able to bring quality players to Ninian Park. His greatest coup was signing Michael Chopra from Newcastle United. Chops responded with 22 league goals and with Kevin McNaughton at full back and Roger Johnson pushing Purse and Loovens for a central defensive role, City shot to the top of the Championship at the end of August 2006, and remained there for three solid months.

28 August 2004, Cardiff City 0 Stoke City 1. Danny Gabbidon gets the better of Stoke's Ade Akinbiye

Peter Whittingham joined from Aston Villa midway through the season to add some additional quality to midfield, but once again City tailed off due mainly to lack of strength in depth and finished just below halfway.

Chopra's success was noted by Premier sides and he joined Sunderland for a £5m fee after just one season with the Bluebirds. The football world was shocked however when Robbie Fowler and Jimmy Floyd Hasselbaink both became Bluebirds in 2007 to get City fans believing that the bad old days were well and truly over. Injury curtailed Fowler's appearances but Hasselbaink proved his worth on numerous occasions, particularly in cup competitions. While the club remained in midtable for most of the season, they seemed to retain their best form for the FA Cup.

Chasetown were the first victims with City's youngest-ever first team player Aaron Ramsey netting one of the goals in a 3-1 victory in the third round.

Hereford United were the next opponents and it took a Steve Thompson penalty to see off the Bulls at Edgar Street.

High-flying Wolves came to Ninian Park in round five and Whittingham and Hasselbaink scored superb early individual goals to send the Bluebirds into a quarter-final meeting at Premier side, Middlesbrough.

Whittingham shone once again, beating five home players before shooting into the far corner, and then Johnson headed the Bluebirds to a brilliant victory and a Wembley semi-final appearance.

On a fantastic afternoon, Joe Ledley hooked in a first half winner against Barnsley and City were in the FA Cup final for the first time in 81 years.

The build-up to the game was superb, even if the match itself was scrappy. Kanu scored for Portsmouth after a mix-up between Peter Enckelman and Johnson and after Loovens had a goal disallowed for a handling offence, it was Pompey who ran out winners. Ridsdale and Jones knew that it would be difficult to top that experience and promotion was high on the agenda for 2008-09, City's last season at Ninian Park. Once again Jones's radar honed in on Scotland and he snapped up Ross McCormack from Motherwell for a small fee. The Scot would more than repay the money laid out by scoring regularly throughout the season.

Did You Know...

The first Welshman to score at the Cardiff City Stadium was David Edwards (Wolves) who netted for Wales against Scotland in November, 2009

Goalkeeper continued to be a problem for the team with a number of players being used after Alexander was allowed to leave for Ipswich Town and that surely unsettled the rest of the defence.

Aaron Ramsey joined Arsenal for £4.8m with best wishes from all supporters, and the same applied to Chris Gunter who joined Spurs for £2m after just a handful of first team games for the Bluebirds. Jay Bothroyd came in to join McCormack up front, and then all fans were delighted when Michael Chopra returned on loan from Sunderland.

Gavin Rae and McCormack were in such good form that both were selected for Scotland and the season ended with Joe Ledley having the honour of captaining Wales.

Sadly, as had happened in so many previous years, City's form deserted them in the final run-in and after being in the top six virtually all season, only one point was gained from the last four matches. They missed out on the play-offs by virtue of scoring one goal less than a Preston side that had beaten the Bluebirds 6-0 in April. Even so, a point at Sheffield Wednesday in the final game would have been enough but they lost 1-0 and 99 years of football at Ninian Park ended like a damp squib.

6 April, 2008 FA Cup semi-final, Cardiff City 1 Barnsley 0. Aaron Ramsey beats Jamal Campbell-Ryce to set up a City attack

The 2009-10 season began at the new Cardiff City Stadium and with it came the optimism that at last, the Bluebirds had the strength both on and off the field to reach their ultimate goal, the Premier Division. The first match at the stadium was a resounding 4-0 defeat of Scunthorpe United and City made a sound start to the new season with newcomers Mark Hudson, the new club skipper, and Anthony Gerrard providing a new centre back partnership while goalkeeper David Marshall had been recruited from relegated Norwich City.

Chopra was in great form early on and scored four times as Derby County were put to the sword in a 6-1 victory in September. The long-standing goalkeeper problems were also settled as Marshall proved a reliable shot-stopper, and with Bothroyd playing the best football of his career up front it was looking good on the field for the Bluebirds.

Sadly, all was not well off the pitch and in December 2009, HMRC issued a winding up order for non-payment of tax. The club agreed a payment plan with the Inland Revenue but were called back a second time when these payments were not met on time. The figure being quoted was £1.9m and in a final act at the High Court, the club were given an eight-week stay of execution during which they had to pay the outstanding amount or face administration.

Did You Know...
The first league goal scored at the Cardiff City Stadium by a Welshman came from Gareth Roberts for Doncaster Rovers in January 2010

To the credit of Dave Jones and the playing squad, they kept the club in the play-off positions during this cash crisis, while behind the scenes there was strenuous activity looking for outside investment to secure the future of the club.

On 17 April the Bluebirds made sure of a play-off place with a 1-0 victory at Queens Park Rangers thanks to a late header from Ledley and two weeks later it was announced that Malaysian investors headed by Tan Sri Vincent Tan Chee Yioun (Vincent Tan) and Datuk Chan Tien Ghee (TG), had agreed a deal to take a large stake in the club, removing any threat of Cardiff City being wound up.

A run of ten matches without defeat up to the last game of the season ensured there was no falling away as had happened over the last couple of years. Whittingham ended the season as joint top scorer in the Championship with 20 goals and with Bothroyd and Chopra also in double figures it was a confident side that travelled to the Walkers Stadium to face fifth placed Leicester City in the opening play-off match

A brilliant free kick by Whittingham secured a 1-0 first leg victory for the Bluebirds, setting up a remarkable night at the Cardiff City Stadium when the Foxes came looking for revenge. In front of the biggest crowd yet seen at the stadium, Chopra put City 2-0 up on aggregate but Nigel Pearson's side had scored three times by early in the second half to put themselves in with a real chance of playing Blackpool at Wembley.

Jay Bothroyd and Michael Chopra celebrate with City chairman Dato Chan Tien Ghee

Up stepped ice-cool Whittingham to bring the aggregate scores level with a spot-kick and after no further scoring, even in extra time, the tie went to penalties.

Chopra, McCormack, Ledley and Mark Kennedy all scored from the spot and as Marshall saved the fourth and fifth penalties from the Leicester players, the Bluebirds were through to face the Seasiders on 22 May in a match described as the richest prize in football.

Bluebirds fans made the M4 their own on a very hot day and one end of the stadium was decked in blue. Sadly, despite taking the lead twice through Chopra and Ledley, Blackpool struck back to score three before half time and with no further scoring in the second half, the Bluebirds missed out on a wonderful opportunity to take the giant leap up to the Premiership. However, outgoing chairman Peter Ridsdale had achieved what he set out to do and that was overseeing the construction of the new stadium, new training facilities, new investment, and a big increase in the average attendance figures. To do all that he sometimes sailed too close to the wind for comfort but without that attitude it is highly unlikely the club would be where it is today.

The new owners were officially in control the week after the Wembley defeat and they confirmed that they wanted only the best for Cardiff City. However it was not clear if this meant providing manager Dave Jones with funds for players, or whether it meant clearing the club's outstanding debts. Further monetary problems arose during the close season leading to a transfer embargo but gradually, the club began moving towards a far more solid financial base although new chairman Datuk Chan Tien Ghee stated a number of times that 'the house has to be in order before guests are invited'.

Did You Know...
The Cardiff City Stadium presently has an all-seater capacity of 26,828 with the possibility of increasing that in the future

The financial re-structuring is certainly taking place but it is a strange coincidence that back in those dimly lit days of 1910 the club also had to find a benefactor in Lord Ninian Crichton-Stuart to help achieve its objectives.

100 years on, with a magnificent new stadium in place, once again it is outside investment that will give Cardiff City, the Bluebirds, the opportunity of strengthening its position both on and off the field.

If the club can achieve anything like the success that came in those first seven years in the Football League then truly great times could be ahead.

2
WARTIME

Cardiff City played league football throughout the 1914-15 season, long after hostilities had started in Europe. The summer of 1915 saw the armed forces increase their recruitment and the Football League decided to disband all fixtures for 1915-16 to allow players to enlist. Although recognised leagues were no longer running, the Football League allowed regional leagues to sprout up, as much for morale purposes as anything else and the Bluebirds took part in the South West Combination between January and April 1916. Because of the undoubted strain on travelling, crowds were very low and the consequent drain on finances became a real cause for concern.

Several Bluebirds remained playing for the club including Jack Kneeshaw, Jack Evans, George Beare and Billy Hardy, who enlisted later, but manager Fred Stewart was left to select sides from local amateurs and any players on leave. At the end of that 1915-16 season, City withdrew from all competitions for the duration of World War One.

It was only after the end of the war in 1918 that players began returning to the club and City were very lucky in that only one player, Tom Witts, failed to return. A big blow however was the loss of Lord Ninian Crichton-Stuart who was killed in action on 2 October 1915. Fred Stewart had remained at the club through the war years building up his corn and coal merchants business in Roath so he was in an ideal position to organise friendly matches during 1918-19 until a resumption of league fixtures in the 1919-20 season.

Stewart had long since departed when once again the Football League was disrupted by World War Two in 1939 and Cyril Spiers was now manager of Cardiff City. The 1939-40 season had actually been started and the Bluebirds won both away fixtures at Norwich City and Swindon Town before losing 4-2 at home to Notts County on 2 September, 1939. The following day it was announced that Great Britain was at war and so the Football League was suspended. The effect on Cardiff City, and all other football clubs, was that contracted players left Ninian Park immediately as the Bluebirds tried to put their house in order financially.

Did You Know...
Guest players were allowed during the wartime matches and Bill Shankly, Raich Carter, Cliff Britton and Johnny Carey all played for Cardiff City

The Government requested once again that regional leagues should be organised to keep up morale so Spiers introduced a number of local amateur players as well as 'guest' players to make up the City's playing staff. This format of regional leagues and friendlies continued through the war years and many famous names appeared for the Bluebirds including Raich Carter, Jimmy Murphy, Johnny Carey and Bill Shankly.

On a positive note, Spiers was helped by the emergence of young players such as Billy Baker, Reg Parker, Ken Hollyman, Beriah Moore, Colin Gibson and Alf Sherwood. Billy James was another who showed great promise at this time but within a few months of the war he was captured by the Japanese while on active service and never fully recovered to resume his playing career.

At the end of the war in the summer of 1945, the Football League decided to use the 1945-46 season to help the clubs reorganise their affairs by keeping the regional leagues in operation. Cardiff City were more fortunate than most because they had kept manager Spiers throughout the hostilities and a number of young players had now become first team regulars.

On 17 November 1945, City entertained the mighty Moscow Dynamo who were on a short tour of Great Britain. A huge crowd totalling 31,000 packed into Ninian Park to watch the Russians rout the Bluebirds 10-1 in a magnificent display of attacking football. The 1945-46 season in Third Division South went well and City finished in second place to give plenty of optimism as the Football League officially returned the following season

World War One

1915-16
South-West Combination

08-Jan	Swindon Town 0 Cardiff City 2	Beare, Coates	
15-Jan	Cardiff City 1 Swindon Town 0	Coates	2,500
22-Jan	Cardiff City 1 Bristol City 0	E Jones	2,500
29-Jan	Cardiff City 1 Bristol Rovers 2	Evans (p)	
12-Feb	Southampton 6 Cardiff City 3	Coates, E Jones, Stone	
04-Mar	Cardiff City 2 Southampton 0	Beare, Durham (og)	1,500
11-Mar	Newport County 1 Cardiff City 5	Jenkins 4, E Jones	
18-Mar	Cardiff City 3 Newport County 1	E Jones 2, Coates	1,500
25-Mar	Portsmouth 4 Cardiff City 0		
01-Apr	Bristol Rovers 0 Cardiff City 2	Beare, E Jones	600
08-Apr	Bristol City 2 Cardiff City 0		2,000
15-Apr	Cardiff City 1 Portsmouth 2	Coates	

1915-16
Friendly Matches

04-Sep	Cardiff City 4 Bristol Rovers 1	Beare 2, Seymour, Stone	3,000
11-Sep	Cardiff City 1 Bristol City 0	Seymour	4,000
18-Sep	Bristol City 1 Cardiff City 1	Beare	2,500
25-Sep	Cardiff City 2 Portsmouth	Seymour, Stone	2,500
02-Oct	Cardiff City 0 Footballers Battalion 1		500
09-Oct	Bristol Rovers 3 Cardiff City 2	Millard, Beare	
16-Oct	Cardiff City 2 Bristol League 0	Davies, Seymour	200
23-Oct	Portsmouth 3 Cardiff City 2	Millard, Beare	2,000
06-Nov	Cardiff City 1 Barry Town 1	Evans	
13-Nov	Southampton 2 Cardiff City 2	Collier, Stone	
20-Nov	Cardiff City 6 Welsh Field Amb. X1 1	Davies 4, Hardy, Stone	1,000
27-Nov	Cardiff City 2 Mid Rhondda 3	Hardy, Davies	
11-Dec	Cardiff City 6 Welsh Regiment X1 3	Hardy 2, Stone 2, Hewitt, Davies	
18-Dec	Barry Town 1 Cardiff City 0		2,000
25-Dec	Merthyr Town 1 Cardiff City 2	Stone, Beare	
27-Dec	Cardiff City 0 Barnsley 0		2,000
01-Jan	Cardiff City 1 Southampton 0	Evans	250
05-Feb	Barry Town 3 Cardiff City 0		3,000
19-Feb	Cardiff City 0 Barry Town 1		
15-Apr	Cardiff City 2 Notts Forest 1	Coates 2	
22-Apr	Cardiff City 3 Swindon Town 2	Coates 2, Jones	

World War Two

1939-40

South West League

21-Oct	Bristol City 1 Cardiff City 1	Corkhill	6,545
28-Oct	Cardiff City 2 Swansea Town 2	Court, Sabin	5,000
04-Nov	Cardiff City 1 Plymouth Argyle 1	Court	4,000
11-Nov	Swindon Town 2 Cardiff City 2	Collins, Marshall	4,161
18-Nov	Cardiff City 0 Bristol Rovers 0		2,000
25-Nov	Newport County 3 Cardiff City 1	Marshall	2,228
02-Dec	Cardiff City 2 Torquay United 2	Anderson, Court	1,500
09-Dec	Cardiff City 7 Bristol City 3	Marshall 2, Court 2, Sabin 2, Egan	1,195
16-Dec	Swansea Town 4 Cardiff City 0		2,500
23-Dec	Plymouth Argyle 6 Cardiff City 2	Egan, og	2,671
30-Dec	Cardiff City 1 Swindon Town 1	James	3,000
06-Jan	Bristol Rovers 7 Cardiff City 0		1,012
13-Jan	Cardiff City 1 Newport County 0	Court	4,000
20-Jan	Torquay United 5 Cardiff City 0		1,200
10-Feb	Cardiff City 0 Plymouth Argyle 0		2,000
24-Feb	Cardiff City 1 Bristol Rovers 1	Pugh	3,000
09-Mar	Cardiff City 1 Torquay United 1	Pugh	3,000
16-Mar	Cardiff City 3 Bristol City 2	Boulter 2, Pugh	4,000
22-Mar	Bristol City 3 Cardiff City 2	Owen, Pugh	3,343
23-Mar	Swansea Town 1 Cardiff City 0		3,000
30-Mar	Plymouth Argyle 4 Cardiff City 1	Morris	3,541
06-Apr	Cardiff City 1 Swindon Town 1	Marshall	3,000
20-Apr	Swindon Town 2 Cardiff City 2	Collins 2	1,665
11-May	Torquay United 2 Cardiff City 4	James, Marshall, Moore, Parker	1,137
13-May	Cardiff City 4 Newport County 1	Parker, Tobin, Pugh, Moore	3,000
18-May	Cardiff City 2 Swansea Town 2	James, Tobin	2,000
25-May	Newport County 4 Cardiff City 1	Baker	600
01-Jun	Bristol Rovers 3 Cardiff City 3	Meads 2, James	1,210

League Cup

13-Apr	Cardiff City 1 Reading 1	Mitchell	3,000
17-Apr	Reading 1 Cardiff City 0		2,750

Welsh Cup

16-Dec	Ebbw Vale 0 Cardiff City 4	Pugh 3, Court	2,000
02-Mar	Cardiff City 1 Newport County 1	Owen	3,000
18-Mar	Newport County 5 Cardiff City 0		800

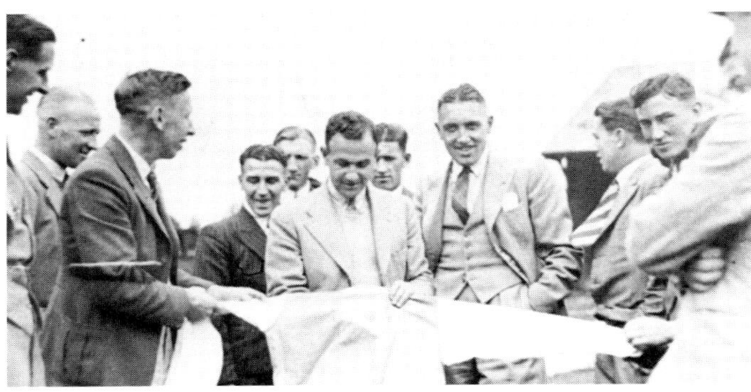

1939-40 season. The players reported for training and were shown their shirts numbered for the first time. Jimmy Kelso is inspecting the no. 3 shirt

1940-41

League South

31-Aug	Reading 2 Cardiff City 0		2,861
07-Sep	Cardiff City 2 Reading 2	James, Moore	3,000
14-Sep	Cardiff City 5 Birmingham City 2	Moore 3, James, Parker	2,175
21-Sep	Birmingham City 3 Cardiff City 2	Pugh, James	3,500
28-Sep	Cardiff City 2 Bristol City 2	James, Wrigglesworth	3,500
05-Oct	Bristol City 1 Cardiff City 0		1,546
12-Oct	Coventry City 5 Cardiff City 2	Parker 2	2,700
19-Oct	Cardiff City 2 Coventry City 2	James, Hollyman	3,000
26-Oct	Cardiff City 8 Swansea Town 0	James 3, Moore 3,Parker 2	4,000
09-Nov	Southampton 1 Cardiff City 3	Moore 2, Parker	2,000
16-Nov	Cardiff City 1 Southampton 1	Moore	1,500
23-Nov	Bristol City 4 Cardiff City 1	James	2,500
30-Nov	Cardiff City 5 Bristol City 1	James 2, Moore, Scott, Wood	2,000
07-Dec	Stoke City 5 Cardiff City 1	Steggles	1,800
14-Dec	Cardiff City 4 Stoke City 0	James 3, Morris	1,000
21-Dec	Bournemouth 2 Cardiff City 5	Moore 2, James, Baker, Parker	800
25-Dec	Swansea Town 1 Cardiff City 3	James 2, Moore	3,000
28-Dec	Cardiff City 1 Bournemouth 3	T Jones	4,000
11-Jan	Cardiff City 5 Bristol City 2	Moore 2, James 2, Joy	2,000
25-Jan	Swansea Town 2 Cardiff City 3	Moore 2, James	1,500
08-Feb	Bristol City 4 Cardiff City 7	Moore 4, Parker, Pugh, Williams	1,500
17-May	Cardiff City 4 West Brom 4	Parker 2, James 2	3,009
24-May	Cardiff City 4 Portsmouth 1	Moore 2, Parker, Walker (og)	2,723
31-May	Cardiff City 5 Wolves 1	James 2, Moore, Parker, T Jones	4,204

League Cup

15-Feb	Cardiff City 3 Swansea Town 2	Moore, Parker, James	4,000
01-Mar	Cardiff City 6 Swansea Town 2	Moore 3, Parker 2, James	4,000
08-Mar	Reading 0 Cardiff City 1	James	5,000
15-Mar	Cardiff City 4 Reading 1	James 2, Baker, Moore	10,000
22-Mar	Spurs 3 Cardiff City 3	Moore 2, Barnes	5,000
29-Mar	Cardiff City 2 Spurs 3	James, Parker	21,000

Western Regional League

05-Apr	Bath City 2 Cardiff City 1	James	1,500
12-Apr	Cardiff City 3 Lovells Athletic	James 2, Parker	2,500
14-Apr	Aberaman 2 Cardiff City 2	Moore, Parker	750
19-Apr	Lovells Athletic 2 Cardiff City 1	Moore	2,000
26-Apr	Cardiff City 5 Bath City 2	James 3, Moore 2	1,700
03-Jun	Cardiff City 1 Lovells Athletic 6	Hollyman	

1941-42

Football League (Southern Section)

Date	Match	Scorers	Attendance
30-Aug	West Brom 6 Cardiff City 3	James 2, Moore	4,462
06-Sep	Cardiff City 1 West Brom 1	Moore	4,647
27-Sep	Cardiff City 5 Southampton 3	Parker 2, Moore, Hollyman, James	3,930
04-Oct	Southampton 1 Cardiff City 3	Parker 2, Moore	2,000
11-Oct	Wolves 0 Cardiff City 3	Lewis, Moore, Perry	4,612
18-Oct	Cardiff City 2 Wolves 0	James, Parker	3,217
25-Oct	Cardiff City 0 Bournemouth 2		2,500
01-Nov	Bournemouth 3 Cardiff City 2	Moore, James	3,000
08-Nov	Cardiff City 6 Luton Town 1	James 3, Moore 2, Dare	2,500
15-Nov	Luton Town 2 Cardiff City 0		2,300
22-Nov	Cardiff City 1 Swansea Town 0	Parker	2,000
29-Nov	Swansea Town 4 Cardiff City 1	Parker	2,500
06-Dec	Cardiff City 8 Bristol City 2	Parker 3, Weir 3, Thomas, Steggles	3,000
13-Dec	Bristol City 2 Cardiff City 6	Weir 2, Wood 2, Parker, Dare	4,000
25-Dec	Cardiff City 2 Swansea Town 1	Moore, Parker	3,750

Football League War Cup Qualifiers and League

Date	Match	Scorers	Attendance
27-Dec	Southampton 2 Cardiff City 5	Parker 3, Morris, Butler	2,500
03-Jan	Cardiff City 9 Southampton 2	Parker 5, Moore 2, Morgan, Wood	5,000
10-Jan	Swansea Town 1 Cardiff City 1	Moore	4,000
17-Jan	Cardiff City 1 Swansea Town 1	Parker	5,000
24-Jan	Bristol City 8 Cardiff City 3	Moore 3	3,312
31-Jan	Cardiff City 0 Bristol City 2		6,000
07-Feb	Bournemouth 2 Cardiff City 1	Parker	2,000
14-Feb	Cardiff City 6 Bournemouth 0	Parker 3, Moore 2, Wood	5,300
21-Feb	Swansea Town 1 Cardiff City 5	Wright 3, Parker, Moore	5,000
28-Feb	Cardiff City 8 Swansea Town 1	Weir 3, Wood 2, Parker 2, Moore	7,000
14-Mar	Cardiff City 2 Luton Town 0	Fenton 2	5,000
21-Mar	Cardiff City 4 Swansea Town 1	Moore 2, Wright, Lewis	4,320
04-Apr	Cardiff City 3 Southampton 1	Moore 2, Fenton	5,000
06-Apr	Southampton 1 Cardiff City 1	Moore	3,600
11-Apr	Cardiff City 1 West Brom 1	Lewis	10,781
18-Apr	West Brom 3 Cardiff City 2	Shelley 2	10,198
25-Apr	Cardiff City 0 Northampton Town 1		3,460
02-May	Northampton Town 6 Cardiff City 1	Moore	2,271
25-May	Cardiff City 4 Swansea Town 1	Moore 3, Griffiths	3,720
30-May	Luton Town 4 Cardiff City 2	Hollyman 2	2,695

Did You Know...

The great Bill Shankly once played for Cardiff City. He was invited to play as a guest for the Bluebirds on 3 October 1942 at Ninian Park against Lovells Athletic. He refused any further offers as his match fee for the game was only 30 shillings (£1.50) and he found out that the Lovells players each received £5 per match

1942-43

Football League West

29-Aug	Bath City 3 Cardiff City 0		2,000
05-Sep	Cardiff City 2 Bath City 0	Moore, Clarke	2,563
12-Sep	Bristol City 9 Cardiff City 1	Clarke	2,743
19-Sep	Cardiff City 0 Bristol City 0		2,500
26-Sep	Cardiff City 4 Lovells Athletic 8	Moore, McAuley, Griffiths, Pugh	2,800
03-Oct	Lovells Athletic 1 Cardiff City 3	Clarke, Moore, McAuley	3,100
10-Oct	Swansea Town 2 Cardiff City 4	Clarke 2, K Griffiths 2	1,200
17-Oct	Cardiff City 5 Swansea Town 0	Clarke 2, Wright, Moore, Parker	2,500
24-Oct	Aberaman 2 Cardiff City 6	Moore 3, Wright 2, Clarke	500
31-Oct	Cardiff City 5 Aberaman 1	Grocott 2, Clarke 2, Moore	3,000
07-Nov	Lovells Athletic 1 Cardiff City 1	Moore	3,000
14-Nov	Cardiff City 0 Lovells Athletic 1		3,500
21-Nov	Cardiff City 1 Aberaman 1	Moore	2,500
28-Nov	Aberaman 2 Cardiff City 4	Clarke 3, Moore	720
05-Dec	Cardiff City 4 Bristol City 3	Morgan 3, Griffiths	3,000
12-Dec	Bristol City 5 Cardiff City 0		1,800
19-Dec	Cardiff City 1 Bath City 3	Morgan	1,000
25-Dec	Swansea Town 3 Cardiff City 1	Clarke	2,426

League Cup Qualifiers, league and League Cup West

26-Dec	Cardiff City 2 Swansea Town 2	K Griffiths, Wright	5,000
02-Jan	Bath City 2 Cardiff City 1	Moore	2,700
09-Jan	Cardiff City 0 Aberaman 1		2,000
16-Jan	Aberaman 3 Cardiff City 1	Handford (og)	640
23-Jan	Lovells Athletic 4 Cardiff City 0		5,000
30-Jan	Cardiff City 1 Lovells Athletic 4	Moore	1,800
06-Feb	Cardiff City 0 Bristol City 3		3,000
13-Feb	Bristol City 1 Cardiff City 1	Clarke	3,000
20-Feb	Swansea Town 1 Cardiff City 2	Clarke, Daly	2,000
27-Feb	Cardiff City 2 Bath City 5	Parker, Daly	3,000
06-Mar	Cardiff City 2 Swansea Town 0	Sparshott 2	2,000
13-Mar	Swansea Town 1 Cardiff City 1	Moore	2,000
20-Mar	Cardiff City 2 Lovells Athletic 5	Nairn 2	3,000
10-Apr	Cardiff City 2 Aberaman 3	Clarke, Evans	2,500
17-Apr	Bath City 4 Cardiff City 3	Clarke 2, Willicombe	1,500
24-Apr	Cardiff City 2 Swansea Town 5	Murphy, Moore	2,500
01-May	Bristol City 3 Cardiff City 0		2,500

Did You Know...

On 14 April, 1945, Cardiff City played Bristol City in a wartime Football League Cup tie. City won the first leg 2-1 at Ashton Gate so when the Robins led 2-1 at the end of full time extra time was needed. The game went on to last 202 minutes of playing time before Cardiff's Billy Rees scored a golden goal winner

1943-44

Football League West

28-Aug	Cardiff City 1 Lovells Athletic 2	K Griffiths	3,500
04-Sep	Lovells Athletic 3 Cardiff City 1	Moore	4,000
11-Sep	Cardiff City 4 Bristol City 1	Steggles, Williams, Sherwood	3,000
18-Sep	Bristol City 2 Cardiff City 1	Raybould	3,310
25-Sep	Bath City 2 Cardiff City 7	Clarke 2, Moore 2, Raybould,Williams, Court	3,500
02-Oct	Cardiff City 1 Bath City 3	Moore	4,000
09-Oct	Cardiff City 3 Aberaman 2	Moore 2, Williams	3,000
16-Oct	Aberaman 1 Cardiff City 2	Wood, Clarke	450
23-Oct	Cardiff City 5 Swansea Town 0	Williams 3, Moore, Clarke	4,500
30-Oct	Swansea Town 1 Cardiff City 3	Moore 2, Raybould	2,000
06-Nov	Cardiff City 1 Bristol City 0	Sherwood	3,000
13-Nov	Bristol City 1 Cardiff City 1	Wood	4,000
20-Nov	Cardiff City 3 Bath City 1	Williams 2, Clarke	3,500
27-Nov	Bath City 2 Cardiff City 1	Williams	2,300
04-Dec	Cardiff City 1 Swansea Town 0	Clarke	2,500
11-Dec	Swansea Town 2 Cardiff City 4	Raybould 2, Williams, Moore	1,000
18-Dec	Lovells Athletic 4 Cardiff City 1	Raybould	2,760
25-Feb	Cardiff City 5 Lovells Athletic 1	Moore 2, Williams 2, Clarke	3,000

League Cup Qualifiers, League

26-Dec	Bath City 3 Cardiff City 2	Clarke, Steggles	6,000
01-Jan	Cardiff City 1 Bath City 2	Sherwood	4,000
08-Jan	Cardiff City 7 Swansea Town 1	Moore 3, Sherwood, Rees, Carless, og	2,500
15-Jan	Swansea Town 1 Cardiff City 2	Rees, Wood	1,200
22-Jan	Aberaman 1 Cardiff City 2	Rees, Carless	200
29-Jan	Cardiff City 4 Aberaman 1	Williams 2, Raybould, Rees	3,000
05-Feb	Cardiff City 2 Bristol City 0	Moore, Rees	5,000
12-Feb	Bristol City 2 Cardiff City 0		4,000
19-Feb	Cardiff City 2 Lovells Athletic 0	Wood, Low (og)	6,000
26-Feb	Lovells Athletic 2 Cardiff City 1	Rees	7,000
04-Mar	Lovells Athletic 2 Cardiff City 0		6,000
11-Mar	Cardiff City 1 Lovells Athletic 0	Rees	10,000
18-Mar	Cardiff City 6 Aberaman 0	Moore 2, Rees 2, Clarke, Gibson	2,000
25-Mar	Aberaman 0 Cardiff City 5	Rees 2, Clarke, Carless, Gibson	1,000
01-Apr	Cardiff City 6 Bristol City 0	Rees 2, Carless, Gibson, Clarke, Preece (og)	1,000
08-Apr	Bristol City 1 Cardiff City 2	Rees, Rowe	2,000
10-Apr	Cardiff City 1 Lovells Athletic 1	Moor	3,000
15-Apr	Lovells Athletic 2 Cardiff City 0		3,000
22-Apr	Swansea Town 2 Cardiff City 4	Gibson 3, Lester	4,000
29-Apr	Cardiff City 3 Swansea Town 1	Rees 2, Carless	2,000

League Cup (West) – Cup Final

06-May	Bath City 4 Cardiff City 2	Gibson, Clarke	5,000
13-May	Cardiff City 0 Bath City 0		8,000

1944-45

Football League (West)

26-Aug	Cardiff City 4 Bristol City 1	Rees 3, Wood	6,000
02-Sep	Bristol City 3 Cardiff City 0		3,920
09-Sep	Cardiff City 2 Bath City 1	Wood, Rees	8,000
16-Sep	Bath City 2 Cardiff City 2	Wood, Rees	3,000
23-Sep	Cardiff City 8 Aberaman 2	Rees 3, Moore 2, Wood 2, Clarke	3,500
30-Sep	Aberaman 0 Cardiff City 6	Clarke 2, Wood 2, Rees, Moore	700
07-Oct	Cardiff City 1 Lovells Athletic 1	Moore	9,500
14-Oct	Lovells Athletic 1 Cardiff City 1	Moore	5,500
21-Oct	Cardiff City 3 Swansea Town 2	Wood, Clarke, Moore	7,000
28-Oct	Swansea Town 0 Cardiff City 4	Clarke 2, Wood, Rees	5,000
04-Nov	Aberaman 0 Cardiff City 3	Rees 2, Wood	800
11-Nov	Cardiff City 3 Aberaman 0	Wood 2, Moore	4,000
18-Nov	Bath City 4 Cardiff City 2	Rees, Raybould	3,000
25-Nov	Cardiff City 6 Bath City 2	Wood 2, Clarke 2, Rees 2	6,000
02-Dec	Swansea Town 1 Cardiff City 3	Wood, Moore, R Moore	3,500
09-Dec	Cardiff City 3 Swansea Town 1	Clarke, Wood, Rees	4,000
16-Dec	Lovells Athletic 2 Cardiff City 3	Clarke, Moore, Rees	4,800
23-Dec	Cardiff City 0 Lovells Athletic 1		10,000

League Cup Qualifiers, Second Championship

25-Dec	Cardiff City 3 Swansea Town 1	Lever, Clarke, Wood	4,000
30-Dec	Swansea Town 1 Cardiff City 3	Clarke, Rees, Wood	4,500
06-Jan	Lovells Athletic 1 Cardiff City 0		7,000
13-Jan	Cardiff City 3 Lovells Athletic 0	Rees 2, Moore	8,000
20-Jan	Cardiff City 4 Bath City 2	Rees 2, Gibson, Clarke	3,600
03-Feb	Aberaman 2 Cardiff City 5	Rees 4, Gibson	1,000
10-Feb	Cardiff City 0 Aberaman 0		3,500
17-Feb	Cardiff City 4 Bristol City 2	Moore 2, Lester, Gibson	11,500
24-Feb	Bristol City 1 Cardiff City 0		11,657
03-Mar	Bath City 1 Cardiff City 4	Rees 2, Gibson, Clarke	3,000
10-Mar	Swansea City 1 Cardiff City 0		4,000
17-Mar	Cardiff City 6 Swansea Town 2	Rees 4, Gibson, Lester	10,000
24-Mar	Cardiff City 1 Lovells Athletic 0	Rees	12,000
31-Mar	Lovells Athletic 0 Cardiff City 0		10,000
02-Apr	Cardiff City 3 Bristol City 2	Carless 2, Gibson	14,000
07-Apr	Bristol City 1 Cardiff City 2	Carless, Lester	20,714
14-Apr	*Cardiff City 2 Bristol City 2	Hollyman,. Rees	23,161
21-Apr	Wolves 3 Cardiff City 0		34,927
28-Apr	Cardiff City 2 Wolves 1	Hollyman, Carless	40,283
12-May	Cardiff City 0 Lovells Athletic 4		5,000

* This is the cup tie that lasted 202 minutes.

Skipper Fred Stansfield receives the Wartime League West trophy at Ninian Park

1945-46

Division Three South (Southern Section League and Cup)

Date	Match	Scorers	Attendance
24-Aug	Cardiff City 9 Bournemouth 3	Rees 4,Clarke 2, Gibson 2, Carless	10,000
31-Aug	Bournemouth 1 Cardiff City 5	Clarke 3, Rees, Wood	7,000
07-Sep	Cardiff City 6 Torquay United 0	Rees 2, Clarke, Wood, Carless, Gibson	12,000
11-Sep	Crystal Palace 3 Cardiff City 0		5,000
14-Sep	Torquay United 0 Cardiff City 7	Rees 3, Clarke 2, Lester, og	5,000
21-Sep	Cardiff City 4 Aldershot 1	Rees 2, Carless, Wood	16,000
28-Sep	Aldershot 1 Cardiff City 5	Rees, Moore, Carless, Clarke, Hollyman	7,000
05-Oct	Bristol City 3 Cardiff City 2	Moore, Rees	18,711
12-Oct	Cardiff City 2 Bristol City 4	Rees, Clarke	28,000
19-Oct	Cardiff City 4 Brighton 0	Rees 2, Clarke, og	22,000
26-Oct	Brighton 2 Cardiff City 3	Moore, Gibson, Clarke	8,500
02-Nov	Exeter City 3 Cardiff City 2	Gibson, Clarke	6,341
09-Nov	Cardiff City 0 Exeter City 0		18,000
30-Nov	Swindon Town 1 Cardiff City 2	Wood, og	11,876
07-Dec	Cardiff City 3 Swindon Town 0	Lever, Clarke, Wood	6,000
14-Dec	Cardiff City 2 Reading 1	Wood 2	8,000
21-Dec	Reading 3 Cardiff City 1	Rees	5,295
24-Dec	Bristol Rovers 2 Cardiff City 2	Unknown	8,000
25-Dec	Cardiff City 4 Bristol Rovers 2	Clarke 2, Hollyman, Allen	18,000
28-Dec	Cardiff City 6 Crystal Palace 2	Wright 2, Allen 2, Hollyman 2	25,000
04-Jan	Cardiff City 1 West Brom 1	Allen	33,000
08-Jan	West Brom 4 Cardiff City 0		18,025
11-Jan	Watford 1 Cardiff City 7	Clarke 2, Wright 2, Allen 2, Tennant	7,800
18-Jan	Cardiff City 0 Watford 2		14,000
25-Jan	Exeter City 2 Cardiff City 1	Haddon	8,000
01-Feb	Cardiff City 5 Exeter City 1	Rees 2, Wright, Lever, Clarke	15,000
08-Feb	Torquay United 1 Cardiff City 0		4,000
15-Feb	Cardiff City 3 Torquay United 0	Rees 2, Allen	14,700
22-Feb	Bristol Rovers 1 Cardiff City 0		11,200
01-Mar	Cardiff City 3 Bristol Rovers 0	Richards 3	18,000
08-Mar	Bristol City 3 Cardiff City 2	Hollyman, Allen	17,375
15-Mar	Cardiff City 3 Bristol City 2	Hill, Allen (p), Clarke	19,000
22-Mar	Swindon Town 3 Cardiff City 2	Rees, Moore	11,779
29-Mar	Cardiff City 2 Swindon Town 0	Allen 2	19,500
05-Apr	Reading 3 Cardiff City 2	Clarke, Richards	11,000
12-Apr	Cardiff City 5 Reading 2	Richards 2, Rees, Clarke, Gibson	21,500
19-Apr	Crystal Palace 1 Cardiff City 1	Clarke	17,500
21-Apr	Cardiff City 3 Crystal Palace 0	Allen, Rees, og	29,000

3
FA CUP

The FA Cup is the oldest and most famous Cup competition in the world and the final, now played at the new Wembley Stadium, is watched by millions all over the globe. Cardiff City made an immediate impact when, in their first season as a League club, they reached the semi-final only to be beaten in a replay by Wolves. It was not long before the Bluebirds did reach the final only to lose 1-0 to Sheffield United in 1925. It was only the third time the final had taken place at the newly built Wembley Stadium. Previous finals were held at various grounds with Old Trafford staging the last one before the onset of World War One, and Stamford Bridge hosting the 1920, 1921 and 1922 finals.

City's greatest achievement came in 1927 with the victory over Arsenal and while that happened many years ago, every Bluebird fan cheered the side on at Wembley against Portsmouth as the Bluebirds went on the march in 2008. So there have been many good memories for the club in the FA Cup, including a record 8-0 victory at Ninian Park over Hendon in 1931, but there have also been a number of dark times brought about by home defeats to Dartford (1935), Weymouth (1982), Bath (1991) and away at Hayes (1990). Billy Hardy played an incredible 56 FA Cup ties for the Bluebirds, while Len Davies bagged 19 cup goals in his 33 appearances.

A portrait of Jack Evans, Cardiff City's first professional player

1910-11

Preliminary Round, 17 September, 1910. Cardiff City 3 Bath City 1 (5,000)

Bluebirds; Ted Husbands; Jim McKenzie, John Duffy; Bob Lawrie, John Ramsay, Davy McDougall; James McDonald, Tom Abley, Bob Peake, Billy Watt, Jack Evans
Scorers; Bob Peake 2, Billy Watt

Round One, 1 October, 1910. Cardiff City 0 Merthyr Town 1 (12,800)

Bluebirds; Ted Husbands; Jim McKenzie, John Duffy; Bob Lawrie, John Ramsay, Davy McDougall; James McDonald, Tom Abley, Bob Peake, Billy Watt, Jack Evans

1911-12

Qualifying Round One, 16 September, 1911. Cardiff City 3 Cardiff Corinthians 0 (3,000)

Bluebirds; George Germaine; Arthur Waters, John Duffy; Bob Lawrie, George Latham, Billy Hardy; Harry Tracey, Jack Burton, Harry Featherstone, Tom Abley, Jack Evans
Scorers; Harry Featherstone, Tom Abley, George Latham

Qualifying Round Two, 30 September, 1911. Cardiff City 2 Mardy 0 (2,900)
Bluebirds; Ted Husbands; Bob Leah, John Duffy; Bob Lawrie, Eddie Thompson, Billy Hardy; Harry Tracey, Jack Burton, Harry Featherstone, Tom Abley, Jack Evans
Scorers; Harry Featherstone, Tom Abley

Qualifying Round Three, 14 October, 1911. Merthyr Town 1 Cardiff City 1 (8,000)
Bluebirds; Ted Husbands; Bob Leah, John Duffy; Bob Lawrie, Eddie Thompson, Billy Hardy; Harry Tracey, Jack Burton, Harry Featherstone, Tom Abley, Jack Evans
Scorer; Jack Evans

Qualifying Round Three (replay), 18 October, 1911. Cardiff City 1 Merthyr Town 2 (5,200)
Bluebirds; Ted Husbands; Bob Leah, John Duffy; Bob Lawrie, George Latham, Billy Hardy; Harry Tracey, Jack Burton, Harry Featherstone, Tom Abley, Jack Evans
Scorer; Jack Evans

1912-13

Qualifying Round One, 12 October, 1912. Merthyr Town 1 Cardiff City 5 (11,500)
Bluebirds; Jack Kneeshaw; Tommy Doncaster, Bob Leah; Henry Harvey, Pat Cassidy, Billy Hardy; Harry Tracey, Jack Burton, Billy Devlin, Harry Keggans, Jack Evans
Scorers; Billy Devlin 3, Henry Harvey, Jack Burton

Qualifying Round Two, 2 November, 1912. Cardiff City 2 Pontypridd 1 (12,000)
Bluebirds; Jack Kneeshaw; Tommy Doncaster, Bob Leah; Henry Harvey, L Saunders, Billy Hardy; Harry Tracey, George Burton, Harry Featherstone, Jack Burton, Billy Gaughan
Scorers; George Burton, Jack Burton

Qualifying Round Three, 16 November, 1912. Llanelly 1 Cardiff City 4 (4,000)
Bluebirds; Jack Kneeshaw; Tommy Doncaster, Bob Leah; Henry Harvey, Pat Cassidy, Billy Hardy; Harry Tracey, George Burton, Billy Devlin, Jack Burton, Jack Evans
Scorers; George Burton, Harry Tracey, Jack Evans, og.

Qualifying Round Four, 30 November, 1912. Cardiff City 5 Exeter City 1 (14,000)
Bluebirds; Billy Douglas; Tommy Doncaster, Bob Leah; Henry Harvey, Pat Cassidy, Billy Hardy; Harry Tracey, George Burton, Billy Devlin, Jack Burton, Jack Evans
Scorers; Billy Devlin 2, Henry Harvey, George Burton, Jack Burton

Qualifying Round Five, 14 December, 1912. Cardiff City 0 Southend 3 (7,000)
Bluebirds; Jack Kneeshaw; Tommy Doncaster, Bob Leah; Henry Harvey, Pat Cassidy, Billy Hardy; Harry Tracey, George Burton, Billy Devlin, Jack Burton, Jack Evans

Did You Know...
When Ninian Park was officially opened on 1 September, 1910, both teams had to use the same changing room and washing facilities, and this continued until 1913-14 when the club installed separate rooms for each team

1913-14

Qualifying Round Four, 29 November, 1913. Swansea Town 2 Cardiff City 0 (12,000)
Bluebirds; Jack Kneeshaw; Tommy Doncaster, Dr JL McBean; Henry Harvey, Pat Cassidy, Billy Hardy; J Bennett, James Henderson, Tom Robertson, Jack Burton, Jack Evans

1914-15

Round One, 9 January, 1915. Bristol City 2 Cardiff City 0 (15,000)
Bluebirds; Jack Kneeshaw; Charlie Brittan, Arthur Layton; Henry Harvey, Pat Cassidy, Billy Hardy; George Beare, Arthur Goddard, Billy Devlin, George West, Jack Evans

1919-20

Round One, 10 January, 1920. Cardiff City 2 Oldham Athletic 0 (21,921)
Bluebirds; Jack Kneeshaw; Arthur Layton, Albert Barnett; Billy Hardy, Bert Smith, Fred Keenor; George Beare, Billy Grimshaw, Billy Cox, George West, Jack Evans
Scorers; George West, Jack Evans

Round Two, 31 January, 1920. Wolverhampton Wanderers 1 Cardiff City 2 (36,475)
Bluebirds; Jack Kneeshaw; Arthur Layton, Albert Barnett; Billy Hardy, Bert Smith, Fred Keenor; George Beare, Billy Grimshaw, Billy Cox, George West, Jack Evans
Scorers; George Beare, Bert Smith

Round Three, 21 February, 1920. Bristol City 2 Cardiff City 1 (32,452)
Bluebirds; Jack Kneeshaw; Arthur Layton, Albert Barnett; Billy Hardy, Bert Smith, Fred Keenor; George Beare, Billy Grimshaw, Billy Cox, George West, Jack Evans
Scorer; George Beare

5 March 1921, FA Cup Quarter final. Cardiff City 1 Chelsea 0. City's centre forward Arthur Cashmore takes a tumble as Chelsea keeper Jimmy Molyneux punches clear

1920-21

Round One, 8 January, 1921. Sunderland 0 Cardiff City 1 (41,923)
Bluebirds; Jack Kneeshaw; Charlie Brittan, Jimmy Blair; Fred Keenor, Bert Smith, Billy Hardy; George Beare, Jimmy Gill, Arthur Cashmore, Albert Barnett, Jack Evans
Scorer; George Beare

Round Two, 29 January, 1921. Brighton 0 Cardiff City 0 (20,260)
Bluebirds; Ben Davies; Charlie Brittan, Jimmy Blair; Fred Keenor, Bert Smith, Billy Hardy; George Beare, Jimmy Gill, Arthur Cashmore, Albert Barnett, Jack Evans

Round Two (replay), 2 February, 1921. Cardiff City 1 Brighton 0 (31,000)
Bluebirds; Ben Davies; Charlie Brittan, Jimmy Blair; Fred Keenor, Bert Smith, Billy Hardy; George Beare, Jimmy Gill, Arthur Cashmore, George West, Jack Evans
Scorer; Arthur Cashmore

Round Three, 19 February, 1921. Southampton 0 Cardiff City 1 (21,363)
Bluebirds; Ben Davies; Charlie Brittan, Jimmy Blair; Fred Keenor, Bert Smith, Billy Hardy; Billy Grimshaw, Jimmy Gill, Arthur Cashmore, George Beare, Joe Clark
Scorer; Jimmy Gill

Round Four (Q/F), 5 March, 1921. Cardiff City 1 Chelsea 0 (50,000)
Bluebirds; Ben Davies; Charlie Brittan, Jimmy Blair; Fred Keenor, Bert Smith, Billy Hardy; George Beare, Jimmy Gill, Arthur Cashmore, Albert Barnett, Jack Evans
Scorer; Arthur Cashmore

Semi-final, Cardiff City 0 Wolverhampton Wanderers 0 (Anfield, 42,000)
Bluebirds; Ben Davies; Charlie Brittan, Jimmy Blair; Fred Keenor, Bert Smith, Billy Hardy; George Beare, Jimmy Gill, Arthur Cashmore, Albert Barnett, Jack Evans

Semi-final (replay), Cardiff City 1 Wolverhampton Wanderers 3 (Old Trafford, 45,000)
Bluebirds; Ben Davies; Charlie Brittan, Jimmy Blair; Fred Keenor, Bert Smith, Billy Hardy; George Beare, Billy Grimshaw, Arthur Cashmore, Albert Barnett, Jack Evans
Scorer; Fred Keenor (p)

1921-22

Round One, 7 January, 1922. Manchester United 1 Cardiff City 4 (25,000)
Bluebirds; Ben Davies; Charlie Brittan, Jack Page; Herbie Evans, Jimmy Blair, Billy Hardy; Billy Grimshaw, Joe Clennell, Len Davies, Harry Nash, Joe Clark
Scorers; Len Davies 2, Harry Nash, Joe Clennell

Round Two, 28 January, 1922. Southampton 1 Cardiff City 1 (19,291)
Bluebirds; Ben Davies; Jack Page, Jimmy Blair; Herbie Evans, Bert Smith, Billy Hardy; Billy Grimshaw, Jimmy Gill, Len Davies, Joe Clennell, Jack Evans
Scorer; Jimmy Gill

Round Two (replay), 1 February, 1922. Cardiff City 2 Southampton 0 (40,000)
Bluebirds; Ben Davies; Jack Page, Jimmy Blair; Herbie Evans, Bert Smith, Billy Hardy; Billy Grimshaw, Jimmy Gill, Len Davies, Joe Clennell, Joe Clark
Scorers; Jimmy Gill, Joe Clennell

Round Three, 18 February, 1922. Cardiff City 4 Nottingham Forest 1 (50,470)
Bluebirds; Ben Davies; Jack Page, Jimmy Blair; Herbie Evans, Bert Smith, Billy Hardy; Billy Grimshaw, Jimmy Gill, Len Davies, Joe Clennell, Jack Evans
Scorers; Len Davies 2, Jimmy Gill, Joe Clennell

Round Four (Q/F), 4 March, 1922. Cardiff City 1 Tottenham Hotspur 1 (51,000)
Bluebirds; Ben Davies; Jack Page, Jimmy Blair; Herbie Evans, Bert Smith, Billy Hardy; Billy Grimshaw, Jimmy Gill, Len Davies, Joe Clennell, Jack Evans
Scorer; Len Davies

9 March 1922, FA Cup Q-final replay. Spurs 2 Cardiff City 1. City keeper Ben Davies punches a Spurs corner clear closely watched by Billy Hardy while Jimmy Nelson guards the goal-line

Round Four (replay), 9 March, 1922. Tottenham Hotspur 2 Cardiff City 1 (53,626)
Bluebirds; Ben Davies; Jack Page, Jimmy Blair; Herbie Evans, Fred Keenor, Billy Hardy; Billy Grimshaw, Jimmy Gill, Len Davies, Joe Clennell, Jack Evans
Scorer; Jimmy Gill

1922-23

Round One, 13 January, 1923. Cardiff City 1 Watford 1 (34,000)
Bluebirds; Tom Farquharson; Jack Page, Jimmy Blair; Fred Keenor, Bert Smith, Billy Hardy; Billy Grimshaw, Jimmy Gill, Ken McDonald, Joe Clennell, Jack Evans
Scorer; Jack Evans (p)

Round One (replay), 17 January, 1923. Watford 2 Cardiff City 2 (12,720)
Bluebirds; Ben Davies; Charlie Brittan, Jimmy Blair; Herbie Evans, Bert Smith, Billy Hardy; Billy Grimshaw, Jimmy Gill, Len Davies, Joe Clennell, Jack Evans
Scorers; Len Davies, Joe Clennell

Round One (second replay), 22 January, 1923. Cardiff City 2 Watford 1 (Villa Park, 15,000)
Bluebirds; Ben Davies; Jimmy Nelson, Jimmy Blair; Herbie Evans, Bert Smith, Fred Keenor; Billy Grimshaw, Jimmy Gill, Len Davies, Joe Clennell, Jack Evans.
Scorers; Herbie Evans, Len Davies

Round Two, 3 February, 1923. Leicester City 0 Cardiff City 1 (35,680)
Bluebirds; Ben Davies; Jimmy Nelson, Jimmy Blair; Herbie Evans, Bert Smith, Fred Keenor; Billy Grimshaw, Jimmy Gill, Len Davies, Joe Clennell, Jack Evans
Scorer; Len Davies

Round Three, 24 February, 1923. Cardiff City 2 Tottenham Hotspur 3 (54,000)
Bluebirds; Ben Davies; Jimmy Nelson, Jimmy Blair; Herbie Evans, Edward Jenkins, Fred Keenor; Billy Grimshaw, Jimmy Gill, Len Davies, Joe Clennell, Jack Evans
Scorers; Jimmy Gill, Jack Evans (p)

1923-24

Round One, 12 January, 1924. Cardiff City 0 Gillingham 0 (20,000)
Bluebirds; Tom Farquharson; Jimmy Nelson, Jimmy Blair; Herbie Evans, Fred Keenor, Billy Hardy; Dennis Lawson, Jimmy Gill, Len Davies, Joe Clennell, Jack Evans

Round One (replay), 16 January, 1924. Gillingham 0 Cardiff City 2 (19,472)
Bluebirds; Tom Farquharson; Jimmy Nelson, Jimmy Blair; Herbie Evans, Fred Keenor, Billy Hardy; Dennis Lawson, Jimmy Gill, Len Davies, Joe Clennell, Jack Evans
Scorers; Jimmy Gill, Len Davies

Round Two, 2 February, 1924. Cardiff City 1 Arsenal 0 (35,000)
Bluebirds; Tom Farquharson; Jimmy Nelson, Jack Page; Herbie Evans, Fred Keenor, Billy Hardy; Dennis Lawson, Jimmy Gill, Len Davies, Joe Clennell, Jack Evans
Scorer; Jimmy Gill

Round Three, 23 February, 1924. Cardiff City 3 Bristol City 0 (50,000)
Bluebirds; Tom Farquharson; Jimmy Nelson, Jimmy Blair; Herbie Evans, Fred Keenor, Billy Hardy; Dennis Lawson, Jimmy Gill, Len Davies, Joe Clennell, Jack Evans
Scorers; Jimmy Gill 2, Joe Clennell

Round Four (Q/F), 8 March, 1924. Manchester City 0 Cardiff City 0 (76,166)
Bluebirds; Tom Farquharson; Jimmy Nelson, Jimmy Blair; Herbie Evans, Fred Keenor, Billy Hardy; Dennis Lawson, Jimmy Gill, Len Davies, Joe Clennell, Jack Evans

Round Four (replay), Cardiff City 0 Manchester City 1 (aet) (50,000)
Bluebirds; Tom Farquharson; Jimmy Nelson, Jimmy Blair; Herbie Evans, Fred Keenor, Billy Hardy; Dennis Lawson, Jimmy Gill, Len Davies, Joe Clennell, Jack Evans

1924-25

Round One, 10 January, 1925. Cardiff City 0 Darlington 0 (21,150)
Bluebirds; Tom Farquharson; Jimmy Nelson, Billy Hardy; Harry Wake, Fred Keenor, Joe Nicholson; Dennis Lawson, Jimmy Gill, Len Davies, Harry Beadles, Jack Evans

Round One (replay), 14 January, 1925. Darlington 0 Cardiff City 0 (aet) (18,808)
Cardiff City; Tom Farquharson; Jimmy Nelson, Jimmy Blair; Harry Wake, Fred Keenor, Billy Hardy; Dennis Lawson, Willie Davies, Len Davies, Harry Beadles, Jack Evans

Round One (second replay), 19 January, 1925. Cardiff City 2 Darlington 0 (Anfield, 22,465)
Bluebirds; Tom Farquharson; Jimmy Nelson, Jimmy Blair; Harry Wake, Fred Keenor, Billy Hardy; Dennis Lawson, Willie Davies, Len Davies, Harry Beadles, Jack Evans
Scorers; Willie Davies, Len Davies

Round Two, 31 January, 1925. Cardiff City 1 Fulham 0 (20,000)
Bluebirds; Tom Farquharson; Jimmy Nelson, Jimmy Blair; Harry Wake, Fred Keenor, Billy Hardy; Willie Davies, Jimmy Gill, Len Davies, Harry Beadles, Jack Evans
Scorer; Len Davies

Round Three, 21 February, 1925. Notts County 0 Cardiff City 2 (39,000)
Bluebirds; Tom Farquharson; Jimmy Nelson, Jimmy Blair; Harry Wake, Fred Keenor, Billy Hardy; Dennis Lawson, Jimmy Gill, Joe Nicholson, Harry Beadles, Jack Evans
Scorers; Joe Nicholson, Jimmy Gill

Round Four (Quarter-final), 7 March, 1925. Cardiff City 2 Leicester City 1 (50,272)
Bluebirds; Tom Farquharson; Jimmy Nelson, Jimmy Blair; Harry Wake, Fred Keenor, Billy Hardy; Dennis Lawson, Jimmy Gill, Joe Nicholson, Harry Beadles, Willie Davies
Scorers; Willie Davies, Harry Beadles

Semi-final, 28 March, 1925. Blackburn Rovers 1 Cardiff City 3 (Meadow Lane, Nottingham, 20,000)
Bluebirds; Tom Farquharson; Jimmy Nelson, Jimmy Blair; Harry Wake, Fred Keenor, Billy Hardy; Willie Davies, Jimmy Gill, Joe Nicholson, Harry Beadles, Jack Evans
Scorers; Harry Beadles, Joe Nicholson, Jimmy Gill

Final, 25 April, 1925. Cardiff City 0 Sheffield United 1 (Wembley Stadium, 91,763)
Bluebirds; Tom Farquharson; Jimmy Nelson, Jimmy Blair; Harry Wake, Fred Keenor, Billy Hardy; Willie Davies, Jimmy Gill, Joe Nicholson, Harry Beadles, Jack Evans

1925-26

Round Three, Cardiff City 2 Burnley 2 (30,000)
Bluebirds; Joe Hills; Jimmy Nelson, Tom Watson; Joe Nicholson, Tom Sloan, Billy Hardy; Willie Davies, Len Davies, Hughie Ferguson, Joe Cassidy, George McLachlan
Scorers; Joe Cassidy, Len Davies

Round Three (replay), 13 January, 1926. Burnley 0 Cardiff City 2 (26,811)
Bluebirds; Joe Hills; Jimmy Nelson, Tom Watson; Joe Nicholson, Jimmy Blair, Tom Sloan; Dennis Lawson, Willie Davies, Hughie Ferguson, Joe Cassidy, George McLachlan
Scorers; Hughie Ferguson 2

23 April 1927, FA Cup Final. Cardiff City 1 Arsenal 0. Man of the match Billy Hardy heads clear from Arsenal skipper Charles Buchan

Round Four, 30 January, 1926, Cardiff City 0 Newcastle United 2 (42,000)
Bluebirds; Joe Hills; Jimmy Nelson, Tom Watson; Joe Nicholson, Tom Sloan, Billy Hardy; Dennis Lawson, Sam Smith, Hughie Ferguson, Joe Cassidy, George McLachlan

1926-27

Round Three, 8 January, 1927. Cardiff City 2 Aston Villa 1 (30,000)
Bluebirds; Tom Farquharson; Jimmy Nelson, Tom Watson; Sam Irving, Tom Sloan, Billy Hardy; Hughie Ferguson, Harry Wake, Len Davies, Ernie Curtis, Percy Richards
Scorers; Len Davies, Ernie Curtis

Round Four, 29 January, 1927. Darlington 0 Cardiff City 2 (12,986)
Bluebirds; Tom Farquharson; Jimmy Nelson, Tom Watson; Sam Irving, Tom Sloan, Billy Hardy; Hughie Ferguson, Harry Wake, Len Davies, Ernie Curtis, George McLachlan
Scorers; George McLachlan, Hughie Ferguson

Round Five, 19 February, 1927. Bolton Wanderers 0 Cardiff City 2 (49,463)
Bluebirds; Tom Farquharson; Jimmy Nelson, Tom Watson; Fred Keenor, Tom Sloan, Billy Hardy; Hughie Ferguson, Sam Irving, Len Davies, Ernie Curtis, George McLachlan
Scorers; Hughie Ferguson (p), Len Davies

Round Six (Q/F), 5 March, 1927. Chelsea 0 Cardiff City 0 (70,184)
Bluebirds; Tom Farquharson; Jimmy Nelson, Tom Watson; Fred Keenor, Tom Sloan, Billy Hardy; Hughie Ferguson, Sam Irving, Len Davies, Ernie Curtis, George McLachlan

Round Six (replay), 9 March, 1927. Cardiff City 3 Chelsea 2 (47,853)
Bluebirds; Tom Farquharson; Jimmy Nelson, Tom Watson; Fred Keenor, Tom Sloan, Billy Hardy; Hughie Ferguson, Sam Irving, Len Davies, Ernie Curtis, George McLachlan
Scorers; Sam Irving, Len Davies, Hughie Ferguson (p)

25 April 1927. Fred Keenor holds the FA Cup outside Cardiff General Station on City's return from Wembley. Club chairman Walter Parker is wearing the bowler hat

Semi-final, 26 March, 1927. Cardiff City 3 Reading 0 (Molineux, 39,476)
Bluebirds; Tom Farquharson; Jimmy Nelson, Tom Watson; Fred Keenor, Tom Sloan, Billy Hardy; Harry Wake, Sam Irving, Hughie Ferguson, Len Davies, George McLachlan
Scorers; Hughie Ferguson 2, Harry Wake

Final, 23 April, 1927. Cardiff City 1 Arsenal 0 (Wembley Stadium, 93,206)
Bluebirds; Tom Farquharson; Jimmy Nelson, Tom Watson; Fred Keenor, Tom Sloan, Billy Hardy; Ernie Curtis, Sam Irving, Hughie Ferguson, Len Davies, George McLachlan
Scorer; Hughie Ferguson

1927-28

Round Three, 14 January, 1928. Cardiff City 2 Southampton 1 (23,000)
Bluebirds; Tom Farquharson; Jimmy Nelson, Billy Hardy; George Blackburn, Fred Keenor, Tom Sloan; Billy Thirlaway, Harry Wake, Hughie Ferguson, Len Davies, George McLachlan
Scorers; Hughie Ferguson, Len Davies

Round Four, 28 January, 1928. Cardiff City 2 Liverpool 1 (20,000)
Bluebirds; Tom Farquharson; Jimmy Nelson, Tom Watson; Harry Wake, Fred Keenor, Billy Hardy; Billy Thirlaway, Sam Irving, Hughie Ferguson, Len Davies, George McLachlan
Scorers; George McLachlan, Jimmy Nelson

Round Five, 18 February, 1928. Nottingham Forest 2 Cardiff City 1 (30,500)
Bluebirds; Tom Farquharson; Jimmy Nelson, Jack Jennings; Harry Wake, Fred Keenor, Billy Hardy; Billy Thirlaway, Sam Irving, Hughie Ferguson, Len Davies, George McLachlan
Scorer; Hughie Ferguson

1928-29

Round Three, 12 January, 1929. Aston Villa 6 Cardiff City 1 (51,242)
Bluebirds; Tommy Hampson; Jack Jennings, Billy Hardy; Tom Helsby, George McLachlan, Fred Keenor; Billy Thirlaway, Harry Wake, Albert Miles, Walter Robbins, Freddie Warren
Scorer; Billy Hardy

1929-30

Round Three, 11 January, 1930. Liverpool 1 Cardiff City 2 (50,141)
Bluebirds; Tom Farquharson; Jack Jennings, Bill Roberts; Harry Wake, Fred Keenor, George Blackburn; Billy Thirlaway, Len Davies, Jim Munro, Matthew Robinson, Jimmy McGrath
Scorer; Len Davies 2

Round Four, 25 January, 1930, Sunderland 2 Cardiff City 1 (49,424)
Bluebirds; Tom Farquharson; Jack McJennett, Bill Roberts; Harry Wake, Fred Keenor, George Blackburn; Billy Thirlaway, Len Davies, Jim Munro, Matthew Robinson, Jimmy McGrath
Scorer; Len Davies

1930-31

Round Three, 10 January, 1931. Brentford 2 Cardiff City 2 (16,500)
Bluebirds; Tom Farquharson; Jock Smith, Tom Ware; Tom Helsby, Fred Keenor, Jimmy McGrath; George Emmerson, Albert Valentine, Ralph Williams, Les Jones, Walter Robbins
Scorers; Les Jones, Albert Valentine

Round Three (replay), 14 January, 1931. Cardiff City 1 Brentford 2 (25,000)
Bluebirds; Tom Farquharson; Jack McJennett, Tom Ware; Tom Helsby, Fred Keenor, Jimmy McGrath; George Emmerson, Albert Valentine, Ralph Williams, Les Jones, Walter Robbins
Scorer; Walter Robbins

Did You Know...
At the end of 1933-34, the Bluebirds finished bottom of Division Three (South) and had to apply for re-election to the league, just seven years after winning the FA Cup at Wembley

1931-32

Round One, 28 November, 1931, Cardiff City 8 Enfield 0 (6,321)
Bluebirds; Tom Farquharson; Jock Smith, Bill Roberts; Frank Harris, Jack Galbraith, Peter Ronan; George Emmerson, Albert Keating, Harry O'Neill, Walter Robbins, Jim McCambridge
Scorers; Albert Keating 3, George Emmerson 2, Harry O'Neill 2, Frank Harris

Round Two, 12 December, 1931. Cardiff City 4 Clapton Orient 0 (10,500)
Bluebirds; Tom Farquharson; Jock Smith, Bill Roberts; Frank Harris, Jack Galbraith, Peter Ronan; George Emmerson, Albert Keating, Harry O'Neill, Walter Robbins, Jim McCambridge
Scorers; Jim McCambridge, Albert Keating, George Emmerson, og

Round Three, 9 January, 1932. Bradford (Park Avenue) 2 Cardiff City 0 (18,343)
Bluebirds; Tom Farquharson; Jock Smith, Bill Roberts; Frank Harris, Jack Galbraith, Peter Ronan; George Emmerson, Albert Keating, Jim McCambridge, Les Jones, Walter Robbins

1932-33

Round One, 26 November, 1932. Cardiff City 1 Bristol Rovers 1 (11,000)
Bluebirds; Tom Farquharson; Eric Morris, Eddie Jenkins; Frank Harris, Jack Galbraith, Peter Ronan; George Emmerson, Freddie Hill, Jim McCambridge, Les Jones, Stan Cribb
Scorer; Frank Harris

Round One (replay), 30 November, 1932. Bristol Rovers 4 Cardiff City 1 (9,000)
Bluebirds; Tom Farquharson; Eric Morris, Eddie Jenkins; Frank Harris, Jack Galbraith, Peter Ronan; George Emmerson, Freddie Hill, Jim McCambridge, Les Jones, Stan Cribb
Scorer; Jim McCambridge

Did You Know...
Billy Hardy spent 21 years as a player with the Bluebirds from 1911-1932. He played in both 1925 and 1927 FA Cup finals and represented the club in Divisions One, Two and Three (South) as well as the Southern League's Division One and Two

1933-34

Round One, 25 November, 1933. Cardiff City 0 Aldershot 0 (12,000)
Bluebirds; Bob Adams; Bob Calder, George Russell; Tom Maidment, Jack Galbraith, Eddie Jenkins; Ted Marcroft, Eli Postin, Jim Henderson, Les Jones, Freddie Hill

Round One (replay), 29 November, 1933. Aldershot 3 Cardiff City 1 (6,000)
Bluebirds; Bob Adams; Bob Calder, George Russell; Tom Maidment, Jack Galbraith, John Duthie; Ted Marcroft, Eli Postin, Jim Henderson, Freddie Hill, Alex Hutchinson
Scorer; Freddie Hill

1934-35

Round One, 24 November, 1934. Cardiff City 1 Reading 2 (16,733)
Bluebirds; Jock Leckie; Edward Lane, Jack Everest; Wally Jennings, Billy Bassett, Billy Moore; Reg Pugh, Tommy Vaughan, Reg Keating, Wilf Lewis, Harry Riley
Scorer; Wilf Lewis

1935-36

Round One, 30 November, 1935. Cardiff City 0 Dartford 3 (9,000)
Bluebirds; Jack Deighton; Wally Jennings, Jack Everest; Cliff Godfrey, Enoch Mort, Harold Smith; Reg Pugh, Freddie Hill, Jack Diamond, Harry Riley, Joe Roberts

1936-37

Round One, 28 November, 1936. Cardiff City 3 Southall 1 (14,000)
Bluebirds; Bill Fielding; Arthur Granville, Bill Scott; George Nicholson, Billy Bassett, Cliff Godfrey; Reg Pugh, Les Talbot, George Walton, Albert Pinxton, James Prescott
Scorers; George Walton, Les Talbot, Reg Pugh

Round Two, 12 December, 1936. Cardiff City 2 Swindon Town 1 (18,833)
Bluebirds; George Poland; Arthur Granville, Bill Scott; George Nicholson, Billy Bassett, Cliff Godfrey; Reg Pugh, Les Talbot, George Walton, Bryn Davies, James Prescott
Scorers; Arthur Granville (p), James Prescott

Round Three, 16 January, 1937. Cardiff City 1 Grimsby Town 3 (36,243)
Bluebirds; George Poland; Arthur Granville, John Mellor; George Nicholson, Billy Bassett, Cliff Godfrey; Reg Pugh, Albert Pinxton, Ted Melaniphy, Les Talbot, George Walton
Scorer; Ted Melaniphy

1937-38

Round One, 27 November, 1937. Northampton Town 1 Cardiff City 2 (14,000)
Bluebirds; Bob Jones; Arthur Granville, Louis Ford; Cecil McCaughey, Billy Bassett, George Nicholson; Reg Pugh, George Walton, Jimmy Collins, Les Talbot, Bert Turner
Scorer; Jimmy Collins 2

Round Two, 11 December, 1937. Cardiff City 1 Bristol City 1 (25,472)
Bluebirds; Bob Jones; Arthur Granville, Ernie Blenkinsop; Cecil McCaughey, Billy Bassett, George Nicholson; Reg Pugh, George Walton, Jimmy Collins, Les Talbot, Bert Turner
Scorer; Bert Turner

Round Two (replay), 15 December, 1937. Bristol City 0 Cardiff City 2 (23,050)
Bluebirds; Bob Jones; Cliff Godfrey, Louis Ford; Cecil McCaughey, Billy Bassett, George Nicholson; Reg Pugh, George Walton, Jimmy Collins, Les Talbot, Bert Turner
Scorers; Jimmy Collins 2

Round Three, 8 January, 1938. Charlton Athletic 5 Cardiff City 0 (34,637)
Bluebirds; Bob Jones; Cliff Godfrey, John Mellor; Cecil McCaughey, Billy Bassett, George Nicholson; Reg Pugh, George Walton, Jimmy Collins, Les Talbot, Bert Turner

1938-39

Round One, 26 November, 1938. Cheltenham Town 1 Cardiff City 1 (8,000)
Bluebirds; Bill Fielding; George Ballsom, Jimmy Kelso; Cecil McCaughey, Billy Bassett, George Nicholson; Tom Rickards, Les Talbot, Jimmy Collins, Ritchie Smith, James Prescott
Scorer; James Prescott

Round One (replay), 30 November, 1938. Cardiff City 1 Cheltenham Town 0 (8,940)
Bluebirds; Bill Fielding; George Ballsom, Jimmy Kelso; Cecil McCaughey, Billy Bassett, George Nicholson; Tom Rickards, Les Talbot, Jimmy Collins, Ritchie Smith, James Prescott
Scorer; James Prescott

Round Two, 10 December, 1938. Cardiff City 1 Crewe Alexandra 0 (19,000)
Bluebirds; Bill Fielding; George Ballsom, Jimmy Kelso; Cecil McCaughey, Billy Bassett, George Nicholson; James McKenzie, George Walton, Jimmy Collins, Les Talbot, Ritchie Smith
Scorer; Les Talbot

Round Three, 7 January, 1939. Cardiff City 1 Charlton Athletic 0 (22,780)
Bluebirds; Bill Fielding; George Ballsom, Jimmy Kelso; Cecil McCaughey, Billy Bassett, George Nicholson; Reg Pugh, George Walton, Jimmy Collins, Les Talbot, Ritchie Smith
Scorer; George Walton

Round Four, 21 January, 1939. Cardiff City 0 Newcastle United 0 (42,060)
Bluebirds; Bill Fielding; George Ballsom, Jimmy Kelso; Cecil McCaughey, Billy Bassett, George Nicholson; Reg Pugh, George Walton, Jimmy Collins, Les Talbot, Harry Egan

Round Four (replay), 25 January, 1939. Newcastle United 4 Cardiff City 1 (44,649)
Bluebirds; Bill Fielding; George Ballsom, Jimmy Kelso; Cecil McCaughey, Billy Bassett, George Nicholson; Reg Pugh, George Walton, Jimmy Collins, Les Talbot, Ritchie Smith
Scorer; Reg Pugh

21 January 1939, FA Cup 4th round. Cardiff City 0 Newcastle United 0
Bill Bassett heads City out of danger in front of 42,060 fans at Ninian Park

1946-47

Round Three, 11 January, 1947. Brentford 1 Cardiff City 0 (32,894)
Bluebirds; Dan Canning; Arthur Lever, Alf Sherwood; Ken Hollyman, Fred Stansfield, Billy Baker; Colin Gibson, Billy Rees, Stan Richards, Bryn Allen, Roy Clarke

1947-48

Round Three, 10 January, 1948. Cardiff City 1 Sheffield Wednesday 2 (48,000)
Bluebirds; Dan Canning; Arthur Lever, Alf Sherwood; Ken Hollyman, Fred Stansfield, Billy Baker; Colin Gibson, Billy Rees, Stan Richards, Dougie Blair, George Wardle
Scorer; Billy Rees

1948-49

Round Three, 8 January, 1949. Oldham Athletic 2 Cardiff City 3 (28,991)
Bluebirds; Phil Joslin; Arthur Lever, Alf Sherwood; Billy Baker, Fred Stansfield, Dougie Blair; Ken Hollyman, Bryn Allen, Billy Rees, Ernie Stevenson, George Edwards
Scorers; Ken Hollyman 2, Bryn Allen

Round Four, 29 January, 1949. Aston Villa 1 Cardiff City 2 (70,718)
Bluebirds; Phil Joslin; Arthur Lever, Ron Stitfall; Billy Baker, Stan Montgomery, Graham Hogg; Ken Hollyman, Bryn Allen, Billy Rees, Ernie Stevenson, George Edwards
Scorers; Ken Hollyman, Billy Rees

Did You Know...
Former City manager Jimmy Scoular was the first player to appear for two different sides in the FA Cup in the same season. While in the Royal Navy he played for Gosport Borough Athletic in the 1945 qualifying rounds then after being transferred to Portsmouth in December 1945, he played in the third round against Birmingham City without anyone realising he should have been cup-tied

Round Five, 12 February, 1949. Derby County 2 Cardiff City 1 (35,746)
Bluebirds; Phil Joslin; Arthur Lever, Alf Sherwood; Billy Baker, Stan Montgomery, Dougie Blair; Ken Hollyman, Bryn Allen, Billy Rees, Ernie Stevenson, George Edwards
Scorer; Ernie Stevenson

1949-50

Round Three, 7 January, 1950. Cardiff City 2 West Bromwich Albion 2 (39,980)
Bluebirds; Phil Joslin; Arthur Lever, Alf Sherwood; Billy Baker, Stan Montgomery, Glyn Williams; Ken Hollyman, Elfed Evans, Ron Stitfall, Dougie Blair, George Edwards
Scorers; Elfed Evans, Glyn Williams

Round Three (replay), 11 January, 1950. West Bromwich Albion 0 Cardiff City 1 (37,358)
Bluebirds; Phil Joslin; Arthur Lever, Alf Sherwood; Billy Baker, Stan Montgomery, Glyn Williams; Ken Hollyman, Elfed Evans, Ron Stitfall, Dougie Blair, George Edwards
Scorer; George Edwards

Round Four, 28 January, 1950. Charlton Athletic 1 Cardiff City 1 (45,829)
Bluebirds; Phil Joslin; Arthur Lever, Alf Sherwood; Billy Baker, Stan Montgomery, Glyn Williams; Ken Hollyman, Elfed Evans, Ron Stitfall, Dougie Blair, George Edwards
Scorer; Elfed Evans

Round Four (replay), 1 February, 1950. Cardiff City 2 Charlton Athletic 0 (37,000)
Bluebirds; Phil Joslin; Arthur Lever, Alf Sherwood; Billy Baker, Stan Montgomery, Glyn Williams; Ken Hollyman, Elfed Evans, Ron Stitfall, Dougie Blair, George Edwards
Scorer; Elfed Evans 2

Round Five, 11 February, 1950. Leeds United 3 Cardiff City 1 (53,099)
Bluebirds; Phil Joslin; Arthur Lever, Alf Sherwood; Billy Baker, Stan Montgomery, Glyn Williams; Ken Hollyman, Elfed Evans, Ron Stitfall, Dougie Blair, George Edwards
Scorer; Alf Sherwood (p)

1950-51

Round Three, 6 January, 1951. West Ham United 2 Cardiff City 1 (30,000)
Bluebirds; Phil Joslin; Glyn Williams, Alf Sherwood; Ken Hollyman, Stan Montgomery, Billy Baker; Mike Tiddy, Derrick Sullivan, Wilf Grant, Elfed Evans, George Edwards
Scorer; Wilf Grant

1951-52

Round Three, 12 January, 1952. Cardiff City 1 Swindon Town 1 (40,000)
Bluebirds; Ron Howells; Charlie Rutter, Crad Wilcox; Billy Baker, Stan Montgomery, Bobby McLaughlin; Mike Tiddy, Dougie Blair, Wilf Grant, Roley Williams, George Edwards
Scorer; Wilf Grant

Round Three (replay), 15 January, 1952. Swindon Town 1 Cardiff City 0 (aet) (24,207)
Bluebirds; Ron Howells; Charlie Rutter, Alf Sherwood; Billy Baker, Stan Montgomery, Bobby McLaughlin; Mike Tiddy, Elfed Evans, Wilf Grant, Derrick Sullivan, George Edwards

1952-53

Round Three, 10 January, 1953. Halifax Town 3 Cardiff City 1 (25,000)
Bluebirds; Ron Howells; Derrick Sullivan, Alf Sherwood; Billy Baker, Stan Montgomery, Dougie Blair; Cliff Nugent, Wilf Grant, Ken Chisholm, Jack Mansell, George Edwards
Scorer; Billy Baker

1953-54

Round Three, 9 January, 1954. Cardiff City 3 Peterborough United 1 (34,000)
Bluebirds; Ron Howells; Charlie Rutter, Derrick Sullivan; Billy Baker, Stan Montgomery, Dougie Blair; Peter Thomas, Cliff Nugent, Trevor Ford, Tommy Northcott, George Edwards
Scorers; Trevor Ford 2, Tommy Northcott

Round Four, 30 January, 1954. Cardiff City 0 Port Vale 2 (27,000)
Bluebirds; Ron Howells; Charlie Rutter, Alf Sherwood; Billy Baker, Colin Gale, Derrick Sullivan; Tommy Northcott, Wilf Grant, Trevor Ford, Dougie Blair, George Edwards

1954-55

Round Three, 8 January, 1955. Arsenal 1 Cardiff City 0 (51,298)
Bluebirds; Ron Howells; Charlie Rutter, Alf Sherwood; Islwyn Jones, Stan Montgomery, Alan Harrington; Mike Tiddy, Cliff Nugent, Trevor Ford, Ron Stockin, Tommy Northcott

1955-56

Round Three, 7 January, 1956. Leeds United 1 Cardiff City 2 (40,000)
Bluebirds; Ron Howells; Ron Stitfall, Alf Sherwood; Alan Harrington, Danny Malloy, Colin Baker; Brian Walsh, Harry Kirtley, Trevor Ford, Gerry Hitchens, Johnny McSeveney
Scorers; Gerry Hitchens, Johnny McSeveney

Round Four, 28 January, 1956. West Ham United 2 Cardiff City 1 (35,500)
Bluebirds; Ron Howells; Ron Stitfall, Alf Sherwood; Alan Harrington, Danny Malloy, Colin Baker; Brian Walsh, Harry Kirtley, Trevor Ford, Gerry Hitchens, Johnny McSeveney
Scorer; Trevor Ford

1956-57

Round Three, 5 January, 1957. Leeds United 1 Cardiff City 2 (34,237)
Bluebirds; Graham Vearncombe; Charlie Rutter, Ron Stitfall; Colin Baker, Danny Malloy, Derrick Sullivan; Brian Walsh, Johnny McSeveney, Gerry Hitchens, Ron Stockin, Cliff Nugent
Scorers; Ron Stockin, Johnny McSeveney

Round Four, 26 January, 1957. Cardiff City 0 Barnsley 1 (32,000)
Bluebirds; Graham Vearncombe; Charlie Rutter, Ron Stitfall; Colin Baker, Danny Malloy, Derrick Sullivan; Brian Walsh, Johnny McSeveney, Gerry Hitchens, Ron Stockin, Cliff Nugent

Did You Know...
Cardiff City were drawn to play Leeds United at Elland Road in the third round of the FA Cup three times in succession in 1956, 1957 and 1958 and each time the Bluebirds won 2-1

1957-58

Round Three, 4 January, 1958. Leeds United 1 Cardiff City 2 (30,374)
Bluebirds; Ken Jones; Ron Stitfall, Alec Milne; Alan Harrington, Danny Malloy, Colin Baker; Brian Walsh, Cliff Nugent, Joe Bonson, Ron Hewitt, Colin Hudson
Scorers; Alan Harrington, Cliff Nugent

Round Four, 25 January, 1958. Cardiff City 4 Leyton Orient 1 (35,849)
Bluebirds; Ken Jones; Ron Stitfall, Alec Milne; Alan Harrington, Danny Malloy, Colin Baker; Brian Walsh, Ron Hewitt, Joe Bonson, Cliff Nugent, Colin Hudson
Scorers; Joe Bonson 2, Brian Walsh, og

Round Five, 15 February, 1958. Cardiff City 0 Blackburn Rovers 0 (45,580)
Bluebirds; Ken Jones; Alec Milne, Ron Stitfall; Alan Harrington, Danny Malloy, Colin Baker; Brian Walsh, Ron Hewitt, Joe Bonson, Cliff Nugent, Colin Hudson

Round Five (replay), 20 February, 1958. Blackburn Rovers 2 Cardiff City 1 (27,000)
Bluebirds; Ken Jones; Alec Milne, Ron Stitfall; Alan Harrington, Danny Malloy, Colin Baker; Brian Walsh, Ron Hewitt, Joe Bonson, Cliff Nugent, Colin Hudson
Scorer; Ron Hewitt

1958-59

Round Three, 3 January, 1959. Plymouth Argyle 0 Cardiff City 3 (36,247)
Bluebirds; Ron Nicholls; Alec Milne, Ron Stitfall; Derrick Sullivan, Danny Malloy, Colin Baker; Brian Walsh, Derek Tapscott, Joe Bonson, Ron Hewitt, Brayley Reynolds
Scorers; Ron Hewitt (p), Brayley Reynolds, Joe Bonson

Danny Malloy

Round Four, 24 January, 1959. Norwich City 3 Cardiff City 2 (38,000)
Bluebirds; Ron Nicholls; Alec Milne, Ron Stitfall; Derrick Sullivan, Danny Malloy, Colin Baker; Brian Walsh, Derek Tapscott, Joe Bonson, Ron Hewitt, Brayley Reynolds
Scorers; Ron Hewitt, Joe Bonson

1959-60

Round Three, 9 January, 1960. Cardiff City 0 Port Vale 2 (25,500)
Bluebirds; Graham Vearncombe; Alec Milne, Ron Stitfall; Alan Harrington, Danny Malloy, Derrick Sullivan; Brian Walsh, Derek Tapscott, Graham Moore, Joe Bonson, Johnny Watkins

1960-61

Round Three, 7 January, 1961. Cardiff City 1 Manchester City 1 (25,640)
Bluebirds; Maurice Swan; Alan Harrington, Ron Stitfall; Steve Gammon, Danny Malloy, Colin Baker; Brian Walsh, Graham Moore, Derek Tapscott, Johnny Watkins, Derek Hogg
Scorer; Derek Tapscott

Round Three (replay), 11 January, 1961. Manchester City 0 Cardiff City 0 aet (40,000)
Bluebirds; Maurice Swan; Alan Harrington, Ron Stitfall; Steve Gammon, Danny Malloy, Colin Baker; Brian Walsh, Graham Moore, Derek Tapscott, Johnny Watkins, Derek Hogg

Round Three (second replay), 16 January, 1961. Cardiff City 0 Manchester City 2 aet (Highbury, 24,168)
Bluebirds; Maurice Swan; Alan Harrington, Ron Stitfall; Steve Gammon, Danny Malloy, Colin Baker; Brian Walsh, Graham Moore, Derek Tapscott, Johnny Watkins, Derek Hogg

1961-62

Round Three, 10 January, 1962. Middlesbrough 1 Cardiff City 0 (29,013)
Bluebirds; Graham Vearncombe; Alan Harrington, Alec Milne; Barry Hole, Frank Rankmore, Colin Baker; Peter King, Derek Tapscott, Johnny King, Dai Ward, Tony Pickrell

1962-63

Round Three, 18 February, 1963. Charlton Athletic 1 Cardiff City 0 (13,448)
Bluebirds; Graham Vearncombe; Alan Harrington, Trevor Edwards; Barry Hole, Mel Charles, Colin Baker; Alan McIntosh, Alan Durban, Derek Tapscott, Ivor Allchurch, Peter Hooper

Did You Know...
Due to the adverse weather conditions, the Bluebirds FA Cup tie at Charlton Athletic on 5 January, 1963 had to be postponed 14 times and was eventually played on 18 February with Charlton winning 1-0

1963-64

Round Three, 4 January, 1964. Leeds United 1 Cardiff City 0 (14,000)
Bluebirds; Dilwyn John; Trevor Edwards, Peter Rodrigues; Gareth Williams, Mel Charles, Colin Baker; Alan McIntosh, Ivor Allchurch, John Charles, Barry Hole, Peter King

1964-65

Round Three, 9 January, 1965. Cardiff City 1 Charlton Athletic 2 (13,500)
Bluebirds; Bob Wilson; Alan Harrington, Peter Rodrigues; Gareth Williams, Don Murray, Barry Hole; Greg Farrell, Peter King, Derek Tapscott, Keith Ellis, Bernard Lewis
Scorer; Derek Tapscott

1965-66

Round Three, 26 January, 1966. Cardiff City 2 Port Vale 1 (18,898)
Bluebirds; Lyn Davies; Colin Baker, Bobby Ferguson; Gareth Williams, Don Murray, Barry Hole; Greg Farrell, George Johnston, Peter King, Terry Harkin, Bernard Lewis
Scorers; Peter King, Barry Hole

Round Four, 12 February, 1966. Southport 2 Cardiff City 0 (14,230)
Bluebirds; Lyn Davies; David Carver, Bobby Ferguson; Gareth Williams, Don Murray, Barry Hole; Greg Farrell, George Johnston, Graham Coldrick, Terry Harkin, Peter King

1966-67

Round Three, 28 January, 1967. Barnsley 1 Cardiff City 1 (21,464)
Bluebirds; Bob Wilson; Graham Coldrick, Bobby Ferguson; Gareth Williams, Don Murray, Brian Harris; Bernard Lewis, George Johnston, Bobby Brown, Peter King, Ronnie Bird
Scorer; Ronnie Bird

Round Three (replay), 31 January, 1967. Cardiff City 2 Barnsley 1 (21,020)
Bluebirds; Bob Wilson; Graham Coldrick, Bobby Ferguson; Gareth Williams, Don Murray, Brian Harris; Bernard Lewis (Bryn Jones), George Johnston, Bobby Brown, Peter King, Ronnie Bird
Scorers; George Johnston (p), Peter King

Round Four, 18 February, 1967. Cardiff City 1 Manchester City 1 (37,205)
Bluebirds; Bob Wilson; Graham Coldrick, Bobby Ferguson; Gareth Williams, Don Murray, Brian Harris; Greg Farrell, George Johnston, Bobby Brown, Peter King, Ronnie Bird
Scorer; Gareth Williams

Round Four (replay), 22 February, 1967. Manchester City 3 Cardiff City 1 (41,616)
Bluebirds; Bob Wilson; Graham Coldrick, Bobby Ferguson; Gareth Williams, Don Murray, Brian Harris; Greg Farrell, George Johnston, Bobby Brown, Peter King, Ronnie Bird
Scorer; George Johnston (p)

1967-68

Round Three, 27 January, 1968. Stoke City 4 Cardiff City 1 (23,563)
Bluebirds; Fred Davies; Steve Derrett, Bobby Ferguson; Malcolm Clarke, Don Murray, Brian Harris (Gary Bell); Barrie Jones, Leslie Lea, John Toshack, Peter King, Ronnie Bird
Scorer; Barrie Jones

1968-69

Round Three, 4 January, 1969. Cardiff City 0 Arsenal 0 (55,136)
Bluebirds; Fred Davies; David Carver, Gary Bell; Mel Sutton, Don Murray, Steve Derrett; Barrie Jones, Brian Clark, Leslie Lea, John Toshack, Ronnie Bird

Did You Know...
The Bluebirds first appeared on BBC's *Match of the Day* on 4 January 1969 in a Round 3 FA Cup tie against Arsenal which ended 0-0 in front of a Ninian Park crowd of 55,136

Round Three (replay), 7 January, 1969. Arsenal 2 Cardiff City 0 (52,681)
Bluebirds; Fred Davies; David Carver, Gary Bell; Mel Sutton, Don Murray, Steve Derrett; Barrie Jones, Brian Clark, Leslie Lea, John Toshack, Ronnie Bird

1969-70

Round Three, 3 January, 1970. York City 1 Cardiff City 1 (8,439)
Bluebirds; Fred Davies; David Carver, Gary Bell, Mel Sutton, Don Murray, Brian Harris, Bobby Woodruff, Peter King, Brian Clark, John Toshack, Ronnie Bird
Scorer; og

Round Three (replay), 12 January, 1970. Cardiff City 1 York City 1 (aet) (21,623)
Bluebirds; Fred Davies; David Carver, Gary Bell, Mel Sutton, Don Murray, Brian Harris, Bobby Woodruff, Peter King, Brian Clark, John Toshack, Ronnie Bird
Scorer; John Toshack

Round Three (second replay), 15 January, 1970. Cardiff City 1 York City 3 (aet) (7,347)
Bluebirds; Fred Davies; David Carver, Gary Bell, Mel Sutton, Don Murray, Steve Derrett, Bobby Woodruff, Brian Clark, Sandy Allan, John Toshack (Graham Coldrick), Peter King
Scorer; Peter King

1970-71

Round Three, 2 January, 1971. Cardiff City 1 Brighton 0 (19,338)
Bluebirds; Jim Eadie; David Carver, Gary Bell, Mel Sutton, Don Murray, Brian Harris, Leighton Phillips, Ian Gibson, Bobby Woodruff (Nigel Rees), Brian Clark, Peter King
Scorer; Peter King

Round Four, 23 January, 1971. Cardiff City 0 Brentford 2 (23,335)
Bluebirds; Jim Eadie; David Carver, Gary Bell, Mel Sutton, Don Murray, Brian Harris, Leighton Phillips, Peter King, Bobby Woodruff, Alan Warboys (Brian Clark), Nigel Rees

1971-72

Round Three, 15 January, 1972. Sheffield United 1 Cardiff City 3 (29,342)
Bluebirds; Bill Irwin; David Carver, Gary Bell, Mel Sutton, Don Murray, Leighton Phillips, Ian Gibson, Brian Clark, Bobby Woodruff, Alan Warboys, Alan Foggon
Scorers; Don Murray, David Carver, Bobby Woodruff

Round Four, 9 February, 1972. Cardiff City 1 Sunderland 1 (27,000)
Bluebirds; Bill Irwin; David Carver, Gary Bell, Mel Sutton, Richie Morgan, Leighton Phillips, Ian Gibson, Brian Clark, Peter King, Alan Warboys, Alan Foggon (Tony Villars)
Scorer; Peter King

Did You Know...
In 1970-71 Cardiff City reached the final of the FA Youth Cup. They were beaten over two legs by an Arsenal side that included Bluebirds coach, Terry Burton

Round Four (replay), 14 February, 1972. Sunderland 1 Cardiff City 1 (aet) (39,348)
Bluebirds; Bill Irwin; David Carver, Gary Bell, Billy Kellock, Don Murray, Leighton Phillips, Ian Gibson, Brian Clark, Peter King, Bobby Woodruff, Brian Rees (Steve Derrett)
Scorer; Brian Clark

Round Four (second replay), 16 February, 1972. Cardiff City 3 Sunderland 1 (Maine Road, 8,868)
Bluebirds; Bill Irwin; David Carver, Gary Bell, Billy Kellock, Don Murray, Leighton Phillips, Ian Gibson, Brian Clark, Peter King, Bobby Woodruff, Alan Foggon (Alan Warboys)
Scorers; Brian Clark, Bobby Woodruff, Billy Kellock

16 February 1971, FA Cup Rd 4 replay at Maine Road. Cardiff City 3 Sunderland 1.
Bobby Woodruff celebrates scoring for City

Round Five, 26 February, 1972. Cardiff City 0 Leeds United 2 (49,180)
Bluebirds; Bill Irwin; David Carver, Gary Bell, Billy Kellock, Don Murray, Leighton Phillips, Ian Gibson, Brian Clark, Peter King, Bobby Woodruff, Alan Foggon (Alan Warboys)

1972-73

Round Three, 13 January, 1973. Scunthorpe United 2 Cardiff City 3 (6,379)
Bluebirds; Bill Irwin; Phil Dwyer, Gary Bell, Leighton Phillips, Richie Morgan, Dave Powell, Billy Kellock, Johnny Vincent, Andy McCulloch, Bobby Woodruff (Nigel Rees), Gil Reece
Scorers; Billy Kellock, Andy McCulloch, Leighton Phillips

Round Four, 3 February, 1973. Bolton Wanderers 2 Cardiff City 2 (24,729)
Bluebirds; Bill Irwin; Phil Dwyer, Gary Bell, Leighton Phillips, Don Murray, Dave Powell, Billy Kellock, Johnny Vincent, Andy McCulloch, Nigel Rees, Gil Reece
Scorers; Billy Kellock, Leighton Phillips

Round Four (replay), 7 February, 1973. Cardiff City 1 Bolton Wanderers 1 (aet) (14,849)
Bluebirds; Bill Irwin; Phil Dwyer, Gary Bell, Leighton Phillips, Don Murray, Peter Morgan, Billy Kellock, Gil Reece, Andy McCulloch, Johnny Vincent, Nigel Rees (Alan Couch)
Scorer; Andy McCulloch

Did You Know...
Cardiff City keeper Bill Irwin won BBC TVs 'Save of the Season' award for his performance in the 2-0 FA Cup defeat by Leeds United in February, 1972

Round Four (second replay), 12 February, 1973. Bolton Wanderers 1 Cardiff City 0 (6,609)
Bluebirds; Bill Irwin; Phil Dwyer, Gary Bell, Leighton Phillips, Don Murray, Dave Powell (Bobby Woodruff), Billy Kellock, Andy McCulloch, Peter King, Derek Showers, Johnny Vincent

1973-74

Round Three, 5 January, 1974. Birmingham City 5 Cardiff City 2 (22,435)
Bluebirds; Bill Irwin; Phil Dwyer, Gary Bell, Leighton Phillips (Gil Reece), Don Murray, John Impey, Tony Villars, John Farrington, Andy McCulloch, Johnny Vincent, Willie Anderson
Scorers; John Impey, Andy McCulloch

1974-75

Round Three, 4 January, 1975. Leeds United 4 Cardiff City 1 (31,572)
Bluebirds; Bill Irwin; Phil Dwyer, Freddie Pethard, John Buchanan, Richie Morgan, Albert Larmour, George Smith, Gil Reece, Derek Showers, Jack Whitham, Willie Anderson
Scorer; Derek Showers

1975-76

Round One, 22 November, 1975. Cardiff City 6 Exeter City 2 (7,532)
Bluebirds; Bill Irwin; Phil Dwyer, Clive Charles, John Buchanan, Mike England, Albert Larmour, Gil Reece, Doug Livermore, Adrian Alston, Tony Evans, Willie Anderson
Scorers; Adrian Alston 3, Gil Reece 2, Tony Evans

Round Two, 13 December, 1975. Cardiff City 1 Wycombe Wanderers 0 (11,607)
Bluebirds; Bill Irwin; Phil Dwyer, Freddie Pethard, John Buchanan, Mike England, Albert Larmour, Gil Reece, Doug Livermore, Adrian Alston, Tony Evans, Willie Anderson
Scorer; Tony Evans

Round Three, 3 January, 1976. Orient 0 Cardiff City 1 (8,031)
Bluebirds; Bill Irwin; Phil Dwyer, Clive Charles, Gil Reece, Richie Morgan, Albert Larmour, Tony Villars, Doug Livermore, Tony Evans, Adrian Alston, Willie Anderson
Scorer; Adrian Alston

20 January 1977, FA Cup 4th Rd. Cardiff City 3 Wrexham 2. John Buchanan strikes City's winner beyond Wrexham keeper Brian Lloyd

Round Four, 24 January, 1976. Southend 2 Cardiff City 1 (12,863)
Bluebirds; Bill Irwin, Phil Dwyer, Clive Charles, Gil Reece, Mike England, Albert Larmour, John Buchanan, Doug Livermore, Tony Evans, Adrian Alston, Willie Anderson
Scorer; Tony Evans

1976-77

Round Three, 8 January, 1977. Cardiff City 1 Tottenham Hotspur 0 (27,868)
Bluebirds; Ron Healey; Phil Dwyer, Brian Attley, John Buchanan, Paul Went, Albert Larmour, Steve Grapes, Doug Livermore, Tony Evans, David Giles, Peter Sayer
Scorer; Peter Sayer

Round Four, 29 January, 1977. Cardiff City 3 Wrexham 2 (28,953)
Bluebirds; Ron Healey; Phil Dwyer, Brian Attley, John Buchanan, Paul Went, Albert Larmour, Steve Grapes, David Giles, Tony Evans, Doug Livermore, Peter Sayer
Scorers; David Giles, Peter Sayer, John Buchanan

26 February 1977, FA Cup 5th Rd Cardiff City 1 Everton 2. Steve Grapes gets in a shot with Everton's Dave Jones attempting a block

Round Five, 26 February, 1977. Cardiff City 1 Everton 2 (35,582)
Bluebirds; Ron Healey; Phil Dwyer, Brian Attley, John Buchanan, Paul Went, Albert Larmour, Steve Grapes, Doug Livermore, Tony Evans, David Giles, Peter Sayer
Scorer; Tony Evans

1977-78

Round Three, 7 January, 1978. Cardiff City 0 Ipswich Town 2 (13,854)
Bluebirds; Ron Healey; Phil Dwyer, Brian Attley (Steve Grapes), Freddie Pethard, Alan Campbell, Keith Pontin, Albert Larmour, David Giles, Peter Sayer, Paul Went, Ray Bishop

1978-79

Round Three, 9 January, 1979. Swindon Town 3 Cardiff City 0 (9,983)
Bluebirds; Ron Healey; Phil Dwyer, Dave Roberts, Rod Thomas, Alan Campbell, Keith Pontin, Albert Larmour, Brian Attley, Ray Bishop (John Buchanan), Tony Evans, John Lewis

1979-80

Round Three, 5 January, 1980. Cardiff City 0 Arsenal 0 (21,972)
Bluebirds; Ron Healey; Phil Dwyer, Colin Sullivan, Rod Thomas, Keith Pontin, John Lewis, Alan Campbell, Ray Bishop (Gary Stevens), Ronnie Moore, Billy Ronson, John Buchanan

Round Three (replay), 8 January, 1980. Arsenal 2 Cardiff City 1 (36,582)
Bluebirds; Ron Healey; Phil Dwyer, Colin Sullivan, Rod Thomas, Keith Pontin, John Lewis, Alan Campbell, Ray Bishop, Ronnie Moore (Gary Stevens), Billy Ronson, John Buchanan
Scorer; John Buchanan

Did You Know...
The Bluebirds and Newport County conducted an unusual transfer deal on 29 September 1983 when Nigel Vaughan and Karl Elsey moved to Ninian Park and Linden Jones, John Lewis and Tarki Micallef made the opposite journey to Somerton Park

1980-81

Round Three, 3 January, 1981. Leicester City 3 Cardiff City 0 (17,527)
Bluebirds; Ron Healey; Linden Jones, John Lewis, Wayne Hughes, Keith Pontin, Rod Thomas (Tarki Micallef), Paul Giles, Peter Kitchen, Gary Stevens, Billy Ronson, John Buchanan

1981-82

Round Three, 2 January, 1982. Manchester City 3 Cardiff City 1 (31,547)
Bluebirds; Ron Healey; Steve Grapes, Phil Dwyer, Paul Maddy, Keith Pontin, Gary Bennett, Dave Bennett, Tarki Micallef, Gary Stevens, Wayne Hughes (Paul Sugrue), John Lewis
Scorer; Paul Maddy

1982-83

Round One, 20 November, 1982. Wokingham Town 1 Cardiff City 1 (3,000)
Bluebirds; Andy Dibble; Linden Jones, Paul Bodin (Godfrey Ingram), Tarki Micallef, Phil Dwyer, Jimmy Mullen, Dave Bennett, David Tong, Roger Gibbins, Jeff Hemmerman, John Lewis
Scorer; David Tong

Round One (replay), 23 November, 1982. Cardiff City 3 Wokingham Town 0 (3,755)
Bluebirds; Andy Dibble; Linden Jones, Paul Bodin, Phil Dwyer, Jimmy Mullen, Dave Bennett (Tarki Micallef), Gary Bennett, Roger Gibbins, Jeff Hemmerman, Godfrey Ingram, John Lewis
Scorers; Linden Jones, Jeff Hemmerman, Godfrey Ingram

Round Two, 11 December, 1982. Cardiff City 2 Weymouth 3 (4,446)
Bluebirds; Andy Dibble; Linden Jones, Paul Bodin, David Tong (Paul Giles), Phil Dwyer, Jimmy Mullen, Dave Bennett, Gary Bennett, Roger Gibbins, Jeff Hemmerman, John Lewis
Scorers; Roger Gibbins, Jeff Hemmerman

Did You Know...
The Bluebirds have played 31 FA Cup ties against non-league opposition since 1920-21 and only lost four of them (Dartford, Weymouth, Hayes and Enfield)

1983-84

Round Three, 7 January, 1984. Cardiff City 0 Ipswich Town 3 (10,118)
Bluebirds; Andy Dibble; Karl Elsey, Paul Bodin, Phil Dwyer, Gary Bennett, David Tong, Gordon Owen, Roger Gibbins, Paul Evans, Nigel Vaughan, Marshall Burke

1984-85

Round Three, 21 January, 1985. Gillingham 2 Cardiff City 1 (5,452)
Bluebirds; Lee Smelt; Karl Elsey, Jimmy Mullen, Phil Dwyer, Mike Ford, David Tong (Tarki Micallef), Brian Flynn, Roger Gibbins, Nigel Vaughan, Graham Withey, Kevin Meacock
Scorer; Graham Withey

1985-86

Round One, 16 November, 1985. Exeter City 2 Cardiff City 1 (2,772)
Bluebirds; Lee Smelt; Jake King, Carleton Leonard, Mike Ford, Nigel Stevenson, Chris Marustik, Jimmy Mullen, Derrick Christie (Paul McLoughlin), Nigel Vaughan, Rob Turner, Tarki Micallef
Scorer; Nigel Stevenson

1986-87

Round One, 15 November, 1986. Ton Pentre 1 Cardiff City 4 (2,700)
Bluebirds; Mel Rees; Andy Kerr, Phil Brignull, Terry Boyle, Mike Ford, Chris Marustik, Paul Wimbleton, Nicky Platnauer, Alan Curtis, Paul Wheeler, Nigel Vaughan
Scorers; Chris Marustik 2, Paul Wimbleton, Paul Wheeler

Round Two, 9 December, 1986. Cardiff City 2 Brentford 0 (2,531)
Bluebirds; Graham Moseley; Chris Marustik, Phil Brignull (Andy Kerr), Terry Boyle, Mike Ford, Paul Wimbleton, Nicky Platnauer, David Giles, Kevin Bartlett, Paul Wheeler, Nigel Vaughan
Scorers; Paul Wimbleton, Kevin Bartlett

Round Three, 10 January, 1987. Millwall 0 Cardiff City 0 (5,615)
Bluebirds; Mel Rees; Chris Marustik, Phil Brignull, Terry Boyle, Mike Ford, Alan Rogers, Nicky Platnauer, David Giles, Alan Curtis, Paul Wheeler, Nigel Vaughan

Round Three (replay), 20 January, 1987. Cardiff City 2 Millwall 2 (aet) (4,585)
Bluebirds; Mel Rees; Chris Marustik, Phil Brignull, Terry Boyle, Mike Ford, Alan Rogers (Paul Wimbleton), Nicky Platnauer, David Giles, Kevin Bartlett, Chris Pike, Nigel Vaughan
Scorers; Nigel Vaughan, Chris Marustik

Round Three (second replay), 26 January, 1987. Cardiff City 1 Millwall 0 (Ninian Park 5,012)
Bluebirds; Graham Moseley; Andy Kerr, Phil Brignull, Terry Boyle, Mike Ford, Paul Wimbleton, Nicky Platnauer, Kevin Bartlett, Chris Pike, Alan Curtis, Chris Marustik
Scorer; Chris Pike

Round Four, 31 January, 1987. Stoke City 2 Cardiff City 1 (20,423)
Bluebirds; Graham Moseley; Andy Kerr, Phil Brignull, Terry Boyle, Mike Ford, Paul Wimbleton, Nicky Platnauer, Kevin Bartlett, Chris Pike (Gary Davies), Alan Curtis, Chris Marustik
Scorer; Paul Wimbleton

1987-88

Round One, 14 November, 1987. Peterborough United 2 Cardiff City 1 (3,600)
Bluebirds; John Roberts; Phil Bater, Terry Boyle, Mike Ford, Nicky Platnauer, Paul Wimbleton, Mark Kelly (Paul Sanderson), Alan Curtis, Jimmy Gilligan, Brian McDermott, Kevin Bartlett (Steve Mardenborough)
Scorer; Kevin Bartlett

1988-89

Round One, 19 November, 1988. Cardiff City 3 Hereford United 0 (4,341)
Bluebirds; George Wood; Ian Rodgerson, Gareth Abraham, Terry Boyle, Nicky Platnauer, Paul Wimbleton, Alan Curtis, Steve Tupling, Steve Lynex, Kevin Bartlett, Jimmy Gilligan
Scorers; Kevin Bartlett, Steve Tupling, Jimmy Gilligan

Did You Know...
Bluebirds favourite Chris Pike played his early football in the Cardiff Combination League with Park Lawn before becoming a professional with Fulham after playing for Maesteg and Barry Town in the Welsh League

Round Two, 11 December, 1988. Enfield 1 Cardiff City 4 (3,604)
Bluebirds; George Wood; Ian Rodgerson, Gareth Abraham, Terry Boyle, Nicky Platnauer, Paul Wimbleton, Alan Curtis, Jason Gummer (Phil Bater), Steve Lynex, Kevin Bartlett, Jimmy Gilligan
Scorers; Jimmy Gilligan 2, Paul Wimbleton (p), Steve Lynex

Round Three, 7 January, 1989. Cardiff City 1 Hull City 2 (7,128)
Bluebirds; George Wood; Ian Rodgerson, Nigel Stevenson, Gareth Abraham, Terry Boyle, Paul Wimbleton (Steve Tupling), Alan Curtis, Mark Kelly, Steve Lynex, Kevin Bartlett (Paul Wheeler), Jimmy Gilligan
Scorer; Jimmy Gilligan

1989-90

Round One, 18 November, 1989. Cardiff City 1 Halesowen Town 0 (3,972)

> **Did You Know...**
> The Bluebirds played an incredible six home league and cup games in succession from 1 November 1988 to 25 November 1988 and won all of them without conceding a single goal

Bluebirds; George Wood; Ian Rodgerson, Gareth Abraham, Roger Gibbins, Ray Daniel, Leigh Barnard, Jon Morgan, Cohen Griffith, Mark Kelly, Jeff Chandler (Chris Fry), Chris Pike
Scorer; Chris Pike (p)

Round Two, 9 December, 1989. Cardiff City 2 Gloucester City 2 (4,531)
Bluebirds; George Wood; Ian Rodgerson, Gareth Abraham, Roger Gibbins, Ray Daniel, Leigh Barnard, Jon Morgan (Richard Haig), Cohen Griffith (Steve Lynex), Mark Kelly, Morrys Scott, Jeff Chandler
Scorer; Morrys Scott 2

Round Two (replay), 12 December, 1989. Gloucester City 0 Cardiff City 1 (3,877)
Bluebirds; George Wood; Ian Rodgerson, Gareth Abraham, Roger Gibbins, Ray Daniel, Leigh Barnard, Jon Morgan, Mark Kelly, Jeff Chandler, Morrys Scott, Chris Pike,
Scorer; Morrys Scott

Round Three, 6 January, 1990. Cardiff City 0 Queens Park Rangers 0 (13,834)
Bluebirds; Roger Hansbury; Ian Rodgerson, Gareth Abraham, Jason Perry, Roger Gibbins, Ray Daniel, Leigh Barnard, Jon Morgan, Cohen Griffith, Chris Pike, Steve Lynex (Mark Kelly)

Round Three (replay), 10 January, 1990. Queens Park Rangers 2 Cardiff City 0 (12,226)
Bluebirds; Roger Hansbury; Ian Rodgerson, Gareth Abraham, Jason Perry, Roger Gibbins, Ray Daniel, Leigh Barnard (Eddie Youds), Jon Morgan, Mark Kelly, Cohen Griffith, Chris Pike

1991-92 Roger Gibbins

1990-91

Round One, 17 November, 1990. Cardiff City 0 Hayes 0 (1,844)
Bluebirds; Roger Hansbury; Neil Matthews, Allan Lewis, Jason Perry, Damon Searle, Leigh Barnard, Mark Jones, Cohen Griffith, Ian Rodgerson, Roger Gibbins, Nathan Blake

Round One (replay), 21 November, 1990. Hayes 1 Cardiff City 0 (4,312)
Bluebirds; Roger Hansbury; Neil Matthews, Allan Lewis, Jason Perry, Damon Searle, Leigh Barnard, Mark Jones, Cohen Griffith, Ian Rodgerson, Roger Gibbins, Nathan Blake (Chris Pike)

1991-92

Round One, 16 November, 1991. Swansea City 2 Cardiff City 1 (9,315)
Bluebirds; Roger Hansbury; Neil Matthews, Jason Perry, Lee Baddeley, Damon Searle, Roger Gibbins, Paul Ramsey, Cohen Griffith (Paul Millar), Chris Pike, Carl Dale, Nathan Blake
Scorer; Chris Pike

1992-93

Round One, 14 November, 1991. Cardiff City 2 Bath City 3 (4,506)
Bluebirds; Gavin Ward; Derek Brazil, Roger Gibbins (Jason Perry), Damon Searle, Robbie James, Neil Matthews, Paul Ramsey, Cohen Griffith, Paul Millar, Nathan Blake, Carl Dale
Scorers; Paul Millar, Nathan Blake

1993-94

Round One, 13 November, 1993. Enfield 0 Cardiff City 0 (2,374)
Bluebirds; Steve Williams; Derek Brazil, Jason Perry, Mark Aizlewood, Damon Searle, Paul Millar, Nick Richardson, Nathan Blake, Cohen Griffith, Garry Thompson (Tony Bird), Phil Stant

Round One (replay), 30 November, 1993. Cardiff City 1 Enfield 0 (3,232)
Bluebirds; Mark Grew; Derek Brazil, Lee Baddeley, Jason Perry (Nathan Wigg), Damon Searle, Nick Richardson, Paul Millar, Nathan Blake, Cohen Griffith, Tony Bird (Garry Thompson), Phil Stant
Scorer; Nathan Blake

Did You Know...
Two former England captains, Frank Moss and Gerry Francis, both played for Cardiff City during their careers

Round Two, 4 December, 1993. Brentford 1 Cardiff City 3 (4,845)
Bluebirds; Mark Grew; Derek Brazil, Mark Aizlewood, Lee Baddeley, Jason Perry, Damon Searle, Nick Richardson, Nathan Blake, Cohen Griffith, Tony Bird, Phil Stant
Scorers; Phil Stant, Tony Bird, og

Round Three, 8 January, 1994. Cardiff City 2 Middlesbrough 2 (13,750)
Bluebirds; Mark Grew; Derek Brazil, Mark Aizlewood, Lee Baddeley, Jason Perry, Damon Searle, Nick Richardson (Cohen Griffith), Nathan Blake, Paul Millar, Garry Thompson, Phil Stant
Scorers; Phil Stant, Gary Thompson

Round Three (replay), 19 January, 1994. Middlesbrough 1 Cardiff City 2 aet (10,769)
Bluebirds; Mark Grew; Derek Brazil, Mark Aizlewood, Jason Perry, Damon Searle, Nick Richardson, Paul Millar, Nathan Blake, Tony Bird, Garry Thompson, Phil Stant (Cohen Griffith)
Scorers; Phil Stant, Nathan Blake

Round Four, 29 January, 1994. Cardiff City 1 Manchester City 0 (20,486)
Bluebirds; Mark Grew; Derek Brazil, Jason Perry, Lee Baddeley, Damon Searle, Mark Aizlewood, Nick Richardson, Paul Millar, Tony Bird, Nathan Blake, Garry Thompson
Scorer; Nathan Blake

Round Five, 20 February, 1994. Cardiff City 1 Luton Town 2 (17,296)
Bluebirds; Mark Grew (Phil Kite); Derek Brazil, Jason Perry, Lee Baddeley, Damon Searle; Nick Richardson, Paul Millar, Tony Bird, Cohen Griffith, Garry Thompson, Carl Dale (Phil Stant)
Scorer; Phil Stant

1994-95

Round One, 12 November, 1994. Enfield 1 Cardiff City 0 (2,345)
Bluebirds; David Williams; Terry Evans, Jason Perry, Lee Baddeley, Andy Scott, Charlie Oatway, Paul Ramsey, Paul Millar, Cohen Griffith, Phil Stant, Carl Dale

1995-96

Round One, 11 November, 1995. Rushden & Diamonds 1 Cardiff City 3 (4,212)
Bluebirds; David Williams; Derek Brazil (Charlie Oatway), Lee Jarman, Scott Young, Damon Searle, Hayden Fleming, Ian Rodgerson, Nathan Wigg, Jimmy Gardner, Carl Dale, Darren Adams (Andy Evans)
Scorers; Carl Dale 2, Lee Jarman

Round Two, 2 December, 1995. Swindon Town 2 Cardiff City 0 (8,274)
Bluebirds; David Williams; Lee Baddeley, Lee Jarman, Scott Young, Damon Searle, Hayden Fleming, Paul Harding (Nathan Wigg), Ian Rodgerson, Jimmy Gardner, Darren Adams (Tony Bird), Carl Dale

1996-97

Round One, 16 November, 1996. Cardiff City 2 Hendon 0 (2,592)
Bluebirds; Tony Elliott; Lee Jarman, Tony Philliskirk, Jeff Eckhardt, Scott Young, Jason Fowler, Ian Rodgerson, Craig Middleton, Mickey Bennett, Steve White, Carl Dale
Scorers; Steve White, Craig Middleton

Round Two, 7 December, 1996. Cardiff City 0 Gillingham 2 (3,474)
Bluebirds; Pat Mountain; Tony Philliskirk, Jason Perry, Jeff Eckhardt, Scott Young, Jason Fowler, Ian Rodgerson, Craig Middleton, Jimmy Gardner, Steve White, Carl Dale

1997-98

Round One, 15 November, 1997. Slough Town 1 Cardiff City 1 (2,262)
Bluebirds; John Hallworth; Craig Middleton, Scott Young, Mark Harris, Chris Beech, Jason Fowler, Wayne O'Sullivan, Gareth Stoker, David Penney, Andy Saville, Carl Dale
Scorer; Wayne O'Sullivan

Round One (replay), 25 November, 1997. Cardiff City 3 Slough Town 2 aet (2,343)
Bluebirds; Tony Elliott; Craig Middleton, Scott Young (Lee Jarman), Mark Harris, Chris Beech, Scott Partridge (Jimmy Rollo), Wayne O'Sullivan, David Penney, Tony Carss, Andy Saville, Carl Dale (Steve White)
Scorers; Carl Dale, Andy Saville, Steve White

Round Two, 6 December, 1997. Cardiff City 3 Hendon 1 (2,578)
Bluebirds; John Hallworth; Craig Middleton, Scott Young, Mark Harris (Lee Jarman), Chris Beech (Jimmy Rollo), Scott Partridge, Wayne O'Sullivan, David Penney (Gareth Stoker), Tony Carss, Andy Saville, Carl Dale
Scorers; Carl Dale 2, Andy Saville

Round Three, 3 January, 1998. Cardiff City 1 Oldham Athletic 0 (6,635)
Bluebirds; John Hallworth; Craig Middleton, Scott Young, Mark Harris, Chris Beech, Jason Fowler (Gareth Stoker), Wayne O'Sullivan, David Penney, Tony Carss, Andy Saville, Carl Dale
Scorer; Jason Fowler

Round Four, 24 January, 1998. Cardiff City 1 Reading 1 (10,174)
Bluebirds; John Hallworth; Craig Middleton, Scott Young, Mark Harris, Chris Beech, Jason Fowler, Jeff Eckhardt, David Penney, Tony Carss, Kevin Nugent (Andy Saville), Carl Dale
Scorer; Kevin Nugent

Round Four (replay), 3 February, 1998. Reading 1 Cardiff City 1 (11,808)
Lost 4-3 on penalties
Bluebirds; John Hallworth; Craig Middleton, Scott Young (Lee Jarman), Mark Harris, Chris Beech, Jeff Eckhardt (Gareth Stoker), Wayne O'Sullivan (Jason Fowler), David Penney, Tony Carss, Kevin Nugent, Carl Dale
Scorer; Carl Dale

1998-99

Round One, 14 November, 1998. Cardiff City 6 Chester City 0 (4,220)
Bluebirds; John Hallworth; Mark Delaney, Graham Mitchell, Scott Young, Mike Ford, Richard Carpenter, Jason Fowler (Christian Roberts), Wayne O'Sullivan, Craig Middleton, John Williams, Kevin Nugent
Scorers; Jason Fowler 2, John Williams 2, Craig Middleton, Mark Delaney

Round Two, 5 December, 1998. Cardiff City 3 Hednesford Town 1 (5,638)
Bluebirds; John Hallworth; Mark Delaney, Graham Mitchell, Scott Young, Mike Ford, Richard Carpenter (Danny Hill), Jason Fowler, Wayne O'Sullivan, Craig Middleton, John Williams (Rob Earnshaw), Kevin Nugent (Dai Thomas)
Scorers; Craig Middleton, Jason Fowler, John Williams

Round Three, 2 January 1999. Cardiff City 1 Yeovil Town 1 (12,561)
Bluebirds; John Hallworth; Mark Delaney, Graham Mitchell, Jeff Eckhardt, Mike Ford, Danny Hill (Andy Legg), Jason Fowler, Wayne O'Sullivan, Craig Middleton, John Williams (Christian Roberts), Kevin Nugent
Scorer; Kevin Nugent

Round Three (replay), 12 January, 1999. Yeovil Town 1 Cardiff City 2 (aet) (8,101)
Bluebirds; John Hallworth; Mark Delaney, Graham Mitchell, Jeff Eckhardt, Mike Ford, Richard Carpenter, Jason Fowler (Andy Legg), Wayne O'Sullivan, Craig Middleton, John Williams (Dai Thomas), Kevin Nugent
Scorers; Jeff Eckhardt, Kevin Nugent

Round Four, 27 January, 1999. Sheffield United 4 Cardiff City 1 (13,296)
Bluebirds; John Hallworth; Mark Delaney, Graham Mitchell, Jeff Eckhardt, Mike Ford, Richard Carpenter, Jason Fowler, Wayne O'Sullivan (Danny Hill), Craig Middleton (Andy Legg), John Williams (Jason Bowen), Kevin Nugent
Scorer; Kevin Nugent

6 January 2001, FA Cup Rd 3. Cardiff City 1 Crewe 1. Leo Fortune-West

1999-00

Round One, 30 October, 1999. Leyton Orient 1 Cardiff City 1 (3,109)
Bluebirds; John Hallworth; Winston Faerber, Russell Perrett, Scott Young, Mike Ford, Jason Fowler, Danny Hill, Andy Legg, Willie Boland (Richard Carpenter), Jason Bowen, Kevin Nugent
Scorer; Kevin Nugent (p)

Round One (replay), 9 November, 1999. Cardiff City 3 Leyton Orient 1 (3,095)
Bluebirds; John Hallworth; Winston Faerber, Russell Perrett, Jeff Eckhardt, Mike Ford, Richard Carpenter, Danny Hill (Willie Boland), Andy Legg, Matt Brazier, Jason Bowen, Kevin Nugent (Christian Roberts)
Scorers; Matt Brazier, Russell Perrett, Kevin Nugent

Round Two, 20 November, 1999. Bury 0 Cardiff City 0 (2,603)
Bluebirds; John Hallworth; Winston Faerber, Russell Perrett, Jeff Eckhardt, Mike Ford, Richard Carpenter, Andy Legg, Mark Bonner, Matt Brazier, Jason Bowen, Christian Roberts

Round Two (replay), 30 November, 1999. Cardiff City 1 Bury 0 (aet) (4,511)
Bluebirds; John Hallworth; Winston Faerber, Russell Perrett, Jeff Eckhardt, Mike Ford, Richard Carpenter, Andy Legg, Mark Bonner, Matt Brazier, Jason Bowen (Jason Fowler), Christian Roberts (Dai Thomas)
Scorer; Mike Ford

Round Three, 21 December, 1999. Bolton Wanderers 1 Cardiff City 0 (5,734)
Bluebirds; John Hallworth; Andy Legg (Winston Faerber), Russell Perrett, Jorn Schwinkendorf (Craig Middleton), Jeff Eckhardt, Mike Ford (Danny Hill), Josh Low, Jason Fowler, Richard Carpenter, Richie Humphreys, Jason Bowen

2000-01

Round One, 19 November, 2000. Cardiff City 5 Bristol Rovers 1 (8,013)
Bluebirds; Mark Walton; Danny Gabbidon, Andy Jordan, Scott Young, Andy Legg (Matt Brazier), Josh Low, Kevin Evans, Mark Bonner, Jason Bowen, Rob Earnshaw (Paul Brayson), Leo Fortune-West (James Collins)
Scorers; Rob Earnshaw 3, Kevin Evans, Leo Fortune-West

Round Two, 9 December, 2000. Cardiff City 3 Cheltenham Town 1 (9,910)
Bluebirds; Mark Walton; Danny Gabbidon, Scott Young, Rhys Weston, Scott McCulloch, Kevin Evans, Andy Legg, Jason Bowen (Paul Brayson), Mark Bonner (Andy Thompson), Rob Earnshaw, Leo Fortune-West
Scorers; Rob Earnshaw 2(1p), Kevin Evans

Round Three, 6 January, 2001. Cardiff City 1 Crewe Alexandra 1 (13,403)
Bluebirds; Mark Walton; Danny Gabbidon, Scott Young, Rhys Weston, Matt Brazier, Scott McCulloch (Willie Boland), Kevin Evans, Andy Legg, Jason Bowen, Rob Earnshaw (Josh Low), Leo Fortune-West
Scorer; Scott Young

Round Three (replay), 16 January, 2001. Crewe Alexandra 2 Cardiff City 1 (5,785)
Bluebirds; Mark Walton; Danny Gabbidon, Scott Young, Rhys Weston, Matt Brazier, Scott McCulloch (James Collins), Andy Legg, Jason Bowen (Paul Brayson), Willie Boland (Josh Low), Rob Earnshaw, Leo Fortune-West
Scorer; Rob Earnshaw

2001-02

Round One, 17 November, 2001. Cardiff City 3 Tiverton Town 1 (6,648)
Bluebirds; Neil Alexander; Rhys Weston, Spencer Prior, Danny Gabbidon, Andy Legg, Des Hamilton, Willie Boland, Paul Brayson, Graham Kavanagh, Leo Fortune-West (James Collins), Rob Earnshaw (Leyton Maxwell)
Scorers; Des Hamilton, Rob Earnshaw, Paul Brayson

Round Two, 8 December, 2001. Cardiff City 3 Port Vale 0 (9,650)
Bluebirds; Neil Alexander; Danny Gabbidon, Spencer Prior, Scott Young, Andy Legg (Rhys Weston), Jason Bowen (Paul Brayson), Willie Boland, Graham Kavanagh, Mark Bonner, Gavin Gordon (Leo Fortune-West), Rob Earnshaw
Scorers; Gavin Gordon, Rob Earnshaw, Leo Fortune-West

Round Three, 6 January, 2002. Cardiff City 2 Leeds United 1 (22,009)
Bluebirds; Neil Alexander; Danny Gabbidon, Spencer Prior, Scott Young, Andy Legg, Willie Boland, Graham Kavanagh, Paul Brayson, Mark Bonner, Rob Earnshaw, Gavin Gordon (Leo Fortune-West)
Scorers; Graham Kavanagh, Scott Young

4 January 2003, FA Cup Rd 3.
Cardiff City 2 Coventry City 2.
Andy Legg in typical action

Round Four, 27 January, 2002. Tranmere Rovers 3 Cardiff City 1 (9,442)
Bluebirds; Neil Alexander; Rhys Weston, Scott Young, Danny Gabbidon, Andy Legg, Des Hamilton (James Collins), Willie Boland, Graham Kavanagh, Mark Bonner (Jason Bowen), Leo Fortune-West, Paul Brayson (Josh Low)
Scorer; Graham Kavanagh (p)

2002-03

Round One, 16 November, 2002. Tranmere Rovers 2 Cardiff City 2 (5,592)
Bluebirds; Neil Alexander; Rhys Weston, James Collins, Spencer Prior, Chris Barker, Leyton Maxwell, Jason Bowen (Leo Fortune-West), Graham Kavanagh, Andy Legg (Des Hamilton), Peter Thorne, Andy Campbell (Rob Earnshaw)
Scorers; James Collins, Graham Kavanagh

Round One (replay), 26 November, 2002. Cardiff City 2 Tranmere Rovers 1 (6,853)
Bluebirds; Martyn Margetson; Rhys Weston, Spencer Prior (Gary Croft), James Collins, Chris Barker, Des Hamilton, Willie Boland (Andy Legg), Graham Kavanagh, Jason Bowen (Leyton Maxwell), Andy Campbell, Leo Fortune-West
Scorers; Andy Campbell, James Collins

Round Two, 7 December, 2002. Margate 0 Cardiff City 3 (1,362)
Bluebirds; Neil Alexander; Gary Croft, Rhys Weston, Spencer Prior, Chris Barker, Des Hamilton (Leyton Maxwell), Willie Boland, Jason Bowen, Andy Legg, Rob Earnshaw (Andy Campbell), Peter Thorne (Leo Fortune-West)
Scorers; Peter Thorne, Willie Boland, Leo Fortune-West

Round Three, 4 January, 2003. Cardiff City 2 Coventry City 2 (16,013)
Bluebirds; Neil Alexander; Gary Croft, Rhys Weston, Spencer Prior (Scott Young), Chris Barker, Jason Bowen, Willie Boland, Graham Kavanagh, Andy Legg (Andy Campbell), Peter Thorne (Leo Fortune-West), Rob Earnshaw
Scorers; Rob Earnshaw, Andy Campbell

Round Three (replay), 15 January, 2003. Coventry City 3 Cardiff City 0 (11,997)
Bluebirds; Neil Alexander; Gary Croft (Andy Campbell), Rhys Weston, Scott Young (James Collins), Chris Barker, Willie Boland, Jason Bowen, Graham Kavanagh, Andy Legg, Rob Earnshaw, Peter Thorne (Leo Fortune-West)

2003-04

Round Three, 3 January, 2004. Cardiff City 0 Sheffield United 1 (10,525)
Bluebirds; Martyn Margetson; Rhys Weston (Gary Croft), Spencer Prior, Danny Gabbidon, Tony Vidmar, Gareth Whalley (Andy Campbell), Graham Kavanagh, Willie Boland, Richard Langley, Rob Earnshaw (Alan Lee), Peter Thorne

2004-05

Round Three, 8 January, 2005. Cardiff City 1 Blackburn Rovers 1 (14,145)
Bluebirds; Tony Warner; Rhys Weston, Danny Gabbidon, James Collins, Chris Barker, Jobi McAnuff, Graham Kavanagh, Junichi Inamoto, Richard Langley (Lee Bullock), Cameron Jerome, Alan Lee (Peter Thorne)
Scorer; Alan Lee

Round Three (replay), 19 January 2005. Blackburn Rovers 3 Cardiff City 2 (9,140)
Bluebirds; Tony Warner; Rhys Weston (Tony Vidmar), Danny Gabbidon, James Collins, Chris Barker, Richard Langley, Graham Kavanagh, Junichi Inamoto (Joe Ledley), Jobi McAnuff, Alan Lee, Peter Thorne (Andy Campbell)
Scorers; Jobi McAnuff, James Collins

2005-06

Round Three, 7 January, 2006. Arsenal 2 Cardiff City 1 (36,552)
Bluebirds; Neil Alexander; Rhys Weston, Glenn Loovens (Toni Koskela), Darren Purse, Chris Barker, Neil Cox, Jeff Whitley, Joe Ledley, Kevin Cooper (Alan Lee), Neil Ardley, Cameron Jerome
Scorer; Cameron Jerome

Did You Know...
In 2007, former Bluebirds keeper Bill Irwin was made head coach of the United States Women's Under 23 side

2006-07

Round Three, 7 January, 2007. Cardiff City 0 Tottenham Hotspur 0 (20,376)
Bluebirds; Neil Alexander; Kerrea Gilbert, Glenn Loovens, Darren Purse, Kevin McNaughton, Willo Flood, Ricci Scimeca, Stephen McPhail, Joe Ledley, Steve Thompson, Michael Chopra

Round Three (replay), 17 January, 2007. Tottenham Hotspur 4 Cardiff City 0 (27,641)
Bluebirds; Neil Alexander; Kerrea Gilbert, Glenn Loovens, Darren Purse, Kevin McNaughton, Willo Flood (Kevin Cooper), Ricci Scimeca, Stephen McPhail, Joe Ledley, Steve Thompson, Michael Chopra (Andrea Ferretti)

2007-08

Round Three, 5 January, 2008. Chasetown 1 Cardiff City 3 (2,420)
Bluebirds; Michael Oakes; Kevin McNaughton, Glenn Loovens, Roger Johnson, Tony Capaldi, Peter Whittingham, Gavin Rae, Aaron Ramsey (Darcy Blake), Joe Ledley, Paul Parry, Steve McLean
Scorers; Peter Whittingham, Aaron Ramsey, Paul Parry

Round Four, 27 January, 2008. Hereford United 1 Cardiff City 2 (6,855)
Bluebirds; Michael Oakes; Kevin McNaughton, Roger Johnson, Glenn Loovens, Tony Capaldi, Peter Whittingham, Gavin Rae, Stephen McPhail, Joe Ledley, Paul Parry, Steve Thompson (Jimmy Floyd Hasselbaink)
Scorers; Kevin McNaughton, Steve Thompson (p)

Did You Know...
City's three Wembley Cup finals were watched by 274,843 fans, but the 2008 attendance was the lowest of the three

Round Five, 16 February, 2008. Cardiff City 2 Wolverhampton Wanderers 0 (15,339)
Bluebirds; Peter Enckelman; Kevin McNaughton, Glenn Loovens, Roger Johnson, Tony Capaldi, Peter Whittingham (Trevor Sinclair), Gavin Rae, Stephen McPhail (Darcy Blake), Aaron Ramsey, Paul Parry, Jimmy Floyd Hasselbaink (Steve Thompson)
Scorers; Peter Whittingham, Jimmy Floyd Hasselbaink

Round Six (Quarter-final), 9 March, 2008. Middlesbrough 0 Cardiff City 2 (32,896)
Bluebirds; Peter Enckelman; Kevin McNaughton (Darcy Blake), Roger Johnson, Glenn Loovens, Tony Capaldi, Aaron Ramsey, Stephen McPhail, Gavin Rae, Peter Whittingham, Paul Parry (Trevor Sinclair), Jimmy Floyd Hasselbaink (Steve Thompson)
Scorers; Peter Whittingham, Roger Johnson

Semi-final, 6 April, 2008. Barnsley 0 Cardiff City 1 (82,752)
Bluebirds; Peter Enckelman; Kevin McNaughton (Aaron Ramsey), Roger Johnson, Glenn Loovens, Tony Capaldi, Peter Whittingham, Gavin Rae, Stephen McPhail, Joe Ledley, Trevor Sinclair (Steve Thompson), Jimmy Floyd Hasselbaink (Ricci Scimeca)
Scorer; Joe Ledley

Final, 17 May, 2008. Cardiff City 0 Portsmouth 1 (89,874)
Bluebirds; Peter Enckelman; Kevin McNaughton, Roger Johnson, Glenn Loovens, Tony Capaldi, Peter Whittingham (Aaron Ramsey), Gavin Rae (Trevor Sinclair), Stephen McPhail, Joe Ledley, Paul Parry, Jimmy Floyd Hasselbaink (Steve Thompson)

2008-09

Round Three, 3 January, 2009. Cardiff City 2 Reading 0 (12,448)
Bluebirds; Peter Enckelman; Kevin McNaughton, Gabor Gyepes, Roger Johnson, Mark Kennedy, Peter Whittingham, Gavin Rae, Joe Ledley, Paul Parry, Jay Bothroyd (Stephen McPhail), Ross McCormack
Scorers; Ross McCormack, Joe Ledley

Round Four, 25 January, 2009. Cardiff City 0 Arsenal 0 (20,079)
Bluebirds; Peter Enckelman; Kevin McNaughton, Gabor Gyepes, Roger Johnson, Mark Kennedy; Chris Burke (Tony Capaldi), Joe Ledley, Gavin Rae, Paul Parry, Jay Bothroyd (Eddie Johnson), Ross McCormack

17 May 2008, FA Cup Final. Cardiff City 0 Portsmouth 1. Jimmy Floyd Hasselbaink breaks clear from a Pompey defender

Round Four (replay), 16 February, 2009. Arsenal 4 Cardiff City 0 (57,237)
Bluebirds; Tom Heaton; Kevin McNaughton, Darren Purse (Darcy Blake), Roger Johnson, Mark Kennedy, Chris Burke, Gavin Rae (Ricci Scimeca), Joe Ledley, Paul Parry (Peter Whittingham), Jay Bothroyd, Ross McCormack

2009-10

Round Three, 12 January, 2010. Bristol City 1 Cardiff City 1 (7,289)
Bluebirds; David Marshall; Adam Matthews, Mark Hudson, Anthony Gerrard, Kevin McNaughton, Joe Ledley, Gavin Rae (Solomon Taiwo), Aaron Wildig, Peter Whittingham, Michael Chopra, Ross McCormack (Warren Feeney)
Scorer; Michael Chopra

Round Three (replay), 19 January, 2010. Cardiff City 1 Bristol City 0 (6,731)
Bluebirds; David Marshall; Paul Quinn, Gabor Gyepes, Anthony Gerrard, Adam Matthews (Mark Kennedy), Chris Burke (Darcy Blake), Joe Ledley, Aaron Wildig (Michael Chopra), Peter Whittingham, Ross McCormack, Jay Bothroyd
Scorer; Bradley Orr (OG)

Did You Know...
Only four players from City's FA Cup Final side of 2008 are still with the club. (Kevin McNaughton, Peter Whittingham, Gavin Rae and Stephen McPhail)

Round Four, 23 January, 2010. Cardiff City 4 Leicester City 2 (10,961)
Bluebirds; David Marshall; Paul Quinn (Chris Burke), Mark Hudson, Anthony Gerrard, Mark Kennedy, Ross McCormack, Joe Ledley, Darcy Blake, Peter Whittingham, Michael Chopra, Jay Bothroyd
Scorers; Jay Bothroyd, Peter Whittingham, Ross McCormack, Chris Burke

Round Five, 13 February, 2010. Chelsea 4 Cardiff City 1 (40,827)
Bluebirds; David Marshall; Kevin McNaughton, Gabor Gyepes, Anthony Gerrard, Mark Kennedy, Chris Burke (Ross McCormack), Gavin Rae (Darcy Blake), Aaron Wildig (Solomon Taiwo), Peter Whittingham, Jay Bothroyd, Michael Chopra
Scorer; Michael Chopra

FA CUP Record

Played	Won	Drawn	Lost	For	Against
246	103	56	87	346	308

Hat-tricks (4)
Billy Devlin (1912), Albert Keating (1933), Adrian Alston (1975), Rob Earnshaw (2000)

Penalties (16)
2 Jack Evans, Hughie Ferguson, George Johnston, 1 Fred Keenor, Arthur Granville, Alf Sherwood, Ron Hewitt, Paul Wimbleton, Chris Pike, Kevin Nugent, Graham Kavanagh, Rob Earnshaw, Steve Thompson

Leading scorers (346 goals)
19 Len Davies, 12 Jimmy Gill, 10 Hughie Ferguson, 9 Rob Earnshaw., 6 Jack Evans, Kevin Nugent, Carl Dale, own goals, 5 Billy Devlin, Joe Clennell, Peter King, 4 Albert Keating, Jimmy Collins, Elfed Evans, Joe Bonson, Adrian Alston, Tony Evans, Paul Wimbleton, Jimmy Gilligan, Nathan Blake, Phil Stant, Jason Fowler, Peter Whittingham

Leading appearances (246 games)
56 Billy Hardy, 42 Jack Evans, 42 Fred Keenor, 34 Tom Farquharson, 33 Len Davies, 31 Jimmy Blair, 30 Jimmy Nelson, 28 Jimmy Gill, 23 Phil Dwyer, Don Murray, 22(1s) Scott Young, 20 Ron Stitfall

Extra Time (12 matches)
Manchester City (1924), Darlington (1925), Swindon Town (1952), Manchester City (1961), Manchester City (1961), York City (1970), York City (1970), Sunderland (1972), Bolton Wanderers (1973), Millwall (1987), Yeovil Town (1999), Bury (1999)

Taken to Penalties (1 match)
Reading (1998)

4
LEAGUE CUP

The Football League Cup was the brainchild of Alan Hardaker who was secretary of the Football League for over 25 years. It was designed specifically for the 92 League clubs with a two-legged final to be played home and away at the grounds of the Finalists. It was met with a certain amount of criticism at the start as it was claimed that it only added more congestion to the clubs who already had full fixture lists. The original plan was for all matches to be played midweek under floodlights but as some clubs were still without lighting, they were forced to play in the afternoons.

It was not until arrangements were made to play the 1967 final on a one-off basis at Wembley Stadium that the competition took on a new improved light. The additional carrot of a place in the Fairs Cup (later the UEFA Cup) for the winners also helped the tournament start to earn a prominent place in the football calendar.

The League Cup has come in many different guises since it began in 1960-61 as sponsorship began to play an important part, and after many changes, it is now known as the Carling Cup. The Bluebirds, then a Division One side, won their first game at Ayresome Park against Middlesbrough of Division Two, only to lose at home to a strong Burnley side in the next round. Results in early seasons were generally poor but City did reach the semi-finals in 1965-66 only to lose heavily, 10-3 on aggregate, to a Bobby Moore-inspired West Ham.

Cardiff City squad 1960-61

It has now become usual for squad players to be used in the competition rather than first-choice sides with clubs making the league a priority. Victory over Division One side Everton (1979) and a thrilling 5-4 win against Plymouth Argyle after being 4-1 down were largely offset by some poor defeats such as at home to Barnet (2006), while the Bluebirds most recent match in the competition ended in a 1-0 loss at Premier club, Aston Villa.

1960-61

Round One, 3 October, 1960. Middlesbrough 3 Cardiff City 4 (15,695)
Bluebirds; Graham Vearncombe; Alan Harrington, Ron Stitfall; Barry Hole, Danny Malloy, Colin Baker; Brian Walsh, Derek Tapscott, Trevor Edwards, Peter Donnelly, Colin Hudson
Scorers; Brian Walsh, Peter Donnelly, Colin Hudson, Trevor Edwards (p)

Round Two, 24 October, 1960. Cardiff City 0 Burnley 2 (12,000)
Bluebirds; Ron Nicholls; Alan Harrington, Ron Stitfall; Steve Gammon, Danny Malloy, Colin Baker; Brian Walsh, Peter King, Trevor Edwards, Barry Hole, Colin Hudson

1961-62

Round One, 13 September, 1961. Cardiff City 2 Wrexham 0 (6,750)
Bluebirds; Graham Vearncombe; Alan Harrington, Alec Milne; Barry Hole, Frank Rankmore, Colin Baker; Brian Walsh, Dai Ward, Johnny King, Graham Moore, Derek Hogg
Scorers; Graham Moore, Dai Ward

Round Two, 5 October, 1961. Mansfield Town 1 Cardiff City 1 (17,100)
Bluebirds; Dilwyn John; Alan Harrington, Ron Stitfall; Barry Hole, Frank Rankmore, Colin Baker; Brian Walsh, Dai Ward, Johnny King, Alan Durban, Danny McCarthy
Scorer; Johnny King

Round Two (replay), 23 October, 1961. Cardiff City 2 Mansfield Town 1 (4,800)
Bluebirds; Dilwyn John; Alan Harrington, Ron Stitfall; Barry Hole, Frank Rankmore, Colin Baker; Peter King, Dai Ward, Johnny King, Alan Durban, Danny McCarthy
Scorers; Johnny King, Dai Ward

Round Three, 15 November, 1961. Bournemouth 3 Cardiff City 0 (12,857)
Bluebirds; Dilwyn John; Alan Harrington, Ron Stitfall; Barry Hole, Gareth Williams, Colin Baker; Peter King, Derek Tapscott, Johnny King, Alan Durban, Tony Pickrell

1962-63

Round Two, 26 September, 1962, Cardiff City 5 Reading 1 (4,500)
Bluebirds; Maurice Swan; Alan Harrington, Ron Stitfall; Barry Hole, Frank Rankmore, Colin Baker; Alan McIntosh, Derek Tapscott, Mel Charles, Alan Durban, Peter Hooper
Scorers; Alan Durban 2, Mel Charles, Peter Hooper (p), Derek Tapscott

Round Three, 23 October, 1962. Bristol City 2 Cardiff City 0 (15,000)
Bluebirds; Graham Vearncombe; Alan Harrington, Ron Stitfall; Barry Hole, Frank Rankmore, Colin Baker; Alan McIntosh, Alan Durban, Mel Charles, Ivor Allchurch, Peter Hooper

1963-64

Round Two, 25 September, 1963. Cardiff City 2 Wrexham 2 (4,600)
Bluebirds; Dilwyn John; Trevor Edwards, Jim Upton; Don Murray, John Charles, Barry Hole; Alan McIntosh, Derek Tapscott, Gareth Williams, Ivor Allchurch, Peter King
Scorer; Derek Tapscott 2

Round Two (replay), 7 October, 1963. Wrexham 1 Cardiff City 1 (11,299)
Bluebirds; Dilwyn John; Ron Stitfall, Peter Rodrigues; Colin Baker, Don Murray, Dick Scott; Alan McIntosh, Peter King, Mel Charles, Ivor Allchurch, Richard Mallory
Scorer; Peter King

Did You Know...
The first Cardiff City substitute was David Summerhayes who replaced an injured Colin Baker against Bury at Ninian Park on 21 August, 1965

Round Two (second replay), 21 October, 1963. Wrexham 3 Cardiff City 0 (8,838)
Bluebirds; Dilwyn John; Colin Baker, Jim Upton; Barry Hole, Don Murray, Phil Watkins; Albert Burns, Peter King, Dick Scott, Ivor Allchurch, Alistair Brack

1964-65

Round Two, 23 September, 1964. Southampton 3 Cardiff City 2 (13,076)
Bluebirds; Bob Wilson; Peter Rodrigues, Trevor Peck; Gareth Williams, John Charles, Barry Hole; Peter King, Clive Lloyd, Derek Tapscott, Ivor Allchurch, Bernard Lewis
Scorers; Bernard Lewis, Peter King

1965-66

Round Two, 22 September, 1965. Crewe Alexandra 1 Cardiff City 1 (5,832)
Bluebirds; Dilwyn John; Peter Rodrigues, Colin Baker; Graham Coldrick, Don Murray, Barry Hole; George Johnston, Gareth Williams, Terry Harkin, Peter King, Bernard Lewis
Scorer; Bernard Lewis

Round Two (replay), 29 September, 1965. Cardiff City 3 Crewe Alexandra 0 (6,939)
Bluebirds; Dilwyn John; Peter Rodrigues, Colin Baker; Graham Coldrick, Don Murray, Barry Hole; George Johnston, Peter King, Gareth Williams, Terry Harkin, Greg Farrell
Scorers; Peter King 2, Terry Harkin

Bluebirds winger Greg Farrell in 1964

Round Three, 13 September, 1965. Cardiff City 2 Portsmouth 0 (8,803)
Bluebirds; Bob Wilson; Don Murray, Peter Rodrigues; David Summerhayes, John Charles, Barry Hole; Greg Farrell, Peter King, George Andrews, Terry Harkin, Bernard Lewis
Scorers; Peter King, George Andrews

Round Four, 3 November, 1965. Cardiff City 5 Reading 1 (6,698)
Bluebirds; Bob Wilson; Alan Harrington, Peter Rodrigues; Barry Hole, Graham Coldrick, David Houston; Greg Farrell, George Johnston, George Andrews, Terry Harkin, Peter King
Scorers; George Johnston 3, Terry Harkin 2

Round Five (Quarter-final), 17 November, 1965. Cardiff City 2 Ipswich Town 1 (8,000)
Bluebirds; Bob Wilson; Alan Harrington, Peter Rodrigues; Barry Hole, Gareth Williams, David Houston; Greg Farrell, George Johnston, George Andrews, John Toshack, Peter King
Scorers; Barry Hole, George Andrews

Semi-final (1st leg), 15 December, 1965. West Ham United 5 Cardiff City 2 (19,980)
Bluebirds; Bob Wilson; Alan Harrington, Peter Rodrigues; Barry Hole, Don Murray, David Houston; Greg Farrell, Terry Harkin, George Andrews, Gareth Williams, Peter King
Scorer; George Andrews 2

Semi-final (2nd leg), 2 February, 1966. Cardiff City 1 West Ham United 5 (14,313)
Bluebirds; Lyn Davies; Graham Coldrick, David Yorath; Gareth Williams, Don Murray, Barry Hole; Bernard Lewis, George Johnston, George Andrews, Peter King, Greg Farrell
Scorer; Bernard Lewis
West Ham United through 10-3 on aggregate

1966-67

Round One, 24 August, 1966. Cardiff City 1 Bristol Rovers 0 (5,574)
Bluebirds; Dilwyn John; Dave Carver, Bobby Ferguson; Gareth Williams, Don Murray, Graham Coldrick; George Johnston, Terry Harkin, Peter King, John Toshack, Bernard Lewis
Scorer; John Toshack

Round Two, 14 September, 1966. Cardiff City 0 Exeter City 1 (5,384)
Bluebirds; Dilwyn John; Dave Carver, Bobby Ferguson; Gareth Williams, Don Murray, Graham Coldrick; George Johnston, Terry Harkin (Ronnie Bird), Peter King, John Toshack, Bernard Lewis

Did You Know...
Cardiff City's longest close-season tour was in the summer of 1968 when they left on a 14-match visit of New Zealand, Australia and Tasmania. They won eleven, drew two and lost only once over the seven weeks they were away

1967-68

Round One, 23 August, 1967. Aldershot 2 Cardiff City 3 (5,133)
Bluebirds; Bob Wilson; Graham Coldrick, Bobby Ferguson; Gareth Williams, Don Murray, Brian Harris; Barrie Jones, Bobby Brown, Norman Dean, Peter King, Ronnie Bird
Scorers; Bobby Brown 2, Peter King

Round Two, 12 September, 1967. Burnley 2 Cardiff City 1 (11,631)
Bluebirds; Bob Wilson; Graham Coldrick, Bobby Ferguson; Gareth Williams, Don Murray, Brian Harris; Barrie Jones, Bobby Brown, Peter King, Malcolm Clarke, Ronnie Bird
Scorer; Graham Coldrick

1968-69

Round Two, 4 September, 1968. Carlisle United 2 Cardiff City 0 (7,714)
Bluebirds; Fred Davies; Graham Coldrick, Steve Derrett; Malcolm Clarke, Don Murray, Brian Harris; Barrie Jones, Brian Clark, Peter King, John Toshack, Mel Sutton

Did You Know...
Between October 1968 and September 1971, Dave Carver never missed a league or cup match for the Bluebirds, playing in 154 consecutive games

1969-70

Round Two, 3 September, 1969. Crystal Palace 3 Cardiff City 1 (18,616)
Bluebirds; Fred Davies; Dave Carver, Gary Bell; Mel Sutton, Don Murray, Brian Harris; Barrie Jones, Brian Clark, Leslie Lea, John Toshack, Peter King
Scorer; Leslie Lea

1970-71

Round Two, 8 September, 1970. Queens Park Rangers 4 Cardiff City 0 (15,086)
Bluebirds; Frank Parsons; Dave Carver, Gary Bell; Mel Sutton, Don Murray, Brian Harris; Ian Gibson, Brian Clark (Ronnie Bird), Bobby Woodruff, John Toshack, Peter King

1971-72

Round Two, 8 September, 1971. West Ham United 1 Cardiff City 1 (24,420)
Bluebirds; Jim Eadie; Ken Jones (John Parsons), Gary Bell; Mel Sutton, Don Murray, Leighton Phillips; Ian Gibson, Brian Clark, Bobby Woodruff, Alan Warboys, Alan Foggon
Scorer; Alan Foggon

Round Two (replay), 22 September, 1971. Cardiff City 1 West Ham United 2 (30,109)
Bluebirds; Jim Eadie; Ken Jones, Gary Bell; Mel Sutton, Don Murray, Leighton Phillips; Ian Gibson, Brian Clark, Bobby Woodruff, Alan Warboys, Roger Hoy
Scorer; Brian Clark

1972-73

Round One, 16 August, 1972. Cardiff City 2 Bristol Rovers 2 (14,540)
Bluebirds; Bill Irwin; Dave Carver, Gary Bell; Leighton Phillips, Don Murray, Albert Larmour; Ian Gibson, Brian Clark, Alan Warboys, Derek Showers, Alan Foggon,
Scorers; Derek Showers, Gary Bell (p)

Round One (replay), 22 August, 1972. Bristol Rovers 3 Cardiff City 1 (14,550)
Bluebirds; Bill Irwin; Dave Carver, Gary Bell; Leighton Phillips, Don Murray, Albert Larmour; Ian Gibson, Brian Clark, Alan Warboys, Derek Showers, Alan Foggon
Scorer; Brian Clark

1973-74

Round One, 29 August, 1973. Cardiff City 2 Hereford United 0 (9,821)
Bluebirds; Bill Irwin; Phil Dwyer, Gary Bell; George Smith, Don Murray, Leighton Phillips; Tony Villars, Andy McCulloch, Derek Showers (John Impey), Johnny Vincent, Willie Anderson
Scorers; John Impey, Andy McCulloch

Round Two, 10 October, 1973. Cardiff City 2 Burnley 2 (8,775)
Bluebirds; Bill Irwin; Phil Dwyer, Gary Bell; George Smith, Richie Morgan, Leighton Phillips; Gil Reece, Andy McCulloch, Derek Showers, Bobby Woodruff, Johnny Vincent
Scorers; Andy McCulloch, Johnny Vincent

Round Two (replay), 16 October, 1973. Burnley 3 Cardiff City 2 (aet) (12,313)
Bluebirds; Bill Irwin; Phil Dwyer, Gary Bell; Peter King, Richie Morgan, Leighton Phillips; Gil Reece, Andy McCulloch, Derek Showers, Johnny Vincent (Dave Powell), Bobby Woodruff
Scorers; Bobby Woodruff, Gary Bell (p)

1974-75

Round One, 19 August, 1974. Bristol City 2 Cardiff City 1 (8,813)
Bluebirds; Bill Irwin; Freddie Pethard, Clive Charles; George Smith, Don Murray, Leighton Phillips; Tony Villars, Derek Showers, Gil Reece (John Impey), Jimmy McInch, Willie Anderson
Scorer; Jimmy McInch

1975-76

Round One (1st leg), 20 August, 1975. Cardiff City 1 Bristol Rovers 2 (6,688)
Bluebirds; Ron Healey; Phil Dwyer, Clive Charles, John Buchanan (Tony Evans), Mike England, Albert Larmour, Freddie Pethard, Steve Derrett, Tony Villars, Brian Clark, Gil Reece
Scorer; Gil Reece (p)

Round One (2nd leg), 26 August, 1975. Bristol Rovers 1 Cardiff City 1 (7,220)
Bluebirds; Ron Healey; Brian Attley, Clive Charles, Phil Dwyer, Mike England, Albert Larmour, Tony Villars, Brian Clark, Gil Reece, Doug Livermore, Tony Evans
Scorer; Brian Clark
Bristol Rovers through 3-2 on aggregate

1976-77

Round One (1st leg), 14 August, 1976. Cardiff City 2 Bristol Rovers 1 (8,496)
Bluebirds; Ron Healey; Freddie Pethard, Clive Charles, Alan Campbell, Keith Pontin, Albert Larmour, Peter Sayer, Doug Livermore, Adrian Alston, Tony Evans, Willie Anderson
Scorers; Tony Evans, Adrian Alston (p)

July 1975. City's new directors.
(L-R) Clive Griffiths, Tony Clemo, Tiny Latner, Stan Stennett, Stefan Terlezski and Julius Hermer

Round One (2nd leg), 17 August, 1976. Bristol Rovers 4 Cardiff City 4 (5,592)
Bluebirds; Ron Healey; Freddie Pethard, Clive Charles, Alan Campbell, Keith Pontin, Albert Larmour, Peter Sayer, Doug Livermore, Tony Evans, Adrian Alston, Willie Anderson
Scorer; Tony Evans 4
Cardiff City through 6-5 on aggregate

Round Two, 1 September, 1976. Cardiff City 1 Queen's Park Rangers 3 (23,618)
Bluebirds; Bill Irwin; Freddie Pethard, Peter Sayer, Alan Campbell, Keith Pontin, Albert Larmour, Doug Livermore, Derek Showers, Adrian Alston (Brian Attley), Tony Evans, Willie Anderson
Scorer; Tony Evans

1977-78

Round One (1st leg), 13 August, 1977. Torquay United 1 Cardiff City 0 (3,925)
Bluebirds; Ron Healey; Brian Attley, Clive Charles, Alan Campbell, Phil Dwyer, Albert Larmour, John Buchanan, Doug Livermore, Tony Evans, Peter Sayer, David Giles

Round One (2nd leg), 17 August, 1977. Cardiff City 3 Torquay United 2 (3,500)
Bluebirds; Ron Healey; Brian Attley, Clive Charles (Keith Pontin), Alan Campbell, Phil Dwyer, Albert Larmour, Steve Grapes, Doug Livermore, Tony Evans, Peter Sayer, David Giles
Scorers; Phil Dwyer, David Giles, Peter Sayer

Round One (replay), 24 August, 1977. Cardiff City 2 Torquay United 1 (1,711)
Bluebirds; Bill Irwin; Brian Attley, Keith Pontin, John Buchanan, Paul Went, Albert Larmour, Steve Grapes, Alan Campbell, Phil Dwyer, Peter Sayer, David Giles
Scorers; Peter Sayer (p), John Buchanan
Cardiff City through after replay

Round Two, 30 August, 1977. Swindon Town 5 Cardiff City 1 (8,919)
Bluebirds; Bill Irwin; Phil Dwyer, Brian Attley, Paul Went, Keith Pontin, Gerry Byrne, Alan Campbell, John Buchanan, Keith Robson (Ray Bishop), Peter Sayer, David Giles
Scorer; John Buchanan

1978-79

Round One (1st leg), 12 August, 1978. Cardiff City 1 Oxford United 2 (4,500)
Bluebirds; Ron Healey; Rod Thomas, Freddie Pethard, Alan Campbell, Phil Dwyer, Albert Larmour (Steve Grapes), Micky Burns, David Giles, Paul Went, Ray Bishop, John Buchanan
Scorer; John Buchanan

Round One (2nd leg), 16 August, 1978. Oxford United 2 Cardiff City 1 (4,760)
Bluebirds; Ron Healey; Brian Attley, Rod Thomas, Alan Campbell, Phil Dwyer (Ray Bishop), Freddie Pethard, Steve Grapes, David Giles, Micky Burns, Paul Went, John Buchanan
Scorer; Ray Bishop
Oxford United through 4-2 on aggregate

1977 Cardiff City squad

1979-80

Round Two (1st leg), 28 August, 1979. Everton 2 Cardiff City 0 (18,061)
Bluebirds; Ron Healey; Linden Jones, Colin Sullivan, Alan Campbell, Dave Roberts, Phil Dwyer, Steve Grapes, Gary Stevens, Ronnie Moore, Billy Ronson, John Buchanan

Round Two (2nd leg), 5 September, 1979. Cardiff City 1 Everton 0 (9,698)
Bluebirds; Ron Healey; Linden Jones, Colin Sullivan, Alan Campbell, Dave Roberts, Phil Dwyer, Ray Bishop, Gary Stevens, Ronnie Moore, Billy Ronson, Mark Elliott (John Buchanan)
Scorer; John Buchanan
Everton through 2-1 on aggregate

1980-81

Round One (1st leg), 9 August, 1980. Torquay United 0 Cardiff City 0 (3,441)
Bluebirds; Peter Grotier; Steve Grapes, John Lewis, Linden Jones, Keith Pontin, Dave Roberts, Ray Bishop, Tarki Micallef (Wayne Hughes), Gary Stevens, Billy Ronson, John Buchanan

Round One (2nd leg), 13 August, 1980. Cardiff City 2 Torquay United 1 (3,149)
Bluebirds; Peter Grotier; Steve Grapes, Phil Dwyer, Keith Pontin, Linden Jones, Dave Roberts, Ray Bishop, Tarki Micallef, Gary Stevens, Billy Ronson, John Buchanan
Scorers; Ray Bishop, Gary Stevens
Cardiff City through 2-1 on aggregate

Round Two (1st leg), 27 August, 1980. Cardiff City 1 Chelsea 0 (6,549)
Bluebirds; Peter Grotier; Steve Grapes, Keith Pontin, Phil Dwyer, John Lewis, Alan Campbell, Ray Bishop, Peter Kitchen, Gary Stevens, Billy Ronson, John Buchanan (Rod Thomas)
Scorer; Ray Bishop

Round Two (2nd leg), 3 September, 1980. Chelsea 1 Cardiff City 1 (12,959)
Bluebirds; Peter Grotier; Steve Grapes, Keith Pontin, Phil Dwyer, John Lewis, Alan Campbell, Ray Bishop, Peter Kitchen, Gary Stevens, Billy Ronson, John Buchanan
Scorer; Peter Kitchen
Cardiff City through 2-1 on aggregate

Round Three, 23 September, 1980. Barnsley 3 Cardiff City 2 (13,135)
Bluebirds; Peter Grotier; Steve Grapes, Keith Pontin, Rod Thomas, John Lewis, Alan Campbell, Ray Bishop, Peter Kitchen, Gary Stevens, Billy Ronson, John Buchanan
Scorers; John Buchanan, John Lewis

1981-82

Round One (1st leg), 2 September, 1981. Cardiff City 2 Exeter City 1 (2,688)
Bluebirds; Ron Healey; Linden Jones, Keith Pontin, Phil Dwyer. Colin Sullivan, Steve Grapes, John Lewis, Peter Kitchen, Gary Stevens, Billy Ronson, John Buchanan
Scorer; Gary Stevens 2

Round One (2nd leg), 16 September, 1981. Exeter City 3 Cardiff City 1 (aet) (4.449)
Bluebirds; Ron Healey; Linden Jones, Keith Pontin, Phil Dwyer, Colin Sullivan, Steve Grapes, John Lewis, Paul Sugrue, Gary Stevens, Billy Ronson, John Buchanan
Scorer; Paul Sugrue
Exeter City through 4-3 on aggregate

1982-83 Milk Cup

Round One (1st leg), 31 August, 1982. Cardiff City 2 Hereford United 1 (1,808)
Bluebirds; Martin Thomas; Linden Jones, Paul Bodin, Gary Bennett (Tarki Micallef), Keith Pontin, Jimmy Mullen, Dave Bennett, David Tong, Roger Gibbins, Jeff Hemmerman, John Lewis
Scorers; Dave Bennett, Roger Gibbins

Round One (2nd leg), 15 September, 1982. Hereford United 1 Cardiff City 2 (3,301)
Bluebirds; Martin Thomas; Linden Jones, Paul Bodin, Jimmy Mullen, Gary Bennett, Tarki Micallef, Dave Bennett, David Tong, Roger Gibbins, Jeff Hemmerman, John Lewis
Scorers; Roger Gibbins, Jeff Hemmerman
Cardiff City through 4-2 on aggregate

Round Two (1st leg), 5 October, 1982. Arsenal 2 Cardiff City 1 (15,115)
Bluebirds; Martin Thomas; Linden Jones, Paul Bodin, Tarki Micallef, Phil Dwyer, Jimmy Mullen, Dave Bennett, David Tong, Roger Gibbins, Jeff Hemmerman, John Lewis
Scorer; Roger Gibbins

Round Two (2nd leg), 26 October, 1982. Cardiff City 1 Arsenal 3 (11,632)
Bluebirds; Martin Thomas; Linden Jones (Godfrey Ingram), Paul Bodin, Tarki Micallef, Phil Dwyer, Gary Bennett, Dave Bennett, David Tong, Roger Gibbins, Jeff Hemmerman, John Lewis
Scorer; Jeff Hemmerman
Arsenal through 5-2 on aggregate)

Did You Know...
City used three goalkeepers in the 4-2 defeat at Bradford City on 16 February, 1983. Andy Dibble went off injured and he was replaced by Phil Dwyer and later, Linden Jones

1983-84

Round One (1st leg), 31 August, 1983. Exeter City 2 Cardiff City 3 (4,005)
Bluebirds; Andy Dibble; Linden Jones, Phil Dwyer, Gary Bennett, Paul Bodin (Jimmy Mullen), Gordon Owen, David Tong, Roger Gibbins, Andy Crawford, Chris Rodon, John Lewis
Scorers; Phil Dwyer, Gordon Owen, Andy Crawford

Round One (2nd leg), 13 September, 1983. Cardiff City 2 Exeter City 1 (2,721)
Bluebirds; Andy Dibble; Chris Rodon, Phil Dwyer, Gary Bennett, Paul Bodin, Gordon Owen, David Tong, Roger Gibbins, Andy Crawford, Jimmy Mullen, John Lewis (Wayne Matthews)
Scorers; Andy Crawford, Gary Bennett
Cardiff City through 5-3 on aggregate

Round Two (1st leg), 4 October, 1983. Cardiff City 0 Norwich City 0 (4,425)
Bluebirds; Andy Dibble; Colin Smith, Phil Dwyer, Jimmy Mullen, Paul Bodin, Gordon Owen, David Tong, Roger Gibbins, Chris Townsend, Andy Crawford, Wayne Matthews

Round Two (2nd leg), 26 October, 1983. Norwich City 3 Cardiff City 0 (9,887)
Bluebirds; Andy Dibble; Colin Smith, Phil Dwyer, Jimmy Mullen, Paul Bodin, David Tong (Chris Townsend), Roger Gibbins, Gary Bennett, Russell Heycock, Gordon Owen, Wayne Matthews
Norwich City through 3-0 on aggregate

1984-85

Round One (1st leg), 29 August, 1984. Exeter City 1 Cardiff City 0 (3,469)
Bluebirds; Lee Smelt; Vaughan Jones, Phil Dwyer, Colin Smith, David Grant, Karl Elsey, David Tong, Roger Gibbins, Nigel Vaughan, John Seasman, Kevin Summerfield

Round One (2nd leg), 4 September, 1984. Cardiff City 2 Exeter City 0 (2,026)
Bluebirds; Lee Smelt; Vaughan Jones, Phil Dwyer, Colin Smith, David Grant, Paul Bodin, Karl Elsey, David Tong, Roger Gibbins, John Seasman, Nigel Vaughan,
Scorers; Roger Gibbins, Marker (og)
Cardiff City through 2-1 on aggregate

Round Two (1st leg), 25 September, 1984. Watford 3 Cardiff City 1 (12,884)
Bluebirds; Gary Plumley; Vaughan Jones, Phil Dwyer, Colin Smith, David Grant, Paul Bodin, Karl Elsey, David Tong, Roger Gibbins, John Seasman, Nigel Vaughan
Scorer; Roger Gibbins

Round Two (2nd leg), 9 October, 1984. Cardiff City 1 Watford 0 (4,607)
Bluebirds; Lee Smelt; Vaughan Jones, Phil Dwyer, David Grant, Paul Bodin, Karl Elsey, David Tong, Kevin Summerfield, Roger Gibbins, John Seasman (Tarki Micallef), Nigel Vaughan
Scorer; David Grant
Watford through 3-2 on aggregate

1985-86

Round One (1st leg), 20 August, 1985. Cardiff City 2 Swansea City 1 (4,218)
Bluebirds; Chris Sander; Jake King, Mike Ford, Roger Gibbins, John Carver, Jimmy Mullen, John Farrington, Brian Flynn, Rob Turner, Nigel Vaughan, Paul McLoughlin (Tarki Micallef)
Scorers; Brian Flynn 2

Round One (2nd leg), 3 September, 1985. Swansea City 3 Cardiff City 1 (4,621)
Bluebirds; Mel Rees; Carleton Leonard, John Carver, Mike Ford, Roger Gibbins, Jimmy Mullen, John Farrington, Brian Flynn (Tarki Micallef), Nigel Vaughan, Kevin Meacock, Paul McLoughlin
Scorer; John Farrington
Swansea City through 4-3 on aggregate

1986-87

Round One (1st leg), 26 August, 1986. Cardiff City 5 Plymouth Argyle 4 (2,503)
Bluebirds; Graham Moseley; Andy Kerr, Steve Sherlock, Phil Brignull, Terry Boyle, Paul Wimbleton, David Giles (Alan Curtis), Rob Turner, Paul Wheeler, Nigel Vaughan, Alan Rogers
Scorers; Nigel Vaughan 2, Terry Boyle, Rob Turner, Paul Wheeler

Round One (2nd leg), 2 September, 1986. Plymouth Argyle 0 Cardiff City 1 (5,829)
Bluebirds; Graham Moseley; Andy Kerr, Phil Brignull, Terry Boyle, Steve Sherlock, Paul Wimbleton, David Giles, Rob Turner, Paul Wheeler, Alan Curtis, Alan Rogers
Scorer; David Giles
Cardiff City through 6-4 on aggregate

Round Two
Bye after being drawn away to Luton Town who withdrew from the competition

Round Three, 28 October, 1986. Cardiff City 2 Chelsea 1 (8,018)
Bluebirds; Mel Rees; Andy Kerr, Steve Sherlock, Phil Brignull, Terry Boyle, Paul Wimbleton, Mike Ford, Nicky Platnauer, Alan Curtis, Paul Wheeler, Nigel Vaughan
Scorer; Nicky Platnauer 2

Round Four, 18 November, 1986. Shrewsbury Town 1 Cardiff City 0 (4,673)
Bluebirds; Mel Rees; Andy Kerr, Phil Brignull, Terry Boyle, Mike Ford, Chris Marustik, Paul Wimbleton, Nicky Platnauer, Alan Curtis (Alan Rogers), Paul Wheeler, Nigel Vaughan

1987-88 Littlewoods Cup

Round One (1st leg), 18 August, 1987. Newport County 2 Cardiff City 1 (3,383) (Played at Ninian Park)
Bluebirds; Graham Moseley; Jason Perry, Gareth Abraham, Terry Boyle, Mike Ford, Brian McDermott, Steve Mardenborough, Alan Curtis, Mark Kelly, Paul Sanderson (Kevin Bartlett), Jimmy Gilligan
Scorer; Alan Curtis

A 'bad hair' day for City's Paul Wimbleton

Round One (2nd leg), 25 August, 1987. Cardiff City 2 Newport County 2 (3,550)
Bluebirds; Graham Moseley; Jason Perry (Kevin Bartlett), Nigel Stevenson, Terry Boyle, Mike Ford, Nicky Platnauer, Alan Curtis, Paul Sanderson, Mark Kelly, Jimmy Gilligan, Brian McDermott
Scorers; Jimmy Gilligan, Paul Sanderson
Newport County through 4-3 on aggregate

1988-89

Round One (1st leg), 30 August, 1988. Cardiff City 0 Swansea City 1 (6,241)
Bluebirds; George Wood; Ian Rodgerson, Nigel Stevenson, Terry Boyle, Nicky Platnauer, Brian McDermott (Ian Walsh), Mark Kelly, Jason Gummer (Steve Lynex), Alan Curtis, Kevin Bartlett, Jimmy Gilligan

Round One (2nd leg), 20 September, 1988. Swansea City 0 Cardiff City 2 (6,987)
Bluebirds; George Wood; Ian Rodgerson, Nigel Stevenson, Terry Boyle, Nicky Platnauer, Paul Wimbleton, Steve Lynex, Jason Gummer, Mark Kelly, Alan Curtis (Paul Wheeler), Jimmy Gilligan
Scorers; Paul Wheeler, Terry Boyle
Cardiff City through 2-1 on aggregate

Round Two (1st leg), 28 September, 1988. Queen's Park Rangers 3 Cardiff City 0 (6,078)
Bluebirds; George Wood; Ian Rodgerson, Nigel Stevenson, Terry Boyle, Phil Bater, Nicky Platnauer, Paul Wimbleton, Mark Kelly, Steve Lynex (Paul Wheeler, Jon Morgan), Alan Curtis, Jimmy Gilligan

Round Two (2nd leg), 11 October, 1988. Cardiff City 1 Queen's Park Rangers 4 (2,692)
Bluebirds; George Wood; Jason Perry, Gareth Abraham, Nigel Stevenson, Terry Boyle, Jon Morgan, Alan Curtis (Allan Lewis), Kevin Bartlett, Jimmy Gilligan, Paul Wheeler, Chris Fry
Scorer; Alan Curtis
Queen's Park Rangers through 7-1 on aggregate

Did You Know...
There have been two cases of fathers and sons both playing league football for the Bluebirds. Jimmy Blair played from 1920-26 while son Dougie played from 1947-54. John Toshack was with City from 1965-70 and son Cameron played in the 1990-91 season

1989-90

Round One (1st leg), 22 August, 1989. Cardiff City 0 Plymouth Argyle 3 (2,620)
Bluebirds; George Wood; Ian Rodgerson, Jason Perry, Gareth Abraham, Roger Gibbins, Alan Curtis, Jon Morgan, Mark Kelly, Steve Lynex, Jimmy Gilligan, Chris Pike (Chris Fry)

5 October 1991 Cardiff City 5 Wrexham 0
Carl Dale is brought down by Wrexham's Joey Jones

Round One (2nd leg), 29 August, 1989. Plymouth Argyle 0 Cardiff City 2 (5,728)
Bluebirds; George Wood; Ian Rodgerson, Gareth Abraham, Jason Perry, Ray Daniel, Alan Curtis (Jason Gummer), Jon Morgan, Mark Kelly, Steve Lynex, Jimmy Gilligan, Chris Pike (Chris Fry)
Scorers; Chris Pike, Steve Lynex
Plymouth Argyle through 3-2 on aggregate

1990-91 Rumbelows Cup

Round One (1st leg), 28 August, 1990. Mansfield Town 1 Cardiff City 1 (2,091)
Bluebirds; Roger Hansbury; Ian Rodgerson, Jason Perry, Gareth Abraham, Ray Daniel, Leigh Barnard, Mark Jones, Cohen Griffith, Pat Heard, Roger Gibbins, Chris Pike (Nathan Blake)
Scorer; Cohen Griffith

Round One (2nd leg), 4 September, 1990. Cardiff City 3 Mansfield Town 0 (2,539)
Bluebirds; Roger Hansbury; Ian Rodgerson, Jason Perry, Nathan Blake, Ray Daniel, Leigh Barnard, Mark Jones, Cohen Griffith, Pat Heard, Roger Gibbins, Chris Pike (Jeff Chandler)
Scorers; Cohen Griffith 2, Chris Pike
Cardiff City through 4-1 on aggregate

Round Two (1st leg), 25 September, 1990. Cardiff City 1 Portsmouth 1 (4,224)
Bluebirds; Roger Hansbury; Ian Rodgerson, Neil Matthews, Jason Perry, Ray Daniel, Leigh Barnard, Mark Jones, Cohen Griffith, Pat Heard, Roger Gibbins, Chris Pike
Scorer; Cohen Griffith

Round Two (2nd leg), 9 October, 1990. Portsmouth 3 Cardiff City 1 aet (6,174)
Bluebirds; Roger Hansbury; Allan Lewis, Neil Matthews, Jason Perry, Ray Daniel, Leigh Barnard, Mark Jones (Jon Morgan), Cohen Griffith, Pat Heard, Roger Gibbins, Nathan Blake (Jeff Chandler)
Scorer; Cohen Griffith
Portsmouth through 4-2 on aggregate

1991-92

Round One (1st leg), 21 August, 1991. Cardiff City 3 Bournemouth 2 (3,439)
Bluebirds; Roger Hansbury; Mark Jones, Gareth Abraham, Jason Perry, Damon Searle, Cohen Griffith (Chris Pike), Neil Matthews, Paul Millar, Pat Heard (Allan Lewis), Roger Gibbins, Carl Dale
Scorers; Paul Millar, Roger Gibbins, Damon Searle

Round One (2nd leg), 27 August, 1991. Bournemouth 4 Cardiff City 1 (4,489)
Bluebirds; Roger Hansbury; Mark Jones, Gareth Abraham, Jason Perry, Damon Searle, Cohen Griffith (Chris Pike), Paul Ramsey, Pat Heard, Paul Millar, Roger Gibbins, Carl Dale
Scorer; Mark Jones (p)
Bournemouth through 6-4 on aggregate

1992-93 Coca Cola Cup

Round One (1st leg), 18 August, 1992. Cardiff City 1 Bristol City 0 (4,066)
Bluebirds; Mark Grew; Robbie James, Jason Perry, Derek Brazil, Damon Searle, Paul Millar, Paul Ramsey, Cohen Griffith, Chris Pike (Roger Gibbins), Carl Dale, Nathan Blake
Scorer; Carl Dale

Round One (2nd leg), 25 August, 1992. Bristol City 5 Cardiff City 1 (9,801)
Bluebirds; Mark Grew; Robbie James, Jason Perry, Derek Brazil, Damon Searle, Paul Millar, Roger Gibbins, Nilson Callaway (Lee Baddeley), Tony Bird, Carl Dale, Nathan Blake
Scorer; Carl Dale
Bristol City through 5-2 on aggregate

1993-94

Round One (1st leg), 17 August, 1993. Bournemouth 3 Cardiff City 1 (3,054)
Bluebirds; Phil Kite; Robbie James, Jason Perry, Kevin Ratcliffe, Derek Brazil, Paul Millar, Tony Bird, Nick Richardson, Cohen Griffith, Garry Thompson, Nathan Blake
Scorer; Tony Bird

Did You Know...
Paul Millar struck a brace of penalties in a game twice during the 1993-94 season, against Rotherham United and Brighton

Round One (2nd leg), 24 August, 1993. Cardiff City 1 Bournemouth 1 (4,459)
Bluebirds; Phil Kite; Robbie James, Derek Brazil, Jason Perry, Damon Searle, Paul Millar, John Cornwell, Nick Richardson, Tony Bird, Garry Thompson, Nathan Blake
Scorer; Morris (og)
Bournemouth through 4-2 on aggregate

1994-95

Round One (1st leg), 16 August, 1994. Cardiff City 1 Torquay United 0 (2,690)
Bluebirds; David Williams; Terry Evans, Mark Aizlewood, Jason Perry, Derek Brazil, Charlie Oatway, Wayne Fereday (Paul Millar), Nick Richardson, Cohen Griffith, Phil Stant, Tony Bird (Carl Dale)
Scorer; Charlie Oatway

Cardiff City forward Phil Stant

Round One (2nd leg), 23 August, 1994. Torquay United 4 Cardiff City 2 (2,709)
Bluebirds; David Williams; Terry Evans, Scott Young, Derek Brazil, Danny Street (Darren Adams), Charlie Oatway, Tony Bird, Nick Richardson, Paul Millar, Phil Stant, Carl Dale
Scorer; Phil Stant 2
Torquay United through 4-3 on aggregate

1995-96

Round One (1st leg), 16 August, 1995. Portsmouth 0 Cardiff City 2 (4,203)
Bluebirds; David Williams; Derek Brazil, Jason Perry, Lee Baddeley, Damon Searle, Paul Harding, Nathan Wigg, Ian Rodgerson, Tony Bird, Simon Haworth (Andy Evans), Carl Dale
Scorers; Carl Dale, Tony Bird

Round One (2nd leg), 22 August, 1995. Cardiff City 1 Portsmouth 0 (4,347)
Bluebirds; David Williams; Derek Brazil, Jason Perry, Lee Baddeley, Damon Searle, Paul Harding (Scott Young), Nathan Wigg, Ian Rodgerson, Tony Bird, Simon Haworth (Keith Downing), Carl Dale
Scorer; Carl Dale
Cardiff City through 3-0 on aggregate

Round Two (1st leg), 19 September, 1995. Cardiff City 0 Southampton 3 (9,041)
Bluebirds; David Williams; Scott Young, Jason Perry, Lee Baddeley, Damon Searle, Paul Harding (Ian Rodgerson), Gerald Dobbs (Darren Adams), Nathan Wigg, Tony Bird, Simon Haworth, Carl Dale

Round Two (2nd leg), 4 October, 1995. Southampton 2 Cardiff City 1 (12,709)
Bluebirds; David Williams; Scott Young, Jason Perry, Lee Baddeley, Damon Searle, Paul Harding, Chris Ingram, Ian Rodgerson, Darren Adams (Andy Evans), Simon Haworth, Carl Dale
Scorer; Ian Rodgerson
Southampton through 5-1 on aggregate

1996-97

Round One (1st leg), 20 August, 1996. Cardiff City 1 Northampton Town 0 (2,294)
Bluebirds; Tony Elliott; Ian Rodgerson, Lee Jarman, Scott Young, Jason Perry, Kevin Lloyd, Mickey Bennett, Jason Fowler, Steve White, Carl Dale (Andy Scott), Tony Philliskirk
Scorer; Carl Dale

Damon Searle in action

Round One (2nd leg), 3 September, 1996. Northampton Town 2 Cardiff City 0 (3,567)
Bluebirds; Tony Elliott; Ian Rodgerson, Lee Jarman (Craig Middleton), Scott Young, Jason Perry, Kevin Lloyd, Mickey Bennett (Jimmy Gardner), Jason Fowler, Steve White, Jeff Eckhardt, Tony Philliskirk
Northampton Town through 2-1 on aggregate

1997-98

Round One (1st leg), 12 August, 1997. Cardiff City 1 Southend United 1 (2,804)
Bluebirds; John Hallworth; Scott Young, Lee Jarman, Mark Harris, Chris Beech, Jason Fowler, Scott Partridge, Craig Middleton (Jimmy Rollo, Kevin Lloyd), Tony Carss (Gareth Stoker), Steve White, Kevin Nugent
Scorer; Jimmy Rollo

Round One (2nd leg), 26 August, 1997. Southend United 2 Cardiff City 1 (3,002)
Bluebirds; John Hallworth; Craig Middleton (Wayne O'Sullivan), Scott Young (Lee Jarman), Mark Harris (Kevin Lloyd), Chris Beech, Jason Fowler, Scott Partridge, Gareth Stoker, David Penney, Tony Carss, Steve White
Scorer; Jason Fowler
Southend United through 2-1 on aggregate

1998-99 Worthington Cup

Round One (1st leg), 11 August, 1998. Fulham 2 Cardiff City 1 (4,305)
Bluebirds; John Hallworth; Mark Delaney, Graham Mitchell (Jeff Eckhardt), Scott Young, Lee Phillips, Richard Carpenter, Mark Bonner (David Penney), Wayne O'Sullivan, Christian Roberts, John Williams, Andy Saville (Kevin Nugent)
Scorer; John Williams

Round One (2nd leg), 18 August, 1998. Cardiff City 1 Fulham 2 (4,768)
Bluebirds; John Hallworth; Mark Delaney, Graham Mitchell, Scott Young, Lee Phillips (Jeff Eckhardt), Richard Carpenter, Mark Bonner, Jason Fowler, John Williams (Rob Earnshaw), Christian Roberts (Wayne O'Sullivan), Kevin Nugent
Scorer; Jeff Eckhardt
Fulham through 4-2 on aggregate

1999-00

Round One (1st leg), 10 August, 1999. Cardiff City 1 Queen's Park Rangers 2 (5,702)
Bluebirds; John Hallworth; Winston Faerber, Jeff Eckhardt, Jason Fowler (Lee Jarman), Mike Ford, Mark Bonner (John Cornforth), Willie Boland, Danny Hill (Matt Brazier), Andy Legg, Jason Bowen, Kevin Nugent
Scorer; Jason Bowen

Round One (2nd leg), 25 August, 1999. Queen's Park Rangers 1 Cardiff City 2 aet (6,185)
Bluebirds; John Hallworth; Winston Faerber (Lee Phillips), Scott Young, Jeff Eckhardt, Mike Ford, Mark Bonner (John Cornforth), Craig Middleton, Matt Brazier, Andy Legg, Jason Bowen (Jamie Hughes), Kevin Nugent
Scorers; Matt Brazier, Jamie Hughes
Cardiff City through 3-2 on penalties

20 January 1999 Cardiff City 4 Brentford 1
Jeff Eckhardt leaps high to head home

Round Two (1st leg), 14 September, 1999. Cardiff City 1 Wimbledon 1 (7,613)
Bluebirds; John Hallworth; Winston Faerber, Scott Young, Jeff Eckhardt, Mike Ford, Jason Fowler (Matt Brazier), Willie Boland, Richard Carpenter, Andy Legg, Jason Bowen (Jamie Hughes), Kevin Nugent
Scorer; Kevin Nugent (p)

Round Two (2nd leg), 21 September, 1999. Wimbledon 3 Cardiff City 1 (2,772)
Bluebirds; John Hallworth; Winston Faerber, Scott Young, Jeff Eckhardt, Mike Ford, Jason Fowler (Matt Brazier), Willie Boland, John Cornforth (Richard Carpenter), Andy Legg, Jason Bowen (Jamie Hughes), Kevin Nugent
Scorer; Jason Bowen
Wimbledon through 4-2 on aggregate

2000-01

Round One (1st leg), 23 August, 2000. Crystal Palace 2 Cardiff City 1 (5,983)
Bluebirds; Mark Walton; Danny Gabbidon, Matt Brazier, David Greene, Scott Young, Josh Low, Willie Boland, Mark Bonner, Andy Legg, Kevin Nugent, Paul Brayson
Scorer; Scott Young

Round One (2nd leg), 5 September, 2000. Cardiff City 0 Crystal Palace 0 (4,904)
Bluebirds; Mark Walton; Danny Gabbidon, Gethin Jones, David Greene, Andy Legg, Scott McCulloch, Mark Bonner (Dai Thomas), Danny Hill, Kevin Evans, Kurt Nogan (Rob Earnshaw), Kevin Nugent
Crystal Palace through 2-1 on aggregate

2001-02

Round One, 21 August, 2001. Millwall 2 Cardiff City 1 (5,516)
Bluebirds; Neil Alexander; Rhys Weston, David Hughes, Danny Gabbidon, Mike Simpkins, Willie Boland, Graham Kavanagh, Paul Brayson (Josh Low), Andy Legg, Leo Fortune-West (Gavin Gordon), Rob Earnshaw
Scorer; Rob Earnshaw

Did You Know...
Rob Earnshaw with ten, has scored the most goals for the Bluebirds in the League Cup

2002-03

Round One, 11 September, 2002. Boston United 1 Cardiff City 5 (2,280)
Bluebirds; Martyn Margetson; Gary Croft, Rhys Weston (Andy Legg), Spencer Prior, Chris Barker, Willie Boland (Des Hamilton), Leyton Maxwell, Graham Kavanagh, Peter Thorne (Andy Campbell), Rob Earnshaw, Leo Fortune-West
Scorers; Rob Earnshaw 3, Peter Thorne, og

Round Two, 1 October, 2002. Tottenham Hotspur 1 Cardiff City 0 (23,723)
Bluebirds; Neil Alexander; Rhys Weston, Danny Gabbidon, Spencer Prior, Gary Croft, Gareth Whalley, Willie Boland (Leyton Maxwell), Graham Kavanagh, Andy Legg (Leo Fortune-West), Andy Campbell, Rob Earnshaw

2003-04 Carling Cup

Round One, 12 August, 2003. Cardiff City 4 Leyton Orient 1 (4,503)
Bluebirds; Martyn Margetson; Tony Vidmar, James Collins, Danny Gabbidon, Chris Barker, Gareth Whalley, Mark Bonner (Willie Boland), Leyton Maxwell, Jason Bowen, Rob Earnshaw (Stuart Fleetwood), Andy Campbell
Scorers; Rob Earnshaw 3, Andy Campbell

12 February 2005, Cardiff City 2 Brighton 0.
Junichi Inamoto beats Brighton defenders Guy Butters (left) and Richard Carpenter (right)

Round Two, 23 September, 2003. Cardiff City 2 West Ham United 3 (10,724)
Bluebirds; Martyn Margetson; Rhys Weston, Tony Vidmar, Danny Gabbidon, Chris Barker, Willie Boland, Mark Bonner, Graham Kavanagh, Jason Bowen (Andy Campbell), Rob Earnshaw, Peter Thorne (Gavin Gordon)
Scorer; Rob Earnshaw 2

2004-05

Round One, 23 August, 2004. Kidderminster Harriers 1 Cardiff City 1 aet (1,897)
Bluebirds; Tony Warner; Rhys Weston, James Collins, Danny Gabbidon, Tony Vidmar, Jobi McAnuff, Lee Bullock (Graham Kavanagh), Willie Boland, Paul Parry, Rob Earnshaw, Andy Campbell (Stuart Fleetwood)
Scorer; Rob Earnshaw
Cardiff City through 5-4 on penalties

15 March 1913, Cardiff City 0 Swansea Town 0. A section of the 10,000 crowd for Swansea Town's first visit to Ninian Park

1913-14. The Cardiff City playing staff. Back row L–R: K McKenzie, George West, Jack Evans, Jack Kneeshaw, Pat Cassidy, J Stephenson, E Milford, W Davidson, Tom Witts, TH Robertson. Centre: Tommy Doncaster, J Bennett, A Holt, Harry Featherstone, John Burton, Henry Harvey, Billy Hardy, H Ward, Bob Leah, Joe Clarke. Front row: George Burton, Harry Tracey, Billy Devlin, Harry Keggans, Billy Gaughan, Jim Henderson, Fred Keenor

26 March 1927, FA Cup semi-final. Cardiff City 3 Reading 0 (at Molineux).
Hughie Ferguson watches as a downward header from Harry Wake gives City a 2-0 lead

25 April 1927. Fred Keenor holds the FA Cup aloft to the massed crowds in Cathays Park, Cardiff

6 October 1945, Bristol City 3 Cardiff City 2.
Dan Canning gathers while Alf Sherwood blocks the Robins attacker

26 April 1947, Cardiff City 3 Ipswich Town 2. Ipswich's Matt O'Mahony slots a spot-kick past City keeper Danny Canning

29 January 1949, Aston Villa 1 Cardiff City 2. FA Cup Rd 4.
City skipper Stan Montgomery leads the Bluebirds out followed by Arthur Lever and Ron Stitfall

15 March 1952, Cardiff City 3 Barnsley 0. Ken Chisholm heads City into the lead on his home debut

12 January 1957, Chelsea 1 Cardiff City 2. Goalmouth action at Stamford Bridge. L–R: Ron Stitfall, Johnny McNicholl (Chelsea), Graham Vearncombe, Ron Tindall (Chelsea) and Danny Malloy

30 April 1959, Welsh Cup Final. Cardiff City 2 Lovells Athletic 0. L–R: Derek Tapscott, Brian Walsh, Joe Bonson, Danny Malloy and Colin Hudson receiving cup

21 November 1959, Cardiff City 4 Stoke City 4. Derek Tapscott with a diving header for the opening goal

9 August 1963. John Charles signs for the Bluebirds watched by manager George Swindin

18 February 1967, FA Cup Round Four. Cardiff City 1 Manchester City 1. Bobby Brown with Ronnie Bird, Graham Coldrick, Bobby Ferguson and Don Murray in tunnel. Spencer Kemp watches the players running out

13 August 1969, Cardiff City 2 Swindon 2. Brian Clark shoots for goal challenged by Frank Burrows

28 December 1974, Cardiff City 3 Aston Villa 1.
Derek Showers scores for City with Jack Whitham waiting to pounce

4 May 1976, Bury 0 Cardiff City 1. Adrian Alston turns
in the winner to give City promotion to Division Two

9 October 1976, Cardiff City 3 Bolton Wanderers 2.
Bolton's Sam Allardyce watches as Tony Evans gathers a high ball

24 September 1977, Cardiff City 3 Fulham 1. John Buchanan is tackled by George Best

Round Two, 21 September, 2004. Milton Keynes Dons 1 Cardiff City 4 (2,266)
Bluebirds; Neil Alexander; Byron Anthony, James Collins, Tony Vidmar, Chris Barker, Jobi McAnuff (Joe Ledley), Lee Bullock, Willie Boland, Paul Parry, Alan Lee, Peter Thorne (Andy Campbell)
Scorers; Peter Thorne 2, Lee Bullock, Byron Anthony

Round Three, 26 October, 2004. Bournemouth 3 Cardiff City 3 aet (8,598)
Bluebirds; Neil Alexander; Rhys Weston (Byron Anthony), James Collins, Tony Vidmar, Chris Barker, Joe Ledley, Lee Bullock, Graham Kavanagh, Nicky Fish (Paul Parry), Alan Lee, Peter Thorne (Cameron Jerome)
Scorers; Alan Lee, Lee Bullock, Cameron Jerome
Cardiff City through 5-4 on penalties

Round Four, 9 November, 2004. Cardiff City 0 Portsmouth 2 (13,555)
Bluebirds; Tony Warner; Tony Vidmar, James Collins, Danny Gabbidon, Chris Barker, Jobi McAnuff (Cameron Jerome), Joe Ledley, Willie Boland, Graham Kavanagh, Alan Lee, Paul Parry (Stuart Fleetwood)

2005-06

Round One, 24 August, 2005. Colchester United 0 Cardiff City 2 (1,904)
Bluebirds; Neil Alexander; Rhys Weston, Darren Purse, Glenn Loovens, Chris Barker (Paul Parry), Jeff Whitley, Jason Koumas, Willie Boland, Kevin Cooper, Alan Lee, Cameron Jerome (Andrea Ferretti)
Scorers; Darren Purse (p), Cameron Jerome

Round Two, 20 September, 2005. Cardiff City 2 Macclesfield Town 1 (3,849)
Bluebirds; Martyn Margetson; Rhys Weston, Darren Purse, Neil Cox, Chris Barker, Joe Ledley, Neil Ardley, Jeff Whitley, Paul Parry (Jason Koumas), Stuart Fleetwood (Andrea Ferretti), Alan Lee
Scorers; Joe Ledley, Jason Koumas

Round Three, 26 October, 2005. Cardiff City 0 Leicester City 1 (8,727)
Bluebirds; Martyn Margetson; Rhys Weston (Neil Ardley), Darren Purse, Glenn Loovens, Chris Barker, Joe Ledley, Jeff Whitley, Jason Koumas, Paul Parry (Andrea Ferretti), Alan Lee, Cameron Jerome

Did You Know...
Loan signing Michael Boulding, who came to the club in March 2005 from Barnsley, was a professional tennis player before taking up full time football

2006-07

Round One, 22 August, 2006. Cardiff City 0 Barnet 2 (3,305)
Bluebirds; Mark Howard; Chris Gunter, Rhys Weston (Darcy Blake), Roger Johnson, Joe Jacobson, Malvin Kamara (Paul Parry), Willo Flood, Nick McKoy, Kevin Cooper (Joe Ledley), Kevin Campbell, Luigi Glombard

2007-08

Round One, 14 August, 2007. Cardiff City 1 Brighton 0 (aet) (3,726)
Bluebirds; Ross Turnbull; Chris Gunter, Darren Purse, Roger Johnson, Tony Capaldi, Paul Parry (Aaron Ramsey), Gavin Rae, Stephen McPhail, Peter Whittingham (Joe Ledley), Steve McLean, Warren Feeney (Matt Green)
Scorer; Roger Johnson

Round Two, 28 August, 2007. Cardiff City 1 Leyton Orient 0 (6,150)
Bluebirds; Ross Turnbull; Chris Gunter, Darren Purse (Darcy Blake), Roger Johnson, Tony Capaldi, Paul Parry, Gavin Rae, Stephen McPhail, Peter Whittingham, Robbie Fowler (Steve McLean), Jimmy Floyd Hasselbaink
Scorer; Peter Whittingham

31 October 2007, Carling Cup Round Four. Liverpool 2 Cardiff 1. Robbie Fowler moves away chased by Steven Gerrard

Round Three, 25 September, 2007. West Bromwich Albion 2 Cardiff City 4 (14,085)
Bluebirds; Michael Oakes; Kevin McNaughton (Chris Gunter), Glenn Loovens, Roger Johnson, Tony Capaldi, Trevor Sinclair (Peter Whittingham), Gavin Rae, Stephen McPhail, Joe Ledley, Robbie Fowler (Paul Parry), Jimmy Floyd Hasselbaink
Scorers; Robbie Fowler 2(1p), Jimmy Floyd Hasselbaink, Trevor Sinclair

Round Four, 31 October, 2007. Liverpool 2 Cardiff City 1 (41,780)
Bluebirds; Michael Oakes; Kevin McNaughton (Chris Gunter), Darren Purse, Roger Johnson, Tony Capaldi, Paul Parry, Gavin Rae, Stephen McPhail (Peter Whittingham), Joe Ledley, Robbie Fowler, Jimmy Floyd Hasselbaink (Steve Thompson)
Scorer; Darren Purse

2008-09

Round One, 12 August, 2008. Bournemouth 1 Cardiff City 2 (3,399)
Bluebirds; Tom Heaton; Kevin McNaughton, Glenn Loovens, Roger Johnson, Mark Kennedy, Peter Whittingham (Ross McCormack), Stephen McPhail, Gavin Rae, Joe Ledley, Jay Bothroyd (Steve Thompson), Paul Parry (Miguel Comminges)
Scorer; Paul Parry 2

Round Two, 26 August, 2008. Cardiff City 2 MK Dons 1 (6,334)
Bluebirds; Tom Heaton; Darcy Blake (Paul Parry), Darren Purse, Roger Johnson, Tony Capaldi (Miguel Comminges), Peter Whittingham, Riccy Scimeca (Aaron Morris), Stephen McPhail, Joe Ledley, Eddie Johnson, Ross McCormack
Scorers; Ross McCormack (p), Peter Whittingham

Round Three, 23 September, 2008. Swansea City 1 Cardiff City 0 (17,411)
Bluebirds; Peter Enckelman; Kevin McNaughton, Darren Purse, Roger Johnson, Miguel Comminges, Paul Parry, Gavin Rae, Stephen McPhail, Joe Ledley (Peter Whittingham), Jay Bothroyd, Eddie Johnson (Ross McCormack)

Did You Know...
The Bluebirds victory over Bristol Rovers in the Carling Cup in August 2009 was their 50th success in the League Cup competition

2009-10

Round One, 11 August, 2009. Cardiff City 3 Dagenham & Redbridge 1 (5,545)
Bluebirds; Peter Enckelman; Paul Quinn, Anthony Gerrard, Mark Hudson, Tony Capaldi, Miguel Comminges (Aaron Wildig), Stephen McPhail, Gavin Rae, Peter Whittingham, Michael Chopra, Jay Bothroyd
Scorers; Gavin Rae, Jay Bothroyd (p), Peter Whittingham

Round Two, 26 August, 2009. Cardiff City 3 Bristol Rovers 1 (9,767)
Bluebirds; Peter Enckelman; Paul Quinn, Anthony Gerrard, Gabor Gyepes, Tony Capaldi, Peter Whittingham, Gavin Rae (Riccy Scimeca), Stephen McPhail, Chris Burke (Aaron Wildig), Kelvin Etuhu (Josh Magennis), Michael Chopra
Scorers; Michael Chopra, Peter Whittingham, Josh Magennis

Did You Know...
Josh Magennis was the 100th player to score for the Bluebirds in the League Cup when he netted the final goal in the 3-1 defeat of Bristol Rovers in August 2009

Round Three, 23 September, 2009. Aston Villa 1 Cardiff City 0 (22,527)
Bluebirds; Peter Enckelman; Adam Matthews, Gabor Gyepes, Anthony Gerrard, Tony Capaldi, Peter Whittingham, Gavin Rae (Aaron Wildig), Joe Ledley, Riccy Scimeca (Michael Chopra), Chris Burke, Jay Bothroyd

Football League Cup Record

Played	Won	Drawn	Lost	For	Against
131	50	21*	60	187	217

* One match drawn (23 August, 2004) but City won on penalties

Hat-tricks (4)
George Johnston (1965), Tony Evans (1976), Rob Earnshaw (2002, 2003)
(Tony Evans scored four goals in a 4-4 draw at Bristol Rovers)

Penalties (13)
2 Gary Bell, 1 Trevor Edwards, Peter Hooper, Gil Reece, Adrian Alston, Peter Sayer, Mark Jones, Kevin Nugent, Darren Purse, Robbie Fowler, Ross McCormack, Jay Bothroyd

Leading scorers (187 goals)
10 Rob Earnshaw, 6 Peter King, Tony Evans, Roger Gibbins, 5 John Buchanan, Cohen Griffith, Carl Dale, 4 George Andrews, Peter Whittingham, 3 Derek Tapscott, Bernard Lewis, Terry Harkin, George Johnston, Brian Clark, Ray Bishop, Gary Stevens, Peter Thorne, own goals

Leading appearances (131 matches)
28 Phil Dwyer, 23 Roger Gibbins, 22 Peter King, Jason Perry, 21 Don Murray, 18 Barry Hole, 15 John Buchanan, Paul Parry, 14 Alan Campbell, Keith Pontin, Ian Rodgerson, Scott Young

5
CUP-WINNERS CUP

Winners of the Welsh Cup were allowed entry into the newly-formed Cup-Winners Cup. The first of the Welsh sides to make an appearance were Swansea Town in 1961 and after the Bluebirds beat Bangor City to win the Welsh Cup in 1964 they entered the competition during the 1964-65 season, a few months after Jimmy Scoular had been appointed manager. They immediately caused a sensation by knocking out holders Sporting Lisbon in the second round but their first season in the competition ended when they were beaten 1-0 at Ninian Park by Real Zaragoza.

It was in the 1967-68 season that the competition came alight after the Bluebirds beat Moscow Torpedo in a play-off in Augsburg, West Germany. The second leg of that tie against the Russian outfit had taken place in Tashkent, a city 300 miles from the Chinese border and it involved a 3,500 mile trek to the Prakhator Stadium, the furthest any club had been asked to travel for a European tie. The first leg of the semi-final against SV Hamburg was drawn 1-1 with Norman Dean netting for the Bluebirds. Over 43,000 crammed into Ninian Park on 1 May, 1968 for the return against a strong German side that contained players such as renowned striker Uwe Seeler and Willie Schultz, who had been voted best sweeper in the 1966 World Cup finals. In a bitter ending for City fans, Hamburg scored the winner in the last minute and dreams of reaching a European final were dashed.

It was not until the 1970-71 tournament was underway that once again Bluebirds fans began dreaming of European success. A 7-2 aggregate victory over French side FC Nantes saw City drawn against the great Real Madrid. On 10 March, 1971 a capacity crowd of 47,500 were in Ninian Park to see Brian Clark head the only goal of the game in possibly one of the Bluebirds' most famous ever victories. Although the away leg was lost 2-0, no one could take away the fact that Cardiff City had beaten Real Madrid in a European competition.

3 February 1965, Cup Winners Cup. Cardiff City 0 Real Zaragoza 1. Peter King with a goal scoring opportunity

The latter years in the cup were difficult as UEFA's ruling over the use of 'foreigners' had serious consequences for all of the Welsh clubs. English players were counted as foreigners and as only four could be used, it meant that youngsters were forced into action. City's last European adventure came in 1993 against crack Belgian side Standard Liege. In the first leg at the Stade de Sclessin, the Bluebirds actually led 2-1 just after half time with a double from Tony Bird but Liege hit back to win 5-2. The home leg in Cardiff also went to the Belgians 3-1 with Robbie James firing City's last goal in Europe. In 1995, Wrexham became the last Welsh Football League side to play in Europe after the FA of Wales decreed that all clubs playing in the English pyramid would be barred from playing in the Welsh Cup.

1964-65

First Round, 1st leg, 9 September, 1964. Esbjerg 0 Cardiff City 0 (Idraetsparken, Copenhagen, 10,000)
Bluebirds; Dilwyn John; Peter Rodrigues, Trevor Peck; Gareth Williams, John Charles, Barry Hole; Peter King, Mel Charles, Tommy Halliday, Ivor Allchurch, Greg Farrell

First Round, 2nd leg, 13 October, 1964. Cardiff City 1 Esbjerg 0 (Ninian Park, 8,784)
Bluebirds; Dilwyn John; Peter Rodrigues, Trevor Peck; Gareth Williams, Don Murray, Barry Hole; Greg Farrell, Peter King, Derek Tapscott, Mel Charles, Bernard Lewis
Scorer; Peter King
Cardiff City through 1-0 on aggregate

Second Round, 1st leg, 16 December, 1964. Sporting Lisbon 1 Cardiff City 2 (Estadio Jose Alvalade, Lisbon, 20,000)
Bluebirds; Dilwyn John; Alan Harrington, Peter Rodrigues; John Charles, Don Murray, Barry Hole; Greg Farrell, Gareth Williams, Derek Tapscott, Peter King, Bernard Lewis
Scorers; Greg Farrell, Derek Tapscott

Second Round, 2nd leg, 23 December, 1964. Cardiff City 0 Sporting Lisbon 0 (Ninian Park, 25,000)
Bluebirds; Dilwyn John; Alan Harrington, Peter Rodrigues; John Charles, Don Murray, Barry Hole; Greg Farrell, Gareth Williams, Derek Tapscott, Peter King, Bernard Lewis
Cardiff City through 2-1 on aggregate

Quarter-final, 1st leg, 20 January, 1965. Real Zaragoza 2 Cardiff City 2 (La Romareda, Zaragoza, 30,000)
Bluebirds; Bob Wilson; Alan Harrington, Peter Rodrigues; John Charles, Don Murray, Barry Hole; Greg Farrell, Gareth Williams, Derek Tapscott, Peter King, Bernard Lewis
Scorers; Gareth Williams, Peter King

Quarter-final, 2nd leg, 3 February, 1965. Cardiff City 0 Real Zaragoza 1 (Ninian Park, 38,458)
Bluebirds; Bob Wilson; Alan Harrington, Peter Rodrigues; John Charles, Don Murray, Barry Hole; Greg Farrell, Gareth Williams, Derek Tapscott, Peter King, Bernard Lewis
Real Zaragoza through 3-2 on aggregate

8 September 1965, Cup Winners Cup. Cardiff City 1 Standard Liege 2. John Charles is bundled to ground during an ill-tempered match

1965-66

First Round, 1st leg, 8 September, 1965. Cardiff City 1 Standard Liege 2 (Ninian Park, 12,738)
Bluebirds; Bob Wilson; Alan Harrington, Peter Rodrigues; Gareth Williams, Don Murray, Barry Hole; Greg Farrell, George Johnston, John Charles, Terry Harkin, Bernard Lewis
Scorer; George Johnston

First Round, 2nd leg, 20 October, 1965. Standard Liege 1 Cardiff City 0 (Stade de Sclessin, Liege, 32,000)
Bluebirds; Bob Wilson; Alan Harrington, Peter Rodrigues; David Summerhayes, Don Murray, Barry Hole; Greg Farrell, George Johnston, John Charles, Peter King, Bernard Lewis
Standard Liege through 3-1 on aggregate

Did You Know...
Sandy Allan never fully established a first team place with the Bluebirds but he did net a hat-trick of headers in the Cup Winners Cup 5-1 victory over Mjondalen of Norway on 1 October 1969

1967-68

First Round, 1st leg. 20 September, 1967, Shamrock Rovers 1 Cardiff City 1 (Dalymount Park, Dublin, 21,883)
Bluebirds; Bob Wilson; Graham Coldrick, Bobby Ferguson; Gareth Williams, Don Murray, Brian Harris; Barrie Jones, Malcolm Clarke, John Toshack, Peter King, Ronnie Bird
Scorer; Peter King

First Round, 2nd leg. 4 October, 1967. Cardiff City 2 Shamrock Rovers 0 (Ninian Park, 14,180)
Bluebirds; Bob Wilson; Graham Coldrick, Dave Carver; Gareth Williams, Don Murray, Brian Harris; Barrie Jones, Bobby Brown, John Toshack, Peter King, Ronnie Bird
Scorers; John Toshack, Bobby Brown (p)
Cardiff City through 3-1 on aggregate

19 March 1968, Cup Winners Cup Q-F. Moscow Torpedo 1 Cardiff City 0 Brian Harris shakes hands with Torpedo skipper Shustikov

Second Round, 1st leg, 15 November, 1967. NAC Breda 1 Cardiff City 1 (Philips Stadium, Eindhoven, 15,000)
Bluebirds; Bob Wilson; Steve Derrett, Bobby Ferguson; Malcolm Clarke, Don Murray, Brian Harris; Barrie Jones, Bobby Brown, Peter King, John Toshack, Ronnie Bird
Scorer; Peter King

Second Round, 2nd leg, 29 November, 1967. Cardiff City 4 NAC Breda 1 (Ninian Park, 16,411)
Bluebirds; Bob Wilson; Graham Coldrick, Bobby Ferguson; Malcolm Clarke, Don Murray, Brian Harris; Barrie Jones, Bobby Brown, Peter King, John Toshack, Gary Bell
Scorers; Bobby Brown, Barrie Jones, Malcolm Clarke, John Toshack
Cardiff City through 5-2 on aggregate

Quarter-final, 1st leg, 6 March, 1968. Cardiff City 1 Moscow Torpedo 0 (Ninian Park, 30,567)
Bluebirds; Bob Wilson; Steve Derrett, Bobby Ferguson; Malcolm Clarke, Don Murray, Brian Harris; Barrie Jones, Bryn Jones, Peter King, John Toshack, Ronnie Bird
Scorer; Barrie Jones

Quarter-final, 2nd leg, 19 March, 1968. Moscow Torpedo 1 Cardiff City 0 (Prakhator Stadium, Tashkent, 65,000)
Bluebirds; Bob Wilson; Steve Derrett, Bobby Ferguson; Malcolm Clarke, Don Murray, Brian Harris; Barrie Jones, Norman Dean, Peter King, John Toshack, Ronnie Bird

Quarter-final, play-off, 3 April, 1968. Moscow Torpedo 0 Cardiff City 1 (Rosenau Stadion, Augsburg, 35,000)
Bluebirds; Bob Wilson; Graham Coldrick, Bobby Ferguson; Malcolm Clarke, Richie Morgan, Brian Harris; Barrie Jones, Norman Dean, Peter King, John Toshack, Ronnie Bird
Scorer; Norman Dean
Cardiff City through after play-off

April 1968, City players at Cardiff Airport before leaving for Cup Winners Cup Q-F play-off against Moscow Torpedo in Tashkent

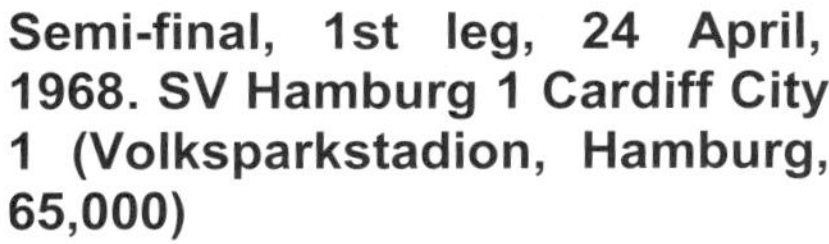

Semi-final, 1st leg, 24 April, 1968. SV Hamburg 1 Cardiff City 1 (Volksparkstadion, Hamburg, 65,000)
Bluebirds; Bob Wilson; Dave Carver, Bobby Ferguson; Norman Dean, Don Murray, Brian Harris; Barrie Jones, Malcolm Clarke, Peter King, John Toshack, Leslie Lea
Scorer; Norman Dean

1 May 1968, Cup Winners Cup S-F. Cardiff City 2 SV Hamburg 3 Norman Dean sends a header over Hamburg defender Hans Schulz

Semi-final, 2nd leg, 1 May, 1968. Cardiff City 2 SV Hamburg 3 (Ninian Park, 43,070)
Bluebirds; Bob Wilson; Dave Carver, Bobby Ferguson; Malcolm Clarke, Don Murray, Brian Harris; Barrie Jones, Norman Dean, Peter King, John Toshack, Leslie Lea
Scorers; Norman Dean, Brian Harris
SV Hamburg through 4-3 on aggregate

1968/69

First Round, 1st leg, 18 September, 1968. Cardiff City 2 FC Porto 2 (Ninian Park, 19,020)
Bluebirds; Fred Davies; Steve Derrett, Gary Bell; Mel Sutton, Don Murray, Brian Harris; Barrie Jones, Brian Clark, Peter King, John Toshack, Ronnie Bird
Scorers; John Toshack, Ronnie Bird (p)

First Round, 2nd leg, 2 October, 1968. FC Porto 2 Cardiff City 1 (Estadio das Antas, Oporto, 60,000)
Bluebirds; Fred Davies; Graham Coldrick, Gary Bell; Mel Sutton, Don Murray, Steve Derrett; Barrie Jones, Brian Clark, Peter King, John Toshack, Leslie Lea (Leighton Phillips)
Scorer; John Toshack
FC Porto through 4-3 on aggregate

Did You Know...
John Toshack scored his 100th first team goal in a Cup Winners Cup match in Nantes on 4 November, 1970, six years after making his debut

1969-70

First Round, 1st leg, 17 September, 1969. Mjoendalen 1 Cardiff City 7 (Neder Eiker Stadium, Mjoendalen, 8,000)
Bluebirds; Fred Davies; Steve Derrett, Dave Carver; Mel Sutton, Don Murray, Brian Harris; Leighton Phillips (Barrie Jones), Brian Clark, Leslie Lea, John Toshack, Peter King
Scorers; Brian Clark 2, John Toshack 2, Leslie Lea, Mel Sutton, Peter King

First Round, 2nd leg, 1 October, 1969. Cardiff City 5 Mjoendalen 1 (Ninian Park, 14,730)
Bluebirds; Fred Davies; Dave Carver, Gary Bell; Mel Sutton, Don Murray, Terry Lewis; Barrie Jones, Brian Clark, Sandy Allan, John Toshack (Leslie Lea), Peter King
Scorers; Sandy Allan 3, Peter King 2
Cardiff City through 12-2 on aggregate

Second Round, 1st leg, 12 November, 1969. Goeztepe Izmir 3 Cardiff City 0 (Alsancak Stadium, Izmir, 20,000)
Bluebirds; Fred Davies; Dave Carver, Gary Bell; Mel Sutton, Don Murray, Brian Harris; Leslie Lea, Brian Clark, Peter King, John Toshack, Frank Sharp (Sandy Allan)

21 October 1970, Cup Winners Cup Rd 2. Cardiff City 5 Nantes 1. Brian Clark surrounded by Nantes defenders

Second Round, 2nd leg, 26 November, 1969. Cardiff City 1 Goeztepe Izmir 0 (Ninian Park, 17,866)
Bluebirds; Fred Davies; Dave Carver, Gary Bell; Mel Sutton, Don Murray, Brian Harris; Sandy Allan, Brian Clark, Leslie Lea (Ronnie Bird), John Toshack (Graham Coldrick), Peter King
Scorer; Ronnie Bird
Goeztepe Izmir through 3-1 on aggregate

1970-71

First Round, 1st leg, 16 September, 1970. Cardiff City 8 PO Larnaca 0 (Ninian Park, 12,984)
Bluebirds; Frank Parsons; Dave Carver, Gary Bell; Mel Sutton, Don Murray, Brian Harris; Ian Gibson, Brian Clark, Peter King, John Toshack, Bobby Woodruff
Scorers; John Toshack 2, Brian Clark 2, Mel Sutton, Ian Gibson, Peter King, Bobby Woodruff

First Round, 2nd leg, 30 September, 1970. PO Larnaca 0 Cardiff City 0 (GSZ Stadium, Larnaca, 5,000)
Bluebirds; Frank Parsons; Dave Carver, Gary Bell; Mel Sutton, Don Murray, Brian Harris; Ian Gibson, Brian Clark, Bobby Woodruff, John Toshack (Leighton Phillips), Peter King
Cardiff City through 8-0 on aggregate

Did You Know...
Cardiff City's first penalty shoot-out came in the Cup Winners Cup second leg against Dynamo Berlin on 29 September, 1971. City lost the shoot-out 4-5

Second Round, 1st leg, 21 October, 1970. Cardiff City 5 FC Nantes 1 (Ninian Park, 17,905)
Bluebirds; Jim Eadie; Dave Carver, Gary Bell; Mel Sutton, Don Murray, Brian Harris; Ian Gibson, Brian Clark (Leighton Phillips), Bobby Woodruff, John Toshack, Peter King
Scorers; John Toshack 2, Ian Gibson, Peter King, Leighton Phillips

Second Round, 2nd leg, 4 November, 1970. FC Nantes 1 Cardiff City 2 (Marcel Saupin Stadium, Nantes, 10,000)
Bluebirds; Jim Eadie; Dave Carver, Gary Bell; Mel Sutton, Don Murray, Brian Harris; Ian Gibson, Leighton Phillips (Brian Clark), Bobby Woodruff, John Toshack, Peter King
Scorers; John Toshack, Brian Clark
Cardiff City through 7-2 on aggregate

March 1971 Jimmy Scoular reads the paper flanked by City players after the defeat of Real Madrid at Ninian Park

Quarter-final, 1st leg, 10 March, 1971. Cardiff City 1 Real Madrid 0 (Ninian Park, 47,500)
Bluebirds; Jim Eadie; Dave Carver, Gary Bell; Mel Sutton, Don Murray, Leighton Phillips; Peter King, Ian Gibson, Brian Clark, Bobby Woodruff, Nigel Rees
Scorer; Brian Clark

Quarter-final, 2nd leg, 24 March, 1971. Real Madrid 2 Cardiff City 0 (Bernabeu, Madrid, 65,000)
Bluebirds; Jim Eadie; Dave Carver, Gary Bell; Mel Sutton, Don Murray, Leighton Phillips; Peter King, Ian Gibson, Brian Clark, Bobby Woodruff, Nigel Rees (Brian Harris)
Real Madrid through 2-1 on aggregate

1971-72

First Round, 1st leg, 15 September, 1971. Dynamo Berlin 1 Cardiff City 1 (Friedrich Ludwig Jahn Stadion, 15,000)
Bluebirds; Jim Eadie; Ken Jones, Gary Bell; Mel Sutton, Don Murray, Leighton Phillips; Peter King, Brian Clark, Bobby Woodruff, Alan Warboys, Ian Gibson
Scorer; Ian Gibson

First Round, 2nd leg, 29 September, 1971. Cardiff City 1 Dynamo Berlin 1 (Ninian Park, 12,676)

Bluebirds; Jim Eadie; Ken Jones, Gary Bell; Mel Sutton, Don Murray, Brian Harris; Ian Gibson, Brian Clark, Bobby Woodruff, Alan Warboys (Alan Foggon), Peter King

Scorer; Brian Clark

Dynamo Berlin through 5-4 after penalty shoot-out

24 March 1971, ECWC Q-F. Real Madrid 2 Cardiff City 0. Gary Bell calls referee after bottle is thrown on pitch

1973-74

First Round, 1st leg, 19 September, 1973. Cardiff City 0 Sporting Lisbon 0 13,300 Ninian Park

Bluebirds; Bill Irwin; Phil Dwyer, Gary Bell; George Smith, Don Murray, Leighton Phillips; Tony Villars (Peter King), Bobby Woodruff, Andy McCulloch, Johnny Vincent, Willie Anderson

First Round, 2nd leg, 3 October, 1973. Sporting Lisbon 2 Cardiff City 1 (Estadio Jose Alvalade, Lisbon, 50,000)

Bluebirds; Bill Irwin; Phil Dwyer, Gary Bell; Peter King, Don Murray, Leighton Phillips; Tony Villars (Gil Reece), Bobby Woodruff, Andy McCulloch, Derek Showers, Johnny Vincent

Scorer; Tony Villars

Sporting Lisbon through 2-1 on aggregate

1974-75

First Round, 1st leg, 18 September, 1974. Ferencvaros 2 Cardiff City 0 (Ulloi Stadion, Budapest, 20,000)

Bluebirds; Ron Healey; Albert Larmour (John Impey), Don Murray, Dave Powell, Freddie Pethard, Clive Charles, Tony Villars, Jimmy McInch, John Farrington, Derek Showers, Willie Anderson

First Round, 2nd leg, 2 October, 1974. Cardiff City 1 Ferencvaros 4 (Ninian Park, 4,228)

Bluebirds; Ron Healey; Phil Dwyer, Don Murray, Dave Powell, Freddie Pethard, George Smith, Tony Villars (John Impey), Johnny Vincent, Gil Reece (John Farrington), Derek Showers, Willie Anderson

Scorer; Phil Dwyer

Ferencvaros through 6-1 on aggregate

1976-77

Preliminary Round, 1st leg, 4 August, 1976. Cardiff City 1 Servette 0 (Ninian Park, 10,226)

Bluebirds; Ron Healey; Clive Charles, Richie Morgan, Albert Larmour, Freddie Pethard, John Buchanan, Doug Livermore, Alan Campbell (David Giles), Tony Evans, Adrian Alston, Derek Showers

Scorer; Tony Evans

Preliminary Round, 2nd leg, 11 August, 1976. Servette 2 Cardiff City 1 (Parc des Sports, Geneva, 21,000)
Bluebirds; Ron Healey; Clive Charles, Richie Morgan (Keith Pontin), Albert Larmour, Freddie Pethard, Alan Campbell, Peter Sayer, Doug Livermore, Adrian Alston, Tony Evans, Derek Showers (Willie Anderson)
Scorer; Derek Showers
Cardiff City through on away goals rule

First Round, 1st leg, 15 September, 1976. Cardiff City 1 Dinamo Tbilisi 0 (Ninian Park, 11,181)
Bluebirds; Bill Irwin; Clive Charles, Richie Morgan, Albert Larmour, Freddie Pethard, Doug Livermore, Adrian Alston (Peter Sayer), John Buchanan, Alan Campbell (Derek Showers), Tony Evans, Willie Anderson
Scorer; Adrian Alston

First Round, 2nd leg, 29 September, 1976. Dinamo Tbilisi 3 Cardiff City 0 (Dinamo Stadium, Tbilisi, 80,000)
Bluebirds; Bill Irwin; Brian Attley, Phil Dwyer, Clive Charles, Freddie Pethard, Albert Larmour, Adrian Alston (Peter Sayer), Doug Livermore, John Buchanan, Derek Showers (Willie Anderson), Tony Evans
Dinamo Tbilisi through 3-1 on aggregate

1977-78

First Round, 1st leg, 14 September, 1977. Cardiff City 0 FK Austria Memphis 0 (Ninian Park, 3,631)
Bluebirds; Bill Irwin; Phil Dwyer, Paul Went, Keith Pontin, Brian Attley, Gerry Byrne, Alan Campbell, Doug Livermore, Peter Sayer, Tony Evans, David Giles (Steve Grapes)

First Round, 2nd leg, 28 September, 1977. FK Austria Memphis 1 Cardiff City 0 (Weststadion, Vienna, 15,000)
Bluebirds; Bill Irwin; Brian Attley, Paul Went, Keith Pontin, Freddie Pethard, Gerry Byrne, Alan Campbell, Peter Sayer, John Buchanan, Phil Dwyer (Ray Bishop), Tony Evans
FK Austria Memphis through 1-0 on aggregate

1988-89

First Round, 1st leg, 7 September, 1988. Derry City 0 Cardiff City 0 (Brandywell Stadium, Derry, 10,500)
Bluebirds; George Wood; Phil Bater, Nigel Stevenson, Terry Boyle, Nicky Platnauer, Paul Wimbleton (Brian McDermott), Alan Curtis, Jason Gummer, Mark Kelly, Ian Walsh (Kevin Bartlett), Jimmy Gilligan

First Round, 2nd leg, 5 October, 1988. Cardiff City 4 Derry City 0 (Ninian Park, 6,933)
Bluebirds; George Wood; Phil Bater (Jason Perry), Terry Boyle, Nigel Stevenson, Nicky Platnauer, Paul Wimbleton (Jon Morgan), Mark Kelly, Brian McDermott, Alan Curtis, Kevin Bartlett, Jimmy Gilligan
Scorers; Jimmy Gilligan 3, Brian McDermott
Cardiff City through 4-0 on aggregate

Second Round, 1st leg, 26 October, 1988. Cardiff City 1 Aarhus 2 (Ninian Park, 6,155)
Bluebirds; George Wood; Nicky Platnauer (Ian Rodgerson), Nigel Stevenson, Terry Boyle, Phil Bater, Paul Wimbleton, Brian McDermott, Mark Kelly, Steve Lynex (Alan Curtis), Kevin Bartlett, Jimmy Gilligan
Scorer; Jimmy Gilligan

Second Round, 2nd leg, 9 November, 1988. Aarhus 4 Cardiff City 0 (Aarhus Stadium, 3,700)
Bluebirds; George Wood; Ian Rodgerson, Gareth Abraham, Terry Boyle, Nicky Platnauer, Paul Wimbleton, Alan Curtis, Mark Kelly, Brian McDermott (Steve Lynex), Kevin Bartlett (Paul Wheeler), Jimmy Gilligan
Aarhus through 6-1 on aggregate

1992-93

First Round, 1st leg, 15 September, 1992. Cardiff City 1 Admira Wacker 1 (Ninian Park, 9,624)
Bluebirds; Mark Grew; Derek Brazil, Lee Baddeley, Gareth Abraham, Damon Searle, Paul Ramsey, Tony Bird (Andy Gorman), Cohen Griffith, Nathan Blake, Chris Pike, Carl Dale
Scorer; Chris Pike

First Round, 2nd leg, 29 September, 1992. Admira Wacker 2 Cardiff City 0 (Sudstadt, Vienna, 4,700)
Bluebirds; Mark Grew; Robbie James, Gareth Abraham (Tony Bird), Lee Baddeley, Damon Searle, Derek Brazil, Paul Ramsey, Cohen Griffith, Nathan Blake, Chris Pike, Carl Dale
Admira Wacker through 3-1 on aggregate

16 September 1992, Cup Winners Cup. Cardiff City 1 Admira Wacker 1 Nathan Blake sends Carl Dale away

1993/94

First Round, 1st Leg, 15 September, 1993. Standard Liege 5 Cardiff City 2 (Stade de Sclessin, Liege, 10,700)
Bluebirds; Phil Kite; Robbie James, Lee Baddeley, Kevin Ratcliffe, Jason Perry, Damon Searle, Nick Richardson, Cohen Griffith, Nathan Blake, Tony Bird, Phil Stant (Terry Evans)
Scorer; Tony Bird 2

First Round, 2nd leg, 28 September, 1993. Cardiff City 1 Standard Liege 3 (Ninian Park, 6,096)
Bluebirds; Steve Williams; Robbie James, Lee Baddeley, Kevin Ratcliffe, Jason Perry, Damon Searle, Tony Bird (Nathan Wigg), Paul Millar (Kevin Bartley), Garry Thompson, Cohen Griffith, Phil Stant
Scorer; Robbie James
Standard Liege through 8-3 on aggregate

Cardiff City Cup Winners Cup record

Played	Won	Drawn	Lost	For	Against
49	16	14	19	67	61

Scorers (67 goals)
11 John Toshack. 9 Peter King. 7 Brian Clark. 4 Jimmy Gilligan. 3 Norman Dean, Sandy Allan, Ian Gibson. 2 Bobby Brown, Barrie Jones, Ronnie Bird, Mel Sutton, Tony Bird. 1 Greg Farrell, Derek Tapscott, Gareth Williams, George Johnston, Malcolm Clarke, Brian Harris, Leslie lea, Bobby Woodruff, Leighton Phillips, Tony Villars, Phil Dwyer, Tony Evans, Derek Showers, Adrian Alston, Brian McDermott, Chris Pike, Robbie James.

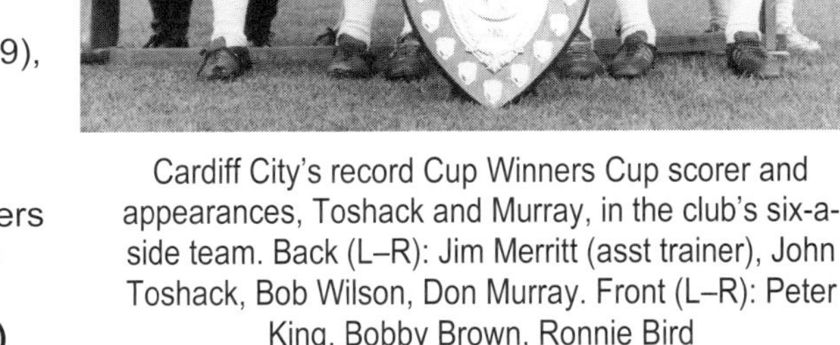

Cardiff City's record Cup Winners Cup scorer and appearances, Toshack and Murray, in the club's six-a-side team. Back (L–R): Jim Merritt (asst trainer), John Toshack, Bob Wilson, Don Murray. Front (L–R): Peter King, Bobby Brown, Ronnie Bird

Hat-tricks (2)
1 Sandy Allan (v Mjoendalen 1969), Jimmy Gilligan (v Derry City 1988)

Penalties (2)
1 Bobby Brown (v Shamrock Rovers 1967), Ronnie Bird (v FC Porto 1968)

Leading Appearances (49 matches)
33 Don Murray. 32 Peter King. 19 John Toshack, Brian Harris, 16 Gary Bell, 14 Mel Sutton, Brian Clark, 13 Bob Wilson, Dave Carver, Barrie Jones, 10 Bobby Woodruff, Leighton Phillips, 9 Gareth Williams, 8 Peter Rodrigues, Barry Hole, Greg Farrell, Bobby Ferguson, Malcolm Clarke, Ian Gibson, Ronnie Bird, 7 John Charles, Bernard Lewis, Freddie Pethard, Leslie Lea, Derek Showers

Did You Know...
The Bluebirds have played a total of 49 matches in the Cup Winners Cup after making their debut in 1964 against Esbjerg of Denmark

6
WELSH CUP

The Welsh Football Association Challenge Cup began in 1877, five years after the FA Cup and four years after the Scottish Cup. It was on 17 August, 1877 that it was proposed and accepted and 19 clubs entered the first competition in the 1877-78 season. Eleven of those clubs came from the Wrexham area so with such a strong bias towards North Wales it is no surprise to find that it was not until 1891-92 that teams from South Wales joined in. By then, Shrewsbury Town and Crewe Alexandra were already regular entrants although it was not until 1909-10 that Cardiff City made their first appearance.

The Bluebirds first won the Welsh Cup in 1912 and they have gone on to lift the trophy on 22 occasions, the last time being in 1993 when they defeated Rhyl 5-0 at the National Stadium. Only Wrexham, with 23, have more Welsh Cup victories than Cardiff City. The trophy was never high on City's list of priorities until 1961 when the winners were given entry into the European Cup Winners Cup. The Bluebirds were then victorious in ten of the following 12 seasons from 1964. Season 1994-95 was their last in the competition as the FA of Wales refused entry for all clubs playing in the English football leagues.

1910-11

Round One, 13 October, 1910. Mardy 0 Cardiff City 1 (3,000)
Bluebirds; Ted Husbands; James McKenzie, John Duffy; Bob Lawrie, John Ramsey, Davy McDougall; W Stewart, Jim Malloch, Tom Abley, Bob Peake, Jack Evans
Scorer; Tom Abley

August 1912. Cardiff City team group

Round Two, 29 October, 1910. Cardiff City 4 Tredegar 1 (4,000)
Bluebirds; Ted Husbands; James McKenzie, John Duffy, Bob Lawrie, John Ramsey, Davy McDougall; James McDonald, Jim Malloch, W Stewart, Billy Watt, Jack Evans
Scorers; Jim Malloch, Billy Watt, Jack Evans, W Stewart

Round Three, 10 December, 1910. Cardiff City 2 Ton Pentre 2 (5,000)
Bluebirds; Ted Husbands; James McKenzie, John Duffy; F Powell, Bob Lawrie, Davy McDougall; James McDonald, Tom Abley, Tommy Niblo, Billy Watt, Jack Evans
Scorers; Tom Abley, F Powell

Round Three replay, 15 December, 1910. Ton Pentre 1 Cardiff City 0 (8,000)
Bluebirds; Ted Husbands; James McKenzie, John Duffy; F Powell, Bob Lawrie, Davy McDougall; James McDonald, Charlie Pinch, Tommy Niblo, Billy Watt, Jack Evans

1911-12

Round Three, 10 January, 1912. Cardiff City 1 Treharris 0 (3,000)
Bluebirds; George Germaine; John Duffy, Arthur Waters; Billy Hardy, Bob Lawrie, Tom Abley; Harry Tracey, George Burton, Harry Featherstone, Jack Burton, Jack Evans
Scorer; Harry Featherstone

Round Four, 3 February, 1912. Wrexham 1 Cardiff City 2 (3,500)
Bluebirds; George Germaine; John Duffy, Arthur Waters; Tom Abley, Bob Lawrie, Billy Hardy; Harry Tracey, George Burton, Harry Featherstone, Jack Burton, Jack Evans
Scorers; Jack Burton, Harry Featherstone

Semi-final, 23 March, 1912. Cardiff City 1 Chester 1 (3,000)
Bluebirds; Ted Husbands; Billy Hardy, Arthur Waters; Tom Abley, Bob Lawrie, Eddie Thompson; Harry Tracey, Charlie Pinch, George Burton, Jack Burton, Jack Evans
Scorer; George Burton

Semi-final replay, 27 March, 1912. Chester 1 Cardiff City 2 (3,000)
Bluebirds; Ted Husbands; Arthur Waters, Billy Douglas; Eddie Thompson, Bob Lawrie, Billy Hardy; Harry Tracey, Tom Abley, George Burton, Jack Burton, Jack Evans
Scorers; George Burton, Harry Tracey

Final, 8 April, 1912. Cardiff City 0 Pontypridd 0 (18,000)
Bluebirds; Ted Husbands; Billy Douglas, Billy Hardy; Tom Abley, Bob Lawrie, Eddie Thompson; Harry Tracey, Charlie Pinch, Harry Featherstone, Jack Burton, Jack Evans

Final replay, 18 April, 1912. Pontypridd 0 Cardiff City 3 (6,648)
Bluebirds; Ted Husbands; George Latham, Arthur Waters; Tom Abley, Eddie Thompson, Billy Hardy; Harry Tracey, George Burton, Harry Featherstone, Jack Burton, Jack Evans
Scorers; Harry Tracey 2, Harry Featherstone

1912-13

Round Three, 4 January, 1913. Cardiff City 4 Ton Pentre 2 (2,000)
Bluebirds; Jack Kneeshaw; Tommy Doncaster, Bob Leah; Henry Harvey, George Latham, Billy Hardy; J Bennett, Harry Featherstone, Billy Douglas, George Burton, Billy Gaughan
Scorers; Billy Douglas 2, George Burton, Harry Featherstone

Round Four, 25 January, 1913. Bangor City 0 Cardiff City 4 (n/a)
Bluebirds; Jack Kneeshaw; Tommy Doncaster, Bob Leah; Henry Harvey, Pat Cassidy, Billy Hardy; Harry Tracey, Harry Featherstone, Billy Devlin, Jack Burton, Jack Evans
Scorers; Jack Burton, Harry Featherstone, Pat Cassidy, Billy Devlin

Semi-final, 15 February, 1913. Cardiff City 2 Swansea Town 4 (12,000)
Bluebirds; Jack Kneeshaw; Tommy Doncaster, Bob Leah; Henry Harvey, Pat Cassidy, Billy Hardy; Harry Tracey, Harry Featherstone, Billy Devlin, Jack Burton, Jack Evans
Scorers; Jack Burton, Pat Cassidy

1913-14

Round Three, 3 January, 1914. Oswestry Town 2 Cardiff City 1 (n/a)
Bluebirds; reserve line-up
Scorer; Billy Gaughan

1914-15

Cardiff City withdrew from the competition this season

1919-20

Round Three, 14 January, 1920. Cardiff City 5 Merthyr Town 0 (5,500)
Bluebirds; Jack Kneeshaw; Charlie Brittan, Alex Stewart; Henry Harvey, Pat Cassidy, Fred Keenor; George Beare, Billy Cox, J Johnstone, Joe Clark, Jack Evans
Scorers; Joe Clark 3, Henry Harvey, Billy Cox

Round Four, 11 February, 1920. Cardiff City 5 Chester 0 (4,000)
Bluebirds; Charlie Hewitt; Billy Hardy, Alex Stewart; Billy Davidson, Bert Smith, Fred Keenor; George Beare, Billy Cox, Arthur Cashmore, George West, Jack Evans
Scorers; Arthur Cashmore 2, Fred Keenor, Jack Evans, Bert Smith

March 1920. The Cardiff City forward line in their last season in the Southern League. L-R George Beare, Billy Grimshaw, Billy Cox, George West and Joe Clarke

Semi-final, 24 March, 1920. Cardiff City 2 Swansea Town 1 (7,000)
Bluebirds; Arthur Layton; Charlie Brittan, Albert Barnett; Fred Keenor, Bert Smith, Billy Hardy; George Beare, Billy Cox, Arthur Cashmore, George West, Jack Evans
Scorers; George West, Jack Evans

Final, 21 April, 1920. Cardiff City 2 Wrexham 1 (10,000)
Bluebirds; Jack Kneeshaw; Charlie Brittan, Arthur Layton; Billy Hardy, Bert Smith, Fred Keenor; Billy Grimshaw, Billy Cox, Arthur Cashmore, George West, Jack Evans
Scorer; George West 2

1920-21

Round Three, 15 January, 1921. Pontypridd 2 Cardiff City 1 (2,000)
Bluebirds; Ben Davies; Jack Page, Tommy Sayles; Billy Newton, Tommy Wilmot, Lol Abram; Sid Evans, Len Hopkins, Len Davies, Charlie Jones, Joe Clark
Scorer; Len Davies

1921-22

Round Three, 18 January, 1922. Cardiff City 7 Newport County 1 (5,500)
Bluebirds; Jack Kneeshaw; Charlie Brittan, Jack Page; Herbie Evans, Bert Smith, Billy Hardy; Billy Grimshaw, Fred Keenor, Len Davies, Harry Nash, Jack Evans
Scorers; Len Davies 4, Billy Grimshaw 2, Fred Keenor

Round Four, 22 February, 1922. Cardiff City 5 Merthyr Town 0 (5,500)
Bluebirds; Ben Davies; Charlie Brittan, Jimmy Blair; Herbie Evans, Bert Smith, Fred Keenor; Sid Evans, Jimmy Gill, Len Davies, Harry Nash, Jack Evans
Scorers; Len Davies 3, Harry Nash, og

Semi-final, 10 April, 1922. Pontypridd 0 Cardiff City 3 (12,000)
Bluebirds; Ben Davies; Charlie Brittan, Jimmy Blair; Herbie Evans, Bert Smith, Fred Keenor; Billy Grimshaw, Jimmy Gill, Len Davies, Joe Clennell, Jack Evans
Scorers; Fred Keenor, Jimmy Gill, Jack Evans

Len Davies

Final, 4 May, 1922. Cardiff City 2 Ton Pentre 0 (12,000)
Bluebirds; Ben Davies; Charlie Brittan, Jimmy Blair; Herbie Evans, Bert Smith, Billy Hardy; Billy Grimshaw, Jimmy Gill, Len Davies, Joe Clennell, Jack Evans
Scorers; Jimmy Gill, Len Davies

1922-23

Round Four, 7 February, 1923. Cardiff City 7 Rhymney 0 (3,000)
Bluebirds; Ben Davies; Jimmy Nelson, Jimmy Blair; Herbie Evans, Bert Smith, Fred Keenor; Sid Evans, Jimmy Gill, Len Davies, Jack Nock, Jack Evans
Scorers; Jimmy Gill 3, Len Davies, Jack Nock, Fred Keenor, Sid Evans

Round Five, 14 March, 1923. Cardiff City 10 Oswestry 0 (3,000)
Bluebirds; Ben Davies; Jimmy Nelson, Jack Page; Herbie Evans, Bert Smith, Fred Keenor; Sid Evans, Jimmy Gill, George Reid, Len Davies, Jack Evans
Scorers; Len Davies 3, Jimmy Gill 3, George Reid 3, Fred Keenor

Semi-final, 11 April, 1923. Swansea Town 2 Cardiff City 3 (12,000)
Bluebirds; Tom Farquharson; Jimmy Nelson, Jimmy Blair; Herbie Evans, Bert Smith, Billy Hardy; Billy Grimshaw, Fred Keenor, Len Davies, Joe Clennell, Jack Evans
Scorers; Joe Clennell 2, Len Davies

Final, 3 May, 1923. Aberdare Athletic 2 Cardiff City 3 (8,000)
Bluebirds; Tom Farquharson; Jimmy Nelson, Jimmy Blair; Herbie Evans, Bert Smith, Fred Keenor; Billy Grimshaw, Jimmy Gill, Len Davies, Joe Clennell, Jack Evans
Scorers; Billy Grimshaw, Jimmy Gill, Len Davies

1923-24

Round Three, 14 February, 1924. Shrewsbury Town 0 Cardiff City 0 (4,000)
Bluebirds; Tom Farquharson; Jimmy Nelson, Jimmy Blair; Herbie Evans, Fred Keenor, Billy Hardy; Dennis Lawson, Jimmy Gill, Len Davies, Joe Clennell, Jack Evans

Round Three replay, 27 February, 1924. Cardiff City 3 Shrewsbury Town 0 (3,500)
Bluebirds; Tom Farquharson; Jimmy Nelson, Jimmy Blair; Herbie Evans, Fred Keenor, Billy Hardy; Dennis Lawson, Alf Hagan, Len Davies, Joe Clennell, Jack Evans
Scorers; Joe Clennell 2, Billy Hardy

Round Four, 17 March, 1924. Newport County 1 Cardiff City 1 (5,500)
Bluebirds; Tom Farquharson; Jack Page, Albert Barnett; Harry Wake, Eddie S Jenkins, Jack Lewis; Elvet Collins, Alf Hagan, Jimmy Jones, Jack Nock, Jack Evans
Scorer; Jimmy Jones

Round Four (replay), 31 March, 1924. Cardiff City 0 Newport County 0 (5,000)
Bluebirds; Tom Farquharson; Jack Page, Jimmy Blair; Jack Lewis, Fred Keenor, Billy Hardy; Elvet Collins, Jimmy Nelson, Jimmy Jones, Alf Hagan, Jack Evans

Round Four (second replay), 31 March, 1924. Newport County 0 Cardiff City 0 (4,000)
Bluebirds; Tom Farquharson; Jimmy Nelson, Jimmy Blair; Jack Lewis, Fred Keenor, Billy Hardy; Elvet Collins, Jimmy Jones, Len Davies, Alf Hagan, Billy Taylor

Round Four (third replay), 10 April, 1924. Newport County 3 Cardiff City 0 (2,000)
Bluebirds; Tom Farquharson; Jimmy Nelson, Jack Page; Jack Lewis, Eddie S Jenkins, Billy Hardy; Jimmy Gill, Alf Hagan, Jimmy Jones, Joe Clennell, Billy Taylor

1924-25

Round Five, 2 March, 1925. Swansea Town 4 Cardiff City 0 (15,000)
Bluebirds; Tom Farquharson; Jimmy Nelson, Jack Page; Harry Wake, George Whitcombe, Tom Sloan; Dennis Lawson, Willie Davies, Joe Nicholson, Harry Beadles, Jack Evans

1925-26

Round Five, 3 March, 1926. Merthyr Town 2 Cardiff City 1 (4,000)
Bluebirds; Tom Farquharson; Jimmy Nelson, Jimmy Blair; Harry Wake, Ebor Reed, Joe Nicholson; Dennis Lawson, Willie Davies, Harry McCracken, Joe Cassidy, George McLachlan
Scorer; og

1926-27

Round Six, 29 March, 1927. Ebbw Vale 0 Cardiff City 0 (10,000)
Bluebirds; Tom Farquharson; Jimmy Nelson, Tom Watson; Fred Keenor, Tom Sloan, Billy Hardy; Harry Wake, Sam Irving, Hughie Ferguson, Len Davies, George McLachlan

Round Six (replay), 4 April, 1927. Cardiff City 6 Ebbw Vale 1 (8,000)
Bluebirds; T Hampson; Jimmy Nelson, Tom Watson; George Blackburn, Tom Pirie, Billy Hardy; Ernie Curtis, Sam Irving, Fred Castle, Len Davies, George McLachlan
Scorers; Len Davies 2, Fred Castle 2, George McLachlan, Ernie Curtis

Did You Know...
Cardiff City achieved a unique treble in 1926-27 when they won the FA Cup, Welsh Cup and Charity Shield

Round Seven, 28 April, 1927. Cardiff City 2 Barry Town 0 (5,000)
Bluebirds; Tom Farquharson; Jimmy Nelson, Tom Watson; Billy Hardy, Tom Pirie, Tom Sloan; Fred Keenor, Sam Irving, Len Davies, Ernie Curtis, George McLachlan
Scorers; George McLachlan, Len Davies

Semi-final, 2 May, 1927. Wrexham 1 Cardiff City 2 (14,600)
Bluebirds; Tom Farquharson; Jimmy Nelson, Tom Watson; George Blackburn, Tom Sloan, Billy Hardy; Fred Keenor, Sam Irving, Len Davies, Ernie Curtis, George McLachlan
Scorer; Len Davies 2

Final, 5 May, 1927. Rhyl 0 Cardiff City 2 (9,600)
Bluebirds; Tom Farquharson; Jimmy Nelson, Tom Watson; George Blackburn, Tom Sloan, Billy Hardy; Fred Keenor, Sam Irving, Len Davies, Ernie Curtis, George McLachlan
Scorers; Len Davies, Sam Irving

1927-28

Round Five, 15 March, 1928. Oswestry 1 Cardiff City 7 (4,000)
Bluebirds; Tom Farquharson; Jack Jennings, Tom Watson; Harry Wake, Fred Keenor, Billy Hardy; Billy Thirlaway, Tom Smith, Fred Castle, Len Davies, Willie Davies
Scorers; Len Davies 3, Fred Castle 2, Tom Smith 2

Round Six, 2 April, 1928. Cardiff City 1 Swansea Town 0 (10,000)
Bluebirds; Tom Farquharson; Jimmy Nelson, Jack Jennings; Fred Keenor, Tom Sloan, George Blackburn; Billy Thirlaway, Tom Smith, Hughie Ferguson, Len Davies, George McLachlan
Scorer; Tom Smith

Semi-final, 18 April, 1928. Rhyl 2 Cardiff City 2 (3,000)
Bluebirds; Tom Farquharson; Jimmy Nelson, Jack Jennings; Fred Keenor, Harry Wake, Billy Hardy; Billy Thirlaway, Tom Smith, Hughie Ferguson, Len Davies, George McLachlan
Scorer; Hughie Ferguson 2

Semi-final (replay), 25 April, 1928. Rhyl 0 Cardiff City 2 (5,000)
Bluebirds; Tom Farquharson; Jimmy Nelson, Jack Jennings; Fred Keenor, Tom Sloan, Billy Hardy; Billy Thirlaway, Harry Wake, Hughie Ferguson, Len Davies, George McLachlan
Scorers; Harry Wake, Len Davies

Final, 2 May, 1928. Bangor City 0 Cardiff City 2 (11,000)
Bluebirds; Tom Farquharson; Jimmy Nelson, Jack Jennings; Fred Keenor, Tom Sloan, Billy Hardy; Billy Thirlaway, Tom Smith, Hughie Ferguson, Len Davies, George McLachlan
Scorer; Hughie Ferguson 2

1928-29

Round Five, 27 February, 1929. Cardiff City 3 Lovells Athletic 1 (5,000)
Bluebirds; Tom Farquharson; Jack Jennings, Bill Roberts; Tom Helsby, Fred Keenor, Billy Hardy; Billy Thirlaway, Frank Harris, Hughie Ferguson, Len Davies, Freddie Warren
Scorers; Hughie Ferguson, Frank Harris, Len Davies

Round Six, 25 March, 1929. Newport County 0 Cardiff City 1 (4,000)
Bluebirds; Tom Farquharson; Jack Jennings, Bill Roberts; Harry Wake, Fred Keenor, George Blackburn; Billy Thirlaway, Stan Davies, Jim Munro, Len Davies, George McLachlan
Scorer; Jim Munro

Semi-final, 25 April, 1929. Rhyl 1 Cardiff City 2 (7,000)
Bluebirds; Tom Farquharson; Jack Jennings, Bill Roberts; Harry Wake, Fred Keenor, George Blackburn; Billy Thirlaway, Frank Matson, Hughie Ferguson, Len Davies, George McLachlan
Scorers; George Blackburn, Len Davies

Final, 1 May, 1929. Connah's Quay Nomads 3 Cardiff City 0 (10,000)
Bluebirds; Tom Farquharson; Jack Jennings, Bill Roberts; Harry Wake, Fred Keenor, George Blackburn; Billy Thirlaway, Frank Matson, Hughie Ferguson, Len Davies, George McLachlan

1929-30

Round Five, 17 March, 1930. Llanelly 1 Cardiff City 4 (5,000)
Bluebirds; Tom Farquharson; Jimmy Nelson, Bill Roberts; Harry Wake, Fred Keenor, George Blackburn; Len Davies, Frank Harris, Albert Miles, Les Jones, Walter Robbins
Scorers; Len Davies 2, Albert Miles, Les Jones

Round Six, 2 April, 1930. Cardiff City 4 Swansea Town 0 (8,000)
Bluebirds; Tom Farquharson; Jimmy Nelson, Bill Roberts; Harry Wake, Fred Keenor, George Blackburn; Billy Thirlaway, Len Davies, Albert Miles, Les Jones, Walter Robbins
Scorers; Billy Thirlaway, Les Jones, Len Davies, Jimmy Nelson

Semi-final, 23 April, 1930. Wrexham 0 Cardiff City 2 (4,000)
Bluebirds; Tom Farquharson; Jimmy Nelson, Bill Roberts; Tom Helsby, Emlyn John, George Blackburn; Len Davies, Frank Harris, Albert Miles, Les Jones, Jimmy McGrath
Scorers; Albert Miles, Les Jones

Final, 3 May, 1930. Rhyl 0 Cardiff City 0 (5,000)
Bluebirds; Tom Farquharson; Jimmy Nelson, Bill Roberts; Tom Helsby, Emlyn John, George Blackburn; Fred Keenor, Harry Wake, Albert Miles, Les Jones, Len Davies

Final (replay), 8 October, 1930. Cardiff City 4 Rhyl 2 (7,000)
Bluebirds; Tom Farquharson; Jock Smith, Billy Hardy; Tom Helsby, Fred Keenor, George Blackburn; George Emmerson, Harry Wake, Len Davies, Les Jones, Walter Robbins
Scorers; Len Davies 3, Les Jones

1930-31

Round Five, 4 March, 1931. Cardiff City 7 Barry Town 1 (3,000)
Bluebirds; Tom Farquharson; Jock Smith, Billy Hardy; Frank Harris, Jack Galbraith, George Blackburn; George Emmerson, Bill Merry, Len Davies, Matthew Robinson, Bobby Weale
Scorers; Matthew Robinson 2, Len Davies 2, Bill Merry 2, George Emmerson

Round Six, 25 March, 1931. Chester 0 Cardiff City 1 (12,000)
Bluebirds; Tom Farquharson; Billy Hardy, Bill Roberts; Frank Harris, Jack Galbraith, George Blackburn; George Emmerson, Bill Merry, Jim McCambridge, Les Jones, Jimmy McGrath
Scorer; Jim McCambridge

Semi-final, 13 April, 1931. Shrewsbury Town 1 Cardiff City 0 (4,000)
Bluebirds; Tom Farquharson; Jock Smith, Billy Hardy; Frank Harris, Jack Galbraith, Eddie Jenkins; George Emmerson, Bill Merry, Jim McCambridge, Les Jones, Jimmy McGrath

1931-32

Round Five, 8 February, 1932. Llanelly 3 Cardiff City 5 (5,000)
Bluebirds; Tom Farquharson; Bill Roberts, Billy Hardy; Frank Harris, Jack Galbraith, Peter Ronan; George Emmerson, Albert Keating, Les Jones, Jim McCambridge, Walter Robbins
Scorers; Walter Robbins 3, Jim McCambridge 2

Round Six, 2 March, 1932. Chester 2 Cardiff City 1 (5,000)
Bluebirds; Tom Farquharson; Billy Hardy, Bill Roberts; Frank Harris, Jack Galbraith, Peter Ronan; George Emmerson, Albert Keating, Les Jones, Jim McCambridge, Walter Robbins
Scorer; George Emmerson

1932-33

Round Seven, 22 February, 1933. Cardiff City 4 Tranmere Rovers 2 (4,000)
Bluebirds; Bob Adams; Bob Pollard, George Russell; Jim McCambridge, Eddie Jenkins, Peter Ronan; George Emmerson, Tom Maidment, Jim Henderson, Les Jones, Jack Collins
Scorers; Les Jones 2, Jim Henderson 2

Round Eight, 9 March, 1933. Swansea Town 1 Cardiff City 1 (3,000)
Bluebirds; Tom Farquharson; Bob Pollard, George Russell; Frank Harris, Jack Galbraith, Eddie Jenkins; George Emmerson, Tom Maidment, Jim McCambridge, Les Jones, Stan Cribb
Scorer; Tom Maidment

Round Eight (replay), 15 March, 1933. Cardiff City 2 Swansea Town 1 (5,000)
Bluebirds; Tom Farquharson; Bob Pollard, George Russell; Frank Harris, Jack Galbraith, Eddie Jenkins; George Emmerson, Tom Maidment, Jim McCambridge, Les Jones, Stan Cribb
Scorers; Tom Maidment, Les Jones

Semi-final, 5 April, 1933. Chester 2 Cardiff City 1 (10,000)
Bluebirds; Tom Farquharson; Bob Pollard, George Russell; Frank Harris, Jack Galbraith, Eddie Jenkins; George Emmerson, Tom Maidment, Jim Henderson, Les Jones, Jim McCambridge
Scorer; Jim Henderson

1933-34

Round Six, 14 February, 1934. Cardiff City 2 Bristol City 2 (1,500)
Bluebirds; Tom Farquharson; Bob Calder, George Russell; Ernie Lewis, Eddie Jenkins, John Duthie; Ted Marcroft, Eli Postin, Jim Henderson, Ernie Curtis, Alex Hutchinson
Scorers; Jim Henderson, Ernie Curtis

Round Six (replay), 26 February, 1934. Bristol City 1 Cardiff City 0 (900)
Bluebirds; Tom Farquharson; Bob Calder, George Russell; Eddie Jenkins, Jack Galbraith, John Duthie; Freddie Hill, Eli Postin, Jim Henderson, Ernie Curtis, Alex Hutchinson

1934-35

Round Six, 13 February, 1935. Cardiff City 3 Newport County 2 (2,000)
Bluebirds; Jock Leckie; Edward Lane, Jack Everest; Wally Jennings, Enoch Mort, Paddy Molloy; Reg Pugh, Freddie Hill, Wilf Lewis, Harry Riley, Phil Griffiths
Scorers; Harry Riley 2, Wilf Lewis

Round Seven, 27 March, 1935. Cardiff City 2 Chester 2 (2,000)
Bluebirds; Jock Leckie; Edward Lane, Jack Everest; Arthur Granville, Billy Bassett, Dai Jones; Reg Pugh, Freddie Hill, Wilf Lewis, Harry Riley, Phil Griffiths
Scorers; Jack Everest, og

Round Seven (replay), 10 April, 1935. Chester 3 Cardiff City 0 (5,000)
Bluebirds; Jock Leckie; Wally Jennings, Jack Everest; Harry Riley, Billy Basset, Dai Jones; Reg Pugh, Reg Keating, Wilf Lewis, Freddie Hill, Phil Griffiths

1935-36

Round Six, 29 January, 1936. Cardiff City 2 Bristol City 1 (6,000)
Bluebirds; George Poland; Arthur Granville, Hugh Hearty; Harold Smith, Billy Bassett, Cliff Godfrey; Reg Pugh, Reg Keating, Dan Williams, Harry Riley, Joe Roberts
Scorers; Reg Pugh, Reg Keating

Round Seven, 12 March, 1936. Rhyl 2 Cardiff City 1 (7,000)
Bluebirds; Jock Leckie; Arthur Granville, Jack Everest; Harry Roper, Cliff Godfrey, Harold Smith; Reg Pugh, Reg Keating, Dan Williams, Wilf Lewis, Jack Diamond
Scorer; Reg Pugh

1936-37

Round Six, 10 March, 1937. Barry Town 3 Cardiff City 1 (5,000)
Bluebirds; Jack Deighton; Louis Ford, John Mellor; James Smith, Harold Smith, Cliff Godfrey; Reg Pugh, Albert Pinxton, Jim McKenzie, George Walton, Arthur Welsby
Scorer; George Walton

1937-38

Round Six, 16 February 1938. Cardiff City 0 Cheltenham Town 1 (5,000)
Bluebirds; Bob Jones; Arthur Granville, Ernie Blenkinsop; Cecil McCaughey, Cliff Godfrey, George Nicholson; Jim Finlay, George Walton, Jimmy Collins, Ted Melaniphy, Bert Turner

1938-39

Round Five, 8 February, 1939. Cardiff City 2 Swansea Town 2 (4,000)
Bluebirds; Bill Fielding; George Ballsom, Jimmy Kelso; Billy Corkhill, Tom Williams, Cecil McCaughey; George Walton, Tom Rickards, Jimmy Collins, Harry Egan, Jim McKenzie
Scorers; James McKenzie, Cecil McCaughey

Round Five (replay), 23 February, 1939. Swansea Town 1 Cardiff City 4 (1,500)
Bluebirds; Bill Fielding; Arthur Granville, Jimmy Kelso; Billy Corkhill, George Ballsom, Cecil McCaughey; Billy Baker, Tom Rickards, Harry Egan, Les Talbot, Ritchie Smith
Scorers; Harry Egan 2, Tom Rickards 2

August 1938. City players at Ninian Park being photographed by George Ballsom with Jimmy Kelso on the roller

Round Six, 8 March, 1939. Cardiff City 5 Newport County 1 (6,000)
Bluebirds; Bill Fielding; George Ballsom, Jimmy Kelso; Billy Corkhill, Billy Bassett, George Nicholson; Billy Baker, Tom Rickards, Harry Egan, Les Talbot, Jim McKenzie
Scorers; Harry Egan 3, Tom Rickards, Jim McKenzie

Semi-final, 30 March, 1939. Oswestry 1 Cardiff City 1 (3,000)
Bluebirds; Bill Fielding; Arthur Granville, Jimmy Kelso; Billy Corkhill, George Ballsom, Cecil McCaughey; George Walton, Tom Rickards, Harry Egan, Les Talbot, Jim Prescott
Scorer; Arthur Granville (p)

Semi-final (replay), 13 April, 1939. Oswestry 2 Cardiff City 2 (3,000)
Bluebirds; Bill Fielding; Louis Ford, Jimmy Kelso; Billy Corkhill, Tom Williams, George Nicholson; Reg Pugh, Les Talbot, Jimmy Collins, Harry Egan, Jim Prescott
Scorers; Les Talbot, Jimmy Collins

Semi-final (second replay), 26 April, 1939. Oswestry 1 Cardiff City 2 (5,000)
Bluebirds; Bill Fielding; George Ballsom, Jimmy Kelso; Billy Corkhill, Billy Bassett, George Nicholson; Reg Pugh, Jim McKenzie, Jimmy Collins, Les Talbot, Charlie Hill
Scorers; Les Talbot, Jimmy Collins

Final, 4 May, 1939. South Liverpool 2 Cardiff City 1 (5,000)
Bluebirds; Bill Fielding; George Ballsom, Jimmy Kelso; Billy Corkhill, Tom Williams, George Nicholson; Reg Pugh, George Walton, Jimmy Collins, Les Talbot, Charlie Hill
Scorer; Jimmy Collins

1946-47

Round Five, 6 February, 1947. Merthyr Tydfil 4 Cardiff City 2 (3,000)
Bluebirds; Wyn Griffiths; Arthur Lever, Alf Sherwood; Ken Hollyman, Glyn Williams, Billy Baker; Colin Gibson, Billy Rees, Billy James, Billy Lewis, Roy Clarke
Scorers; Billy Rees, Billy James

1947-48

Round Five, 15 January, 1948. Lovells Athletic 2 Cardiff City 1 (5,000)
Bluebirds; Dan Canning; Ron Stitfall, Arthur Lever; Beriah Moore, Fred Stansfield, Billy Baker; Billy Foulkes, Billy James, A Davies, Bobby Tobin, Dougie Blair
Scorer; Beriah Moore

8 January 1948. Training at Coney Beach, Porthcawl. L-R Ken Hollyman, Ron Stitfall, Billy Baker, Danny Canning, Arthur Lever, Colin Gibson, George Wardle, Fred Stansfield and Alf Sherwood

1948-49

Round Six, 12 January, 1949. Cardiff City 3 Troedyrhiw 1 (500)
Bluebirds; Ted Morris; Arthur Lever, Alf Sherwood; Billy Baker, Fred Stansfield, Dougie Blair; Ken Hollyman, Ted Gorin, Tommy Best, George Wardle, Gordon Pembrey
Scorers; Ted Gorin, George Wardle, Tommy Best

Round Seven, 3 March, 1949. Milford United 1 Cardiff City 2 (7,500)
Bluebirds; Phil Joslin; Arthur Lever, Ken Hollyman; Glyn Williams, Stan Montgomery, Billy Baker; Bryn Allen, Tommy Best, Alf Rowland, Ernie Stevenson, George Edwards
Scorers; Alf Rowland, George Edwards

Semi-final, 7 April, 1949. Merthyr Tydfil 3 Cardiff City 1 (22,000)
Bluebirds; Ted Morris; Ron Stitfall, Albert Stitfall; Ken Hollyman, Stan Montgomery, Glyn Williams; Ted Gorin, Bryn Allen, Billy Rees, Ernie Stevenson, George Edwards
Scorer; Ernie Stevenson

1949-50

Round Six, 18 January, 1950. Cardiff City 3 Ebbw Vale 0 (2,500)
Bluebirds; Bob Stitfall; Arthur Lever, Ken Devonshire; Billy Baker, Stan Montgomery, Glyn Williams; Roley Williams, Elfed Evans, Ted Gorin, Ron Stitfall, George Edwards
Scorers; George Edwards 2, Billy Baker

Round Seven, 23 February, 1950. Swansea Town 3 Cardiff City 0 (11,000)
Bluebirds; Phil Joslin; Arthur Lever, Ken Devonshire; Ken Hollyman, Stan Montgomery, Billy Baker; Elfed Evans, Dougie Blair, Ron Stitfall, Ernie Stevenson, George Edwards

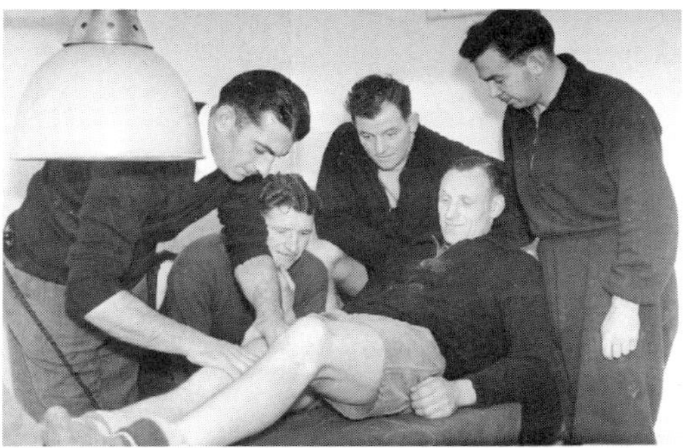
26 January, 1950. In the treatment room with trainer/physio Walter Robbins

1950-51

Round Five, 31 January, 1951. Cardiff City 8 Barry Town 0 (1,500)
Bluebirds; Phil Joslin; Ron Stitfall, Glyn Williams; Ken Hollyman, Stan Montgomery, Billy Baker; Les Evans, Marwood Marchant, Wilf Grant, Dougie Blair, Mike Tiddy
Scorers; Les Evans 4, Marwood Marchant 2, Wilf Grant, og

Round Six, 7 March, 1951. Bangor City 1 Cardiff City 7 (12,000)
Bluebirds; Phil Joslin; Crad Wilcox, Glyn Williams; Ken Hollyman, Derrick Sullivan, Billy Baker; Mike Tiddy, Marwood Marchant, Wilf Grant, Dougie Blair, George Edwards
Scorers; George Edwards 3, Mike Tiddy 2, Wilf Grant, Marwood Marchant

Semi-final, 16 April, 1951. Wrexham 0 Cardiff City 1 (5,000)
Bluebirds; Phil Joslin; Charlie Rutter, Crad Wilcox; Ken Hollyman, Stan Montgomery, Billy Baker; Mike Tiddy, Marwood Marchant, Wilf Grant, Bobby McLaughlin, George Edwards
Scorer; George Edwards

Final, 7 May, 1951. Merthyr Tydfil 1 Cardiff City 1 (18,000)
Bluebirds; Phil Joslin; Glyn Williams, Alf Sherwood; Ken Hollyman, Stan Montgomery, Billy Baker; Mike Tiddy, Bobby McLaughlin, Wilf Grant, Dougie Blair, George Edwards
Scorer; Wilf Grant

Final (replay), 17 May, 1951. Merthyr Tydfil 3 Cardiff City 2 (18,000)
Bluebirds; Ron Howells; Glyn Williams, Charlie Rutter; Ken Hollyman, Derrick Sullivan, Billy Baker; Mike Tiddy, Bobby McLaughlin, Wilf Grant, Dougie Blair, George Edwards
Scorers; George Edwards, Mike Tiddy

1951-52

Round Five, 3 January, 1952. Milford United 1 Cardiff City 3 (2,500)
Bluebirds; Ron Howells; Ron Stitfall, Charlie Rutter; Glyn Williams, Stan Montgomery, Don Moss; Cliiff Nugent, Crad Wilcox, Elfed Evans, Derrick Sullivan, George Edwards
Scorers; Crad Wilcox 2, Elfed Evans

Round Six, 2 February, 1952. Merthyr Tydfil 3 Cardiff City 1 (13,000)
Bluebirds; Iorrie Hughes; Charlie Rutter, Alf Sherwood; Ken Hollyman, Derrick Sullivan, Glyn Williams; Cliff Nugent, Bobby McLaughlin, Dougie Blair, Roley Williams, George Edwards
Scorer; George Edwards

1952-53

Round Six, 15 January, 1953. Merthyr Tydfil 2 Cardiff City 5 (8,000)
Bluebirds; Graham Vearncombe; John Frowen, Jack Mansell; Alan Harrington, Stan Montgomery, Bobby McLaughlin; George Hazlett, Roley Williams, Tommy Northcott, Ken Chisholm, Cliff Nugent
Scorers; Ken Chisholm 2, Tommy Northcott 2, George Hazlett

Round Seven, 31 January, 1953. Barry Town 2 Cardiff City 3 (9,000)
Bluebirds; Ron Howells; John Frowen, Jack Mansell; Bobby McLaughlin, Stan Montgomery, Derrick Sullivan; Mike Tiddy, Alan Harrington, Tommy Northcott, Ken Chisholm, Cliff Nugent
Scorers; Tommy Northcott 2, Mike Tiddy

Semi-final, 21 March, 1953. Rhyl 1 Cardiff City 0 (10,000)
Bluebirds; Ron Howells; Alf Sherwood, Jack Mansell; Alan Harrington, Stan Montgomery, Billy Baker; Mike Tiddy, Roley Williams, Wilf Grant, Ken Chisholm, George Edwards

1953-54

Round Five, 20 January, 1954. Barry Town 1 Cardiff City 1 (2,500)
Bluebirds; Graham Vearncombe; Ron Stitfall, Charlie Rutter; Alan Harrington, Colin Gale, Tommy Bevan; Mike Tiddy, Wilf Grant, Ken Oakley, Peter Thomas, Clive Burder
Scorer; Clive Burder

Round Five (replay), 10 February, 1954. Cardiff City 4 Barry Town 2 (4,500)
Bluebirds; Graham Vearncombe; Colin Gale, Alf Sherwood; Billy Baker, Stan Montgomery, Derrick Sullivan; Mike Tiddy, Cliff Nugent, Trevor Ford, Peter Thomas, George Edwards
Scorers; Cliff Nugent 2, Mike Tiddy, Trevor Ford

Round Six, Bye
Note: several clubs were awarded byes, reasons not known

Round Seven, 20 February, 1954. Merthyr Tydfil 3 Cardiff City 5 (7,000)
Bluebirds; Graham Vearncombe; Ron Stitfall, Harry Parfitt; Dennis Callan, Stan Montgomery, Derrick Sullivan; Mike Tiddy, Cliff Nugent, Wilf Grant, Alan Harrington, Tommy Northcott
Scorers; Wilf Grant 3, Cliff Nugent, og

Semi-final, 24 March, 1954. Flint Town 2 Cardiff City 1 (10,500)
Bluebirds; Graham Vearncombe; Colin Gale, Alf Sherwood; Dennis Callan, Stan Montgomery, Derrick Sullivan; Mike Tiddy, Cliff Nugent, Trevor Ford, Tommy Northcott, Wilf Grant
Scorer; Tommy Northcott

1954-55

Round Five, 12 January, 1955. Pembroke 0 Cardiff City 7 (4,000)
Bluebirds; Ron Howells; Ron Stitfall, Charlie Rutter; Billy Baker, Derrick Sullivan, Islwyn Jones; Mike Tiddy, Ron Stockin, Trevor Ford, Cliff Nugent, Gordon Nutt
Scorers; Trevor Ford 4, Mike Tiddy, Cliff Nugent, Ron Stockin

Round Six, 17 February,1955. Newport County 1 Cardiff City 3 (10,223)
Bluebirds; Ron Howells; Charlie Rutter, Alf Sherwood; Alan Harrington, Stan Montgomery, Derrick Sullivan; Gordon Nutt, Roley Williams, Trevor Ford, Ron Stockin, Tommy Northcott
Scorers; Derrick Sullivan, Trevor Ford, Ron Stockin

30 April 1956, Cardif City 3 Swansea Town 2. Welsh Cup Final. Trevor Ford shakes hands with Swansea skipper Ivor Allchurch in front of referee BM Griffiths

Semi-final, 13 April, 1955. Chester 2 Cardiff City 0 (7,961)
Bluebirds; Ron Howells; Charlie Rutter, Harry Parfitt; Billy Baker, Stan Montgomery, Islwyn Jones; Gordon Nutt, Tommy Northcott, Gerry Hitchens, Ron Stockin, George Edwards

1955-56

Round Five, 1 February, 1956. Pembroke 2 Cardiff City 2 (5,000)
Bluebirds; Ron Howells, Ron Davies, Ron Stitfall; Derrick Sullivan, Danny Malloy, Colin Baker; Brian Walsh, Harry Kirtley, Trevor Ford, Gerry Hitchens, Johnny McSeveney
Scorers; Trevor Ford, Gerry Hitchens

Round Five (replay), 8 February, 1956. Cardiff City 9 Pembroke 0 (4,549)
Bluebirds; Graham Vearncombe; Ron Stitfall, Alf Sherwood; Derrick Sullivan, Danny Malloy, Colin Baker; Colin Dixon, Harry Kirtley, Trevor Ford, Gerry Hitchens, Johnny McSeveney
Scorers; Trevor Ford 4, Gerry Hitchens 3, Colin Baker, Johnny McSeveney

Round Six, 28 February, 1956. Cardiff City 5 Wrexham 3 (5,300)
Bluebirds; Graham Vearncombe; Ron Davies, Derrick Sullivan; Alan Harrington, John Frowen, Colin Baker; Brian Walsh, Harry Kirtley, Trevor Ford, Gerry Hitchens, Johnny McSeveney
Scorers; Gerry Hitchens 3, Trevor Ford, Johnny McSeveney

Did You Know...
When Cardiff City met Swansea Town in the Welsh Cup Final at Ninian Park on 30 April, 1956, a new attendance record for the competition was set when 37,500 fans saw the Bluebirds win 3-2

Semi-final, 17 March, 1956. Oswestry 0 Cardiff City 7 (11,418)
Bluebirds; Graham Vearncombe; Ron Stitfall, Alan Harrington; Derrick Sullivan, John Frowen, Colin Baker; Cliff Nugent, Harry Kirtley, Trevor Ford, Gerry Hitchens, Johnny McSeveney
Scorers; Gerry Hitchens 5, Trevor Ford 2

Final, 30 April, 1956. Cardiff City 3 Swansea Town 2 (37,500)
Bluebirds; Graham Vearncombe; Ron Stitfall, Alan Harrington; Derrick Sullivan, Danny Malloy, Colin Baker; Brian Walsh, Harry Kirtley, Trevor Ford, Gerry Hitchens, Johnny McSeveney
Scorers; Brian Walsh 2, Johnny McSeveney

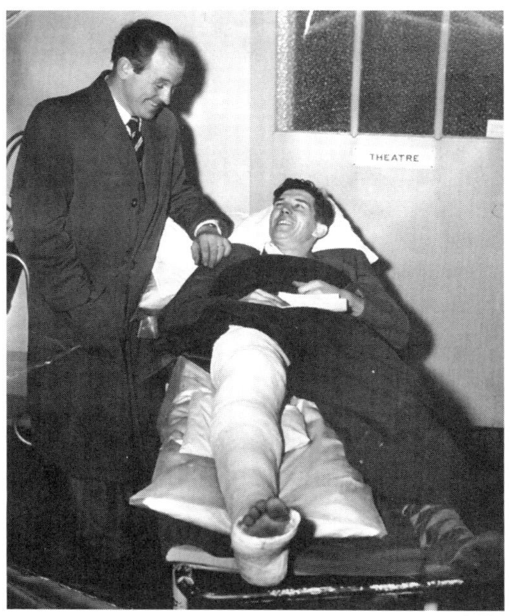

30 April 1956, Cardiff City 3 Swansea Town 2. Welsh Cup Final. City's Harry Kirtley lies in St David's Hospital after breaking his leg during the match

1956-57

Round Five, 31 January, 1957. Haverfordwest 3 Cardiff City 3 (1,800)
Bluebirds; Graham Vearncombe; Ron Davies, Ron Stitfall; Colin Baker, Danny Malloy, Derrick Sullivan; Brian Walsh, Harry Kirtley, Gerry Hitchens, Ron Stockin, Johnny McSeveney
Scorers; Gerry Hitchens 2, Harry Kirtley

Round Five (replay), 6 February, 1957. Cardiff City 8 Haverfordwest 1 (3,500)
Bluebirds; Ron Howells; Ron Davies, Ron Stitfall; Colin Baker, John Frowen, Derrick Sullivan; Brian Walsh, Harry Kirtley, Gerry Hitchens, Ron Stockin, Don Godwin
Scorers; Gerry Hitchens 2, Brian Walsh 2, Harry Kirtley, Ron Stockin, Derrick Sullivan, og

Round Six, 27 February, 1957. Cardiff City 0 Chester 2 (5,000)
Bluebirds; Ron Howells; Charlie Rutter, Ron Stitfall; Alan Harrington, Danny Malloy, Colin Baker; Colin Dixon, Harry Kirtley, Gerry Hitchens, Derrick Sullivan, Johnny McSeveney

1957-58

Round Five, 29 January, 1958. Cardiff City 0 Hereford United 2 (1,500)
Bluebirds; Ken Jones; Charlie Rutter, Ron Stitfall; Ray Daniel, Danny Malloy, Derrick Sullivan; Colin Hudson, Brayley Reynolds, Joe Bonson, Cliff Nugent, Ken Tucker

1958-59

Round Five, 5 February, 1959. Gloucester City 1 Cardiff City 1 (5,000)
Bluebirds; Ron Nicholls; Alec Milne, Ron Stitfall; Derrick Sullivan, Danny Malloy, Colin Baker; Brian Walsh, George Kelly, Joe Bonson, Ron Hewitt, Brian Jenkins
Scorer; Ron Hewitt

Round Five (replay), 11 February, 1959. Cardiff City 3 Gloucester City 0 (5,000)
Bluebirds; Graham Vearncombe; Alec Milne, Ron Stitfall; Colin Baker, Danny Malloy, Derrick Sullivan; Colin Hudson, Derek Tapscott, Joe Bonson, Brayley Reynolds, Brian Jenkins
Scorers; Alec Milne, Joe Bonson, Colin Hudson

Did You Know...
In three successive Welsh Cup matches during the 1955-56 season, the Bluebirds scored 21 goals with Gerry Hitchens netting 11 of them

Round Six, 25 February, 1959. Cardiff City 3 Rhyl 1 (4,000)
Bluebirds; Ron Nicholls; Alec Milne, Ron Stitfall; Colin Baker, Danny Malloy, Derrick Sullivan; Brian Walsh, Derek Tapscott, Harry Knowles, Brayley Reynolds, Colin Hudson
Scorers; Brayley Reynolds, Derek Tapscott, Harry Knowles

Semi-final, 19 March, 1959, Wrexham 0 Cardiff City 6 (3,621)
Bluebirds; Graham Vearncombe; Alan Harrington, Alec Milne; Colin Baker, Danny Malloy, Derrick Sullivan; Brian Walsh, Derek Tapscott, Harry Knowles, Ron Hewitt, Colin Hudson
Scorers; Harry Knowles 3, Derek Tapscott 2, Ron Hewitt

Final, 30 April, 1959. Lovells Athletic 0 Cardiff City 2 (8,000)
Bluebirds; Graham Vearncombe; Alec Milne, Ron Stitfall; Steve Gammon, Danny Malloy, Colin Baker; Brian Walsh, Derek Tapscott, Joe Bonson, Graham Moore, Colin Hudson
Scorers; Joe Bonson, Colin Hudson

1959-60

Round Five, 20 January, 1960. Cardiff City 5 Lovells Athletic 0 (2,000)
Bluebirds; Graham Vearncombe; Alec Milne, Ron Stitfall; Derrick Sullivan, Danny Malloy, Colin Baker; Brian Walsh, Derek Tapscott, Graham Moore, Joe Bonson, Johnny Watkins
Scorers; Colin Baker, Derek Tapscott, Graham Moore, Johnny Watkins, Joe Bonson

Round Six, 25 February, 1960. Swansea Town 1 Cardiff City 2 (11,000)
Bluebirds; Ron Nicholls; A Monk, Alan Harrington; Steve Gammon, Trevor Peck, Barry Hole; Colin Hudson, Steve Mokone, Harry Knowles, Mike Hughes, Brian Jenkins
Scorers; Harry Knowles, og

Semi-final, 28 March, 1960. Bangor City 1 Cardiff City 1 (3,600)
Bluebirds; Graham Vearncombe; Alec Milne, Ron Stitfall; Steve Gammon, Danny Malloy, Colin Baker; Brian Walsh, Derek Tapscott, Graham Moore, Joe Bonson, Johnny Watkins
Scorer; Graham Moore

Semi-final (replay), 25 April, 1960. Cardiff City 4 Bangor City 1 (2,500)
Bluebirds; Graham Vearncombe; Alan Harrington, Ron Stitfall; Colin Baker, Danny Malloy, Barry Hole; Brian Walsh, Steve Mokone, Graham Moore, Alan Durban, Brian Jenkins
Scorers; Brian Jenkins 2(1p), Graham Moore, Steve Mokone

Final, 2 May, 1960. Cardiff City 1 Wrexham 1 (11,172)
Bluebirds; Graham Vearncombe; Alan Harrington, Ron Stitfall; Colin Baker, Danny Malloy, Barry Hole; Brian Walsh, Derek Tapscott, Graham Moore, Johnny Watkins, Brian Jenkins
Scorer; Brian Jenkins

Final (replay), 5 May, 1960. Wrexham 1 Cardiff City 0 (5,800)
Bluebirds; Graham Vearncombe; Alan Harrington, Ron Stitfall; Steve Gammon, Danny Malloy, Colin Baker; Colin Hudson, Derek Tapscott, Graham Moore, Brian Jenkins, Johnny Watkins

1960-61

Round Five, 28 January, 1961. Cardiff City 16 Knighton 0 (1,800)
Bluebirds; Maurice Swan; Alan Harrington, Ron Stitfall; Steve Gammon, Danny Malloy, Colin Baker; Brian Walsh, Graham Moore, Derek Tapscott, Peter Donnelly, Derek Hogg
Scorers; Derek Tapscott 6, Graham Moore 4, Brian Walsh 2, Peter Donnelly 2, Danny Malloy, Derek Hogg.

Round Six, 16 February, 1961. Cardiff City 2 Newport County 1 (12,192)
Bluebirds; Maurice Swan; Trevor Edwards, Ron Stitfall; Barry Hole, Danny Malloy, Colin Baker; Brian Walsh, Graham Moore, Derek Tapscott, Peter Donnelly, Derek Hogg
Scorers; Graham Moore, Derek Hogg

Did You Know...
The most goals scored by the Bluebirds in one match was the 16 netted against Knighton in the Welsh Cup on 28 January, 1961

Semi-final, 22 March, 1961. Swansea Town 1 Cardiff City 1 (10,470) Somerton Park
Bluebirds; Ron Nicholls; Alan Harrington, Ron Stitfall; Barry Hole, Danny Malloy, Colin Baker; Brian Walsh, Graham Moore, Derek Tapscott, Peter Donnelly, Derek Hogg
Scorer; Derek Tapscott

Semi-final (replay), 28 March, 1961. Swansea Town 2 Cardiff City 1 (20,000) Llanelli
Bluebirds; Graham Vearncombe; Alan Harrington, Ron Stitfall; Barry Hole, Danny Malloy, Colin Baker; Derek Hogg, Derek Tapscott, Brian Edgley, Dai Ward, Peter Donnelly
Scorer; Derek Tapscott

1961-62

Round Five, 30 January, 1962. Cardiff City 4 Newport County 1 (5,715)
Bluebirds; Graham Vearncombe; Alan Harrington, Alec Milne; Steve Gammon, Frank Rankmore, Colin Baker; Peter King, Alan Durban, Johnny King, Dai Ward, Derek Hogg
Scorers; Johnny King 2, Alan Durban, Peter King

Round Six, 20 February, 1962. Bristol City 0 Cardiff City 2 (13,579)
Bluebirds; Dilwyn John; Ron Stitfall, Alec Milne; Barry Hole, Frank Rankmore, Colin Baker; Peter King, Derek Tapscott, Johnny King, Dai Ward, Alan McIntosh
Scorer; Dai Ward 2

Semi-final, 20 March, 1962. Bangor City 2 Cardiff City 0 (5,482) Wrexham
Bluebirds; Graham Vearncombe; Trevor Edwards, Alec Milne; Barry Hole, Alan Harrington, Colin Baker; Peter King, Dai Ward, Derek Tapscott, Johnny King, Danny McCarthy

1962-63

Round Five, 26 March, 1963. Cardiff City 7 Abergavenny Thursdays 1 (2,200)
Bluebirds; Graham Vearncombe; Ron Stitfall, Trevor Edwards; Colin Baker, Frank Rankmore, Barry Hole; Alan McIntosh, Alan Durban, Derek Tapscott, Ivor Allchurch, Peter Hooper
Scorers; Ivor Allchurch 2, Alan Durban 2, Derek Tapscott, Peter Hooper, Barry Hole

Round Six, 11 April, 1963. Swansea Town 2 Cardiff City 0 (11,500)
Bluebirds; Graham Vearncombe; Ron Stitfall, Trevor Edwards; Alan Harrington, Frank Rankmore, Barry Hole; Alan McIntosh, Derek Tapscott, Mel Charles, Ivor Allchurch, Peter Hooper

1963-64

Round Five, 25 January, 1964. Ebbw Vale 1 Cardiff City 6 (5,000)
Bluebirds; Graham Vearncombe; Trevor Edwards, Alec Milne; Gareth Williams, John Charles, Dick Scott; Bernard Lewis, Derek Tapscott, Mel Charles, Ivor Allchurch, Peter King
Scorers; Mel Charles 2, Peter King 2, Bernard Lewis 2

1 February 1963. Two of Cardiff City's most famous players Billy Hardy on left with Fred Keenor at Ninian Park

Round Six, 19 February, 1964. Cardiff City 3 Chester 1 (3,120)
Bluebirds; Dilwyn John; Trevor Peck, Peter Rodrigues; Gareth Williams, John Charles, Dick Scott; Bernard Lewis, Barry Hole, Mel Charles, Ivor Allchurch, Derek Tapscott
Scorers; Mel Charles, Barry Hole, Derek Tapscott

Semi-final, 11 March, 1964. Newport County 2 Cardiff City 2 (5,200)
Bluebirds; Dilwyn John; Trevor Peck, Trevor Edwards; Gareth Williams, John Charles, Barry Hole; Peter King, Dick Scott, Mel Charles, Ivor Allchurch, Derek Tapscott
Scorers; Ivor Allchurch, Mel Charles

Semi-final (replay), 25 March, 1964. Cardiff City 1 Newport County 0 (8,400) (Swansea)
Bluebirds; Dilwyn John; Trevor Peck, Peter Rodrigues; Gareth Williams, John Charles, Barry Hole; Bernard Lewis, Dick Scott, Mel Charles, Ivor Allchurch, Peter King
Scorer; Mel Charles

Final (first leg), 22 April, 1964. Bangor City 2 Cardiff City 0 (10,000)
Bluebirds; Dilwyn John; Trevor Peck, Peter Rodrigues; Dick Scott, John Charles, Barry Hole; Bernard Lewis, Peter King, Mel Charles, Ivor Allchurch, Greg Farrell

Final (second leg), 29 April, 1964. Cardiff City 3 Bangor City 1 (6,000)
Bluebirds; Grahan Vearncombe; Colin Baker, Peter Rodrigues; Gareth Williams, Don Murray, Barry Hole; Bernard Lewis, Mel Charles, John Charles, Ivor Allchurch, PeterKing
Scorers; Bernard Lewis, Ivor Allchurch, Mel Charles
(Play-off required after both sides with two points each for a win)

Final (play-off), 4 May, 1964. Cardiff City 2 Bangor City 0 (10,014) (Wrexham)
Bluebirds; Graham Vearncombe; Colin Baker, Peter Rodrigues; Gareth Williams, Don Murray, Barry Hole; Bernard Lewis, Mel Charles, John Charles, Ivor Allchurch, Peter King
Scorer; Peter King 2

1964-65

Round Five, 26 January, 1965. Merthyr Tydfil 1 Cardiff City 3 (6,000)
Bluebirds; Bob Wilson; Alan Harrington, Peter Rodrigues; Gareth Williams, Don Murray, Barry Hole; Greg Farrell, Peter King, Derek Tapscott, Keith Ellis, Bernard Lewis
Scorers; Peter King 2, Derek Tapscott

Round Six, 17 February, 1965. Cardiff City 3 Hereford United 1 (8,000)
Bluebirds; Bob Wilson; Trevor Peck, Peter Rodrigues; Gareth Williams, Don Murray, Barry Hole; Greg Farrell, Mel Charles, Keith Ellis, Ivor Allchurch, Peter King
Scorers; Ivor Allchurch, Keith Ellis, Greg Farrell (p)

Semi-final, 10 March, 1965. Swansea Town 0 Cardiff City 1 (7,500)
Bluebirds; Bob Wilson; Trevor Peck, Peter Rodrigues; John Charles, Don Murray, Barry Hole; Greg Farrell, Gareth Williams, Keith Ellis, Ivor Allchurch, Peter King
Scorer; Greg Farrell (p)

Final (first leg), 12 April, 1965. Cardiff City 5 Wrexham 1 (7,000)
Bluebirds; Bob Wilson; Peter Rodrigues, Colin Baker; Gareth Williams, Don Murray, Barry Hole; George Johnston, Ivor Allchurch, Mel Charles, Peter King, Bernard Lewis
Scorers; George Johnston 2, Peter King 2, Ivor Allchurch

Did You Know...
City went out of three cup competitions in the space of ten days by losing to Southport (FA Cup) on 12 February 1965 after losing to West Ham (Football League Cup) on 2 February and Swansea Town (Welsh Cup) on 8 February

Final (second leg), 26 April, 1965. Wrexham 1 Cardiff City 0 (8,000)
Bluebirds; Bob Wilson; Gordon Harris, Colin Baker; Gareth Williams, Don Murray, Barry Hole; George Johnston, Ivor Allchurch, John Charles, Peter King, Bernard Lewis
(Play-off required after both sides with two points for a win)

Final (play-off), 5 May, 1965. Cardiff City 3 Wrexham 0 (7,840) (Shrewsbury)
Bluebirds; Bob Wilson; Graham Coldrick, Colin Baker; Gareth Williams, Don Murray, Barry Hole; George Johnston, Ivor Allchurch, John Charles, Peter King, Bernard Lewis
Scorers; Ivor Allchurch 2, og

1965-66

Round Five, 4 January, 1966. Swansea Town 2 Cardiff City 2 (10,275)
Bluebirds; Lyn Davies; Alan Harrington, Colin Baker; Gareth Williams, Don Murray, Barry Hole; Greg Farrell, George Johnston, George Andrews, Terry Harkin, Peter King
Scorers; Peter King, George Andrews

Round Five (replay), 8 February, 1966. Cardiff City 3 Swansea Town 5 aet (9,836)
Bluebirds; Lyn Davies; Graham Coldrick, Colin Baker; Gareth Williams, Don Murray, Barry Hole; Greg Farrell, George Johnston, George Andrews, Terry Harkin, Bernard Lewis
Scorers; George Johnston 2, Gareth Williams

1966-67

Round Five, 17 January, 1967. Swansea Town 0 Cardiff City 4 (11,816)
Bluebirds; Bob Wilson; Graham Coldrick, Bobby Ferguson; Gareth Williams, Don Murray, Brian Harris; Bernard Lewis, George Johnston, Bobby Brown, Peter King, Greg Farrell
Scorers; George Johnston 2, Bernard Lewis, Greg Farrell

Round Six, 8 February, 1967. Cardiff City 6 Hereford United 3 (11,190)
Bluebirds; Bob Wilson; Graham Coldrick, Bobby Ferguson; Gareth Williams, Don Murray, Brian Harris; Greg Farrell, George Johnston, Bobby Brown, Peter King, Ronnie Bird
Scorers; George Johnston 2, Peter King, Graham Coldrick, Bobby Ferguson, Bobby Brown

Semi-final, 15 March, 1967. Newport County 1 Cardiff City 2 (8,500)
Bluebirds; Bob Wilson; Dave Carver, Bobby Ferguson; Gareth Williams, Don Murray, Brian Harris; Bryn Jones, John Toshack, Bobby Brown, Peter King, Ronnie Bird
Scorers; Bobby Brown, Peter King

Final (first leg), 17 April, 1967. Wrexham 2 Cardiff City 2 (11,437)
Bluebirds; Bob Wilson; Graham Coldrick, Bobby Ferguson; Gareth Williams, Don Murray, Brian Harris; Barrie Jones, Bobby Brown, Norman Dean, Peter King, Ronnie Bird
Scorers; Bobby Brown, Peter King

Final (second leg), 3 May, 1967. Cardiff City 2 Wrexham 1 (8,299)
Bluebirds; Bob Wilson; Graham Coldrick, Bobby Ferguson; Gareth Williams, Don Murray, Brian Harris; Barrie Jones, Bobby Brown, Norman Dean, Peter King, Ronnie Bird
Scorers; Norman Dean, og
(Cardiff City winners by three points to one point)

16 May 1968, Welsh Cup Final. Cardiff City 4 Hereford Utd.
City players celebrate victory

1967-68

Round Five, 16 January, 1968. Cardiff City 8 Ebbw Vale 0 (3,542)
Bluebirds; Lyn Davies; Graham Coldrick, Bobby Ferguson; Malcolm Clarke, Don Murray, Brian Harris (Steve Derrett); Barrie Jones, Leslie Lea, Peter King, John Toshack, Ronnie Bird
Scorers; John Toshack 3, Ronnie Bird 3(1p), Peter King, Leslie Lea

Round Six, 12 February, 1968. Wrexham 1 Cardiff City 3 (7,671)
Bluebirds; Fred Davies; Steve Derrett, Bobby Ferguson (Gary Bell); Malcolm Clarke, Don Murray, Brian Harris; Barrie Jones, Leslie Lea, Peter King, John Toshack, Ronnie Bird
Scorers; Barrie Jones, Leslie Lea, Ronnie Bird

Semi-final, 27 March, 1968. Chester 0 Cardiff City 3 (5,488)
Bluebirds; Fred Davies; Graham Coldrick, Bobby Ferguson; Malcolm Clarke, Don Murray, Brian Harris; Leslie Lea, Brian Clark, Peter King, John Toshack, Ronnie Bird
Scorers; Peter King, John Toshack, Leslie Lea

Final (first leg), 6 May, 1968. Hereford United 0 Cardiff City 2 (5,442)
Bluebirds; Fred Davies; Dave Carver, Bobby Ferguson; Malcolm Clarke, Don Murray, Brian Harris; Barrie Jones, Peter King, Norman Dean, John Toshack, Leslie Lea
Scorers; Barrie Jones, Peter King

Final (second leg), 16 May, 1968. Cardiff City 4 Hereford United 1 (6,036)
Bluebirds; Fred Davies; Dave Carver, Bobby Ferguson; Malcolm Clarke, Don Murray, Brian Harris; Barrie Jones, Norman Dean, Peter King, John Toshack, Leslie Lea
Scorers; Norman Dean, Malcolm Clarke, Leslie Lea, og
(Cardiff City winners by four points to nil)

1968-69

Round Five, 15 January, 1969. Aberystwyth Town 0 Cardiff City 3 (5,000)
Bluebirds; Fred Davies; Dave Carver, Gary Bell; Mel Sutton, Richie Morgan, Steve Derrett; Leslie Lea, Brian Clark, Peter King, John Toshack, Barrie Jones
Scorers; Leslie Lea, John Toshack, Barrie Jones

Round Six, 5 February, 1969. Cardiff City 6 Bethesda Athletic 0 (6,749)
Bluebirds; Fred Davies; Dave Carver, Gary Bell; Mel Sutton, Don Murray, Steve Derrett; Barrie Jones, Brian Clark, Leslie Lea, John Toshack, Peter King
Scorers; Brian Clark 2, Leslie Lea, Barrie Jones, John Toshack, Gary Bell

Semi-final, 19 March, 1969. Chester 0 Cardiff City 2 (8,404)
Bluebirds; Fred Davies; Dave Carver, Steve Derrett; Mel Sutton (Ronnie Bird), Don Murray, Brian Harris; Barrie Jones, Brian Clark, Peter King, John Toshack, Frank Sharp
Scorer; John Toshack 2

Final (first leg), 22 April, 1969. Swansea Town 1 Cardiff City 3 (10,207)
Bluebirds; Fred Davies; Dave Carver, Steve Derrett; Peter King, Don Murray, Brian Harris; Barrie Jones, Brian Clark, Leslie Lea, John Toshack, Frank Sharp
Scorers; John Toshack 2, og

Final (second leg), 29 April, 1969. Cardiff City 2 Swansea Town 0 (12,617)
Bluebirds; Fred Davies; Dave Carver, Steve Derrett; Peter King, Don Murray, Brian Harris; Barrie Jones, Brian Clark, Leslie Lea, John Toshack, Frank Sharp
Scorers; Leslie Lea, John Toshack
(Cardiff City winners by four points to nil)

1969-70

Round Five, 21 January, 1970. Cardiff City 6 Barmouth 1 (4,901)
Bluebirds; Fred Davies; Dave Carver, Gary Bell, Mel Sutton, Don Murray, Bobby Woodruff, Peter King, Brian Clark, Brian Harris, John Toshack, Ronnie Bird
Scorers; Brian Clark 5, John Toshack

Round Six, 4 February, 1970. Cardiff City 3 Wrexham 0 (12,332)
Bluebirds; Fred Davies; Dave Carver, Gary Bell, Mel Sutton, Don Murray, Bobby Woodruff, Leslie Lea, Brian Clark, Brian Harris, John Toshack (Ronnie Bird), Peter King
Scorers; Brian Clark 2, Peter King

Semi-final, 11 March, 1970. Cardiff City 2 Swansea City 2 (18,050)
Bluebirds; Fred Davies; Dave Carver, Gary Bell, Mel Sutton, Don Murray, Bobby Woodruff, Peter King, Brian Clark, Brian Harris, John Toshack, Leslie Lea
Scorers; Bobby Woodruff, John Toshack

Semi-final (replay), 2 May, 1970. Swansea City 0 Cardiff City 2 (16,000)
Bluebirds; Fred Davies; Dave Carver, Gary Bell, Mel Sutton, Don Murray, Brian Harris, Peter King, Bobby Woodruff, Leslie Lea (John Toshack), Brian Clark, Ronnie Bird
Scorers; Ronnie Bird, Peter King

Final (first leg), 8 May, 1970. Chester 0 Cardiff City 1 (3,087)
Bluebirds; Fred Davies; Dave Carver, Gary Bell, Mel Sutton, Don Murray, Brian Harris, Leslie Lea, Bobby Woodruff, Brian Clark, Peter King, Ronnie Bird
Scorer; Ronnie Bird

Final (second leg), 13 May, 1970. Cardiff City 4 Chester 0 (5,567)
Bluebirds; Fred Davies; Dave Carver, Gary Bell, Mel Sutton, Don Murray, Brian Harris, Leslie Lea, Bobby Woodruff, Brian Clark, Peter King, Ronnie Bird
Scorers; Bobby Woodruff, Peter King, Leslie Lea, Brian Clark
(Cardiff City winners by four points to nil)

1970-71

Round Five, 2 February, 1971. Newport County 1 Cardiff City 1 (6,162)
Bluebirds; Jim Eadie; Dave Carver, Gary Bell, Mel Sutton, Don Murray, Brian Harris, Peter King, Ian Gibson (John Parsons), Brian Clark, Leighton Phillips, Nigel Rees
Scorer; Brian Clark

Did You Know...
From May 1967 to May 1972, the Bluebirds won five consecutive Welsh Cup finals during which time they were unbeaten in 31 ties

Round Five (replay), 10 February, 1971. Cardiff City 4 Newport County 0 (10,350)
Bluebirds; Jim Eadie; Dave Carver, Gary Bell, Leighton Phillips, Don Murray, Brian Harris (Ian Gibson), Peter King, John Parsons, Bobby Woodruff, Brian Clark, Ronnie Bird
Scorers; Don Murray, Ian Gibson, Peter King, John Parsons

Round Six, 17 February, 1971. Cardiff City 5 Bangor City 0 (5,019)
Bluebirds; Jim Eadie; Dave Carver, Gary Bell, Bobby Woodruff, Don Murray, Leighton Phillips, Ian Gibson, John Parsons, Peter King, Brian Clark, Nigel Rees
Scorers; Brian Clark, Ian Gibson, Peter King, John Parsons, Nigel Rees

Semi-final, 31 March, 1971. Cardiff City 0 Chester 0 (5,522)
Bluebirds; Jim Eadie; Dave Carver, Gary Bell, Mel Sutton, Don Murray, Leighton Phillips, Ian Gibson, Brian Clark (Peter King), Bobby Woodruff, Alan Warboys, Ronnie Bird

Semi-final (replay), 19 April, 1971. Chester 1 Cardiff City 2 (7,352)
Bluebirds; Jim Eadie; Dave Carver, Gary Bell, Steve Derrett, Don Murray, Leighton Phillips, Ian Gibson, Brian Clark, Alan Warboys, Bobby Woodruff, Peter King
Scorers; Brian Clark, Steve Derrett

Final (first leg), 10 May, 1971. Wrexham 0 Cardiff City 1 (14,101)
Bluebirds; Jim Eadie; Dave Carver, Gary Bell, Mel Sutton, Don Murray, Leighton Phillips, Peter King, Ian Gibson, Alan Warboys, Bobby Woodruff, Ronnie Bird
Scorer; Bobby Woodruff

Final (second leg), 12 May, 1971. Cardiff City 3 Wrexham 1 (4,987)
Bluebirds; Jim Eadie; Dave Carver, Gary Bell, Mel Sutton, Don Murray, Leighton Phillips, Peter King, Ian Gibson, Brian Clark, Bobby Woodruff, Ronnie Bird
Scorers; Ian Gibson 2, Ronnie Bird
(Cardiff City winners by four points to nil)

1971-72

Round Five, 3 January, 1972. Swansea City 0 Cardiff City 2 (14,391)
Bluebirds; Bill Irwin; Dave Carver, Gary Bell, Mel Sutton, Don Murray, Leighton Phillips, Ian Gibson, Brian Clark, Bobby Woodruff, Alan Warboys, Nigel Rees
Scorers; Alan Warboys, Brian Clark

Round Six, 22 February, 1972. Llanelli 0 Cardiff City 1 (6,000)
Bluebirds; Bill Irwin; Dave Carver, Gary Bell, Billy Kellock, Don Murray, Leighton Phillips, Ian Gibson, Brian Clark, Peter King, Bobby Woodruff, Alan Foggon
Scorer; Alan Foggon

Semi-final, 14 March, 1972. Rhyl 1 Cardiff City 2 (5,000)
Bluebirds; Bill Irwin; Dave Carver, Freddie Pethard, Mel Sutton, Don Murray, Leighton Phillips, Ian Gibson, Brian Clark, Billy Kellock (Nigel Rees), Alan Warboys, Peter King
Scorers; Brian Clark, Alan Warboys

Final (first leg), 8 May, 1972. Wrexham 2 Cardiff City 1 (6,984)
Bluebirds; Bill Irwin; Dave Carver, Gary Bell, Billy Kellock, Richie Morgan, Leighton Phillips, Tony Villars, Brian Clark, Ian Gibson (Bobby Woodruff), Alan Warboys, Peter King
Scorer; Bobby Woodruff

Final (second leg), 12 May, 1972. Cardiff City 1 Wrexham 1 (6,508)
Bluebirds; Bill Irwin; Dave Carver, Gary Bell, Mel Sutton, Don Murray, Leighton Phillips, Alan Foggon, Brian Clark, Peter King, Alan Warboys, Tony Villars
Scorer; Alan Foggon
(Wrexham winners by three points to one)

1972-73

Round Four, 3 January, 1973. Aberystwyth Town 1 Cardiff City 7 (3,500)
Bluebirds; Bill Irwin; Phil Dwyer, Gary Bell, Leighton Phillips, Richie Morgan, Peter Morgan, Billy Kellock, Andy McCulloch, Bobby Woodruff, Johnny Vincent, Gil Reece
Scorers; Andy McCulloch 2, Gil Reece 2, Bobby Woodruff 2, Johnny Vincent

Round Five, 20 February, 1973, Newport County 1 Cardiff City 3 (11,350)
Bluebirds; Bill Irwin; Phil Dwyer, Gary Bell, Leighton Phillips, Don Murray, Peter Morgan, Billy Kellock, Andy McCulloch, Bobby Woodruff, Derek Showers, Johnny Vincent
Scorers; Johnny Vincent, Leighton Phillips, Derek Showers

Semi-final, 21 March, 1973. Chester 0 Cardiff City 1 (2,158)
Bluebirds; Bill Irwin; Phil Dwyer, Gary Bell, Alan Couch, Don Murray, Leighton Phillips, Billy Kellock, Andy McCulloch, Derek Showers, Johnny Vincent (Bobby Woodruff), Willie Anderson
Scorer; Andy McCulloch

Final (first leg), 4 April, 1973. Bangor City 1 Cardiff City 0 (5,005)
Bluebirds; Bill Irwin; Phil Dwyer, Gary Bell, Alan Couch, Don Murray, Leighton Phillips, Billy Kellock, Andy McCulloch, Derek Showers (Dave Powell), Bobby Woodruff, Willie Anderson

Final (second leg), 11 April, 1973. Cardiff City 5 Bangor City 0 (4,679)
Bluebirds; Bill Irwin; Phil Dwyer, Gary Bell, Albert Larmour, Don Murray, Dave Powell, Gil Reece, Andy McCulloch, Leighton Phillips, Johnny Vincent, Willie Anderson
Scorers; Gil Reece 3, Leighton Phillips, Gary Bell
(Cardiff City winners 5-1 on aggregate)

1973-74

Round Four, 9 January, 1974. Cardiff City 1 Ton Pentre 0 (856)
Bluebirds; Bill Irwin; Phil Dwyer, Gary Bell, John Impey, Don Murray, George Smith, John Farrington, Willie Carlin, Derek Showers (Jimmy McInch), Johnny Vincent, Tony Villars
Scorer; John Impey

Round Five, 21 February, 1974. Oswestry Town 1 Cardiff City 3 (2,500)
Bluebirds; Bill Irwin; Phil Dwyer, Freddie Pethard, John Impey, Don Murray, Dave Powell, John Farrington, Andy McCulloch, Leighton Phillips, Tony Villars, Gil Reece (Peter Sayer)
Scorers; Gil Reece 2(1p), John Farrington

Semi-final, 13 March, 1974. Shrewsbury Town 1 Cardiff City 2 (1,193)
Bluebirds; Bill Irwin; Phil Dwyer, Freddie Pethard, Dave Powell, Don Murray, Tony Villars, John Farrington, Derek Showers, Leighton Phillips, Willie Carlin, Jack Whitham
Scorers; Derek Showers, Don Murray

Final (first leg), 24 April, 1974. Stourbridge 0 Cardiff City 1 (5,729)
Bluebirds; Bill Irwin; Albert Larmour, Freddie Pethard, Richie Morgan, Don Murray, Clive Charles, John Farrington, George Smith, Jack Whitham, Derek Showers, Bobby Woodruff
Scorer; Derek Showers

Final (second leg), 6 May, 1974. Cardiff City 1 Stourbridge 0 (4,030)
Bluebirds; Ron Healey; Phil Dwyer, Freddie Pethard (Derek Showers), Clive Charles, Richie Morgan, Leighton Phillips, Gil Reece, Tony Villars, Johnny Vincent, John Impey, Willie Anderson
Scorer; Gil Reece
(Cardiff City winners 2-0 on aggregate)

1974-75

Round Four, 14 January, 1975. Cardiff City 2 Hereford United 0 (3,515)
Bluebirds; Bill Irwin; Phil Dwyer, Freddie Pethard, John Buchanan, Richie Morgan, Albert Larmour, Tony Villars, George Smith, Derek Showers, Gil Reece, Willie Anderson
Scorers; Derek Showers, Gil Reece

Round Five, 19 February, 1975. Cardiff City 4 Oswestry Town 0 (1,296)
Bluebirds; Bill Irwin; Phil Dwyer, Freddie Pethard, John Buchanan, Richie Morgan, Albert Larmour, Tony Villars, David Giles, Derek Showers, Peter Sayer, Willie Anderson
Scorers; John Buchanan, Derek Showers, David Giles, og.

Semi-final, 11 March, 1975. Newport County 0 Cardiff City 1 (3,808)
Bluebirds; Bill Irwin; Brian Attley, Freddie Pethard, John Buchanan, Richie Morgan, Albert Larmour, David Giles, Phil Dwyer, Gil Reece, Johnny Vincent, Willie Anderson
Scorer; Phil Dwyer

Final (first leg), 5 May, 1975. Wrexham 2 Cardiff City 1 (6,862)
Bluebirds; Bill Irwin; Brian Attley, Freddie Pethard, John Buchanan, Keith Pontin (Tony Villars), Albert Larmour, David Giles, Phil Dwyer, Gil Reece, John McClelland, Willie Anderson
Scorer; John Buchanan

Final (second leg), 12 May, 1975. Cardiff City 1 Wrexham 3 (5,280)
Bluebirds; Bill Irwin; Brian Attley, Freddie Pethard, John Buchanan, Keith Pontin, Albert Larmour, Tony Villars, Phil Dwyer, Derek Showers, John McClelland (Gil Reece), Willie Anderson
Scorer; Albert Larmour
(Wrexham winners 5-2 on aggregate)

Did You Know...
Albert Larmour played over 200 league and cup games for the Bluebirds but his only goal for the club came in the second leg of the Welsh Cup final of 1975 when City lost 5-2 to Wrexham on aggregate

1975-76

Round Four, 14 January, 1976. Cardiff City 5 Sully 0 (3,260)
Bluebirds; Bill Irwin; Phil Dwyer, Clive Charles, Peter Sayer, Mike England, Albert Larmour, John Buchanan, Doug Livermore (Martin Morgan), Tony Evans, Adrian Alston, Willie Anderson
Scorers; Tony Evans 3, Doug Livermore, John Buchanan

Round Five, 17 February, 1976. Cardiff City 1 Swansea City 1 (5,812)
Bluebirds; Ron Healey; Phil Dwyer, Clive Charles, Freddie Pethard (Peter Sayer), Richie Morgan, Albert Larmour, John Buchanan, Doug Livermore, Gil Reece, Adrian Alston, Willie Anderson
Scorer; og

Round Five (replay), 2 March, 1976. Swansea City 0 Cardiff City 3 (10,056)
Bluebirds; Ron Healey; Phil Dwyer, Clive Charles, Freddie Pethard, Richie Morgan, Mike England, John Buchanan, Doug Livermore, Brian Clark, Adrian Alston, Gil Reece
Scorers; Adrian Alston 2, Brian Clark

Semi-final, 23 March, 1976. Chester 0 Cardiff City 0 (3,743)
Bluebirds; Ron Healey; Freddie Pethard, Clive Charles, Alan Campbell, Keith Pontin, Phil Dwyer, David Giles, Doug Livermore, Brian Clark, Adrian Alston, Gil Reece

Semi-final (replay), 1 April, 1976. Cardiff City 1 Chester o (4,244)
Bluebirds; Ron Healey; Freddie Pethard, Clive Charles (John Buchanan), Alan Campbell, Mike England, Phil Dwyer, Peter Sayer, Doug Livermore, Brian Clark, Adrian Alston, Gil Reece
Scorer; og

17 February 1976, Welsh Cup Round. 5 Cardiff City 1 Swansea City 1. Swans keeper Steve Potter dives at the feet of Tony Evans

Final, *29 April, 1976*
(This was drawn 2-2 but declared void as Hereford United played an ineligible player)

Final (first leg), 18 May, 1976. Hereford United 3 Cardiff City 3 (3,709)
Bluebirds; Ron Healey; Freddie Pethard, Clive Charles, David Giles, Phil Dwyer, Albert Larmour, Peter Sayer, Doug Livermore, Brian Clark, Derek Showers, Tony Evans
Scorers; Phil Dwyer 2, Tony Evans

Final (second leg), 19 May, 1976. Cardiff City 3 Hereford United 2 (2,648)
Bluebirds; Bill Irwin; Freddie Pethard, Clive Charles, David Giles, Phil Dwyer, Albert Larmour, Peter Sayer, Doug Livermore, Brian Clark, Tony Evans, Willie Anderson
Scorers; Freddie Pethard, Brian Clark, Tony Evans
(Cardiff City winners 6-5 on aggregate)

1976-77

Round Four, 19 January, 1977. Cardiff City 2 Stourbridge 0 (1,782)
Bluebirds; Ron Healey; Phil Dwyer, Brian Attley (Willie Anderson), David Giles, Paul Went, Albert Larmour, Steve Grapes, Doug Livermore, Tony Evans, Robin Friday, Peter Sayer
Scorers; Phil Dwyer, David Giles

Round Five, 16 February, 1977. Bangor City 0 Cardiff City 2 (5,000)
Bluebirds; Ron Healey; Phil Dwyer, Brian Attley, John Buchanan, Paul Went (David Giles), Albert Larmour, Steve Grapes, Doug Livermore, Tony Evans, Robin Friday, Peter Sayer
Scorers; David Giles, Steve Grapes

Semi-final, 16 March, 1977. Bridgend Town 1 Cardiff City 2 (2,000)
Bluebirds; Ron Healey; Phil Dwyer, Clive Charles, David Giles, Paul Went, Albert Larmour, Steve Grapes, Doug Livermore, Tony Evans, Peter Sayer, John Buchanan
Scorers; Peter Sayer, Tony Evans

Final (first leg), 16 May, 1977. Cardiff City 2 Shrewsbury Town 1 (2,907)
Bluebirds; Ron Healey; Phil Dwyer, Freddie Pethard, Alan Campbell, Keith Pontin, Albert Larmour, Steve Grapes, Doug Livermore (Derek Showers), Peter Sayer, Robin Friday, John Buchanan
Scorers; Freddie Pethard, Robin Friday

Final (second leg), 18 May, 1977. Shrewsbury Town 3 Cardiff City 0 (3,178)
Bluebirds; Ron Healey; Phil Dwyer, Freddie Pethard, Alan Campbell, Keith Pontin, Albert Larmour, David Giles, Peter Sayer, Derek Showers (Steve Grapes), Robin Friday, John Buchanan
(Shrewsbury Town winners 4-2 on aggregate)

19 May 1976, Welsh Cup Final (2nd leg). Cardiff City 3 Hereford 2. Albert Larmour goes for goal watched by Brian Clark (2nd rt) playing in his last match for the Bluebirds

1977-78

Round Four, 21 December, 1977. Worcester City 2 Cardiff City 2 (2,915)
Bluebirds; Bill Irwin; Phil Dwyer, Freddie Pethard, Alan Campbell, Paul Went, Albert Larmour, David Giles, John Buchanan, Keith Robson, Ray Bishop, Steve Grapes
Scorers; Paul Went (p), Ray Bishop

Round Four (replay), 11 January, 1978. Cardiff City 3 Worcester City 0 (963)
Bluebirds; Ron Healey; Phil Dwyer, Freddie Pethard, Alan Campbell, Keith Pontin, Albert Larmour, Steve Grapes, David Giles, Keith Robson, Ray Bishop, Peter Sayer
Scorers; Ray Bishop, Keith Robson, og

Round Five, 1 March, 1978. Cardiff City 1 Kidderminster Harriers 1 (1,639)
Bluebirds; Ron Healey; Phil Dwyer, Freddie Pethard, Alan Campbell, Keith Pontin, Albert Larmour, Steve Grapes, David Giles, Paul Went, Ray Bishop (Tony Evans), John Buchanan
Scorer; John Buchanan

Round Five (replay), 15 March, 1978. Kidderminster Harriers 1 Cardiff City 3 (3,000)
Bluebirds; Ron Healey; Rod Thomas, Freddie Pethard, Alan Campbell, Keith Pontin, Albert Larmour, Steve Grapes, David Giles, Phil Dwyer, Ray Bishop (Paul Went), John Buchanan
Scorers; David Giles 2, John Buchanan (p)

Semi-final, 13 April, 1978. Cardiff City 0 Wrexham 2 (8,928)
Bluebirds; Ron Healey; Rod Thomas, Freddie Pethard, Alan Campbell, Keith Pontin, Albert Larmour, Brian Attley (Tony Evans), Phil Dwyer, Ray Bishop, Paul Went, John Buchanan

1978-79

Round Four, 17 January, 1979. Cardiff City 2 Merthyr Tydfil 1 (694)
Bluebirds; Ron Healey; Phil Dwyer, Rod Thomas, John Lewis, Keith Pontin, Albert Larmour, Steve Grapes, Ray Bishop, Tony Evans, Gary Stevens, John Buchanan
Scorers; Gary Stevens, Tony Evans (p)

Round Five, 12 February, 1979. Worcester City 3 Cardiff City 2 (2,500)
Bluebirds; Ron Healey; Phil Dwyer, Freddie Pethard, Steve Grapes, Keith Pontin, Rod Thomas, Ray Bishop, John Buchanan, Tony Evans, Gary Stevens, John Lewis
Scorers; Phil Dwyer, John Buchanan

1979-80

Round Four, 22 January, 1980. Newport County 2 Cardiff City 0 (7,709)
Bluebirds; Ron Healey; Phil Dwyer, Colin Sullivan, Alan Campbell, Keith Pontin, Rod Thomas, John Lewis, Ray Bishop, Ronnie Moore, Gary Stevens, John Buchanan

1980-81

Round Three, 3 December, 1980. Cardiff City 6 Cardiff Corinthians 0 (1,080)
Bluebirds; Ron Healey; Linden Jones, Rod Thomas, Wayne Hughes, Keith Pontin, Phil Dwyer (Ray Bishop), Paul Giles, Peter Kitchen, Gary Stevens, John Lewis, John Buchanan
Scorers; Peter Kitchen 5, Wayne Hughes

Round Four, 27 January, 1981. Wrexham 3 Cardiff City 0 (4,880)
Bluebirds; Ron Healey; Linden Jones, Rod Thomas, Wayne Hughes, Keith Pontin, Paul Maddy, Paul Giles, Peter Kitchen, Gary Stevens, Billy Ronson, John Buchanan

1981-82

Round Three, 6 December, 1981. Bridgend Town 1 Cardiff City 4 (1,000)
Bluebirds; Ron Healey; Steve Grapes, Phil Dwyer, Paul Maddy, Keith Pontin, Gary Bennett, Paul Sugrue, Tarki Micallef, Gary Stevens, Wayne Hughes, John Lewis
Scorers; Tarki Micallef 2, John Lewis, Paul Sugrue

Round Four, 15 December, 1981. Cardiff City 3 Newport County 1 (3,915)
Bluebirds; Ron Healey; Steve Grapes, Phil Dwyer, Paul Maddy, Keith Pontin, Gary Bennett, Dave Bennett, Tarki Micallef, Gary Stevens, Wayne Hughes, John Lewis
Scorers; Dave Bennett, Phil Dwyer, Gary Stevens

Round Five, 9 January, 1982. Cardiff City 4 Wrexham 1 (2,767)
Bluebirds; Ron Healey; Linden Jones, Tim Gilbert, Steve Grapes, Keith Pontin, Gary Bennett, Dave Bennett, Tarki Micallef, Gary Stevens, Phil Dwyer, Peter Kitchen
Scorers; Peter Kitchen 3, Gary Stevens

Semi-final, 8 April, 1982. Hereford United 0 Cardiff City 0 (4,832)
Bluebirds; Ron Healey; Linden Jones, Mick Henderson, Steve Grapes, Keith Pontin, Gary Bennett (Paul Maddy), Dave Bennett, Andy Polycarpou, Gary Stevens, Peter Kitchen, Tarki Micallef

Semi-final (replay), 19 April, 1982. Cardiff City 2 Hereford United 1 (3,635)
Bluebirds; Ron Healey; Linden Jones, Andy Polycarpou, Keith Pontin, Wayne Hughes, Tarki Micallef, Steve Grapes, Mick Henderson, Peter Kitchen, Dave Bennett, Gary Stevens
Scorers; Tarki Micallef, Gary Stevens

Final (first leg), 11 May, 1982. Cardiff City 0 Swansea City 0 (11,960)
Bluebirds; Andy Dibble; Linden Jones, Mick Henderson, Keith Pontin, Gary Bennett (Stan McEwan), Jimmy Mullen, **Lythgoe, Tim Gilbert, Tarki Micallef, Dave Bennett, Gary Stevens

Final (second leg), 19 May, 1982. Swansea City 2 Cardiff City 1 (15,828)
Bluebirds; Andy Dibble; Linden Jones, Mick Henderson, Keith Pontin (Gary Stevens), Gary Bennett, Jimmy Mullen, ** Lythgoe, Tim Gilbert, Tarki Micallef, Dave Bennett, Stan McEwan
Scorer; Gary Bennett
(Swansea winners 2-1 on aggregate)

1982-83

Round Three, 30 November, 1982. Newport County 1 Cardiff City 0 (7,800)
Bluebirds; Andy Dibble; Linden Jones, Paul Bodin, Tarki Micallef, Phil Dwyer (Paul Giles), Jimmy Mullen, Gary Bennett, David Tong, Roger Gibbins, Jeff Hemmerman, John Lewis

1983-84

Round Three, 22 November, 1983. Cardiff City 5 Taffs Well 0 (894)
Bluebirds; Gary Plumley; Colin Smith, Paul Bodin, Phil Dwyer, Gary Bennett, David Tong, Gordon Owen (Chris Townsend), Roger Gibbins, Waynew Matthews, Nigel Vaughan, Karl Elsey
Scorers; Wayne Matthews, Gordon Owen, Roger Gibbins, Nigel Vaughan, Chris Townsend

Round Four, 18 January, 1984. Cardiff City 4 Maesteg Park 0 (905)
Bluebirds; Gary Plumley; Karl Elsey, Paul Bodin, Phil Dwyer (Colin Smith), Gary Bennett, David Tong, Gordon Owen, Roger Gibbins, Ian Baird, Nigel Vaughan, Trevor Lee
Scorers; Gordon Owen 2(2p), Ian Baird, Trevor Lee

Round Five, 7 February, 1984. Cardiff City 1 Hereford United 3 (2,033)
Bluebirds; Andy Dibble; Karl Elsey, Colin Smith, Phil Dwyer, Gary Bennett, David Tong, Gordon Owen, Roger Gibbins, Ian Baird, Nigel Vaughan, Paul Bodin (Wayne Matthews)
Scorer; Nigel Vaughan

1984-85

Round Three, 27 November, 1984. Cardiff City 5 Merthyr Tydfil 0 (1,399)
Bluebirds; Lee Smelt; Colin Smith, Jimmy Mullen, Phil Dwyer, Mick Martin (Vaughan Jones), David Tong, Brian Flynn, Roger Gibbins, Nigel Vaughan, Tarki Micallef, Karl Elsey
Scorers; Nigel Vaughan 2, David Tong, Tarki Micallef, Karl Elsey

Did You Know...
The Bluebirds and Newport County conducted an unusual transfer deal on 29 September 1983 when Nigel Vaughan and Karl Elsey moved to Ninian Park and Linden Jones, John Lewis and Tarki Micallef made the opposite journey to Somerton Park

Round Four, 30 January, 1985. Cardiff City 0 Hereford United 4 (2,075)
Bluebirds; Lee Smelt; Jake King, Jimmy Mullen, Phil Dwyer, Mike Ford, Roger Gibbins, Brian Flynn, Kevin Meacock, Nigel Vaughan, Graham Withey, Karl Elsey

1985-86

Round Three, 26 November, 1985. Caerleon 2 Cardiff City 3 (500)
Bluebirds; Lee Smelt; Wayne Curtis, Jimmy Mullen, Mike Ford, Chris Marustik, Derrick Christie (Mark Farrington), David Giles, Rob Turner, Nigel Vaughan, Graham Withey, Tarki Micallef
Scorers; Nigel Vaughan 2, Chris Marustik

Round Four, 8 January, 1986. Cardiff City 4 Mold Alexandra 1 (604)
Bluebirds; Lee Smelt; Wayne Curtis, Mike Ford, Jimmy Mullen, Carleton Leonard, Derrick Christie, David Giles, Nigel Vaughan, Rob Turner (Paul Wheeler), Jeff Hemmerman, Kevin Meacock
Scorers; Nigel Vaughan 2, Rob Turner, Jeff Hemmerman

Round Five, 11 March, 1986. Cardiff City 0 Barry Town 0 (2,053)
Lee Smelt; Wayne Curtis, Chris Marustik, Mike Ford, Jimmy Mullen, Derrick Christie, David Giles, Nigel Vaughan, Rob Turner, Paul Wheeler, Paul McLoughlin

Round Five (replay), 13 March, 1986. Barry Town 0 Cardiff City 2 (1,750)
Bluebirds; Lee Smelt; Wayne Curtis, Chris Marustik, Mike Ford, Jimmy Mullen, Paul McLoughlin, Nigel Vaughan, David Giles, Jeff Hemmerman, Paul Wheeler (Mark Farrington), Tarki Micallef
Scorers; David Giles, Jeff Hemmerman

Semi-final (first leg), 15 April, 1986. Wrexham 4 Cardiff City 1 (1,639)
Bluebirds; Lee Smelt; Wayne Curtis, Mike Ford, Jimmy Mullen, Chris Marustik, Paul McLoughlin, Nigel Vaughan, David Giles, Paul Wheeler, Tarki Micallef, AD Price
Scorer; Nigel Vaughan

Semi-final (second leg), 22 April, 1986. Cardiff City 1 Wrexham 2 (1,255)
Bluebirds; Lee Smelt; Wayne Curtis, Mike Ford, Jimmy Mullen, Chris Marustik, Paul McLoughlin, David Giles, Nigel Vaughan, Robbie Turner, Jeff Hemmerman, Tarki Micallef (Jason Gummer)
Scorer; Chris Marustik
(Wrexham through 6-2 on aggregate)

1986-87

Round Three, 25 November, 1986. Cardiff City 4 Taffs Well 0 (581)
Bluebirds; Mel Rees; Andy Kerr, Mike Ford, Terry Boyle, Wayne Curtis, Paul Wimbleton, Nicky Platnauer, Nigel Vaughan, Kevin Bartlett, Paul Wheeler, Chris Marustik (Alan Rogers)
Kevin Bartlett 2, Paul Wheeler, Terry Boyle

Round Four, 3 February, 1987. Wrexham 1 Cardiff City 0 (1,915)
Bluebirds; Graham Moseley; Andy Kerr, Phil Brignull, Terry Boyle, Mike Ford, Paul Wimbleton (Nigel Vaughan), Nicky Platnauer, Alan Curtis, Kevin Bartlett, Chris Pike, Chris Marustik

1987-88

Round Three, 18 November, 1987. Cardiff City 0 Ebbw Vale 0 (935)
Bluebirds; Jon Roberts; Phil Bater, Mike Ford, Terry Boyle, Nicky Platnauer, Paul Wimbleton, Alan Curtis (Steve Mardenborough), Mark Kelly, Jimmy Gilligan, Kevin Bartlett, Brian McDermott (Paul Sanderson)

18 November 1987, Welsh Cup Round 3. Ebbw Vale 0 Cardiff City 0 (Ninian Park). Jimmy Gilligan on the attack

Round Three (replay), 5 December, 1987. Cardiff City 1 Ebbw Vale 0 (975)
Bluebirds; Alan Judge; Phil Bater, Mike Ford, Terry Boyle, Nicky Platnauer, Paul Wimbleton, Alan Curtis (Steve Mardenborough), Mark Kelly, Jimmy Gilligan, Kevin Bartlett, Brian McDermott
Scorer; Kevin Bartlett
(Both matches played at Ninian Park)

Round Four, 9 January, 1988. Cardiff City 3 Port Talbot 0 (1,382)
Bluebirds; Scott Endersby; Phil Bater, Nigel Stevenson, Terry Boyle (Mark Kelly), Nicky Platnauer, Paul Wimbleton, Alan Curtis, Mike Ford, Jimmy Gilligan, Kevin Bartlett, Brian McDermott (Steve Mardenborough)
Scorers; Mike Ford 2, Jimmy Gilligan

Round Five, 24 February, 1988. Cardiff City 3 Merthyr Tydfil 1 (7,213)
Bluebirds; Jon Roberts; Phil Bater, Nigel Stevenson, Terry Boyle, Nicky Platnauer (Mark Kelly), Paul Wimbleton, Alan Curtis, Mike Ford, Jimmy Gilligan, Ian Walsh (Paul Wheeler), Brian McDermott
Scorers; Paul Wimbleton 2, Jimmy Gilligan

Semi-final (first leg), 19 April, 1988. Cardiff City 2 Caernarfon Town 1 (2,750)
Bluebirds; George Wood; Phil Bater, Nigel Stevenson, Terry Boyle, Nicky Platnauer, Paul Wimbleton (Brian McDermott), Alan Curtis, Mike Ford, Mark Kelly, Jimmy Gilligan, Kevin Bartlett (Paul Wheeler)
Scorers; Paul Wimbleton (p), Mark Kelly

Semi-final (second leg), 27 April, 1988. Caernarfon Town 0 Cardiff City 1 (3,000)
Bluebirds; George Wood; Phil Bater, Nigel Stevenson, Terry Boyle, Nicky Platnauer, Mike Ford, Alan Curtis, Brian McDermott, Mark Kelly, Jimmy Gilligan, Kevin Bartlett (Paul Wheeler)
Scorer; Brian McDermott (p)
(Cardiff City through 3-1 on aggregate)

Final, 17 May, 1988. Cardiff City 2 Wrexham 0 (5,645) Swansea
Bluebirds; George Wood; Phil Bater, Nigel Stevenson, Terry Boyle, Nicky Platnauer, Mike Ford, Alan Curtis, Brian McDermott, Mark Kelly, Jimmy Gilligan, Kevin Bartlett (Paul Wheeler)
Scorers; Alan Curtis, Jimmy Gilligan

1988-89

Round Three, 15 November, 1988. Cardiff City 3 Bath City 0 (1,517)
Bluebirds; George Wood; Ian Rodgerson, Gareth Abraham, Terry Boyle, Nicky Platnauer, Paul Wimbleton, Alan Curtis, Steve Ketteridge, Mark Kelly (Phil Bater), Kevin Bartlett, Jimmy Gilligan
Scorers; Kevin Bartlett 2, Paul Wimbleton

Round Four, 17 January, 1989. Cardiff City 1 Worcester City 0 (1,522)
Bluebirds; George Wood; Ian Rodgerson, Gareth Abraham, Nigel Stevenson, Phil Bater, Paul Wimbleton, Chris Fry (Paul Wheeler), Mark Kelly, Steve Lynex, Kevin Bartlett, Jimmy Gilligan
Scorer; Mark Kelly

Round Five, 8 February, 1989. Kidderminster Harriers 3 Cardiff City 1 (3,012)
Bluebirds; George Wood; Ian Rodgerson, Terry Boyle, Nicky Platnauer, Phil Bater, Paul Wimbleton, Jon Morgan, Mark Kelly (Paul Wheeler), Steve Lynex, Kevin Bartlett, Jimmy Gilligan
Scorer; Kevin Bartlett

1989-90

Round Three, 25 October, 1989. Cardiff City 1 Newport AFC 0 (2,929)
Bluebirds; Roger Hansbury; Ian Rodgerson (Allan Lewis), Gareth Abraham, Roger Gibbins, Ray Daniel, Leigh Barnard, Jon Morgan (Morrys Scott), Mark Kelly, Chris Fry, Cohen Griffith, David Kevan
Scorer; Gareth Abraham

Round Four, 16 January, 1990. Cardiff City 4 Port Talbot 1 (1,128)
Bluebirds; Roger Hansbury; Ian Rodgerson, Eddie Youds, Jason Perry, Roger Gibbins, Ray Daniel, Leigh Barnard, Mark Kelly, Jeff Chandler (Gareth Abraham), Cohen Griffith, Chris Pike (Steve Lynex),
Scorers; Chris Pike 2, Ian Rodgerson, Leigh Barnard

Round Five, 6 February, 1990. Cardiff City 2 Aberystwyth Town 0 (1,319)
Bluebirds; Roger Hansbury; Ian Rodgerson, Gareth Abraham, Jason Perry (Steve Lynex), Ray Daniel, Leigh Barnard, Roger Gibbins, Jeff Chandler, Mark Kelly, Cohen Griffith, Chris Pike
Scorers; Ian Rodgerson, Mark Kelly

Semi-final (first leg), 2 April, 1990. Cardiff City 0 Hereford United 3 (2,393)
Bluebirds; Roger Hansbury; Ian Rodgerson, Jason Perry, Roger Gibbins, Ray Daniel, Leigh Barnard, Mark Kelly, Chris Fry (Jon Morgan), Jeff Chandler (Nathan Blake), Cohen Griffith, Chris Pike

Semi-final (second leg), 4 April, 1990. Hereford United 1 Cardiff City 3 (2,955)
Bluebirds; Roger Hansbury; Ian Rodgerson (Nathan Blake), Jason Perry, Gareth Abraham, Ray Daniel (Jon Morgan), Leigh Barnard, Roger Gibbins, Mark Kelly, Cohen Griffith, Chris Pike, Morrys Scott
Scorers; Chris Pike, Gareth Abraham, Cohen Griffith
(Hereford United through 4-3 on aggregate)

1990-91

Round Three, 6 November, 1990, Cardiff City 1 Merthyr Tydfil 4 (3,204)
Bluebirds; Roger Hansbury; Ian Rodgerson (Nathan Blake), Jason Perry, Neil Matthews, Damon Searle, Leigh Barnard, Mark Jones, Pat Heard, Cohen Griffith, Roger Gibbins, Chris Pike
Scorer; Chris Pike (p)

1991-92

Round Three, 29 October, 1991. Cardiff City 3 Newport AFC 0 (2,433)
Bluebirds; Roger Hansbury; Mark Jones (Jamie Unsworth), Allan Lewis, Jason Perry, Damon Searle, Roger Gibbins, Robin Semark, Cohen Griffith, Nathan Blake, Chris Pike, Carl Dale
Scorers; Chris Pike, Cohen Griffith, Carl Dale

7 December 1991, Welsh Cup Round 4. Cardiff City 3 Stourbridge 3. Chris Pike in action

Round Four, 7 December, 1991. Cardiff City 3 Stourbridge 3 (1,495)
Bluebirds; Gavin Ward; Jason Perry, Lee Baddeley, Neil Matthews, Damon Searle, Roger Gibbins, Robin Semark (Pat Heard), Cohen Griffith, Nathan Blake, Chris Pike (Cameron Toshack), Carl Dale
Scorer; Carl Dale 3(1p)

Round Four (replay), 17 December, 1991. Stourbridge 1 Cardiff City 2 (1,004)
Bluebirds; Gavin Ward; Neil Matthews, Lee Baddeley, Jason Perry, Damon Searle, Roger Gibbins, Paul Ramsey, Andy Gorman, Cohen Griffith, Chris Pike (Allan Lewis), Carl Dale
Scorers; Carl Dale, Cohen Griffith

Round Five, 18 February, 1992. Swansea City 0 Cardiff City 1 (7,303)
Bluebirds; Gavin Ward; Jason Perry, Gareth Abraham, Damon Searle, Roger Gibbins, Eddie Newton, Paul Ramsay, Gerry Harrison (Cohen Griffith), Nathan Blake, Chris Pike, Carl Dale
Scorer; Chris Pike

Semi-final (first leg), 24 March, 1992. Cardiff City 0 Maesteg Park 0 (3,308)
Bluebirds; Roger Hansbury; Neil Matthews (Andy Gorman), Lee Baddeley, Damon Searle, Roger Gibbins, Eddie Newton, Paul Ramsey, Mark Jones (Paul Millar), Cohen Griffith, Tony Bird, Carl Dale

Semi-final (second leg), 18 April, 1992. Cardiff City 4 Maesteg Park 0 (3,578)
Bluebirds; Roger Hansbury; Mark Jones, Lee Baddeley, Jason Perry, Damon Searle, Roger Gibbins (Andy Gorman), Paul Ramsey, Eddie Newton, Cohen Griffith, Chris Pike (Tony Bird), Carl Dale
Scorers; Carl Dale, Damon Searle, Mark Jones, og
(Cardiff City through 4-0 on aggregate – both legs at Ninian Park)

Final, 7 May, 1992. Cardiff City 1 Hednesford Town 0 (11,000) National Stadium
Bluebirds; Roger Hansbury; Jason Perry, Gary Bellamy, Gareth Abrahyam, Damon Searle, Roger Gibbins (Gary Gill), Paul Ramsay, Nathan Blake, Cohen Griffith (Tony Bird), Chris Pike, Carl Dale
Scorer; Carl Dale

1992-93

Round Three, 27 October, 1992. Ton Pentre 0 Cardiff City 2 (1,700)
Bluebirds; Mark Grew; Robbie James, Jason Perry, Derek Brazil, Damon Searle, Nick Richardson, Paul Ramsey, Paul Millar, Chris Pike (Roger Gibbins), Carl Dale, Nathan Blake
Scorers; Paul Millar, Paul Ramsey (p)

Round Four, 5 December, 1992. Caerau 0 Cardiff City 9 (2,579)
Bluebirds; Gavin Ward; Robbie James (Roger Gibbins), Jason Perry, Derek Brazil, Damon Searle, Nick Richardson, Paul Ramsey, Paul Millar, Chris Pike, Carl Dale, Nathan Blake (Cohen Griffith)
Scorers; Carl Dale 4, Nick Richardson 3, Chris Pike, Nathan Blake

Round Five, 16 January, 1993. Cardiff City 4 Maesteg Park 0 (2,867)
Bluebirds; Gavin Ward; Robbie James, Jason Perry, Derek Brazil, Damon Searle, Nathan Blake, Nick Richardson, Paul Ramsey, Phil Stant, Tony Bird (Carl Dale, Neil Matthews), Cohen Griffith
Scorers; Phil Stant 3, Paul Ramsey

Semi-final (first leg), 16 March, 1993. Cardiff City 2 Wrexham 0 (10,251)
Bluebirds; Gavin Ward; Robbie James, Jason Perry, Derek Brazil, Damon Searle, Kevin Ratcliffe, Neil Matthews, Nick Richardson, Cohen Griffith (Paul Ramsey), Chris Pike (Carl Dale), Phil Stant,
Scorers; Cohen Griffith, Carl Dale

Semi-final (second leg), 17 April, 1993. Wrexham 1 Cardiff City 0 (5,735)
Bluebirds; Gavin Ward; Robbie James, Jason Perry, Derek Brazil, Damon Searle, Kevin Ratcliffe, Nick Richardson, Paul Ramsey, Phil Stant (Carl Dale), Nathan Blake, Cohen Griffith
(Cardiff City through 2-1 on aggregate)

Final, 16 May, 1993. Cardiff City 5 Rhyl 0 (16,443) National Stadium
Bluebirds; Gavin Ward; Robbie James, Jason Perry, Derek Brazil (Chris Pike), Damon Searle, Neil Matthews (Carl Dale), Nick Richardson, Paul Ramsey, Phil Stant, Nathan Blake, Cohen Griffith
Scorers; Phil Stant 3, Cohen Griffith 2

1993-94

Round Three, 25 October, 1993, Cardiff City 2 Afan Lido 0 (1,451)
Bluebirds; Phil Kite; Terry Evans (Nathan Wigg), Lee Baddeley, Jason Perry (Garry Thompson), Derek Brazil, Paul Millar, Nick Richardson, Cohen Griffith, Phil Stant, Nathan Blake, Tony Bird
Scorers; Tony Bird, Garry Thompson

Round Four, 7 December, 1993. Wrexham 0 Cardiff City 2 (2,143)
Bluebirds; Mark Grew; Derek Brazil, Mark Aizlewood, Lee Baddeley, Jason Perry, Damon Searle, Nick Richardson, Tony Bird, Phil Stant (Garry Thompson), Nathan Blake, Cohen Griffith
Scorers; Phil Stant, Tony Bird

Round Five, 9 February, 1994. Ebbw Vale 1 Cardiff City 1 (3,500)
Bluebirds; Mark Grew; Derek Brazil, Mark Aizlewood (Darren Adams), Lee Baddeley, Damon Searle, Nathan Wigg, Garry Thompson, Nick Richardson, Tony Bird (Carl Dale), Nathan Blake, Cohen Griffith
Scorer; Darren Adams

Round Five (replay), 22 February, 1994. Cardiff City 3 Ebbw Vale 0 (1,850)
Bluebirds; Steve Williams; Derek Brazil, Lee Baddeley, Jason Perry, Damon Searle, Paul Millar, Nick Richardson, Garry Thompson (Darren Adams), Phil Stant, Tony Bird (Carl Dale), Cohen Griffith
Scorers; Garry Thompson, Tony Bird, Phil Stant

Semi-final (first leg), 14 April, 1994. Swansea City 1 Cardiff City 2 (3,286)
Bluebirds; Phil Kite; Wayne Fereday, Damon Searle, Jason Perry, Mark Aizlewood, Paul Millar, Kevin Brock, Nick Richardson, Phil Stant, Garry Thompson (Nathan Wigg), Cohen Griffith
Scorer; Phil Stant 2

Semi-final (second leg), 28 April, 1994. Cardiff City 4 Swansea City 1 (5,606)
Bluebirds; Steve Williams; Terry Evans (Scott Young), Mark Aizlewood, Jason Perry, Wayne Fereday, Paul Millar, Garry Thompson, Tony Bird, Phil Stant, Carl Dale, Darren Adams (Nathan Wigg)
Scorers; Wayne Fereday, Tony Bird, Paul Millar (p), Phil Stant
(Cardiff City through 6-2 on aggregate)

Final, 15 May, 1994. Barry Town 2 Cardiff City 1 (14,130) National Stadium
Bluebirds; Steve Williams; Terry Evans, Mark Aizlewood, Jason Perry, Damon Searle, Paul Millar, Garry Thompson (Darren Adams), Nick Richardson (Tony Bird), Phil Stant, Kevin Brock, Cohen Griffith
Scorer; Phil Stant

1994-95

Round Three, 7 November, 1994. Ebbw Vale 1 Cardiff City 1 (1,346)
Bluebirds; David Williams; Derek Brazil (Scott Young), Jason Perry, Lee Baddeley, Andy Scott; Nathan Wigg, Mark Aizlewood, Paul Millar, Cohen Griffith (Garry Thompson); Tony Bird, Phil Stant
Scorer; Paul Millar

Round Three (replay), 22 November, 1994. Cardiff City 2 Ebbw Vale 0 (1,343)
Bluebirds; David Williams; Scott Young (Nick Richardson), Lee Baddeley, Jason Perry, Damon Searle; Paul Ramsey, Mark Aizlewood, Charlie Oatway, Paul Millar; Garry Thompson, Phil Stant
Scorers; Garry Thompson, Nick Richardson

Round Four, 14 February, 1995. Cardiff City 4 Risca 0 (1,294)
Bluebirds; David Williams; Wayne Fereday, Lee Baddeley, Scott Young, Damon Searle; Nathan Wigg, Mark Aizlewood, Cohen Griffith, Paul Millar (Derek Brazil); Carl Dale, Tony Bird (Andy Evans)
Scorers; Carl Dale 3, Derek Brazil

Round Five, 28 February, 1995. Llandudno 0 Cardiff City 1 (700)
Bluebirds; David Williams; Derek Brazil, Lee Baddeley, Jason Perry, Damon Searle; Nathan Wigg, Mark Aizlewood, Nick Richardson, Wayne Fereday (Cohen Griffith); Andy Evans, Carl Dale
Scorer; Carl Dale

Semi-final (first leg), 11 April, 1995. Swansea City 0 Cardiff City 1 (2,634)
Bluebirds; David Williams (Steve Williams); Derek Brazil, Lee Baddeley, Jason Perry, Damon Searle; Nathan Wigg, Nick Richardson, Paul Millar, Cohen Griffith; Tony Bird, Carl Dale
Scorer; Paul Millar

Semi-final (second leg), 2 May, 1995. Cardiff City 0 Swansea City 0 (4,227)
Bluebirds; Steve Williams; Derek Brazil, Lee Baddeley, Jason Perry, Damon Searle; Nathan Wigg, Nick Richardson, Paul Millar, Cohen Griffith; Paul Milsom (Scott Young), Carl Dale

Final, 21 May, 1995. Cardiff City 1 Wrexham 2 (12,840)
Bluebirds; Steve Williams; Derek Brazil, Lee Baddeley, Jason Perry, Damon Searle; Nathan Wigg, Paul Millar (Charlie Oatway), Nick Richardson, Cohen Griffith; Tony Bird (Scott Young), Carl Dale
Scorer; Carl Dale

Welsh Cup Record

Played	Won	Drawn	Lost	For	Against
281	179	45	57	689	284

Hat-tricks (35 – including one double hat-trick*)
5 Len Davies, 3 Gerry Hitchens, Carl Dale, 2 Trevor Ford, Derek Tapscott*, Peter Kitchen, Phil Stant, 1 Joe Clarke, Jimmy Gill, George Reid, Walter Robbins, Harry Egan, Les Evans, George Edwards, Wilf Grant, Harry Knowles, Graham Moore, John Toshack, Ronnie Bird, Brian Clark, Gil Reece, Tony Evans, Nick Richardson

Penalties (17)
2 Greg Farrell, Gordon Owen
1 Arthur Granville, Brian Jenkins, Ronnie Bird, Gil Reece, Paul Went, John Buchanan, Tony Evans, Paul Wimbleton, Brian McDermott, Chris Pike, Carl Dale, Paul Ramsey, Paul Millar

Leading scorers (689 goals)
35 Len Davies, 21 Peter King, 17 Brian Clark, 16 Gerry Hitchens, own goals, 15 Derek Tapscott, 14 Trevor Ford, Carl Dale, 13 John Toshack, 12 Phil Stant, 10 Chris Pike, 9 George Edwards, Gil Reece, Nigel Vaughan, 8 Graham Moore, Ivor Allchurch, George Johnston, Leslie Lea, 7 Jimmy Gill, Les Jones, Ronnie Bird, Peter Kitchen

Leading appearances (281 matches)
49 Don Murray, 48 Peter King, 44 Phil Dwyer, 38 Tom Farquharson, 36 Billy Hardy, 33 Colin Baker, 32 Fred Keenor, Len Davies, Ron Stitfall, 28 Jack Evans, Brian Clark, 26 Graham Vearncombe, Dave Carver, Ron Healey, 26 Gary Bell, 24 Jimmy Nelson, Derrick Sullivan, Alan Harrington, Barry Hole, Freddie Pethard, 24 Cohen Griffith, 23 Jason Perry, 22 Albert Larmour, John Buchanan

7
Other Cups and Play-offs

Division Three South Cup

This was a new competition and it took some time before the Bluebirds won a match. In fact it was the club's only success because when World War Two put an end to organised football, this particular competition also ended.

1933-34

Round One. 1 January 1934, Cardiff City 0 Aldershot 1 (3,000)
Bluebirds; Tom Farquharson; Bob Calder, George Russell; Tom Maidment, Jack Galbraith, John Duthie; Thomas Rogers, Jim Henderson, Eli Postin, Les Jones, Ernie Curtis

1934-35

Round One, 17 October, 1934. Crystal Palace 3 Cardiff City 1 (attendance unknown)
Bluebirds; Jock Leckie; Edward Lane, Jack Everest; Paddy Molloy, Enoch Mort, Jack Galbraith; Billy Jackson, Tommy Vaughan, Fred Whitlow, Freddie Hill, Dai Jones
Scorer; Tommy Vaughan

1935-36

Round One, 30 September, 1935. Crystal Palace 2 Cardiff City 1 (8,000)
Bluebirds; Jock Leckie; Billy Bassett, Jack Everest; Wally Jennings, Enoch Mort, Harold Smith; Reg Pugh, Harry Roper, Jack Diamond, Harry Riley, Reg Keating
Scorer; Jack Diamond

The City team before a League game at Walsall, 29 August 1936. Back Row L-R: Jack Kneeshaw (trainer), George Nicholson, Arthur Granville, Bill Fielding, Bill Scott, Bill Bassett, Harold Smith. Front: Reg Pugh, Les Talbot, Cliff Godfrey (capt), Cecil Smith, Albert Pinxton, Dai Ovenstone

1936-37

Round One, 28 October, 1936. Cardiff City 0 Exeter City 1 (3,000)
Bluebirds; Bill Fielding; Louis Ford, Bill Scott; George Nicholson, Billy Bassett, Bill Main; Reg Pugh, Albert Pinxton, George Walton, Les Talbot, Davie Ovenstone

1937-38

Round One, 27 November, 1937. Northampton Town 0 Cardiff City 1 (3,689)
Bluebirds; Bob Jones; Arthur Granville, John Mellor; Cecil McCaughey, Enoch Mort, Cliff Godfrey; Reg Pugh, George Walton, Jimmy Collins, Andrew Brown, Bert Turner
Scorer; Bert Turner

Round Two, 10 November, 1937. Bristol City 2 Cardiff City 1 (2,130)
Bluebirds; Bob Jones; Arthur Granville, Louis Ford; Cecil McCaughey, Cliff Godfrey, George Nicholson; Reg Pugh, George Walton, Jimmy Collins, Les Talbot, Bert Turner
Scorer; Jimmy Collins

1938-39

Round 1, 16 November, 1938, Bristol City 6 Cardiff City 0 (670)
Bluebirds; Bob Jones; Arthur Granville, Jimmy Kelso; Billy Corkhill, George Ballsom, Bill Main; Jimmy Mitchell, Les Talbot, Jimmy Collins, Charlie Hill, James McKenzie

Division Three South Cup Record

Played	Won	Drawn	Lost	For	Against
7	1	0	6	4	15

Scorers (4)
1 Tommy Vaughan, Jack Diamond, Bert Turner, Jimmy Collins

Leading appearances (7 matches)
4 Reg Pugh, 3 Enoch Mort, George Walton, Les Talbot, Bob Jones, Arthur Granville, Jimmy Collins. 2 Jock Leckie, Jack Everest, Jack Galbraith, Billy Bassett, Louis Ford, George Nicholson, Bill Main, Cecil McCaughey, Cliff Godfrey, Bert Turner

Did You Know...
The Grange End covered stand that replaced an earth bank behind the goal was opened on 1 September, 1928. It lasted 50 years until demolished for safety reasons in 1978

Anglo-French Friendship Cup

The Bluebirds played against the French side from Lens, but met no other opposition so these two home and away fixtures were virtually friendly matches.

1961-62

13 December, 1961, RC Lensois 2 Cardiff City 4 (1,500)
Bluebirds; Dilwyn John; Alan Harrington, Alec Milne; Barry Hole, Frank Rankmore, Steve Gammon; Peter King, Derek Tapscott, Johnny King, Graham Moore, Tony Pickrell
Scorers; Peter King 2, Johnny King, Graham Moore

7 March, 1962, Cardiff City 2 RC Lensois 0 (3,000)
Bluebirds; Graham Vearncombe; Trevor Edwards, Alec Milne; Alan Harrington, Trevor Peck, Colin Baker; Derek Tapscott, Mel Charles, Johnny King, Dai Ward, Peter King
Scorers; Derek Tapscott, Mel Charles

Anglo-French Cup Record

Played	Won	Drawn	Lost	For	Against
2	2	0	0	6	2

Scorers (6)
2 Peter King, 1 Johnny King, Graham Moore, Derek Tapscott, Mel Charles

Appearances (2 Matches)
2 Alan Harrington, Alec Milne, Peter King, Derek Tapscott, Johnny King. 1 Dilwyn John, Barry Hole, Frank Rankmore, Steve Gammon, Graham Moore, Tony Pickrell, Graham Vearncombe, Trevor Edwards, Trevor Peck, Colin Baker, Mel Charles, Dai Ward

Did You Know...
The Bluebirds played three matches in the Anglo-Scottish Cup during 1978-79 yet none of their opponents were from Scotland

Anglo-Scottish Cup

This was yet another ill-fated idea to give clubs more games in an effort to bring in much-needed revenue. The Bluebirds played only three matches in the competiton, none of them against a side from Scotland.

1978-79

Qualifying Group, 1 August, 1978. Bristol Rovers 1 Cardiff City 0 (5,095)
Bluebirds; John Davies; Rod Thomas, Freddie Pethard, Alan Campbell, Keith Pontin, Phil Dwyer, Steve Grapes, David Giles, Ray Bishop, Paul Went, John Buchanan

Preliminary Competition Group C, 5 August, 1978. Cardiff City 1 Fulham 0 (4,149).
Bluebirds; John Davies; Rod Thomas, Freddie Pethard, Alan Campbell, Keith Pontin, Phil Dwyer, Linden Jones, David Giles, Mickey Burns, Ray Bishop, John Buchanan
Scorer; Phil Dwyer

Preliminary Competition Group C, 8 August, 1978. Bristol City 1 Cardiff City 0 (6,916)
Bluebirds; Ron Healey; Rod Thomas, Freddie Pethard, Alan Campbell, Keith Pontin, Linden Jones, David Giles, Phil Dwyer, Paul Went, Ray Bishop, John Buchanan

Did You Know...
Cardiff-born Phil Dwyer holds the record for most first team appearances for the Bluebirds with 575 senior games for the club, including 471 league matches

Anglo-Scottish Cup Record

Played	Won	Drawn	Lost	For	Against
3	1	0	2	1	2

Scorer (1)
1 Phil Dwyer

Appearances (3 Matches)
3 Rod Thomas, Freddie Pethard, Alan Campbell, Keith Pontin, Phil Dwyer, David Giles, Ray Bishop, John Buchanan. 2 John Davies, Paul Went, Linden Jones, 1 Steve Grapes, Mickey Burns, Ron Healey

Associate Members Cup

This competition was initially for clubs in Divisions Three and Four. The Bluebirds were relegated from Division Two in the 1984-85 season so were not eligible until the following term. The format has changed a number of times over the seasons as has the sponsors of the trophy (Freight Rover Trophy, Sherpa Van Trophy, Leyland DAF Trophy, AutoGlass Trophy, Auto Windscreen Shield and LDV Vans Trophy), but many clubs chasing promotion, including City, tended to use reserves or young players in their starting line-ups. Attendances have historically been very poor, reaching an all-time low at Ninian Park on 14 January, 1997 when only 793 hardy fans turned up to watch Exeter City hold the Bluebirds to a 1-1 draw.

City played their last game in this competition in December 2002, the season they won promotion to Division Two (Championship) after beating Queen's Park Rangers in the play-off final at the Millennium Stadium.

Did You Know...
The Bluebirds failed to score a goal in their four matches in the Freight Rover Trophy from 1985-87

1985-86 Freight Rover Trophy

Preliminary Group, 21 January, 1986. Newport County 1 Cardiff City 0 (1,863)
Bluebirds; Lee Smelt; Chris Marustik, Mike Ford, Jimmy Mullen, Paul McLoughlin, Nigel Vaughan, John Farrington, David Giles, Tarki Micallef, Robbie Turner, Paul Wheeler (Graham Withey)

Preliminary Group, 28 January, 1986, Cardiff City 0 Swansea City 2 (1,006)
Bluebirds; Lee Smelt; Wayne Curtis, Chris Marustik, Mike Ford, Jimmy Mullen, Nigel Vaughan, Tarki Micallef, David Giles, Paul Wheeler, Derrick Christie, Paul McLoughlin

1986-87

Preliminary Group, 2 December, 1986. Cardiff City 0 Wolverhampton Wanderers 1 (1,201)
Bluebirds; Graham Moseley; Nicky Platnauer, Phil Brignull, Terry Boyle (Andy Kerr), Mike Ford, Paul Wimbleton, David Giles, Alan Rogers, Nigel Vaughan, Paul Wheeler (Gary Davies), Kevin Bartlett

Preliminary Group, 6 January, 1987. Bournemouth 1 Cardiff City 0 (1,482)
Bluebirds; Graham Moseley; Chris Marustik, Phil Brignull, Terry Boyle, Mike Ford, Nicky Platnauer, Paul Wimbleton, Alan Curtis, Nigel Vaughan, Alan Rogers, Gary Davies (Paul Wheeler),

1987-88 Sherpa Van Trophy

Preliminary Group, 13 October, 1987. Cardiff City 3 Wrexham 2 (1,102)
Bluebirds; Graham Moseley; Phil Bater, Nigel Stevenson, Nicky Platnauer, Mike Ford, Mark Kelly, Jason Gummer, Steve Mardenborough, Brian McDermott, Paul Wheeler (Kevin Bartlett), Jimmy Gilligan (Paul Sanderson)
Scorers; Paul Wheeler, Brian McDermott, Jimmy Gilligan

Preliminary Group, 24 November, 1987, Walsall 3 Cardiff City 1 (2,420)
Bluebirds; Alan Judge; Phil Bater, Terry Boyle, Mike Ford, Nicky Platnauer, Paul Wimbleton, Mark Kelly, Alan Curtis, Jimmy Gilligan, Kevin Bartlett (Steve Mardenborough), Paul Sanderson
Scorer; Jimmy Gilligan

Round One, 20 January, 1988. Notts County 2 Cardiff City 0 (2,704)
Bluebirds; Jon Roberts; Mark Kelly, Nigel Stevenson, Terry Boyle, Nicky Platnauer, Paul Wimbleton, Alan Curtis (Paul Wheeler), Mike Ford, Brian McDermott, Kevin Bartlett (Paul Sanderson), Jimmy Gilligan

Did You Know...
In the three matches of the 1987-88 Sherpa Van Trophy the Bluebirds used three goalkeepers, Graham Moseley, Alan Judge and Jon Roberts

1988-89

Preliminary Group, 6 December, 1988. Cardiff City 2 Swansea City 0 (2,986)
Bluebirds; George Wood; Ian Rodgerson, Terry Boyle, Gareth Abraham, Nicky Platnauer, Paul Wimbleton, Alan Curtis, Jason Gummer (Phil Bater), Steve Lynex, Kevin Bartlett, Jimmy Gilligan
Scorers; Alan Curtis, Jimmy Gilligan

Preliminary Group, 20 December, 1988. Torquay United 3 Cardiff City 1 (1,187)
Bluebirds; George Wood; Ian Rodgerson, Terry Boyle, Gareth Abraham (Phil Bater), Nicky Platnauer, Paul Wimbleton, Alan Curtis, Jason Gummer, Steve Lynex, Kevin Bartlett, Jimmy Gilligan
Scorer; Paul Wimbleton (p)

Round One, 24 January, 1989. Bristol Rovers 2 Cardiff City 1 (4,029)
Bluebirds; George Wood; Ian Rodgerson, Gareth Abraham, Nigel Stevenson, Nicky Platnauer, Paul Wimbleton, Phil Bater, Mark Kelly (Jon Morgan), Steve Lynex, Kevin Bartlett, Jimmy Gilligan
Scorer; Paul Wimbleton

1989-90 Leyland DAF Trophy

Preliminary Group, 7 November, 1989. Cardiff City 3 Walsall 5 (1,487)
Bluebirds; Gavin Ward; Ian Rodgerson, Gareth Abraham, Roger Gibbins, Ray Daniel, Leigh Barnard, Jon Morgan (Chris Fry), Cohen Griffith, Mark Kelly, Jeff Chandler, Chris Pike (Cliff Powell)
Scorers; Cohen Griffith, Leigh Barnard, Gareth Abraham

Preliminary Group, 19 December, 1989. Shrewsbury Town 4 Cardiff City 0 (1,058)
Bluebirds; Gavin Ward; Ian Rodgerson, Jason Perry, Allan Lewis, Damon Searle, Leigh Barnard (Jon Roberts), Jon Morgan, Mario Meithig, Richard Haig (Nathan Blake), Steve Lynex, Morrys Scott

1990-91

Preliminary Group, 13 November, 1990. Cardiff City 0 Exeter City 1 (1,024)
Bluebirds; Roger Hansbury; Neil Matthews, Jason Perry, Allan Lewis, Damon Searle, Leigh Barnard, Lee Stephens (Chris Summers), Cohen Griffith, Pat Heard, Roger Gibbins, Chris Pike (Nathan Blake)

Preliminary Group, 11 December, 1990, Hereford United 1 Cardiff City 1 (2,007)
Bluebirds; Roger Hansbury; Neil Matthews, Jason Perry, Allan Lewis, Damon Searle, Nathan Blake, Mark Jones (Jon Morgan), Cohen Griffith (Chris Fry), Pat Heard, Roger Gibbins, Chris Pike
Scorer; Cohen Griffith

1991-92 Autoglass Trophy

Preliminary Group, 19 November, 1991. Swansea City 0 Cardiff City 0 (2,955)
Bluebirds; Roger Hansbury; Neil Matthews, Lee Baddeley, Jason Perry (Andy Gorman), Damon Searle, Roger Gibbins (Paul Millar), Paul Ramsey, Allan Lewis, Chris Pike, Carl Dale, Nathan Blake

Preliminary Group, 10 December, 1991, Cardiff City 3 Bournemouth 3 (1,337)
Bluebirds; Gavin Ward; Neil Matthews, Lee Baddeley, Jason Perry, Damon Searle, Roger Gibbins, Robin Semark (Allan Lewis), Cohen Griffith, Nathan Blake, Chris Pike, Carl Dale
Scorers; Carl Dale 2, Chris Pike

Round One, 14 January, 1992. Stoke City 3 Cardiff City 0 (4,551)
Bluebirds; Gavin Ward; Mark Jones (Jamie Unsworth), Lee Baddeley, Allan Lewis, Damon Searle, Roger Gibbins, Paul Ramsey, Cohen Griffith, Nathan Blake, Chris Pike, Carl Dale (Cameron Toshack)

1992-93

Round One Group, 1 December, 1992. Shrewsbury Town 1 Cardiff City 3 (936)
Bluebirds; Gavin Ward; Robbie James, Jason Perry, Derek Brazil, Damon Searle, Paul Millar, Paul Ramsey, Nick Richardson, Nathan Blake, Chris Pike, Carl Dale
Scorers; Paul Millar, Nick Richardson, Carl Dale

Round One Group, 8 December, 1992, Cardiff City 3 Hereford United 2 (3,246)
Bluebirds; Gavin Ward; Robbie James, Jason Perry, Derek Brazil, Damon Searle, Paul Millar, Paul Ramsey, Nick Richardson, Nathan Blake, Phil Stant, Carl Dale
Scorers; Paul Ramsey (p), Phil Stant, Carl Dale

Round Two, 18 January, 1993. Cardiff City 1 Swansea City 2 aet (13,516)
Bluebirds; Gavin Ward; Robbie James, Neil Matthews, Jason Perry, Damon Searle, Kevin Ratcliffe, Nick Richardson, Paul Ramsey (Derek Brazil), Cohen Griffith (Tony Bird), Nathan Blake, Phil Stant
Scorer; Nathan Blake

1993-94

Round One Group, 20 October, 1993. Bristol Rovers 3 Cardiff City 0 (2,035)
Bluebirds; Phil Kite; Derek Brazil, Lee Baddeley, Jason Perry, Damon Searle (Tony Bird), Mark Aizlewood, Paul Millar, Nick Richardson, Garry Thompson, Nathan Blake, Cohen Griffith

Round One Group, 9 November, 1993. Cardiff City 2 Torquay United 0 (1,642)
Bluebirds; Steve Williams; Derek Brazil, Mark Aizlewood, Jason Perry, Damon Searle, Tony Bird (Garry Thompson), Nathan Blake, Cohen Griffith, Paul Millar (Nathan Wigg) Nick Richardson, Phil Stant
Scorers; Garry Thompson, Phil Stant

Round Two, 14 December, 1993. Wycombe Wanderers 3 Cardiff City 2 aet (2,703)
Bluebirds; Mark Grew; Terry Evans (Paul Millar), Lee Baddeley, Jason Perry, Damon Searle, Mark Aizlewood, Tony Bird (Garry Thompson), Nick Richardson, Phil Stant, Nathan Blake, Cohen Griffith
Scorers; Cohen Griffith, Phil Stant

1994-95 Auto Windscreens Shield

Round One Group, 27 September, 1994. Cardiff City 2 Plymouth Argyle 0 (1,299)
Bluebirds; David Williams; Jason Perry, Lee Baddeley, Mark Aizlewood, Damon Searle, Charlie Oatway, Paul Millar, Cohen Griffith, Tony Bird, Carl Dale, Darren Adams (Nick Richardson)
Scorers; Cohen Griffith, Carl Dale

Round One Group, 15 November, 1994, Exeter City 1 Cardiff City 1 (1,203)
Bluebirds; David Williams; Scott Young, Mark Aizlewood, Lee Baddeley, Damon Searle, Paul Millar, Paul Ramsey, Cohen Griffith, Phil Stant, Garry Thompson, Darren Adams (Nathan Wigg)
Scorer; Scott Young

Round Two, 29 November, 1994. Exeter City 1 Cardiff City 0 (1,452)
Bluebirds; Steve Williams; Terry Evans (Cohen Griffith), Lee Baddeley, Derek Brazil, Damon Searle, Charlie Oatway, Paul Ramsey, Nick Richardson, Phil Stant, Garry Thompson, Wayne Fereday (Carl Dale)

1995-96

Round One Group, 26 September, 1995. Hereford United 3 Cardiff City 3 (1,411)
Bluebirds; David Williams; Scott Young, Lee Baddeley, Jason Perry, Damon Searle, Paul Harding, Chris Ingram, Ian Rodgerson, Simon Haworth (Andy Evans), Carl Dale, Darren Adams (Terry Evans)
Scorers; Carl Dale 2, Darren Adams

Round One Group, 17 October, 1995. Cardiff City 3 Gillingham 2 (1,034)
Bluebirds; David Willliams; Scott Young, Lee Baddeley (Lee Jarman), Derek Brazil, Damon Searle, Paul Harding, Nathan Wigg, Tony Bird (Darren Adams), Jimmy Gardner, Simon Haworth (Chris Ingram), Carl Dale
Scorers; Carl Dale 2, Darren Adams

Round Two, 28 November, 1995. Cardiff City 1 Northampton Town 2 (1,450)
Bluebirds; David Williams; Scott Young (Tony Bird), Lee Baddeley, Lee Jarman, Damon Searle, Ian Rodgerson, Hayden Fleming, Alan Harper, Jimmy Gardner, Darren Adams, Carl Dale
Scorer; Carl Dale (p)

1996-97

Round One, 10 December, 1996. Gillingham 1 Cardiff City 2 aet (1,193)
Bluebirds; Pat Mountain; Jason Perry, Scott Young, Tony Philliskirk, Jeff Eckhardt, Keith O'Halloran (Lee Jarman), Ian Rodgerson, Craig Middleton, Jimmy Gardner, Steve White (Mickey Bennett), Carl Dale
Scorers; Jeff Eckhardt, Carl Dale
Cardiff City through on golden goal

Did You Know...
On 14 January 1997, only 793 fans saw the Bluebirds draw 1-1 with Exeter City in the Associate Members Cup (Southern Section). Exeter went on to win 4-2 on penalties

Round Two, 14 January, 1997. Cardiff City 1 Exeter City 1 aet (793)
Bluebirds; Pat Mountain; Jason Perry, Jeff Eckhardt (Craig Middleton), Lee Baddeley, Kevin Lloyd (Steve White), Scott Young, Jason Fowler, Keith O'Halloran, Jimmy Gardner, Carl Dale (Tony Philliskirk), Deon Burton
Scorer; Carl Dale
Exeter City won 4-2 on penalties

1997-98

Round One, 9 December, 1997. Cardiff City 0 Millwall 2 (1,219)
Bluebirds; Tony Elliott; Marvin Harriott (Lee Phillips), Scott Young, Lee Jarman, Jimmy Rollo, Scott Partridge (Rob Earnshaw), Wayne O'Sullivan, Gareth Stoker, Tony Carss, Glen Crowe, Steve White

1998-99

Round One, 9 December, 1998. Millwall 2 Cardiff City 0 (1,858)
Bluebirds; John Hallworth; Chris Allen, Jeff Eckhardt, Graham Mitchell, Lee Jarman, Mark Bonner, Danny Hill (Nathan Cadette), Wayne O'Sullivan, Craig Middleton, John Williams (Christian Roberts), Dai Thomas

1999-00

Round One, 7 December, 1999. Northampton Town 2 Cardiff City 0 (2,431)
Bluebirds; John Hallworth; Winston Faerber (Josh Low), Scott Young, Russell Perrett, Tony Vaughan, Richard Carpenter, Willie Boland, Danny Hill (Craig Middleton), Matt Brazier, Jason Bowen (Christian Roberts), Richie Humphries

2000-01 LDV Vans Trophy

Round One, 5 December, 2000. Brighton 2 Cardiff City 0 (2,364)
Bluebirds; Mark Walton; Rhys Weston, James Collins, David Greene, Andy Thompson, Josh Low, Scott McCulloch, Mark Bonner (Kevin Evans), Danny Hill, Paul Brayson, Kurt Nogan

2001-02

Round One, 16 October, 2001. Cardiff City 7 Rushden & Diamonds 1 (2,052)
Bluebirds; Mark Kendall; Andy Thompson (Gethin Jones), Scott Young, David Hughes, Matt Brazier, Des Hamilton, Josh Low, Mark Bonner, Leyton Maxwell (Martin Giles), Gavin Gordon, Kevin Nugent (James Collins)
Scorers; Gavin Gordon 5, Mark Bonner, Martin Giles

Round Two, 30 October, 2001. Cardiff City 1 Peterborough United 3 (2,584)
Bluebirds; Mark Walton; Gethin Jones (Andy Thompson), Scott Young, David Hughes, Scott McCulloch (Martin Giles), Josh Low, Des Hamilton, Mark Bonner, Leyton Maxwell (Kevin Nugent), Leo Fortune-West, James Collins
Scorer; Kevin Nugent (p)

2002-03

Southern Section, Round One, Bye
Bye given as odd number of clubs in competition

Round Two, 12 November, 2002. Exeter City 0 Cardiff City 3 (1,360)
Bluebirds; Martyn Margetson; Ryan Green, James Collins, Mike Simpkins, Chris Barker, Des Hamilton, Jason Bowen, Mark Bonner, Andy Legg, Leo Fortune-West, Andy Campbell
Scorers; Jason Bowen, Andy Campbell (p), Leo Fortune-West

Quarter-finals, 10 December, 2002. Bournemouth 2 Cardiff City 1 (3,615)
Bluebirds; Martyn Margetson; Rhys Weston, James Collins, Mike Simpkins, Fan Zhiyi, Des Hamilton, Mark Bonner, Leyton Maxwell, Andy Campbell, Leo Fortune-West (Gavin Gordon), Peter Thorne
Scorer; Gavin Gordon

Associate Members Cup Record

Played	Won	Drawn	Lost	For	Against
39	10	6	23	51	70

Hat-tricks (1)
1 Gavin Gordon (5 goals)

Penalties (5)
1 Paul Wimbleton, Paul Ramsey, Carl Dale, Kevin Nugent, Andy Campbell

Leading scorers (51 goals)
12 Carl Dale, 6 Gavin Gordon, 4 Cohen Griffith, 3 Jimmy Gilligan, Phil Stant, 2 Paul Wimbleton, Darren Adams

Leading appearances (39 matches)
18 Damon Searle, 15 Jason Perry, 12 Lee Baddeley, Cohen Griffith, Carl Dale, Nathan Blake, 10 Scott Young, 8 Nicky Platnauer, Ian Rodgerson, Nick Richardson, Paul Millar

Did You Know...
Neil Alexander was the first goalkeeper to go through the play-offs without conceding a goal. In the 2003 semi-final the Bluebirds beat Bristol City 1-0 at Ninian Park and then drew 0-0 with the Robins at Ashton Gate. In the final they defeated QPR 1-0

The Play-offs

The Football League play-offs began at the end of season 1986-87. They were initially brought in to stimulate interest while each season drew to a close, and they have become such an important part of league football that the Championship play-off final is now reputed to be worth in excess of £50m to the winners.

When it was first introduced, the Division Two play-off consisted of clubs that finished in third, fourth and fifth place along with the club from Division One that ended the season fourth from bottom. In that first season Charlton Athletic, managed by Lennie Lawrence, maintained their status in Division One when they beat Leeds United in a replay after the first two matches had ended 1-1 on aggregate. Within a couple of seasons that plan was scratched and it was the top four sides outside the promotion places that contested the play-offs in each division. At the end of the 1989-90 season the finals were played out on a one-match basis at Wembley Stadium and that has been the case ever since, apart from the period when the Millennium Stadium hosted the matches here in Cardiff.

The Bluebirds took the seventh, and lowest, position in the 1996-97 play-offs and so had to play against Northampton Town who were the highest rated club after finishing in fourth spot. In the corresponding league matches during the season, goals from Tony Philliskirk and Craig Middleton had given City a 2-2 draw at Ninian Park but in the return at the County Ground, Northampton had won by a convincing 4-0. The first leg at Ninian Park looked to be heading for a scoreless draw until Sean Parrish scored late in the game to give the Cobblers a priceless advantage. The Bluebirds were rarely in the hunt in the away leg and when Jeff Eckhardt was red-carded it spelled the end of City's promotion hopes. Northampton went on to beat Swansea City 1-0 in the final at Wembley with a 90th minute goal from John Frain.

Andy Campbell celebrates scoring the 2003 play-off winner

It was in the early part of Sam Hamman's reign at the club that City were next involved in the end of season lottery that were the play-offs. After a 2001-02 league programme that flattered to deceive, the Bluebirds ended in fourth place, just one point off automatic promotion. Opponents Stoke, who were fifth and three points behind City, had been beaten 2-0 at Ninian Park in the league meeting while at the Britannia Stadium the sides had finished all-square at 1-1. A magnificent 2-1 victory in the first leg in Stoke gave City a tremendous chance of making the Millennium Stadium final but it was not to be. Just as an announcement was made over the tannoy that the City players would do a lap of honour at the end of the game, James O'Connor scored a last minute goal to take the tie into extra time. That goal seemed to knock the stuffing out of the Bluebirds and when substitute Souleymane Oulare made it 2-0 in the final minutes, City's dreams had been shattered for another season.

A chance to make amends came within a year but once again the Bluebirds had tossed away a possible automatic promotion place by dropping to sixth spot after ending the season with just two points and no goals from their last five league matches. They were drawn to play Severnside rivals Bristol City in what was generally thought to be the toughest draw possible. The Robins had done the double over the Bluebirds during the season and they were confident of making the final. City were magnificent in the first leg at Ninian Park and they gained the advantage so desperately needed when Peter Thorne rose high to head home a cross from Mark Bonner late in the second half.

The return at Ashton Gate was a tense affair with the Bluebirds defence in superb form, particularly Neil Alexander who made one save from a Brian Tinnion header that looked a goal all the way. There were wild celebrations from players and fans alike when the final whistle blew and City were through to the final.

The occasion ended up bigger than the match when the Bluebirds met Queen's Park Rangers at the Millennium Stadium. In fact Rangers had more chances than City to score but in extra time Andy Campbell lobbed in that never to be forgotten winner and the Bluebirds were promoted.

It was the 2009-10 season when the Bluebirds once again tasted the play-offs and they earned the right with two games to spare by finishing in fourth place. Leicester City, who ended the season on 76 points as did the Bluebirds, hosted the first meeting between the sides at the Walkers Stadium and on a very tense afternoon, a Peter Whittingham free kick in the 78th minute gave the Bluebirds a valuable advantage to take back to the Cardiff City Stadium.

If the first game was tense, the second leg was even more so despite Michael Chopra giving us an early lead. In no time at all City were 3-1 down on the night, 3-2 on aggregate and facing an agonising defeat in front of the largest crowd ever assembled at the new ground. Up stepped Whittingham to dispatch a penalty and take the game into extra time. With no further score it was down to penalties. Michael Chopra, Ross McCormack, Joe Ledley and Mark Kennedy all scored and with David Marshall saving spot kicks from Yann Kermorgant and Martyn Waghorn, the Bluebirds were through to Wembley to face a Blackpool side managed by Ian Holloway, who was Queen's Park Rangers manager when City beat them 1-0 at the Millennium Stadium.

Did You Know...
The nine players booked during the Championship play-off against Leicester City on 12 May, 2010 (three Bluebirds and six for Leicester) are the most in any match at the Cardiff City Stadium to date

Once again the M4 was alive with blue flags and scarves waving from the many cars and coaches that made the trip to Wembley. On a very hot day Chopra put the Bluebirds ahead but a superb free kick from Charlie Adam brought the sides level. Once again City forged ahead with another superbly worked goal with Joe Ledley firing home after running on to a Whittingham through ball. Elation soon turned to despair as poor defending allowed the Tangerines to strike twice in four minutes just before half time to go in at the interval 3-2 ahead. The loss of Jay Bothroyd through injury in the opening minutes had proved a desperate blow to Bluebird hopes and though the Blackpool crossbar was struck twice during the match, it was Ian Holloway's side that took the honours and promotion to the Premiership.

1996-97

Division Three Semi-final (first leg), 11 May, 1997. Cardiff City 0 Northampton Town 1 (11,369)

Bluebirds; Steve Williams; Lee Jarman, Jason Perry, Scott Young, Kevin Lloyd; Jason Fowler, Jeff Eckhardt (Jimmy Rollo), Gareth Stoker (Steve White), Craig Middleton; Carl Dale, Simon Haworth

Northampton Town; Andy Woodman; Ian Clarkson, John Frain, Ian Sampson, Ray Warburton, David Rennie, Sean Parrish, Mark Cooper, Roy Hunter, Neil Grayson (Chris Lee), John Gayle (Dean Peer)
Scorer; Sean Parrish 77

Division Three Semi-final (second leg), 14 May, 1997. Northampton Town 3 Cardiff City 2 (7,302)
Northampton Town; Andy Woodman; Ian Clarkson, John Frain, Ian Sampson, Ray Warburton, David Rennie (Dean Peer), Sean Parrish, Chris Lee, Roy Hunter, Neil Grayson, John Gayle (White)
Scorers; Ian Sampson 23, Ray Warburton 68, John Gayle 77

Bluebirds; Steve Williams; Lee Jarman, Jason Perry, Scott Young, Kevin Lloyd (Gareth Stoker); Jason Fowler, Jeff Eckhardt, Craig Middleton (Jimmy Gardner); Carl Dale, Simon Haworth, Steve White
Scorers; Jason Fowler 36, Simon Haworth 90
Northampton Town through 4-2 on aggregate

2001-02

Division Two Semi-final (first leg), 28 April, 2002. Stoke City 1 Cardiff City 2 (21,245)
Stoke City; Neil Cutler; Wayne Thomas, Peter Handyside, Sergei Shtanyuk, Clive Clarke; Tony Dinning, Bjarni Gudjonsson (Jurgen Vandeurzen), James O'Connor, Marc Goodfellow (Deon Burton); Andy Cooke, Chris Iwelumo (Rikhardur Dadason)
Scorer; Deon Burton 84

Bluebirds; Neil Alexander; Rhys Weston, Scott Young, Spencer Prior, Gary Croft; Mark Bonner, Graham Kavanagh, Willie Boland, Peter Thorne (James Collins); Rob Earnshaw (Andy Campbell), Leo Fortune-West
Scorers; Rob Earnshaw 12, Leo Fortune-West 59

Division Two Semi-final (second leg), 1 May, 2002. Cardiff City 0 Stoke City 2 aet (19,367)
Bluebirds; Neil Alexander; Rhys Weston, Scott Young, Spencer Prior, Gary Croft; Mark Bonner (Leyton Maxwell), Graham Kavanagh, Willie Boland, Peter Thorne (Jason Bowen); Rob Earnshaw (Andy Campbell), Leo Fortune-West

Stoke City; Neil Cutler; Wayne Thomas, Peter Handyside, Sergei Shtanyuk, Clive Clarke; Tony Dinning (Jurgen Vandeurzen), Bjarni Gudjonsson, James O'Connor, Arnar Gunnlaugsson (Andy Cooke); Deon Burton, Chris Iwelumo (Souleymane Oulare)
Scorers; James O'Connor 90, Souleymane Oulare 115
Stoke City through 3-2 on aggregate

25 May 2003, Play-off final. Cardiff City 1 QPR 0. The Bluebirds celebrate their play-off victory

2002-03

Division Two Semi-final (first leg), 10 May, 2003. Cardiff City 1 Bristol City 0 (19,146)
Bluebirds; Neil Alexander; Rhys Weston, Spencer Prior, Danny Gabbidon, Chris Barker; Gareth Whalley, Willie Boland, Graham Kavanagh, Andy Legg (Mark Bonner); Rob Earnshaw (Andy Campbell), Peter Thorne
Scorer; Peter Thorne 74

Bristol City; Steve Phillips; Louis Carey, Tony Butler, Danny Coles, Mickey Bell; Scott Murray, Joe Burnell, Tom Doherty (Brian Tinnion), Matt Hill; Christian Roberts (Liam Rosenior), Lee Peacock

Division Two Semi-final (second leg), 13 May, 2003. Bristol City 0 Cardiff City 0 (16,307)
Bristol City; Steve Phillips; Louis Carey, Tony Butler, Danny Coles, Matt Hill (Peter Beadle); Scott Murray, Joe Burnell, Tom Doherty, Brian Tinnion; Christian Roberts (Leroy Lita), Lee Peacock

Bluebirds; Neil Alexander; Rhys Weston (Gary Croft), Spencer Prior, Danny Gabbidon, Chris Barker; Gareth Whalley, Willie Boland, Graham Kavanagh, Andy Legg (Mark Bonner); Rob Earnshaw (Andy Campbell), Peter Thorne
Bluebirds through 1-0 on aggregate

Division Two final Millennium Stadium, 25 May, 2003. Cardiff City 1 Queen's Park Rangers 0 aet (66,096)
Bluebirds; Neil Alexander; Rhys Weston (Gary Croft), Spencer Prior, Danny Gabbidon, Chris Barker; Gareth Whalley, Willie Boland, Graham Kavanagh, Andy Legg (Mark Bonner); Rob Earnshaw (Andy Campbell), Peter Thorne
Scorer; Andy Campbell 114

Queen's Park Rangers; Chris Day; Stephen Kelly, Clark Carlisle, Danny Shittu, Gino Padula (Tom Williams); Marc Bircham, Kevin Gallen, Steve Palmer, Kevin McLeod; Richard Pacquette (Andy Thomson), Paul Furlong

12 May 2010, Play-off semi final 2nd leg. Cardiff City 2 Leicester City 1. Peter Whittingham strokes home the vital spot-kick to bring the aggregate scores level

2009-10

Championship Semi-final (first leg), 9 May, 2010. Leicester City 0 Cardiff City 1 (29,165)
Leicester City; Chris Weale; Nolberto Solano, Jack Hobbs, Alex Bruce, Bruno Berner; Paul Gallagher, Andy King, Richie Wellens (Dany N'Guessan), Jay Spearing, Lloyd Dyer (Matt Fryatt); Martyn Waghorn (Yann Kermorgant)

Bluebirds; David Marshall; Kevin McNaughton, Mark Hudson, Darcy Blake, Mark Kennedy; Chris Burke (Kelvin Etuhu), Joe Ledley, Stephen McPhail, Peter Whittingham; Michael Chopra (Ross McCormack), Jay Bothroyd
Scorer; Peter Whittingham (78)

Championship Semi-final (second leg), 12 May, 2010. Cardiff City 2 Leicester City 3 aet (26,033)

Bluebirds; David Marshall; Kevin McNaughton (Paul Quinn), Mark Hudson, Darcy Blake, Mark Kennedy; Chris Burke (Kelvin Etuhu), Stephen McPhail, Joe Ledley, Peter Whittingham (Ross McCormack); Michael Chopra, Jay Bothroyd

Scorers; Michael Chopra (21), Peter Whittingham (69p)

Play-off final, Blackpool 3 Cardiff City 2. Joe Ledley scores City's second goal at Wembley

Leicester City; Chris Weale; Nolberto Solano, Jack Hobbs, Alex Bruce, Bruno Berner; Lloyd Dyer (Martyn Waghorn), Andy King, Richie Wellens, Paul Gallagher (Jay Spearing); Steve Howard, Matt Fryatt (Yann Kermorgant)

Scorers; Matt Fryatt (25), Mark Hudson (36og), Andy King (49)

Score level 3-3 after extra time. Bluebirds win 4-3 on penalties

Championship Final, 22 May, 2010. Blackpool 3 Cardiff City 2 (82,244)

Blackpool; Matt Gilks; Stephen Crainey, Ian Evatt, Alex Baptiste, Seamus Coleman; Keith Southern, David Vaughan (Barry Bannan), Charlie Adam, Gary Taylor-Fletcher (Ben Burgess); Brett Ormerod (Stephen Dobbie), DJ Campbell

Scorers; Charlie Adam (13), Gary Taylor-Fletcher (41), Brett Ormerod (45)

Bluebirds; David Marshall; Kevin McNaughton (Anthony Gerrard), Mark Hudson, Darcy Blake, Mark Kennedy; Peter Whittingham, Joe Ledley, Stephen McPhail, Chris Burke (Ross McCormack); Michael Chopra, Jay Bothroyd (Kelvin Etuhu)

Scorers; Michael Chopra (9), Joe Ledley (35)

Did You Know...
Cardiff City's match against Blackpool at Wembley on 22 May, 2010 was the first play-off final to be broadcast around the country in 3D

Bluebirds full record in the Play-offs

Played	Won	Drawn	Lost	For	Against
10	4	1	5	11	13

Scorers (11 goals)

2 Michael Chopra, Peter Whittingham

1 Jason Fowler, Simon Haworth, Rob Earnshaw, Leo Fortune-West, Peter Thorne, Andy Campbell, Joe Ledley

Appearances (10 matches)

5 Neil Alexander, Rhys Weston, Spencer Prior, Graham Kavanagh, Willie Boland, Peter Thorne, Rob Earnshaw, Mark Bonner, Andy Campbell, 4 Scott Young, Gary Croft, 3 Danny Gabbidon, Chris Barker, Gareth Whalley, Andy Legg, David Marshall, Kevin McNaughton, Mark Hudson, Darcy Blake, Mark Kennedy, Chris Burke, Joe Ledley, Stephen McPhail, Peter Whittingham, Michael Chopra, Jay Bothroyd, Andy Campbell, Ross McCormack, Kelvin Etuhu, 2 Steve Williams, Lee Jarman, Jason Perry, Kevin Lloyd, Jason Fowler, Jeff Eckhardt, Craig Middleton, Carl Dale, Simon Haworth, Leo Fortune-West, Gareth Stoker, Steve White, 1Jimmy Rollo, Jimmy Gardner, James Collins, Leyton Maxwell, Jason Bowen, Paul Quinn, Anthony Gerrard

8
MANAGERS (1910–2009)

1. Davy McDougall (August 1910–April 1911)

Davy McDougall became Cardiff City's first professional skipper when he joined the club from Glasgow Rangers in 1910. The left half took over as player-manager in the 1910-11 season which was the first for the Bluebirds in the Second Division of the Southern League and they finished in a creditable fourth place.

McDougall had experience of playing in Ireland and Scotland, and he had also spent time with Bristol City. He recruited most of his players from the North and Scotland and it proved to be an expensive business but he knew that the club could not prosper in the Southern League with home-grown players alone.

1910 An early Cardiff City squad photograph with player manager Davy McDougall in the centre of the bottom row

Cardiff also had a team in the Glamorgan League at the same time and Davy played in many of City's matches in that league. When Fred Stewart arrived at the club in the summer of 1911 to take over as secretary-manager McDougall was retained as a player but did not seem part of the new manager's plans and never played a first team game in City's second season. At the start of the 1912-13 season, he accepted the post of player-manager with Newport County.

Bluebirds Manager's League record: 22 matches (12–4–6) = 54.5% win ratio.

2. Fred Stewart (May 1911–May 1933)

Fred Stewart had been with Stockport County since 1893 and manager for 11 years when in May 1911 he was asked to take over at Cardiff City. The Board of Directors had realised the need for a full-time manager and advertised the position in the *Athletic News*, a widely read sports publication. Stewart's application was far and away the best received and he was given the job initially on a three-year contract at the princely sum of £4 a week plus bonuses. He appointed George Latham as trainer but one of his greatest captures was the signing of Billy Hardy from Hearts. Hardy was well known to Stewart as he had played for him at Stockport. It was rumoured at the time that the City manager wanted Hardy so badly that he paid the £25 transfer fee out of his own pocket.

Stewart was so busy in the transfer market in the summer of 1911 that only four players remained from Davy McDougall's one year at the club when the new term began. The Bluebirds did well in the Southern League and even better when they joined the Football League for the 1920-21 season. It was in the summer of 1920 that Stewart completed the club's most expensive signing at the time when he paid The Wednesday £750 for inside forward Jimmy Gill. That record didn't last long as he returned to The Wednesday to set a league record fee for a full back by signing Scottish international Jimmy Blair for a staggering £3,500. There was one black spot during Stewart's tenure and that was in 1921 as City were about to begin life in Division One. The club were fined £50 for allegedly making an illegal approach to a Wolverhampton Wanderers player though Stewart claimed his innocence.

Every new season players were recruited and Stewart worked the transfer market to good effect both in obtaining players and letting others go for fees. With City averaging over 30,000 at Ninian Park for league games, the directors were happy enough to allow him to wheel and deal whenever necessary.

22 April 1927. City manager Fred Stewart puts mascot Trixie in her basket at the Imperial Hotel in Southport watched closely by Hughie Ferguson

City's Cup Final appearances in 1925 and 1927 were testament to the shrewd manner in which Stewart managed the club but after the victory over Arsenal at Wembley, a downward spiral began. He was forced to shop for players more prudently as relegation sent the Bluebirds tumbling back into Division Two. Another relegation quickly followed and with the club in a poor state both on and off the field, it was no surprise when Stewart tendered his resignation in May 1933. He had started a number of businesses in the Roath district of Cardiff, including coal and corn merchants, and on his retirement from football he concentrated on those interests until his death on 1 February,1954 at the age of 81. He had been secretary-manager of the club for 22 years.

Bluebirds Manager's League record: 672 matches (285–146–241) = 42.4% win ratio.

3. Bartley Wilson (May 1933–March 1934)

The vacant post was taken up by Cardiff City founder and secretary, Bartley Wilson. His first appointment was making Jimmy Blair player-coach but although both men scoured the leagues for new recruits they had little money to spend. Wilson struggled to keep the club on a tight rein but when the directors realised the prospect of applying for re-election was becoming ever more probable, they invited Ben Watts-Jones to take over from Wilson in March 1934.

Bluebirds Manager's League record: 30 matches (8–3–19) = 26.6% win ratio.

4. Ben Watts-Jones (March 1934–April 1937)

Ben Watts-Jones was a former chairman of Swansea Town and a committee member of the Football Association of Wales. Despite being known and respected throughout football, it was a strange choice and he could do little to stop City's slide to the basement. The club only won one more game that season and finished rock-bottom of Division Three South just seven years after winning the FA Cup. They were forced to go cap-in-hand to the Football League but were duly re-elected.

In readiness for the new season, Watts-Jones released all but five of his professionals and brought back George Latham as trainer in place of Jimmy Blair. It was one of the busiest close-seasons ever seen at the club as Watts-Jones completely rebuilt the first team. City did a little better in 1934-35 but he was still not satisfied and yet another clear out happened in the summer of 1935.

When Latham retired through ill-health in 1936, Watts-Jones replaced him with former Wales international, Bill Jennings. There were seven debutants for the start of the 1936-37 season as the manager continued to bring new players in and release others. But with little change in the club's fortunes, he finally called it a day in April 1937 by tendering his resignation while also taking up a position on the Board.
Bluebirds Manager's League record: 131 matches (38–29–64) = 28.9% win ratio.

5. Bill Jennings (April 1937–April 1939)

Bill Jennings was a Wales international with 11 caps for the senior side. He was also capped at schoolboy level in 1907 while still a player with Bethel Baptists in his home town of Barry. In 1912 he signed for Bolton Wanderers but it was not until after World War One that he gained a regular place with the Trotters. He won his first FA Cup winners medal in the 1923 Wembley final victory over West Ham and another three years later when Bolton beat Manchester City. He retired in 1931 to become coach at Notts County and in 1936 became coach with the Bluebirds, taking over as secretary-manager one year later.

Jennings used his contacts in the game to strengthen the playing staff in readiness for the 1937-38 season. The side now had an experienced look about it and they made a blistering start with only two defeats in the first 12 matches. The signing of Jimmy Collins from Liverpool proved a trump card as he banged in ten goals in those opening dozen games. Although the club ended the season in mid-table, their performances were a marked improvement on the previous four. Attendances were also up and the opening game of the 1938-39 season brought a crowd of 30,000 to Ninian Park. It seemed that Jennings was winning the battle to restore City's fortunes yet they were inconsistent and had to be content with a mid-table finish as the storm clouds gathered over Europe.

There was a major development behind the scenes in March 1939 when Herbert Merrett was elected to the Board. Within weeks he became club chairman and his first task was to relieve Bill Jennings of his duties and appoint a new manager.
Bluebirds Manager's League record: 82 matches (30–20–32) = 36.5% win ratio.

6. Cyril Spiers (April 1939–June 1946)

Despite the ever-increasing prospect of war breaking out, Cyril Spiers set about the task of bringing new players into the club. Spiers was a former goalkeeper with Aston Villa, Tottenham Hotspur and Wolves, and he had also represented the Football League as well as playing in an international trial in 1931. As soon as he had settled in at the club he began moving players out and bringing others in, including a certain Trevor Morris from Ipswich Town.

The Football League was stopped when war broke out and all the contracted players were allowed to leave as the government decreed that only friendly matches and regional leagues could take place. Football carried on during the war years with most clubs using guest players to supplement their staff. Cardiff City were no different and over 70 players represented the club in wartime including Bill Shankly and Jimmy Murphy.

The 1945-46 season was used to help clubs get back on their feet and the Football League resumed the season after. But Spiers would not be in charge when league football resumed because on 7 June, 1946, he resigned to take over the manager's role at Norwich City.

Did You Know...
Cyril Spiers, Len Ashurst, Eddie May, Frank Burrows and Kenny Hibbitt have all managed Cardiff City on two separate occasions

Bluebirds Manager's League record: 9 matches (3–3–3) = 33.3% win ratio.

7. Billy McCandless (June 1946–November 1947)

Billy McCandless had a distinguished playing career winning three Irish Cup finals with Linfield before moving to Scotland where he won seven league titles with Glasgow Rangers. He also played nine times for Ireland after gaining his first cap in 1919 in a 1-1 draw against England. He left Rangers in 1930 to return to Ireland as player-manager of Ballymena United where he stayed four years before making his way back to Scotland. This time he settled in Dundee as manager but after only three years he left for Wales and took charge of Newport County. He guided County to the Third Division (South) title in 1938-39 only for World War Two to cause the cessation of all league football. County's playing staff had been decimated by the war years and in April, 1946 he resigned, two months later becoming manager at Ninian Park.

In his first season with City he took the side to the Division Three (South) title, finishing nine points clear of Queen's Park Rangers, their nearest rivals. In November, 1947 he took up another challenge by moving west to manage Swansea Town and in a unique treble, helped the Swans to the Division Three (South) title in 1948-49.

Bluebirds Manager's League record: 58 matches (37–11–10) = 63.8% win ratio.

8. Cyril Spiers December 1947–May 1954

Cyril Spiers took over for his second spell in charge at Ninian Park on 3 December, 1947 after being coaxed from Norwich City by chairman Herbert Merrett. His appointment led to a good run by the Bluebirds with four wins and two draws from the first six matches under his management. The good times didn't last long however, and after a mid-season slump in fortunes City finished their first season back in Division Two in fifth position.

The following 1948-49 season the Bluebirds moved up to finish fourth and it was expected that a tilt for promotion would be made the following season. That turned out to be a disappointment as the club finished down in tenth spot despite the shrewd signing of Wilf Grant who came from Southampton in exchange for record signing Ernie Stevenson.

Spiers signed popular winger Mike Tiddy the following term and his arrival meant that Grant could switch to centre forward. This proved to be a clever move by the manager as City's fortunes took a turn for the better. The club finished the season two points behind second-placed Manchester City to just miss out on promotion but established themselves as favourites for 1951-52. They did not disappoint as Spiers kept faith with his players, bringing only Ken Chisholm in from Coventry City to make sure of promotion and the burly striker did just that with eight goals from 11 league matches.

Spiers never made any new signings for the return to Division One even though attendances went above 50,000 on a couple of occasions. Stan Montgomery and Alf Sherwood were ever-present in a defence that conceded only 46 goals, easily the best in the division and the club ended their first year back in the top flight in twelfth place.

It was during the next season that Spiers shook the football world by paying £30,000 to Sunderland for Wales international Trevor Ford. It appears that Spiers was at odds with chairman Herbert Merrett over the signing as it was later revealed that the chairman at first refused to countersign the cheque. Ford's arrival failed to improve the goals for column and City ended the season in tenth place with their tally of 51 goals in 42 matches the lowest in the division. Spiers tendered his resignation on 10 May, 1954 and accepted a post with Crystal Palace.

Bluebirds Manager's League record: 275 matches (114–75–86) = 41.0% win ratio.

9. Trevor Morris (May 1954–July 1958)

Caerphilly-born Trevor Morris had been signed by Cyril Spiers but in a wartime match for City he broke his leg and was forced into retirement. He took over as secretary of the

Bluebirds on the resumption of league football after the war and was a surprise appointment to follow Spiers as he had no managerial experience. He made his first major signing by recruiting inside forward Ron Stockin from Wolves for £12,000, but an inconsistent City just evaded relegation in his first season in charge.

The following year was a little better as Morris made a unique transfer deal by recruiting three players from Sunderland for a joint fee of £9,000. Harry Kirtley and Johnny McSeveney instantly made their marks at Ninian Park but Howard Sheppeard remained a fringe player. The season could not have started any worse as Wolves thrashed the Bluebirds 9-1 at Ninian Park in September to equal a Football League record. Stan Montgomery had departed the club in the summer and it was not until December that Morris made his most important signing when he brought in Danny Malloy from Dundee to replace the long-serving centre half. During the season he also promoted a young centre forward called Gerry Hitchens to the first team. A run of only one defeat in 14 games helped the Bluebirds to finish the season four points above relegation.

Did You Know...
Bluebirds manager Trevor Morris was awarded the Distinguished Flying Medal for his services during World War Two

Unfortunately for Morris, it was only a temporary reprieve as the following 1956-57 season brought relegation with only ten victories from the 42 matches. He wasn't helped by the ban imposed on Trevor Ford which left the scoring burden on the shoulders of the young Hitchens. Despite this, safety seemed on the cards even as late as February, but they could only manage one victory in their remaining 14 games and finished three points adrift of third from bottom Sunderland.

Morris took the club into Division Two intent on winning promotion straight back but with attendances dropping to around 16,000 and the club only managing a mid-table spot, it was no surprise when he accepted an invitation in July 1958 to go west and manage Swansea Town.

Bluebirds Manager's League record: 168 matches (52–38–78) = 30.9% win ratio.

10. Bill Jones (August 1958–September 1962)

Bill Jones had a short playing career with Newport County where he made only seven league appearances before going non-league with Barry Town. When he hung up his boots he joined Ipswich Town as chief scout before being appointed manager of Barry Town in 1950. He moved to Ninian Park in 1957 as assistant to Trevor Morris so he knew the set-up of the club when appointed to replace Morris on a temporary basis in August, 1958.

Jones had a disastrous opening as the Bluebirds lost their first three matches without even scoring a goal. George Kelly, a signing from Stoke City, began to find his form and with Ron Nicholls recruited from Bristol Rovers to replace Graham Vearncombe who was doing his National Service in the Merchant Navy, City began to recover. Then Kelly lost his place to new young star Graham Moore and with City staggering around near the bottom of the division, Jones made one of the Bluebirds finest ever signings when he paid Arsenal £10,000 for Derek Tapscott.

Fortunes were soon on the up and Jones was offered the post full-time in October. Inspired by Tapscott's tenacity, the Bluebirds surged up the table but after losing to Swansea at Ninian Park for the first time in a league match, a run of indifferent results left them in ninth place, way off a promotion spot.

The 1959-60 season began in fine fashion and big crowds returned in anticipation that this might be City's season. By the time Easter 1960 arrived it was all over bar the shouting and 52,364 crammed into Ninian Park to see the match against Division Two championship contenders Aston Villa. A Graham Moore goal gave City victory in a pulsating game and took them to the top of the division but they were unable to hold on and Villa pipped them for the title. After an absence of three years, City made their return to Division One and seven goals in the opening ten games from Tapscott kept the club ticking over. Jones knew he needed some more experience in the side so he signed Derek Hogg from West Brom for a £12,000 fee. Jones suffered a bitter blow when promising wing half Steve Gammon was forced into early retirement after breaking his leg in a clash with Manchester City's Denis Law. After a superb victory over double-winners Spurs in March, 1961 City's season fizzled out and they lost six of their remaining nine league matches.

Jones made one major signing for 1961-62 in centre forward Johnny King from Stoke City, but that left room for the introduction of youngsters such as Gareth Williams, Tony Pickrell and Alan McIntosh. To offset that, Jones lost the services of Malloy who left the club under a cloud after a contract dispute. This was to prove disastrous as the popular Malloy had been the kingpin in City's defence ever since his arrival from Dundee. Worse was to befall Jones as Moore was transferred to relegation-rivals Chelsea for a record fee of £35,000. Although Mel Charles was brought to Ninian Park from Arsenal, the heart had been knocked out of the club and they were relegated at the end of the season, just one point from safety.

The following year an inconsistent start cost Jones his job and he was sacked, along with trainer Wilf Grant, on 10 September 1962.

Bluebirds Manager's League record: 173 matches (65–45–63) = 37.5% win ratio.

11. George Swindin (November 1962–April 1964)

George Swindin made his name as a goalkeeper with Arsenal but he had previously played for Rotherham United and Bradford City before joining the Gunners in 1936. He won three Championship medals and a Cup winners medal while at Highbury and after four years as Peterborough's player-manager, he returned to the marble halls as manager of Arsenal in 1958. He had little success however, and resigned in May 1962 to take charge of Norwich City.

December 1962. City manager George Swindin with coach Ernie Curtis and new trainer Stan Montgomery

He only stayed at Carrow Road for 20 games before accepting an offer from Cardiff City and in November 1962 he took over at Ninian Park. One of Swindin's first jobs was to bring former Bluebird Stan Montgomery back to Cardiff as trainer-coach. Monty had been at Norwich with Swindin. The new manager was unhappy that City settled for a mid-table position in his first season, particularly as they could field as many as six Wales internationals in their line-up. He gave a young 17 year-old ground staff boy called Don Murray his debut at Middlesbrough in the last away game of the season but then shocked the soccer world by transfer-listing 13 players, half of them internationals. It led to a summer of discontent amongst players and fans alike.

During the close season, Swindin sold Alan Durban, Peter Hooper and Maurice Swan, while Frank Rankmore was allowed to leave after the great John Charles signed for the club. City ended the 1963-64 season in 15th place but it was a great surprise when the Club announced that they had dispensed with Swindin's services on the morning of a Welsh Cup final replay. It emerged later that Swindin had refused to resign so had his contract terminated. In his defence he did introduce a number of youngsters to the first team in

addition to Murray for future captain Gareth Williams, Peter Rodrigues and Bernard Lewis all began their careers under his managership.
Bluebirds Manager's League record: 68 matches (24–15–29) = 35.3% win ratio.

12. Jimmy Scoular (June 1964–November 1973)

Jimmy Scoular became a steel foundry worker when he left school but he had already been capped at junior level by Scotland. He joined the Royal Navy in 1943 and was posted to Portsmouth and at the end of WW2 he signed professional forms for Pompey.

For seven years he helped form one of the greatest half back lines in League football. Alongside Reg Flewin and Jimmy Dickinson he won Championship medals in 1949 and 1950 along with nine senior caps for Scotland. He moved to Newcastle United for a fee of £22,500 and captained the Magpies when they won the FA Cup in 1955. As he was coming to the end of his playing career he joined Bradford as player-manager but hung up his boots in March 1964. Three months later he was in the manager's seat at Ninian Park in time for the 1964-65 season and he would fill that position for over nine years.

4 February 1966. Ronnie Bird with City manager Jimmy Scoular after signing for City

Goalkeeper Bob Wilson was Scoular's first signing yet the Bluebirds went 12 matches before gaining their first victory under the craggy Scot. The season was saved by City's first foray into Europe in the Cup-Winners Cup but the following two league terms saw the Bluebirds finish just one place off relegation. In 1967-68, Derby County won 5-1 at Ninian Park and it was widely reported that Scoular and Brian Clough had to be separated following a set-to in the tunnel after the match.

Season 1968-69 saw a big improvement, no doubt sparked by the exciting Cup-Winners Cup run to the semi-finals, though Crystal Palace won the opening game of the season at Ninian Park by 4-0. A fifth place finish that season was followed by seventh place in 1969-70 but it was the following season that had fans dreaming of promotion. That was until news broke in November 1970 that John Toshack had been sold to Liverpool. By the time Alan Warboys, his replacement, had been brought in the momentum was lost and the Bluebirds finished third, three points behind second-placed Sheffield United.

Once again Europe proved a major counter attraction with the quarter-final tie against Real Madrid becoming part of Ninian Park folk lore, but it was back to a depressing set of results in 1971-72 as it took the Bluebirds until their seventh match before recording a victory. A run of 12 matches with only one defeat helped pull City out of the mire.

The following season Scoular swapped Alan Warboys for Sheffield United's Dave Powell and Gil Reece, and shortly after accepted an offer of £100,000 from Bournemouth for fans favourites, Brian Clark and Ian Gibson. With the money received he signed Andy McCulloch from Queen's Park Rangers but once again the Bluebirds finished in 20th place, perilously

close to relegation. Scoular knew he was on borrowed time but 1973-74 saw a good start and the Bluebirds were in a heady fifth spot only for form to desert them. On the 9 November, 1973 chairman David Goldstone dismissed Scoular. He was in his tenth year as manager of the club.
Bluebirds Manager's League record: 391 matches (131–109–151) = 33.5% win ratio.

13. Frank O'Farrell (November 1973–April 1974)

Frank O'Farrell had a distinguished playing career with West Ham and also won seven caps for the Republic of Ireland. After six years at Upton Park, he joined Preston and scored on his debut against Manchester City but he only had a short stay there before linking up with non-league side Weymouth as player-manager in May 1961.

He won the Southern League championship with Weymouth before joining Torquay United in 1965 and gaining promotion in his first season in charge.

He was on the move again three years later to take control of Leicester City, taking them to the FA Cup final in 1969. Those successes led him to one of the top jobs in football when he was invited to become manager of Manchester United in 1971. Unfortunately for O'Farrell, he was unable to follow in the footsteps of the legendary Sir Matt Busby and he left after a short time.

On 13 November, 1973 he was appointed manager of Cardiff City and his first job was to bring in Jimmy Andrews as first team coach. After a 0-0 draw at home to Luton Town, City lost 3-0 at Middlesbrough in his second game in charge and he acted swiftly by signing Willie Carlin on loan from Notts County before paying a club record fee of £62,000 for Leicester City's winger, John Farrington.

Did You Know...
Frank O'Farrell replaced Jimmy Scoular as City manager in 1974 but only lasted 158 days before taking up a lucrative offer to manage the Iran national team

City's fortunes fluctuated and O'Farrell acted by signing Ron Healey from Manchester City and Clive Charles from West Ham but after just 158 days in charge and the club flirting with relegation, it was announced that he was leaving Ninian Park to take up an appointment in Iran.
Bluebirds Manager's League record: 24 matches (8–7–9) = 33.3% win ratio.

14. Jimmy Andrews (May 1974–November 1978)

When O'Farrell left the club rather abruptly, first team coach Jimmy Andrews was appointed caretaker-manager. Andrews had played Scottish League football for Dundee before joining West Ham in November, 1951. He went on to play for Leyton Orient and Queen's Park Rangers where he began coaching.

His reputation as a coach grew and he worked at Chelsea, Luton, Coventry and Spurs before O'Farrell brought him to Ninian Park in 1973. He was appointed full time manager after saving the club from relegation in 1973-74 but they dropped into Division Three the following season only to bounce straight back up the following year.

After struggling for some time with little or no funds, Andrews set a new club transfer record of £75,000 when he signed Micky Burns from Newcastle, following that by paying Hull City £70,000 for Dave Roberts. Despite this massive spending, the Bluebirds just staved off relegation over the next couple of seasons and on 6 November 1978, after a disastrous 4-1 home defeat by Charlton Athletic, Andrews was dismissed.
Bluebirds Manager's League record: 189 matches (60–54–75) = 31.7% win ratio.

15. Richie Morgan (November 1978–November 1981)

Richie Morgan was a one-club man unlucky enough to spend ten years as a player at Ninian Park while the great Don Murray was first-choice centre half. During that time

Morgan played only 68 league matches but he did play an important part in the Bluebirds Cup Winners Cup exploits of 1968 when he took over from the injured Murray in City's epic quarter-final play-off against Moscow Torpedo in Augsburg. When he hung up his boots, Morgan joined the club's administrative staff and was a shock choice to take over from Jimmy Andrews although at first the appointment was in a caretaker capacity.

On 9 December, he was officially appointed team manager and at 34 years of age, became the youngest in City's history. He brought in some experienced assistants in Doug Livermore, Brian Harris and Dave Elliott and signed a number of players including Colin Sullivan from Norwich City and Ronnie Moore who was brought to the club from Tranmere Rovers for a new record fee of £100,000. An 11-match unbeaten run to the end of the season saw the Bluebirds finish in a creditable ninth place in Division Two.

Morgan's transfer dealings went to a new high when Billy Ronson joined from Blackpool for a fee of £130,000, but most of that outlay was recouped when the popular striker Tony Evans departed for Birmingham City for just £10,000 less. That made the fee received for Evans the highest ever received by the club, eclipsing the £110,000 Liverpool paid for John Toshack.

1979-80 turned out to be a poor season for the club and the following term was even worse as City slumped to 19th in the league. The lack of funds available to Morgan became very evident at the start of the 1981-82 season as the Bluebirds withdrew from the Football Combination and the Welsh League for financial reasons. Despite all these problems, and Cardiff Blue Dragons playing rugby league at Ninian Park, Morgan masterminded a better start to the new term and the club were in the top half of the division when Graham Williams was appointed first team coach on 9 November and Morgan was relieved of his duties and moved upstairs.

Williams reign in charge lasted until March when he was dismissed along with Morgan, who received a lot of sympathy from the fans for the way he had been so harshly treated by the club.

Bluebirds Manager's League record: 126 matches (45–30–51) = 35.7% win ratio.

16. Graham Williams (November 1981–March 1982)

Graham Williams had been out of football for some time and was running a health club in Weymouth when City appointed him as first team coach, although he was effectively the team manager. Williams was a full back who played over 300 games for West Brom and he was capped 26 times by Wales. He had coached extensively abroad but showed a lack of experience of managing in English League football while at Ninian Park. After a run of eight matches without a victory and City tumbling down the table, Williams was dismissed on 3 March, taking the unfortunate Morgan with him.

Bluebirds Manager's League record: 13 matches (2–2–9) = 15.3% win ratio.

17. Len Ashurst (March 1982–March 1984)

City's board knew they had to come up with an experienced candidate to replace Williams and they didn't have far to go when appointing Len Ashurst on 3 March, 1982. He had all the right credentials having managed Hartlepool, Gillingham and Sheffield Wednesday before taking Newport County to their highest position in years. Liverpool-born Ashurst made over 400 appearances for Sunderland before going into management with Hartlepool. While at Newport, Ashurst won promotion and took the club into Europe in the Cup Winners Cup.

He was unable to stem the tide in that 1981-82 season and City were relegated to Division Three, but the following year they bounced back in great style to win promotion with Jeff Hemmerman and Dave Bennett netting 34 league goals between them.

The following season was a struggle for Ashurst with Bob Hatton's retirement, Hemmerman's loss through injury, and then Dave Bennett being allowed to join Coventry for a fee of £120,000. He had to raid the free-transfer market but with the tide turning against him, resigned on 4 March 1984 to take up the manager's position at Sunderland before later going abroad to coach in Kuwait and Qatar.
Bluebirds Manager's League record: 91 matches (41–17–33) = 45.0% win ratio.

18. Jimmy Goodfellow/Jimmy Mullen (March 1984–May 1984 and September 1984)

> **Did You Know...**
> Jimmy Goodfellow scored for Crook Town against Enfield in the 1964 Amateur Cup Final at Wembley

Jimmy Goodfellow was a left winger who played amateur football for the famous Crook Town and Bishop Auckland clubs before joining Port Vale in 1966. He went on to play for Workington Town, Rotherham United and Stockport County before hanging up his boots. He became trainer and coach at Newport County and when Len Ashurst moved to the Bluebirds, he joined him as assistant.

After Ashurst left to manage Sunderland, the City board put Goodfellow and club skipper Jimmy Mullen in temporary charge.

Mullen began his career with Sheffield Wednesday and then captained Rotherham United to the Division Three title before joining the Bluebirds in March 1982. He was made club skipper and though City were relegated in his first full season, he was one of the driving forces as they won promotion at the first attempt in 1982-83.

Their joint reign started with two victories against Cambridge United and Shrewsbury Town but when the Bluebirds were beaten 4-0 at Huddersfield Town, the Board decided on a change of approach.
Bluebirds Joint Managers League record: 10 matches (4–2–4) = 40.0% win ratio.

19. Jimmy Goodfellow (May 1984–September 1984)

On 4 May 1984, Goodfellow was given sole responsibility for management of the side with Mullen reverting to player-coach. With City deep in debt, all the summer transfer activity involved players leaving the club and Andy Dibble, Dave Bennett and Gordon Owen were all allowed to leave with little or no money being made available to obtain replacements. Dibble's transfer fee from Luton Town of £125,000 was a new record incoming amount for the club.

Six defeats and only one victory from the opening seven matches of 1984-85 equalled the Bluebirds worst ever start which came way back in the 1921-22 season. The result was that on 27 September, 1984 Goodfellow was dismissed from his post.
Bluebirds Managers League record: 10 matches (1–2–7) = 10.0% win ratio.

20. Alan Durban (September 1984–May 1986)

Alan Durban began his career with Cardiff City but it was with Derby County that he built a reputation as a fine inside forward. He was signed by the Rams in July 1963 for a £10,000 fee and went on to play over 350 games for Derby and win 27 caps for Wales. He left the Baseball Ground to join Shrewsbury as player-manager and won two promotions with the Shrews. He left them to take charge of Stoke City where another promotion came his way but then followed two difficult years as manager of Sunderland which ended with his dismissal in March 1984. He had been out of football for six months when the call came to manage the Bluebirds.

From the beginning, results were poor and only one victory came in Durban's opening six matches. There was little or no improvement during the season and the manager incensed fans when he released the long-serving Phil Dwyer who ended the season at

Rochdale. Dean Saunders arrived on loan from Swansea City but after four matches was not offered a contract and left the club. The Bluebirds lost their last three league matches and were relegated in 23rd position, just two points above bottom club Wolverhampton Wanderers.

The club began the 1985-86 season without any shirt sponsorship and consequently, Durban had little money to play the transfer market. It was a great shock when the opening game of the season at Notts County was won 4-1, the best opening day victory since the win at Stockport County in 1920. The good times didn't last long as City plummeted from a top ten position to bottom of Division Three with just one win from 17 matches. Players came and went with remarkable speed but it was not until December that the Bluebirds strung three victories together. Three victories and two defeats from the final five matches were not enough and Durban's turbulent reign came to an end on 1 May, 1986 as the Bluebirds plunged into the basement division along with Swansea City and Wolves.

Did You Know...
Alan Durban won a First Division championship medal with Derby County in 1971-72

Bluebirds Manager's League record: 81 matches (20–17–44) = 24.7% win ratio.

22. Frank Burrows (May 1986–August 1989)

Frank Burrows was coach at Sunderland when the new club chairman, Tony Clemo, approached them about his availability. The deal was quickly arranged and Burrows became manager of the Bluebirds on 21 May, 1986.

A tough-tackling centre half in his playing days, Burrows had begun his career in his native Scotland with Raith Rovers before joining Scunthorpe United in 1965. Three years later he moved to Swindon Town and helped the Robins to promotion as well as a shock League Cup final victory over Arsenal in 1969. When his career ended in October, 1976, he became Swindon's assistant manager. He went into coaching and joined Portsmouth, later succeeding Jimmy Dickinson as Pompey manager. Spells as coach at Southampton and Sunderland followed before he arrived at Ninian Park.

After suffering successive relegations under Durban, the Burrows reign began in fine style as City lost only once in their opening nine matches. New players were brought into the club including Terry Boyle, Paul Wimbleton, Nicky Platnauer and the speedy Kevin Bartlett. Jason Perry became one of the youngest debutants for the club when he appeared at full back against Exeter City on 31 March,1987 but public apathy came to the fore when only 1,510 fans showed up for the 4-0 victory over Hartlepool on 7 May. This was the lowest recorded home League attendance for the Bluebirds. City finished in mid-table and Burrows knew that a big improvement was needed in 1987-88.

Once again there was a lot of transfer activity but little money was paid out. Over £100,000 came into the club after Mel Rees's move to Watford but Burrows was once again expected to deal in free transfers. Nigel Stevenson, Brian McDermott, Paul Sanderson, Ian Walsh and Phil Bater all arrived on frees. Bater would later become the first City player to be sent off on his debut. Despite a few ups and downs, the Bluebirds ended the season with five straight wins to secure promotion in second place, five points behind champions Wolverhampton Wanderers. The popular Jimmy Gilligan was top scorer with 19 league goals while his front partner Bartlett weighed in with another 12 strikes.

Did You Know...
Frank Burrows was centre half in the Swindon Town team that beat Arsenal in the 1969 League Cup final at Wembley. Bobby Gould was centre forward for the Gunners

Optimism for the new 1988-89 season was jolted when Oxford United paid £150,000 for Mike Ford, City's longest-serving player. It was a new outgoing record fee for the club. Unfortunately for Burrows, none of that money was made available to him but he did sign George Wood and Steve Lynex on free transfers, while Ian Rodgerson cost only £35,000 from Hereford United.

A 6-1 defeat at Port Vale early on in the season was another bitter blow but Burrows steadied the side and it was a big surprise when City accepted an offer of £125,000 for Kevin Bartlett. At the same time, chairman Clemo announced that the club was up for sale. This affected performances on the field and it was only when they beat Chester 2-0 on 9 May that they clambered out of the relegation places. Only 14 goals scored away from home all season told its own story.

Once again season 1989-90 started in turmoil as Burrows was forced to sell several players in an effort to balance the books. Terry Boyle, Nicky Platnauer and Paul Wimbleton all departed Ninian Park but Cardiff-born Chris Pike did arrive from Fulham on a free transfer. The inevitable happened and they didn't chalk up their first league victory until 7 October, making it the worst start to a season in Bluebirds history. However, Burrows was no longer at the club by then because on 28 August, 1989 just two games into the season, he accepted an offer to become John Gregory's assistant at Portsmouth.

Bluebirds Manager's League record: 140 matches (53–44–43) = 37.8% win ratio.

22. Len Ashurst (August 1989–May 1991)

Len Ashurst was quickly installed as manager for his second spell with the club on 31 August, 1989 but early results were poor. There was more gloom around Ninian Park when a bid of £215,000 for Jimmy Gilligan was accepted from Portsmouth, no doubt at the request of Frank Burrows. At least Ashurst was given some money to spend and he paid Kettering £65,000 for Cohen Griffith, and Swindon £25,000 for Leigh Barnard. He also brought in keeper Gavin Ward for what was a successful trial period. Despite this change of personnel, City remained rooted to the foot of the table. Griffith and Chris Pike became a potent partnership up front and fortunes improved but a poor home record of eight defeats at Ninian Park proved too much and after just two seasons in Division Three it was back to the basement.

The 1990-91 season began with a seven match unbeaten run, ended when Rochdale won 1-0 at Ninian Park in October. Ashurst had recruited Pat Heard and Neil Matthews but one of his best appointments was bringing Eddie May to the club as coach to replace Bobby Smith who had resigned before joining Hereford United. Following a run of poor results, Ashurst decided to give youth a fling and Damon Searle and Lee Baddeley made their debuts alongside youngsters such as Nathan Blake and Jason Perry.

Rick Wright, the owner of Barry Island's Majestic Holiday Camp complex became a financial benefactor and offered to provide funds for new recruits but no one was brought into the club and City failed to win any of their last eight games. It was another mid-table finish for the Bluebirds after the season had promised so much. It became farcical when Ashurst selected reserve keeper Ward as substitute in the final two league games. Ward actually went on for Roger Hansbury in the final match of the season, a 0-0 home draw against Maidstone United.

It came as no surprise when Ashurst left his post after the final game as his frustration at the club's situation had caused him to be sent from the touchline twice during the season.

Bluebirds Manager's League record: 90 matches (27–29–34) = 30.0% win ratio.

23. Eddie May (July 1991–November 1994)

Eddie May was a big centre half for both Wrexham and Swansea during a distinguished playing career that saw him make over 500 league appearances. Born in Epping, he joined Southend United from Dagenham in January 1965 and made his league debut later that season. He moved to Wrexham from the Shrimpers in June 1968, staying at the Racecourse for eight years before travelling south to Swansea City in 1976. He had spent the summer of 1975 in the NASL with Chicago Sting. After a further 90 games for the

Swans, May retired from playing and became coach at Leicester City. A number of coaching appointments followed in this country and also in Saudi Arabia, Kenya, Iceland and Norway.

In July 1991 he was appointed manager of Cardiff City and led them to the Division Three title and Welsh Cup in 1993. Cash-strapped City struggled in Division Two over the next couple of seasons and May was relieved of his post on 28 November, 1994 when a new consortium moved in to take over the club.

Bluebirds Manager's League record: 148 matches (59–42–47) = 39.8% win ratio.

24. Terry Yorath (November 1994–March 1995)

Terry Yorath was born in Cardiff but his playing career took off at Leeds United after he signed professional forms in 1967. He joined Coventry City in August 1976 for £125,000 and three years later went to White Hart Lane for a fee of £275,000. Injuries took a toll and Yorath moved to Vancouver Whitecaps before finishing his playing career with Bradford City. He was then appointed manager of Swansea City and took the club to promotion in 1988 but left the Vetch Field in controversial circumstances to return to Bradford City before becoming the national team manager of Wales.

In November 1994 he became involved in a consortium trying to buy Cardiff City but only stayed four months as the attempted buy-out never materialised. After working at Huddersfield and Bradford City, Yorath had a spell out of football before offering to help out at non-league Margate.

Bluebirds Manager's League record: 20 matches (3–5–12) = 15.0% win ratio.

25. Eddie May (March 1995–May 1995)

After leaving Ninian Park in November, 1994, Eddie May took over as manager of Barry Town but on 30 March, 1995 he was re-instated as Bluebirds manager following the collapse of the intended take-over. He left in the summer of 1995 and after another short spell with Barry Town he took over the reins at Torquay United for a season before another lengthy spell coaching overseas in a number of countries.

Bluebirds Manager's League record: 8 matches (1–3–4) = 12.5% win ratio.

26. Kenny Hibbitt (July 1995–January 1996)

Bradford-born Kenny Hibbitt made his reputation as a skilful midfield player for Wolves from 1968-84. During his 16 years at the club he won two League Cups (1974 and 1980) and was a finalist in the 1972 UEFA Cup final when Wolves were beaten by Spurs. He played over 500 games for Wolves, scoring 114 goals, before switching to Coventry City but his career ended four years later following a broken leg playing for Bristol Rovers against Southend. He went behind the scenes at Rovers as an assistant before being appointed manager at Walsall who reached the 1993-94 play-offs.

On 21 July,1995 he took over at Cardiff City officially as team coach but to all intents and purposes as team manager. After only a few months in the role he was moved upstairs as director of football when Phil Neal was brought in as the new team manager.

Bluebirds Manager's League record: 26 matches (7–8–11) = 26.9% win ratio.

27. Phil Neal (January 1996–October 1996)

Phil Neal began his much-decorated career at Northampton Town but it was with Liverpool that he won more medals than any other player of the era. With the Anfield club he had eight League titles, four European Cups, one UEFA Cup and one European Super Cup amongst others, as well as winning 50 caps for England. Neal left Anfield after 11 years in December 1985 to join Bolton Wanderers as player-manager and he stayed with the

Trotters for seven years. An infamous spell with England as assistant to Graham Taylor followed before a year at Coventry City.

He joined Cardiff City 26 January 1996 but to everyone's amazement, left very abruptly 7 October 1996 to become Steve Coppell's assistant at Manchester City.

Bluebirds Manager's League record: 29 matches (8–6–15) = 27.5% win ratio.

28. Russell Osman (November 1996–December 1996)

Russell Osman was the son of a former Derby County footballer but it was with his first club, Ipswich Town, that he made his name. He played almost 300 league games for Ipswich and represented England on 11 occasions before moving on to various other clubs. He joined the Bluebirds as a non-contract player in February 1996 making his debut in a 1-0 defeat at Scarborough and appeared in 15 matches that season. He became City's manager 11 November, 1996 after the club had played eight matches with no one officially at the helm but enraged Bluebirds fans when he appeared on a Sports West TV programme commenting on Bristol City and referring to the Robins as 'our' club. He was only manager until 24 December, 1996 when Hibbitt was asked to take over once again and Osman was demoted to assistant manager.

Did You Know...
The shortest official time for a manager at Cardiff City is the 43 days by Russell Osman 11 November to 24 December, 1996

Bluebirds Manager's League record: 5 matches (2–0–3) = 40.0% win ratio

29. Kenny Hibbitt (December 1996–February 1998)

Hibbitt had remained upstairs as director of football but it was no secret that he was equally responsible for team selection along with Osman. It was therefore a surprise when Osman was sacked and Hibbitt re-instated as manager although later events proved that as Hibbitt was on a long contract, it was better to keep him at the club than pay up his contract. A promising position at the end of the 1996-97 season was not maintained and Hibbitt was finally relieved of the post 16 February, 1998.

Bluebirds Manager's League record: 55 matches (16–22–17) = 29.0% win ratio.

30. Frank Burrows (16 February 1998–31 January 2000)

Frank Burrows had left Portsmouth following a number of poor performances and in March 1991 he was appointed Swansea City manager. He had a four-year spell at the Vetch Field before leaving in July 1995 after falling out with the board. He was then on the coaching staff at West Ham under Harry Redknapp before taking over from Kenny Hibbitt in February, 1998.

Under Burrows, City won promotion to Division Two in 1998-99 but lack of finances left the team struggling to avoid relegation and he resigned for a second time at the end of January, 2000.

Bluebirds Manager's League record: 89 matches (30–30–29) = 33.7% win ratio.

31. Billy Ayre (February 2000–August 2000)

Billy Ayre played over 300 league games for a number of lower division clubs before becoming caretaker-manager of Halifax Town in October, 1984, but this lasted only one month before Mick Jones was installed. In December 1986 he returned to Halifax on a full time basis but after failing to lift the Shaymen out of the league basement during his three years at the club he was sacked.

Ayre was soon snapped up by Blackpool and in 1990 was appointed manager, becoming the most popular and successful boss of the Seasiders since the Stan Mortensen days. They won promotion at Wembley in 1991-92 after defeating Scunthorpe on penalties but with the club failing to maintain their improvement at the higher level over the next two seasons, Ayre was replaced by Sam Allardyce in June 1994.

After short spells at Scarborough and Southport, he joined Jan Molby at Swansea City in March 1996 but when the Swans were beaten by Northampton in the play-off final at Wembley, both men were sacked.

Ayre then joined Frank Burrows at Cardiff and 31 January, 2000 he was installed firstly as temporary manager after Burrows resigned and then given the post full time. He had already taken a break from football to have a tumour removed. City were relegated at the end of the season and he stayed at the club even though he was demoted to assistant when Sam Hamman appointed Bobby Gould 25 August, 2000. Two months later he was relieved of all duties when Alan Cork was put in charge of team affairs and Gould became general manager. Sadly, Billy Ayre died when only 49 years old.

Bluebirds Manager's League record: 20 matches (5–8–7) = 25.0% win ratio.

32. Bobby Gould (August 2000–October 2000)

Bobby Gould had a distinguished playing career appearing in over 400 league games and scoring 160 goals. He started at home-town club Coventry City and made his debut at the age of 16 in 1963. After playing for a number of clubs including Arsenal, West Brom and Wolves, he joined Chelsea briefly as assistant to Geoff Hurst but began his full managerial career at Bristol Rovers in 1981. Gould returned to Coventry in May, 1983 but his most famous achievement in management was winning the FA Cup with Wimbledon in 1988. He left the Dons two years later and after various jobs found himself back at Coventry where he remained until 1993.

His appointment as Wales team manager in June 1995 was met with surprise in many quarters and his spell in the job was not without controversy. He quit in 1999 after a 4-0 defeat to Italy. On 25 August 2000 he was made manager of the Bluebirds but less than two months later handed over the duties to Alan Cork after being promoted to the role of general manager. When City won promotion in 2000-01 he left the club.

Bluebirds Manager's League record: 9 matches (2–5–2) = 22.2% win ratio.

33. Alan Cork (October 2000–February 2002)

Alan Cork started his playing career with Derby County but it was with Wimbledon that he made his name, playing over 400 games for the club, including the 1988 FA Cup final, and scoring 145 goals. After ending his playing career at Fulham, he joined Swansea City as assistant to Micky Adams in September 1997 but when Adams left the job after only two weeks, Cork took over until the end of the 1997-98 season.

He returned to management with the Bluebirds 16 October, 2000 and guided them to promotion from Division Three that season. He only lasted until February 2002 when he was fired by impatient chairman Sam Hamman just a few weeks after City's famous FA Cup victory over Premier Division leaders Leeds United. Cork has since worked for both Leicester City and Bolton Wanderers.

Bluebirds Manager's League record: 68 matches (33–18–17) = 48.5% win ratio.

34. Lennie Lawrence (February 2002–May 2005)

Lennie Lawrence never played league football having turned out for non-league clubs, Croydon, Carshalton and Sutton United. He began his managerial career at Plymouth Argyle, moved on to Lincoln City, and then became full-time boss of Charlton Athletic in 1982. He won promotion to the top flight in 1986 and stayed at the Valley until 1991 when he took over at Middlesbrough. After taking Middlesbrough into the Premier League in 1991-92 they struggled, and in 1994 he left the club to manage Bradford City for a season.

Luton Town was his next post and he stayed at Kenilworth Road for five seasons. An unproductive spell with Grimsby came before he joined Cardiff on a consultancy basis as director of football 4 January, 2002 but when Alan Cork was dismissed, Lawrence quickly moved into the hot seat. He took City up via the 2003 play-offs and remained in charge at Ninian Park until May 2005, by which time a fire-sale had seen most of the Bluebirds best players leave the club. He is one of the few people to have managed clubs for over 1,000 matches and was director of football at Bristol Rovers.

Did You Know...
Kenny Hibbitt, Lennie Lawrence and Dave Jones have all taken the Bluebirds into the play-offs

Bluebirds Manager's League record: 151 matches (63–44–44) = 41.7% win ratio.

35. Dave Jones (May 2005–

Dave Jones began his playing career with Everton and stayed on Merseyside for seven years, during which time he represented England at Youth and under-21 level. He left Everton for Coventry in 1981 but suffered a knee injury that threatened his career. After regaining fitness he had a spell in Hong Kong with Seiko before joining Preston for a season but was forced into early retirement in 1984 at the age of 28.

After managing at non-league level, he took over as Stockport County's manager in March 1995, taking the club into the First Division (Championship) and also the semi-finals of the Coca Cola Cup. His achievements at Stockport led to him managing Southampton in the Premier Division from 1997-98 but in January 2000 he was effectively dismissed after being suspended on full pay while personal issues were being successfully concluded.

He took over at Wolves in January 2001 and in 2003 they were promoted to the top flight after winning the Championship play-off at the Millennium Stadium. Due to lack of finance and support, Wolves' stay in the Premier Division never lasted long and he was dismissed in November 2004.

17 May 2008, FA Cup Final. Dave Jones lines up with his team before the kick off

It was in May 2005 that he was appointed manager of the Bluebirds and he used his extensive contacts in the game to bring in a number of players including Darren Purse, Riccy Scimeca, Glenn Loovens and loan-signing Jason Koumas. City finished in 11th place in 2005-06 and Jones continued to improve the quality of players at Ninian Park by signing Michael Chopra from Newcastle United, Stephen McPhail from Barnsley, Roger Johnson from Wycombe and Peter Whittingham from Aston Villa. He also gave Aaron Ramsey his debut in the last game of the 2006-07 season. Even with this influx of players, the Bluebirds finished the season two places lower despite leading the division at the end of November.

Although Chopra left the club in a big-money move to Sunderland, Jones used some of the money to bring three veteran former internationals to Ninian Park for the 2007-08 season. Robbie Fowler, Jimmy Floyd Hasselbaink and Trevor Sinclair all joined the club but league success paled into insignificance as Jones masterminded the Bluebirds' march to Wembley and the FA Cup final. Another mid-table finish in the league was disappointing but with affairs off the pitch looking better, there was every optimism that 2008-09 would see a big improvement.

That optimism seemed well-placed when the Bluebirds firmly lodged themselves in amongst the top six sides for most of the season. New signing Ross McCormack proved to have a magic scoring touch by knocking in 21 league and two cup goals going into the final games of the season. Aided by the return of Michael Chopra and the fine form of a rejuvenated Jay Bothroyd, City looked certainties for a play-off place but only one point from their last four matches spelled disaster and the Bluebirds ended their last season at Ninian Park in seventh place.

> **Did You Know...**
> At the end of the 2009-10 season, Dave Jones had managed Cardiff City for 230 league matches, still well short of third-placed Cyril Spiers who was in control for 284

Jones was determined to go one better as the club moved across the road to the superb Cardiff City Stadium. The season opened with a 4-0 victory over Scunthorpe and the opening two months went well apart from a home defeat to eventual champions Newcastle United followed by a 2-0 defeat at the hands of Queen's Park Rangers.

Jones had brought David Marshall and Mark Hudson to the club but it was the form of Jay Bothroyd and Michael Chopra up front that was proving to be the ace card along with Peter Whittingham who suddenly found a scoring touch that would eventually see him joint Championship top scorer.

The Bluebirds were hardly ever out of the top six and victory at Rangers thanks to a late Joe Ledley header confirmed a place in the play-offs. Leicester City were beaten 1-0 away through a fantastic free kick by Whittingham but the second leg was on a knife edge and the Bluebirds scraped through on penalties with Marshall saving two of Leicester's spot kicks. So the Bluebirds were back at Wembley for the third time in a little over two years to play sixth placed Blackpool but it wasn't to be Cardiff's day and the Seasiders were promoted to the Premier Division by virtue of a 3-2 victory.

For the last few seasons the final league position has improved and Jones will be hoping that the new owners will allow him to spend a little money to improve a squad that has come so near to realising the dream of top flight football.

Bluebirds Manager's League record: 230 matches (90–68–72) = 39.1% win ratio.

230 matches (90–68–72) signifies 230 league matches in charge of which 90 were wins, 68 were draws, and 72 were defeats.

The win ratio percentage does not take into consideration the division in which the league matches were played.

9
Internationals

International players who have appeared for their country whilst playing for Cardiff City

A represents Austria; Alb, Albania; Arg, Argentina; Arm, Armenia; Az, Azerbaijan; Bel, Belgium; Bl, Belarus; Bos, Bosnia; Br, Brazil; Bul, Bulgaria; Ca, Canada; Ch, Chile; Cr, Costa Rica; Cro, Croatia; Cy, Cyprus; CZ, Czechoslovakia; CzR, Czech Republic; D, Denmark, E, England; Ei, Republic of Ireland; EG, East Germany; Est, Estonia; F, France; Fa, Faroes; Fi, Finland; Fij, Fiji; G, Germany; Ge, Georgia; Gr, Greece; H, Hungary; Ho, Holland; I, Italy; Ic, Iceland; Ind, Indonesia; Ir, Iran; Ira, Iraq; Is, Israel; J, Japan; Jam, Jamaica; K, Kuwait; L, Luxembourg; La, Latvia; Lie, Liechtenstein; M, Mexico; Ma, Malta; Mol, Moldova; N, Norway; Ni, Northern Ireland; Nig, Nigeria; Nz, New Zealand; P, Portugal; Para, Paraguay; Pol, Poland; R, Romania; RCS, Republic of Czechs and Slovaks; R of E, Rest of Europe; R of UK, Rest of United Kingdom; Ru, Russia; Sa, South Africa; SAr, Saudi Arabia; S, Scotland; Se, Sweden; Ser, Serbia & Montenegro; Slo, Slovakia; Slv, Slovenia; Sm, San Marino; Sol, Solomon Islands; Sp, Spain; Sw, Switzerland; Tah, Tahiti; T, Turkey; Tr, Trinidad & Tobago; Tun, Tunisia; Uk, Ukraine; USSR, Soviet Union; Van, Vanuata; Ven, Venezuela; W, Wales; WG, West Germany; Y, Yugoslavia

The year indicated is the year in which the match was played. Asterisk shows that player was a substitute.

> **Did You Know...**
> Four Bluebirds were in the Wales squad that reached the quarter-finals of the 1958 World Cup in Sweden. Derrick Sullivan, Colin Baker and Ron Hewitt all played in matches while Ken Jones was the reserve goalkeeper

Wales

Mark Aizlewood (1)	1994: Bul
Ivor Allchurch (12)	1962: S, H, E, 1963: H, Ni, E, 1964: S, E, 1965: Gr, Ni, I, USSR
Colin Baker (7)	1958: M, 1959: S, 1960: Ni, Ei, S, E, 1961: S
Billy Baker (1)	1948: Ni
Harry Beadles (2)	1925: S, E
John Charles (3)	1963: S, 1964: S, 1965: USSR
Mel Charles (4)	1962: Ni, Br, S, H
James Collins (6)	2004: N, Ca, La*, Ni, Pol, 2005: A
Alan Curtis (1)	1987: USSR
Ernie Curtis (1)	1927: S
Len Davies (23)	1922: S, E, Ni, 1923: E, S, Ni, 1924: S, E, Ni,1925: S, Ni, 1926: Ni, E, 1927: E, Ni, S, E, 1928: Ni, S, E, 1929: Ni, S, E
Willie Davies (8)	1925: S, E, Ni, S, 1926: Ni, E, S, 1928: Ni
Steve Derrett (4)	1969: WG, S, I, 1971: Fi
Phil Dwyer (10)	1978: Ir, E, S, Ni, 1979: T, S, E, Ni, Ma*, 1980: WG
Rob Earnshaw (13)	2002: G, Cro, Az, 2003: Bos, Ser*, I*, Fi, Ser, USSR*, 2004: S, H, N, Ca*
George Edwards (6)	1949: Ni, P, Bel, Sw, E, S
Herbie Evans (6)	1922: S, E, Ni, 1924: S, E, Ni
Jack Evans (8)	1912: Ni, 1913: Ni, 1914: S, 1920: Ni, S, 1922: Ni, 1923: E, Ni

Did You Know...
When Wales met Scotland at Ninian Park on 16 February, 1924, Fred Keenor captained Wales and team-mate Jimmy Blair skippered the Scots

Len Evans (2) 1930: E, S
Trevor Ford (10) 1954: A, Y, S, E, 1955: Ni, E, S, A, 1956: Ni, S
Danny Gabbidon (19) 2002: CzR, Cro, Fi, I, 2003: Ser, Ser, Ru, Ru
2004: S, H, N, Ca, Az, Ni, E, Pol, 2005: H, A, A
Chris Gunter (3) 2007: NZ, Ei, G
Alan Harrington (11) 1956: Ni, S, E, 1957: S, 1958: Is, Is, Ni, 1960: S, E, 1961: E, S
Simon Haworth (1) 1997: S*
Ron Hewitt (5) 1958: Ni, Is, Se, H, Br
Barry Hole (18) 1963: Ni, 1964: Ni, 1965: S, E, Ni, D, Gr, Gr, USSR, I,
1966: E, S, Ni, USSR, D, Br, Br, Ch
Ron Howells (2) 1954: E, S
Barrie Jones (7) 1969: S, E, Ni, I*, WG, EG, 1970: R of UK
Les Jones (1) 1933: F
Fred Keenor (31) 1920: E, Ni, 1921: E, Ni, S, 1922: Ni, 1923: E, Ni, S,
1924: E, Ni, S, 1925: E, Ni, S, 1926: S, 1927: E, Ni, S,
1928: E, Ni, S, 1929: E, Ni, S, 1930: E, Ni, S, 1931: E, Ni, S
George Latham (1) 1913: Ni
Joe Ledley (32) 2006: Pol*, Para*, Tr, Bul*, CzR*, Br*, Slo*, Cy*,
2007: Lie*, Ei, NZ*, CzR, Bul, G, Slo, Cy, Sm, Ei, G,
2008: N, Ic, H, Az, Ru, 2009: Pol, Fi, G, Est, Az, 2009: Mon, Ru, S
Andy Legg (2) 1999: D*, 2001: Arm
Jack Lewis (1) 1926: S
Martyn Margetson (1) 2004: Ca*
Graham Moore (5) 1960: E, S, Ni, 1961: Ei, Sp
Jack Nicholls (2) 1925: E, S
Robert Page (3) 2005: La, Az, H
Paul Parry (10) 2004: S*, N, Ca, 2005: Ni*, Pol*, 2006: Slv*, Cy*, 2007: Ni, Sm*,
2008: Ge
Jason Perry (1) 1994: N
Leighton Phillips (12) 1971: Cz, S, E, Ni, 1972: Cz, R, S, Ni, 1973: E 1974, Pol*, Ni:
1975: A
Keith Pontin (2) 1980: E*, S
Kevin Ratcliffe (1) 1993: Bel
Gil Reece (13) 1973: E*, Ni, 1974: Pol*, E, S, Ni, 1975: A, H, H, L, L, S, Ni
Billy Rees (3) 1949: Ni, Bel, Sw
Stan Richards (1) 1947: E
Walter Robbins (5) 1931: E, S, 1932: Ni, E, S
Peter Rodrigues (7) 1965: Ni, Gr, Gr, 1966: USSR, E, S, D
Peter Sayer (7) 1977: Cz, S, E, Ni, 1978: K, K, S
Alf Sherwood (39) 1947: E, Ni, 1948: S, Ni, 1949: E, S, Ni, P, Sw,
1950: E, S, Ni, Bel, 1951: E, S, Ni, P, Sw,
1952: E, S, Ni, R of UK, 1953: S, E, Ni, F, Y, 1954: E, S, Ni, A,
1955: S, E, Y, Ni, 1956: E, S, Ni, A
Derek Showers (2) 1975: E*, Ni
Fred Stansfield (1) 1949: S
Ron Stitfall (2) 1953: E, 1957: Cz
Derrick Sullivan (17) 1953: Ni, F, Y, 1954: Ni, 1955: E, Ni, 1957: E, S,
1958: Ni, H, H, Se, Br, 1959: S, Ni, 1960: E, S

Derek Tapscott (2)	1959: E, Ni
Rod Thomas (1)	1978: Cz
John Toshack (8)	1969: S, E, Ni, WG, EG, 1970: R of UK, EG, I
Nigel Vaughan (7)	1984: R, Bul, Y, Ni*, N, Is, 1985: Sp*
Graham Vearncombe (2)	1958: EG, 1961: Ei
Tony Villars (3)	1974: E, S, Ni*
Dai Ward (1)	1962: E
Freddie Warren (1)	1929: Ni
Rhys Weston (6)	2003: Cro*, Az*, Bos, 2004: Fi, Ser, 2005: H*
Glyn Williams (1)	1951: Sw

Scotland

Neil Alexander (3)	2006: Sw*, Bul, J
Jimmy Blair (6)	1921: E, 1922: E, 1923: E, W, Ni, 1924: W
David Marshall (3)	2009: N, Ho, W
Ross McCormack (3)	2009: Ho, Ic, W*
Jimmy Nelson (4)	1925: W, Ni, 1928: E, 1930: F
Gavin Rae (2)	2009: Cro, CzR, 2009: Ic

Northern Ireland

Tony Capaldi (1)	2007: Se
Tom Farquharson (7)	1923: S, W, 1924: E, S, W, 1925: E, S
Warren Feeney (14)†	2007: Lie, Lat, Ic, D, Sp, 2008: Ge*, S, H, Sm*, 2009: Sm*, Pol, Slv, CzR, Ser
Sam Irving (6)	1927: S, E, W, 1928: S, E, W
Josh Magennis (2)	2010: T*, Ch
Jim McCambridge (2)	1931: W, 1932: E
George Reid (1)	1923: S
Tom Sloan (8)	1926: S, W, E, 1927: W, S, 1928: E, W, 1929: E
Bert Smith (4)	1921: S, 1923: W, E, 1924: E
Tom Watson (1)	1926: S
Phil Mulryne (1)	2005: Ma*
Jeff Whitley (1)	2005: Ma

† *Warren Feeney has been capped while on loan at Swansea City and Dundee United.*

Republic of Ireland

Tom Farquharson (4)	1929: Bel, 1930: Bel, 1931: Sp, 1932: Sp
Ron Healey (2)	1977: Pol, 1980: E*
Graham Kavanagh (7)	2004: Ca, Br, 2005: Bul*, Cy, Sw*, Cro, P*
Alan Lee (6)	2004: CzR, Pol, Nig, Jam, H, Cy

Australia

Tony Vidmar (15)	2003: Ei*, Jam, 2004: Ven*, T, T, Nz, Tah, Fij, Van, Sol, Sol, N, 2005: Sa, Ira*, Ind

Hungary

Gabor Gyepes (3)	2009: Se, Ho, P

Jamaica

Richard Langley (2)	2003: Br, 2004: Ei

Did You Know...

In May 2004, City's James Collins created a new Wales international record when he appeared in a senior international against Norway after being capped at every other level: schoolboy, various youth levels, Under-21, B and then senior

10
LEGENDS

There are many players who have left their mark with Bluebirds fans throughout the years and some of them have achieved legendary status among the faithful followers. Every City fan will have a favourite player but only those with more than 290 appearances and 50 goals are included below.

League appearances date from entry into the League in the 1920-21 season and cup appearances include all FA Cup, Football League Cup, Welsh Cup, Cup Winners Cup, Associate Members Cup, play-offs and the other cup competitions found listed elsewhere.

Billy BAKER

Billy joined the Bluebirds in 1938 and made his debut against Northampton in February 1939 but the Second World War curtailed his progress. He played a number of wartime matches for the club before being called up for army duty but was captured by the Japanese and interned for four years.

On the resumption of League football in 1946-47 Billy became a regular first team member and won his only cap for Wales against Northern Ireland in 1948. He remained a first team player for nine seasons, racking up the appearances, until leaving for Ipswich in June 1955.

Bluebirds record: 325 apps (292 lge + 33 cup) and 7 goals (5 lge + 2 cup)

Colin BAKER

Colin made his Bluebirds debut against Sheffield Wednesday at Ninian Park on the final day of the 1953-54 season. Although he took some time to establish a place in the team, he went on to become a regular over the next ten seasons. During that period he won seven caps for Wales and played in the 1958 World Cup finals in Sweden. He was the injured player replaced when the Bluebirds made their first-ever substitution in the 1965-66 season.

Bluebirds record: 361 apps (298 lge + 63 cup) and 20 goals (18 lge + 2 cup)

Gary BELL

Gary was originally a left winger when signed from West Midlands League outfit Lower Gornal. In his debut for the Bluebirds in 1967 he conceded two penalties as Wolves romped to a 7-1 victory at Molineux. Jimmy Scoular converted him to left back and his career at the club took off. He only missed two games in three seasons from 1970-73. One of the penalty-takers at the club, Gary had a spot-kick saved by Hull keeper Jeff Wealands only to head the rebound into the net. He had a loan spell at Hereford United before joining Newport County in 1974.

Bluebirds record: 291 apps (223 lge + 68 cup) and 14 goals (10 lge + 4 cup)

27 September 1969, Cardiff City 4 QPR 2. Gary Bell in action with Terry Venables watching

John BUCHANAN

After playing for Ross County in the Highland League, John moved south to join Northampton Town in 1970. He stayed four years at the County Ground before moving to Ninian Park in exchange for John Farrington and made his debut against York City in October 1974.

He was a regular in the promotion-winning side of 1975-76 and topped the Bluebirds scoring charts for two seasons, scoring 16 league goals in 1978-79 as City finished in the top half of Division Two. It was during that season he notched a hat-trick in a 4-0 victory over Sheffield United at Ninian Park. He returned to Northampton Town in 1981 after just over seven seasons with the Bluebirds.

Bluebirds record: 286 apps (231 lge + 55 cup) and 67 goals (54 lge + 13 cup)

Michael CHOPRA

Chops was a product of the Newcastle United youth system and signed professional forms in 2000. He joined the Bluebirds in June 2006 for a fee of £500,000 and netted his first hat-trick in January 2007 against Leicester City. In his first season he scored 22 goals to prompt Sunderland into paying £5m and he scored the opening goal of the 2007-08 Premier season.

3 April 2010, Cardiff City 2 Swansea City 1. Michael Chopra wheels away after netting against the Swans

In November 2008 he rejoined Cardiff on a two month loan deal and was eventually re-signed permanently in July 2009 for a fee in the region of £3m. He scored four goals against Derby County at the Cardiff City Stadium and opened the scoring in the play-off final at Wembley against Blackpool.

Bluebirds record: 118 apps (106 lge + 12 cup) and 52 goals (47 lge + 5 cup)

Brian CLARK

Brian will always be remembered as the player who scored the winning goal for the Bluebirds against Real Madrid in 1971, but he started his career with Bristol City where his father Don still holds the record for most league goals in a season.

> Did You Know...
> Brian Clark was the leading scorer for the Bluebirds in three successive seasons, 1969-70, 1970-71, and 1971-72

He switched to Huddersfield Town in 1966 but failed to settle and Jimmy Scoular brought him to Ninian Park for a bargain £8,000 in 1968 and he netted a double on his debut in a 4-3 victory over Derby County. He was the club's leading scorer over a number of seasons, striking five goals in a Welsh Cup tie against Barmouth in 1970.

He was allowed to leave the club along with Ian Gibson in 1972 but after short spells at Bournemouth and Millwall he returned to the Bluebirds in the 1975-76 season to help the club to promotion before ending his league career with Newport County.

Bluebirds record: 267 apps (204 lge + 63 cup) and 108 goals (79 lge + 29 cup)

Carl DALE

Carl played Welsh League football before joining Chester in May, 1988. In three seasons he netted 48 goals in 139 games and the Bluebirds paid £100,000 to bring him to Cardiff City. He scored on his debut at Crewe in August 1991 and went on to form a potent partnership with Chris Pike, leading City to promotion in 1992-93.

Injury problems limited his appearances over the next couple of seasons but he was back to his best in 1995-96 when scoring 30 league and cup goals, including a hat-trick in a 3-2 Ninian Park victory over Doncaster Rovers. His last league goal came at Colchester in 1998 and at the end of the season he joined Yeovil Town.

Bluebirds record: 274 apps (212 lge + 62 cup) and 108 goals (71 lge + 37 cup)

Len DAVIES

Len holds the record for the most goals scored for the club. He joined in 1919 before the Bluebirds were elected to the Football League and made his Division Two debut in the inaugural 1920-21 season in a 2-0 win over Barnsley. The following season he netted 17 goals in just 25 league games including a hat-trick in a 6-2 victory over Bradford City. In 1922 he made his international debut against England and went on to complete 23 appearances for Wales, scoring six goals.

He regularly topped the Bluebirds scoring charts but missed a penalty against Birmingham City in the final game of the 1923-24 season. That miss cost City the Division One championship. The arrival of Hughie Ferguson meant a reshuffle and Len moved out wide where he played in the 1927 FA Cup victory over Arsenal. He continued to be first-choice until 1930-31 when he left to join the ill-fated Thames Association and he was in their side when the Bluebirds defeated them 9-2 for their record league success.

Bluebirds record: 371 apps (305 lge + 66 cup) and 182 goals (128 lge + 54 cup)

Phil DWYER

Phil holds the club record for appearances. He made his debut for the Bluebirds in a goalless draw at Leyton Orient in 1972 and held his place for the rest of the season. He appeared in 76 consecutive matches before injury brought the run to an end. He missed only one match as City won promotion in 1975-76 and then earned the first of his ten Wales caps when selected to play against Iran in 1978.

16 November 1974, Cardiff City 2 Notts Forest 1. Phil Dwyer heads City's opening goal

Phil, or Joe as he was known, was mainly used as a full back or centre half but he also played as a bustling centre forward. In a controversial move, manager Alan Durban allowed him to leave for Rochdale in 1985

Bluebirds record: 575 app (471 lge + 104 cup) and 51 goals (41 lge + 10 cup)

Robert EARNSHAW

Earnie won his first YTS contract in 1997 and became a full time professional one year later. After scoring against Hartlepool on the opening day of the 1998-99 season he was sent on loan to Morton in the Scottish League while he also spent a week with Bryan Robson's Middlesbrough.

29 November 2003, Cardiff City 2 Ipswich 3. A typical Earnie strike on goal

It was not until two years later that Earnie won a regular place in the starting line-up and he responded with 19 league goals before hitting the jackpot in 2002-03 when he scored 31 league goals to beat Stan Richards' record of 30 that had stood since 1947. He also scored another four cup goals to break John Toshack's record by netting 35 goals in a season.

In 2004, with City suffering financial problems, he was transferred to West Brom in a deal reported to be worth £3m and when he scored a hat-trick for the Baggies, he became the first player to have scored hat-tricks in all four levels of English football as well as in an international match. He has since played for Norwich City, Derby County and is at present with Notts Forest.

Bluebirds record: 105 goals (85 lge + 20 cup) in 205 apps (178 lge + 27 cup)

Tony EVANS

Joining the Bluebirds from Blackpool in 1975, Tony made his debut in a 1-0 victory at Brighton in the opening match of the 1975-76 season. He scored 21 goals to shoot City to promotion that first season and was again top scorer the following season including netting all four in a 4-4 draw at Bristol Rovers in a League Cup tie.

Tony was hampered by injury and left to join Birmingham City in 1979 for a £120,000 fee. He later went on to play for Crystal Palace, Wolves, Bolton and Swindon before retiring.

Bluebirds record: 62 goals (47 lge + 15 cup) in 154 apps (124 lge + 30 cup)

Tom FARQUHARSON

Irish-born Tom joined City from Abertillery and made his debut in a 3-1 home win over Manchester United on the final day of the 1921-22 season. He became first choice in 1923-24 and held that position for the next 11 seasons. He is one of the few players to have won caps for Northern Ireland (7) and also the Republic of Ireland (4). He was the last line of defence as the Bluebirds reached the 1925 and 1927 cup finals.

He is reputed to be one of the reasons why the law regarding penalties was changed as his tactic was to charge from out of the back of the net towards the penalty taker. His final appearance for the club was against Bristol City at the end of the 1934-35 season.

Bluebirds record: 519 apps (445 lge + 74 cup)

25 April 1925, FA Cup final. Cardiff City 0 Sheffield United 1. Another Blades attack is beaten off by City keeper Tom Farquharson

Hughie FERGUSON

The Bluebirds paid £5,000 to Motherwell for Hughie who had scored a remarkable 362 goals for the Scottish outfit over a nine-year period. He joined in November 1925, scoring on his home debut against Leicester City, and ended the season with 19 goals from only 26 league games including a hat-trick against Notts County.

In the 1926-27 season he set a new club record with 26 goals in 39 matches and scored the winner in the FA Cup final against Arsenal at Wembley. His prolific run continued until the 1929-30 season when he suffered from injuries yet still managed to score five in a league match against Burnley.

Dundee came in for him and with City short of cash they let Ferguson leave the club but the move ended in tragic circumstances when he took his own life just three years after netting that Wembley winner.

Bluebirds record: 93 goals (77 lge + 16 cup) in 139 apps (117 lge + 22 cup)

Trevor FORD

Did You Know...
The fastest goal ever scored by the Bluebirds came from Trevor Ford just 15 seconds into the match at Charlton Athletic on 23 October, 1954

Fordy's controversial career began at Swansea Town but he soon joined Aston Villa for a fee of £10,000 in 1947. After a successful couple of seasons he joined Sunderland in October 1950 and it was from there that he joined the Bluebirds for a club record fee of £30,000 in December, 1953.

He soon became a firm fans favourite with his bustling style but eventually fell out with manager Trevor Morris after being asked to play out wide. Revelations of illegal payments during his Sunderland days led to him being banned so he joined PSV Eindhoven before ending his career at Newport County.

Bluebirds record: 59 goals (42 lge + 17 cup) in 110 apps (96 lge +14 cup)

Roger GIBBINS

Roger had a number of clubs before arriving at Ninian Park including a spell in the USA with the New England Teamen. He was with Cambridge United before joining the Bluebirds and made his debut in a 2-1 defeat by Wrexham on the opening day of the 1982-83 season. He went on to become the only ever-present as City won promotion and played 91 consecutive league games following his debut.

In October 1985 he joined Swansea City in exchange for Chris Marustik. Spells at Newport County and Torquay United followed but he returned to Ninian Park in March 1989 for a second time with the club. He stayed a further couple of years before going non-league with Newport AFC in 1991.

Bluebirds record: 345 apps (281 lge and 64 cup) and 33 goals (25 lge + 8 cup)

Jimmy GILL

Jimmy scored City's first goal in the Football League. He started with Wednesday but transferred to the Bluebirds in 1920 for a fee of £750. He became top scorer as City won promotion in their first season and scored consistently during the next four years including claiming a couple of hat-tricks.

Did You Know...
Jimmy Gill was Cardiff City's first signing after the club was elected to the Football League in May 1920

After being left out of the Bluebirds side that lost to Sheffield United in the 1925 cup final he decided to leave the club and the following year joined Blackpool. He later played for Derby County and Crystal Palace but his best times were at Ninian Park.

Bluebirds record: 101 goals (82 lge + 19 cup) in 220 apps (184 lge + 36 cup)

Wilf GRANT

Wilf was instrumental in helping the club win promotion in 1951-52 with 26 goals. He joined from Southampton as an outside right but was switched to the middle after Mike Tiddy joined the Bluebirds. He made his debut against Coventry City in 1950 and was virtually ever-present throughout his career. He added another 26 league goals in City's first season back in Division One and was rewarded with an England B cap.

He left for Ipswich Town in October 1954 but returned to Ninian Park in a coaching capacity at the end of his playing career.

Bluebirds record: 73 goals (65 lge + 8 cup) in 168 apps (154 lge + 14 cup)

Cohen GRIFFITH

Cohen became a firm favourite with the fans soon after arriving from non-league Kettering Town in October 1989. The Bluebirds paid £60,000 for his services and it was money well spent. He scored on his league debut at Huddersfield Town, ending the season with ten goals. He was a regular member of the side that won promotion in 1991-92 but was given a free transfer in 1995.

Bluebirds record: 299 apps (234 lge and 65 cup) and 54 goals (39 lge + 15 cup)

Billy HARDY

Billy was probably one of the finest club men never to win a full cap. He was brought to Ninian Park by Fred Stewart in time for the 1911-12 season and he remained at the club until the end of the 1932-33 season. Born in Bedlington, Billy played for Hearts in the Scottish League before moving south to sign for Stockport County. He made his debut for the Bluebirds against Kettering Town in the Southern League and played in 144 matches before the club won Football League status in 1920. He appeared in both City's Wembley cup finals and represented the Football League in 1927-28. His last game for the Bluebirds was in March 1932 when at the age of 41 he played in a 1-0 victory over Gillingham at Ninian Park. He managed Bradford for a number of seasons before becoming a scout for the club.

Bluebirds record: 447 apps (354 lge and 93 cup) and 8 goals (6 lge + 2 cup)

Alan HARRINGTON

Broken legs cost Alan dearly as they caused him to miss the entire 1963-64 season as well as bring his career to a close in 1966. A local lad, he made his debut for the Bluebirds in 1952 in a 0-0 draw with Spurs. He took some time to win a regular place in the starting line-up but once he had done that, he became a virtual ever-present for the next 12 seasons. His career took off when he was switched from wing half to full back after dislocating his shoulder and he won his first cap for Wales in 1956 against Northern Ireland. He later managed at non-league level and still lives in the Cardiff area.

Bluebirds record: 405 apps (348 lge + 57 cup) and 7 goals (6 lge + 1 cup)

Gerry HITCHENS

Gerry signed from Kidderminster Harriers in January 1955 and made his debut against Wolves in the last match of that season, scoring a goal to help save City from relegation. He formed a feared partnership with Trevor Ford over the next couple of seasons and was top scorer in both 1955-56 and 1956-57 but in December 1957 he was transferred to Aston Villa for £22,500.

In 1959-60, Villa pipped City to the Division Two title and Hitchens topped his side's scoring chart with 23 league goals. He scored on his England debut against Mexico but then moved to Italian giants Inter Milan, spending many successful years in Italy by also playing for Torino, Atalanta and Cagliari.

He returned to England only to collapse and die while playing in a charity match in North Wales in 1983. He was only 48 years old.

Bluebirds record: 57 goals (40 lge and 17 cup) in 108 apps (95 lge + 13 cup)

Fred KEENOR

Fred began his schoolboy career as a forward and joined the Bluebirds in 1911. He became a professional a year later, made his debut at Ninian Park against Exeter City in the Southern League in December 1913, and soon made a half back position his own.

21 April 1925 Jack Evans, Joe Nicholson and Fred Keenor keeping fit shortly before the FA Cup final

After twice being wounded during hostilities in World War One, Fred returned to Cardiff and scored in the club's first Football League game at Stockport County. He was capped by Wales, played in the 1925 losing FA Cup final side and then captained the Bluebirds in their 1927 victory over Arsenal.

He was an inspirational skipper, a strong tackler, and one of the reasons why the club became so established after just a few years in the League. He spent 19 years at Ninian Park before joining Crewe in 1931.

Bluebirds record: 446 apps (371 lge + 75 cup) and 19 goals (13 lge + 6 cup)

Peter KING

Peter arrived at Ninian Park in 1960 as part of a swap deal with Harry Knowles who went in the opposite direction. He became probably the most versatile player in Bluebirds history after making his debut in a Division One match at Burnley in 1961 but his early career was hampered by a chest complaint that caused him to miss most of the 1962-63 season. He netted a league hat-trick against Middlesbrough in 1964-65 and scored City's first goal in Europe against Danish side, Esbjerg.

Injury began to take its toll late in his career and after 13 seasons at the club, Peter was forced to retire from the game in 1974.

Bluebirds record: 479 apps (356 lge + 123 cup) and 110 goals (67 lge + 43 cup)

Jim McCAMBRIDGE

Irishman Jim joined the Bluebirds in January 1931 from Everton where he understudied the great Dixie Dean. He finished with 18 goals, including a hat-trick in his first season with City during which he was also capped by Ireland. In the 1931-32 season he equalled the Bluebirds scoring record with 26 league goals. After netting better than a goal every other game, Jim was allowed to join Bristol Rovers in 1933 and he continued to score at regular intervals.

Bluebirds record: 55 goals (51 lge + 4 cup) in 108 apps (95 lge + 13 cup)

Don MURRAY

Don was one of the finest centre halves ever to play for the club. He was only 17 years old when he made his debut at Middlesbrough in May, 1963 and he soon established himself as first choice, a position he held for the next ten seasons. Rarely troubled by injury, the tough-tackling Scot played in 146 consecutive league matches between 1968 and 1971 for a club record. Don played a prominent part in City's Cup-Winners Cup exploits but was always overlooked by the Scottish selectors and only gained one Under-23 cap.

He had a short loan spell with Swansea City in 1974 before briefly joining Hearts in the Scottish League, playing there for a season before rejoining Jimmy Scoular at Newport County where he ended his career.

21 December 1968, Bolton Wdrs 1 Cardiff City 2. Don Murray heads clear

Bluebirds record: 532 apps (406 lge + 126 cup) and 9 goals (6 lge + 3 cup)

Jimmy NELSON

Jimmy was in the famous Scotland 'Wembley Wizards' side but he started his career in Ireland with Crusaders. He joined the Bluebirds in 1921 and soon became a fixture in City's starting line-up. He was ever-present in the season that the Bluebirds were pipped to the First Division championship on goal average. Jimmy had the unenviable record of being the first Cardiff City player to be sent off in a league match when he was dismissed in the last minute at Maine Road against Manchester City on 29 August, 1925. He played in both of City's FA Cup finals and was capped four times by Scotland.

Just before the start of the 1930-31 season, the club accepted a bid from Newcastle United and Jimmy was back at Wembley two years later as skipper of Newcastle's 1932 cup-winning side.

He was the father-in-law of long-serving centre half Stan Montgomery and returned to Cardiff when his playing days were over to become a licensee.

Did You Know...

Jimmy Nelson skippered the Irish Alliance against England and was about to be capped by Ireland when they found that he had been born in Greenock, Scotland in 1901. He was later capped four times by Scotland

Bluebirds record: 295 apps (240 lge and 55 cup) and 4 goals (2 lge + 2 cup)

Jason PERRY

Jason came through the ranks at Ninian Park and made his debut against Exeter City in March 1987. It was sometime before he established himself in the first team but after helping the club to promotion in 1992-93 he rarely missed a match until December 1995 when he suffered a serious injury.

Known as 'Psycho' by the fans, he was back in the side the following season when the Bluebirds were beaten in the play-offs but was then surprisingly offered a free transfer and joined Bristol Rovers.

Bluebirds record: 361 apps (281 lge and 80 cup) and 5 goals (5 lge)

Chris PIKE

Chris began his career in the Cardiff Combination League before moving up to the Welsh League. He joined Fulham but injury hampered his progress and he was allowed to join the Bluebirds on loan in December 1986. He was recalled by the Cottagers but eventually made a permanent move to the City for the start of the 1989-90 season and netted 18 goals in 41 matches. The designated penalty taker during his time at the club, he scored regularly over the next three seasons but left for Hereford United in 1993 after City's promotion to Division Two.

Bluebirds record: 84 goals (67 lge + 17 cup) in 197 apps (154 lge + 43 cup)

Damon SEARLE

Cardiff-born Damon made his first league start for the Bluebirds against Peterborough United in October 1990 and kept his place for the remaining matches that season, going on to make 124 successive league appearances. He netted his first league goal for the club in a 2-1 victory over Walsall in March 1992 but although he represented Wales at Youth, Under-21 and B levels, he never earned a deserved full cap.

At the end of the 1995-96 season he joined Stockport County and later came back to south Wales to play non-league for Newport County.

Bluebirds record: 297 apps (234 lge + 63 cup) and 5 goals (3 lge + 2 cup)

Alf SHERWOOD

Training at Ninian Park during 1949-50 season. L to R: Phil Joslin, Stan Montgomery, Ted Gorin, Billy Baker, Alf Sherwood, Ken Hollyman

Alf signed for Cardiff City in 1941 and played in over 100 wartime games for the club. He made his league debut against Norwich City in the opening match of the 1946-47 season and missed just one game as the club won promotion. The first of his 41 caps for Wales came in 1946 against England at Manchester, and as well as being an ever-present for his club, Alf rarely missed selection for Wales, captaining them on occasions. He also skippered the Bluebirds and led them to promotion in 1951-52.

He was the stand-in keeper before substitutes were allowed and even went in goal in place of the injured Jack Kelsey for Wales against England at Wembley in 1956.

At the end of the 1955-56 season, Alf joined Newport County where he finished a distinguished league career before becoming manager of Barry Town.

Bluebirds record: 379 apps (354 lge and 25 cup) and 15 goals (14 lge + 1 cup)

Phil STANT

Phil joined the Bluebirds in December 1992 when the club paid Mansfield Town £100,000 for his services and he immediately became a cult favourite among City fans with his whole-hearted displays. After a military career during which he fought in the Falklands War, he was bought out of the army by Hereford United. Several league clubs followed until he arrived at Ninian Park where he averaged a goal every other game during his three seasons as a Bluebird.

An ongoing argument over bonuses with City chairman Rick Wright overshadowed Phil's last season at the club and he joined Bury in January 1995 before managing Lincoln City.

Bluebirds record: 55 goals (34 lge + 21 cup) in 106 apps (79 lge + 27 cup)

Gary STEVENS

Gary was playing non-league football for Evesham United when he signed for the Bluebirds in the summer of 1978 for a £4,000 fee. He scored a goal on his first home start against Blackburn Rovers and netted 14 in all competitions in that first season. The following year he was top scorer for the club and again in 1981-82 but at the end of that season he transferred to Shrewsbury Town for a fee of £20,000.
Bluebirds record: 51 goals (44 lge + 7 cup) in 175 apps (150 lge + 25 cup)

Ron STITFALL

Ron joined his hometown club as a schoolboy during World War Two and played in a wartime competition for City when only 14 years old. After army service he rejoined City in 1947 and made his debut at full back against Brentford in place of Alf Sherwood who was away on international duty.

Ron played in almost every position, including up front, and won two Wales caps against Czechoslovakia in 1957 and England in 1962. His brother Albert also played in the league for the Bluebirds while another brother Bob played mainly in the Reserves.
Bluebirds record: 453 apps (398 lge and 55 cup) and 8 goals (8 lge)

Derrick SULLIVAN

Derrick was known as a utility player and he made his debut in April 1948 against Newcastle United when still only 17 years old. He scored his first goal for the club in a 1-1 draw at Barnsley in September, 1948. Derek played in all the forward positions but eventually made a half back slot his own during the 1952-53 season. He made his international debut against Northern Ireland in 1953 and went on to win 17 caps, including playing in the 1958 World Cup finals in Sweden. He left the Bluebirds in September 1961 to join Exeter City but soon returned to Newport County where he ended his league career.
Bluebirds record: 309 apps (275 lge and 34 cup) and 21 goals (19 lge + 2 cup)

Derek TAPSCOTT

Tappy started his league career at Arsenal where he was leading scorer for three successive seasons. He joined the Bluebirds in September 1958 in one of City's best ever deals. He was leading scorer when the club won promotion to Division One in 1959-60 and followed that with 21 goals in the top flight, including a hat-trick against West Brom. He continued scoring on a regular basis and netted a club record six goals against Knighton in the Welsh Cup. In July 1965 he joined Newport County for a season before going into non-league football.
Bluebirds record: 101 goals (79 lge + 22 cup) in 234 apps (193 lge + 41 cup)

Did You Know...
The Bluebirds team coach was on the way to Northampton for a league match in February, 1964 when it was stopped by the police. Derek Tapscott's wife had gone into labour and the police took Tappy back to Cardiff where his wife gave birth later that day

Peter THORNE

When Peter joined the Bluebirds from Stoke City for the 2001-02 season he became the club's record signing at £1.7m. He scored eight league goals in his first season but was ever-present the following year when he scored 13 times. His play-off semi-final winner at Ninian Park against Bristol City paved the way for promotion. Injury restricted him to only 23 appearances in 2003-04 yet he still managed to score another 13 goals. He top-scored the

following year with 12 goals but then became a victim of the deepening financial crisis at the club and was allowed to leave for Norwich City on a free transfer.
Bluebirds record: 51 goals (46 lge + 5 cup) in 143 apps (126 lge + 17 cup)

John TOSHACK

22 April 1967 Cardiff City 1 Coventry City 1. John Toshack misses from the spot watched by Peter King and Ronnie Bird

Tosh's career took off the moment he left the substitute's bench in November 1965 to score in a 3-1 victory over Leyton Orient. At the time he was the youngest player to represent the club. He continued to score with great regularity and netted his first league hat-trick in a 4-2 victory over QPR at Ninian Park in 1969-70.

There was great uproar when the City board accepted an offer of £110,000 from Liverpool in November 1970 and, because of a delay in signing a replacement, the club finished third in Division Two and missed out on promotion.

Tosh went on to have a superb career with Liverpool, managed Swansea all the way from Division Four to Division One, and later took the head job at Real Madrid. He is now manager of the Wales national side.
Bluebirds record: 100 goals (74 lge + 26 cup) in 208 apps (162 lge + 46 cup)

Nigel VAUGHAN

Caerleon-born Nigel began his career with Newport County but joined City in an amazing deal in September 1983 that saw five players change clubs. He scored nine goals in his first season but topped the score chart during the following two seasons. He remained a regular member of the side until the end of 1986-87 when he joined Wolves for £12,000 after a lengthy dispute with the club.
Bluebirds record: 53 goals (41 lge + 12 cup) in 182 apps (149 lge +33 cup)

Scott YOUNG

Scott will be best remembered for his winning goal in the 2-1 defeat of Leeds United in the FA Cup match of January, 2002 but he was handed his league debut when just 16 years old by Eddie May in a 3-1 victory over Stockport County at Ninian Park in November, 1993. He had come through the youth ranks at the club and would go on to serve the Bluebirds for the next nine seasons.

A tough, no-nonsense central defender, his career was cut short through a persistent back injury and he was forced into premature retirement at the end of the 2003-04 season while still only 28 years old.

He attempted a comeback at Newport County but was unable to overcome the injury and became a Football in the Community Officer for Cardiff City.
Bluebirds record: 327 apps (276 lge and 51 cup) and 26 goals (22 lge + 4 cup)

11
Matches to Remember

There were many matches at Ninian Park that will live long in the memory for Bluebirds fans. For some it may be the first game they ever saw, for others perhaps when their favourite player scored, or it could be a famous cup victory. Some games decided promotion or relegation while events in others will never be forgotten. Perhaps these notable matches will bring back some memories.

Did You Know...
The first known colours of Cardiff City were chocolate and amber quartered shirts and black shorts

1 September, 1910

Friendly, Cardiff City 1 Aston Villa 2 (0-2) (7,000)
Bluebirds; Ted Husbands; James McKenzie, John Duffy; Bob Lawrie, John Ramsey, Davy McDougall; James McDonald, Tom Abley, Jim Malloch, Billy Watt, Jack Evans
Scorer; Jack Evans (88)

Aston Villa; Billy George; Arthur Layton, John Kearns; Jeffries, George Hunter, Walter Kimberley, Samson Whittaker, Walter Jones, William Renneville, Walker, Eddie Eyre
Scorers; Samson Whittaker (8), Walker (44)

Aston Villa were the reigning Football League champions when they agreed to play in a friendly match to open Ninian Park. Kick-off was performed by club benefactor Lord Ninian Crichton-Stuart at 5.00pm on a Thursday evening. It turned out to be an exciting game with Villa made to work hard for their narrow victory.

August 1910. A roll call of Cardiff City's first professional football squad

The honour of scoring Cardiff's first goal at Ninian Park went to outside left Jack Evans who would go on to have a fine career with the City either side of World War One. He scored a consolation goal for the Bluebirds two minutes from time after Villa led 2-0 at the interval. He fired in a low ground shot from 15yds after beating Arthur Layton for speed.

9 March, 1927

FA Cup (round six replay), Cardiff City 3 Chelsea 2 (2-1) (47,853)
Bluebirds; Tom Farquharson; Jimmy Nelson, Tom Watson; Fred Keenor, Tom Sloan, Billy Hardy; Ernie Curtis, Sam Irving, Len Davies, Hughie Ferguson, George McLachlan
Scorers; Sam Irving (10), Len Davies (20), Hughie Ferguson (56p)

Chelsea; Sam Millington; George Smith, Tommy Law; Jock Priestley, Harry Wilding, Willie Ferguson; Jackie Crawford, Bert Thain, Bobby Turnbull, Andy Wilson, George Pearson
Scorers; Jock Priestley (45), Bobby Turnbull (50)

The game was played in the background of the General Strike but that did not stop over 11,000 Cardiff City fans travelling to Stamford Bridge for the first match between the clubs which was drawn 0-0 in front of 70,184 fans. The replay at Ninian Park proved to be one of the most dramatic and controversial matches ever played at the ground. The Bluebirds were noted for their short-passing game but they surprised the visitors by also using the long ball to good effect. Only ten minutes had passed when Len Davies's shot struck the post and Sam Irving drove home the rebound. A further ten minutes later the ball was once again in the Chelsea net when Davies sped in to score.

Nine minutes before the interval Chelsea were awarded a penalty but when Andy Wilson ran up to take the spot kick, Tom Farquharson advanced from goal so quickly that he saved the ball on his own six yard line. Soon after the law was changed so that a goalkeeper couldn't move until the kick was taken.

Right on half time Chelsea levelled in unusual circumstances. A shot from Jock Priestley appeared to have drifted wide of the post but the referee signalled a goal, claiming that the pegs holding down the net had worked loose allowing the ball to pass through. This took the steam out of the Bluebirds and Chelsea were level five minutes into the second half when Bobby Turnbull headed home from a George Pearson free kick.

City were now struggling and Bert Thain hit the bar just before Ernie Curtis had to leave the field for attention. When the teenager returned to the action he played on the right wing and with seven minutes remaining crossed into the danger area where Chelsea's Harry Wilding handled. Hughie Ferguson sent the spot kick wide of Sam Millington to send the Bluebirds into the semi-finals of the FA Cup for the third time in only seven years as a Football League club.

1 September, 1928

Division One, Cardiff City 7 Burnley 0 (4-0) (20,174)

Bluebirds; Tom Farquharson; Jimmy Nelson, Jack Jennings; Fred Keenor, Tom Sloan, Billy Hardy; Billy Thirlaway, Stan Davies, Hughie Ferguson, Len Davies, George McLachlan

Scorers; Len Davies (1, 25), Hughie Ferguson (15, 20, 62, 70, 75)

1 September 1928, Cardiff City 7 Burnley 0. The match Hughie Ferguson netted five goals. Back row L–R Tom Sloan, George McLachlan, Tom Farquharson, Stan Davies, Jack Jennings, Jimmy Nelson. Front row: Billy Thirlaway, Len Davies, Fred Keenor (capt), Hughie Ferguson, Billy Hardy

Burnley; Billy Down; Andy McCluggage, George Waterfield; John Steel, Jack Hill, George Parkin; Jack Bruton, Billy Stage, George Beel, Joe Devine, Louis Page

This was City's biggest ever Division One victory and it came on the day that the 18,000 capacity Grangetown Stand was officially opened at the start of the 1928-29 season. Hughie Ferguson struck five league goals for a Cardiff City league record that has never been bettered, while Stan Davies played one of his finest matches for the Bluebirds and had a hand in four of the goals.

No one thought after this first home match of the season that it would turn so sour. But City won only one of their last 16 matches to suffer relegation to Division Two. The club's meteoric rise to the top was over and a poor season was reflected in a big drop in attendances with only 5,738 watching the last match of that 1928-29 season.

30 December 1988, Cardiff City 2 Wigan 2.
Kevin Bartlett goes for a corner with Gareth Abraham (centre) and Alan Curtis (far left)

8 September 1990, Cardiff City 3 Torquay United 3.
Cohen Griffith races past two defenders with Roger Gibbins far left

3 January 1998, FA Cup Round Three. Cardiff City 1 Oldham Athletic 0.
Jason Fowler shoots for goal

19 August 2000, Cardiff City 1 Blackpool 1. Kevin Nugent is congratulated by
Willie Boland and Paul Brayson with Josh Low in background

8 November 2003, Cardiff City 3 Stoke City 1. Rob Earnshaw scoring to set City on the way to victory. John Robinson lies injured in the background

14 January 2006, Cardiff City 3 Burnley 0. Steve Thompson turns, shoots and scores

10 March 2007, Cardiff City 1 Norwich City 0. Chris Gunter clears from Dickson Etuhu with Riccy Scimeca in background

31 October 2007, Carling Cup Round 3. Liverpool 2 Cardiff City 1. Roger Johnson rises above Peter Crouch to win the ball for Cardiff

31 October 2007, Carling Cup Round 3. Liverpool 2 Cardiff City 1. Darren Purse celebrates scoring at Anfield with Joe Ledley and Roger Johnson

29 March 2008, Cardiff City 1 Southampton 0.
Cardiff's Aaron Ramsey takes the ball past Youssef Safri

12 April 2008, Cardiff City 3 Blackpool 1.Trevor Sinclair scores City's second goal of the game

16 May 2008. City players in thoughtful mood waiting for coach at Cardiff General Station L–R: Stephen McPhail, Tony Capaldi, Trevor Sinclair, Joe Ledley, Aaron Ramsey, Peter Whittingham and Darcy Blake

17 May 2008, FA Cup Final. Cardiff City 0 Portsmouth 1.
Aaron Ramsey is consoled after defeat by Paul Wilkinson

25 April 2009, Cardiff City 0 Ipswich 3. The end of an era, the final game at Ninian Park

8 August 2009, Cardiff City 4 Scunthorpe 0. A new chapter begins with an emphatic win in the first game at the Cardiff City Stadium

12 May 2010, Play-off s/f (2nd leg). Cardiff City 2 Leicester City 3. David Marshall gathers as Matt Fryatt tumbles between Mark Kennedy and Kevin McNaughton

P/O final, Blackpool 3 Cardiff City 2. Fans from both sides making their way into Wembley Stadium

P/O final, Blackpool 3 Cardiff City 2. City's Michael Chopra is in tears as he salutes the fans after the final whistle

28 November, 1931

FA Cup (round one), Cardiff City 8 Enfield Town 0 (2-0) (6,321)

Bluebirds: Tom Farquharson; Jock Smith, Bill Roberts; Frank Harris, Jack Galbraith, Peter Ronan; George Emmerson, Albert Keating, Harry O'Neill, Jim McCambridge, Walter Robbins

Scorers; Albert Keating (33, 50, 54) Harry O'Neill (40, 86), Frank Harris (60), George Emmerson (70, 76)

Enfield Town; F Holmes; JE Dyson, J Lawrence; WC Heale, FR Johnson, J Walton; W Green, GB Gaunt,, WS Magner, JT Wilton, SW Irons

City's relegation the previous season meant they now had to enter the competition in the first round. Only just over 6,000 supporters were in the ground to see the Bluebirds register their highest ever FA Cup victory and Albert Keating, who had joined the club earlier in the season from Blackburn Rovers, net the first hat-trick in the competition by a Cardiff City player.

Harry O'Neill scored twice but after failing to hold down a regular spot would later join Swiss side, Berne.

6 February, 1932

Division Three (South), Cardiff City 9 Thames 2 (5-0) (6,698)

Bluebirds; Tom Farquharson; Eric Morris, Bill Roberts; Frank Harris, Jack Galbraith, Peter Ronan; George Emmerson, Albert Keating, Les Jones, Jim McCambridge, Walter Robbins

Scorers; Jim McCambridge (2), Walter Robbins (20, 22, 25, 80, 88), George Emmerson (40), Albert Keating (46), Les Jones (89)

Thames; Harry Bailey; Jim Donnelly, George Smith; Jack Warner, Tommy Pritchard, Riddock; Ernie Brown, Len McCarthy, Len Davies, Charlie Handley, Jimmy Dimmock

Scorers; Len McCarthy (50), Len Davies (65)

Former Bluebird Len Davies was in the Thames line-up that was on the receiving end of City's record league victory. The visitors were on the brink of extinction and it was reported that they could not afford a change of strip for the match against City. Davies came to the rescue and Thames played in ten of his Wales international shirts.

Walter Robbins scored five goals from the left wing to equal the City individual league record while Davies scored one of the goals for Thames on his last appearance at Ninian Park. Also in the Thames side was Jimmy Dimmock who had three England caps and scored 100 goals for Spurs in 400 appearances.

City had dropped to 19th position in the table following three straight defeats but Thames finished bottom and their two-season stint in league football came to an immediate end in 1932 when they were disbanded.

3 May, 1952

Division Two, Cardiff City 3 Leeds United 1 (2-0) (45,925)

Bluebirds: Ron Howells; Glyn Williams, Alf Sherwood; Bobby McLaughlin, Stan Montgomery, Billy Baker; Roley Williams, Dougie Blair, Wilf Grant, Ken Chisholm, George Edwards

Scorers; Wilf Grant (28, 45), Ken Chisholm (58)

Leeds United; John Scott; James Milburn, Grenville Hair; Eric Kerfoot, Jimmy McCabe, Tom Burden; Peter Harrison, Don Mills, Frank Fidler, Ray Iggleden, Harold Williams
Scorer; Ray Iggleden (88)

The match was played on Cup Final day when Arsenal met Newcastle United, but queues started to form four hours before kick-off despite the pouring rain and a huge crowd filled Ninian Park for what proved to be a momentous occasion. In the visitors line-up was former Bluebird Don Mills, while Wales international Harold Williams was on the wing.

3 May 1952, Cardiff City 3 Leeds Utd 1. Wilf Grant shoots past Leeds keeper John Scott to send City into Division One

The Bluebirds went close early on with shots from Wilf Grant and Dougie Blair but they had a lucky escape when Frank Fidler struck the home crossbar with a header. Just before the half hour, Grant settled home nerves when he drifted past Jimmy McCabe and Grenville Hair before scoring at the Canton Stand end.

With the referee about to blow up for half time, Grant struck again with a brilliant individual strike for his 26th league goal of the season.

The Bluebirds sealed the victory needed midway through the second half when Roley Williams centred and Ken Chisholm beat the keeper to head home. The signing of Chisholm for the final run-in had been a masterstroke as he scored eight goals in the last 11 league matches.

Ray Iggleden scored a consolation for Leeds in the dying moments but the scenes when the final whistle blew were incredible as supporters raced on to the field to salute their heroes. Alf Sherwood, chairman Sir Herbert Merrett, and manager Cyril Spiers all took turns to address the fans from the directors box and every City player came out to wild cheers from the massed crowd. The Bluebirds had regained their place in the top flight after an absence of 23 years.

3 September, 1955

Division One, Cardiff City 1 Wolves 9 (0-5) (42,546)
Bluebirds; Ron Howells; Ron Stitfall, Alf Sherwood; Alan Harrington, Colin Gale, Derrick Sullivan; Colin Dixon, Harry Kirtley, Gerry Hitchens, Ron Stockin, Johnny McSeveney
Scorer; Ron Stockin (89)

Wolves; Bert Williams; Eddie Stuart, Bill Shorthouse; Bill Slater, Billy Wright, Eddie Clamp; Johnny Hancocks, Peter Broadbent, Roy Swinbourne, Colin Booth, Jimmy Mullen
Scorers; Johnny Hancocks (1, 10. 35), Alf Sherwood (14og), Roy Swinbourne (19, 55, 82), Peter Broadbent 65, 72)

This was Cardiff City's worst ever home defeat and it equalled the record away win in Division One posted way back in 1908 when Sunderland won by the same score at Newcastle United. Four months earlier the Bluebirds had ended Wolves' hopes of a title win but they exacted heavy revenge in what was City's third home match of the season. Within just 15 seconds, Johnny Hancocks had fired the visitors in front and they led 5-0 at the interval.

It was not until they were leading 9-0 that City scored a consolation goal when Ron Stockin forced the ball home. By a quirk of fate, Stockin had been signed from Wolves a year earlier.

Despite that crushing defeat, the Bluebirds went to Molineux for the return on 31 December, 1955 and took their ground record with a 2-0 win. Wolves were beaten at home for the first time in 1955 and goals from Trevor Ford and Gerry Hitchens gave City only their second away victory of the season.

28 December, 1957

Division Two, Cardiff City 6 Liverpool 1 (5-0) (30,622)

> **Did You Know...**
> Three successive home games during December 1957 brought no less than 18 goals for the Bluebirds. They beat Barnsley 7-0, Stoke City 5-2 on Boxing Day, and then swamped Liverpool 6-1

Bluebirds; Ken Jones; Ron Stitfall, Alec Milne; Alan Harrington, Danny Malloy, Colin Baker; Brian Walsh, Ron Hewitt, Brayley Reynolds, Joe Bonson, Colin Hudson
Scorers; Colin Hudson (5), Ron Hewitt (18), Brayley Reynolds (30, 43), Joe Bonson (32, 77)

Liverpool; Tommy Younger; John Molyneux, Ronnie Moran; John Wheeler, Dick White, Don Campbell; Tony McNamara, Tony Rowley, Billy Liddell, Bobby Murdoch, Alan A'Court
Scorer; John Wheeler (90)

The Bluebirds had gone on to beat Stoke City 5-2 at Ninian Park on Boxing Day after a 7-0 hammering of Barnsley, but no one expected them to continue the goal glut against a Liverpool side pushing for promotion to Division One.

Colin Hudson had spent the morning of the game getting married in Newport and straight after the ceremony raced to Ninian Park along with best man Alan Harrington. The Bluebirds led 5-0 at half time with Hudson on the score sheet and they went on to a convincing victory to make it a staggering 18 goals in three successive home matches.

16 April, 1960

Division Two, Cardiff City 1 Aston Villa 0 (52,364)

Bluebirds; Ron Nicholls; Ron Stitfall, Alec Milne; Steve Gammon, Danny Malloy, Colin Baker; Brian Walsh, Derek Tapscott, Graham Moore, Colin Hudson, Johnny Watkins
Scorer; Graham Moore (12)

Aston Villa; Nigel Sims; John Neal, Stan Lynn; Vic Crowe, Jimmy Dugdale, Pat Saward; Jimmy Adam, Bobby Thomson, Johnny Dixon, Ron Wylie, Peter McParland

16 April 1960, Cardiff City 1 Aston Villa 0. Danny Malloy talks to the crowd after City had won promotion

By March, 1960, Villa and the Bluebirds had opened up an eight point gap at the top of the division but two big home defeats by Portsmouth and Brighton meant that City still needed to beat the Midland side to make promotion a certainty.

The only goal came in the 12th minute when Brian Walsh played the ball wide down the right for Colin Hudson to chase. Hudson was playing his first league match since October and was a late replacement for the injured Joe Bonson. Hudson slipped as he attempted to cross the ball but it ran kindly for Graham Moore who hammered a shot beyond Nigel Sims and into the top corner of the net. Villa were without the injured former City star Gerry Hitchens and though they made a number of forays into the City danger area, the Bluebirds defended solidly.

There were great celebrations at the end of the match but City missed the chance of winning the title when they lost 1-0 at home to Plymouth after Danny Malloy and Brian Walsh had both missed from the penalty spot. Villa finished one point ahead of Cardiff who in turn were eight points clear of third-placed Liverpool.

28 January, 1961

Welsh Cup (round five), Cardiff City 16 Knighton 0 (7-0) (1,800)
Bluebirds; Maurice Swan; Alan Harrington, Ron Stitfall; Steve Gammon, Danny Malloy, Colin Baker; Brian Walsh, Graham Moore, Derek Tapscott, Peter Donnelly, Derek Hogg
Scorers; Derek Tapscott (22, 40, 44, 56, 59, 62), Graham Moore (15, 34, 39, 49), Brian Walsh (64, 85), Peter Donnelly (38, 60), Danny Malloy (78), Derek Hogg (84)

Knighton; Cunnington; I Price, K Price; Crump, Draycott, Francis; G Price, Mayle, Reece, Bodenham, Jones

This was one of the most farcical cup ties ever played when the Bluebirds were forced to put out their first team against the amateurs of Mid-Wales League outfit, Knighton.

City had been fined and censured by the FA of Wales after playing a reserve side at Swansea Town in the Welsh Cup the previous season. City had requested a change of date for the Swans match because they were due to play Leyton Orient in the league two days later but the FA of Wales refused the request and so manager Bill Jones played his reserves. The fact that the Bluebirds actually beat the Swans 2-1 meant nothing to the governing body who imposed a £350 penalty on the club and then ordered them to play their strongest team in all future Welsh Cup games.

The result made a mockery of both the game and the cup competition, because under normal circumstances the club would have played a mixture of first team players along with a number of reserves. To make it even more bizarre, City played some of the game with only ten men after Alan Harrington left the field injured, while for part of the second half, six-goal Derek Tapscott played in central defence with Danny Malloy up front. The six goals scored by Tappy is still a Cardiff City individual record, and of course the 16 goals are never likely to be beaten in a recognised first team fixture.

11 March, 1961

Division One, Cardiff City 3 Tottenham Hotspur 2 (1-2) (45,463)
Bluebirds; Ron Nicholls; Alan Harrington, Ron Stitfall; Barry Hole, Danny Malloy, Colin Baker; Brian Walsh, Graham Moore, Derek Tapscott, Peter Donnelly, Derek Hogg
Scorers; Derek Hogg (11), Brian Walsh (50), Derek Tapscott (51)

Tottenham Hotspur; Bill Brown; Peter Baker, Ron Henry; Danny Blanchflower, Maurice Norman, Dave Mackay; Cliff Jones, John White, Bobby Smith, Les Allen, Terry Dyson
Scorers; Terry Dyson (3), Les Allen (16)

This match was played under the Ninian Park floodlights on a Saturday night after Wales had beaten Ireland 9-0 in an afternoon rugby international at Cardiff Arms Park. Spurs were chasing a cup and league double and they made a great start when Terry Dyson put them ahead early on but it was then that balding winger Derek Hogg came into his own by outwitting a number of Spurs defenders before lashing a shot into the top corner of the net.

11 March 1961, Cardiff City 3 Tottenham Hotspur 2. Alan Harrington keeps Graham Moore away from Dave Mackay after Ron Nicholls is injured. Ron Stitfall and Danny Malloy are on the left

Hogg had been signed earlier in the season from West Brom for a fee of £12,000 and he actually put pen to paper in the TV studios of TWW (Television Wales and West) in front of the television cameras. Spurs were far from finished and before the interval Les Allen restored their lead.

The half time break was just what the Bluebirds needed and five minutes after the restart, Brian Walsh levelled the scores when he prodded home through a crowded goalmouth. The visitors were wilting under the strain and the huge crowd went wild when Derek Tapscott met a cross at the near post and swept the ball home for the winner. Skipper Danny Malloy was superb in a City defence that held out even though Ron Nicholls was given a severe bruising by Spurs players Bobby Smith and Dave Mackay.

The boys from White Hart Lane went on to claim a cup and league double that 1960-61 season, suffering only seven league defeats while the Bluebirds finished in 13th place.

6 April, 1965

Division Two, Cardiff City 5 Swansea Town 0 (2-0) (15,896)
Bluebirds; Bob Wilson; Peter Rodrigues, Gordon Harris; Gareth Williams, Don Murray, Barry Hole; George Johnston, Ivor Allchurch, John Charles, Peter King, Bernard Lewis
Scorers; Ivor Allchurch (6, 19, 75), John Charles (84, 88)

Swansea City; John Black; Roy Evans, Brian Hughes; Herbie Williams, Mike Johnson, Peter Davies; Willie Humphries, Keith Todd, George Kirby, John McGuigan, Jim McLaughlin

This was as comprehensive a victory as the scoreline suggests. The Swans had been struggling all season and although they managed to win three of their last four matches, they were relegated to Division Three just one point from safety. To make matters worse, former Swan Ivor Allchurch netted a superb hat-trick and City's other two goals came from Swansea-born John Charles.

The result helped the Bluebirds to a mid-table finish and a slight improvement on the previous season.

3 May, 1966

Division Two, Cardiff City 5 Middlesbrough 3 (3-2) (12,935)
Bluebirds; Dilwyn John; Dave Carver, Bobby Ferguson; Gareth Williams, Don Murray, Barry Hole; Greg Farrell, Graham Coldrick, George Andrews, Peter King, Bernard Lewis
Scorers; George Andrews (35, 86), Barry Hole (25), Peter King (65), Greg Farrell (29p)

Middlesbrough; Bob Appleby; Geoff Butler, Frank Spraggon, Billy Horner, Dickie Rooks, Andy Davidson, Derrick Downing, Ian Gibson, Jimmy Irvine, Eric McMordie, Gordon Jones
Scorer; Dickie Rooks (7, 27p, 90)

When Boro came to Ninian Park for their last match of a poor season, they needed a win to have any chance of avoiding relegation to Division Three. City required two points to be sure of safety after a run of only one victory in seven games had sent them hurtling towards the bottom reaches of the table.

The game became known as 'Farrell's Match' due to the fact that the Scottish-born winger gave his finest performance in a Bluebirds shirt. The visitors started well and centre half Dickie Rooks headed in a seventh minute corner. Farrell began tormenting the Boro defence and Barry Hole equalised midway in the opening period. Two minutes later, however, City were behind once again when Rooks slammed home from the penalty spot but a handling offence in the Boro area led to a City spot-kick five minutes later and Farrell coolly dispatched it to bring the scores level. The Bluebirds went ahead for the first time just before the interval when George Andrews brilliantly headed home a Bernard Lewis corner.

The second half was all Cardiff, and in particular Farrell as he continually mesmerised the visitors defence with some superb wing play. Peter King made it 4-2 following neat build-up play by skipper Gareth Williams and Barry Hole, before Farrell laid a fifth on a plate for Andrews late in the game. There was just time for Rooks to complete a remarkable hat-trick but despite a determined effort, Middlesbrough were relegated and City had the two points required for safety.

The following Saturday was one of the blackest in Bluebirds history as they went to Deepdale and were beaten 9-0 by Preston. The display was such a shambles that City manager Jimmy Scoular was reported as saying that if he was a Cardiff City player he would be ashamed to walk down the street.

1 May, 1968

Cup Winners Cup (semi-final-second leg), Cardiff City 2 SV Hamburg 3 (1-1) (43,070)
Bluebirds; Bob Wilson; Dave Carver, Bobby Ferguson; Malcolm Clarke, Don Murray, Brian Harris; Barrie Jones, Norman Dean, Peter King, John Toshack, Leslie Lea
Scorers; Norman Dean (10), Brian Harris (75)

SV Hamburg; Ankos Oezcan; Helmut Sandeman, Juergen Kurbjuhn; Klaus Hellfitz, Egon Horst, Willi Schulz; Hans Schulz, Werner Kraemer, Uwe Seeler, Franz-Josef Hoenig, Gert Doerfel
Scorers; Franz-Josef Hoenig (17, 90) Uwe Seeler (60)

A superb performance in front of 65,000 fans at the Volksparkstadion saw City come back from Hamburg with a 1-1 draw. Norman Dean scored an early goal but Helmut Sandeman equalised midway through the second half.

The Germans were strengthened for the second leg by the return of 1966 World Cup heroes, Willi Schulz and Uwe Seeler while the Bluebirds kept the same side. Dean opened the scoring for Cardiff but Franz-Josef Hoenig equalised soon after and there was no more scoring in the first half although Ankos Oezcan was forced to make smart saves from Barrie Jones, Leslie Lea and Peter King.

Soon after the restart, Bob Wilson allowed a speculative shot from Seeler to drift over him and under the bar but City were far from finished. A Barrie Jones corner was headed in by Brian Harris for his only City goal. Exuberant youngsters raced onto the pitch and play was held up while the playing area was cleared. The price of that invasion would become clear as the match drew to a close. Before that however, Dean had a shot cleared off the line as the Bluebirds went looking for outright victory. Under UEFA rules away goals did not count double in semi-finals so a drawn second leg would necessitate a play-off.

Three minutes into injury time, Hoenig tried a 25 yard effort more as a time waster than a serious goal attempt. The shot deceived Wilson and the ball evaded his grasp and nestled in the corner of the net. No sooner did the game restart than the referee blew the final whistle.

Hamburg were beaten in the final 2-0 by AC Milan.

31 October, 1970

Division Two, Cardiff City 5 Hull City 1 (2-0) (21,856)
Bluebirds; Jim Eadie; Dave Carver, Gary Bell, Mel Sutton, Don Murray, Brian Harris, Ian Gibson, John Toshack, Leighton Phillips, Bobby Woodruff, Peter King
Scorers; John Toshack (6, 14, 60), Ian Gibson (67), Leighton Phillips (84)

Hull City; Ian McKechnie; Don Beardsley, Roger de Vries, Billy Wilkinson, Terry Neill, Chris Simpkin, Alan Jarvis, Ken Houghton, Stuart Pearson, Ken Wagstaff, Geoff Barker
Scorer; Geoff Barker (18)

This would prove to be John Toshack's final appearance at Ninian Park and he went out displaying the opportunism that would lead Liverpool to spend £110,000 for his services within a matter of days.

The Bluebirds were near the top of Division Two for this match and they were two ahead, thanks to Toshack, within the opening 15 minutes. On the hour he linked with Bobby Woodruff and netted his hat-trick with a spectacular volley before flicking on Peter King's corner for Ian Gibson to score the fourth. Towards the end Leighton Phillips piled even more agony on the visitors with the fifth but the game belonged to Toshack.

The transfer remains one of the most controversial in Bluebirds history as it undoubtedly cost the club promotion to Division One at the end of that season.

10 March, 1971

Cup Winners Cup (quarter final-first leg), Cardiff City 1 Real Madrid 0 (1-0) (47,500)
Bluebirds; Jim Eadie; Dave Carver, Gary Bell, Mel Sutton, Don Murray, Leighton Phillips, Peter King, Ian Gibson, Brian Clark, Bobby Woodruff, Nigel Rees
Scorer; Brian Clark (31)

Real Madrid; Borja; Zunzunegui, Sanchis (De Felipe), Grande, Benito, Zoco, Amancio, Pirri, Grosso (Fleitas), Velasquez, Perez

Since they first took part in the Cup Winners Cup, City had longed to draw one of Europe's giants and no club came bigger than Real Madrid. Real were one point off the top of La Liga following successive victories over Atletico Madrid, Barcelona and Athletic Bilbao, and none of those sides had even managed a goal.

City had climbed back to the top of Division Two after the 4-0 victory over Carlisle four days earlier but Alan Warboys was ineligible for the tie. Jimmy Scoular selected teenage winger Nigel Rees who defied FA of Wales rules by opting to play for City rather than for Wales against Scotland in a Youth International match in Wrexham.

The flight carrying the Real party to Wales was delayed due to a freak blizzard and that caused a change to their training routine. Senor Santiago Bernabeu, in his 28th year as president of the club, was among the Real party in Cardiff.

The Spanish side rarely threatened the City goal in a match denied the opportunity of flowing by a fussy Belgian referee, Vital Loraux, who blew his whistle for every slight infringement. On the half hour, Bobby Woodruff slipped a pass down City's left flank to Rees. He wriggled past a couple of defenders before crossing to Brian Clark who headed home one of Cardiff City's most famous goals. Mel Sutton and Don Murray had chances to increase City's lead in the second half but the Bluebirds had to be content with their solitary goal success.

A 2-0 defeat in Spain proved the end for the Bluebirds but Real Madrid went on to beat PSV Eindhoven in the semi-final only to lose to Chelsea in the final.

14 April, 1976

Division Three, Cardiff City 2 Hereford United 0 (0-0) (35,501)
Bluebirds; Ron Healey; Phil Dwyer, Freddie Pethard, Alan Campbell, Mike England, Albert Larmour, Peter Sayer, Doug Livermore, Tony Evans, Adrian Alston, Willie Anderson
Scorers; Doug Livermore (55), Alan Campbell (88)

Hereford United; Kevin Charlton; Stephen Emery, Steve Ritchie, John Layton, John Galley, Jimmy Lindsay, Eric Redrobe (Terry Paine), Dudley Tyler, Steve Davey, Dixie McNeil, Roy Carter

This was the meeting of the heavyweights in Division Three with league leaders Hereford at Ninian Park. The Bluebirds were in second spot right behind the Bulls and victory would leave City virtually certain of promotion back to Division Two.

Did You Know...
When the Bluebirds won promotion in 1975-76 they started the season with only two wins from the opening ten games, yet had eight clean sheets from their final nine matches

A huge crowd packed Ninian Park and it was scoreless at the interval but ten minutes into the second period City went ahead with a superb goal. Ron Healey threw the ball out to Freddie Pethard who played it down the line to Tony Evans. The centre forward steadied himself before putting over a chest-high cross which was met by a diving header from Doug Livermore who had run half the length of the field in support of the attack. Once ahead, the Bluebirds controlled the game and two minutes from time Livermore slipped a pass to Alan Campbell who sidestepped Hereford keeper Kevin Charlton before slotting into an empty net.

The Bulls went up as champions, six points ahead of second-placed City and no attendance figure since has matched the crowd that day.

31 March, 1984

Division Two, Cardiff City 3 Chelsea 3 (3 - 0) (11,060)
Bluebirds; Andy Dibble; Karl Elsey, David Grant (Martin Goldsmith), Phil Dwyer, Colin Smith, David Tong, Gordon Owen, Roger Gibbins, Nigel Vaughan, Jeff Hemmerman, Trevor Lee
Scorers; Roger Gibbins (17), Gordon Owen (22p), Nigel Vaughan (24)

Chelsea; Eddie Niedzwiecki, Colin Lee, Joey Jones, Colin Pates, Dale Jasper, Tony McAndrew, Pat Nevin, Nigel Spackman, Kerry Dixon, David Speedie, Mickey Thomas
Scorers; Kerry Dixon (81), Colin Lee (87), Nigel Spackman (90p)

This was a sensational match played in very intimidating circumstances against high-flying Chelsea who would end the season as Division Two champions.

There was a large following from London but they were kept quiet as the Bluebirds overwhelmed their visitors to move into a 3-0 lead with time running out. Kerry Dixon scored what was thought to be a consolation goal for the Londoners nine minutes from time but it spurred Chelsea into action. Colin Lee pulled another back to make the closing stages hectic and the match was in injury time when David Tong was pulled up for an alleged handling offence inside the area. The visitors scored from the spot and City had blown a three goal lead in less than ten minutes.

There were scenes of violence, mainly outside the ground, after the match which possibly would have been worse had Chelsea been beaten.

25 August, 1986

Football League Cup (round one first leg), Cardiff City 5 Plymouth Argyle 4 (1-4) (2,503)

Bluebirds; Graham Moseley; Andy Kerr, Phil Brignull, Terry Boyle, Steve Sherlock, Paul Wimbleton, David Giles (Alan Curtis), Nigel Vaughan, Alan Rogers, Rob Turner, Paul Wheeler

Scorers; Nigel Vaughan (29, 56), Rob Turner (54), Terry Boyle (68), Paul Wheeler (83)

Plymouth Argyle; Geoff Crudgington; Gordon Nisbet, Leigh Cooper, John Uzzell, Gerry McElhinney (Clive Goodyear), John Matthews, Kevin Hodges, Russell Coughlin, Kevin Summerfield (Steve Cooper), John Clayton, Gary Nelson

Scorers; John Matthews (4), Russell Coughlin (22, 38), Kevin Summerfield (44)

Frank Burrows had re-shaped the City side which included no less than six summer signings but they were given a shock when John Matthews struck a 30 yard free kick beyond Graham Moseley in the Bluebirds goal. Russell Coughlin doubled their lead before Nigel Vaughan pulled one back. With the sparse crowd expecting City to push on, Argyle scored a third when Coughlin netted his second from 35 yards and the visitors went in at half time after former Bluebird Kevin Summerfield nipped in to put his side three goals ahead.

The Bluebirds received a stern lecture from Burrows at the interval and a different side emerged after the break. Two goals in three minutes from Rob Turner and Vaughan brought City back into the match and Terry Boyle forced the ball home from an Alan Rogers free kick to square the match at 4-4. Still the Bluebirds weren't finished and seven minutes from time Paul Wheeler rammed in a close range shot to give City an unlikely victory.

In the away leg at Home Park, a freak goal from David Giles saw the Bluebirds through 6-4 on aggregate.

7 May, 1987

Division Four, Cardiff City 4 Hartlepool United 0 (0-2) (1,510)

Bluebirds; Mel Rees; Nigel Vaughan, Mike Ford, Paul Wimbleton, Terry Boyle, Nicky Platnauer, Alan Rogers, Paul Wheeler, Steve Mardenborough (Kevin Bartlett), Alan Curtis, Jason Gummer

Scorers; Alan Curtis (20), Jason Gummer (32), Kevin Bartlett (76), Paul Wimbleton (86)

Hartlepool United; Eddie Blackburn; Tony Barratt, Rob McKinnon, David McLean, Tony Smith, Keith Nobbs, Roy Hogan, Alan Shoulder, John Borthwick (Keith Dixon), Brian Honour, Dean Gibb

Did You Know...

The lowest total for the Bluebirds leading scorer for the season is eight goals by Cecil Smith (1936-37), Elfed Evans (1949-50) and Paul Wimbleton (1986-87)

Crowds were at an all time low and the visit of Hartlepool for the final game of the 1986-87 season registered the lowest ever Ninian Park attendance for a league match. Only one fixture that season went into five figures with just over 11,000 in the ground on Boxing Day 1986 to watch the derby match against Swansea City end in a 0-0 draw.

The average attendance dipped below the 3,000 mark for the first time since the days when City were in freefall down into the basement divisions in the mid 1930s. Finishing in 13th place in the bottom division was hardly likely to inspire the fans but the victory over Hartlepool did bring hope for the following season and that hope was fully justified one year later.

4 April, 1988

Division Four, Cardiff City 4 Newport County 0 (1-0) (6,536)
Bluebirds; George Wood; Phil Bater, Nigel Stevenson, Terry Boyle, Nicky Platnauer, Paul Wimbleton, Alan Curtis, Mike Ford, Brian McDermott, Jimmy Gilligan, Kevin Bartlett (Steve Mardenborough)
Scorers; Nigel Stevenson (37), Paul Wimbleton (66), Brian McDermott (71), Mike Ford (75)

Newport County; David Coles; David Abbruzzese, Ryan Preece, Kevin Hamer, Richard Jones, Steve Tupling, Glynne Millett, Andy Thackeray, Richard Thompson (Anthony Hopkins), Robbie Taylor, Norman Parselle (Simon Morgan)

The Bluebirds lost their next match at Torquay but then won their last five games to clinch promotion, five games to clinch promotion, five points adrift of champions Wolves and seven points ahead of third-placed Bolton Wanderers.

County, who were in financial meltdown, would end the season bottom of the division and dispatched out of the Football League. They were unable to complete their Conference fixtures the following season and were disbanded.

28 September, 1993

Cup Winners Cup (round one second leg), Cardiff City 1 Standard Liege 3 (0-2) (6,096)
Bluebirds; Steve Williams; Robbie James, Jason Perry, Lee Baddeley, Damon Searle, Kevin Ratcliffe, Paul Millar (Kevin Bartley), Cohen Griffith, Garry Thompson, Phil Stant, Tony Bird (Nathan Wigg)
Scorer; Robbie James (59)

Standard Liege; Gilbert Bodart (Jacques Munaron); Roberto Bisconti, Philippe Leonard, Patrick Vervoort (Axel Smeets), Andre Cruz, Thierry Pister, Guy Hellers, Patrick Asselman, Mohamed Lashaf, Franz van Rooy, Marc Wilmots
Scorers; Marc Wilmots (14), Mohamed Lashaf (36), Roberto Bisconti (50)

The Bluebirds were without the injured Nathan Blake and that had resulted in a loss of league form with eight matches having been played since their last victory. With the amount of 'foreign' players now reduced to only three, Eddie May had a selection dilemma which was eased when he brought teenager Steve Williams into goal in place of Phil Kite. This freed an extra outfield place which he gave to Garry Thompson who became one of the three permitted 'foreigners' along with Paul Millar and Phil Stant. Cohen Griffith had fortunately been classified as a Welshman for the European campaign.

The classy Belgians were two up at the interval through Marc Wilmots, who headed home from a corner, and Moroccan international Mohamed Lashaf who was on hand to bundle in a loose ball after City's defence had failed to clear. Early in the second half Roberto Bisconti added the third but the biggest cheer of the evening came when Robbie James smashed a drive into the net from 25 yards. It would turn out to be the last goal scored in European competition by a Welsh Football League club.

6 January, 2002

FA Cup (round three), Cardiff City 2 Leeds United 1 (1-1) (22,009)
Bluebirds; Neil Alexander; Danny Gabbidon, Spencer Prior, Scott Young, Andy Legg, Willie Boland, Paul Brayson, Graham Kavanagh, Mark Bonner, Rob Earnshaw, Gavin Gordon (Leo Fortune-West)
Scorers; Graham Kavanagh (21), Scott Young (87)

Leeds United; Nigel Martyn; Danny Mills, Rio Ferdinand (Michael Duberry), Jonathan Woodgate, Ian Harte, David Batty, Gary Kelly, Lee Bowyer, Alan Smith, Robbie Fowler, Mark Viduka
Scorer; Mark Viduka (12)

This brilliant victory over the Premier Division leaders will forever be soured by the reaction to the end of match celebrations. Comments from Leeds manager David O'Leary only increased the notoriety that Cardiff City received following this match.

The game itself began with Mark Viduka belting a shot beyond Neil Alexander and it seemed only time before the visitors would increase their lead. Up stepped skipper Graham Kavanagh to curl a delightful free kick high into the net beyond Nigel Martyn and it was game on.

6 January 2002, Cardiff City 2 Leeds 1. Scott Young beats David Batty to hook in City's winner after a knockdown from Leo Fortune-West

Leeds were down to ten men after Alan Smith was red-carded for a foul on Andy Legg and the Bluebirds used the one man advantage to good effect. Just as it seemed that a replay at Elland Road was on the cards, substitute Leo Fortune-West flicked a pass goalwards and there was Scott Young to slam the ball in the net for an unforgettable winner.

1 May, 2002

Division Two play-off (second leg), Cardiff City 0 Stoke City 2 (0-0) aet (19,367)
Bluebirds; Neil Alexander; Rhys Weston, Spencer Prior, Scott Young, Gary Croft, Willie Boland, Graham Kavanagh, Peter Thorne (Jason Bowen), Mark Bonner (Leyton Maxwell), Leo Fortune-West, Rob Earnshaw (Andy Campbell)

Stoke City; Neil Cutler; Wayne Thomas, Clive Clarke, Peter Handyside, Sergei Shtanyuk, Tony Dinning (Jurgen Vandeurzen), Bjarni Gudjonsson, James O'Connor, Deon Burton, Arnar Gunnlaugsson (Andy Cooke), Chris Iwelumo (Souleymane Oulare)
Scorers; James O'Connor (89), Souleymane Oulare (115)

The Bluebirds were confident of success after winning the away leg 2-1 though a late goal from Stoke's Deon Burton, a former Cardiff City loan player, would prove decisive.

An almost capacity crowd were on tenterhooks as the score remained 0-0 with just five minutes remaining. It was about this time that an announcement on the PA declared that the City players would be doing a lap of honour after the match to celebrate reaching the play-off final. Sadly, no one told Stoke of this arrangement because James O'Connor, a long-time pal of Bluebirds skipper Graham Kavanagh, scored in the last minute to take the game into extra time.

Cardiff somehow managed to miss out when substitute Souleymane Oulare scored a scrappy goal with just five minutes of extra time remaining.

10 May, 2003

Division Two play-off (first leg), Cardiff City 1 Bristol City 0 (0-0) (19,146)

Bluebirds; Neil Alexander; Rhys Weston, Spencer Prior, Danny Gabbidon, Chris Barker, Gareth Whalley, Willie Boland, Graham Kavanagh, Andy Legg (Mark Bonner), Rob Earnshaw (Andy Campbell), Peter Thorne
Scorer; Peter Thorne (74)

Bristol City; Steve Phillips; Louis Carey, Matt Hill, Joe Burnell, Tony Butler, Danny Coles, Tom Doherty (Brian Tinnion), Mickey Bell, Scott Murray, Christian Roberts (Liam Rosenior), Lee Peacock

The Bluebirds had let a chance of automatic promotion slip by and almost missed out on the play-offs. After holding on to sixth place they were paired with a Bristol City side that had done the double over the Bluebirds that season. In a superbly fought game, Peter Thorne rose high to head the only goal beyond Steve Phillips to give City a slight advantage to take to Ashton Gate for the second leg.

A brilliant team performance with Neil Alexander outstanding saw the Bluebirds book a Millennium Stadium final by holding out for a 0-0 draw. Alexander would go on to become the first keeper not to concede a goal in the three play-off matches.

26 August, 2006

Championship, Cardiff City 2 Birmingham City 0 (1-0) (20,109)

Bluebirds; Neil Alexander; Kerrea Gilbert, Roger Johnson, Glenn Loovens, Kevin McNaughton, Paul Parry, Riccy Scimeca, Stephen McPhail, Joe Ledley, Steve Thompson (Kevin Campbell), Michael Chopra
Scorers; Joe Ledley (12), Paul Parry (75)

Birmingham City; Colin Doyle; Stephen Kelly (Sebastien Larsson), Bruno N'Gotty, Radhi Jaidi, Matt Sadler, Damien Johnson, Mehdi Nafti, David Dunn, Gary McSheffrey, Niklas Bendtner, DJ Campbell (Cameron Jerome)

When these two clubs met, the Bluebirds were lying in second place while visitors Birmingham were top of the Championship. By the end of the game Cardiff City were top of the table and they stayed there until 28 November when they were beaten at Stoke. At one time the Bluebirds held a 12 point advantage at the top but despite 22 goals from Michael Chopra, they slipped away in the second half of the season to finish in a disappointing 13th place.

Did You Know...
The last Bluebird to be ever-present during a season was Joe Ledley who played in all 46 matches of the 2006-07 season

16 February, 2008

FA Cup (round five), Cardiff City 2 Wolves 0 (2-0) (15,349)
Bluebirds; Peter Enckelman; Kevin McNaughton, Roger Johnson, Glenn Loovens, Tony Capaldi, Peter Whittingham (Trevor Sinclair), Gavin Rae, Stephen McPhail (Darcy Blake), Aaron Ramsey, Paul Parry, Jimmy Floyd Hasselbaink (Steve Thompson)
Scorers; Peter Whittingham (2), Jimmy Floyd Hasselbaink (11)

Wolves; Wayne Hennessey; Neil Foley (Darron Gibson), Gary Breen, Jody Craddock, Michael Bridge, Darren Potter, Seyi Olofinjana (Freddy Eastwood), Karl Henry, Kevin Kyle, Jay Bothroyd, Andy Keogh

City's only home FA Cup game during their march to Wembley was over after just 11 minutes. Peter Whittingham started it off in the second minute when he was put through the middle to slot past Wales international Wayne Hennessey in the visitors goal. Wolves had little of the ball during the opening stages and a superb shot from Jimmy Floyd Hasselbaink doubled the lead after only eleven minutes play.

Mick McCarthy's men never looked likely to claw back that lead and the Bluebirds ran out comfortable winners to put themselves just one match away from a Wembley appearance.

25 April, 2009

Championship, Cardiff City 0 Ipswich Town 3 (0-1) (19,129)
Bluebirds; Tom Heaton; Kevin McNaughton, Gabor Gyepes, Roger Johnson, Mark Kennedy, Paul Parry (Stephen McPhail), Joe Ledley, Gavin Rae (Eddie Johnson), Chris Burke, Jay Bothroyd, Ross McCormack (Michael Chopra)

Ipswich Town; Richard Wright; Alex Bruce (Jonathan Stead), Pim Balkestein, Ivan Campo, Matt Richards, Owen Garvan, David Norris, Jaime Peters (Alan Quinn), Giovani, Kevin Lisbie, Pablo Counago (Danny Haynes)
Scorers; Pablo Counago (34), David Norris (51), Jonathan Stead (90)

The last match at Ninian Park and it all but ended City's hopes of making the play-offs. Needing just one point from the last two matches, the Bluebirds self-destructed but when Roy Keane brought the Tractor Boys to Cardiff there was still hope.

After an hour the visitors led 2-0 with City unable to make any headway and in the final minute Jonathan Stead scored to give Ipswich a convincing victory. Defeat in the last match at Sheffield Wednesday left the Bluebirds in seventh place.

Appendix 1. League Records Season by Season

1910-11 4th in Southern League Division Two

Date	Att	Home	Score	Away	Scorers	1	2	3	4	5	6	7	8	9	10	11	12	13	14	15	16	17	18	19	20	21	22	23	24	25	26
24-Sep	8,000	CARDIFF CITY	4-1	Ton Pentre	Peake 2, Watt, Evans	8			3	11		1		4		7	6	2						9			5		10		
08-Oct	4,500	Treharris	0-0	CARDIFF CITY					3	11		1		5	8	7	6	2		9				10		4					
05-Nov	4,500	Aberdare	1-1	CARDIFF CITY	McDonald	8		9	3	11				4		7	6	2				10					5				
12-Nov	6,000	CARDIFF CITY	2-1	Treharris	Evans 2	8			3	11				4		7	6	2				10			9		5				1
03-Dec	4,000	Salisbury City	1-4	CARDIFF CITY	Evans 2, Cant, Pinch			9	3	11		1		4		7	6	2				10			8		5				1
07-Dec	6,000	CARDIFF CITY	1-2	Aberdare	Pinch			9	3	11		1		4				2				10		7	8		5	6			
24-Dec	5,000	Kettering	4-7	CARDIFF CITY	Peake 3, Pinch 2, McDonald, Evans				3	11		1		4		7	6	2						9	8		5		10		
26-Dec	8,000	Reading	0-0	CARDIFF CITY				10	3	11		1		4		7	6	2						9	8		5				
27-Dec	9,000	Stoke	5-0	CARDIFF CITY					3	11		1		4	9	7	6	2							8		5		10		
07-Jan	8,000	CARDIFF CITY	2-0	Kettering	Peake, Ramsey		10		3	11		1		4		7	6	2						9	8		5				
14-Jan	2,500	Chesham	1-7	CARDIFF CITY	Peake 4, Evans 3		10		3	11		1		4		7	6	2						9	8		5				
21-Jan	4,100	CARDIFF CITY	3-1	Salisbury	Peake 2, Ball		10		3	11		1		4		7	6	2						9	8		5				
28-Jan	8,500	CARDIFF CITY	1-0	Croydon Common	Pinch	10			3	11		1		4		7	6	2						9	8		5				
04-Feb	6,200	Croydon Common	1-3	CARDIFF CITY	Abley 2, Peake	10			3	11		1		4		7	6	2						9	8		5				
11-Feb	4,000	Walsall	1-1	CARDIFF CITY	Pinch	10			3	11		1		4		7	6						2	9	8		5				
04-Mar	6,000	CARDIFF CITY	2-1	Walsall	Peake, Abley	10				11		1		4		7	6	2	3					9	8		5				
11-Mar	14,000	Ton Pentre	4-2	CARDIFF CITY	Peake, Abley	10						1	2	4		7	6		3					9	8		5			11	
18-Mar	5,000	CARDIFF CITY	1-0	Merthyr Town	Peake	8	10					1	5	4		7	6	2	3					9						11	
25-Mar	8,000	Merthyr Town	1-0	CARDIFF CITY		8	10		3	11		1	5	4		7	6	2						9							
01-Apr	4,000	CARDIFF CITY	6-0	Chesham	Evans 2, Pinch 2, Peake, Latham	10			3	11		1	5	4		7	6	2						9	8						
17-Apr	10,000	CARDIFF CITY	0-2	Reading		10			3	11	9	1	5	4		7	6	2							8						
18-Apr	6,000	CARDIFF CITY	1-2	Stoke	Ramsey	8			3	11		1	4	6		7		2						9			5		10		
					Appearances	13	5	4	19	20	1	20	6	22	2	21	20	20	3	1	0	4	1	17	16	1	17	1	4	2	2
					Goals	4	1	1		11			1			2								17	7		2		1		

1 Tom Abley
2 H Ball
3 J Cant
4 John Duffy
5 Jack Evans
6 Haggard
7 Ted Husbands
8 George Latham
9 Bob Lawrie
10 Jim Malloch
11 James McDonald
12 Davy McDougall
13 James McKenzie
14 E Milford
15 T Mudie
16 L Nash
17 Tommy Niblo
18 C Norton
19 Bob Peake
20 Charlie Pinch
21 F Powell
22 John Ramsey
23 W Stewart
24 Billy Watt
25 Westall
26 White

Glamorgan League

Date	Att	Home	Score	Away	Scorers
05-Sep	4,800	Ton Pentre	2-3	CARDIFF CITY	Peake 2, Watt
10-Sep	5,000	CARDIFF CITY	1-1	Mardy	Ramsey
12-Sep	3,000	Aberdare	2-2	CARDIFF CITY	Peake 2
26-Sep	1,200	Cwm Albion	1-0	CARDIFF CITY	
10-Oct	6,000	Merthyr Town	1-0	CARDIFF CITY	
17-Oct	1,000	Cwmparc	2-2	CARDIFF CITY	Peake 2
19-Nov	4,000	Barry	1-2	CARDIFF CITY	Niblo, Evans (p)
26-Nov	6,000	CARDIFF CITY	5-0	Cwm Albion	Niblo 3, Cant 2
17-Dec	2,500	CARDIFF CITY	3-0	Cwmparc	Lawrie, Peake, Pinch
31-Dec	1,500	CARDIFF CITY	2-1	Tredegar	Ramsey, Peake
02-Jan	4,000	CARDIFF CITY	5-1	Barry Town	Ball 2, Lawrie, Peake, Pinch
08-Feb	5,000	CARDIFF CITY	1-1	Aberdare	Evans (p)
25-Feb	2,500	Treharris	2-0	CARDIFF CITY	
01-Mar	5,500	CARDIFF CITY	1-1	Merthyr Town	Evans
06-Apr	2,000	Mardy	1-1	CARDIFF CITY	Peake
15-Apr	1,000	Tredegar	0-2	CARDIFF CITY	Watt, Cant
19-Apr	3,000	CARDIFF CITY	2-1	Treharris	Abley, Cant
28-Apr	4,000	CARDIFF CITY	0-0	Ton Pentre	

1911-12 3rd in Southern League Division Two

Date	Att	Home	Score	Away	Scorers	1	2	3	4	5	6	7	8	9	10	11	12	13	14	15	16	17	18	19	20	21
02-Sep	6,200	CARDIFF CITY	3-1	Kettering	Tracey, J Burton, Abley	10			8			11	9			6		1		4	3			5	7	2
23-Sep	4,000	Pontypridd	3-2	CARDIFF CITY	J Burton 2		10		9		3	11	8			6	7	1		4				5		2
07-Oct	5,000	CARDIFF CITY	5-1	Cwm Albion	Featherstone 4, J Burton	10			8		3	11	9			6		1		4	2			5	7	
21-Oct	3,500	CARDIFF CITY	0-0	Portsmouth				9	8		3	11	10			6		1	5	4	2				7	
28-Oct	2,000	Cwm Albion	2-4	CARDIFF CITY	Evans 2, J Burton, G Burton	4		9	8		2	11	10			6		1		5	3				7	
11-Nov	2,200	Ton Pentre	3-4	CARDIFF CITY	Featherstone 2, Evans 2	4		8	10		3	11	9			6		1		5	2				7	
18-Nov	4,000	CARDIFF CITY	0-0	Treharris		4		8	10		3	11	9			6		1		5	2				7	
16-Dec	3,000	Chesham	4-0	CARDIFF CITY	Evans 2, J Burton, G Burton	4		8	10		3	11	9			6		1		5	2				7	
23-Dec	5,000	Kettering	0-2	CARDIFF CITY	Featherstone, Evans	4		8	10		3	11	9		1	6				5	2				7	
25-Dec	8,000	CARDIFF CITY	4-0	Croydon Common	J Burton, G Burton, Featherstone, Abley	4		8	10		3	11	9		1	6				5	2				7	
26-Dec	2,500	Croydon Common	2-0	CARDIFF CITY		4		8	10		3	11	9		1	6								5	7	2
13-Jan	5,000	CARDIFF CITY	3-1	Aberdare	Thompson, Featherstone, G Burton	4		8	10		2	11	9		1					5				6	7	3
20-Jan	6,000	CARDIFF CITY	1-1	Mardy	Featherstone	4		8	10		2	11	9		1	6				5					7	3
27-Jan	4,000	Aberdare	0-2	CARDIFF CITY	Evans, G Burton	4		8	10		2	11	9		1	6				5					7	3
10-Feb	7,000	CARDIFF CITY	3-0	Ton Pentre	Tracey 2, Lawrie	4		8	10		2	11	9		1	6				5					7	3
17-Feb	11,000	Portsmouth	3-2	CARDIFF CITY	Tracey, Evans	4		8	10		2	11	9		1	6				5					7	3
24-Feb	14,000	CARDIFF CITY	1-2	Merthyr Town	Evans			8	10		2	11	9		1	6				5				4	7	3
29 Feb	2,000	Mardy	0-1	CARDIFF CITY	Douglas	4		8	10	9	2	11				6		1				5			7	3
09-Mar	2,000	CARDIFF CITY	5-0	Chesham	Douglas 3, Tracey, Abley	4		8	10	9	2	11				6		1		5					7	3
16-Mar	7,100	CARDIFF CITY	0-0	Pontypridd		4			10	9	2	11	8			6		1				5			7	3
18-Mar	4,000	Walsall	0-3	CARDIFF CITY	G Burton 2, Duffy	4		8	10	9	2	11				6		1		5					7	3
05-Apr	10,000	CARDIFF CITY	0-2	Southend		8		9	10	2		11						1		4		5		6	7	3
06-Apr	9,000	Merthyr Town	2-0	CARDIFF CITY		4		9	10	3				11				1	2			5	8	6	7	
10-Apr	5,000	CARDIFF CITY	5-1	Walsall	Pinch 2, G Burton, Tracey, J Burton	4		9	10	2				11				1	3	5			8	6	7	
24-Apr	2,000	Southend United	0-1	CARDIFF CITY	Featherstone	4		8	10	2		11	9			6		1						5	7	3
27-Apr	2,000	Treharris	2-0	CARDIFF CITY		4		8	10	2			9	11	1	6								5	7	3
					Appearances	23	1	22	26	9	20	23	20	3	10	22	1	16	3	20	9	4	2	11	25	16
					Goals	3		8	8	4	1	10	11							1			2	1	6	

1 Tom Abley
2 J Bates
3 George Burton
4 John Burton
5 W Douglas
6 John Duffy
7 Jack Evans
8 Harry Featherstone
9 Billy Gaughan
10 George Germaine
11 Billy Hardy
12 J Hiftle
13 Ted Husbands
14 George Latham
15 Bob Lawrie
16 Bob Leah
17 L Newton
18 Charlie Pinch
19 Eddie Thompson
20 Harry Tracey
21 Arthur Waters

1912-13 Champions of Southern League Division Two (Promoted)

Date	Att	Home	Score	Away	Scorers	1	2	3	4	5	6	7	8	9	10	11	12	13	14	15	16	17	18	19	20	21	22	23	24
07-Sep	8,000	Swansea Town	1-1	CARDIFF CITY	J Burton				8			2				11	9		6	4		10	1		3			5	7
12-Sep	4,000	Mid Rhondda	0-1	CARDIFF CITY	Keggans				8	5				2		11	9		6	4		10	1		3				7
14-Sep	8,000	CARDIFF CITY	2-0	Newport County	Tracey, Featherstone				8	5				2		11	9		6	4		10	1		3				7
21-Sep	6,000	Ton Pentre	0-1	CARDIFF CITY	J Burton				8	5				2	9			11	6	4		10	1		3				7
28-Sep	7,000	CARDIFF CITY	3-1	Croydon Common	J Burton 2, Keggans				8	5			9	2		11			6	4		10	1		3				7
05-Oct	2,000	Treharris	0-2	CARDIFF CITY	Keggans, Devlin				8	5			9	2		11			6	4		10	1		3				7
19-Oct	6,500	CARDIFF CITY	5-2	Mardy	J Burton, G Burton, Cassidy, Evans, Devlin	6		8	10	5			9	2		11				4			1		3				7
09-Nov	6,000	Croydon Common	1-2	CARDIFF CITY	G Burton, Evans			8	10	5				2		11	9		6	4			1		3				7
07-Dec	8,000	CARDIFF CITY	2-1	Treharris	Tracey, Cassidy			8	10	5			9	2	1	11			6	4					3				7
21-Dec	8,000	CARDIFF CITY	1-0	Southend United	Evans			8	10	5			9	2		11			6	4			1		3				7
25-Dec	11,000	CARDIFF CITY	1-1	Pontypridd	Featherstone			8	10	5				2		11	9		6	4			1		3				7
26-Dec	6,000	Luton Town	2-0	CARDIFF CITY				8	10	5				2		11	9		6	4			1		3				7
01-Jan	3,000	CARDIFF CITY	5-0	Llanelly	J Burton 2, Featherstone 2, Devlin				10	5			9	2		11	8		6	4			1		3				7
15-Jan	3,000	CARDIFF CITY	9-0	Ton Pentre	Devlin 3, Tracey 2, Cassidy 2, J Burton, Evans				10	5			9	2		11	8		6	4			1		3				7
08-Feb	8,000	Newport County	1-3	CARDIFF CITY	G Burton, Cassidy, Tracey			10		5			9	2		11	8		6	4			1		3				7
12-Feb	4,000	CARDIFF CITY	3-0	Aberdare	Harvey, Tracey, Devlin				10	5			9	2		11	8		6	4			1		3				7
22-Feb	7,000	Southend United	1-1	CARDIFF CITY	G Burton		7	8	10	5	9			2					6	4			1		3				11
01-Mar	6,000	CARDIFF CITY	1-0	Mid Rhondda	G Burton			8	10	5	9			2		11			6	4			1		3				7
08-Mar	3,000	Mardy	1-2	CARDIFF CITY	G Burton, Clarke			8	10	5	9			2		11			6		7		1	3			4		
15-Mar	10,000	CARDIFF CITY	0-0	Swansea Town				8		5	10		9	2		11			6	4	7		1		3				
21-Mar	22,000	CARDIFF CITY	3-0	Luton Town	J Burton 2, G Burton			8	10	5			9	2		11			6	4			1		3				7
24-Mar	7,500	Pontypridd	1-1	CARDIFF CITY	Hardy		7	8	10	5			9	2		11			6	4			1		3				
29-Mar	1,500	Llanelly	0-2	CARDIFF CITY	J Burton, Devlin			8	10	5			9			11			6	4			1	2	3				7
05-Apr	2,000	Aberdare	2-3	CARDIFF CITY	Devlin, Evans, G Burton			10	8	5			9	2		11			6	4			1		3				7
					Appearances	1	2	15	22	23	4	1	14	22	2	22	10	1	23	23	2	6	23	2	23	0	1	1	21
					Goals			8	11	5	1		9			5	4		1	1		3							6

1 Tom Abley
2 J Bennett
3 George Burton
4 John Burton
5 Pat Cassidy
6 J Clarke
7 R Croft
8 Billy Devlin
9 Tommy Doncaster
10 W Douglas
11 Jack Evans
12 Harry Featherstone
13 Billy Gaughan
14 Billy Hardy
15 Henry Harvey
16 A Holt
17 Harry Keggans
18 Jack Kneeshaw
19 George Latham
20 Bob Leah
21 Lewis
22 C McKechnie
23 L Saunders
24 Harry Tracey

Southern Alliance

Date	Att	Home	Score	Away	Scorers
03-Oct		Millwall	3-2	CARDIFF CITY	J Burton, Evans, Devlin
23-Oct		Brighton	4-1	CARDIFF CITY	Evans
12-Nov		CARDIFF CITY	1-2	Southampton	J Burton
20-Nov		CARDIFF CITY	4-2	Brentford	G Burton, Tracey, Featherstone, og
11-Dec	500	Southampton	3-1	CARDIFF CITY	Devlin
01-Feb	3,000	CARDIFF CITY	1-1	Portsmouth	Featherstone
05-Feb		Croydon Common	3-0	CARDIFF CITY	
26-Feb	3,500	CARDIFF CITY	0-1	Brighton	
12-Mar	5,000	CARDIFF CITY	1-2	Croydon Common	Holt
22-Mar		CARDIFF CITY	1-1	Southend United	J Burton
09-Apr		CARDIFF CITY	3-2	Millwall	Tracey 2, Clarke
12-Apr		Southend United	1-0	CARDIFF CITY	
14-Apr		Brentford	4-2	CARDIFF CITY	Bennett, Evans
19-Apr		Luton Town	2-0	CARDIFF CITY	
23-Apr	2,000	Portsmouth	3-1	CARDIFF CITY	Devlin
26-Apr		CARDIFF CITY	5-2	Luton Town	Devlin 2, G Burton 2, Hardy

1913-14 10th in Southern League Division One

Date	Att	Home	Score	Away	Scorers	1	2	3	4	5	6	7	8	9	10	11	12	13	14	15	16	17	18	19	20	21	22	23	24	25	26	27	28
01-Sep	7,000	Bristol Rovers	1-0	CARDIFF CITY				8	10	5			9	2	11		6	4		7			12	1	3								
06-Sep	13,463	Plymouth Argyle		CARDIFF CITY	Harvey				10	5			9	2	11		6	4		7			8	1	3								
13-Sep	15,000	CARDIFF CITY		Southampton	Devlin				10	5			9	2	11	3	6	4					8	1						7			
20-Sep	4,000	Reading	1-0	CARDIFF CITY				8	10	5			9	2	11		6	4						1	3					7			
27-Sep	12,000	CARDIFF CITY		Crystal Palace	Devlin			8	10	5			9	2	11		6	4		7				1	3								
04-Oct	7,000	Coventry City		CARDIFF CITY	Robertson 2	7			10	5				2	11		6	4	8					1	3		9						
11-Oct	14,000	CARDIFF CITY	2-0	Watford	Robertson, Henderson	7				5	11		10	2			6	4	8					1	3		9						
18-Oct	7,000	Norwich City		CARDIFF CITY	Robertson 2	7			10	5				2	11		6	4	8					1	3		9						
25-Oct	13,000	CARDIFF CITY	2-0	Gillingham	Henderson, Evans	7			10	5				2	11		6	4	8					1	3		9						
01-Nov	6,000	Northampton Town		CARDIFF CITY	J Burton	7		9	10					2	11		6	4	8					1	3	5							
08-Nov	14,500	CARDIFF CITY	3-0	Southend United	Hopkins 2, Harvey	7			10					2	11		6	4	8		9			1	3	5							
15-Nov	7,000	Brighton		CARDIFF CITY	Hopkins	7			10					2	11		6	4	8		9			1	3	5							
22-Nov	15,000	CARDIFF CITY		Portsmouth	J Burton	7			10	5			9	2	11		6	4	8					1									3
06-Dec	8,000	CARDIFF CITY		Exeter City	Hopkins					5	11		7	2			3	4			9	6					8		1		10		
13-Dec	12,000	CARDIFF CITY	3-0	QPR	G West 3					5			8	2	11		6	4			9				3				1	7	10		
20-Dec	10,000	Swindon Town		CARDIFF CITY	G West, Devlin		2			5		4	9		11		6				8				3				1	7	10		
25-Dec	20,000	CARDIFF CITY		Merthyr Town	Evans		2			5			9		11		6	4			8				3				1	7	10		
26-Dec	12,000	Merthyr Town		CARDIFF CITY	J Burton, Hopkins		3		8	5		4		2	11		6				9								1	7	10		
27-Dec	27,000	CARDIFF CITY		Plymouth Argyle	G West, Tracey				8			4		2	11		5				9	6			3				1	7	10		
01-Jan	16,000	CARDIFF CITY	2-0	Bristol Rovers	J Burton, G West		3		8	5	11	4		2			6				9								1	7	10		
03-Jan	9,000	Southampton	2-0	CARDIFF CITY			3		8	5		4		2	11		6				9								1	7	10		
17-Jan	13,000	CARDIFF CITY	1-0	Reading	G West		3			5			8	2	11		6	4	7		9								1		10		
24-Jan	11,000	Crystal Palace	4-0	CARDIFF CITY			3			5			8	2	11		6	4	7		9								1		10		
07-Feb	8,500	CARDIFF CITY		Coventry City	Harvey, G West		3		8	5				2	11		6	4	7		9								1		10		
14-Feb	4,000	Watford		CARDIFF CITY	Cassidy, Hopkins		2			5					11		6	4	8		9				3			7	1		10		
21-Feb	14,000	CARDIFF CITY	3-0	Norwich City	J Burton, Robertson, G West		2	8		5					11		6	4							3		9	7	1		10		
28-Feb	8,000	Gillingham	0-0	CARDIFF CITY			2			5	11	4					6				8				3		9	7	1		10		
07-Mar	12,000	CARDIFF CITY	0-0	Northampton Town			2			5					11		6	4			8				3		9	7	1		10		
14-Mar	12,000	Southend United		CARDIFF CITY	G West		2			5					11		6	4			8				3		9	7	1		10		
21-Mar	12,000	CARDIFF CITY	0-0	Brighton			2			5			8	3	11		6	4			9							7	1		10		
28-Mar	12,470	Portsmouth		CARDIFF CITY	Evans		2			5			8	3	11		6	4									9	7	1		10		
04-Apr	9,000	Millwall	3-0	CARDIFF CITY			2			5			8	3	11		6	4			9							7	1		10		
10-Apr	20,000	CARDIFF CITY	2-0	West Ham United	Devlin 2		2			5			9	3	11		6	4						1				7			10	8	
11-Apr	5,000	Exeter City	0-1	CARDIFF CITY	Devlin		2			5			9	3	11		6	4						1				7			10	8	
13-Apr	15,000	West Ham United		CARDIFF CITY	Doncaster		2		8	5				3	11		6	4			9			1				7			10		
18-Apr	10,000	QPR	0-2	CARDIFF CITY	Evans, JF West		2			5				3	11		6	4									9	7	1		10	8	
25-Apr	25,000	CARDIFF CITY	0-0	Swindon Town			2			5			9	3	11		6	4										7	1		10	8	
29-Apr	6,500	CARDIFF CITY	0-0	Millwall			2							3	11		6	4			9	5						7	1		10	8	
						8	22	5	18	33	4	6	19	31	34	1	38	32	12	3	21	3	3	16	20	3	11	14	22	9	25	5	1
									5	1			6	1	4			3	2		6						6			1	10	1	

1 J Bennett
2 Charlie Brittan
3 George Burton
4 Jack Burton
5 Pat Cassidy
6 J Clarke
7 Billy Davidson
8 Billy Devlin
9 Tommy Doncaster
10 Jack Evans
11 Harry Featherstone
12 Billy Hardy
13 Henry Harvey
14 John Henderson
15 A Holt
16 L Hopkins
17 Fred Keenor
18 Harry Keggans
19 Jack Kneeshaw
20 Bob Leah
21 K McKenzie
22 T Robertson
23 T Seymour
24 J Stephenson
25 Harry Tracey
26 George West
27 JF West
28 Tom Witts

1914-15 3rd in Southern League Division One

Date	Att	Home	Score	Away	Scorers	1	2	3	4	5	6	7	8	9	10	11	12	13	14	15	16	17	18	19	20	21
02-Sep	8,000	Watford	2-1	CARDIFF CITY	Cassidy		7	2			5				11		6	4		9		1	3		10	8
05-Sep	8,000	CARDIFF CITY	1-0	Norwich City	Evans		7	2			5				11		6	4		9	8	1	3			10
12-Sep	6,000	Gillingham	1-1	CARDIFF CITY	J Burton		7	2		9	5				11		6	4	8			1	3			10
19-Sep	10,000	CARDIFF CITY	0-1	Brighton			7	2		9					11		6	4	8		5	1	3			10
26-Sep	9,000	Crystal Palace	0-2	CARDIFF CITY	Evans, Hopkins		7	2			5				11	8	6			9	4	1	3			10
03-Oct	3,000	Exeter City	2-0	CARDIFF CITY			7	2			5				11	8	6			9	4	1	3			10
10-Oct	8,000	CARDIFF CITY	3-0	Luton Town	G West, Hopkins, Cassidy		7	2			5				11	8	6			9	4	1	3		10	
17-Oct	16,887	Portsmouth	0-1	CARDIFF CITY	G West		7	2			5				11	8	6	4		9		1	3		10	
24-Oct	16,000	CARDIFF CITY	3-0	Swindon Town	G West, Evans, Cassidy		7	2			5				11	8	6	4		9		1	3		10	
31-Oct	7,000	Southend United	2-1	CARDIFF CITY	Beare		7				5		9	2	11	8	6	4				1	3		10	
07-Nov	9,000	CARDIFF CITY	2-0	QPR	Beare, Evans		7	2			5		9		11	8	6	4				1	3		10	
14-Nov	6,000	Millwall	2-1	CARDIFF CITY	Beare		7	2			5				11	8	6	4		9		1	3		10	
21-Nov	10,000	CARDIFF CITY	7-0	Bristol Rovers	Devlin 3, Evans, Goddard, G West, Beare		7	2			5		9		11	8	6	4				1	3		10	
28-Nov	2,000	Croydon Common	0-1	CARDIFF CITY	Cassidy		7	2			5		9		11	8	6	4				1	3		10	
05-Dec	12,000	CARDIFF CITY	3-2	Reading	Devlin 2, og		7	2			5		9		11	8	6	4				1	3		10	
12-Dec	8,000	Southampton	1-1	CARDIFF CITY	G West		7	2			5		9		11	8	6	4				1	3		10	
19-Dec	12,000	CARDIFF CITY	5-0	Northampton Town	Devlin 2, Goddard 2, Beare		7	2			5		9	3	11	8	6	4				1			10	
25-Dec	8,000	Plymouth Argyle	2-0	CARDIFF CITY			7	2			5		9	3	11	8	6	4				1			10	
26-Dec	9,000	CARDIFF CITY	2-0	Plymouth Argyle	Goddard, Beare		7	2			5		9		11	8	6	4				1	3		10	
01-Jan	1,900	CARDIFF CITY	2-3	Watford	Evans, Beare		7	2			5		9		11	8	6	4				1	3		10	
02-Jan	4,000	Norwich City	2-1	CARDIFF CITY	Beare		7	2					9		11		6	4	8		5	1	3		10	
16-Jan	8,000	CARDIFF CITY	3-1	Gillingham	G West 2, Devlin		7	2			5		9	3	11	8	6	4				1			10	
23-Jan	6,000	Brighton	2-1	CARDIFF CITY	Evans	10	7	2							11	8	6	4			5	1	3		9	
30-Jan	10,000	CARDIFF CITY	5-0	Crystal Palace	G West 2, Barnett, Beare, Evans	10	7	2							11	8	6	4			5	1	3		9	
06-Feb	5,000	CARDIFF CITY	1-0	Exeter City	Barnett	10	7							2	11	8	6	4			5	1	3		9	
13-Feb	9,000	Luton Town	2-1	CARDIFF CITY	G West	10	7				5		8	2	11		6				4		3	1	9	
20-Feb	6,000	CARDIFF CITY	3-2	Portsmouth	Barnett, Keenor, Evans	10	7				5			2	11	8	6				4	1	3		9	
27-Feb	5,000	Swindon Town	0-0	CARDIFF CITY		10	7	2			5				11	8	6	4			9	1	3			
06-Mar	10,000	CARDIFF CITY	3-0	Southend United	Goddard, Keenor, Evans	10	7	2			5				11	8	6	4			9	1	3			
13-Mar	7,000	QPR	3-0	CARDIFF CITY		10	7	2				5			11	8	6	4			9	1	3			
20-Mar	11,000	CARDIFF CITY	4-1	Millwall	Hopkins 3, Goddard	10			7		5				11	8	2	4		9	6	1	3			
27-Mar	11,000	Bristol Rovers	0-1	CARDIFF CITY	Beare	10	7	2							11	8	6	4		9	5	1	3			
02-Apr	10,000	West Ham United	2-1	CARDIFF CITY	Goddard	10	7	2							11	8	6	4		9	5	1	3			
03-Apr	9,000	CARDIFF CITY	1-0	Croydon Common	G West	10	7				5				11		2	4		9	6	1	3		8	
05-Apr	13,000	CARDIFF CITY	1-2	West Ham United	Barnett, Goddard	10	11	2	7		5					8		4			6	1	3		9	
10-Apr	6,000	Reading	1-2	CARDIFF CITY	Evans, G West	10	7	2							11	8	6	4			5	1	3		9	
17-Apr	12,000	CARDIFF CITY	1-1	Southampton	Barnett	10	7	2							11	8	6	4			5	1	3		9	
24-Apr	5,000	Northampton Town	2-5	CARDIFF CITY	Barnett, Evans, G West, Beare, Cassidy	10	7	2			5				11	8	6	4				1	3		9	
					Appearances	16	37	32	2	2	28	1	13	7	37	31	37	33	3	12	21	37	35	1	27	6
					Goals	6	11			1	5		8		12	8				5	2				13	

1 Albert Barnett
2 George Beare
3 Charlie Brittan
4 George Burton
5 Jack Burton
6 Pat Cassidy
7 Billy Davidson
8 Billy Devlin
9 Tommy Doncaster
10 Jack Evans
11 A Goddard
12 Billy Hardy
13 Henry Harvey
14 John Henderson
15 L Hopkins
16 Fred Keenor
17 Jack Kneeshaw
18 Arthur Layton
19 J Stephenson
20 George West
21 JF West

1919-20 4th in Southern League Division One

Date	Att	Home	Score	Away	Scorers	1	2	3	4	5	6	7	8	9	10	11	12	13	14	15	16	17	18	19	20	21	22	23
30-Aug	8,000	Reading	2-0	CARDIFF CITY			7	2		5					11	8		4				10	6	1	3			9
01-Sep	6,000	Bristol Rovers	4-4	CARDIFF CITY	Grimshaw 2, Jones, Evans		7	2							11	8		4		9		10	6	1	3	5		
06-Sep	11,000	CARDIFF CITY	3-0	Southampton	Keenor, West, Evans		7	2							11	8	6	4					9	1	3	5		10
08-Sep	7,500	CARDIFF CITY	0-0	Bristol Rovers			7	2						8	11	10	6	4					9	1	3	5		
13-Sep	10,000	Luton Town	2-2	CARDIFF CITY	Grimshaw 2	10		2					7	9	11	8		4					6	1	3	5		
20-Sep	12,500	CARDIFF CITY	5-0	Gillingham	Grimshaw 2, Evans 2, Devlin	10	7	2						9	11	8		4					6	1	3	5		
27-Sep	15,500	Swansea Town	2-1	CARDIFF CITY	Evans	10	7	2						9	11	8		4					6	1	3	5		
04-Oct	12,500	CARDIFF CITY	1-0	Exeter City	Cox	10	7			2		9			11	8		4					6	1	3	5		
11-Oct	8,000	Watford	0-0	CARDIFF CITY		3	7	2		6	11	9		10		8		4						1		5		
18-Oct	10,000	QPR	0-0	CARDIFF CITY		3	7	2		6		9		10	11	8		4						1		5		
25-Oct	13,500	CARDIFF CITY	3-3	Swindon Town	Clarke 2, Cox	10	7	2		3	11	9				8		4					6	1		5		
01-Nov	12,000	Millwall	1-2	CARDIFF CITY	Grimshaw 2	3	7	2				9			11	8		4					6	1		5		10
08-Nov	14,000	CARDIFF CITY	2-0	Brighton	Harvey, Grimshaw	3	7	2			11	9				8		4		9			6	1		5		10
15-Nov	10,500	Newport County	1-3	CARDIFF CITY	West, Smith, Hopkins	3	7	2			11					8		4		9			6	1		5		10
22-Nov	16,000	CARDIFF CITY	0-1	Portsmouth			7	2			11					8		4					6	1	3	5		10
29-Nov	7,000	Northampton Town	2-2	CARDIFF CITY	Grimshaw, West		7	2				9			11	8		4					6	1	3	5		10
06-Dec	13,000	CARDIFF CITY	2-1	Crystal Palace	Evans, Cashmore		7	2	9						11	8		4					6	1	3	5		10
13-Dec	9,000	Southend United	1-1	CARDIFF CITY	Cashmore	3			9			8			11	7		4					6	1	2	5		10
25-Dec	10,000	Merthyr Town	1-1	CARDIFF CITY	Cashmore		7	2	9						11	8		4					6	1	3	5		10
26-Dec	18,000	CARDIFF CITY	3-2	Merthyr Town	Beare, Evans, og	3	7		9			8			11		4						6	1	2	5		10
27-Dec	10,000	Brentford	1-2	CARDIFF CITY	Evans, Cashmore	3	7		9			8			11		6				4		10	1	2	5		
01-Jan	14,000	CARDIFF CITY	1-0	Norwich City	Hardy	3	7	2	9			8			11		4					10	6	1		5		
03-Jan	15,000	CARDIFF CITY	4-0	Reading	Clarke 2, Cox 2		7	2	9		10	8			11		4						6	1	3	5		
17-Jan	10,000	Southampton	2-2	CARDIFF CITY	Cashmore, Beare	3	7	2	9		10	8			11		4						6	1		5		
24-Jan	15,000	CARDIFF CITY	2-1	Luton Town	Cashmore, West	3	7	2	9						11	8		4					6	1		5		10
07-Feb	21,371	CARDIFF CITY	1-0	Swansea Town	Beare	3	7		9			8			11		2	4					6	1		5		10
14-Feb	8,000	Exeter City	1-1	CARDIFF CITY	Clarke		7	2	9		11	8					6	4						1		5	3	10
28-Feb	17,000	CARDIFF CITY	4-0	QPR	Beare 2, Cashmore, West	3	7		9						11	8	4						6	1	2	5		10
06-Mar	9,000	Swindon Town	2-2	CARDIFF CITY	Cashmore 2	3	7		9						11	8	4						6	1	2	5		10
13-Mar	12,000	CARDIFF CITY	4-2	Millwall	Grimshaw 2, West, Clarke		7	2			11	9				8	46	4						1	3	5		10
17-Mar	8,000	Gillingham	3-0	CARDIFF CITY			7	2	9						11	8	4						6	1	3	5		10
20-Mar	13,000	Brighton	1-1	CARDIFF CITY	Cashmore	3	7	2	9		10				11	8	6						4		1	5		
27-Mar	20,000	CARDIFF CITY	0-0	Newport County		3	7		9		10	8			11		6		1				4		2	5		
02-Apr	19,000	Plymouth Argyle	1-0	CARDIFF CITY			7	2	9						11	8	6						4	1	3	5		10
03-Apr	24,606	Portsmouth	0-0	CARDIFF CITY			7	2	9						11	8	6						4	1	3	5		10
05-Apr	25,000	CARDIFF CITY	0-2	Plymouth Argyle		3	7	2	9		11					8	6						4	1		5		10
10-Apr	12,000	CARDIFF CITY	6-1	Northampton Town	Hopkins 2, Grimshaw, West, Keenor, Evans			2				8			11	7	6	4	1	9			5				3	10
14-Apr	11,000	CARDIFF CITY	0-1	Watford			7	2							11	8		4	1	9			6			5	3	10
17-Apr	16,000	Crystal Palace	1-1	CARDIFF CITY	Cashmore		7	2	9			8			11	4	6							1	3	5		10
24-Apr	16,000	CARDIFF CITY	1-0	Southend United	West		7	2	9			8			11		6						4	1	3	5		10
29-Apr	5,000	Norwich City	1-1	CARDIFF CITY	West			2	9						11	7	6		1	8			4		3	5		10
01-May	12,000	CARDIFF CITY	2-0	Brentford	Evans, Cashmore	3	7	2	9						11		6			8			4	1		5		10
					Appearances	23	38	34	23	5	12	20	1	6	34	32	23	25	4	7	1	3	37	37	27	40	3	27
					Goals		5		12		6	4		1	10	13	1	1		3		1	2			1		9

1 Albert Barnett
2 George Beare
3 Charlie Brttan
4 Arthur Cashmore
5 Pat Cassidy
6 J Clarke
7 Billy Cox
8 Len Davies
9 Billy Devlin
10 Jack Evans
11 Billy Grimshaw
12 Billy Hardy
13 Henry Harvey
14 Charlie Hewitt
15 L Hopkins
16 Eddie Jenkins
17 C Jones
18 Fred Keenor
19 Jack Kneeshaw
20 Arthur Layton
21 Bert Smith
22 A Stewart
23 George West

1920-21 2nd in Division Two (Promoted)

Date	Att	Home	Score	Away	Scorers	1	2	3	4	5	6	7	8	9	10	11	12	13	14	15	16	17	18	19	20	21	22	23	24	25	26
28-Aug	13,000	Stockport County	5-2	CARDIFF CITY	Gill 2, J Evans, Grimshaw, Keenor					2	9					11			8	7	6		4	1	3					5	10
30-Aug	25,000	CARDIFF CITY	0-0	Clapton Orient		6	3			2	9					11		8	10	7	4			1						5	
04-Sep	22,000	CARDIFF CITY	3-0	Stockport County	Grimshaw 2, Cashmore		3			2	9					11			8	7	6		4	1						5	10
06-Sep	12,000	Clapton Orient	2-0	CARDIFF CITY			3			2	9					11			8	7	6		4	1						5	10
11-Sep	30,000	CARDIFF CITY	2-1	Birmingham	Gill, Cashmore					2	9					11			8	7	6		4	1	3					5	10
18-Sep	45,000	Birmingham	1-1	CARDIFF CITY	Gill		3			2	9					11			8	7	6		4	1						5	10
25-Sep	30,000	CARDIFF CITY	0-0	West Ham United			3			2	9					11		10	8	7	6		4	1						5	
02-Oct	26,000	West Ham United	1-1	CARDIFF CITY	Gill		3	7		2	9					11			8		6		4	1						5	10
09-Oct	28,000	Fulham	0-3	CARDIFF CITY	Beare, Gill, West		3	7		2	9					11			8		6		4	1						5	10
16-Oct	25,000	CARDIFF CITY	3-0	Fulham	Cashmore 2, Keenor		3	7		2	9					11			8		6		4	1						5	10
23 Oct	22,000	Notts County	1-2	CARDIFF CITY	Cashmore, Gill		3	7		2	9					11			8		6		4	1						5	10
30-Oct	30,000	CARDIFF CITY	1-1	Notts County	Gill		3	7		2	9					11			8		6		4	1						5	10
06-Nov	21,000	Leicester City	0-2	CARDIFF CITY			3	7			9					11			8		6		4	1				2		5	10
13-Nov	20,000	CARDIFF CITY	2-0	Leicester City	Cashmore, Gill		3	7		2	9					11			8		6		4	1						5	10
20-Nov	10,000	Blackpool	2-4	CARDIFF CITY	Gill, West, Cashmore, og			7	3	2	9					11			8		6		4	1						5	10
27-Nov	28,000	CARDIFF CITY	0-0	Blackpool				7	3	2	9					11			8		6		4	1						5	10
04-Dec	12,000	Sheffield Wednesday	0-1	CARDIFF CITY	West			7	3	2	9					11			8		6		4	1						5	10
11-Dec	28,500	CARDIFF CITY	1-0	Sheffield Wednesday	West			7	3	2	9					11			8		6		4	1						5	10
18-Dec	27,500	CARDIFF CITY	2-1	Bury	Gill, Cashmore			7	3	2	9					11			8		6		4	1						5	10
25-Dec	22,000	Coventry City	2-4	CARDIFF CITY	Gill 2, Cashmore, Beare			7	3	2	9					11			8		6		4	1						5	10
27-Dec	42,000	CARDIFF CITY	0-1	Coventry City				7	3	2	9					11			8		6		4	1						5	10
01-Jan	25,000	Bury	3-1	CARDIFF CITY	Cashmore			7	3	2	9					11			8		6		4	1						5	10
15-Jan	35,000	Bristol City	0-0	CARDIFF CITY			10	7	3	2	9					11			8		6		4	1						5	
22-Jan	42,000	CARDIFF CITY	1-0	Bristol City	Barnett		10	7	3	2	9		1			11			8		6		4							5	
05-Feb	27,000	CARDIFF CITY	0-1	Stoke City					3	2	9		1			11			8	7	6	10	4							5	
12-Feb	17,000	Barnsley	0-2	CARDIFF CITY	Gill, Nash				3	2		11	1	9					8	7	6					10	4			5	
14-Feb	15,000	Stoke	0-0	CARDIFF CITY					3	2		11	1	9					8	7	6		4			10				5	
26-Feb	22,000	Nottingham Forest	1-2	CARDIFF CITY	Gill, Keenor				3	2		11	1	9					8	7	6		5			10	4				
09-Mar	20,000	CARDIFF CITY	3-2	Barnsley	Gill, Beare, Pagnam			7	3	2			1			11			8		6		4			10			9	5	
12-Mar	18,000	Rotherham County	2-0	CARDIFF CITY			3	7		2			1			11			8		6		4			10			9	5	
26-Mar	30,000	CARDIFF CITY	1-2	Port Vale	Grimshaw				3	2	8		1			11				7	6		5			10	4		9		
28-Mar	25,000	CARDIFF CITY	1-0	Leeds United	Pagnam		10		3			11	1		8		7				6		4					2	9	5	
29-Mar	20,000	Leeds United	1-2	CARDIFF CITY	Pagnam, Keenor			7	3			11	1		8						6		4			10		2	9	5	
02-Apr	18,000	Port Vale	0-0	CARDIFF CITY				7	3			11	1		8						6		4			10		2	9	5	
04-Apr	27,000	CARDIFF CITY	3-0	Nottingham Forest	Pagnam 2, S Evans				3	2		11	1		8		7				6		4			10			9	5	
09-Apr	30,000	CARDIFF CITY	1-0	South Shields	Gill					2		11	1				7		8		6					10	4	3	9	5	
11-Apr	30,000	CARDIFF CITY	1-0	Rotherham County	Pagnam				3			11	1		10		7		8		6		4					2	9	5	
16-Apr	17,000	South Shields	0-1	CARDIFF CITY	Hardy			7	3	2		11	1						8		6		4			10			9	5	
23-Apr	30,000	CARDIFF CITY	0-0	Hull City				7	3			11	1						8		6					10	4	2	9	5	
30-Apr	10,000	Hull City	2-0	CARDIFF CITY					3	2			1			11			8	7	6		4						9	5	10
02-May	40,000	CARDIFF CITY	2-0	Wolves	Gill, Pagnam				3			11	1						8	7	6		4			10		2	9	5	
07-May	10,000	Wolves	1-3	CARDIFF CITY	Pagnam, Nash, Gill					2		11	1						8	7	6		4			10		3	9	5	
					Appearances	1	16	23	25	35	26	13	19	3	5	29	4	2	37	15	42	1	38	23	2	14	5	9	14	40	21
					Goals		1	3			10					1	1		19	4	1		4			2			8		4

1 Lol Abram
2 Albert Barnett
3 George Beare
4 Jimmy Blair
5 Charlie Brittan
6 Arthur Cashmore
7 Joe Clark
8 Ben Davies
9 Len Davies
10 Herbic Evans
11 Jack Evans
12 Sid Evans
13 Ernie Gault
14 Jimmy Gill
15 Billy Grimshaw
16 Billy Hardy
17 Charlie Jones
18 Fred Keenor
19 Jack Kneeshaw
20 Arthur Layton
21 Harry Nash
22 Billy Newton
23 Jack Page
24 Fred Pagnam
25 Bert Smith
26 George West

1921-22 4th in Division One

Date	Att	Home	Score	Away	Scorers	1	2	3	4	5	6	7	8	9	10	11	12	13	14	15	16	17	18	19	20	21	22	23	24	25	26	27	28	29	30	31
27-Aug	56,000	CARDIFF CITY	0-1	Tottenham Hotspur			2								11		8	7	6		4	1							3	9	5	10				
29-Aug	30,000	Aston Villa	21	CARDIFF CITY	Smith		2		8						11			7	6		4	1								9	5	10		3		
03-Sep	45,000	Tottenham Hotspur	41	CARDIFF CITY	West		2		8						11			7	6		4	1		3						9	5	10				
05-Sep	40,000	CARDIFF CITY	0-4	Aston Villa			2	11	9					8		7			6		4	1							3	10	5					
10-Sep	20,000	CARDIFF CITY	0-1	Oldham Athletic		3	2	11				1	9	8				7			4				10						5					6
17-Sep	18,000	Oldham Athletic	21	CARDIFF CITY	Grimshaw	3	2		10			1			11		8	7		5	4				6					9						
24-Sep	35,000	CARDIFF CITY	31	Middlesbrough	Gill 2, Nash	3	2					1		4	11		8	7		6	5				10					9						
01-Oct	30,000	Middlesbrough	0-0	CARDIFF CITY		3	2					1		4	11		8	7	6		5									9		10				
08-Oct	40,000	CARDIFF CITY	12	Bolton Wanderers	Gill	3	2					1		4	11		8	7	6		5				10					9						
15-Oct	25,486	Bolton Wanderers	12	CARDIFF CITY	Gill 2	3	2					1		4	11		8	7		6	5				10					9						
22-Oct	20,000	West Brom	22	CARDIFF CITY	Gill, Keenor	3	2				10	1		4	11		8	7		6	5									9						
29-Oct	35,000	CARDIFF CITY	2-0	West Brom	Gill 2	3					10	1		4	11		8	7		6	5					2				9						
05-Nov	38,000	CARDIFF CITY	0-2	Manchester City		3					10	1		4	11		8	7		6	5					2				9						
12-Nov	25,000	Manchester City	11	CARDIFF CITY	Gill	3	2				10	1		4	11		8	7		6	5									9						
19-Nov	35,000	CARDIFF CITY	21	Everton	L Davies 2	3	2				10	1	9	4	11		8	7		6	5															
26-Nov	30,000	Everton	0-1	CARDIFF CITY	L Davies	3	2				10	1	9	4	11		8	7	6												5					
03-Dec	35,000	CARDIFF CITY	2-0	Sunderland	L Davies, Gill		2				10	1	9	4	11		8	7	6										3		5					
10-Dec	20,000	Sunderland	41	CARDIFF CITY	Gill		2				10	1	9	4	11		8	7	6										3		5					
17-Dec	25,000	CARDIFF CITY	0-0	Huddersfield Town		3	2				10	1	9	4	11	7	8		6												5					
24-Dec	20,000	Huddersfield Town	0-1	CARDIFF CITY	Grimshaw	3					10	1	9	4	11		8	7	6										2		5					
26-Dec	35,000	Arsenal	0-0	CARDIFF CITY		3					10	1	9	4	11		8	7	6										2		5					
27-Dec	41,000	CARDIFF CITY	43	Arsenal	Clennell, Grimshaw, Gill, L Davies	3					10	1	9	4	11		8	7	6										2		5					
31-Dec	30,000	Birmingham	0-1	CARDIFF CITY	L Davies	3					10	1	9	4	11		8	7	6										2		5					
02-Jan	30,000	Blackburn Rovers	13	CARDIFF CITY	L Davies 2, Grimshaw	3					10	1	9	4				7	6						11				2		5		8			
14-Jan	37,000	CARDIFF CITY	31	Birmingham	Clennell 2, Grimshaw	3					10		9	4	11			7	6		8	1							2		5					
21-Jan	27,000	CARDIFF CITY	63	Bradford City	L Davies 3, Gill 2, Clennell	3					10	1	9		11		8	7	6								4		2		5					
04-Feb	27,000	CARDIFF CITY	3-0	Preston North End	McDonald, Grimshaw, Gill	3	2				10	1			11		8	7	6		4		9								5					
08-Feb	25,000	CARDIFF CITY	2-0	Chelsea	Clennell, Gill	3	2				10	1	9		11		8	7	6		4										5					
11-Feb	20,000	Preston North End	11	CARDIFF CITY	L Davies		2				10	1	9		11		8	7	6		4								3		5					
25-Feb	47,000	Chelsea	1-0	CARDIFF CITY			2				10	1	9	4	11		8	7	6										3		5					
11-Mar	35,000	Sheffield United	0-2	CARDIFF CITY	McDonald, Clennell	3	2				8	1		4	11			7	6		5		9		10											
15-Mar	15,000	Bradford City	1-0	CARDIFF CITY		3	2				8	1			11			7	6		4		9		10						5					
18-Mar	30,000	Burnley	11	CARDIFF CITY	Hardy		2				10	1	9	4	11	7	8		6		5								3							
25-Mar	35,000	CARDIFF CITY	42	Burnley	L Davies 2, J Evans, Gill	3	2				10	1	9	4	11	7	8				6										5					
01-Apr	25,000	Newcastle United	0-0	CARDIFF CITY		3				11	10	1					8	7	6	4			9						2		5					
08-Apr	25,000	CARDIFF CITY	1-0	Newcastle United	L Davies		2				10	1	9		11		8	7	6		4								3		5					
15-Apr	45,000	Liverpool	51	CARDIFF CITY	Clennell	3					10	1	9	4	11		8	7	6										2		5					
17-Apr	30,000	CARDIFF CITY	13	Blackburn Rovers	Clennell	3	2				10	1	9	4	11		8	7	6		5															
22-Apr	37,000	CARDIFF CITY	2-0	Liverpool	Gill, L Davies	3					10	1	9		11		8	7	6		4								2		5					
26-Apr	15,000	CARDIFF CITY	11	Sheffield United	Clennell	3					10		9	4			8	7	6			1						11	2		5					
29-Apr	15,000	Manchester United	11	CARDIFF CITY	L Davies	3					10		9		11		8	7	6		4	1							2		5					
06-May	19,000	CARDIFF CITY	31	Manchester United	Clennell 2, Gill	3					10		9	4			8	7	6									11	2		5				1	
					Appearances	32	27	2	4	1	32	34	25	29	36	4	34	38	32	9	27	7	4	1	8	2	1	2	21	13	29	4	1	1	1	1
					Goals						10		17		1		20	6	1		1		2		1						1	1				

1 Jimmy Blair
2 Charlie Brittan
3 TH Brown
4 Arthur Cashmore
5 Joe Clark
6 Joe Clennell
7 Ben Davies
8 Len Davies
9 Herbie Evans
10 Jack Evans
11 Sid Evans
12 Jimmy Gill
13 Billy Grimshaw
14 Billy Hardy
15 Eddie Jenkins
16 Fred Keenor
17 Jack Kneeshaw
18 Ken McDonald
19 J Melville
20 Harry Nash
21 Jimmy Nelson
22 W Newton
23 Jack Nock
24 Jack Page
25 Fred Pagnam
26 Bert Smith
27 George West
28 George Latham
29 Albert Barnett
30 Tom Farquharson
31 Frank Anderson

1922-23 9th in Division One

Date	Att	Home	Score	Away	Scorers	1	2	3	4	5	6	7	8	9	10	11	12	13	14	15	16	17	18	19	20	21	22	23	24	25	26
26-Aug	40,000	Tottenham Hotspur	1-1	CARDIFF CITY	Gill		3	2	10	1	9		11			8	7	6		4									5		
28-Aug	45,000	CARDIFF CITY	3-0	Aston Villa	Clennell 2, Grimshaw		3		10	1	9		11			8	7	6		4							2		5		
02-Sep	50,000	CARDIFF CITY	2-3	Tottenham Hotspur	L Davies 2		3		10	1	9	4	11			8	7			6							2		5		
04-Sep	25,000	Aston Villa	1-3	CARDIFF CITY	Grimshaw 2, Nash		3			1	9	4	11			8	7			6				10			2		5		
09-Sep	30,000	CARDIFF CITY	4-1	Arsenal	L Davies 2, Grimshaw, Nash		3			1	9	4	11			8	7			6				10			2		5		
16-Sep	45,000	Arsenal	2-1	CARDIFF CITY	L Davies			2		1	9		11			8	7	6		4				10			3		5		
23-Sep	30,000	CARDIFF CITY	0-2	Everton			3		10	1	9		11			8	7	6		4							2		5		
30-Sep	35,000	Everton	3-1	CARDIFF CITY	Smith		3		10	1	9		11			8	7	6		4							2		5		
07-Oct	37,000	CARDIFF CITY	2-4	Sunderland	Clennell 2		3		10	1	9	4	11				7	6		8					2				5		
14-Oct	35,000	Sunderland	2-1	CARDIFF CITY	McDonald			2	8			4	11		1		7	6		5			9	10			3				
21-Oct	35,000	Liverpool	3-1	CARDIFF CITY	Clennell (p)			2	8		9	4	11		1		7	6		5				10			3				
28-Oct	40,000	CARDIFF CITY	3-0	Liverpool	Grimshaw, McDonald, Clennell		3	2	10			4	11		1	8	7	6		5			9								
04-Nov	30,000	Birmingham	0-0	CARDIFF CITY			3		10		8	4	11		1		7	6		5			9				2				
11-Nov	25,000	CARDIFF CITY	1-1	Birmingham	Gill		3		10		9	4	11		1	8	7	6		5							2				
18-Nov	15,000	Huddersfield Town	1-0	CARDIFF CITY			3		8	1		4	11			9	7	6		5						10	2				
25-Nov	27,000	CARDIFF CITY	0-1	Huddersfield Town			3	2	10	1	9	8	11				7	6		4									5		
02-Dec	27,000	CARDIFF CITY	2-1	Stoke City	Gill, Clennell			2	10	1		4	11			8	7	6		5			9				3				
09-Dec	15,000	Stoke City	3-1	CARDIFF CITY	McDonald			2	10			4	11		1	8	7	6		5			9				3				
16-Dec	20,000	CARDIFF CITY	3-1	Manchester City	McDonald 2, Gill	7		2					11		1	8		6		4			9	10			3		5		
23-Dec	16,000	Manchester City	5-1	CARDIFF CITY	Reid	7	3	2					11		1	8		6		4			9					10	5		
26-Dec	35,000	CARDIFF CITY	3-0	West Brom	Gill 2, Reid		3		10				11		1	8	7	6		4							2	9	5		
27-Dec	14,898	West Brom	3-0	CARDIFF CITY			3						11		1	8	7	6		4				10			2	9	5		
30-Dec	15,829	Bolton Wanderers	0-0	CARDIFF CITY			3		10				11		1	8	7	6		4					2			9	5		
06-Jan	25,000	CARDIFF CITY	1-0	Bolton Wanderers	Reid		3		10				11		1	8	7	6		4					2			9	5		
20-Jan	20,000	Blackburn Rovers	3-1	CARDIFF CITY	Nash			2		1			11			8	7	6		4				10			3	9	5		
27-Jan	25,000	CARDIFF CITY	5-0	Blackburn Rovers	Gill 3, L Davies 2		3		10	1	9	4	11			8	7			6					2				5		
10-Feb	27,000	CARDIFF CITY	5-0	Newcastle United	L Davies 2, Gill 2, Grimshaw		3		10	1	9	4	11			8	7			6					2				5		
17-Feb	10,000	Nottingham Forest	3-2	CARDIFF CITY	L Davies, Gill		3		10	1	9	4	11			8	7			6					2				5		
28-Feb	10,000	Newcastle United	3-1	CARDIFF CITY	L Davies		3		10	1	9	4	11			8	7	6		5					2						
03-Mar	20,000	Chelsea	1-1	CARDIFF CITY	Gill				10	1	9	4	11			8	7			6					2		3		5		
10-Mar	25,000	CARDIFF CITY	6-1	Chelsea	L Davies 3, Gill 2, J Evans		3		10		9	4	11		1	8	7			6					2				5		
17-Mar	22,000	CARDIFF CITY	2-0	Middlesbrough	Gill, Reid				10			4	11		1	8	7	6							2		3	9	5		
24-Mar	15,000	Middlesbrough	0-1	CARDIFF CITY	Gill		3		10		9		11		1	8	7	6		4					2				5		
30-Mar	22,000	Burnley	1-5	CARDIFF CITY	Clennell 3, Keenor, L Davies		3		10		9	4	11		1		7	6		8					2				5		
31-Mar	20,000	CARDIFF CITY	1-0	Preston North End	L Davies		3		10		9	4	11		1		7	6		8					2				5		
02-Apr	35,000	CARDIFF CITY	2-2	Burnley	Keenor 2		3		10			4	11		1		7	6		8					2		9		5		
07-Apr	20,000	Preston North End	3-0	CARDIFF CITY			3		10		9	4	11		1		7	6	9	8					2				5		
14-Apr	15,000	CARDIFF CITY	1-0	Sheffield United	Clennell				10			4		7			8	6			1	3			2		5			11	
21-Apr	20,000	Sheffield United	0-0	CARDIFF CITY			3		10	1	9		11			8	7	6		4					2				5		
25-Apr	18,000	CARDIFF CITY	3-1	Nottingham Forest	L Davies 2, Clennell		3		10	1	9	4	11			8	7	6									2		5		
28-Apr	15,000	CARDIFF CITY	2-0	Oldham Athletic	Clennell 2 (p)		3	2	10		9		11		1		7	6		4									5		8
05-May	6,000	Oldham Athletic	3-1	CARDIFF CITY	L Davies		3	2	10		9	4	11		1	8	7	6											5		
					Appearances	2	32	13	35	20	27	27	41	1	21	31	40	34	1	38	1	1	7	8	17	1	23	7	32	1	1
					Goals				14		19		1			17	6			3			5	3				4	1		

1 Fergie Aitken
2 Jimmy Blair
3 Charlie Brittan
4 Joe Clennell
5 Ben Davies
6 Len Davies
7 Herbie Evans
8 Jack Evans
9 Sid Evans
10 Tom Farquharson
11 Jimmy Gill
12 Billy Grimshaw
13 Billy Hardy
14 Vince Jones
15 Fred Keenor
16 Jack Kneeshaw
17 Frank Mason
18 Ken McDonald
19 Harry Nash
20 Jimmy Nelson
21 Jack Nock
22 Jack Page
23 George Reid
24 Bert Smith
25 Billy Taylor
26 Billy Turnbull

1923-24 2nd in Division One

Date	Att	Home	Score	Away	Scorers	1	2	3	4	5	6	7	8	9	10	11	12	13	14	15	16	17	18	19	20	21
25-Aug	30,000	CARDIFF CITY	3-2	Bolton Wanderers	Gill 2, Clennell	3	10		9		11	1	8	7		6			4			2		5		
27-Aug	25,000	CARDIFF CITY	2-1	Sunderland	Gill, J Evans (p)	3	10		9	4	11	1	8	7		6			5			2				
01-Sep	20,013	Bolton Wanderers	2-2	CARDIFF CITY	Davies, Hardy	3	10		9	4	11	1	8	7		6			5			2				
05-Sep	30,000	Sunderland	0-3	CARDIFF CITY	Gill, Clennell, Davies	3	10		9	4	11	1	8	7		6			5			2				
08-Sep	30,000	West Ham United	0-0	CARDIFF CITY		3	10		9	4	11	1	8	7		6			5			2				
15-Sep	35,000	CARDIFF CITY	1-0	West Ham United	Davies	3	10		9	4	11	1	8	7		6			5			2				
22-Sep	40,000	Newcastle United	1-1	CARDIFF CITY	Davies	3	10		9	4	11	1	8	7		6			5			2				
29-Sep	46,000	CARDIFF CITY	1-0	Newcastle United	Davies	3	10		9	4	11	1	8	7		6			5			2				
06-Oct	40,000	Chelsea	1-2	CARDIFF CITY	Clennell, Gill	3	10		9	4	11	1	8	7		6			5			2				
13-Oct	40,000	CARDIFF CITY	1-1	Chelsea	Davies	3	10		9	4	11	1	8	7		6			5			2				
20-Oct	35,000	CARDIFF CITY	1-1	Preston North End	Davies	3	10		9	4	11		8	7		6			5	1		2				
27-Oct	20,000	Preston North End	3-1	CARDIFF CITY	Davies	3	10		9	4	11	1	8	7		6			5			2				
03-Nov	25,000	CARDIFF CITY	3-0	West Brom	Gill 2, H Evans	3	8		9	4	11	1	10	7		6			5			2				
10-Nov	20,000	West Brom	2-4	CARDIFF CITY	Davies 4	3	8		9	4	11	1	10	7		6			5			2				
17-Nov	20,000	Manchester City	1-1	CARDIFF CITY	Grimshaw	3	8		9	4	11	1	10	7					5			2		5		
24-Nov	35,000	CARDIFF CITY	1-1	Manchester City	Davies	3	8		9	4	11	1	10						5		7	2		5		
01-Dec	10,000	Nottingham Forest	0-1	CARDIFF CITY	J Evans	3	10		9	4	11	1	8			6			5		7	2				
08-Dec	22,000	CARDIFF CITY	4-1	Nottingham Forest	Gill 2, Clennell, Davies	3	10		9	4		1	8			6			5		7	2			11	
15-Dec	40,000	Liverpool	0-2	CARDIFF CITY	Clennell, Gill	3	10		9	4	11	1	8			6			5		7	2				
22-Dec	25,000	CARDIFF CITY	2-0	Liverpool	Davies 2	3	10		9	4	11	1	8			6			5		7	2				
25-Dec	45,000	Sheffield United	1-1	CARDIFF CITY	Hardy	3	10		9	4	11	1	8			6			5		7	2				
26-Dec	50,000	CARDIFF CITY	3-1	Sheffield United	Davies 2, Keenor	3	10		9	4	11	1			8	6			5		7	2				
29-Dec	52,000	Aston Villa	1-2	CARDIFF CITY	Davies	3			9	4		1	8		10				5		7	2		5	11	
01-Jan	30,000	Middlesbrough	0-1	CARDIFF CITY	Clennell	3	10		9	4		1				6		8	5		7	2			11	
05-Jan	40,000	CARDIFF CITY	0-2	Aston Villa		3	10		9	4		1	8			6			5		7	2			11	
19-Jan	30,000	Arsenal	1-2	CARDIFF CITY	Davies, Clennell		10		9	4	11	1	8			6			5		7	2	3			
26-Jan	35,000	CARDIFF CITY	4-0	Arsenal	Gill 3, Davies		10		9	4	11	1	8			6			5		7	2	3			
09-Feb	20,000	CARDIFF CITY	2-0	Blackburn Rovers	Gill, Hardy	3	10		9	4	11	1	8			6			5		7	2				
16-Feb	35,000	Tottenham Hotspur	1-1	CARDIFF CITY	Hagan		10				11	1			8	6	5	9			7	2	3			4
01-Mar	25,000	Huddersfield Town	2-0	CARDIFF CITY		3	10		9	4	11		8			6			5	1	7	2				
15-Mar	19,800	CARDIFF CITY	0-2	Notts County		3					11		8		10	6	5	9		1	7	2				4
20-Mar	12,000	Blackburn Rovers	2-1	CARDIFF CITY	Clennell	3	10	7		4	11	1	8			6		9	5			2				
22-Mar	20,000	Notts County	1-0	CARDIFF CITY		3	10	7			11	1	8			6		9	5			2				4
29-Mar	20,000	CARDIFF CITY	0-0	Everton		3			9		11	1	8		10	6			5		7	2				4
05-Apr	45,000	Everton	0-0	CARDIFF CITY		3	10		9		11	1	8			6	5				7	2				4
07-Apr	25,000	CARDIFF CITY	2-1	Tottenham Hotspur	Jones, Clennell		10		9		11	1	7			6		8	5			2	3			4
12-Apr	10,000	CARDIFF CITY	2-0	Burnley	Gill, Davies		10		9		11	1	7			6		8	5			2	3			4
14-Apr	30,000	CARDIFF CITY	0-0	Huddersfield Town			10		9		11	1	7			6		8	5			2	3			4
19-Apr	15,000	Burnley	1-2	CARDIFF CITY	J Evans, Davies	3	10		7		11	1	8			6		9	5			2				4
21-Apr	30,000	CARDIFF CITY	1-0	Middlesbrough	Clennell	3	10		7		11	1	8			6		9	5			2				4
26-Apr	18,000	CARDIFF CITY	2-0	Birmingham City	Jones, Clennell	3	10		7		11	1	8			6		9	5			2				4
03-May	50,000	Birmingham	0-0	CARDIFF CITY		3	10		7		11	1	8			6		9	5			2				4
					Appearances	36	39	2	38	29	38	39	39	15	5	39	3	12	39	3	18	42	6	4	4	12
					Goals		11		23	1	3		15	1	1	3		2	1							

1 Jimmy Blair
2 Joe Clennell
3 Elvet Collins
4 Len Davies
5 Herbie Evans
6 Jack Evans
7 Tom Farquharson
8 Jimmy Gill
9 Billy Grimshaw
10 Alfie Hagan
11 Billy Hardy
12 Eddie Jenkins
13 Jimmy Jones
14 Fred Keenor
15 Jack Kneeshaw
16 Denis Lawson
17 Jimmy Nelson
18 Jack Page
19 Bert Smith
20 Billy Taylor
21 Harry Wake

1924-25 11th in Division One

Date	Att	Home	Score	Away	Scorers	1	2	3	4	5	6	7	8	9	10	11	12	13	14	15	16	17	18	19	20	21	22	23
30-Aug	17,000	Burnley	0-0	CARDIFF CITY			3	10		9		11	1	8		6		5	7			2						4
01-Sep	35,000	CARDIFF CITY	1-1	Sheffield United	L Davies		3	10		9		11	1	8		6		5	7			2						4
06-Sep	30,000	CARDIFF CITY	3-0	Leeds United	L Davies 2, Lawson		3	10		9		11	1	8		6		5	7			2		4				
08-Sep	22,000	Sheffield United	1-0	CARDIFF CITY			3	10		9		11	1	8		6		5	7			2		4				
13-Sep	20,000	Birmingham	2-1	CARDIFF CITY	Gill		3	10		9	11		1	8		6		5	7			2		4				
15-Sep	12,000	Preston North End	1-3	CARDIFF CITY	I Davies, Gill, Clennell		3	10		9	11		1	8		6		5	7					4	2			
20-Sep	20,000	CARDIFF CITY	0-1	West Brom			3	10			11		1	8		6		5	7		9			4	2			
27-Sep	40,000	Tottenham Hotspur	1-1	CARDIFF CITY	McIlvenny	10	3				7	11	1	8		6		5			9	2		4				
04-Oct	30,000	CARDIFF CITY	1-2	Bolton Wanderers	W Davies		3	10			7	11	1	8		6					9	2		5				4
11-Oct	20,000	Notts County	3-0	CARDIFF CITY			3	10		9	7	11	1	8		6		5				2		4				
18-Oct	20,000	CARDIFF CITY	2-1	Everton	L Davies 2	10	3	8		9	7	11	1			6		5				2		4				
25-Oct	20,000	Newcastle United	1-2	CARDIFF CITY	L Davies 2	10				9	7	11	1			6		5				2	8	4	3			
08-Nov	10,000	Nottingham Forest	2-1	CARDIFF CITY	Beadles	10				9	7	11	1			6		5				2	8	4	3			
15-Nov	20,000	CARDIFF CITY	4-1	Bury	Beadles 2, L Davies 2	10	3			9	8	11	1					5	7			2		6				4
22-Nov	15,000	Manchester City	2-2	CARDIFF CITY	Beadles, L Davies	10	3			9	8	11	1					5	7			2		6				4
29-Nov	20,000	CARDIFF CITY	1-1	Arsenal	Beadles	10	3			9	8	11	1			6		5	7			2						4
06-Dec	30,000	Aston Villa	1-2	CARDIFF CITY	L Davies 2	10	3			9	8	11	1			6		5	7			2						4
13-Dec	25,000	CARDIFF CITY	2-2	Huddersfield Town	W Davies, Beadles	10	3			9	8	11	1			6		5	7			2						4
15-Dec	17,000	CARDIFF CITY	1-3	Liverpool	Gill			10		9			1	8				5	7			2		6	3		11	4
20-Dec	20,000	Blackburn Rovers	3-1	CARDIFF CITY	Beadles	10				9	8	11	1			3		5	7			2		6				4
25-Dec	27,000	West Ham United	3-2	CARDIFF CITY	W Davies, Beadles	10	3			9	7	11	1	8				5				2		6				4
26-Dec	31,000	CARDIFF CITY	2-1	West Ham United	Beadles, L Davies	10	3			9	7	11	1	8				5				2		6				4
01-Jan	18,000	Sunderland	1-0	CARDIFF CITY		10	3			9		11		8			1	5	7			2		6				4
03-Jan	13,000	Leeds United	0-0	CARDIFF CITY		10				9	7	11		8		3	1	5				2		6				4
17-Jan	16,000	CARDIFF CITY	1-0	Birmingham	L Davies	10	3			9	8	11	1			6		5	7			2						4
24-Jan	20,000	West Brom	1-0	CARDIFF CITY		10	3			9	7	11	1	8		6		5				2						4
07-Feb	17,374	Bolton Wanderers	3-0	CARDIFF CITY		10	3			9	7	11	1	8		6		5				2						4
11-Feb	8,000	CARDIFF CITY	4-0	Burnley	L Davies 2, Nelson (p), Gill	10	3			9	7	11	1	8		6		5				2						4
14-Feb	20,000	CARDIFF CITY	1-1	Notts County	Nicholson		3	10				11	1	8		5			7					9	2	6		4
25-Feb	8,000	Everton	1-2	CARDIFF CITY	Beadles, W Davies	10	3				11		1	8		6		5	7			2		9				4
28-Feb	25,000	CARDIFF CITY	3-0	Newcastle United	Nicholson 2, McIlvenny		3					11		8		5	1		7		10			9	2	6		4
14-Mar	15,000	CARDIFF CITY	2-0	Nottingham Forest	Nelson (p), Gill	10	3				11		1	8		6		5	7			2		9				4
18-Mar	27,000	CARDIFF CITY	0-2	Tottenham Hotspur			3			9	10	11	1	8		6		5	7			2						4
21-Mar	20,000	Bury	4-1	CARDIFF CITY	Nicholson		3			9	7	11	1	8		5				4				10	2	6		
01-Apr	15,000	CARDIFF CITY	0-2	Manchester City		10					7	11	1	8		6		5			9	2			3			4
04-Apr	25,000	Arsenal	1-1	CARDIFF CITY	Beadles	9	3				8	11		10		6	1	5	7			2						4
11-Apr	18,000	CARDIFF CITY	2-1	Aston Villa	Nicholson, Gill	10	3				7	11		8		6	1	5				2		9				4
13-Apr	25,000	CARDIFF CITY	2-0	Sunderland	L Davies 2		3			11	7		1	8	10	6		5				2		9				4
15-Apr	12,000	CARDIFF CITY	3-0	Blackburn Rovers	Gill, W Davies. Nicholson		3				11		1	8	10	6		5	7			2		9				4
18-Apr	16,000	Huddersfield Town	0-0	CARDIFF CITY			3		7				1	8	10	6			11			2		9		5		4
29-Apr	20,000	Liverpool	1-2	CARDIFF CITY	Beadles, Gill	10	3			9		11	1	8		5			7			2		6				4
02-May	17,000	CARDIFF CITY	0-0	Preston North End		10	3			9		11	1	8		6		5	7			2						4
					Appearances	25	36	12	1	30	31	33	37	32	3	36	5	36	26	1	5	37	2	29	9	4	1	31
					Goals	10		1		20	4			9					1		2	2		6				

1 Harry Beadles
2 Jimmy Blair
3 Joe Clennell
4 Elvet Collins
5 Len Davies
6 Willie Davies
7 Jack Evans
8 Tom Farquharson
9 Jimmy Gill
10 Alfie Hagan
11 Billy Hardy
12 Joe Hills
13 Fred Keenor
14 Denis Lawson
15 Jack Lewis
16 Paddy McIlvenny
17 Jimmy Nelson
18 Jack Nicholls
19 Joe Nicholson
20 Jack Page
21 Tom Sloan
22 Billy Taylor
23 Harry Wake

1925-26 16th in Division One

Date	Att	Home	Score	Away	Scorers	1	2	3	4	5	6	7	8	9	10	11	12	13	14	15	16	17	18	19	20	21	22	23	24	25	26	27
29-Aug	42,529	Manchester City	3-2	CARDIFF CITY	Gill, Beadles	10	3			9	11			1		8		6			5	7		2							4	
31-Aug	16,129	West Ham United	3-1	CARDIFF CITY	Nicholson		3			9	11			1		8		6			5	7		2	10						4	
05-Sep	13,914	CARDIFF CITY	2-1	Everton	Gill, Beadles	10	3			9	11			1		8		6			5	7		2							4	
07-Sep	19,462	CARDIFF CITY	0-1	West Ham United		10				9	11			1		8		6			5	7		2							4	3
12-Sep	19,033	Huddersfield Town	1-1	CARDIFF CITY	W Davies		3			9	10		11	1		8		6			5	7		2							4	
14-Sep	26,716	Tottenham Hotspur	1-2	CARDIFF CITY	W Davies. Lawson		3			9	10		11			8		6	1		5	7		2							4	
21-Sep	20,698	CARDIFF CITY	0-1	Tottenham Hotspur			3			9	10		11			8		6	1		5	7		2							4	
23-Sep	18,316	CARDIFF CITY	0-1	Sunderland			3			9	10		11			8		6	1		5	7				2					4	
26-Sep	18,042	Blackburn Rovers	6-3	CARDIFF CITY	Nicholson 2, Beadles	10	3				11			1		8					5	7			9	2		6			4	
03-Oct	20,281	CARDIFF CITY	3-2	Bury	Nicholson, L Davies, Beadles	10	3			11	8			1				2			5	7			9			6			4	
10-Oct	24,335	Birmingham	3-2	CARDIFF CITY	Keenor, W Davies		3			11	8			1		10		2		4	9	7					5	6				
17-Oct	38,130	Arsenal	5-0	CARDIFF CITY		10				11	7			1		8					5				9	2		6			4	3
24-Oct	15,846	CARDIFF CITY	0-2	Manchester United				10		9			11	1			8	6			5	7		2	4							3
31-Oct	33,161	Aston Villa	0-2	CARDIFF CITY	Nicholson, S Smith			10		11				1				4				7		2	9		6	5	8			3
07-Nov	25,089	CARDIFF CITY	5-2	Leicester City	Cassidy 3, W Davies, Ferguson			10		8	7			1	9			4					11	2			6	5				3
14-Nov	19,360	Leeds United	1-0	CARDIFF CITY				10		8	7			1	9			4					11	2			6	5				3
21-Nov	25,539	CARDIFF CITY	0-0	Newcastle United				10		8	7				9			4	1				11	2			6	5				3
28-Nov	21,520	Bolton Wanderers	0-1	CARDIFF CITY	Ferguson			10		8	7			1	9			4					11	2	6			5				3
05-Dec	17,856	CARDIFF CITY	2-1	Notts County	Ferguson 2			10		8	7			1	9			4					11	2	6			5				3
12-Dec	31,373	Liverpool	0-2	CARDIFF CITY	L Davies, Ferguson			10		8	7			1	9			4					11	2	6			5				3
19-Dec	17,678	CARDIFF CITY	2-3	Burnley	L Davies, Ferguson			10		8	7			1	9			4					11	2	6			5				3
25-Dec	13,683	CARDIFF CITY	3-2	West Brom	Ferguson 2, L Davies			10		8	7			1	9			4					11	2	6			5				3
26-Dec	35,504	West Brom	3-0	CARDIFF CITY				10		8	7			1	9			4					11	2	6			5				3
01-Jan	21,943	Sheffield United	1-2	CARDIFF CITY	W Davies, L Davies		3	10		8	7			1	9			4					11	2	6			5				
02-Jan	10,242	CARDIFF CITY	2-2	Manchester City	Cassidy 2			10		8	7			1	9			4					11	2	6			5				3
16-Jan	26,553	Everton	1-1	CARDIFF CITY	McLachlan		3	10			8				9				1			7	11		4		5	6				2
23-Jan	13,049	CARDIFF CITY	1-2	Huddersfield Town	Ferguson		3	10			8				9			5	1			7	11		4			6				2
06-Feb	16,484	CARDIFF CITY	4-1	Blackburn Rovers	McLachlan 2, L Davies, Cassidy			10	7	8		4			9			6	1			7	11	2				5				3
13-Feb	16,777	Bury	4-1	CARDIFF CITY	Ferguson			10				4			9			6	1		5		11	2					8			3
20-Feb	18,862	CARDIFF CITY	2-0	Birmingham	L Davies, Ferguson			10		8	7	4		1	9						5		11	2				6				3
27-Feb	21,684	CARDIFF CITY	0-0	Arsenal			3	10		8	7			1	9					4	5		11	2	6							
13-Mar	21,982	CARDIFF CITY	2-0	Aston Villa	Ferguson 2					8	7			1	9			4			5		11	2				6		10		3
20-Mar	24,095	Leicester City	1-2	CARDIFF CITY	W Davies 2					8	7			1	9			4			5		11	2				6		10		3
27-Mar	15,300	CARDIFF CITY	0-0	Leeds United				10		8	11			1	9			4			5	7		2				6				3
31-Mar	4,315	Sunderland	1-3	CARDIFF CITY	W Davies, L Davies, Ferguson					8	11			1	9			4			5	7		2				6		10		3
03-Apr	26,205	Newcastle United	0-1	CARDIFF CITY	Ferguson					8	11			1	9			6			5	7		2						10	4	3
05-Apr	22,241	CARDIFF CITY	0-1	Sheffield United			3	10		8			11		9			6	1		5	7									4	2
10-Apr	13,787	CARDIFF CITY	0-1	Bolton Wanderers			3	10	7				11	1				4			5			8	9			6				2
17-Apr	8,712	Notts County	2-4	CARDIFF CITY	Ferguson 3, Keenor				7	8	11			1	9			6			5			2						10	4	3
24-Apr	14,868	CARDIFF CITY	2-2	Liverpool	Hardy, Ferguson				7	8	11			1	9			4			5			2				6		10		3
28-Apr	9,116	Manchester United	1-0	CARDIFF CITY				4	7	8	11			1	9			6						2				5		10		3
01-May	16,381	Burnley	4-1	CARDIFF CITY	L Davies			10	7	9	11			1				6						2				5		8	4	3
					Appearances	6	16	24	6	37	36	3	7	33	26	11	1	37	9	2	25	20	19	34	18	3	6	28	2	8	15	30
					Goals	4		6		8	9				19	2		1			2	1	2		6				1			

1 Harry Beadles
2 Jimmy Blair
3 Joe Cassidy
4 Elvet Collins
5 Len Davies
6 Willie Davies
7 Herbie Evans
8 Jack Evans
9 Tom Farquharson
10 Hughie Ferguson
11 Jimmy Gill
12 Alfie Hagan
13 Billy Hardy
14 Joe Hills
15 Jack Jennings
16 Fred Keenor
17 Denis Lawson
18 George McLachlan
19 Jimmy Nelson
20 Joe Nicholson
21 Jack Page
22 Ebor Reed
23 Tom Sloan
24 Sam Smith
25 Tom Smith
26 Harry Wake
27 Tom Watson

1926-27 14th in Division One

Date	Att	Home	Score	Away	Scorers	1	2	3	4	5	6	7	8	9	10	11	12	13	14	15	16	17	18	19	20	21	22	23	24	25	26
28-Aug	19,985	Burnley	4-3	CARDIFF CITY	Ferguson 2, L Davies		6				8	7	1	9		2			5		11						10			4	3
30-Aug	14,242	Leeds United	0-0	CARDIFF CITY			6				8	7	1	9		2	4		5		11						10				3
04-Sep	19,213	CARDIFF CITY	1-1	West Brom	L Davies		6				8	7	1	9		2	4		5		11						10				3
06-Sep	13,653	CARDIFF CITY	3-1	Leeds United	T Smith, Ferguson, W Davies		6				8	7	1	9		2	4		5		11						10				3
11-Sep	20,081	CARDIFF CITY	2-3	Aston Villa	Ferguson 2(p)		6				8	7	1	9		3	4		5		11	2					10				
18-Sep	18,737	Bolton Wanderers	2-0	CARDIFF CITY			6				8	7	1	9		3	4		5		11	2					10				
20-Sep	14,048	CARDIFF CITY	1-1	Newcastle United	W Davies		6				8	7	1	9		3	4		5		11	2					10				
25-Sep	17,267	CARDIFF CITY	0-2	Manchester United		4	6			10	11	7	1	8		3						2	9		5						
02-Oct	21,216	Derby County	6-3	CARDIFF CITY	L Davies, Ferguson, Curtis					10	8	7	1	9		6	4		5		11	2									3
09-Oct	12,282	CARDIFF CITY	3-0	Sheffield United	W Davies, Irving, Ferguson					10	8	7	1	9		6	4		5		11	2									3
16-Oct	17,705	Huddersfield Town	0-0	CARDIFF CITY						10	8	7	1	9		6	4		5		11	2									3
23-Oct	15,870	CARDIFF CITY	3-0	Sunderland	Ferguson 2, Curtis	8				10		7	1	9		6	4		5		11	2									3
30-Oct	15,182	Bury	2-3	CARDIFF CITY	Ferguson 2, McLachlan		6		7	10	8		1	9		4					11	2			5						3
06-Nov	10,598	CARDIFF CITY	1-0	Birmingham	McLachlan		6			10	8	7	1	9		4			5		11	2									3
13-Nov	15,350	Tottenham Hotspur	4-1	CARDIFF CITY	Curtis		6			10	8	7	1	9		4			5		11	2									3
20-Nov	10,736	CARDIFF CITY	1-2	West Ham United	W Davies					10	8	7	1	9		6			5		11	2								4	3
29-Nov	16,986	Sheffield Wednesday	3-0	CARDIFF CITY		7	4			10	8		1	9		6			5		11	2									3
04-Dec	13,627	CARDIFF CITY	0-1	Leicester City		4	6		7	10	8		1	9					5		11	2									3
11-Dec	27,181	Everton	0-1	CARDIFF CITY	Ferguson				7		10		1	9		6			4		11	2			5	8					3
18-Dec	12,254	CARDIFF CITY	0-1	Blackburn Rovers							10		1	9		6	4		5	7	11	2				8					3
25-Dec	36,250	Newcastle United	5-0	CARDIFF CITY				8			10		1	9		6			4	7	11	2			5						3
27-Dec	25,387	CARDIFF CITY	2-0	Arsenal	Ferguson, Curtis					10	9		1	7		6	4					2		11	5					8	3
01-Jan	31,000	Arsenal	3-2	CARDIFF CITY	Curtis, L Davies					10	9		1	7		6	4					2		11	5					8	3
15-Jan	14,647	CARDIFF CITY	0-0	Burnley						10	9			7	1	6			4			2		11	5					8	3
31-Jan	10,481	Aston Villa	0-0	CARDIFF CITY						10	9		1	7		6	4				11	2			5		8				3
05-Feb	12,721	CARDIFF CITY	1-0	Bolton Wanderers	L Davies					10	9		1	7		6	8		4		11	2			5						3
12-Feb	26,213	Manchester United	1-1	CARDIFF CITY	Ferguson					10			1	9		6	8				11	2			5				7	4	3
21-Feb	12,820	West Brom	1-2	CARDIFF CITY	McLachlan, og					10	9		1	7		6	8		4		11	2			5						3
26-Feb	25,658	Sheffield United	3-1	CARDIFF CITY	L Davies					10	8		1	9		6			5		11	2							7	4	3
12-Mar	17,194	Sunderland	2-2	CARDIFF CITY	Irving 2						10		1	9		6	8		4		11	2			5			7			3
16-Mar	10,057	CARDIFF CITY	2-0	Derby County	Ferguson 2						10		1	9		6	8	3	4		11	2			5			7			
19-Mar	17,594	CARDIFF CITY	2-1	Bury	Ferguson, McLachlan						10		1	9		6	8	3	4		11	2			5			7			
21-Mar	17,051	CARDIFF CITY	2-0	Huddersfield Town	Ferguson 2						10		1	9		6	8	3	4		11	2			5			7			
02-Apr	13,384	CARDIFF CITY	1-2	Tottenham Hotspur	og		6				10		1	9		6	8				11	2			5			7			3
07-Apr	10,994	Leicester City	3-1	CARDIFF CITY	Ferguson						10		1	9		6	8	3	4		11	2			5			7			
09-Apr	14,777	West Ham United	2-2	CARDIFF CITY	Ferguson, Wake		4			10			1	9		6		3			11	2	5					7		8	
15-Apr	35,247	Liverpool	5-0	CARDIFF CITY				9		10					1	6	8		4		11	2			5			7			3
16-Apr	13,426	CARDIFF CITY	3-2	Sheffield Wednesday	Ferguson, Wake, og		6			10			1	9					4		11	2			5			7		8	3
18-Apr	21,668	CARDIFF CITY	2-0	Liverpool	Irving, Ferguson		4			7	10		1	9		6	8				11	2	5								3
27-Apr	23,681	Birmingham	1-2	CARDIFF CITY	Ferguson 2					10			1	9		6	8		4		11	2	5					7			3
30-Apr	18,341	CARDIFF CITY	1-0	Everton	Keenor		4			10			1			6			5	8	11	2			5			7			3
07-May	11,786	Blackburn Rovers	1-0	CARDIFF CITY						10			1			6	8		4	9	11	2	5					7			3
					Appearances	4	18	2	3	26	34	15	40	39	2	40	27	5	33	4	38	38	5	3	20	2	8	12	2	9	33
					Goals					5	7	3		26			3		1		5						2			2	

1 Jim Baillie
2 George Blackburn
3 Fred Castle
4 Elvet Collins
5 Ernie Curtis
6 Len Davies
7 Willie Davies
8 Tom Farquharson
9 Hughie Ferguson
10 Tommy Hampson
11 Billy Hardy
12 Sam Irving
13 Jack Jennings
14 Fred Keenor
15 Frank Matson
16 George McLachlan
17 Jimmy Nelson
18 Tom Pirie
19 Percy Richards
20 Tom Sloan
21 Sam Smith
22 Tom Smith
23 Billy Thirlaway
24 Frank Tysoe
25 Harry Wake
26 Tom Watson

1927-28 6th in Division One

Date	Att	Home	Score	Away	Scorers	1	2	3	4	5	6	7	8	9	10	11	12	13	14	15	16	17	18	19	20	21	22	23	24
27-Aug	24,107	CARDIFF CITY	2-1	Bolton Wanderers	McLachlan, L Davies				10	8		1	9	6		4		5		11			2			7			3
03-Sep	19,218	Sheffield Wednesday	3-3	CARDIFF CITY	Ferguson, Curtis, Thirlaway				10	8		1	9	6		4		5		11			2			7			3
05-Sep	14,343	Blackburn Rovers	0-0	CARDIFF CITY					10	8		1	9	6		4		5		11			2			7			3
10-Sep	23,033	CARDIFF CITY	1-1	Middlesbrough	McLachlan				10	8		1	9	6		4		5		11			2			7			3
12-Sep	15,955	CARDIFF CITY	1-1	Blackburn Rovers	L Davies				10	8		1	9	6		4		5		11			2			7			3
17-Sep	23,723	Birmingham	1-3	CARDIFF CITY	Ferguson 2, Thirlaway				10	8		1	9	6		4		5		11			2			7			3
24-Sep	30,590	CARDIFF CITY	3-1	Newcastle United	Curtis, L Davies, Ferguson				10	8		1	9	6		4		5		11			2			7			3
01-Oct	12,975	Huddersfield Town	8-2	CARDIFF CITY	Ferguson 2				10	8		1	9	6		4		5		11			2			7			3
08-Oct	21,811	CARDIFF CITY	2-1	Tottenham Hotspur	L Davies, Ferguson				10	8		1	9	6		4		5		11			2			7			3
15-Oct	31,090	Manchester United	2-2	CARDIFF CITY	Thirlaway, Curtis		6		10	8		1	9	3		4		5		11			2			7			
22-Oct	9,060	CARDIFF CITY	3-1	Portsmouth	Thirlaway, Ferguson, McLachlan		6		10	8		1	9	3				5		11			2			7	4		
29-Oct	25,634	Leicester City	4-1	CARDIFF CITY	Smith							1	9	6		4			8	11			2	5	10	7			3
05-Nov	12,735	CARDIFF CITY	1-1	Liverpool	Smith					8		1	9	6		4		5		11			2		10	7			3
12-Nov	18,189	West Ham United	2-0	CARDIFF CITY					10	8		1	9	6		4		5		11			2			7			3
19-Nov	6,606	CARDIFF CITY	4-4	Derby County	L Davies 2, W Davies, Matson					10	7	1	9	6		4		5	8	11			2						3
26-Nov	22,999	Sheffield United	3-4	CARDIFF CITY	McLachlan 2, L Davies, Ferguson					10	8	1	9	6		4		5		11			2			7			3
03-Dec	14,264	CARDIFF CITY	2-1	Aston Villa	Ferguson 2		4			10	8	1	9	6				5		11			2			7			3
10-Dec	16,450	Sunderland	0-2	CARDIFF CITY	Thirlaway, L Davies					10	8	1	9	6		4		5		11			2			7			3
17-Dec	11,961	CARDIFF CITY	0-1	Bury						10	8	1	9	6		4				11			2	5		7			3
24-Dec	13,159	Burnley	2-1	CARDIFF CITY	Thirlaway				8	10		1	9	6		4		5		11			2			7			3
26-Dec	56,305	Everton	2-1	CARDIFF CITY	Wake		6		8	10		1	9					5		11			2			7	4		3
27-Dec	25,387	CARDIFF CITY	2-0	Everton	L Davies, Wake		4			10				6	1		3			11	9		2	5		7	8		
31-Dec	15,745	Bolton Wanderers	2-1	CARDIFF CITY	Miles		4			10				6	1		3			11	9		2	5		7	8		
07-Jan	9,208	CARDIFF CITY	1-1	Sheffield Wednesday	Ferguson		4			10		1	9	3				5		11			2	6		7	8		
21-Jan	21,728	Middlesbrough	1-2	CARDIFF CITY	Thirlaway, Ferguson					10		1	9	6		8		5		11			2			7	4		3
04-Feb	26,439	Newcastle United	2-0	CARDIFF CITY			6		8			1	9	5			3			11			2		10	7	4		
11-Feb	21,073	CARDIFF CITY	4-0	Huddersfield Town	Thirlaway 2, L Davies, og				10	9		1		6		8	3	5		11			2			7	4		
22-Feb	10,758	CARDIFF CITY	2-1	Birmingham	Ferguson, McLachlan		4		8	10		1	9	6			3	5		11			2			7			
25-Feb	15,579	CARDIFF CITY	2-0	Manchester United	L Davies, Ferguson				8	10		1	9	6			3	5		11			2			7	4		
03-Mar	25,157	Portsmouth	3-0	CARDIFF CITY					8	10		1	9	6			3	5		11			2			7	4		
05-Mar	6,250	Tottenham Hotspur	1-0	CARDIFF CITY					10	9		1		6			3	5	8	11			2			7	4		
10-Mar	13,178	CARDIFF CITY	3-0	Leicester City	Ferguson 2, McLachlan					10		1	9	6			3	5		11			2		8	7	4		
17-Mar	34,532	Liverpool	1-2	CARDIFF CITY	L Davies, Thirlaway			9		10		1		6			3	5		11			2		8	7	4		
24-Mar	14,529	CARDIFF CITY	5-1	West Ham United	Ferguson	4				10		1	9	6			3	5		11			2		8	7			
31-Mar	15,565	Derby County	7-1	CARDIFF CITY	Thirlaway		4			10		1	9	6			2	5		11					8	7			3
06-Apr	36,828	Arsenal	3-0	CARDIFF CITY			4							6	1		3			11	9	10	2	5	8	7			
07-Apr	11,283	CARDIFF CITY	2-2	Sheffield United	McLachlan 2								9	6	1		3	4		11			2	5	10	7	8		
09-Apr	17,699	CARDIFF CITY	2-2	Arsenal	Smith, Wake								9	6	1		3	4	7	11			2	5	10		8		
14-Apr	22,428	Aston Villa	3-1	CARDIFF CITY	McLachlan					10		1		6			3	4		9			2	5		7	8	11	
21-Apr	10,268	CARDIFF CITY	3-1	Sunderland	Warren, L Davies, McLachlan					10		1		6			3	4		9			2	5		7	8	11	
28-Apr	13,375	Bury	3-0	CARDIFF CITY						10		1		6			3	4		9			2	5	8	7		11	
05-May	8,663	CARDIFF CITY	3-2	Burnley	L Davies 2, Warren					10		1		6			3	4		9			2	5	8	7		11	
					Appearances	1	11	1	20	37	5	37	32	41	5	20	19	36	4	42	3	1	41	12	12	40	17	4	21
					Goals				3	15	1		18						1	11	1				3	11	3	2	

1 Jim Baillie
2 George Blackburn
3 Fred Castle
4 Ernie Curtis
5 Len Davies
6 Willie Davies
7 Tom Farquharson
8 Hughie Ferguson
9 Billy Hardy
10 Joe Hillier
11 Sam Irving
12 Jack Jennings
13 Fred Keenor
14 Frank Matson
15 George McLachlan
16 Albert Miles
17 Jerry Murphy
18 Jimmy Nelson
19 Tom Sloan
20 Tom Smith
21 Billy Thirlaway
22 Harry Wake
23 Freddie Warren
24 Tom Watson

1928-29 22nd in Division One (Relegated)

Date	Att	Home	Score	Away	Scorers	1	2	3	4	5	6	7	8	9	10	11	12	13	14	15	16	17	18	19	20	21	22	23	24	25	26	27	28	29	30
25-Aug	36,964	Newcastle United	1-1	CARDIFF CITY	Ferguson (p)			10	1	9		6			3		4		11				2				5		7	8					
01-Sep	20,174	CARDIFF CITY	7-0	Burnley	Ferguson 5, L Davies 2		10	8	1	9		6			3		4		11				2				5		7						
08-Sep	20,462	Derby County	2-0	CARDIFF CITY			10	8	1	9		6			3		4		11				2				5		7						
10-Sep	17,189	CARDIFF CITY	3-2	West Ham United	Ferguson 2, Thirlaway		10	8	1	9		6			3		4		11				2				5		7						
15-Sep	24,207	Sheffield United	3-1	CARDIFF CITY	S Davies		10	8	1	9		6			3		4		11				2				5		7						
17-Sep	13,750	West Ham United	1-1	CARDIFF CITY	Ferguson		10	8	1	9		6			3		4		11				2				5		7						
22-Sep	18,739	CARDIFF CITY	4-0	Bury	L Davies 2, Ferguson, Thirlaway		10	8	1	9		6			3		4		11				2				5		7						
29-Sep	30,190	Aston Villa	1-0	CARDIFF CITY			10		1	9		6	8		3		4		11				2				5		7						
06-Oct	19,477	CARDIFF CITY	1-2	Leicester City	Harris		10		1			6	8		3		4		11				2			9	5		7						
13-Oct	26,010	Manchester United	1-1	CARDIFF CITY	McLachlan	6	10				1	3	8		2		4		11							9	5		7						
20-Oct	15,361	CARDIFF CITY	0-1	Sunderland		6	10	8			1	3	9		2		4		11								5		7						
27-Oct	20,116	Sheffield Wednesday	1-0	CARDIFF CITY		6		9	1			3		4	2				10								5	8	7		11				
03-Nov	18,757	CARDIFF CITY	1-1	Arsenal	Sloan	6	10		1	9		3	8		2		4		11								5		7						
10-Nov	25,994	Everton	1-0	CARDIFF CITY		6	10		1	9		3	8	4	2		5		11										7						
17-Nov	13,845	CARDIFF CITY	0-0	Huddersfield Town		6			1	9		5		4	2			8	10						3				7		11				
24-Nov	13,691	Manchester City	1-1	CARDIFF CITY	Smith		10		1			6		4	2		5		9						3			8	7		11				
01-Dec	19,649	CARDIFF CITY	1-4	Birmingham	Thirlaway	4	9	10	1			6			2		5		11						3			8	7						
08-Dec	19,649	Portsmouth	0-1	CARDIFF CITY	Miles	6			1			3		4	2		5			9				10				8	7		11				
15-Dec	11,286	CARDIFF CITY	1-1	Bolton Wanderers	Robbins	6			1			3		4	2		5			9				10				8	7		11				
22-Dec	11,040	Blackburn Rovers	2-0	CARDIFF CITY		6	9		1			3		4	2		5		11					10				8	7						
25-Dec	28,188	Leeds United	3-0	CARDIFF CITY		6	9		1			3		4	2		5		11					10				8	7						
26-Dec	20,439	CARDIFF CITY	2-1	Leeds United	Thirlaway, Wake	6				9	1			4	2		5		10						3				7	8	11				
29-Dec	12,254	CARDIFF CITY	2-0	Newcastle United	Thirlaway, Wake	6				9	1			4	3				5				2					10	7	8	11				
01-Jan	33,651	Bolton Wanderers	1-0	CARDIFF CITY						9	1			4	2		6		5						3			10	7	8	11				
05-Jan	10,966	Burnley	3-0	CARDIFF CITY						9	1			4	2		6		5						3			10	7	8	11				
19-Jan	14,647	CARDIFF CITY	3-0	Derby County	Ferguson 2, McLachlan			10	1	9					2		5		11		6				3			8	7	4					
26-Jan	17,334	CARDIFF CITY	0-0	Sheffield United				10	1	9					2		5		11		6				3			8	7	4					
02-Feb	9,954	Bury	4-1	CARDIFF CITY	Ferguson			10	1	9					2				11		5				3			8	7	4				6	
09-Feb	15,978	CARDIFF CITY	0-2	Aston Villa			8		1	9					2				11		6			10	3		5		7	4					
21-Feb	12,938	Leicester City	2-0	CARDIFF CITY			10		1						2		5		11		6	9			3			8	7	4					
23-Feb	13,070	CARDIFF CITY	2-2	Manchester United	Ferguson, S Davies	6		10	1	9					2		5		11		4	8			3				7						
02-Mar	21,546	Sunderland	1-0	CARDIFF CITY		6	10		1				8		2		5					9			3				7	4	11				
09-Mar	18,636	CARDIFF CITY	3-1	Sheffield Wednesday	Thirlaway, L Davies, Warren	6	10		1				8		2		5					9			3				7	4	11				
16-Mar	28,393	Arsenal	2-1	CARDIFF CITY	L Davies	6	10		1				8		2		5					9			3				7	4	11				
23-Mar	14,681	CARDIFF CITY	0-2	Everton		6	10		1				8		2		5				4	9			3				7		11				
29-Mar	30,927	Liverpool	2-0	CARDIFF CITY		6	10		1				8		2		5	7				9			3					4	11				
30-Mar	13,332	Huddersfield Town	1-1	CARDIFF CITY	L Davies	6	9		1						2		5	7	10		4				3					8	11				
01-Apr	16,849	CARDIFF CITY	1-2	Liverpool	Wake	6	9		1					4	2			7	10						3		5			8	11				
06-Apr	11,392	CARDIFF CITY	1-3	Manchester City	Munro	6			1				8		2		5					9		10					7	4	11	3			
13-Apr	12,997	Birmingham	0-0	CARDIFF CITY		6	10		1						2		5	8	7		4	9			3						11				
20-Apr	10,834	CARDIFF CITY	1-1	Portsmouth	Munro	6	10								2	5	4	8	7			9			3								1		11
04-May	5,738	CARDIFF CITY	1-1	Blackburn Rovers	Harris				1			6	8		3	5	4					9	2	10					7		11				
					Appearances	24	27	14	35	20	6	22	13	13	42	2	36	6	33	2	9	11	11	7	21	2	15	14	37	17	19	1	1	1	1
					Goals		8	2		14			2						2	1		2		1			1	1	5	3	1				

1 George Blackburn
2 Len Davies
3 Stan Davies
4 Tom Farquharson
5 Hughie Ferguson
6 Tommy Hampson
7 Billy Hardy
8 Frank Harris
9 Tom Helsby
10 Jack Jennings
11 Emlyn John
12 Fred Keenor
13 Frank Matson
14 George McLachlan
15 Albert Miles
16 Frank Moss
17 Jim Munro
18 Jimmy Nelson
19 Walter Robbins
20 Bill Roberts
21 William Shaw
22 Tom Sloan
23 Tom Smith
24 Billy Thirlaway
25 Harry Wake
26 Freddie Warren
27 Tom Watson
28 Joe Hillier
29 Jimmy McGrath
30 Matthew Robinson

1929-30 8th in Division Two

Date	Att	Home	Score	Away	Scorers	1	2	3	4	5	6	7	8	9	10	11	12	13	14	15	16	17	18	19	20	21	22	23	24	25	26	27	28	29
31-Aug	24,173	Charlton Athletic	4-1	CARDIFF CITY	Robbins			1	6				2			4	8	7						2	10				9		11			5
02-Sep	13,510	CARDIFF CITY	2-0	Preston North End	Robbins 2	6		1					2			5	8	7							10	3			9	4	11			
07-Sep	12,664	CARDIFF CITY	0-1	Hull City		6		1					2			5	8	7							10	3			9	4	11			
09-Sep	5,963	Preston North End	2-3	CARDIFF CITY	Matson, Warren, Harris		9	1	6	8			2			5		7							10	3				4	11			
14-Sep	19,065	Stoke City	1-1	CARDIFF CITY	Davies		9	1	6	8			2			5		7							10	3				4	11			
16-Sep	11,533	CARDIFF CITY	3-1	Notts County	Matson, Warren, Harris	6	9	1		8			2			5		7								3	10			4	11			
21-Sep	13,314	CARDIFF CITY	0-0	Wolves			9	1	6	8			2			5		7								3	10			4	11			
25-Sep	7,778	Notts County	2-1	CARDIFF CITY	Warren	6	9	1		8			2			5		7								3	10			4	11			
28-Sep	18,886	Bradford City	0-1	CARDIFF CITY	Warren	10	9	1	6	8			2			5		7								3				4	11			
05-Oct	29,093	CARDIFF CITY	0-0	Swansea Town		6	9	1		8			2			5		7							10	3				4	11			
12-Oct	15,900	Blackpool	3-0	CARDIFF CITY		6	9	1		8			2			5		7							10	3				4	11			
19-Oct	12,058	CARDIFF CITY	1-0	Barnsley	Harris		9	1	6	8			2			5		7							10	3				4	11			
26-Oct	18,455	Bradford	2-0	CARDIFF CITY		6		1		8			2	5				7			11	9			10	3				4				
02-Nov	11,916	CARDIFF CITY	3-2	West Brom	Davies, Miles, Thirlaway	6	10	1		8			2			5					11	9				3		7		4				
09-Nov	23,071	Tottenham Hotspur	1-2	CARDIFF CITY	Miles, Robinson	6	8	1					2			5					11	9				3	10	7		4				
16-Nov	10,969	CARDIFF CITY	5-2	Southampton	Thirlaway 3, Roberts, Davies	6	8	1					2			5					11	9				3	10	7		4				
23-Nov	14,208	Millwall	2-0	CARDIFF CITY		6				8		1	2			5					11	9				3	10	7		4				
30-Nov	12,112	CARDIFF CITY	5-0	Oldham Athletic	Miles 3, Thirlaway, McLachlan	6	8					1	2			5					11	9				3	10	7		4				
07-Dec	4,385	Nottingham Forest	3-1	CARDIFF CITY	McLachlan	6	8					1	2			5					11	9				3	10	7		4				
14-Dec	10,536	CARDIFF CITY	1-0	Chelsea	Davies	6	8	1					2			5					11	9				3	10	7		4				
21-Dec	9,249	Bury	4-2	CARDIFF CITY	Thirlaway, Warren	6	8	1					2			5							9		10	3		7		4	11			
25-Dec	17,140	Bristol City	2-0	CARDIFF CITY		6	8	1					2			5						9				3	10	7		4	11			
26-Dec	25,244	CARDIFF CITY	1-1	Bristol City	Wake	11	8	1	6				2			5						9		2		10		7		4				
28-Dec	5,793	CARDIFF CITY	1-0	Charlton Athletic	Miles	6	8	1	4				2			5			11			9			10	3		7						
04-Jan	11,695	Hull City	2-2	CARDIFF CITY	Davies, Munro	6	8	1					2			5			11				9			3	10	7		4				
18-Jan	13,888	CARDIFF CITY	1-2	Stoke City	Robinson	6	8	1					3			5			11				9	2			10	7		4				
01-Feb	8,287	CARDIFF CITY	0-1	Bradford City		6	8	1						5					11	2					10	3		7		4		9		
08-Feb	22,121	Swansea Town	1-0	CARDIFF CITY		6	8	1							10	5								2		3	11	7		4		9		
15-Feb	12,730	CARDIFF CITY	4-2	Blackpool	Williams, Blackburn, Davies, Harris	6	7	1		8					10	5								2		3	11			4		9		
22-Feb	7,345	Barnsley	2-2	CARDIFF CITY	Williams 2	6	7	1		8					10	5								2		3	11			4		9		
01-Mar	11,442	CARDIFF CITY	2-0	Bradford	Williams, Jones		7	1		8	6				10	5								2	11	3				4		9		
08-Mar	15,310	West Brom	0-2	CARDIFF CITY	Robbins, Harris		7	1		8	6				10	5								2	11	3				4		9		
15-Mar	15,404	CARDIFF CITY	1-0	Tottenham Hotspur	Jones	6	7	1		8					10	5								2	11	3				4		9		
22-Mar	13,725	Southampton	1-1	CARDIFF CITY	Williams	6	7	1		8					10	5								2	11	3				4		9		
29-Mar	12,219	CARDIFF CITY	3-1	Millwall	Williams 2, Jones	6	8	1							10	5								2	11	3		7		4		9		
05-Apr	18,596	Oldham Athletic	4-1	CARDIFF CITY	Robbins	6	8	1							10	5								2	11	3		7		4		9		
12-Apr	9,328	CARDIFF CITY	1-1	Nottingham Forest	Davies	6	8	1			4				10	5								2	11	3		7				9		
14-Apr	5,210	Wolves	4-0	CARDIFF CITY		6	7	1		8					10	5								2	11	3				4		9		
18-Apr	12,656	CARDIFF CITY	2-1	Reading	Williams, Davies	6	7	1		8				5	10									2	11	3				4		9		
19-Apr	23,100	Chelsea	1-0	CARDIFF CITY		6	7	1		8				5	10									2		3		11		4		9		
21-Apr	18,112	Reading	2-0	CARDIFF CITY		6	7	1		8				5	10				11					2		3				4		9		
26-Apr	7,136	CARDIFF CITY	5-1	Bury	Williams 3, Bird, Davies	6	7	1		8	4			5	10									2		3						9	11	
					Appearances	35	37	39	8	23	4	3	26	6	15	36	3	13	5	1	8	11	3	18	21	40	15	19	3	38	14	16	1	1
					Goals	1	9			5					3			2			2	6	1		5	1	2	6		1	5	11	1	

1 George Blackburn
2 Len Davies
3 Tom Farquharson
4 Billy Hardy
5 Frank Harris
6 Tom Helsby
7 Joe Hillier
8 Jack Jennings
9 Emlyn John
10 Les Jones
11 Fred Keenor
12 Wilf Lievesley
13 Frank Matson
14 Jimmy McGrath
15 Jack McJennett
16 George McLachlan
17 Albert Miles
18 Jim Munro
19 Jimmy Nelson
20 Walter Robbins
21 Bill Roberts
22 Matthew Robinson
23 Billy Thirlaway
24 Albert Valentione
25 Harry Wake
26 Freddie Warren
27 Ralph Williams
28 Don Bird
29 Paddy Moore

1930-31 22nd in Division Two (Relegated)

Date	Att	Home	Score	Away	Scorers	1	2	3	4	5	6	7	8	9	10	11	12	13	14	15	16	17	18	19	20	21	22	23	24	25	26	27	28	29	30	31	32
30-Aug	20,363	Swansea Town	3-2	CARDIFF CITY	Williams 2		6		7	1			8				10	5			2			11	3				4			9					
03-Sep	9,488	Bury	3-0	CARDIFF CITY			6		7	1			8	4			10	5			2			11	3							9					
06-Sep	10,987	CARDIFF CITY	3-6	West Brom	Jones, Bird, Helsby	11	6		7	1		2	8	4			10	5							3							9					
08-Sep	11,463	CARDIFF CITY	1-2	Everton	Bird	11	6		7	1				4		3	8	5						10	2							9					
13-Sep	9,693	Port Vale	2-0	CARDIFF CITY		11	6	7		1			8	4				5						10	3		2					9					
17-Sep	17,464	Everton	1-1	CARDIFF CITY	Williams	11	6		7	1				8		5								10	3		2		4			9					
20-Sep	5,839	CARDIFF CITY	1-1	Bradford City	Bird	11	6		7	1				8		5		6						10			2		4			9					
22-Sep	6,615	CARDIFF CITY	4-1	Plymouth Argyle	Robbins 2, Williams, Davies	11	6	8	7	1				4		3		5						10			2					9					
27-Sep	12,279	Charlton Athletic	4-1	CARDIFF CITY	Williams	11		8	7	1				4		3		5		6				10			2					9					
04-Oct	9,884	CARDIFF CITY	2-0	Barnsley	Helsby, Jones		6	9	7	1				4		3	8	5						11			2					10					
11 Oct	19,447	Bristol City	1-0	CARDIFF CITY		11	6		7	1				4			8	5						10	3		2					9					
18-Oct	11,663	Oldham Athletic	4-2	CARDIFF CITY	Harris, Emmerson		6		7	1			9	8			10	4						11	3		2						5				
25-Oct	8,955	CARDIFF CITY	1-1	Nottingham Forest	Jones	11	6		8	1				5			10						7		3		2	9	4								
01-Nov	12,182	Southampton	0-1	CARDIFF CITY	Keenor	11	6		7	1				8			10	5							3		2	9	4								
08-Nov	10,902	CARDIFF CITY	5-0	Reading	Robbins 2, Valentine 2, Jones		6		7	1				8			11	5						10	3		2	9	4								
15-Nov	8,666	Stoke City	1-0	CARDIFF CITY			6		7	1				8			11	5						10	3		2	9	4								
22-Nov	5,475	CARDIFF CITY	0-3	Bradford		11	6		7	1			8	5			10								3		2	9	4								
29-Nov	6,995	Wolves	4-1	CARDIFF CITY	Valentine		6		7	1		3		8			11	5						10			2	9	4								
06-Dec	6,400	CARDIFF CITY	4-4	Millwall	Robbins 3, Emmerson		6		7			3		4			10	5						11			2	9	8						1		
13-Dec	13,457	Preston North End	7-0	CARDIFF CITY			6		8	1				4				5					7	11		10	2	9		3							
20-Dec	7,485	CARDIFF CITY	4-0	Burnley	Robbins 2, Jones, Emmerson		6		7	1				4			10	5						11			2	8		3		9					
26-Dec	31,106	Plymouth Argyle	5-1	CARDIFF CITY	Williams		6		7	1				4			10	5						11			2	8		3		9					
27-Dec	24,232	CARDIFF CITY	1-0	Swansea Town	Jones		6		7	1				4			10	5						11			2	8		3		9					
03-Jan	13,792	West Brom	3-2	CARDIFF CITY	McCambridge 2				7	1				4			10	5	9	6				11			2	8		3							
17-Jan	8,028	CARDIFF CITY	2-1	Port Vale	Robbins 2				7	1				4			8	5	10	6	2			9						3	11						
31-Jan	4,470	CARDIFF CITY	0-2	Charlton Athletic			6		7	1			5				8	4	10					9			2			3	11						
04-Feb	4,799	Bradford City	2-1	CARDIFF CITY	McCambridge				7	1				4	5		10		9	6				11			2	8		3							
07-Feb	5,399	Barnsley	4-0	CARDIFF CITY					7	1				4			10	5	9	6				11			2			3						8	
14-Feb	11,780	CARDIFF CITY	0-1	Bristol City				10	7	1	5			4				6	9					11			2			3						8	
21-Feb	8,911	CARDIFF CITY	0-0	Oldham Athletic			6	9	7	1	5			4					10								2			3	11					8	
28-Feb	3,565	Nottingham Forest	3-1	CARDIFF CITY	Davies			9	7	1	5	6	4						10			8					2			3	11						
07-Mar	5,555	CARDIFF CITY	0-1	Southampton			6	11	7	1	5	3	9	4			10					8					2										
14-Mar	9,555	Reading	3-0	CARDIFF CITY		11		8	7	1		3	4					5	9	6						10	2										
21-Mar	5,372	CARDIFF CITY	3-2	Stoke City	McCambridge 3		6		7	1	5	2	4				10		9	11		8			3												
28-Mar	6,557	Bradford	3-0	CARDIFF CITY					7	1	5	2	4		6		10		9	11		8			3												
03-Apr	41,547	Tottenham Hotspur	2-2	CARDIFF CITY	McCambridge 2				7	1	5	2	4		6		10		9			8			3												
04-Apr	6,659	CARDIFF CITY	0-3	Wolves					7	1	5	2	4		6		10		9	11		8			3												
06-Apr	6,666	CARDIFF CITY	0-0	Tottenham Hotspur			6	9	7	1		3	4				10	5		11		8					2				11						
11-Apr	14,328	Millwall	0-0	CARDIFF CITY					7	1	5	3	4		6		10		9	11		8					2										
18-Apr	4,082	CARDIFF CITY	0-0	Preston North End					7	1	5	3	4		6		10		9	11							2									8	
25-Apr	4,125	Burnley	1-0	CARDIFF CITY					7		5	3	4		6		10		9	11							2								1	8	
02-May	3,841	CARDIFF CITY	1-3	Bury	Jones						5		4		6		10			11			7				2							9	1	8	3
					Appearances	12	27	10	40	39	12	14	19	29	8	6	32	27	16	14	3	8	3	25	17	2	33	13	10	12	5	14	1	1	3	6	1
					Goals	3		2	3				1	2			7	1	8					11				3				6					

1 Don Bird
2 George Blackburn
3 Len Davies
4 George Emmerson
5 Tom Farquharson
6 Jack Galbraith
7 Billy Hardy
8 Frank Harris
9 Tom Helsby
10 Eddie Jenkins
11 Emlyn John
12 Les Jones
13 Fred Keenor
14 Jim McCambridge
15 Jimmy McGrath
16 Jack McJennett
17 Bill Merry
18 Idris Miles
19 Walter Robbins
20 Bill Roberts
21 Matthew Robinson
22 Jock Smith
23 Albert Valentine
24 Harry Wake
25 Tom Ware
26 Bobby Weale
27 Ralph Williams
28 Tom Wilson
29 Albert Mayo
30 Len Evans
31 Albert Keating
32 Ralph Blakemore

1931-32 9th in Division Three (South)

Date	Att	Home	Score	Away	Scorers	1	2	3	4	5	6	7	8	9	10	11	12	13	14	15	16	17	18	19	20	21	22
29-Aug	13,448	Northampton Town	1-0	CARDIFF CITY		7			1			4	5					10			8		9	11	3	6	2
31-Aug	10,435	CARDIFF CITY	1-1	Brighton	O'Neill	7			1	5		4						10			8		9	11	3	6	2
05-Sep	9,562	CARDIFF CITY	5-1	Reading	Robbins 3, Jones, McCambridge	7			1	5	6	4				10		9			8			11	3		2
07-Sep	11,648	Coventry City	2-1	CARDIFF CITY	McCambridge	7		1		5	6	4						9			8		10	11	3		2
12-Sep	7,494	Southend United	1-1	CARDIFF CITY	og	7			1	5	6	4				10		9	11		8				3		2
14-Sep	7,105	CARDIFF CITY	6-1	Coventry City	Keating 2, Robbins 2, Jones, McCambridge	7			1	5	6	4				10	8	9						11	3		2
19-Sep	13,233	CARDIFF CITY	0-3	Fulham		7			1	5	6	4				10	8	9						11	3		2
26-Sep	3,528	Thames	1-2	CARDIFF CITY	McCambridge, Keating	7			1	5		4					8	10	6		9			11	3		2
03-Oct	9,521	CARDIFF CITY	3-2	Brentford	Emmerson, Robbins, Keating	7			1	5		4				10	8	9	6					11	3		2
10-Oct	8,160	Exeter City	3-1	CARDIFF CITY	Emmerson	7	4	1		5		8				10		9	6					11	3		2
17-Oct	7,688	CARDIFF CITY	2-0	Mansfield Town	Emmerson, Robbins	7		1		5		4				10	8		6				9	11	3		2
24-Oct	11,526	Watford	3-0	CARDIFF CITY		7		1		5	2	4				10	8		6				9	11	3		
31-Oct	6,757	CARDIFF CITY	1-3	Crystal Palace	Emmerson	7			1	5	2	4			6	10	8	9	11						3		
07-Nov	6,562	Bournemouth	3-0	CARDIFF CITY		7	8		1	5	6	4				10		11						9	3		2
14-Nov	3,491	CARDIFF CITY	0-4	Queen's Park Rangers		7	8		1			4	5					10		2			9	11	3	6	
21-Nov	9,047	Bristol Rovers	2-2	CARDIFF CITY	O'Neill, Ronan (p)	7	8		1	5		4						10					9	11	3	6	2
05-Dec	6,524	Clapton Orient	1-1	CARDIFF CITY	Keating	7	8		1	5		4				11	10						9		3	6	2
19-Dec	7,904	Norwich City	2-0	CARDIFF CITY		7			1	5		4					8	10					9	11	3	6	2
25-Dec	11,609	Luton Town	2-1	CARDIFF CITY	Keating	7			1	5		4				10	8	9						11	3	6	2
26-Dec	13,515	CARDIFF CITY	4-1	Luton Town	Robbins 2, Keating, McCambridge	7			1	5		4				10	8	9						11	3	6	2
02-Jan	3,917	CARDIFF CITY	5-0	Northampton Town	McCambridge 2, Robbins, Emmerson, Harris	7			1	5		4				10	8	9				2		11	3	6	
13-Jan	3,890	CARDIFF CITY	5-2	Torquay United	Emmerson 2, McCambridge, Keating, Robbins	7			1	5		4				10	8	9						11	3	6	2
16-Jan	7,065	Reading	5-1	CARDIFF CITY	McCambridge	7			1	5				4		10	8	9				2		11	3	6	
23-Jan	6,831	CARDIFF CITY	2-3	Southend United	Robbins, og	7			1			4		5		10	9	9						11	3	6	2
30-Jan	14,690	Fulham	4-0	CARDIFF CITY		7	8		1	5		4				10	8							11	3	6	2
06-Feb	6,698	CARDIFF CITY	9-2	Thames	Robbins 5, Jones, McCambridge, Emmerson, Keating	7			1	5		4				9	8	10				2		11	3	6	
13-Feb	16,239	Brentford	2-3	CARDIFF CITY	McCambridge, Keating, Robbins	7			1	5		4				9	8	10				2		11	3	6	
20-Feb	8,817	CARDIFF CITY	5-2	Exeter City	Robbins 2, Jones, Emmerson, McCambridge	7			1	5		4				9	8	10				2		11	3	6	
27-Feb	8,316	Mansfield Town	1-2	CARDIFF CITY	McCambridge 2	7			1	5		4				9	8	10				2		11	3	6	
05-Mar	10,019	CARDIFF CITY	2-1	Watford	Robbins, Jones	7			1	5		4				9	8	10				2		11	3	6	
12-Mar	13,206	Crystal Palace	5-0	CARDIFF CITY		7			1	5		4				9	8	10				2		11	3	6	
19-Mar	6,863	CARDIFF CITY	0-0	Bournemouth		7			1	5		4				9	8	10				2		11	3	6	
25-Mar	8,015	Gillingham	1-1	CARDIFF CITY	Keating	7			1	5		4				9	8	10						11	3	6	2
26-Mar	8,324	Queen's Park Rangers	2-3	CARDIFF CITY	McCambridge 3	7			1	5		4				9	8	10						11	3	6	2
28-Mar	10,455	CARDIFF CITY	1-0	Gillingham	McCambridge	7			1	5	4					9	8	10				2		11	3	6	
02-Apr	6,773	CARDIFF CITY	3-1	Bristol Rovers	Keating 2, McCambridge	7			1	5		4				9	8	10	6			2		11	3		
09-Apr	3,437	Torquay United	2-2	CARDIFF CITY	McCambridge 2	7			1	5		4		6		11	8	10							3	10	2
13-Apr	4,018	CARDIFF CITY	3-0	Swindon Town	Keating 2, Emmerson	7			1	5		4		6		10	8	9	11						3		2
16-Apr	5,290	CARDIFF CITY	5-0	Clapton Orient	McCambridge 3, Keating 2	7			1	5		4		6		10	8	9	11						3		2
23-Apr	3,728	Swindon Town	1-4	CARDIFF CITY	McCambridge 2, Keating 2	7			1	5		4				10	8	9	11						3	6	2
30-Apr	6,487	CARDIFF CITY	0-2	Norwich City		7			1	5		4				10	8	9	11						3	6	2
07-May	5,447	Brighton	0-0	CARDIFF CITY		7	8		1	5		4				10		9	11						3	6	2
					Appearances	42	7	4	38	39	9	40	2	5	1	35	32	38	13	1	6	11	9	33	42	27	28
					Goals	10						1				5	19	26					2	21		1	

1 George Emmerson
2 Albert Evans
3 Len Evans
4 Tom Farquharson
5 Jack Galbraith
6 Billy Hardy
7 Frank Harris
8 Stan Holt
9 Eddie Jenkins
10 Emlyn John
11 Les Jones
12 Albert Keating
13 Jim McCambridge
14 Jimmy McGrath
15 Jack McJennett
16 Owen McNally
17 Eric Morris
18 Harry O'Neill
19 Walter Robbins
20 Bill Roberts
21 Peter Ronan
22 Jock Smith

1932-33 19th in Division Three (South)

Date	Att	Home	Score	Away	Scorers	1	2	3	4	5	6	7	8	9	10	11	12	13	14	15	16	17	18	19	20	21	22	23	24	25	26	27
27-Aug	13,867	Reading	4-2	CARDIFF CITY	Cribb, McCambridge			11	7	4			1	5			8			10			9			2		3	6			
29-Aug	8,351	CARDIFF CITY	3-0	Bournemouth	Keating, Cribb, Jones			11	7	6			1	5	4					10	8		9			2		3				
03-Sep	9,767	CARDIFF CITY	4-2	Norwich City	McCambridge 2, Emmerson, Cribb			11	7	6			1	5	4		8			10			9			2		3				
07-Sep	6,264	Bournemouth	3-2	CARDIFF CITY	McCambridge 2			11	7	6			1	5	4		8			10			9			2		3				
10-Sep	7,790	Brighton	1-0	CARDIFF CITY				11	7	8			1	5	4		9		6				10			2		3				
17-Sep	9,104	CARDIFF CITY	4-3	Bristol Rovers	McCambridge 2, Keating, Cribb			11	7	6			1	5	4		10				8		9			2		3				
24-Sep	7,172	Aldershot Town	1-0	CARDIFF CITY				11	7	6			1	5	4		10				8		9			2		3				
01-Oct	7,842	CARDIFF CITY	2-5	Queen's Park Rangers	Jones 2			11	7	6			1	5	4					10	8		9			2		3				
08-Oct	3,590	Southend United	2-2	CARDIFF CITY	Keating, McCambridge			11	7	6			1	5	4		10		3		8		9	2								
15-Oct	7,144	CARDIFF CITY	1-1	Crystal Palace	McCambridge			11	7				1	5	4		10		2	6	8		9					3				
22-Oct	10,163	CARDIFF CITY	1-3	Newport County	McCambridge			11	7				1	5	4		10		2	6	8		9					3				
29-Oct	6,002	Luton Town	8-1	CARDIFF CITY	McCambridge			11	7	6			1	5	4		8			10			9	2			3					
05-Nov	4,881	CARDIFF CITY	1-3	Exeter City	Emmerson				7	6		1		5	4		10		3	11			9	2								8
12-Nov	3,911	Torquay United	4-1	CARDIFF CITY	Cribb			11	7	6			1	5	4		8		3	10			9	2								
19-Nov	5,274	CARDIFF CITY	2-1	Brentford	Jones, Cribb			11	7				1	5	4		8		3	10			9	2					6			
03-Dec	6,115	CARDIFF CITY	1-1	Bristol City	Jones		11		7	6			1	5	4			8	3	10			9							2		
17-Dec	4,433	CARDIFF CITY	6-1	Clapton Orient	McCambridge 2, Hill, Harris, Jones, Cribb			11	7	6			1	5	4		8		3	10			9			2						
24-Dec	6,145	Swindon Town	6-2	CARDIFF CITY	McCambridge 2			11	7	6			1	5	4		8		3	10			9			2						
26-Dec	11,178	CARDIFF CITY	1-0	Gillingham	Jones		11		7				1	5	4		8		6	10			9			2				3		
27-Dec	10,449	Gillingham	1-1	CARDIFF CITY	Jones		11						1	5	4		8		6	10			9			2				3	7	
31-Dec	6,773	CARDIFF CITY	0-1	Reading			11		7				1	5	4		8		6	10			9			2				3		
07-Jan	9,486	Norwich City	3-1	CARDIFF CITY	Jones (p)			11					1	5	4		8		6	10			9			2				3	7	
14-Jan	9,752	Coventry City	5-0	CARDIFF CITY				11	7				1	5	4				6	10			9		8	2				3		
21-Jan	4,185	CARDIFF CITY	1-2	Brighton	McCambridge			11	7				1	5					4	10		8	9			2			6	3		
28-Jan	6,249	Bristol Rovers	0-0	CARDIFF CITY				11					1	5	4		10		3	9		8	6		7					2		
04-Feb	4,287	CARDIFF CITY	2-1	Aldershot Town	Maidment, Henderson				7		6		1	5	4	9			3	11		8	10							2		
11-Feb	5,347	Queen's Park Rangers	5-1	CARDIFF CITY	Maidment			11	7				1	5		9			3	6		8	10			4				2		
18-Feb	5,275	CARDIFF CITY	2-0	Southend United	Jones 2	1	11		7					5		9			6	10		8	4			2				3		
25-Feb	5,805	Crystal Palace	4-1	CARDIFF CITY	Maidment	1	11		7					5		9			6	10		8	4			2				3		
04-Mar	7,933	Newport County	4-2	CARDIFF CITY	Emmerson, Henderson		11		7				1	5		9			6	10		8	4			2				3		
11-Mar	5,919	CARDIFF CITY	3-2	Luton Town	Jones, Cribb, Maidment			11	7				1	5	4				6	10		8	9			2				3		
18-Mar	8,146	Exeter City	1-0	CARDIFF CITY				11	7				1	5	4	9			6	10		8				2				3		
25-Mar	6,630	CARDIFF CITY	2-1	Torquay United	Henderson 2				7				1	5	4	9			6	10		8	11			2				3		
01-Apr	10,831	Brentford	7-3	CARDIFF CITY	Henderson 3				7				1	5	4	9			6	10		8	11			2				3		
08-Apr	5,902	CARDIFF CITY	2-2	Coventry City	Henderson, McCambridge			11	7				1	5	4	9			6	10			8			2				3		
10-Apr	2,304	Northampton Town	2-0	CARDIFF CITY					7				1	5	4	9			6	10		8	11			2				3		
14-Apr	9,451	CARDIFF CITY	1-1	Watford	Jones				7				1	5	4	9			6	10		8	11			2				3		
15-Apr	7,176	Bristol City	3-1	CARDIFF CITY	Russell	1			7					5	4	9			6	11		8	10			2				3		
17-Apr	7,713	Watford	2-1	CARDIFF CITY	Jones								1	5		9	7		6	11		4	10		8	2				3		
22-Apr	6,631	CARDIFF CITY	6-0	Northampton Town	Henderson 5, Cribb			11	7				1	5	4	9				8		6	10			2				3		
29-Apr	3,739	Clapton Orient	3-0	CARDIFF CITY				11	7				1		4	9			5	8		6	10			2				3		
06-May	7,871	CARDIFF CITY	3-0	Swindon Town	Cribb 2, Maidment			11	7				1	5	4	9			3	8		6	10							2		
					Appearances	3	7	27	38	15	1	1	38	41	35	16	21	1	33	38	7	18	41	5	3	31	1	10	3	25	2	1
					Goals			11	3						1	13	1			13	3	6	17							1		

1 Bob Adams
2 Jack Collins
3 Stan Cribb
4 George Emmerson
5 Albert Evans
6 Rollo Evans
7 Len Evans
8 Tom Farquharson
9 Jack Galbraith
10 Frank Harris
11 Jim Henderson
12 Freddie Hill
13 Ralph Horton
14 Eddie Jenkins
15 Les Jones
16 Albert Keating
17 Tom Maidment
18 Jim McCambridge
19 Eric Morris
20 Tommy Paget
21 Bob Pollard
22 Len Richards
23 Bill Roberts
24 Peter Ronan
25 George Russell
26 Jim Tennant
27 Ernie Carless

1933-34 22nd in Division Three (South) Re-Elected

Date	Att	Home	Score	Away	Scorers	1	2	3	4	5	6	7	8	9	10	11	12	13	14	15	16	17	18	19	20	21	22	23	24	25	26	27	28
26-Aug	11,561	Watford	1-2	CARDIFF CITY	Hutchinson 2			2				1		5	9		11	6	10			4	7						8		3		
28-Aug	13,824	CARDIFF CITY	2-0	Reading	Henderson 2 (p)			2				1		5	9		11	6	10			4	7						8		3		
02-Sep	15,513	CARDIFF CITY	1-1	Charlton Athletic	Postin			2				1		5	9		11	6	10			4	7						8		3		
06-Sep	9,198	Reading	3-1	CARDIFF CITY	Maidment			2			6	1		5	9	8			10			4	7					11			3		
09-Sep	9,315	Bournemouth	1-3	CARDIFF CITY	Henderson 2, Postin			2				1		5	9			6	10			4	7					11	8		3		
16-Sep	13,666	CARDIFF CITY	0-1	Torquay United				2				1		5	9			6	10			4	7					11	8		3		
23-Sep	10,241	CARDIFF CITY	2-1	Exeter City	Marcroft. Hutchinson			2				1		5	9		11	6	10			4	7				8				3		
30-Sep	8,907	Gillingham	6-2	CARDIFF CITY	Hutchinson, Henderson			2				1		5	9		11	6	10			4	7				8				3		
07-Oct	9,022	CARDIFF CITY	4-0	Crystal Palace	Postin 2, Jones, Henderson	1		2						5	11	9		6	10			4	7						8		3		
14-Oct	11,860	Bristol Rovers	3-1	CARDIFF CITY	Marcroft	1		2						5	9	11			10			4	7	6					8		3		
21-Oct	12,169	Queen's Park Rangers	4-0	CARDIFF CITY								1		5		11		6	10			8	7	4					9		2		3
28-Oct	16,175	CARDIFF CITY	1-1	Newport County	Jones	1		2						5			11	6	10			8	7	4					9		3		
04-Nov	10,698	Norwich City	2-0	CARDIFF CITY		1		2						5			11	6	10			8	7	4					9		3		
11-Nov	9,090	CARDIFF CITY	1-5	Bristol City	Galbraith	1		2						5		9	11	6	10				7	4					8		3		
18-Nov	8,402	Clapton Orient	4-2	CARDIFF CITY	Hill, Henderson			2				1		5	9	11		6	10			4	7						8		3		
02-Dec	5,612	Brighton	4-0	CARDIFF CITY		1		2	10		6			5		8						4	7					11			3	9	
16-Dec	5,984	Luton Town	3-1	CARDIFF CITY	West	1		2	10		6			5			11		8			4	7								3	9	
23-Dec	6,168	CARDIFF CITY	1-3	Northampton Town	Curtis (p)	1	6	2	10					5			11		8			4	7								3	9	
25-Dec	27,589	Coventry City	4-1	CARDIFF CITY	Maidment		4	2	10		6	1					11	5	8			9	7								3		
26-Dec	10,729	CARDIFF CITY	3-3	Coventry City	Curtis, Postin, og		4	2	11		6	1		5					10			8	7						9		3		
30-Dec	6,010	CARDIFF CITY	4-1	Watford	Postin, Rogers. Curtis, Jones		4	2	11		6	1		5					10			8							9	7	3		
06-Jan	11,020	Charlton Athletic	2-0	CARDIFF CITY				2	11		6	1		5				4	10				7				8		9		3		
17-Jan	2,859	CARDIFF CITY	0-1	Swindon Town				2	11		6	1		5		9		4	8			10	7								3		
20-Jan	4,261	CARDIFF CITY	4-2	Bournemouth	Henderson 2, West, Curtis			2	10		6	1		5	9		11	4											8		3	7	
27-Jan	3,091	Torquay United	3-1	CARDIFF CITY	Marshalsey			2	10		6	1		5	9		11							4					8		3	7	
03-Feb	6,091	Exeter City	4-0	CARDIFF CITY				2	10		6	1		5	9		11								4				8	7	3		
10-Feb	5,194	CARDIFF CITY	1-3	Gillingham	Postin			2	10		6	1		5	9		11					8			4				7		3		
17-Feb	6,290	Crystal Palace	3-2	CARDIFF CITY	Henderson, Curtis			2	11	3		1			9		10	5			4		7		6				8				
24-Feb	6,591	CARDIFF CITY	1-5	Bristol Rovers	Postin			2	10	3		1			9		11	5			4		7		6				8				
03-Mar	6,140	CARDIFF CITY	3-1	Queen's Park Rangers	Henderson 2, Curtis			2	11			1			9			4		7	10				6	5			8		3		
10-Mar	10,438	Newport County	2-2	CARDIFF CITY	Postin 2			2	11			1			9			4		7	10				6	5			8		3		
17-Mar	8,630	CARDIFF CITY	0-2	Norwich City				2				1			9		11	4		7	10				6	5			8		3		
24-Mar	7,186	Bristol City	3-0	CARDIFF CITY				2				1		4	8		11			9	10				6	5		7			3		
30-Mar	7,890	CARDIFF CITY	1-1	Southend United	Postin			2				1		4			11	3		9	10		7		6	5			8				
31-Mar	5,154	CARDIFF CITY	1-2	Clapton Orient	Postin			2				1	6	4			11	3		9	10		7			5			8				
02-Apr	9,303	Southend United	1-1	CARDIFF CITY	Postin			2				1	6	4	10		11	3		9				7		5			8				
07-Apr	7,163	Swindon Town	6-3	CARDIFF CITY	Keating 2, Lewis			2				1	6	4	10			3		9	7	11				5			8				
14-Apr	4,237	CARDIFF CITY	1-4	Brighton	Keating			2			6	1		4			11	3		9	10	7				5			8				
21-Apr	2,484	Aldershot Town	1-3	CARDIFF CITY	Keating 3					2		1		4	8			3		9	6	7				5		11	10				
25-Apr	2,660	CARDIFF CITY	1-2	Aldershot Town	Perks					2		1		4	8			3		9	6	7				5		11	10				
28-Apr	3,080	CARDIFF CITY	0-4	Luton Town						2		1		4	8			3		9	6		7			5		11	10				
05-May	2,992	Northampton Town	2-0	CARDIFF CITY						2		1		4	8			3			6		7			5		11	10			9	
					Appearances	8	4	37	16	6	13	34	3	36	27	8	23	31	22	12	14	26	28	7	9	13	3	9	33	2	31	6	1
					Goals				6					1	12	1	4		3	6	1	2	2	1				1	13	1		2	

1 Bob Adams
2 Les Adlam
3 Bob Calder
4 Ernie Curtis
5 Jack Durkin
6 John Duthie
7 Tom Farquharson
8 Harold Friend
9 Jack Galbraith
10 Jim Henderson
11 Freddie Hill
12 Alex Hutchinson
13 Eddie Jenkins
14 Les Jones
15 Reg Keating
16 Ernie Lewis
17 Tom Maidment
18 Ted Marcroft
19 Bill Marshalsey
20 Paddy Molloy
21 Enoch Mort
22 Tommy Paget
23 Harry Perks
24 Eli Postin
25 Tom Rogers
26 George Russell
27 Joe West
28 John Bartlett

1934-35 19th in Division Three (South)

Date	Att	Home	Score	Away	Scorers	1	2	3	4	5	6	7	8	9	10	11	12	13	14	15	16	17	18	19	20	21	22	23	24	25	26	27
25-Aug	17,193	CARDIFF CITY	2-1	Charlton Athletic	Riley, Keating		5	2	3	1		6		7			11	4			9								10		8	
27-Aug	18,608	CARDIFF CITY	1-0	Luton Town	P Griffiths		5	2	3	1		6		7			11	4			9								10		8	
01-Sep	17,641	Crystal Palace	6-1	CARDIFF CITY	Everest		5	2	3	1		6		7			11	4			9								10			8
03-Sep	9,392	Luton Town	4-0	CARDIFF CITY			5	4	3	1		6			11						8	2		9					10			7
08-Sep	12,663	CARDIFF CITY	2-1	Queen's Park Rangers	Riley, Keating		5	4	3	1		6				8			11		7	2							10			9
10-Sep	11,922	CARDIFF CITY	2-0	Southend United	Riley, Keating		5	4	3	1		6		7					11		8	2							10			9
15-Sep	4,309	Torquay United	5-2	CARDIFF CITY	Hill, Lewis		5	4	3	1		6		7		11					8	2		9					10			
22-Sep	7,111	CARDIFF CITY	1-3	Swindon Town	P Griffiths		5		3	1	6			7			11	4			8	2		9					10			
29-Sep	4,996	Aldershot Town	2-0	CARDIFF CITY			5		3		6						11	4			9	2	1	8					10		7	
06-Oct	5,053	CARDIFF CITY	2-1	Bournemouth	Riley, Bassett		5		3			6		7			11	4			9	2	1	8					10			
13-Oct	8,957	CARDIFF CITY	0-0	Brighton			5	4	3			6		7			10		11		9	2	1	8								
20-Oct	7,844	Watford	1-3	CARDIFF CITY	Vaughan 2, Hill		5		3							10	11				9	2	1		6		4	7			8	
27-Oct	16,131	CARDIFF CITY	3-4	Newport County	Hill, Keating, Vaughan		5		3							10	11				9	2	1		6		4	7			8	
03-Nov	8,272	Reading	1-1	CARDIFF CITY	Keating		5		3							10	11				9	2	1		6		4	7			8	
10-Nov	9,378	CARDIFF CITY	2-2	Northampton Town	Riley, Hill		5		3							10		2			9		1		6		4	7	11		8	
17-Nov	11,047	Millwall	2-2	CARDIFF CITY	Pugh, Keating		5		3									4			9	2	1	10		6		7	11		8	
01-Dec	8,145	Clapton Orient	0-1	CARDIFF CITY	Whitlow		5		3							8	11	4				2	1	10		6		7				9
08-Dec	8,463	CARDIFF CITY	0-2	Gillingham			5		3							8	11	4				2	1			6		7	10			9
15-Dec	3,439	Exeter City	2-1	CARDIFF CITY	Pugh		5		3			4							11		9	2	1	10		6		7	8			
22-Dec	7,043	CARDIFF CITY	3-3	Bristol City	Riley, Bassett, Keating		5		3			4								11	9	2	1	8		6		7	10			
26-Dec	9,438	Southend United	2-1	CARDIFF CITY	Galbraith		5		3			4								11	9	2	1	8		6		7	10			
29-Dec	12,101	Charlton Athletic	3-1	CARDIFF CITY	Keating		5		3			6						4		11	9	2	1	8				7	10			
05-Jan	9,648	CARDIFF CITY	2-0	Crystal Palace	Pugh, og		5		3				2					4		11	9		1	10		6		7			8	
16-Jan	7,235	CARDIFF CITY	2-4	Coventry City	Keating 2		5		3									4		11	9	2	1		6			7	10		8	
19-Jan	5,548	Queen's Park Rangers	2-2	CARDIFF CITY	Hill, Pugh		5		3			4				8				11	9	2	1		6			7	10			
26-Jan	8,034	CARDIFF CITY	1-1	Torquay United	Hill		5		3							8				11	9	2	1		4	6		7	10			
02-Feb	6,043	Swindon Town	2-1	CARDIFF CITY	Everest		5		3							8		4		11	9	2	1	10	6			7				
09-Feb	6,563	CARDIFF CITY	1-1	Aldershot Town	Hill				3							11		4			9	2	1		6		5	7	10		8	
16-Feb	4,764	Bournemouth	3-1	CARDIFF CITY	Everest (p)		5		3					11		8		4				2	1	9	6			7	10			
23-Feb	5,828	Brighton	3-1	CARDIFF CITY	Pugh				3							8		4		11		2	1	9	6		5	7	10			
02-Mar	9,247	CARDIFF CITY	2-1	Watford	Riley, Lewis		5		3				4			8				11		2	1	9	6			7	10			
09-Mar	8,461	Newport County	4-0	CARDIFF CITY			5		3				4			8				11		2	1	9	6			7	10			
16-Mar	8,684	CARDIFF CITY	1-1	Reading	S Griffiths		5		3				4		11	8						2	1	9		6		7	10			
23-Mar	3,476	Northampton Town	3-0	CARDIFF CITY			5		3				4			8		6				2	1		11			7	10			9
30-Mar	7,282	CARDIFF CITY	3-1	Millwall	Lewis 2, Attley	10	5		3									4	6		9	2	1	8				7	11			
06-Apr	8,176	Coventry City	0-0	CARDIFF CITY			5		3					11		8		2	6		9		1	10				7	4			
13-Apr	7,453	CARDIFF CITY	3-0	Clapton Orient	Keating, Lewis, Attley	10	5		3	1				11				2	6		9			8				7	4			
19-Apr	14,392	CARDIFF CITY	4-1	Bristol Rovers	Keating 2, Pugh, Hill	10	5		3	1						11		2	6		9			8				7	4			
20-Apr	5,820	Gillingham	1-0	CARDIFF CITY		10			3	1				11				2	6		9			8			5	7	4			
22-Apr	10,222	Bristol Rovers	4-1	CARDIFF CITY	Keating 2		5		3	1		6				10		2			9							7	4	11	8	
27-Apr	7,016	CARDIFF CITY	5-0	Exeter City	Keating 4, og	10	5		3	1						11		2			9			8		6		7	4			
04-May	5,558	Bristol City	4-0	CARDIFF CITY		10	5		3	1						11		2			9			8		6		7	4			
					Appearances	6	39	8	42	14	2	15	5	12	2	23	12	26	9	11	34	30	28	26	14	11	7	31	35	1	12	7
					Goals	2	2		3			1		2	1	8					19			5				6	7		3	1

1 Len Attley
2 Billy Bassett
3 Harry Bland
4 Jack Everest
5 Tom Farquharson
6 Syd Fursland
7 Jack Galbraith
8 Arthur Granville
9 Phil Griffiths
10 Stan Griffiths
11 Freddie Hill
12 Billy Jackson
13 Wally Jennings
14 Dai Jones
15 Glyn Jones
16 Reg Keating
17 Edward Lane
18 Jock Leckie
19 Wilf Lewis
20 Paddy Molloy
21 Billy Moore
22 Enoch Mort
23 Reg Pugh
24 Harry Riley
25 Sid Taylor
26 Tommy Vaughan
27 Fred Whitlow

1935-36 20th in Division Three (South)

Date	Att	Home	Score	Away	Scorers	1	2	3	4	5	6	7	8	9	10	11	12	13	14	15	16	17	18	19	20	21	22	23	24	25	26
31-Aug	16,694	Crystal Palace	3-2	CARDIFF CITY	Riley, Hill		5				3	4		2	11			9	1						7		10		8	6	
02-Sep	18,774	CARDIFF CITY	0-0	Bristol Rovers			5			9	3	4		2	11				1						7		10		8	6	
07-Sep	16,850	CARDIFF CITY	2-3	Reading	Roper, og	10	5				3	4		2	11			9	1						7				8	6	
11-Sep	11,209	Bristol Rovers	1-1	CARDIFF CITY	Pugh	10	2				3	4			11			9	1				5		7				8	6	
14-Sep	15,858	Newport County	0-0	CARDIFF CITY			2	10			3	4			11			9	1				5		7				8	6	
16-Sep	7,239	CARDIFF CITY	4-1	Clapton Orient	Hill 2, Roper, Riley		2				3	4			9				1				5		7		10	11	8	6	
21-Sep	5,663	Gillingham	3-0	CARDIFF CITY			2				3	4			9				1				5		7		10	11	8	6	
28-Sep	11,844	CARDIFF CITY	1-1	Bournemouth	Smith		2				3	4						9	1				5		7		10	11	8	6	
05-Oct	12,288	Luton Town	2-2	CARDIFF CITY	Diamond 2		2			9	3	4							1				5		7		10	11	8	6	
12-Oct	11,458	CARDIFF CITY	3-2	Notts County	Hill, Diamond, og		2			9	3	4			10				1				5		7		11		8	6	
19-Oct	12,239	CARDIFF CITY	1-0	Coventry City	Roberts		2			9	3	4			10				1				5		7			11	8	6	
26-Oct	8,224	Swindon Town	2-1	CARDIFF CITY	Pugh		2			9	3	4			10				1				5		7			11	8	6	
02-Nov	8,506	CARDIFF CITY	0-1	Aldershot Town			2			9	3	4							1				5		7		10	11	8	6	
09-Nov	4,590	Exeter City	2-0	CARDIFF CITY			2		1	9	3	4			8					10			5		7			11		6	
16-Nov	8,185	CARDIFF CITY	3-1	Millwall	Roberts 2, Diamond				1	9	3	10			8	2							5		7		4	11		6	
23-Nov	10,350	Bristol City	0-2	CARDIFF CITY	Diamond, Roberts				1	9	3	4			8	2							5		7		10	11		6	
07-Dec	5,048	Queen's Park Rangers	5-1	CARDIFF CITY	Diamond		2		1	9		4		3									5		7		10	11	8	6	
25-Dec	8,478	Southend United	3-1	CARDIFF CITY	Everest	10			1	9	3	4	2					8					5		7			11		6	
26-Dec	11,574	CARDIFF CITY	1-1	Southend United	Diamond					9		4		3		2		8	1				5		7		10	11		6	
28-Dec	7,411	CARDIFF CITY	1-1	Crystal Palace	Diamond				1	9		6	2	3	11			8		10	4		5		7						
04-Jan	8,713	Reading	4-1	CARDIFF CITY	Keating				1	9		6	2	3				8		10	4		5		7	11					
11-Jan	3,560	Torquay United	2-1	CARDIFF CITY	Keating					9		6	2	3				8		10			5	1	7	11			4		
15-Jan	3,765	CARDIFF CITY	0-2	Watford		10				9		6	2	3				8					5	1	7	11			4		
18-Jan	10,981	CARDIFF CITY	2-0	Newport County	Smith, Riley		5					4	2	3						10				1	7	11	8			6	9
25-Jan	5,998	CARDIFF CITY	4-0	Gillingham	Williams 2, Riley, Roberts		5					6	2	3				8						1	7		10	11		4	9
01-Feb	7,058	Bournemouth	4-4	CARDIFF CITY	Keating 2, Williams, Pugh							6	2	3		5		8						1	7		10	11		4	9
08-Feb	12,142	CARDIFF CITY	2-3	Luton Town	Williams 2		5					6	2	3				8						1	7	11	10			4	9
15-Feb	4,639	Notts County	2-0	CARDIFF CITY			5					6	2	3				8	1						7		10	11		4	9
22-Feb	11,257	Coventry City	5-1	CARDIFF CITY	Everest		5				11	6	2	3				8	1						7				10	4	9
29 Feb	6,390	CARDIFF CITY	5-2	Exeter City	Lewis, Pugh, Smith, Diamond, Williams					11	3	5	2					8	1	10					7				4	6	9
07-Mar	8,198	Brighton	1-0	CARDIFF CITY						11	3	5	2					8	1	10					7				4	6	9
14-Mar	8,637	CARDIFF CITY	2-1	Swindon Town	Keating 2		5		1		3	6	2					8		10					7	11				4	9
18-Mar	4,268	CARDIFF CITY	1-0	Brighton	Williams		5		1		3	6	2				10	8							7			11		4	9
21-Mar	11,774	Millwall	2-4	CARDIFF CITY	Keating 3, Williams				1		3	5	2					8							7		10	11	4	6	9
28-Mar	9,755	CARDIFF CITY	1-0	Bristol City	Keating				1		3	5	2					8							7		10	11	4	6	9
04-Apr	5,165	Watford	4-0	CARDIFF CITY					1		3	5	2					8							7		10	11	4	6	9
10-Apr	11,302	CARDIFF CITY	0-0	Northampton Town			5		1		3	4	2					8							7		10	11		6	9
11-Apr	8,571	CARDIFF CITY	3-2	Queen's Park Rangers	Riley 2, Pugh		5	8	1		2	6		3											7		10	11	4		9
13-Apr	7,890	Northampton Town	2-0	CARDIFF CITY			5	8	1		2	6		3						10					7		11		4		9
18-Apr	4,271	Aldershot Town	1-1	CARDIFF CITY	Williams	11		8	1		2	5		3											7		10		4	6	9
25-Apr	4,206	CARDIFF CITY	1-2	Torquay United	Pugh	11		8	1		3	5	2												7		10		4	6	9
02-May	5,460	Clapton Orient	2-1	CARDIFF CITY	Hill			8	1		3	5	2		11							9			7		10		4	6	
					Appearances	6	25	6	18	18	31	42	21	18	15	4	1	24	18	9	2	1	20	6	42	6	26	22	27	36	18
					Goals					9	2				5			10		1					6		6	5	2	3	9

1 Len Attley
2 Billy Bassett
3 Bryn Davies
4 Jack Deighton
5 Jack Diamond
6 Jack Everest
7 Cliff Godfrey
8 Arthur Granville
9 Hugh Hearty
10 Freddie Hill
11 Wally Jennings
12 Glyn Jones
13 Reg Keating
14 Jock Leckie
15 Wilf Lewis
16 Charles McDonagh
17 James McKenzie
18 Enoch Mort
19 George Poland
20 Reg Pugh
21 Doug Redwood
22 Harry Riley
23 Joe Roberts
24 Harry Roper
25 Harold Smith
26 Dan Williams

1936-37 18th in Division Three (South)

Date	Att	Home	Score	Away	Scorers	1	2	3	4	5	6	7	8	9	10	11	12	13	14	15	16	17	18	19	20	21	22	23	24	25	26	27	28	29	30	31
29-Aug	10,268	Walsall	1-0	CARDIFF CITY		5		1		6	2						4	11	10			7			3	9			8							
31-Aug	16,698	CARDIFF CITY	2-1	Clapton Orient	Pugh, C Smith	5		1		6	2						4		10			7			3	9			8		11					
05-Sep	17,915	CARDIFF CITY	3-0	Luton Town	C Smith 2, Pugh	5		1		6	2						4	11	8			7			3	9			10							
10-Sep	5,471	Clapton Orient	0-1	CARDIFF CITY	Pugh	5		1		6	2						4	11	8			7			3	9			10							
12-Sep	16,732	Newport County	2-3	CARDIFF CITY	Ovenstone, Talbot, C Smith	5		1		6	2						4	11	8			7			3	9			10							
14-Sep	24,936	CARDIFF CITY	3-1	Bristol City	Pugh, Pinxton, Talbot	5		1		6	2						4	11	8			7			3	9			10							
19-Sep	18,348	Crystal Palace	2-2	CARDIFF CITY	C Smith, Pugh	5		1		6	2							11	8			7			3	9	4		10							
26-Sep	21,749	CARDIFF CITY	3-1	Exeter City	Ovenstone, Talbot, C Smith	5		1		6	2						4	11	8			7			3	9			10							
28-Sep	26,094	CARDIFF CITY	1-1	Southend United	Pinxton	5		1		6	2						4	11	8			7			3	9			10							
03-Oct	13,209	Reading	3-0	CARDIFF CITY		5		1		6	2						4	11	8			7			3	9			10							
10-Oct	21,897	CARDIFF CITY	2-0	Queen's Park Rangers	Talbot, Williams	5		1		6	2						4	11	8			7			3				10			9				
24-Oct	14,015	Watford	2-0	CARDIFF CITY		5		1		6	2						4	11	8			7			3				10			9				
31-Oct	17,805	CARDIFF CITY	1-2	Brighton	Granville (p)	5		1			2						4	11				7			3	9	6		10	8						
07-Nov	9,231	Bournemouth	0-2	CARDIFF CITY	Talbot, Walton	5		1		6	2						4	11	10			7			3				8	9						
14-Nov	18,200	CARDIFF CITY	2-1	Northampton Town	Pugh, Walton	5		1		6	2						4	11	10			7			3				8	9						
21-Nov	17,171	Bristol Rovers	5-1	CARDIFF CITY	Talbot	5		1		6	2						4	11	10			7			3				8	9						
05-Dec	10,532	Swindon Town	4-2	CARDIFF CITY	Prescott, C Smith	5	8	1	2	6							4				11	7			3	9				10						
19-Dec	8,361	Gillingham	0-0	CARDIFF CITY		5				6	2						4			1	9	7							8	10	11					3
25-Dec	4,582	Torquay United	1-0	CARDIFF CITY						5	2		6		9		4			1	11	7							8	10						3
26-Dec	31,594	CARDIFF CITY	2-2	Walsall	Walton, Melaniphy					5	2		6		9		4	11		1		7							8	10					3	
28-Dec	12,048	CARDIFF CITY	0-2	Torquay United					2	6					9		4			1		7	11					5	8	10						3
02-Jan	12,368	Luton Town	8-1	CARDIFF CITY	Prescott					6		3			9	2	4			1	7	11						5	8	10						
09-Jan	24,681	CARDIFF CITY	0-1	Newport County						6	2				9	3	4			1	11	7					5		8	10						
23-Jan	9,415	CARDIFF CITY	1-1	Crystal Palace	Talbot					5	2				9	3	4		8	1		7					6		10	11						
03-Feb	2,298	Exeter City	3-1	CARDIFF CITY	Pinxton					5	2		6		9	3	4		8	1			11							10	7					
06-Feb	10,569	CARDIFF CITY	1-1	Reading	Walton							2				3	4		10	1		7	11	6			5		8	9						
13-Feb	11,408	Queen's Park Rangers	6-0	CARDIFF CITY			4					2			7	3			8	1				6		9		5	11	10						
20-Feb	7,100	Southend United	8-1	CARDIFF CITY	C Smith			1				2	6			3	4					7	11			9			8	10					5	
27-Feb	6,283	CARDIFF CITY	2-2	Watford	Granville (p), Walton						2			9		3	4			1		7	11				6	5	8	10						
06-Mar	10,632	Brighton	7-2	CARDIFF CITY	McKenzie, Granville (p)					6	3			9		2	4			1		7	11					5	8	10						
13-Mar	8,582	CARDIFF CITY	2-1	Bournemouth	McKenzie 2			1		5	2			10		3	4				11	7		6					8	9						
20-Mar	7,334	Northampton Town	2-0	CARDIFF CITY				1	2	5				10	8	3	4				11	7		6						9						
26-Mar	17,664	Notts County	4-0	CARDIFF CITY					2	5				8		3	4			1	11	7					6			9						
27-Mar	9,666	CARDIFF CITY	3-1	Bristol Rovers	McKenzie, Pugh, Granville (p)					5	2			10		3	4			1	11	7				9	6			8						
29-Mar	20,245	CARDIFF CITY	0-2	Notts County						5	2		4	10		3			10	1		7	11			9	6			8						
03-Apr	19,489	Millwall	3-1	CARDIFF CITY	Granville (p)	5			9	6	2			10		3	4			1	11	7								8						
10-Apr	9,066	CARDIFF CITY	1-2	Swindon Town	Walton	5				6	2			10	9	3	4	11		1		7								8						
12-Apr	6,775	CARDIFF CITY	0-1	Millwall					3	5	2			10	9		4	11		1		7					6			8						
17-Apr	3,084	Aldershot Town	0-1	CARDIFF CITY	Melaniphy			1	3	5	2			10	9		4	11				7					6			8						
19-Apr	5,940	CARDIFF CITY	4-1	Aldershot Town	Meaniphy 2, Walton, Ovenstone			1	3	5	2			10	9		4	11				7					6			8						
24-Apr	8,358	CARDIFF CITY	2-0	Gillingham	Melaniphy, Ovenstone			1	2	5				10	9		4	11				7					6	3		8						
01-May	4,360	Bristol City	2-1	CARDIFF CITY	(og)			1	3	5					9		4				11						6	2		10			7	8		
					Appearances	20	2	24	10	37	32	4	5	13	15	16	39	21	20	18	11	39	7	4	17	16	14	7	29	30	3	2	1	1	2	3
					Goals						5			4	5			4	3		2	7				8			7	7		1				

1 Billy Bassett
2 Bryn Davies
3 Bill Fielding
4 Louis Ford
5 Cliff Godfrey
6 Arthur Granville
7 Bob MacAuley
8 Bill Main
9 Jim McKenzie
10 Ted Melaniphy
11 John Mellor
12 George Nicholson
13 Davie Ovenstone
14 Albert Pinxton
15 George Poland
16 Jim Prescott
17 Reg Pugh
18 Doug Redwood
19 Harry Roper
20 Bill Scott
21 Cecil Smith
22 Harold Smith
23 James Smith
24 Les Talbot
25 George Walton
26 Arthur Welsby
27 Dan Williams
28 Hugh Campbell
29 Andrew Brown
30 Charlie Turner
31 Jack Estor

1937-38 10th in Division Three (South)

Date	Att	Home	Score	Away	Scorers	1	2	3	4	5	6	7	8	9	10	11	12	13	14	15	16	17	18	19	20	21	22	23	24	25	26
28-Aug	14,598	Clapton Orient	1-1	CARDIFF CITY	Collins	5			9					6	2		1	4			3					7		10	11	8	
30-Aug	20,796	CARDIFF CITY	5-2	Torquay United	Collins 3, Walton, Turner	5			9					6	2		1	4			3					7		10	11	8	
04-Sep	22,912	CARDIFF CITY	5-0	Southend United	Talbot 2, Walton, Turner, Granville (p)	5			9					6	2		1	4			3					7		10	11	8	
08-Sep	5,970	Torquay United	0-1	CARDIFF CITY	Collins	5			9					6	2		1	4			3					7		10	11	8	
11-Sep	15,300	Queen's Park Rangers	2-1	CARDIFF CITY	Turner	5			9					6	2		1	4			3					7		10	11	8	
13-Sep	20,693	CARDIFF CITY	4-1	Northampton Town	Collins 2, Godfrey, Turner	5			9					6			1	4			3					7	2	10	11	8	
18-Sep	28,034	CARDIFF CITY	4-1	Brighton	Collins 2, Walton, Turner	5			9					6	2		1	4		7	3							10	11	8	
25-Sep	10,320	Bournemouth	3-0	CARDIFF CITY		5			9					6	2		1	4			3					7		10	11	8	
02-Oct	35,468	CARDIFF CITY	2-2	Notts County	Turner 2	5			9					6	2		1	4			3					7		10	11	8	
09-Oct	19,086	CARDIFF CITY	3-1	Walsall	Collins, Turner, Pugh	5			9					6			1	4			3					7	3	10	11	8	
16-Oct	24,268	Newport County	1-1	CARDIFF CITY	Talbot	5			9				2	6			1	4			3					7		10	11	8	
23-Oct	17,858	CARDIFF CITY	0-0	Bristol City		5			9					6	2		1	4			3					7		10	11	8	
30-Oct	11,183	Watford	4-0	CARDIFF CITY					9					6	2		1	4					5			7	3	10	11	8	
06-Nov	14,818	CARDIFF CITY	4-0	Gillingham	Turner, Collins, Walton, Talbot				9				3	5	2		1	4						6		7		10	11	8	
13-Nov	9,541	Exeter City	2-1	CARDIFF CITY	Collins				9				3	6	2		1	4					5			7		10	11	8	
20-Nov	15,404	CARDIFF CITY	2-2	Swindon Town	Collins, McCaughey				9				3		2		1	4					5	6		7		10	11	8	
04-Dec	16,160	CARDIFF CITY	3-2	Millwall	Pugh, McCaughey, Walton	5	3		9						2		1	4						6		7		10	11	8	
18-Dec	18,374	CARDIFF CITY	4-2	Crystal Palace	Turner 2(1p), Collins, Talbot	5			9				3	2			1	4						6		7		10	11	8	
25-Dec	12,114	Mansfield Town	3-0	CARDIFF CITY		5			9				3	2			1	4						6		7		10	11	8	
27-Dec	37,726	CARDIFF CITY	4-1	Mansfield Town	Turner 2(1p), Pugh, Collins	5			9				3	2			1	4						6		7		10	11	8	
01-Jan	19,580	CARDIFF CITY	2-0	Clapton Orient	Melaniphy 2	5							3		2		1	4		9				6		7		10	11	8	
12-Jan	2,711	Aldershot	1-1	CARDIFF CITY	Collins	5			9				3	2			1	4						6		7		10	11	8	
15-Jan	6,061	Southend United	3-1	CARDIFF CITY	Turner	5			9				3	2			1	4						6		7		10	11	8	
22-Jan	26,268	CARDIFF CITY	2-2	Queen's Park Rangers	Walton, Turner	5			9				3		2		1	4						6		7		10	11	8	
29-Jan	9,802	Brighton	2-1	CARDIFF CITY	Collins	5			9				3	4	2		1	10						6		7			11	8	
05-Feb	17,563	CARDIFF CITY	3-0	Bournemouth	Walton, Melaniphy, Collins	5	3		9						2		1	4		10				6	7				11	8	
12-Feb	13,278	Notts County	2-0	CARDIFF CITY			3		9			7		5	2		1	4		10				6					11	8	
19-Feb	4,638	Walsall	1-0	CARDIFF CITY					9	8			3		2		1	4				7		6					11	10	5
26-Feb	25,608	CARDIFF CITY	3-1	Newport County	Turner 2(1p), Pugh	5			9				3		2		1	4						6		7		10	11	8	
05-Mar	38,953	Bristol City	0-1	CARDIFF CITY	Collins	5			9				3		2		1	4						6		7		10	11	8	
12-Mar	25,349	CARDIFF CITY	1-1	Watford	McCaughey	5	3		9						2		1	4	10					6		7		8	11		
19-Mar	6,710	Gillingham	1-0	CARDIFF CITY		5	3		9						2		1	4	8					6	7			10	11		
26-Mar	12,065	CARDIFF CITY	1-1	Exeter City	Collins	5	3		9						2		1	4		8		7		6				10	11		
02-Apr	8,797	Swindon Town	2-0	CARDIFF CITY		5			9						2		1		8					6		7	3	10	11		4
09-Apr	7,761	CARDIFF CITY	0-1	Aldershot		5		10	9						2		1	4						6		7	3	8	11		
15-Apr	10,384	CARDIFF CITY	1-1	Bristol Rovers	Collins	5			9						2	10	1	4						6		7	3	8	11		
16-Apr	25,647	Millwall	1-0	CARDIFF CITY		5							3	6	2		1	4	9						8	7		10	11		
18-Apr	9,851	Bristol Rovers	2-1	CARDIFF CITY	Prescott	5			9				3	6	2		1	4	8						11	7		10			
23-Apr	8,281	CARDIFF CITY	4-1	Reading	Turner 2, Collins 2		3		9				2	6			1	4	8							7		10	11		5
30-Apr	9,018	Crystal Palace	1-0	CARDIFF CITY		5	3		9				2				1	4	8					6		7		10	11		
04-May	4,597	Reading	0-0	CARDIFF CITY		5	3		9				2				1	4	8					6		7		10	11		
07-May	6,410	Northampton Town	0-0	CARDIFF CITY		5	3		9		11		2				1	4	8					6		7		10			
					Appearances	35	10	1	40	1	1	1	21	25	30	1	42	41	9	5	12	2	3	25	4	36	6	38	40	30	3
					Goals				23					1	1			3		3					1	4		5	19	7	

1 Billy Bassett
2 Ernie Blenkinsop
3 Andrew Brown
4 Jimmy Collins
5 Bryn Davies
6 Trevor Evans
7 Jim Finlay
8 Louis Ford
9 Cliff Godfrey
10 Arthur Granville
11 Jim Harrison
12 Bob Jones
13 Cecil McCaughey
14 Jim McKenzie
15 Ted Melaniphy
16 John Mellor
17 Jimmy Mitchell
18 Enoch Mort
19 George Nicholson
20 Jim Prescott
21 Reg Pugh
22 James Smith
23 Les Talbot
24 Bert Turner
25 George Walton
26 Tom Williams

1938-39 13th in Division Three (South)

Date	Att	Home	Score	Away	Scorers	1	2	3	4	5	6	7	8	9	10	11	12	13	14	15	16	17	18	19	20	21	22	23	24	25	26	27	28	29
27-Aug	24,645	CARDIFF CITY	1-2	Exeter City	Turner			5		9	4						3		1	2					6		7				10	11	8	
31-Aug	6,959	Mansfield Town	2-2	CARDIFF CITY	Collins 2			5		9	4						2		1	3					6				7	11	10		8	
03-Sep	18,387	Newport County	3-0	CARDIFF CITY				2	5	9	4								1	3					6				7	11	10		8	
05-Sep	15,697	CARDIFF CITY	2-1	Walsall	Collins 2			2	5	9	4								1	3					6		7		8		10	11		
10-Sep	16,179	Ipswich Town	1-2	CARDIFF CITY	Rickards, Prescott			2	5	9									1	3		4			6	11	7		8		10			
17-Sep	15,843	CARDIFF CITY	0-1	Reading				2	5	9									1	3		4			6	11	7		8				10	
24-Sep	10,046	Bristol Rovers	1-1	CARDIFF CITY	Talbot			2	5	9									1	3		4			6	11	7		8		10			
01-Oct	17,393	CARDIFF CITY	4-1	Brighton	Collins 2, Prescott, Rickards			2	5	9									1	3		4			6	11	7		8		10			
08-Oct	7,211	Bournemouth	0-0	CARDIFF CITY				2	5	9									1	3		4			6	11	7		8		10			
15-Oct	16,317	CARDIFF CITY	1-2	Clapton Orient	Talbot			2	5	9									1	3		4			6	11	7		8		10			
22-Oct	10,262	Northampton Town	2-1	CARDIFF CITY	Prescott				5	9						2		10	1	3		4			6	11			7		8			
29-Oct	14,313	CARDIFF CITY	2-1	Swindon Town	Rickards, Collins				5	9						2		10	1	3		4			6	11			7		8			
05-Nov	12,521	Port Vale	1-1	CARDIFF CITY	Collins			2	5	9								10	1	3		4			6	11			7		8			
12-Nov	11,646	CARDIFF CITY	5-3	Watford	Collins 3, McCaughey, Hill			2	5	9								10	1	3		4			6	11			7		8			
19-Nov	17,898	Crystal Palace	2-0	CARDIFF CITY				2	5	9					1			10		3		4	11		6				7		8			
03-Dec	5,699	Aldershot	1-1	CARDIFF CITY	Collins			2	5	9			11		1					3		4			6	7				8	10			
17-Dec	2,257	Torquay United	1-3	CARDIFF CITY	Talbot 2, Collins			2	5	9	4				1					3			7		6					11	10		8	
24-Dec	4,242	Exeter City	1-1	CARDIFF CITY	Egan			2	5	9	4			10	1					3					6			7		11			8	
26-Dec	26,744	CARDIFF CITY	1-0	Queen's Park Rangers	Collins				5	9				10	1		2			3		4			6			7		11			8	
27-Dec	14,799	Queen's Park Rangers	5-0	CARDIFF CITY					5	9				10	1		2			3		4			6			7		11			8	
31-Dec	40,187	CARDIFF CITY	1-2	Newport County	Smith			2	5	9				10	1					3	6	4						7		11			8	
11-Jan	8,645	CARDIFF CITY	2-1	Bristol City	Smith, Walton			2	5	9					1					3		4			6		7			11	10		8	
14-Jan	15,312	CARDIFF CITY	2-1	Ipswich Town	Collins, og			2	5	9	6			11	1					3		4					7				10		8	
28-Jan	12,659	CARDIFF CITY	0-2	Bristol Rovers				2	5	9					1					3		4			6		7			11	10		8	
01-Feb	3,623	Reading	0-0	CARDIFF CITY				2	5	9	4			10	1					3			11		6		7						8	
04-Feb	9,770	Brighton	1-2	CARDIFF CITY	Egan, Collins			2	5	9	4			10	1					3			11		6				8				7	
11-Feb	12,309	CARDIFF CITY	5-0	Bournemouth	Egan 2, Rickards, Walton, McKenzie			2	5	99	4			10	1					3			11		6				8				7	
18-Feb	9,035	Clapton Orient	1-1	CARDIFF CITY	Egan			2	5	9	4			10	1					3			11		6				8				7	
25-Feb	10,282	CARDIFF CITY	2-0	Northampton Town	Rickards, McCaughey		7		5		4			9	1		2			3		6							8	11	10			
04-Mar	8,861	Swindon Town	4-1	CARDIFF CITY	Egan			2	5	10	4			9	1					3		6	11						8				7	
11-Mar	9,145	CARDIFF CITY	2-4	Port Vale	Egan, Talbot		7	2	5	11	4			9	1					3					6				8		10			
18-Mar	6,714	Watford	1-0	CARDIFF CITY			7		5		4			9	1		2	10		3			11		6								8	
25-Mar	11,910	CARDIFF CITY	0-1	Crystal Palace					5	9	4	8		10	1		2			3					6	11							7	
01-Apr	10,003	Bristol City	1-1	CARDIFF CITY	Egan			5			4			9	1		2	10		3			7		6	11							8	
07-Apr	9,299	Southend United	2-0	CARDIFF CITY				5		9	4					3	2	10	1			6				11		7			8			
08-Apr	9,060	CARDIFF CITY	2-4	Aldershot	Prescott, Egan			5						9	1		2	10		3				8	6	11							7	4
10-Apr	8,220	CARDIFF CITY	1-0	Southend United	Pugh					9	4			10	1	2				3					6	11	7						8	5
15-Apr	7,640	Notts County	1-1	CARDIFF CITY	McKenzie	8		2	5		4				1			11		3		6	9				7				10			
17-Apr	5,070	CARDIFF CITY	4-1	Notts County	Talbot 2, Anderson, Pugh	8		2	5		4				1			11		3		6	9				7				10			
22-Apr	7,277	CARDIFF CITY	3-1	Torquay United	Collins, Talbot, Hill			2	5	9	4							11	1	3			8		6		7				10			
29-Apr	5,886	CARDIFF CITY	0-0	Mansfield Town				2		9					1			11		3		4			6		7				10		8	5
06-May	6,246	Walsall	6-3	CARDIFF CITY	Collins, Talbot, Hill			2	5	9	4				1			11		3		6					7				10		8	
					Appearances	2	3	34	35	36	23	1	1	17	26	4	10	14	16	41	1	25	12	1	34	16	18	5	20	11	27	2	24	3
					Goals	1				18				9				3				2	2			4	2		2	2	9	1	2	

1 Reg Anderson
2 Billy Baker
3 George Ballsom
4 Billy Bassett
5 Jimmy Collins
6 Billy Corkhill
7 Jack Court
8 Jim Davies
9 Harry Egan
10 Bill Fielding
11 Louis Ford
12 Arthur Granville
13 Charlie Hill
14 Bob Jones
15 Jimmy Kelso
16 Bill Main
17 Cecil McCaughey
18 Jim McKenzie
19 Jimmy Mitchell
20 George Nicholson
21 Jim Prescott
22 Reg Pugh
23 Arthur Rhodes
24 Tom Rickards
25 Ritchie Smith
26 Les Talbot
27 Bert Turner
28 George Walton
29 Tom Williams

1946-47 1st in Division Three South (Promoted)

Date	Att	Home	Score	Away	Scorers	1	2	3	4	5	6	7	8	9	10	11	12	13	14	15	16	17	18	19	20	21
31-Aug	20,678	Norwich City	2-1	CARDIFF CITY	Richards	10			11	7		4		3				1	8	9		2	5			6
04-Sep	14,354	Swindon Town	3-2	CARDIFF CITY	Richards, Allen	10			11	7		4		3				1	8	9		2	5			6
07-Sep	24,779	CARDIFF CITY	2-1	Notts County	James, Gibson	10		1	11	7		4	8	2		6				9		3	5			
09-Sep	19,239	CARDIFF CITY	2-0	Bournemouth	James, Allen	10		1	11	7		4	9	2					8			3	5			6
14-Sep	8,853	Northampton Town	0-2	CARDIFF CITY	Allen 2	10	4	1	11	7	6		9	2					8			3	5			
18-Sep	8,926	Bournemouth	2-0	CARDIFF CITY		8	6	1	11	7	10	4	9	2								3	5			
21-Sep	22,475	CARDIFF CITY	2-1	Aldershot	Baker, Clarke	8	6	1	11	7		4	9	2								3	5			10
23-Sep	19,172	CARDIFF CITY	5-0	Swindon Town	Gibson 3, Richards, Allen	10	6	1	11	7		4		2					8	9		3	5			
28-Sep	13,193	Brighton	0-4	CARDIFF CITY	Richards 2, Rees, Allen	10	6	1	11	7		4		2					8	9		3	5			
05-Oct	27,585	CARDIFF CITY	5-0	Exeter City	Richards 2, Allen, Baker, Clarke	10	6	1	11	7		4		2					8	9		3	5			
12-Oct	10,724	Port Vale	0-4	CARDIFF CITY	Richards 2, Clarke, Rees	10	6	1	11	7		4		2					8	9		3	5			
19-Oct	44,010	CARDIFF CITY	2-2	Queen's Park Rangers	Richards, Clarke	10	6	1	11	7		4		2			3		8	9			5			
26-Oct	12,973	Southend United	0-2	CARDIFF CITY	Gibson, Rees	10	6	1	11	7		4		2					8	9		3	5			
02-Nov	28,699	CARDIFF CITY	4-0	Bristol Rovers	Richards 2, Allen, Rees	10	6	1	11	7		4		2					8	9		3	5			
09-Nov	9,827	Mansfield Town	1-3	CARDIFF CITY	Rees 2, Richards	10	6	1	11	7		4		2					8	9		3	5			
16-Nov	27,259	CARDIFF CITY	1-0	Torquay United	Rees	10	6	1	11	7		4		2					8	9		3	5			
23-Nov	25,296	Crystal Palace	1-2	CARDIFF CITY	Richards 2	10	6	1	11	7		4		2					8	9		3	5			
07-Dec	16,386	Walsall	2-3	CARDIFF CITY	Allen 2, Rees	10	6	1	11	7		4		2					8	9		3	5			
21-Dec	12,398	Ipswich Town	0-1	CARDIFF CITY	Gibson	10	6	1	11	7		4		2					8	9		3	5			
25-Dec	12,947	Leyton Orient	0-1	CARDIFF CITY	Rees	10	6	1	11	7		4		2					8	9		3	5			
28-Dec	36,285	CARDIFF CITY	6-1	Norwich City	Richards 3, Rees, Allen, Clarke	10	6	1	11	7		4		2					8	9		3	5			
04-Jan	28,450	Notts County	1-1	CARDIFF CITY	Allen	10	6	1	11	7		4		2					8	9		3	5			
18-Jan	29,426	CARDIFF CITY	6-2	Northampton Town	Allen 3, Rees 2, Richards	10	6	1		7		4		2	11				8	9		3	5			
22-Jan	28,534	CARDIFF CITY	3-0	Reading	Richards 2, Clarke	10	6	1	11			4		2	7				8	9		3	5			
25-Jan	7,239	Aldershot	0-1	CARDIFF CITY	Richards	10	6	1	11					2	7				8	9		3	5		4	
01-Feb	20,533	CARDIFF CITY	4-0	Brighton	Richards 2, Rees, Clarke	10	6	1	11					2	7				8	9		3	5		4	
01-Mar	33,698	CARDIFF CITY	3-1	Southend United	Clarke 2, Allen	10	6	1	11			4		2	7				8	9		3	5			
08-Mar	30,455	Bristol Rovers	1-0	CARDIFF CITY		10	6	1	11	7		4		2					8	9		3	5			
15-Mar	9,384	CARDIFF CITY	5-0	Mansfield Town	Richards 2, Hollyman, Gibson, Clarke	10	6	1	11	7		4		2					8	9		3	5			
22-Mar	9,352	Torquay United	0-0	CARDIFF CITY		10	6	1	11	7		4	9	2			2		8			3				
29-Mar	24,214	CARDIFF CITY	0-0	Crystal Palace		10	6	1	11	7		4		2					8	9		3	5			
04-Apr	32,535	Bristol City	2-1	CARDIFF CITY	Rees	10	6	1	11	7		8		2					9			3	5		4	
05-Apr	21,627	Reading	0-0	CARDIFF CITY		10	6	1	11	7		4		2	8							3	5		9	
07-Apr	49,310	CARDIFF CITY	1-1	Bristol City	Richards	8	6	1	11	7	10	4		2						9		3	5			
12-Apr	33,195	CARDIFF CITY	3-0	Walsall	Hill 2, Gibson	8	6	1	11	7	10	4		2						9		3	5			
19-Apr	20,030	Watford	2-0	CARDIFF CITY		10	6	1	9	8	11	4		2	7							3	5			
26-Apr	31,219	CARDIFF CITY	3-2	Ipswich Town	Gibson, Richards, Allen	10	6	1	11	7		4		2					8	9		3	5			
03-May	30,368	CARDIFF CITY	1-0	Watford	Richards	10	6	1	11	7		4		2					8	9		3	5			
10-May	36,732	CARDIFF CITY	1-0	Port Vale	Richards	10	6	1	11	7		4		2					8	9		3	5			
17-May	12,031	Exeter City	0-2	CARDIFF CITY	Gibson, Rees		6	1	11	7				2					8	9	10	3	5		4	
24-May	23,272	Queen's Park Rangers	2-3	CARDIFF CITY	Ross 2, Wardle		6	1		7				2					8	9	10	3	5	11	4	
07-Jun	24,572	CARDIFF CITY	1-0	Leyton Orient	Rees		6	1		7				2					8	9	10	3	5	11	4	
					Appearances	39	38	40	39	38	5	36	6	42	7	1	2	2	35	34	3	41	41	2	7	4
					Goals	17	2		10	10		1	3						17	30	2			1		

1 Bryn Allen
2 Billy Baker
3 Dan Canning
4 Roy Clarke
5 Colin Gibson
6 Charlie Hill
7 Ken Hollyman
8 Billy James
9 Arthur Lever
10 Billy Lewis
11 Ernie Marshall
12 Joe Phillips
13 George Poland
14 Billy Rees
15 Stan Richards
16 Bernard Ross
17 Alf Sherwood
18 Fred Stansfield
19 George Wardle
20 Glyn Williams
21 Terry Wood

1947-48 5th in Division Two

Date	Att	Home	Score	Away	Scorers	1	2	3	4	5	6	7	8	9	10	11	12	13	14	15	16	17	18	19	20	21	22	23	24	25
23-Aug	38,028	CARDIFF CITY	0-0	Chesterfield		10		6		1	7		4		2					8	9		3	5				11		
25-Aug	44,415	CARDIFF CITY	3-0	Doncaster Rovers	Wardle 2, Richards			6	10	1			4		2		7			8	9		3	5				11		
30-Aug	28,703	Millwall	0-1	CARDIFF CITY	Wardle			6	10	1			4		2	7				9		8	3	5				11		
04-Sep	27,760	Doncaster Rovers	2-2	CARDIFF CITY	Wardle, Blair			6	10	1	7		4		2					9		8	3	5				11		
06-Sep	48,894	CARDIFF CITY	0-3	Tottenham Hotspur		8		6	10	1			4		2	7				9			3	5				11		
08-Sep	39,363	CARDIFF CITY	5-1	Southampton	Moore 2, Richards, Rees, og			6	10	1					2			11		8	9		3	5				7		4
13-Sep	36,489	Sheffield Wednesday	2-1	CARDIFF CITY	Rees			6	10	1			4		2	7		11		8	9		3	5						
17-Sep	16,495	Southampton	2-2	CARDIFF CITY	McBennett 2			6	10	1			4		2		7			8	9		3	5				11		
20-Sep	33,060	CARDIFF CITY	3-0	Plymouth Argyle	Blair, Rees, Lever (p)			6	10	1			4		2		7			8	9		3	5				11		
27-Sep	39,796	CARDIFF CITY	1-0	Bradford	Rees			6	10	1			4		2		7			8	9		3	5				11		
04-Oct	30,618	Nottingham Forest	1-2	CARDIFF CITY	Gibson 2			6	10	1	7		4		2					8	9		3	5				11		
11-Oct	39,505	CARDIFF CITY	1-0	Luton Town	Rees			6	10	1	7		4		2					8	9		3	5				11		
18-Oct	34,483	Brentford	0-0	CARDIFF CITY				6	10	1	7		4		2					8	9			5	3			11		
25-Oct	36,940	Leicester City	2-1	CARDIFF CITY	og			6	10	1	7		4		2					8	9		3	5				11		
01-Nov	36,851	CARDIFF CITY	0-0	Leeds United					10	1	7		4		2					8	9		3	5				11		6
08-Nov	34,778	Fulham	4-1	CARDIFF CITY	Gibson				10	1	7		4		2						9	8	3	5				11		6
15-Nov	35,835	CARDIFF CITY	1-1	Coventry City	Richards				10	1	7		4		2					8	9		3	5				11	6	
22-Nov	56,904	Newcastle United	4-1	CARDIFF CITY	Lever (p)			6	11	1	7		4		2					8	9		3	5				10		
29-Nov	39,646	CARDIFF CITY	2-0	Birmingham City	Richards 2			6	11	1	7		4		2					8	9		3	5				10		
06-Dec	38,914	West Brom	2-3	CARDIFF CITY	Blair 2, Gibson			6	11	1	7		4		2					8	9			5	3			10		
13-Dec	33,538	CARDIFF CITY	1-0	Barnsley	Wardle			6	11	1	7		4		2						9		3	5			8	10		
20-Dec	18,959	Chesterfield	2-2	CARDIFF CITY	Stitfall, Blair			6	11	1	7		4		2					8			3	5	9			10		
26-Dec	43,805	CARDIFF CITY	2-2	Bury	Wardle, Gibson			6	11	1	7		4		2					8			3	5	9			10		
01-Jan	12,382	Bury	1-2	CARDIFF CITY	Rees, Richards			6	11	1	7		4		2					8	9		3	5				10		
03-Jan	29,483	CARDIFF CITY	6-0	Millwall	Rees 2, Richards 2, Blair, Gibson			6	11	1	7		4		2					8	9		3	5				10		
17-Jan	57,386	Tottenham Hotspur	2-1	CARDIFF CITY	Rees			6	8	1	7				5			11		9			3		2			10		4
31-Jan	33,147	CARDIFF CITY	2-1	Sheffield Wednesday	Richards, Rees			6	11	1	7				2					8	9		3	5	10					4
07-Feb	26,396	Plymouth Argyle	3-0	CARDIFF CITY				6	11	1	7		4	9	2					8			3	5				10		
14-Feb	14,756	Bradford	0-1	CARDIFF CITY	Hullett			6	11	1	7			9	2					8			3	5				10		4
21-Feb	28,929	CARDIFF CITY	4-1	Nottingham Forest	Hullett 2, Wardle 2			6		1	7			9	2					8			3	5	10			11		4
28-Feb	22,112	Luton Town	1-1	CARDIFF CITY	Hullett			6		1	7			9	2					8			3	5	10			11		4
06-Mar	41,032	CARDIFF CITY	1-0	Brentford	Hullett			6		1	7			9	2					8			3	5	10			11		4
13-Mar	39,100	CARDIFF CITY	3-0	Leicester City	Hullett 2, Wardle			6	10	1	7			9	2					8			3	5	4			11		
20-Mar	34,276	Leeds United	4-0	CARDIFF CITY				6	10	1	7			9	2					8			3	5	4			11		
26-Mar	41,700	CARDIFF CITY	0-3	West Ham United				6	10	1	7			9	2					8			3	5	4			11		
27-Mar	33,786	CARDIFF CITY	0-0	Fulham				6	11	1	7			9	2							10	3	5	4			8		
29-Mar	31,667	West Ham United	4-2	CARDIFF CITY	Hullett, Wardle			6	11	1				9	2				8			10		5	3			7		4
03-Apr	26,175	Coventry City	1-0	CARDIFF CITY					11	1	7			9	6					8	10		2	5	3					4
10-Apr	49,209	CARDIFF CITY	1-1	Newcastle United	Lever (p)				10		7	1			6					8	9		2	5	3	11				4
17-Apr	52,276	Birmingham City	2-0	CARDIFF CITY					10	1	7			9	6					8			2	5	3			11		4
24-Apr	26,179	CARDIFF CITY	0-5	West Brom				6	11	1	7			9	5					8			2		3		10			4
01-May	14,979	Barnsley	1-2	CARDIFF CITY	Rees, Moore		1	6			7				3			11	9	8			2	5	10					4
					Appearances	2	1	36	37	40	33	1	25	13	42	3	4	4	2	38	23	5	39	40	19	1	2	36	1	15
					Goals				6		6			8	3		2	3		11	9				1			10		

1 Bryn Allen
2 Roger Ashton
3 Billy Baker
4 Dougie Blair
5 Dan Canning
6 Colin Gibson
7 Wyn Griffiths
8 Ken Hollyman
9 Bill Hullett
10 Arthur Lever
11 Billy Lewis
12 Seamus MacBennett
13 Beriah Moore
14 Reg Parker
15 Billy Rees
16 Stan Richards
17 Bernard Ross
18 Alf Sherwood
19 Fred Stansfield
20 Ron Stitfall
21 Derrick Sullivan
22 Bobby Tobin
23 George Wardle
24 Bill Watson
25 Glyn Williams

1948-49 4th in Division Two

Date	Att	Home	Score	Away	Scorers	1	2	3	4	5	6	7	8	9	10	11	12	13	14	15	16	17	18	19	20	21	22	23	24	25	26	27	28
21-Aug	15,048	Bradford	3-0	CARDIFF CITY		10	6		11		7			4		1	3						9		2	5			8				
23-Aug	35,687	CARDIFF CITY	3-3	Luton Town	Hollyman, Hullett, Moore	10	6							4	9	1	3		11				8		2	5			7				
28-Aug	37,189	CARDIFF CITY	2-1	Southampton	Hullett 2	10	6							4	9	1	2						8		3	5			7	11			
30-Aug	20,185	Luton Town	3-0	CARDIFF CITY		10	6							4	9	1	2						8		3	5			7	11			
04-Sep	18,542	Barnsley	1-1	CARDIFF CITY	Sullivan				6					8	9	1	2								3	5			7	11	10	4	
09-Sep	25,337	Queen's Park Rangers	0-0	CARDIFF CITY			4		6					8	9	1	2						10		3	5			7	11			
11-Sep	32,156	CARDIFF CITY	3-0	Grimsby Town	Hollyman, Rees, og		4		6					8	9	1	2						10		3	5			7	11			
13-Sep	36,223	CARDIFF CITY	3-0	Queen's Park Rangers	Rees 2, Hullett		4		6					8	9	1	2						10		3	5			7	11			
18-Sep	20,417	Nottingham Forest	0-0	CARDIFF CITY			4		6					8	9	1	2						10		3	5			7	11			
25-Sep	38,423	CARDIFF CITY	2-1	Fulham	Hullett 2		4		6					8	9	1	2						10		3	5			7	11			
02-Oct	27,371	Plymouth Argyle	0-1	CARDIFF CITY	Hollyman		4		6					8	9	1	2						10		3	5			7		11		
09-Oct	56,018	CARDIFF CITY	0-1	Tottenham Hotspur			4		6					8	9	1	2						10		3	5			7	11			
16-Oct	29,433	West Ham United	3-1	CARDIFF CITY	Lever (p)				6					8	9	1	2					11	10		3	5			7			4	
30-Oct	46,036	West Brom	2-0	CARDIFF CITY			4	8	6						9	1	2		11						3	5	10		7				
06-Nov	36,359	CARDIFF CITY	3-4	Chesterfield	Rees, Blair, Stansfield		4	8	6					7		1	2						9		3	5	10		11				
13-Nov	14,438	Lincoln City	0-0	CARDIFF CITY				8	6					7	9	1	2				11				3	5	10		4				
20-Nov	30,084	CARDIFF CITY	1-1	Sheffield Wednesday	Stevenson		4	9	6					8		1	2								3	5	10	11	7				
27-Nov	22,121	Coventry City	0-1	CARDIFF CITY	Stevenson		4	8	6			9		7		1	2								3	5	10	11					
04-Dec	31,972	CARDIFF CITY	2-1	Leeds United	Allen, Stevenson	9	4		6					7		1	2						8		3	5	10			11			
11-Dec	24,343	Leicester City	2-2	CARDIFF CITY	Rees, Gorin	8	4		6	11		7				1	2						9		3	5	10						
18-Dec	28,002	CARDIFF CITY	6-1	Bradford	Stevenson 2, Edwards, Allen, Hollyman, Lever (p)	8	4		6	11				7		1	2						9		3	5	10						
25-Dec	22,813	Brentford	1-1	CARDIFF CITY	Allen	8	4		6	11				7		1	2						9		3	5	10						
27-Dec	49,236	CARDIFF CITY	2-0	Brentford	Allen, Stevenson	8	4		6	11				7		1	2						9		3	5	10						
01-Jan	20,937	Southampton	2-0	CARDIFF CITY		8	4		6	11				7		1	2						9		3	5	10						
15-Jan	29,116	CARDIFF CITY	0-3	Barnsley		8	4	10	6	11				7		1	2						9		3	5							
22-Jan	15,210	Grimsby Town	2-2	CARDIFF CITY	Rees, Montgomery	8	4		6	11				7			2	5		1			9		3		10						
05-Feb	31,522	CARDIFF CITY	1-0	Nottingham Forest	Rees	8	4		6	11				7		1	2	5					9		3		10						
19-Feb	40,795	Fulham	4-0	CARDIFF CITY		8	4			11				7		1	2	6					9	5	3		10						
26-Feb	29,006	CARDIFF CITY	1-0	Plymouth Argyle	Hollyman	8	7			11				4		1	2	5					9		3		10					6	
05-Mar	51,183	Tottenham Hotspur	0-1	CARDIFF CITY	Hollyman	8	7	9		11				4		1	2	5							3		10					6	
12-Mar	28,271	CARDIFF CITY	4-0	West Ham United	Stevenson 2, Hollyman, Best	8	7	9		11				4		1		5							2		10		3			6	
19-Mar	15,836	Bury	0-3	CARDIFF CITY	Blair, Best, Edwards			9	10	11			7	4		1		5							3		8		2			6	
26-Mar	47,649	CARDIFF CITY	2-2	West Brom	Blair, Best		7	9	10	11				4		1		5							3		8		2			6	
02-Apr	14,299	Chesterfield	0-2	CARDIFF CITY	Best, Edwards			9	8	11				4		1		5					7		3		10		2			6	
04-Apr	34,161	CARDIFF CITY	2-1	Bury	Blair, Best			9	8	11				4		1		5					7		3		10		2			6	
09-Apr	32,585	CARDIFF CITY	3-1	Lincoln City	Stevenson 2, Edwards		7	9	8	11				4		1	3	5									10		2			6	
15-Apr	23,468	Blackburn Rovers	2-1	CARDIFF CITY	Edwards		7	9	8	11				4		1		5							3		10		2			6	
16-Apr	32,297	Sheffield Wednesday	1-1	CARDIFF CITY	Best		7	9		11				4		1	3	5									10		2			6	8
18-Apr	33,325	CARDIFF CITY	1-0	Blackburn Rovers	Lever		7	9	6	11						1	3	5					10						2			4	8
23-Apr	26,441	CARDIFF CITY	3-0	Coventry City	Stevenson 2, Edwards		7	9	6	11								5							3		10		2			4	8
30-Apr	19,945	Leeds United	0-0	CARDIFF CITY				9	6	11								5							3		10	7	2			4	8
07-May	33,496	CARDIFF CITY	1-1	Leicester City	Baker		7	9	6	11								5					8		3		10		2			4	
					Appearances	17	35	19	34	23	1	2	1	36	14	38	33	17	2	1	1	1	28	1	39	25	27	3	29	10	2	16	4
					Goals	4	1	6	4	6		1		7	7		3	1	1				6			1	12			1			

1 Bryn Allen
2 Billy Baker
3 Tommy Best
4 Dougie Blair
5 George Edwards
6 Alex Gilchrist
7 Ted Gorin
8 Graham Hogg
9 Ken Hollyman
10 Bill Hullett
11 Phil Joslin
12 Arthur Lever
13 Stan Montgomery
14 Beriah Moore
15 Ted Morris
16 Joe Nibloe
17 Cecil Price
18 Billy Rees
19 Alf Rowland
20 Alf Sherwood
21 Fred Stansfield
22 Ernie Stevenson
23 Albert Stitfall
24 Ron Stitfall
25 Derrick Sullivan
26 George Wardle
27 Glyn Williams
28 Roley Williams

1949-50 10th in Division Two

Date	Att	Home	Score	Away	Scorers	1	2	3	4	5	6	7	8	9	10	11	12	13	14	15	16	17	18	19	20	21	22	23	24	25	26
20-Aug	28,265	Blackburn Rovers	1-0	CARDIFF CITY			9	6	11				7	1		2						5	3		10					4	8
22-Aug	37,913	CARDIFF CITY	1-0	Sheffield Wednesday	Stevenson	6	9	8	11				7	1		2			5				3		10					4	
27-Aug	60,855	CARDIFF CITY	1-0	Swansea Town	Best	6	9	8	11				7	1		2			5				3		10					4	
29-Aug	32,765	Sheffield Wednesday	1-1	CARDIFF CITY	Stevenson (p)	6	8		11	9			7	1		2			5				3		10					4	
03-Sep	42,649	CARDIFF CITY	0-1	Tottenham Hotspur		6	9		11				7	1		2			5				3		10					4	8
05-Sep	40,254	CARDIFF CITY	2-0	Hull City	Best 2	6	9	10	11					1		2			5				3		8					4	7
10-Sep	17,371	Bury	2-2	CARDIFF CITY	Best, R Williams	6	9	10	11				8	1		2			5				3							4	7
17-Sep	32,044	CARDIFF CITY	2-4	Leicester City	Best, Edwards	6	9	10	11				8	1		2			5				3							4	7
24-Sep	13,187	Bradford	3-3	CARDIFF CITY	R Stitfall 2, Edwards	6		10	11				4			2			5	1			3		8		9				7
01-Oct	29,619	CARDIFF CITY	2-0	Chesterfield	Blair, Stevenson	6		10	11				4	1		2			5				3		8		9				7
08-Oct	25,523	Leeds United	2-0	CARDIFF CITY		6		10	11				4	1		2						5	3		8		9				7
22-Oct	23,042	Coventry City	2-1	CARDIFF CITY	Blair	6		10	11				4	1		2			5				3		8		9				7
29-Oct	24,011	CARDIFF CITY	0-0	Luton Town		10		9	11				8	1		2			5				6				3			4	7
05-Nov	18,564	Barnsley	1-0	CARDIFF CITY				6	11		9			1					5				2		10		3		8	4	7
12-Nov	21,644	CARDIFF CITY	0-1	West Ham United				6			9			1	11				5				2		10		3		8	4	7
19-Nov	24,702	Sheffield United	2-0	CARDIFF CITY		6	9	11					8	1					5				2		10		3			4	7
26-Nov	22,664	CARDIFF CITY	1-0	Grimsby Town	R Stitfall			6	11				7	1		2			5				3		10		9			4	8
03-Dec	15,954	Queen's Park Rangers	0-1	CARDIFF CITY	R Stitfall	4		6	11				7	1		2			5				3		10		9				8
10-Dec	21,922	CARDIFF CITY	3-2	Preston North End	Edwards 2, R Stitfall	4		6	11				7	1		2			5				3		10		9				8
17-Dec	19,882	CARDIFF CITY	2-1	Blackburn Rovers	R Stitfall, Edwards	4		6	11					1		2			5				3		10	7	9				8
24-Dec	27,264	Swansea Town	5-1	CARDIFF CITY	R Stitfall	4		6			11			1		2			5				3		10	7	9				8
26-Dec	28,585	Plymouth Argyle	0-0	CARDIFF CITY		4		6	11				7	1		2			5				3		10		9				8
27-Dec	32,499	CARDIFF CITY	1-0	Plymouth Argyle	Evans	4		10		7				1		2			5		11		3				9			6	8
31-Dec	59,780	Tottenham Hotspur	2-0	CARDIFF CITY		4		10					7	1		2			5				3		8		9	11		6	
14-Jan	27,883	CARDIFF CITY	1-0	Bury	R Williams	4			11	10				1	7	2			5				3				9			6	8
21-Jan	27,300	Leicester City	1-0	CARDIFF CITY		4		10	11	8						2	9		5				3	1			7			6	
04-Feb	25,164	CARDIFF CITY	1-2	Bradford	Evans	4		10	11	8			7	1		2			5				3				9			6	
18-Feb	15,042	Chesterfield	0-1	CARDIFF CITY	Evans	4		9	11	8				1		7			5				3		10		2			6	
25-Feb	28,423	CARDIFF CITY	1-0	Leeds United	Evans	4		10	11	9			6	1		7			5				3		8		2				
04-Mar	23,475	Southampton	3-1	CARDIFF CITY	Evans	4		10	11	9			6	1		7			5				3		8		2				
11-Mar	22,875	CARDIFF CITY	1-0	Coventry City	Edwards	4			11	10		7	6	1		9			5				3				2	8			
18-Mar	15,071	Luton Town	0-0	CARDIFF CITY		4		10	11	9		7	6	1				8	5				3				2				
25-Mar	19,987	CARDIFF CITY	3-0	Barnsley	Evans, Grant, og	4		10	11	8		7	6	1		9			5				3				2				
01-Apr	14,922	Grimsby Town	0-0	CARDIFF CITY		4		10	11	8		7	6			9			5				3	1			2				
07-Apr	24,584	Brentford	1-0	CARDIFF CITY		4		10	11	8		7	6			9			5				3	1		2					
08-Apr	21,102	CARDIFF CITY	4-0	Queen's Park Rangers	Evans 2, Lever, Sherwood (p)	4		10	11	8		7				9			5				3	1			2			6	
10-Apr	16,260	CARDIFF CITY	0-0	Brentford		4		10	11	8		7				9			5				3	1			2			6	
15-Apr	14,109	West Ham United	0-1	CARDIFF CITY	Lever				11	8		7	4			9			5				3	1			2			6	10
17-Apr	21,247	CARDIFF CITY	1-1	Southampton	Edwards	4			11	8		7	6			9							3	1			2			5	10
22-Apr	33,382	CARDIFF CITY	1-2	Sheffield United	Lever	4			11	8		7				9			5				3	1			2			6	10
29-Apr	13,799	Preston North End	3-0	CARDIFF CITY		4			11	8		7	6			9							3	1			2			5	10
06-May	18,213	Hull City	1-1	CARDIFF CITY	Gorin	4				8	9	7	6		11								3	1			2			5	10
					Appearances	37	9	33	36	20	4	12	30	31	3	37	1	1	37	1	1	2	42	10	23	3	33	2	2	26	26
					Goals		5	2	7	8	1	1				3							1		3	1	6				2

1 Billy Baker
2 Tommy Best
3 Dougie Blair
4 George Edwards
5 Elfed Evans
6 Ted Gorin
7 Wilf Grant
8 Ken Hollyman
9 Phil Joslin
10 Bob Lamie
11 Arthur Lever
12 Harry May
13 Bob McLaren
14 Stan Montgomery
15 Ted Morris
16 Gordon Pembrey
17 Alf Rowland
18 Alf Sherwood
19 Alf Steel
20 Ernie Stevenson
21 Albert Stitfall
22 Ron Stitfall
23 Derrick Sullivan
24 Bobby Taggart
25 Glyn Williams
26 Roley Williams

1950-51 3rd in Division Two

Date	Att	Home	Score	Away	Scorers	1	2	3	4	5	6	7	8	9	10	11	12	13	14	15	16	17	18	19	20	21	22	23	24
19-Aug	20,083	Grimsby Town	0-0	CARDIFF CITY		6		11	10			4	1				8		5		9		3		2				7
23-Aug	18,242	Manchester City	2-1	CARDIFF CITY	R Williams		6	11	10			4	1		5		8				9		3		2				7
26-Aug	36,646	CARDIFF CITY	2-0	Notts County	Oakley, Edwards	6		11				4	1				8				9		3		2	10		5	7
28-Aug	32,817	CARDIFF CITY	1-1	Manchester City	E Evans	6		11	8			4	1								9		3		2	10		5	7
02-Sep	25,900	Preston North End	1-1	CARDIFF CITY	Edwards	6		11	8			4	1								9		3		2	10		5	7
04-Sep	32,292	CARDIFF CITY	2-1	West Ham United	E Evans, Blair	6	10	11	9			4	1	7									3		2			5	8
09-Sep	29,797	CARDIFF CITY	2-2	Bury	Lamie, E Evans	6	10	11	9			4	1	7									3		2			5	8
16-Sep	19,236	Queen's Park Rangers	3-2	CARDIFF CITY	E Evans, og	6	10	11	9			4	1	7			8						3		2			5	
23-Sep	27,754	CARDIFF CITY	1-0	Chesterfield	og	6		11	9			4	1				8		5				3		2	10			7
30-Sep	22,696	Leicester City	1-1	CARDIFF CITY	Blair	6	9	11	10			4	1				8		5				3		2	7			
07-Oct	24,831	Blackburn Rovers	2-0	CARDIFF CITY		6	9	11	8		7	4	1				10		5				3		2				
14-Oct	26,409	CARDIFF CITY	2-2	Southampton	Blair, og	6	9		10		7	4	1				11		5				3		2			8	
21-Oct	26,356	Doncaster Rovers	0-0	CARDIFF CITY		6	10		9		7	4					11		5	1		2			3			8	
28-Oct	22,885	CARDIFF CITY	1-1	Brentford	Blair	6	10		9		7	4					11		5	1			3		2			8	
04-Nov	26,393	Swansea Town	1-0	CARDIFF CITY			10	11			8	6					4		5	1			3		2			9	7
11-Nov	25,007	CARDIFF CITY	2-1	Hull City	R Williams, Blair		10	11			7	9	1				4		5				3		2			6	8
18-Nov	21,818	Barnsley	0-0	CARDIFF CITY			10	11			9	4	1						5				3		2		7	6	8
25-Nov	25,622	CARDIFF CITY	2-0	Sheffield United	Edwards, R Williams		10	11			9	4	1						5			2	3				7	6	8
02-Dec	13,062	Luton Town	1-1	CARDIFF CITY	Grant		10	11			9	4	1						5			2	3				7	6	8
09-Dec	23,716	CARDIFF CITY	1-0	Leeds United	Edwards		10	11			9	4	1						5			2	3				7	6	8
16-Dec	15,364	CARDIFF CITY	5-2	Grimsby Town	Grant 3, R Williams		10	11			9	4	1						5			2	3				7	6	8
23-Dec	27,634	Notts County	1-2	CARDIFF CITY	Grant, R Williams		10	11			9	4	1						5			2	3				7	6	8
25-Dec	32,778	CARDIFF CITY	2-1	Coventry City	Edwards 2		10	11			9	4	1						5			2	3				7	6	8
26-Dec	33,194	Coventry City	2-1	CARDIFF CITY	Grant	6		11	10		9	4	1						5			2					7	3	8
30-Dec	26,717	CARDIFF CITY	0-2	Preston North End				11	10		9	4	1						5			2	3				7	6	8
13-Jan	10,726	Bury	1-2	CARDIFF CITY	Edwards, og	6		11	10		9	4	1				8		5				3				7	2	
20-Jan	21,017	CARDIFF CITY	4-2	Queen's Park Rangers	Grant 2, McLaughlin, Tiddy	6	10	11			9	4	1				8		5				3				7	2	
03-Feb	12,998	Chesterfield	0-3	CARDIFF CITY	Grant 2, Marchant	6	10	11			9	4	1			8						2	3				7	5	
17-Feb	23,583	CARDIFF CITY	2-2	Leicester City	Marchant, Baker	6	10	11			9	4	1			8			5				3	2			7		
24-Feb	32,811	CARDIFF CITY	1-0	Blackburn Rovers	Grant	6	10	11			9	4	1			8			5				3				7	2	
03-Mar	24,233	Southampton	1-1	CARDIFF CITY	Edwards	6	10	11			9	4	1						5				3				7	2	8
10-Mar	27,724	CARDIFF CITY	0-0	Doncaster Rovers		6	10	11			9	4	1			8			5				3				7	2	
17-Mar	19,663	Brentford	4-0	CARDIFF CITY		6	10	11			9	4	1			8			5				3				7	2	
23-Mar	15,054	Birmingham City	0-0	CARDIFF CITY		6		11			9	4	1			8	10		5				3				7	2	
24-Mar	41,074	CARDIFF CITY	1-0	Swansea Town	Marchant	6		11			9	4	1			8	10		5				3				7	2	
26-Mar	36,992	CARDIFF CITY	2-1	Birmingham City	McLaughlin, Grant	6		11			9	4	1			8	10		5				3				7	2	
31-Mar	20,239	Hull City	2-0	CARDIFF CITY		6		11			9	4	1			8	10		5				3				7	2	
07-Apr	27,631	CARDIFF CITY	1-1	Barnsley	Grant	6	10	11			9	4	1					8	5				3				7	2	
14-Apr	20,747	Sheffield United	1-2	CARDIFF CITY	Tiddy, Edwards	6		11			9	4	1			8	10		5				3				7	2	
21-Apr	28,022	CARDIFF CITY	2-1	Luton Town	Grant, og	6		11			9	4	1			8	10		5				3				7	2	
28-Apr	14,765	Leeds United	2-0	CARDIFF CITY		6		11		10	9	4	1				8		5				3				7	2	
05-May	17,942	West Ham United	0-0	CARDIFF CITY		6	10	11			9	4	1			8			5				3				7	2	
					Appearances	31	27	39	16	1	32	42	39	3	1	12	21	1	34	3	5	10	40	1	17	5	26	36	20
					Goals	1	5	9	4		14			1		3	2				1						2		6

1 Billy Baker
2 Dougie Blair
3 George Edwards
4 Elfed Evans
5 Leslie Evans
6 Wilf Grant
7 Ken Hollyman
8 Phil Joslin
9 Bob Lamie
10 Arthur Lever
11 Marwood Marchant
12 Bobby McLaughlin
13 Don Mills
14 Stan Montgomery
15 Ted Morris
16 Ken Oakley
17 Charlie Rutter
18 Alf Sherwood
19 Albert Stitfall
20 Ron Stitfall
21 Derrick Sullivan
22 Mike Tiddy
23 Glyn Williams
24 Roley Williams

1951-52 2nd in Division Two (Promoted)

Date	Att	Home	Score	Away	Scorers	1	2	3	4	5	6	7	8	9	10	11	12	13	14	15	16	17	18	19	20	21
18-Aug	28,973	CARDIFF CITY	4-0	Leicester City	Grant 2, Edwards, R Williams	4	10		11			9			1					2	3		5	7	6	8
20-Aug	32,442	CARDIFF CITY	2-4	Rotherham United	Grant 2	4	10		11			9			1					2	3		5	7	6	8
25-Aug	31,776	Nottingham Forest	2-3	CARDIFF CITY	Edwards 2, R Williams	6	10		11			9	4		1		5			2				7	3	8
27-Aug	17,062	Rotherham United	2-0	CARDIFF CITY		6	10		11			9	4		1		5			2				7	3	8
01-Sep	27,772	CARDIFF CITY	2-0	Brentford	Grant 2	6	10		11	8		9	4		1		5				3			7	2	
08-Sep	19,676	Doncaster Rovers	1-0	CARDIFF CITY		6	10		11	8		9	4		1		5				3			7	2	
12-Sep	12,680	Leeds United	2-1	CARDIFF CITY	E Evans	6			11	10		9			1		5				3		4	7	2	8
15-Sep	23,923	CARDIFF CITY	3-1	Everton	Grant 2, E Evans	4			11	10		9			1		5			2	3			7	6	8
17-Sep	29,176	CARDIFF CITY	1-1	Sheffield United	Grant	4			11	10		9			1		5			2	3			7	6	8
22-Scp	21,672	Southampton	1-1	CARDIFF CITY	Tiddy	4				10		9			1		5	11		2	3			7	6	8
29-Sep	30,352	CARDIFF CITY	2-1	Sheffield Wednesday	Grant 2	4	10		11			9			1		5			2	3			7	6	8
06-Oct	26,277	CARDIFF CITY	4-1	Coventry City	Grant 2, Edwards, Tiddy	4			11			9	8		1		5			2	3			7	6	10
13-Oct	24,103	West Ham United	1-1	CARDIFF CITY	McLaughlin	4			11			9			1	8	5			2	3			7	6	10
27-Oct	11,168	Barnsley	2-0	CARDIFF CITY		4			11			9			1	8				2	3		5	7	6	10
03-Nov	23,459	CARDIFF CITY	1-0	Hull City	Grant	6			11			9	4		1	8	5		7	2	3					10
10-Nov	22,477	Blackburn Rovers	0-1	CARDIFF CITY	Edwards	6			11			9	4		1	8	5			2	3			7		10
17-Nov	21,211	CARDIFF CITY	3-1	Queen's Park Rangers	Blair 2, Sherwood (p)	6	8		11			9	4		1		5			2	3			7		10
24-Nov	19,452	Notts County	1-1	CARDIFF CITY	Montgomery	6	8		11			9	4		1		5			2	3			7		10
01-Dec	26,106	CARDIFF CITY	3-0	Luton Town	Blair 2, Grant	6	8		11			9	4		1		5			2	3			7		10
08-Dec	7,887	Bury	1-1	CARDIFF CITY	Edwards	6	8		11			9			1		5			2	3			7	4	10
15-Dec	26,021	Leicester City	3-0	CARDIFF CITY		6	8		11			9			1		5			2	3			7	4	10
22-Dec	19,860	CARDIFF CITY	4-1	Nottingham Forest	Blair 2, Grant, Sherwood (p)	4	8		11			9			1	6	5				3			7	2	10
25-Dec	19,260	Swansea Town	1-1	CARDIFF CITY	Tiddy	4	8		11			9			1	6	5				3			7	2	10
26-Dec	46,003	CARDIFF CITY	3-0	Swansea Town	Baker, Grant, Tiddy	4	8		11			9		1		6	5			2			10	7	3	
29-Dec	27,547	Brentford	1-1	CARDIFF CITY	Tiddy		8		11			9		1		6	5			2	3		10	7	4	
05-Jan	28,404	CARDIFF CITY	2-1	Doncaster Rovers	Sherwood 2		8		11			9		1		6	5			2	3		10	7	4	
19-Jan	49,230	Everton	3-0	CARDIFF CITY		4	8					9			1	6	5			2	3		10	7		11
26-Jan	23,205	CARDIFF CITY	1-0	Southampton	Grant	4			11			9			1	8	5			2	3			7	6	10
09-Feb	42,867	Sheffield Wednesday	4-2	CARDIFF CITY	E Evans 2	4			11	10		9		1		6	5			2	3		8	7		
16-Feb	26,410	Coventry City	2-1	CARDIFF CITY	Sullivan	4			11	10		9		1		6	5			2	3		8	7		
01-Mar	29,495	CARDIFF CITY	1-1	West Ham United	Blair	4	10		11			9		1			5				3	2	8	7	6	
12-Mar	16,398	Sheffield United	6-1	CARDIFF CITY	Grant	6	8	10				9	4	1			5			2			11	7	3	
15-Mar	24,542	CARDIFF CITY	3-0	Barnsley	Chisholm 2, L Evans		8	10			11	9		1		4	5			2	3			7	6	
22-Mar	27,009	Hull City	0-0	CARDIFF CITY			8	10			11	9		1		4	5			2	3			7	6	
05-Apr	19,738	Queen's Park Rangers	1-1	CARDIFF CITY	Grant	6		10	11			9		1		4	5				3	2		7		8
11-Apr	32,941	Birmingham City	3-2	CARDIFF CITY	Grant, Chisholm	6		10	11			9			1	4	5			2	3			7		8
12-Apr	24,178	CARDIFF CITY	1-0	Notts County	Chisholm	6	8	10				9		1		4	5			2	3		11			7
14-Apr	25,470	CARDIFF CITY	3-1	Birmingham City	Chisholm 2, Grant	6	8	10	11			9		1		4	5				3				2	7
19-Apr	14,186	Luton Town	2-2	CARDIFF CITY	R Williams, Sherwood (p)	6	8	10	11			9		1		4	5				3	2				7
21-Apr	31,169	CARDIFF CITY	3-1	Blackburn Rovers	Grant, Chisholm, Sherwood (p)	6	8	10	11			9		1		4	5				3				2	7
26-Apr	39,907	CARDIFF CITY	3-0	Bury	Blair 2, Grant	6	8	10	11			9		1		4	5				3				2	7
03-May	45,925	CARDIFF CITY	3-1	Leeds United	Grant 2, Chisholm	6	8	10	11			9		1		4	5				3				2	7
					Appearances	38	28	11	36	8	2	42	11	16	26	23	39	1	1	30	38	3	13	35	30	31
					Goals	1	9	8	6	4	1	26				1	1				6		1	5		3

1 Billy Baker
2 Dougie Blair
3 Ken Chisholm
4 George Edwards
5 Elfed Evans
6 Les Evans
7 Wilf Grant
8 Ken Hollyman
9 Ron Howells
10 Iorrie Hughes
11 Bobby McLaughlin
12 Stan Montgomery
13 Griff Norman
14 Cliff Nugent
15 Charlie Rutter
16 Alf Sherwood
17 Ron Stitfall
18 Derrick Sullivan
19 Mike Tiddy
20 Glyn Williams
21 Roley Williams

1952-53 12th in Division One

Date	Att	Home	Score	Away	Scorers	1	2	3	4	5	6	7	8	9	10	11	12	13	14	15	16	17	18	19	20	21	22
23-Aug	52,309	Wolves	1-0	CARDIFF CITY		6	8	10	11		9				1			5		3		4		7		2	
27-Aug	42,159	Middlesbrough	3-0	CARDIFF CITY		6	8	10	11		9		7		1		4	5		3	2						
30-Aug	43,478	CARDIFF CITY	4-0	Sheffield Wednesday	Chisholm 2, Hazlett, Grant	4	8	10	11		9		7		1			5		3	2					6	
03-Sep	51,512	CARDIFF CITY	1-1	Middlesbrough	Blair	4	8	10	11		9		7		1			5		3	2					6	
06-Sep	62,150	Tottenham Hotspur	2-1	CARDIFF CITY	Chisholm	4	8	10	11		9		7		1			5		3	2					6	
10-Sep	23,343	West Brom	1-0	CARDIFF CITY		4	10	9	11	2	7				1			5		3						6	8
13-Sep	45,182	CARDIFF CITY	0-0	Burnley		4	8	10	11	2	9		7		1			5		3						6	
17-Sep	40,338	CARDIFF CITY	1-2	West Brom	Thomas	4		10	11	2	9		7		1			5		3			8			6	
20-Sep	29,337	Preston North End	2-3	CARDIFF CITY	Blair, R Williams, Chisholm	4	9	10	11						1			5		3	2			7		6	8
27-Sep	39,223	CARDIFF CITY	2-0	Stoke City	R Williams 2	4	9	10	11						1			5		3	2			7		6	8
04-Oct	33,551	Manchester City	2-2	CARDIFF CITY	Chisholm, Tiddy	4	9	10	11						1			5		3	2			7		6	8
11-Oct	30,583	Charlton Athletic	3-1	CARDIFF CITY	Edwards	4		10	11		9				1			5		3	2			7		6	8
25-Oct	23,208	Derby County	1-1	CARDIFF CITY	Chisholm	4	8	10	11						1			5	9	3	2			7		6	
01-Nov	43,662	CARDIFF CITY	2-2	Blackpool	Northcott, Chisholm	4		10	11						1			5	9	3	2	8		7		6	
08-Nov	52,139	Chelsea	0-2	CARDIFF CITY	Edwards, Sherwood	4		10	11						1			5	9	3	2	8		7		6	
15-Nov	40,096	CARDIFF CITY	1-2	Manchester United	Chisholm	4	6	10	11						1			5	9	3	2	8		7			
22-Nov	31,258	Portsmouth	0-2	CARDIFF CITY	Northcott, Grant	4	6	10	11		8				1	3		5	9		2			7			
13-Dec	42,518	CARDIFF CITY	4-1	Sunderland	Grant 2, Edwards, Chisholm	4	6	10	11		8				1				9	3	2	5		7			
20-Dec	25,598	CARDIFF CITY	0-0	Wolves		4	6	10	11		8				1				9	3	2	5		7			
25-Dec	36,143	Newcastle United	3-0	CARDIFF CITY		4	6	10	11		8				1				9	3	2	5		7			
27-Dec	52,202	CARDIFF CITY	0-0	Newcastle United		4		10	11		8		7		1		6	5	9	3	2						
03-Jan	39,652	Sheffield Wednesday	2-0	CARDIFF CITY		4	6	10	11		8				1			5	9	3	2			7			
17-Jan	36,423	CARDIFF CITY	0-0	Tottenham Hotspur			6	10	11			4			1			5	9	3	2	8		7			
24-Jan	29,491	Burnley	0-0	CARDIFF CITY		4		10	11			8			1			5	9	3	2	6		7			
07-Feb	32,445	CARDIFF CITY	0-2	Preston North End		4	6	10			9	8			1			5	11	3	2			7			
14-Feb	21,626	Stoke City	0-0	CARDIFF CITY			10		11		9	4			1		6	5		3	2	8		7			
21-Feb	24,886	CARDIFF CITY	6-0	Manchester City	Thomas 2, Grant 2, R Williams, Edwards	4	10		11		9				1			5		3	2	6	7				8
28-Feb	35,248	CARDIFF CITY	0-1	Charlton Athletic		4	10		11		9				1			5		3	2	6	7				8
07-Mar	59,780	Arsenal	0-1	CARDIFF CITY	Blair		10				9	4			1			5	11	3	2	6		7			8
11-Mar	31,099	CARDIFF CITY	1-0	Bolton Wanderers	Chisholm			10			9	4			1			5	11	3	2	6		7			8
14-Mar	33,670	CARDIFF CITY	2-0	Derby County	Northcott, R Williams			10			9	4			1	3		5	11	2		6		7			8
25-Mar	15,227	Blackpool	0-1	CARDIFF CITY	Northcott	6	10				9	4			1	3		5	11			2		7			8
28-Mar	19,830	CARDIFF CITY	3-3	Chelsea	Tiddy 2, Blair	6	10			2	9	4			1	3		5					11	7			8
03-Apr	52,259	Liverpool	2-1	CARDIFF CITY	Northcott	4	10				9				1			5	11	3	2	6		7			8
04-Apr	38,987	Manchester United	1-4	CARDIFF CITY	Grant 2, Tiddy, Chisholm		6	10			9			4	1	3		5	11	2				7			8
06-Apr	35,419	CARDIFF CITY	4-0	Liverpool	Grant 2, Chisholm 2		6	10			9			4	1	3		5	11	2				7			8
11-Apr	35,945	CARDIFF CITY	0-1	Portsmouth			6	10			9			4	1	3		5	11	2				7			8
18-Apr	18,037	Bolton Wanderers	0-1	CARDIFF CITY	Sherwood			10			9			4	1	3		5	11	2		6		7			8
22-Apr	57,893	CARDIFF CITY	0-0	Arsenal			11	10			9			4	1	3		5		2		6		7			8
25-Apr	29,917	CARDIFF CITY	1-2	Aston Villa	Grant			10	11		9			4	1	3		5		2		6		7			8
27-Apr	7,469	Sunderland	4-2	CARDIFF CITY	Thomas, Tiddy		10			5		4			1	3		9		2		6	11	7			8
29-Apr	18,876	Aston Villa	2-0	CARDIFF CITY			6	10		2				4				5	9	3			11	7	1		8
					Appearances	29	32	34	28	6	31	10	7	7	41	11	3	39	23	39	27	21	6	32	1	14	21
					Goals		4	13	4		11		1						5	2			4	5			5

1 Billy Baker
2 Dougie Blair
3 Ken Chisholm
4 George Edwards
5 John Frowen
6 Wilf Grant
7 Alan Harrington
8 George Hazlett
9 Ken Hollyman
10 Ron Howells
11 Jack Mansell
12 Bobby McLaughlin
13 Stan Montgomery
14 Tommy Northcott
15 Alf Sherwood
16 Ron Stitfall
17 Derrick Sullivan
18 Keith Thomas
19 Mike Tiddy
20 Graham Vearncombe
21 Glyn Williams
22 Roley Williams

1953-54 10th in Division One

Date	Att	Home	Score	Away	Scorers	1	2	3	4	5	6	7	8	9	10	11	12	13	14	15	16	17	18	19	20	21	22	23	24	25	26	27	28	29	30
19-Aug	33,726	Middlesbrough	0-0	CARDIFF CITY		4									9			1			5		11			10		3	2	6			7		8
22-Aug	36,671	CARDIFF CITY	2-1	Aston Villa	Rainford, P Thomas	4									9			1			5		11			10		3	2	6		7			8
26-Aug	30,089	Huddersfield Town	2-0	CARDIFF CITY											9	4		1			5					10		3	2	6	11	7			8
29-Aug	33,221	Wolves	3-1	CARDIFF CITY	Grant				10				2		9	8	4	1		11	5							3		6					7
02-Sep	29,446	CARDIFF CITY	2-1	Huddersfield Town	Grant, Chisholm	6		8	10		11				9	4		1	3		5								2						7
05-Sep	42,002	CARDIFF CITY	1-1	Sunderland	Chisholm	6		8	10		11				9	4		1	3		5								2						7
07-Sep	34,043	Sheffield United	0-1	CARDIFF CITY	Chisholm	4		8	10		11				9			1	3		5						6		2						7
12-Sep	31,915	Manchester City	1-1	CARDIFF CITY	Edwards	6		8	10		11				9	4		1	3		5								2						7
16-Sep	27,350	CARDIFF CITY	2-0	Sheffield United	Edwards, Grant	4		8	10		11				9	6		1	3		5						2				7				
19-Sep	35,788	CARDIFF CITY	1-1	Bolton Wanderers	Chisholm	6		8	10		11				9	4		1	3		5						2				7				
26-Sep	49,137	CARDIFF CITY	0-3	Arsenal		6		8	10		11				9	4		1	3		5							2				7			
03-Oct	31,766	Portsmouth	1-1	CARDIFF CITY	Sullivan	6					11				8	4		1	3		5	9						2		10			7		
10-Oct	23,500	Preston North End	2-1	CARDIFF CITY	Chisholm 2	4			10		11				8				3		5	9		7					2	6				1	
17-Oct	41,083	CARDIFF CITY	1-0	Tottenham Hotspur	Grant (p)	4			10		11				8			1	3		5	9							2	6			7		
24-Oct	29,539	Burnley	3-0	CARDIFF CITY					10	9	11				8		4	1	3		5	7							2	66					
31-Oct	25,340	CARDIFF CITY	5-0	Charlton Athletic	Chisholm 3, Dudley, Tiddy	4			10	9	11							1	3		5	8						2		6			7		
07-Nov	42,355	Newcastle United	4-0	CARDIFF CITY		4		10		9	11							1	3		5	8						2		6			7		
14-Nov	26,844	CARDIFF CITY	1-6	Manchester United	Chisholm	4			10	9	11				7			1	3		5	8					2			6					
21-Nov	39,444	West Brom	6-1	CARDIFF CITY	Chisholm	4		6	10	8	11				9	2		1			5									3			7		
28-Nov	21,284	CARDIFF CITY	3-1	Liverpool	Grant, Chisholm, Edwards	6		8	10		11				9	4		1			5						2			3			7		
05-Dec	26,597	Sheffield Wednesday	2-1	CARDIFF CITY	Chisholm	4			10		11	9			8			1			5						3		2	6			7		
12-Dec	31,776	CARDIFF CITY	1-0	Middlesbrough	Ford	4			10		11	9						1			5		8				3		2	6			7		
19-Dec	27,012	Aston Villa	1-2	CARDIFF CITY	Northcott 2	4		6			11	9						1			5	10	8				2			3			7		
26-Dec	61,336	Chelsea	2-0	CARDIFF CITY		4		6			11	9						1			5	10	8				2			3			7		
28-Dec	36,958	CARDIFF CITY	0-0	Chelsea		4		6			11	9						1			5	10	8				2		3				7		
02-Jan	42,521	CARDIFF CITY	1-3	Wolves	Nugent	4					11	9						1			5	10	8				2		3	6		7			
16-Jan	40,629	Sunderland	5-0	CARDIFF CITY							11	9	2		10	4		1			5		8				3			6			7		
23-Jan	22,516	CARDIFF CITY	0-3	Manchester City		4					11			3		8					5	10		9					2	6			7	1	
06-Feb	30,777	Bolton Wanderers	3-0	CARDIFF CITY		4					11	9		10							5		8		2			3		6			7	1	
13-Feb	45,497	Arsenal	1-1	CARDIFF CITY	Ford	4						9		2	11						5	10	8					3		6			7	1	
27-Feb	30,502	CARDIFF CITY	2-1	Preston North End	Grant 2	4						9		2	11						5	10	8					3		6			7	1	
03-Mar	17,842	CARDIFF CITY	3-2	Portsmouth	Nugent, Tiddy, Grant	4						9		2	11						5	10	8					3		6			7	1	
06-Mar	45,248	Tottenham Hotspur	0-1	CARDIFF CITY	Tiddy	4						9		2	11						5	10	8					3		6			7	1	
13-Mar	33,413	CARDIFF CITY	1-0	Burnley	Sullivan	4						9		2	11						5	10	8					3		6			7	1	
20-Mar	20,717	Charlton Athletic	3-2	CARDIFF CITY	Grant, Ford	4						9	5	2	11							10	8					3		6			7	1	
27-Mar	26,242	CARDIFF CITY	2-1	Newcastle United	Nugent, Tiddy	4					11				9			1			5	10	8					3	2	6			7		
03-Apr	24,616	Manchester United	2-3	CARDIFF CITY	Grant 2, Sullivan	4					11				9			1			5		8				6	3	2	10			7		
10-Apr	43,614	CARDIFF CITY	2-0	West Brom	Grant, Ford	4						9			11			1			5	10	8					3	2	6			7		
16-Apr	26,194	Blackpool	4-1	CARDIFF CITY	Ford	4						9			11			1			5	10	8					3	2	6			7		
17-Apr	41,340	Liverpool	0-1	CARDIFF CITY	Northcott	4					11	9			7			1			5	10	8					3	2	6					
19-Apr	44,508	CARDIFF CITY	0-1	Blackpool		4						9			11						5	10	8				6	3	2				7	1	
24-Apr	15,777	CARDIFF CITY	2-2	Sheffield Wednesday	Sherwood, Ford		6				11	9		5		4						8	7					3	2	10				1	
					Appearances	37	1	13	17	5	29	19	3	9	32	14	2	31	14	1	40	24	22	2	1	3	14	22	22	33	3	4	26	11	8
					Goals				12	1	4	6			12							3	3			1		1		3		1	4		

1 Billy Baker
2 Colin Baker
3 Dougie Blair
4 Ken Chisholm
5 Frank Dudley
6 George Edwards
7 Trevor Ford
8 John Frowen
9 Colin Gale
10 Wilf Grant
11 Alan Harrington
12 Ken Hollyman
13 Ron Howells
14 Jack Mansell
15 Bobby McLaughlin
16 Stan Montgomery
17 Tommy Northcott
18 Cliff Nugent
19 Ken Oakley
20 Harry Parfitt
21 Johnny Rainford
22 Charlie Rutter
23 Alf Sherwood
24 Ron Stitfall
25 Derrick Sullivan
26 Keith Thomas
27 Peter Thomas
28 Mike Tiddy
29 Graham Vearncombe
30 Roley Williams

1954-55 20th in Division One

Date	Att	Home	Score	Away	Scorers	1	2	3	4	5	6	7	8	9	10	11	12	13	14	15	16	17	18	19	20	21	22	23	24
21-Aug	27,836	Burnley	1-0	CARDIFF CITY			4			9			11			1		5	10				3	2		6	7		8
25-Aug	39,448	CARDIFF CITY	2-5	Preston North End	Tiddy, Ford		4			9			11	6		1			10				3	2		5	7		8
28-Aug	25,938	CARDIFF CITY	2-1	Leicester City	Northcott, Ford		6		11	9	5			4					10			2	3				7	1	8
01-Sep	29,057	Preston North End	7-1	CARDIFF CITY	Grant		6		11		5		9	4					10			2	3				7	1	8
04-Sep	42,688	Chelsea	1-1	CARDIFF CITY	Tiddy		6		11				9	4		1		5		10			3	2			7		8
08-Sep	28,511	CARDIFF CITY	1-1	Sheffield United	Tiddy		6		11	9			8	4		1		5					3	2	10		7		
11-Sep	21,840	CARDIFF CITY	1-1	Huddersfield Town	Sherwood (p)		6			9		5		4		1			11				3	2	10	8	7		
13-Sep	18,090	Sheffield United	1-3	CARDIFF CITY	Sullivan, Ford, Stockin					9				4		1	6	5	11				3	2	10	8	7		
18-Sep	28,847	CARDIFF CITY	3-0	Manchester City	Sherwood, Stockin, og					9				4		1	6	5		11			3	2	10	8	7		
25-Sep	54,248	Everton	1-1	CARDIFF CITY	Nugent			7		9				4		1	6	5		11			3	2	10	8			
02-Oct	34,760	CARDIFF CITY	4-2	Newcastle United	Ford 2, Sullivan, Stockin					9				4		1	6	5		11			3	2	10	8	7		
09-Oct	41,159	Manchester United	5-2	CARDIFF CITY	Ford, Stockin					9				4		1	6	5		11			3	2	10	8	7		
16-Oct	30,166	Wolves	1-1	CARDIFF CITY	Stockin									4		1	6	5	9	11		3		2	10	8	7		
23-Oct	26,376	Charlton Athletic	4-1	CARDIFF CITY	Ford					9				4		1	6	5		11		2	3		10	8	7		
30-Oct	31,698	CARDIFF CITY	2-2	Bolton Wanderers	Nugent, og			7		9						1	6	5	8	11			3	2	10	4			
06-Nov	38,805	Tottenham Hotspur	0-2	CARDIFF CITY	Stockin 2					9				4		1		5	8	11		2	3		10	6	7		
13-Nov	15,998	CARDIFF CITY	5-3	Sheffield Wednesday	Nugent 2, Northcott, Sullivan, Tiddy					9				4		1		5	10	11		2	3			6	7		8
20-Nov	31,292	Portsmouth	1-3	CARDIFF CITY	Northcott 2, Ford					9						1	6	5	10	11		2	3			4	7		8
27-Nov	19,823	CARDIFF CITY	1-2	Blackpool	Montgomery			7		9							6	5		11		2	3		10	4		1	8
04-Dec	25,186	Aston Villa	0-2	CARDIFF CITY	Ford 2					9						1	6	5	8	11		2	3		10	4	7		
11-Dec	32,098	CARDIFF CITY	0-1	Sunderland						9						1	6	5	8	11		2	3		10	4	7		
18-Dec	22,035	CARDIFF CITY	0-3	Burnley						9				4		1		5	8	11	7	2	3		10	6			
25-Dec	22,845	CARDIFF CITY	3-2	West Brom	Ford 2, Montgomery					9						1	4	5		11	7	2	3		10	6			8
27-Dec	50,885	West Brom	1-0	CARDIFF CITY						9				6		1	4			11	7	2	3		10	5			8
01-Jan	25,408	Leicester City	1-2	CARDIFF CITY	Nutt									6		1	4	9		11	7	2	3		10	5			8
05-Feb	31,922	Manchester City	4-1	CARDIFF CITY	Ford (p)		4			9						1	6		11		7		3	2	10	5			8
12-Feb	17,108	CARDIFF CITY	4-3	Everton	Ford 2, Stockin 2					9				4		1	6		11		7		3	2	10	5			8
26-Feb	16,329	CARDIFF CITY	3-0	Manchester United	Stockin 2, Nutt					9		3		4		1		5	11		7	2			10	6			8
05-Mar	41,096	Sunderland	1-1	CARDIFF CITY	Stockin	6				9				4		1		5	11		7	3		2	10				8
12-Mar	20,261	CARDIFF CITY	4-3	Charlton Athletic	Nutt, Ford, Williams, Northcott					9	5			4		1			11		7	2		3	10	6			8
19-Mar	25,321	Bolton Wanderers	0-0	CARDIFF CITY						9	5			4		1			11	8	7	2		3	10	6			
23-Mar	16,649	CARDIFF CITY	0-1	Chelsea						9	5			4		1			11		7	2		3	10	6			8
26-Mar	14,461	CARDIFF CITY	1-2	Tottenham Hotspur	Ford					9	5			4		1			10	11	7	2	3			6			8
02-Apr	19,541	Sheffield Wednesday	1-1	CARDIFF CITY	Nutt					9				4		1		5	10	11	7		3	2		6	8		
08-Apr	39,052	Arsenal	2-0	CARDIFF CITY										4		1		5	9	11	7		3	2		6	8		10
09-Apr	20,720	CARDIFF CITY	0-1	Aston Villa						9	5			4		1	6				11			2	10	3	7		8
11-Apr	29,080	CARDIFF CITY	1-2	Arsenal	Harrington					9	5			4		1				11	7		3	2		6	8		10
16-Apr	21,832	Blackpool	0-0	CARDIFF CITY						9	5			4		1			11				3	2	10	6	7		8
23-Apr	21,185	CARDIFF CITY	1-1	Portsmouth	Williams					9	5			4		1			11				3	2	10	6	7		8
27-Apr	19,252	Newcastle United	3-0	CARDIFF CITY						9	5			4					11			2		3	10	6	7	1	8
30-Apr	30,903	CARDIFF CITY	3-2	Wolves	Ford 2, Hitchens					9				4	8		6		11				3	2	10	5	7	1	
02-May	10,473	Huddersfield Town	2-0	CARDIFF CITY		5								4	9		6		10	11		2	3				7	1	8
					Appearances	2	8	3	4	36	11	2	5	34	2	36	20	24	29	24	16	22	34	26	30	36	27	6	25
					Goals					19			1	1	1			2	5	4	4		2		12	3	4		2

1 Colin Baker
2 Billy Baker
3 Cecil Dixon
4 George Edwards
5 Trevor Ford
6 John Frowen
7 Colin Gale
8 Wilf Grant
9 Alan Harrington
10 Gerry Hitchens
11 Ron Howells
12 Islwyn Jones
13 Stan Montgomery
14 Tommy Northcott
15 Cliff Nugent
16 Gordon Nutt
17 Charlie Rutter
18 Alf Sherwood
19 Ron Stitfall
20 Ron Stockin
21 Derrick Sullivan
22 Mike Tiddy
23 Graham Vearncombe
24 Roley Williams

1955-56 17th in Division One

Date	Att	Home	Score	Away	Scorers	1	2	3	4	5	6	7	8	9	10	11	12	13	14	15	16	17	18	19	20	21	22	23	24	25	26
20-Aug	36,098	CARDIFF CITY	3-1	Sunderland	McSeveney 2, Ford				7	9			4		1		6	8		11				2		3	10	5			
23-Aug	31,361	Arsenal	3-1	CARDIFF CITY	Stockin				7		5		4	9	1		6	8		11				2			10	3			
27-Aug	32,893	Aston Villa	2-0	CARDIFF CITY					7	9			4		1		6	8		11				2		3	10	5			
31-Aug	26,973	CARDIFF CITY	1-0	Bolton Wanderers	Harrington			2	7			5	4	9	1			8		11		10				3		6			
03-Sep	42,546	CARDIFF CITY	1-9	Wolves	Stockin				7			5	4	9	1			8		11					2	3	10	6			
07-Sep	25,012	Bolton Wanderers	4-0	CARDIFF CITY				2	7				4	9	1		6	8		11				3				5			10
10-Sep	33,240	Manchester City	3-1	CARDIFF CITY	Williams				7				4	9	1		6	10		11				2		3		5			8
17-Sep	23,337	CARDIFF CITY	3-2	Sheffield United	Harrington, Ford, Hitchens				7	9			4	8	1		6	10		11				2		3		5			
24-Sep	25,117	CARDIFF CITY	1-2	Huddersfield Town	Kirtley		6		7	9			4	8	1			10		11				2		3		5			
01-Oct	33,451	Blackpool	2-1	CARDIFF CITY	Ford				7	9			4		1			10		11				6	3	2		5			8
08-Oct	19,433	Preston North End	1-2	CARDIFF CITY	Ford, Stockin					9			6		1			8		11				4	3	2	10	5		7	
15-Oct	24,338	CARDIFF CITY	2-2	Burnley	Ford 2					9			6		1			8		11				4	3	2	10	5		7	
22-Oct	22,131	West Brom	2-1	CARDIFF CITY	Kirtley			2			5		6	9	1			8		11				4		3	10			7	
29-Oct	27,795	CARDIFF CITY	0-1	Manchester United						9			6		1			8		11				4	3	2	10	5		7	
05-Nov	34,368	Tottenham Hotspur	1-1	CARDIFF CITY	Walsh						5			9	1			8		11				4	3	2	10	6		7	
12-Nov	22,439	CARDIFF CITY	3-1	Everton	McSeveney 2, Walsh						5			9	1			8		11				4	3	2	10	6		7	
19-Nov	35,603	Newcastle United	4-0	CARDIFF CITY							5		4	9	1			8		11				2	3		10	6		7	
26-Nov	23,638	CARDIFF CITY	2-1	Birmingham City	Kirtley, Dixon	6			11				4	9	1			8		10					3	2		5		7	
03-Dec	21,827	Luton Town	3-0	CARDIFF CITY		4							6	9	1			8		11					3	2	10	5		7	
10-Dec	23,132	CARDIFF CITY	3-1	Charlton Athletic	O'Halloran 3	6							4	9	1			8	5	11			10		3	2				7	
17-Dec	29,823	Sunderland	1-1	CARDIFF CITY	og	6							4	9	1			8	5	11			10		3	2				7	
24-Dec	20,384	CARDIFF CITY	1-0	Aston Villa	Hitchens	6		2					4	9	1			8	5	11			10		3					7	
26-Dec	26,794	CARDIFF CITY	1-1	Chelsea	Sherwood (p)	6		2					4	9	1			8	5	11			10		3					7	
27-Dec	36,740	Chelsea	2-1	CARDIFF CITY	Hitchens	6				9			4	8	1			7	5		11		10		3	2					
31-Dec	36,772	Wolves	0-2	CARDIFF CITY	Hitchens, Ford	6				9			4	10	1			8	5	11					3	2				7	
14-Jan	26,329	CARDIFF CITY	4-1	Manchester City	Hitchens 2, McSeveney, Ford	6				9			4	10	1			8	5	11					3	2				7	
21-Jan	22,921	Sheffield United	2-1	CARDIFF CITY	Sherwood	6				9			4	10	1			8	5	11					3	2				7	
04-Feb	12,586	Huddersfield Town	1-2	CARDIFF CITY	Hitchens, Ford	6				9			4	10				8	5	11						2		3	1	7	
11-Feb	36,019	CARDIFF CITY	1-0	Blackpool	Ford	6				9			4	10				8	5	11					3	2			1	7	
18-Feb	25,300	CARDIFF CITY	3-1	Preston North End	Hitchens, Kirtley, Ford	6				9			4	10				8	5	11						2		3	1	7	
25-Feb	18,549	Burnley	0-2	CARDIFF CITY	Hitchens 2	6				9			4	10				8	5	11						2		3	1	7	
07-Mar	31,265	CARDIFF CITY	1-1	Newcastle United	Baker	6				9				10				8	5	11				2		3		4	1	7	
10-Mar	44,914	Manchester United	1-1	CARDIFF CITY	Hitchens	6				9			4	10				8	5	11						2		3	1	7	
24-Mar	29,959	Everton	2-0	CARDIFF CITY		6				9			4	10				8	5	11						2		3	1	7	
30-Mar	26,443	Portsmouth	1-1	CARDIFF CITY	Ford	6				9			4	10					5	11						2	8	3	1	7	
31-Mar	31,641	CARDIFF CITY	1-3	West Brom	Hitchens	6				9				10				8	5	11			4			2		3	1	7	
02-Apr	27,018	CARDIFF CITY	2-3	Portsmouth	McSeveney, Ford	6			7	9			4	10					5	11						2	8	3	1		
07-Apr	37,154	Birmingham City	2-1	CARDIFF CITY	Hitchens	6		2		9			4	10				8	5	11								3	1	7	
14-Apr	16,086	CARDIFF CITY	2-0	Luton Town	Hitchens, Walsh					9			4	10				8	5	11					3	2		6	1	7	
21-Apr	17,726	Charlton Athletic	0-0	CARDIFF CITY		6				9			4	8		10			5	11						2		3	1	7	
23-Apr	19,684	CARDIFF CITY	0-0	Tottenham Hotspur		6				9			4	8		10			5	11						2		3	1	7	
28-Apr	23,169	CARDIFF CITY	1-2	Arsenal	Hitchens	6				9			4	10				8	5	11						2		3	1	7	
					Appearances	24	1	6	12	27	5	2	38	36	27	2	6	38	23	41	1	1	6	16	20	36	14	32	15	30	3
					Goals	1			1	13			2	15				4		6					2		3			3	1

1 Colin Baker
2 Dennis Callan
3 Ron Davies
4 Cecil Dixon
5 Trevor Ford
6 John Frowen
7 Colin Gale
8 Alan Harrington
9 Gerry Hitchens
10 Ron Howells
11 Bernard Jones
12 Islwyn Jones
13 Harry Kirtley
14 Danny Malloy
15 Johnny McSeveney
16 Cliff Nugent
17 Gordon Nutt
18 Neil O'Halloran
19 Charlie Rutter
20 Alf Sherwood
21 Ron Stitfall
22 Ron Stockin
23 Derrick Sullivan
24 Graham Vearncombe
25 Brian Walsh
26 Roley Williams

1956-57 21st in Division One (Relegated)

Date	Att	Home	Score	Away	Scorers	1	2	3	4	5	6	7	8	9	10	11	12	13	14	15	16	17	18	19	20	21	22	23
18-Aug	51,069	Arsenal	0-0	CARDIFF CITY		6			9			4	10				5	8	11			2	3				1	7
22-Aug	35,833	CARDIFF CITY	5-2	Newcastle United	Ford 2, Nugent 2, McSeveney				9			4	10				5	8	11			2	3		6		1	7
25-Aug	30,769	CARDIFF CITY	3-3	Burnley	McSeveney, Hitchens, Ford				9			4	10				5	8	11			2	3		6		1	7
29-Aug	34,859	Newcastle United	1-0	CARDIFF CITY		6			9			4	10				5	8	11				2		3		1	7
01-Sep	22,102	Preston North End	6-0	CARDIFF CITY		6	2		9			4	10				5	8	11						3		1	7
05-Sep	12,983	CARDIFF CITY	2-1	Sheffield Wednesday	Hitchens, McSeveney		2		9	5			10				4	8	11				3		6		1	7
08-Sep	26,568	CARDIFF CITY	1-1	Chelsea	og		2		9	5			10				4	8	11				3		6		1	7
12-Sep	37,235	Sheffield Wednesday	5-3	CARDIFF CITY	McSeveney 2(p), Walsh		2		9	5			10				4	8	11				3		6		1	7
15-Sep	28,738	Bolton Wanderers	2-0	CARDIFF CITY			2	7	9			4	10				5	8	11				3		6		1	
22-Sep	39,931	Birmingham City	2-1	CARDIFF CITY	O'Halloran		2		7			4	9				5	8	11	10			3		6		1	
29-Sep	22,362	CARDIFF CITY	0-0	West Brom			2		9			4	8				5		11	10			3		6		1	7
06-Oct	38,333	CARDIFF CITY	4-1	Leeds United	Hitchens 2, Ford, McSeveney		2		9			4	10				5	11			8		3		6		1	7
13-Oct	52,429	Tottenham Hotspur	5-0	CARDIFF CITY			2		9			4	10				5	11			8		3		6		1	7
27-Oct	34,935	Wolves	3-1	CARDIFF CITY	Hitchens		2					4	10				5	8	11	9			3		6		1	7
03-Nov	23,820	CARDIFF CITY	1-1	Manchester City	Reynolds	6			9			4	10				5	11			8		2		3		1	7
10-Nov	17,642	Charlton Athletic	0-2	CARDIFF CITY	Hitchens, Reynolds	6						4	9				5	10	11		8		2		3		1	7
17-Nov	20,017	CARDIFF CITY	1-0	Sunderland	Nugent					2		4	9				5	10	11		8		3		6		1	7
24-Nov	13,674	Luton Town	3-0	CARDIFF CITY						2		4	9				5	10	11		8		3		6		1	7
01-Dec	15,600	CARDIFF CITY	1-0	Everton	McSeveney					2		4					5	11	10	9	8		3		6		1	7
08-Dec	16,623	Blackpool	3-1	CARDIFF CITY	Walsh					2		4	9				5	8	11				3	10	6		1	7
15-Dec	11,302	CARDIFF CITY	2-3	Arsenal	Hitchens 2	4						2	9				5		11		8		3	10	6		1	7
22-Dec	10,118	Burnley	6-2	CARDIFF CITY	Hitchens 2	4						2	9				5		11		8		3	10	6		1	7
26-Dec	28,810	Manchester United	3-1	CARDIFF CITY	Malloy (p)	6						4	9				5		11		8		3	10	3		1	7
29-Dec	15,474	CARDIFF CITY	2-3	Preston North End	Stockin, McSeveney	6		7				4	9				5		11		8		3	10	3		1	
12-Jan	28,828	Chelsea	1-2	CARDIFF CITY	McSeveney, Hitchens	4							9				5	8	11			2	3	10	6		1	7
19-Jan	12,810	CARDIFF CITY	2-0	Bolton Wanderers	Hitchens, Walsh	4							9				5	8	11			2	3	10	6		1	7
02-Feb	16,854	CARDIFF CITY	1-2	Birmingham City	McSeveney	4	2						9				5	8	11				3	10	6		1	7
09-Feb	23,522	West Brom	1-2	CARDIFF CITY	Hitchens, Baker	4	2				11		9	1			5				8		3	10	6			7
16-Feb	21,695	Leeds United	3-0	CARDIFF CITY		4	2				11		9	1			5				8		3	10	6			7
23-Feb	13,879	CARDIFF CITY	2-2	Wolves	Hitchens, Baker	4	2	7					9	1			5	11			8		3	10	6			
09-Mar	15,724	CARDIFF CITY	3-4	Blackpool	Hitchens 2, McSeveney (p)	4	2	7				8	9	1		10	5	11					3		6			
13-Mar	12,567	Aston Villa	4-1	CARDIFF CITY	Hitchens	4		7		2		8	9			10	5	11					3		6		1	
16-Mar	26,395	Manchester City	4-1	CARDIFF CITY	McSeveney (p)	6						4	9			10	5	8				2	3			11	1	7
23-Mar	17,047	CARDIFF CITY	2-3	Charlton Athletic	Hitchens, Baker	6				5		8	9			10	4	11				2	3				1	7
30-Mar	40,100	Sunderland	1-1	CARDIFF CITY	Hitchens	6		7				4	9				5	8	11			2	3	10			1	
03-Apr	18,354	CARDIFF CITY	1-0	Aston Villa	McSeveney	6						4	9		10		5	8	7			2	3			11	1	
06-Apr	18,730	CARDIFF CITY	0-0	Luton Town		6						4	9		10		5	8	7			2	3			11	1	
13-Apr	24,397	Everton	0-0	CARDIFF CITY		6						4	9		10		5	8	7			2	3			11	1	
19-Apr	31,223	Portsmouth	1-0	CARDIFF CITY		6						4	9		10		5	8				2	3			11	1	7
20-Apr	25,181	CARDIFF CITY	0-3	Tottenham Hotspur		6	2					4	9			10	5	8				3				11	1	7
22-Apr	22,197	CARDIFF CITY	0-2	Portsmouth		6	2					4	9			10	5					3		8		11	1	7
27-Apr	17,708	CARDIFF CITY	2-3	Manchester United	Hitchens 2	6						4	9			10	5	8				2	3			11	1	7
					Appearances	27	17	6	14	9	2	33	41	4	4	7	42	34	28	4	14	15	39	13	31	8	38	32
					Goals	3			4				21				1	13	3	1	2			1				3

1 Colin Baker
2 Ron Davies
3 Cecil Dixon
4 Trevor Ford
5 John Frowen
6 Don Godwin
7 Alan Harrington
8 Gerry Hitchens
9 Ron Howells
10 Brian Jenkins
11 Bernard |Jones
12 Danny Malloy
13 Johnny McSeveney
14 Cliff Nugent
15 Neil O'Halloran
16 Brayley Reynolds
17 Charlie Rutter
18 Ron Stitfall
19 Ron Stockin
20 Derrick Sullivan
21 Ken Tucker
22 Graham Vearncombe
23 Brian Walsh

1957-58 15th in Division Two

Date	Att	Home	Score	Away	Scorers	1	2	3	4	5	6	7	8	9	10	11	12	13	14	15	16	17	18	19	20	21	22	23	24	25	26
24-Aug	42,482	CARDIFF CITY	0-0	Swansea Town							4	8	9	7				5				10			2		3	6	11	1	
27-Aug	18,429	Grimsby Town	1-1	CARDIFF CITY	og						4	8	9	7				5				10			2		3	6	11	1	
31-Aug	45,698	Liverpool	3-0	CARDIFF CITY					4		6	8	9	7				5				10			2		3		11	1	
04-Sep	13,433	CARDIFF CITY	1-3	Grimsby Town	Nicholls	6			8		4		9	7				5				10	11		2		3			1	
07-Sep	14,013	CARDIFF CITY	0-2	Middlesbrough		6			4	5		8	9	7							3	10	11		2					1	
11-Sep	10,073	CARDIFF CITY	1-0	Huddersfield Town	Davies	6			9		4	8						5			3		10				2		11	1	7
14-Sep	16,719	Leyton Orient	4-2	CARDIFF CITY	Davies, Nugent	6			9		4	8						5			3		10				2		11	1	7
18-Sep	9,821	Huddersfield Town	1-1	CARDIFF CITY	Reynolds	6					4	10	9					5			3		11	8			2			1	7
21-Sep	14,439	CARDIFF CITY	0-3	Charlton Athletic					6		4	10	9					5			3		11	8			2			1	7
28-Sep	9,909	Doncaster Rovers	0-1	CARDIFF CITY	Davies				8		4	10	9					5			3		11				2	6		1	7
05-Oct	14,390	CARDIFF CITY	2-2	Rotherham United	Walsh, Hewitt (p)				8		4	10	9					5			3		11				2	6		1	7
12-Oct	15,513	CARDIFF CITY	3-2	Derby County	Hitchens, Hewitt, Walsh	6					4	10	9					5			3	11		8	2					1	7
19-Oct	23,366	Bristol Rovers	0-2	CARDIFF CITY	Hitchens 2	4		5				10	9								3		11	8			2	6		1	7
26-Oct	14,515	CARDIFF CITY	3-2	Lincoln City	Hewitt, Nugent, Reynolds	4		5				10	9								3		11	8			2	6		1	7
02-Nov	14,911	Notts County	5-2	CARDIFF CITY	Reynolds, Nicholls			5			4	10										9	11	8	2		3	6		1	7
04-Nov	20,016	Stoke City	3-0	CARDIFF CITY				5			4	10										9	11	8	2		3	6		1	7
09-Nov	16,490	CARDIFF CITY	1-1	Ipswich Town	Bonson		10	5			4	9			11			8			3						2	6		1	7
16-Nov	24,642	Blackburn Rovers	4-0	CARDIFF CITY		6	9	5			4		10		11						3			8			2			1	7
23-Nov	15,215	CARDIFF CITY	0-0	Sheffield United		6	9				4	8	10				1	5			3		11				2				7
30-Nov	23,954	West Ham United	1-1	CARDIFF CITY	Bonson		9				4	8	10	11			1	5			3					6	2				7
07-Dec	8,941	CARDIFF CITY	7-0	Barnsley	Nugent 3, Hewitt 2(p), Bonson, Hudson		9				4	8		11			1	5			3		10			6	2				7
14-Dec	16,024	Fulham	2-0	CARDIFF CITY			10				4	8	9	11			1	5			3					6	2				7
21-Dec	19,483	Swansea Town	0-1	CARDIFF CITY	Hudson	6	9				4	8		11			1	5			3		10				2				7
26-Dec	23,638	CARDIFF CITY	5-2	Stoke City	Bonson 2, Hudson, Reynolds, Walsh	6	9				4			11			1	5			3		10	8			2				7
28-Dec	30,622	CARDIFF CITY	6-1	Liverpool	Reynolds 2, Bonson 2, Hudson, Hewitt	6	10				4	10		11			1	5			3			9			2				7
11-Jan	23,115	Middlesbrough	4-1	CARDIFF CITY	Walsh	6	9				4	10		11			1	5			3		8				2				7
18-Jan	13,387	CARDIFF CITY	1-1	Leyton Orient	Hewitt	6	9				4	10		11			1	5			3			8			2				7
01-Feb	20,556	Charlton Athletic	3-1	CARDIFF CITY	Nugent		9				4	8		11			1	5		6	3		10				2				7
08-Feb	13,277	CARDIFF CITY	3-1	Doncaster Rovers	Walsh, Nugent, Hewitt				9		4	8		11			1	5			2		10				3	6			7
22-Feb	19,368	Sheffield United	3-0	CARDIFF CITY			9				4	8		7			1	5			2		11	10			3	6			
15-Mar	11,116	CARDIFF CITY	2-0	Notts County	Bonson, Hewitt	6	9				4	8		11			1	5						10			2	3			7
22-Mar	13,469	Ipswich Town	3-1	CARDIFF CITY	Bonson	6	9				4			11			1	5					8	10			2	3			7
26-Mar	5,867	CARDIFF CITY	0-2	Bristol Rovers		6	9				4			11			1	5			2		8	10				3			7
29-Mar	10,335	CARDIFF CITY	4-3	Blackburn Rovers	Hewitt 3(p), Bonson	6	9				4	10		7				5					11	8			2	3		1	
04-Apr	15,567	CARDIFF CITY	2-3	Bristol City	Hewitt 2	6	9				4	8		11			1	5					10				2	3			7
05-Apr	15,529	Derby County	0-2	CARDIFF CITY	Bonson, Jenkins		9				4	8		7	11		1	5	6				10				2	3			
07-Apr	25,723	Bristol City	2-0	CARDIFF CITY			9				4	8		7	11		1	5	6				10				2	3			
12-Apr	17,596	CARDIFF CITY	0-3	West Ham United		6	9				4	8		11			1	5					10		2			3			7
19-Apr	8,948	Barnsley	1-1	CARDIFF CITY	Hudson		9							11			1	5	6				8	10	2		3	4			7
21-Apr	8,147	Rotherham United	3-1	CARDIFF CITY	Walsh		9				4	8		11		1		5	6				10		2			3			7
26-Apr	11,846	CARDIFF CITY	3-0	Fulham	Sullivan 2, Baker	4	9					8		11			1	5			3		10				2	6			7
30-Apr	18,001	Lincoln City	3-1	CARDIFF CITY	Nugent	4	9					8		11			1	5			3		10				2	6			7
					Appearances	23	25	6	9	1	36	36	16	28	4	1	22	36	4	1	27	8	31	17	11	3	37	23	5	19	33
					Goals	1	12		3			14	3	4	1							2	8	6				2			6

1 Colin Baker
2 Joe Bonson
3 Ray Daniel
4 Ron Davies
5 John Frowen
6 Alan Harrington
7 Ron Hewitt
8 Gerry Hitchens
9 Colin Hudson
10 Brian Jenkins
11 Alan Jones
12 Ken Jones
13 Danny Malloy
14 George McGuckin
15 Ross Menzies
16 Alec Milne
17 Johnny Nicholls
18 Cliff Nugent
19 Brayley Reynolds
20 Charlie Rutter
21 Bob Scott
22 Ron Stitfall
23 Derrick Sullivan
24 Ken Tucker
25 Graham Vearncombe
26 Brian Walsh

1958-59 9th in Division Two

Date	Att	Home	Score	Away	Scorers	1	2	3	4	5	6	7	8	9	10	11	12	13	14	15	16	17	18	19	20	21	22	23
23-Aug	23,731	CARDIFF CITY	0-1	Barnsley			9			4	8	11			1	10		5	3					2	6			7
27-Aug	13,267	Huddersfield Town	3-0	CARDIFF CITY						4		11			1	8		5	3			10	9	2	6			7
30-Aug	11,474	Rotherham United	1-0	CARDIFF CITY						4		11				8		5	3		1	10	9	2	6			7
03-Sep	13,078	CARDIFF CITY	3-2	Huddersfield Town	Baker, Walsh (p), Nugent	4								11		8		5	3		1	10	9	2	6			7
06-Sep	16,079	CARDIFF CITY	3-1	Sheffield United	Kelly 2, Reynolds	4								11		8		5	3		1	10	9	2	6			7
08-Sep	20,579	Bristol Rovers	2-0	CARDIFF CITY		4								11		8		5	3		1	10	9	2	6			7
13-Sep	26,662	Brighton	2-2	CARDIFF CITY	Hewitt, Moore	6	9			4	10	7		11				5	3	8	1			2				
17-Sep	14,495	CARDIFF CITY	2-4	Bristol Rovers	Hudson, Moore	6	9			4		7		11				5	3	8	1	10		2				
20-Sep	15,646	CARDIFF CITY	4-1	Grimsby Town	Hewitt 2, Bonson, Jenkins	6	9	4			10			11				5	3		1				2	8		7
27-Sep	41,866	Liverpool	1-2	CARDIFF CITY	Bonson, Hewitt	6	9	4			10			11				5	2		1				3	8		7
04-Oct	20,560	CARDIFF CITY	3-2	Middlesbrough	Jenkins, Hewitt, Walsh	6	9	4			10			11				5	2		1				3	8		7
11-Oct	20,357	CARDIFF CITY	1-2	Ipswich Town	Tapscott	6	9	4			10			11				5	2		1				3	8		7
25-Oct	18,359	CARDIFF CITY	2-1	Stoke City	Tapscott, Stitfall	6	9	4			10			11				5	2		1			3		8		7
01-Nov	17,532	Derby County	1-3	CARDIFF CITY	Reynolds, Hewitt (p), Walsh	6		4			10			11				5	2		1		9	3		8		7
08-Nov	15,689	CARDIFF CITY	3-0	Lincoln City	Hewitt, Jenkins, Walsh	6					10			11				5	2		1		9	3	4	8		7
15-Nov	24,078	Fulham	2-1	CARDIFF CITY	Walsh	6				2	10			11				5	3		1		9		4	8		7
22-Nov	20,195	CARDIFF CITY	2-2	Sheffield Wednesday	Jenkins, Tapscott	6					10			11				5	2		1		9	3	4	8		7
06-Dec	15,184	CARDIFF CITY	2-1	Leyton Orient	Hewitt 2 (p)	6					10			11				5	2		1		9	3	4	8		7
13-Dec	30,097	Sunderland	0-2	CARDIFF CITY	Tapscott, Bonson	6	9				10							5	2		1		11	3	4	8		7
18-Dec	10,365	Scunthorpe United	1-0	CARDIFF CITY		6	9				10							5	2		1		11	3	4	8		7
20-Dec	7,798	Barnsley	3-2	CARDIFF CITY	Hewitt, Walsh	6	9		3		10							5	2		1		11		4	8		7
26-Dec	27,570	Bristol City	2-3	CARDIFF CITY	Bonson 2, Walsh	6	9				10							5	2		1		11	3	4	8		7
27-Dec	27,146	CARDIFF CITY	1-0	Bristol City	og	6	9		3		10							5	2		1		11		4	8		7
03-Jan	17,115	CARDIFF CITY	1-0	Rotherham United	Reynolds	6	9				10							5	3		1		11	2	4	8		7
31-Jan	15,891	CARDIFF CITY	3-1	Brighton	Jenkins, Bonson, Tapscott	6	9				10			11				5	2		1			3	4	8		7
07-Feb	9,969	Grimsby Town	5-1	CARDIFF CITY	Reynolds	6					10			11			9	5	2		1		7	3	4	8		
14-Feb	18,313	CARDIFF CITY	3-0	Liverpool	Tapscott 2, Reynolds	4						11					9	5	2		1		10	3	6	8		7
21-Feb	12,986	Middlesbrough	1-1	CARDIFF CITY	Walsh	4						11					9	5	2		1		10	3	6	8		7
28-Feb	8,736	Lincoln City	4-2	CARDIFF CITY	Reynolds, Jenkins	6				2				11				5	3	10	1		9		4	8		7
07-Mar	24,450	CARDIFF CITY	0-1	Swansea Town		4	10			2		11					9	5	3		1				6	8		7
14-Mar	11,931	Stoke City	0-1	CARDIFF CITY	Hewitt	4	9			2	10	11						5	3		1				6	8		7
21-Mar	14,011	CARDIFF CITY	0-0	Derby County		6				2	10	11					9	5	3		1				4	8		7
28-Mar	12,159	Ipswich Town	3-3	CARDIFF CITY	Tapscott, Hewitt (p), Hudson	4	9			2	10	11						5	3		1				6	8		7
30-Mar	16,344	Charlton Athletic	0-0	CARDIFF CITY		4	9			2	10	11						5	3		1				6	8		7
31-Mar	16,045	CARDIFF CITY	1-2	Charlton Athletic	Sullivan	4	9			2	10	11						5	3		1				6	8		7
04-Apr	23,217	CARDIFF CITY	1-2	Fulham	Walsh	6				2	10			11				5	3	8	1				4	9		7
11-Apr	22,665	Sheffield Wednesday	3-1	CARDIFF CITY	Tapscott	6				2	10	11						5	3		1		9		4	8		7
15-Apr	14,893	Swansea Town	1-3	CARDIFF CITY	Kelly 2, og	6				2		11				8		5	2		1			3	10	9		7
18-Apr	13,003	CARDIFF CITY	0-2	Scunthorpe United		6				2		11				8		5	2		1			3	10	9		7
22-Apr	10,734	CARDIFF CITY	2-1	Sunderland	Hewitt, Walsh	6				2	10		8				9	5	2		1		11	3				7
25-Apr	11,351	Leyton Orient	3-0	CARDIFF CITY		6				2	10						9	5	2		1		11	3		8		7
27-Apr	12,733	Sheffield United	1-1	CARDIFF CITY	Tapscott	6	9	4		2								5	3	10			11			8	1	7
					Appearances	39	21	7	2	20	29	16	1	19	2	8	7	42	42	5	39	6	24	25	35	33	1	39
					Goals	1	6				13	2		6		4				2		1	6	1	1	10		10

1 Colin Baker
2 Joe Bonson
3 Steve Gammon
4 Alec Gray
5 Alan Harrington
6 Ron Hewitt
7 Colin Hudson
8 Mike Hughes
9 Brian Jenkins
10 Ken Jones
11 George Kelly
12 Harry Knowles
13 Danny Malloy
14 Alec Milne
15 Graham Moore
16 Ron Nicholls
17 Cliff Nugent
18 Brayley Reynolds
19 Ron Stitfall
20 Derrick Sullivan
21 Derek Tapscott
22 Graham Vearncombe
23 Brian Walsh

1959-60 2nd in Division Two (Promoted)

Date	Att	Home	Score	Away	Scorers	1	2	3	4	5	6	7	8	9	10	11	12	13	14	15	16	17	18	19	20	21
22-Aug	23,744	CARDIFF CITY	3-2	Liverpool	Mokone, Moore, Watkins	6				2					5	3	10	9				4	8	1	7	11
26-Aug	23,052	CARDIFF CITY	2-0	Middlesbrough	Moore, Watkins	6				2					5	3	10	9				4	8	1	7	11
29-Aug	18,513	Charlton Athletic	2-1	CARDIFF CITY	Moore	6				2					5	3	10	9				4	8	1	7	11
02-Sep	29,122	Middlesbrough	1-1	CARDIFF CITY	Watkins	6	10			2		7			5	3		9			8	4		1		11
05-Sep	22,545	CARDIFF CITY	4-2	Bristol City	Hudson 2, Watkins, Baker	6	10		4	2		7			5	3		9			8			1		11
09-Sep	17,959	Derby County	1-2	CARDIFF CITY	Sullivan 2	6		8	4	2		7			5	3		9				10		1		11
12-Sep	10,933	Scunthorpe United	1-2	CARDIFF CITY	Moore, Watkins	6		8	4	2		7			5	3		9				10		1		11
16-Sep	21,548	CARDIFF CITY	2-0	Derby County	Sullivan 2	6		8	4	2		7			5	3		9				10		1		11
19-Sep	24,392	CARDIFF CITY	1-4	Rotherham United	Sullivan	6			4	2		7			5	3		9				10	8	1		11
26-Sep	8,401	Lincoln City	3-2	CARDIFF CITY	Sullivan, Watkins, Harrington	6		8	4	2		7			5			9			3	10		1		11
03-Oct	14,933	Hull City	0-0	CARDIFF CITY		6		8	4	2		7			5			9			3	10		1		11
10-Oct	18,794	CARDIFF CITY	5-1	Leyton Orient	Moore 2, Tapscott 2, Sullivan	6			4	2					5			9			3	10	8	1	7	11
17-Oct	18,367	Huddersfield Town	0-1	CARDIFF CITY	Tapscott	6	10		4					9	5	2					3		8	1	7	11
24-Oct	20,223	CARDIFF CITY	3-2	Ipswich Town	Baker, Tapscott, Sullivan	6			4	2					5	3		9				10	8	1	7	11
31-Oct	27,630	Bristol Rovers	1-1	CARDIFF CITY	Moore	6			4	2					5			9			3	10	8	1	7	11
07-Nov	34,881	CARDIFF CITY	2-1	Swansea Town	Sullivan, Bonson		10		4	2					5			9			3	6	8	1	7	11
14-Nov	16,253	Brighton	2-2	CARDIFF CITY	Bonson 2		10		4	2					5			9			3	6	8	1	7	11
21-Nov	21,793	CARDIFF CITY	4-4	Stoke City	Bonson 2, Tapscott, Gammon		10		4	2					5			9			3	6	8	1	7	11
28-Nov	14,018	Portsmouth	1-1	CARDIFF CITY	Walsh		10		4	2					5			9			3	6	8	1	7	11
05-Dec	20,016	CARDIFF CITY	2-1	Sunderland	Watkins, Tapscott		10		4	2					5			9			3	6	8	1	7	11
12-Dec	50,039	Aston Villa	2-0	CARDIFF CITY			10		4						5	2		9			3	6	8	1	7	11
19-Dec	27,291	Liverpool	0-4	CARDIFF CITY	Tapscott 2, Watkins, Bonson	6	10								5	2		9			3	4	8	1	7	11
26-Dec	29,515	CARDIFF CITY	2-0	Sheffield United	Tapscott, Bonson	6	10								5	2		9			3	4	8	1	7	11
28-Dec	18,590	Sheffield United	2-1	CARDIFF CITY	Tapscott	6	10								5	2		9			3	4	8	1	7	11
02-Jan	20,619	CARDIFF CITY	5-1	Charlton Athletic	Baker 2, Tapscott, Bonson, Walsh	6	10								5	2		9			3	4	8	1	7	11
16-Jan	18,184	Bristol City	0-3	CARDIFF CITY	Bonson, Moore, og	6	10								5	2		9			3	4	8	1	7	11
23-Jan	16,759	CARDIFF CITY	4-2	Scunthorpe United	Watkins, Bonson, Tapscott, Moore	6	10								5	2		9			3	4	8	1	7	11
30-Jan	21,923	Plymouth Argyle	1-1	CARDIFF CITY	Tapscott	6	10								5	2		9			3	4	8	1	7	11
06-Feb	16,525	Rotherham United	2-2	CARDIFF CITY	Tapscott 2, Watkins, Bonson	6	10								5	2		9			3	4	8	1	7	11
13-Feb	16,231	CARDIFF CITY	6-2	Lincoln City	Bonson 2, Watkins 2, Tapscott, Walsh	6	10								5	2		9			3	4	8	1	7	11
20-Feb	21,580	CARDIFF CITY	3-2	Hull City	Bonson 2, Watkins 2, Tapscott, Walsh	6	10								5	2		9			3	4	8	1	7	11
27-Feb	22,918	Leyton Orient	3-4	CARDIFF CITY	Tapscott 2, Bonson 2	4	10				6				5	2		9			3		8	1	7	11
05-Mar	32,733	CARDIFF CITY	2-1	Huddersfield	Moore, Watkins	6	10				4				5	2		9			3		8	1	7	11
12-Mar	18,776	Ipswich Town	1-1	CARDIFF CITY	Bonson	6	10				4				5	2		9			3		8	1	7	11
19-Mar	21,011	CARDIFF CITY	1-4	Portsmouth	Tapscott	6	10				4				5	2		9			3		8	1	7	11
26-Mar	24,004	Swansea Town	3-3	CARDIFF CITY	Bonson, Moore, Walsh	6	10				4				5	2		9			3		8	1	7	11
02-Apr	19,523	CARDIFF CITY	1-4	Brighton	Tapscott	6	10		4						5	2		9	1		3		8		7	11
09-Apr	9,548	Stoke City	0-1	CARDIFF CITY	Watkins	6			4							2		9	1	5	3	10	8		7	11
16-Apr	52,364	CARDIFF CITY	1-0	Aston Villa	Moore	6			4			10			5	2		9	1		3		8		7	11
19-Apr	28,890	CARDIFF CITY	0-1	Plymouth Argyle		6			4			10			5	2		9	1		3		8		7	11
23-Apr	20,663	Sunderland	1-1	CARDIFF CITY	Baker	6	10			2	4	7			5			9	1		3		8			11
30-Apr	17,624	CARDIFF CITY	2-2	Bristol Rovers	Moore, Watkins	6				2	4		11		5			9			3		8	1	7	11
					Appearances	36	26	5	21	21	7	11	1	1	41	31	3	41	5	1	34	30	35	37	33	42
					Goals	6	18		1	1		2						13				8	20		4	

1 Colin Baker
2 Joe Bonson
3 Alan Durban
4 Steve Gammon
5 Alan Harrington
6 Barry Hole
7 Colin Hudson
8 Brian Jenkins
9 Harry Knowles
10 Danny Malloy
11 Alec Milne
12 Steve Mokone
13 Graham Moore
14 Ron Nicholls
15 Trevor Peck
16 Ron Stitfall
17 Derrick Sullivan
18 Derek Tapscott
19 Graham Vearncombe
20 Brian Walsh
21 Johnny Watkins

1960-61 15th in Division One

Date	Att	Home	Score	Away	Scorers	1	2	3	4	5	6	7	8	9	10	11	12	13	14	15	16	17	18	19	20	21	22	23	24	25
20-Aug	30,911	Fulham	2-2	CARDIFF CITY	Walsh, Moore	6	10				4	2					5		3	9						8	1	7		11
24-Aug	31,335	CARDIFF CITY	0-1	Sheffield Wednesday					10		4	2		6			5		3	9						8	1	7		11
27-Aug	27,213	CARDIFF CITY	2-0	Preston North End	Tapscott 2	6	8				4	2					5		3	9						10	1	7		11
31-Aug	27,537	Sheffield Wednesday	2-0	CARDIFF CITY		6	10				4	2					5		3	9						8	1	7		11
03-Sep	19,695	Burnley	1-2	CARDIFF CITY	Tapscott, Watkins	6	10		9		4	2					5		3							8	1	7		11
07-Sep	34,716	CARDIFF CITY	1-1	Aston Villa	Tapscott	6	8		9		4	2					5		3							10	1	7		11
10-Sep	24,037	CARDIFF CITY	1-3	Nottingham Forest	Tapscott	6	9				4	2					5		3	10						8	1	7		11
12-Sep	32,901	Aston Villa	2-1	CARDIFF CITY	Donnelly	6	10				4	2					5		3	9						8	1	7		11
17-Sep	30,932	Manchester City	4-2	CARDIFF CITY	Tapscott, Durban	6		9		3		2			11		5			10				4		8	1	7		
24-Sep	32,775	CARDIFF CITY	1-0	Arsenal	Tapscott	6	9			3	4	2			7		5			10						8	1			11
01-Oct	17,627	Newcastle United	5-0	CARDIFF CITY		6	9			3		2		4	7		5			10						8	1			11
08-Oct	23,800	Wolves	2-2	CARDIFF CITY	Hudson, Edwards		10			9	4	2		6	7		5		3		1					8				11
15-Oct	22,672	CARDIFF CITY	0-1	Bolton Wanderers			10			9	4	2		6	7		5		3		1					8				11
28-Oct	19,136	CARDIFF CITY	2-1	Leicester City	Donnelly, Hogg	6	9			3	4	2	11				5							8		10	1	7		
02-Nov	47,605	Tottenham Hotspur	3-2	CARDIFF CITY	Donnelly 2	6	10			3	4	2	11				5							8		9	1	7		
05-Nov	13,457	Blackpool	6-1	CARDIFF CITY	Tapscott	6	10			3	4	2	11	8			5									9	1	7		
12-Nov	19,234	CARDIFF CITY	1-1	Everton	Watkins	6	9				4	2	11				5						3			8	1	7		10
19-Nov	15,132	Blackburn Rovers	2-2	CARDIFF CITY	Tapscott, og	6			8		4	2	11				5						3			9	1	7		10
26-Nov	21,122	CARDIFF CITY	3-0	Manchester United	Hogg 2, Edgley	6			8		4	2	11				5						3			9	1	7		10
03-Dec	13,967	West Ham United	2-0	CARDIFF CITY		6			8		4	2	11				5						3			9	1	7		10
10-Dec	21,840	CARDIFF CITY	2-1	Chelsea	Walsh, Baker	6			8		4	2	11				5						3			9	1	7		10
17-Dec	16,807	CARDIFF CITY	2-0	Fulham	Baker, Tapscott	6			8		4	2	11				5						3			9	1	7		10
26-Dec	25,214	CARDIFF CITY	3-1	West Brom	Tapscott 3	6			8		4	2	11				5						3			9	1	7		10
27-Dec	30,131	West Brom	1-1	CARDIFF CITY	Baker	6			8		4	2	11				5						3		1	9		7		10
31-Dec	11,048	Preston North End	1-1	CARDIFF CITY	Tapscott	6					4	2	11				5			8			3		1	9		7		10
14-Jan	25,670	CARDIFF CITY	2-1	Burnley	Tapscott 2	6					4	2	11				5			8			3		1	9		7		10
21-Jan	19,227	Nottingham Forest	2-1	CARDIFF CITY	Tapscott	6	10				4	2	7				5			8			3		1	9				11
04-Feb	15,218	CARDIFF CITY	3-3	Manchester City	Moore, Tapscott, Baker	6	10			2	4		11				5			8			3		1	9		7		
11-Feb	33,534	Arsenal	2-3	CARDIFF CITY	Moore, Walsh, Donnelly	6	10			2			11	4			5			8			3		1	9		7		
22-Feb	22,502	CARDIFF CITY	3-2	Newcastle United	Moore 2, Walsh	6	10					2	11	4			5			8			3		1	9		7		
25-Feb	24,396	CARDIFF CITY	3-2	Wolves	Walsh, Donnelly, Tapscott	6	10					2	11	4			5			8	1		3			9		7		
04-Mar	21,815	Bolton Wanderers	3-0	CARDIFF CITY		6	10					2	11	4			5			8	1		3			9		7		
11-Mar	45,463	CARDIFF CITY	3-2	Tottenham Hotspur	Hogg, Walsh, Tapscott	6	10					2	11	4			5			8	1		3			9		7		
24-Mar	19,754	CARDIFF CITY	0-2	Blackpool		6	10					2	11	4			5			8	1		3			9		7		
31-Mar	16,339	CARDIFF CITY	0-2	Birmingham City		6	10					2		4			5		3			11				9	1	7	8	
01-Apr	22,697	Chelsea	6-1	CARDIFF CITY	Durban	4		8		9		2		6			5		3			11					1	7	10	
03-Apr	20,065	Birmingham City	2-1	CARDIFF CITY	Moore	6		10		9				4		11	5		3	8			2			7	1			
08-Apr	16,192	CARDIFF CITY	1-1	Blackburn Rovers	Edwards	6		10		9		2	11	4			5			8			3				1	7		
10-Apr	32,042	Leicester City	3-0	CARDIFF CITY		6	10			9		2	11	4			5	7	3	8	1									
15-Apr	34,382	Everton	5-1	CARDIFF CITY	Ward	6						2	11	4			5	7	3	8					1	9			10	
22-Apr	9,549	CARDIFF CITY	1-1	West Ham United	Donnelly	6	10					2	11	4			5		3	8						9	1	7		
29-Apr	30,420	Manchester United	3-3	CARDIFF CITY	Hogg 2, Tapscott	6	10					2	11	4			5		3	9						8	1	7		
					Appearances	39	27	4	10	14	26	39	26	19	5	1	42	2	17	25	7	2	20	3	8	39	27	34	3	23
					Goals	4	7	2	1	2			6		1					6						20		7	1	2

1 Colin Baker
2 Peter Donnelly
3 Alan Durban
4 Brian Edgley
5 Trevor Edwards
6 Steve Gammon
7 Alan Harrington
8 Derek Hogg
9 Barry Hole
10 Colin Hudson
11 Brian Jenkins
12 Danny Malloy
13 John McMillan
14 Alec Milne
15 Graham Moore
16 Ron Nicholls
17 Tony Pickrell
18 Ron Stitfall
19 Derrick Sullivan
20 Maurice Swan
21 Derek Tapscott
22 Graham Vearncombe
23 Brian Walsh
24 Dai Ward
25 Johnny Watkins

1961-62 21st in Division One (Relegated)

Date	Att	Home	Score	Away	Scorers	1	2	3	4	5	6	7	8	9	10	11	12	13	14	15	16	17	18	19	20	21	22	23	24
19-Aug	18,428	Blackburn Rovers	0-0	CARDIFF CITY		6						2	11	4		9				3	10		5				1	7	8
23-Aug	24,662	CARDIFF CITY	1-1	Sheffield United	J King	6						2	11	4		9				3	10		5				1	7	8
26-Aug	22,701	CARDIFF CITY	3-2	Blackpool	Ward 2, Hogg	6						2	11	4		9				3	10		5				1	7	8
28-Aug	19,193	Sheffield United	1-0	CARDIFF CITY		6						2	11	4		9				3	10		5				1	7	8
02-Sep	37,834	Tottenham Hotspur	3-2	CARDIFF CITY	J King, Ward	6						2	11	4		9				3	10		5			7	1		8
06-Sep	20,853	CARDIFF CITY	5-2	Chelsea	Ward 2, Tapscott, Moore, og	6						2	11	4		9				3	10		5			7	1		8
09-Sep	22,076	CARDIFF CITY	1-2	Bolton Wanderers	Ward	6						2		4		9				3	10	11	5			7	1		8
16-Sep	29,251	CARDIFF CITY	1-2	Manchester United	Ward	6		11				2		4		9				3	10		5			7	1		8
20-Sep	15,804	Chelsea	2-3	CARDIFF CITY	Baker, Ward, Donnelly	6		11	10			2		4	1	9				3			5			7			8
23-Sep	26,643	Wolves	1-1	CARDIFF CITY	Harrington	6		11	10			2		4	1	9				3			5			7			8
30-Sep	20,502	CARDIFF CITY	2-2	Nottingham Forest	Ward, J King	6		11	10			2		4	1	9				3			5			7			8
07-Oct	20,143	Manchester City	1-2	CARDIFF CITY	J King, Hole	6			10			2	11	4	1	9		7		3			5						8
18-Oct	16,819	CARDIFF CITY	2-2	West Brom	Durban, Ward	6			10			2		4	1	9		11		3			5					7	8
21-Oct	22,765	Burnley	2-1	CARDIFF CITY	Ward	6			10			2	11	4	1	9	7			3			5						8
28-Oct	25,096	CARDIFF CITY	1-1	Arsenal	Pickrell	6						2		4	1	9	7			3	10	11	5						8
04-Nov	20,077	Fulham	0-1	CARDIFF CITY	Tapscott	6						2		4	1	9	7			3	10	11	5			8			
11-Nov	17,987	CARDIFF CITY	2-1	Sheffield Wednesday	Tapscott 2	6						2		4	1	9	7			3	10	11	5			8			
18-Nov	16,992	Leicester City	3-0	CARDIFF CITY		6			10			2		4	1	9	7			3		11	5						8
25-Nov	22,823	CARDIFF CITY	0-3	Ipswich Town		6						2	11	4	1	9	7			3			5			8			10
02-Dec	20,959	Birmingham City	3-0	CARDIFF CITY		5				9	4	2		6		11	7			3	10				1				8
09-Dec	15,782	CARDIFF CITY	0-0	Everton		6						2		4	1	9	7			3	10	11	5			8			
16-Dec	13,799	CARDIFF CITY	1-1	Blackburn Rovers	Moore	6						2		4	1	9	7			3	10	11	5			8			
23-Dec	13,961	Blackpool	3-0	CARDIFF CITY		4					6	2		10	1	9	7			3		11	5			8			
26-Dec	18,394	CARDIFF CITY	1-0	Aston Villa	Tapscott	4					6	2		10	1		7			3		11	5			8			9
13-Jan	33,606	CARDIFF CITY	1-1	Tottenham Hotspur	J King (p)	6			8		4	2	11			9	7			3			5				1		10
20-Jan	11,231	Bolton Wanderers	1-1	CARDIFF CITY	Ward	6			8		4	2	11			9	7			3			5				1		10
03-Feb	29,200	Manchester United	3-0	CARDIFF CITY		6			10		4	2	11			9	7			3			5				1		8
09-Feb	18,372	CARDIFF CITY	2-3	Wolves	Ward, Milne	6			10			2		4		9	7			3		11	5				1		8
17-Feb	19,227	Nottingham Forest	2-1	CARDIFF CITY	J King	6			10			2		4	1	9	7		11	3			5						8
24-Feb	19,347	CARDIFF CITY	0-0	Manchester City		6	9							4	1	10	7		11	3			5	2					8
03-Mar	13,894	West Brom	5-1	CARDIFF CITY	P King	6	9		10			2	11	4	1		7			3			5			8			
14-Mar	15,416	CARDIFF CITY	1-1	Burnley	M Charles	6	9			2		5	11	4		10	7			3							1		8
17-Mar	25,059	Arsenal	1-1	CARDIFF CITY	Ward	6	9			2		5		4		10	7	11		3							1		8
23-Mar	16,758	CARDIFF CITY	0-3	Fulham		6	9		10	2		5	11	4			7			3						8	1		
03-Apr	17,475	Sheffield Wednesday	2-0	CARDIFF CITY		6	5			2		4				9	7	11		3						8	1		10
07-Apr	11,058	CARDIFF CITY	0-4	Leicester City		6	9			2		4				10		11		3			5			7	1		8
14-Apr	17,693	Ipswich Town	1-0	CARDIFF CITY		4	9		10					6	1		8	7		3		11	5	2					
20-Apr	25,459	West Ham United	4-1	CARDIFF CITY	Pickrell	4	9		10					6	1		8	7		3		11	5	2					
21-Apr	8,608	CARDIFF CITY	3-2	Birmingham City	Tapscott 3	4	9		10	7				6	1					3		11	5	2		8			
23-Apr	11,274	CARDIFF CITY	3-0	West Ham United	Ward 2, Tapscott	6			10					4			7			3		11	5	2		8	1		9
28-Apr	31,186	Everton	8-3	CARDIFF CITY	Pickrell 2, M Charles	4	9		10					6			7			3		11	5	2		8	1		
01-May	22,174	Aston Villa	2-2	CARDIFF CITY	Ward, M Charles	6	9		8			2		4						3		11	5			7	1		10
					Appearances	42	12	4	20	7	6	36	15	37	21	33	26	7	2	42	14	16	37	6	1	22	20	5	31
					Goals	1	3	1	1			1	1	1		6	1			1	2	4				9			17

1 Colin Baker
2 Mel Charles
3 Peter Donnelly
4 Alan Durban
5 Trevor Edwards
6 Steve Gammon
7 Alan Harrington
8 Derek Hogg
9 Barry Hole
10 Dilwyn John
11 Johnny King
12 Peter King
13 Danny McCarthy
14 Alan McIntosh
15 Alec Milne
16 Graham Moore
17 Tony Pickrell
18 Frank Rankmore
19 Ron Stitfall
20 Maurice Swan
21 Derek Tapscott
22 Graham Vearncombe
23 Brian Walsh
24 Dai Ward

1962-63 10th in Division Two

Date	Att	Home	Score	Away	Scorers	1	2	3	4	5	6	7	8	9	10	11	12	13	14	15	16	17	18	19	20	21	22
18-Aug	27,569	CARDIFF CITY	4-4	Newcastle United	Hole 2, Hooper, M Charles	10	6		9	8			2	4	11	1		7	3			5					
22-Aug	25,360	Norwich City	0-0	CARDIFF CITY		10	6			8		9	2	4	11	1		7	3		5						
25-Aug	14,538	Derby County	1-2	CARDIFF CITY	Hooper (p), Allchurch	10	6			8		9	2	4	11	1		7				5	3				
29-Aug	26,103	CARDIFF CITY	2-4	Norwich City	Hooper 2	10	6		9	8			2	4	11	1		7	3			5					
01-Sep	18,940	CARDIFF CITY	1-2	Middlesbrough	og	10	6	2				9		4	11			7	3			5		1	8		
04-Sep	24,687	Swansea Town	2-1	CARDIFF CITY	M Charles	10	6		9				2	4	11			7				5	3	1	8		
08-Sep	17,573	Huddersfield Town	1-0	CARDIFF CITY		10	6		9				2	4	11			7				5	3	1	8		
12-Sep	14,426	CARDIFF CITY	5-3	Grimsby Town	M Charles 2, Allchurch, Hooper, McIntosh	10	6		9				2	4	11			7				5	3	1	8		
15-Sep	23,454	CARDIFF CITY	5-2	Swansea Town	M Charles 2, McIntosh, Hooper, og	10	6		9				4		11	1		7	2			5	3		8		
18-Sep	10,962	Grimsby Town	1-2	CARDIFF CITY	Hooper 2	10	6		9				2	4	11	1		7				5	3		8		
22-Sep	22,302	CARDIFF CITY	1-2	Portsmouth	Tapscott	10	6		9				2	4	11	1		7				5	3		8		
29-Sep	11,994	Preston North End	2-6	CARDIFF CITY	Hooper 2, M Charles 2, Tapscott, Durban		6		9	10			2	4	11			7				5	3	1	8		
06-Oct	25,434	Chelsea	6-0	CARDIFF CITY		10	6		9				2	4	11			7				5	3	1	8		
13-Oct	15,901	CARDIFF CITY	1-0	Luton Town	Hooper		6		9	10			2	4	11			7				5	3		8	1	
27-Oct	12,003	CARDIFF CITY	4-0	Scunthorpe United	Allchurch 2, Tapscott, McIntosh	10	6		5	8	2		4		11			7					3		9	1	
31-Oct	16,616	Southampton	3-5	CARDIFF CITY	Allchurch 2, Hole, McIntosh, Durban	10	6		5	8	3		4	11				7					2		9	1	
03-Nov	9,915	Bury	1-0	CARDIFF CITY		10	6		4	8	3		2	11				7				5			9	1	
10-Nov	14,199	CARDIFF CITY	4-1	Rotherham United	Durban 2, Hooper 2	10	6			8	3		2	4	11			7				5			9	1	
17-Nov	11,509	Charlton Athletic	2-4	CARDIFF CITY	Tapscott 3, Hooper	10	6		5	8	3		2	4	11			7							9	1	
24-Nov	21,543	CARDIFF CITY	1-1	Stoke City	McIntosh	10	6		5	8	3		2	4	11			7							9	1	
01-Dec	37,603	Sunderland	2-1	CARDIFF CITY	Allchurch	10	6		5	8	3		2	4	11			7							9	1	
08-Dec	11,334	CARDIFF CITY	0-0	Leeds United		10	6		9		3		2		11			7				5			8	1	4
15-Dec	27,916	Newcastle United	2-1	CARDIFF CITY	Hooper	10	6		5	8	3		2		11			7							9	1	4
22-Dec	12,027	CARDIFF CITY	1-0	Derby County	Hooper	10	6		5	8	3		2		11			7							9	1	4
26-Dec	18,992	Plymouth Argyle	4-2	CARDIFF CITY	Durban 2	10				8	3		4		11			7				5	2		9	1	6
23-Feb	16,108	CARDIFF CITY	1-0	Chelsea	Harrington	10	4		9		3		2	6	11			7				5			8	1	
09-Mar	12,427	CARDIFF CITY	3-1	Southampton	Allchurch, Tapscott, McIntosh	10	4		9		3		2	6	11			7				5			8	1	
15-Mar	8,060	Scunthorpe United	2-2	CARDIFF CITY	Allchurch 2	10	4		9	8	3		2	6	11			7				5				1	
23-Mar	15,565	CARDIFF CITY	3-1	Bury	Hooper, M Charles, og	10	4		9	8	3		2	6	11			7				5				1	
29-Mar	9,131	Rotherham United	2-1	CARDIFF CITY	Allchurch	10	4		9	8	3		2	6	11			7				5				1	
06-Apr	12,619	CARDIFF CITY	1-2	Charlton Athletic	Hole	10	4		9	8	3		2	6	11			7				5				1	
13-Apr	30,453	Stoke City	1-0	CARDIFF CITY			4		9	10	7		2	6	11	1						5	3		8		
15-Apr	11,257	CARDIFF CITY	2-2	Walsall	Edwards, Tapscott		4			8	3			6	11	1	10	7			5		2		9		
16-Apr	10,381	Walsall	2-1	CARDIFF CITY	King						3	9		6	11	1	10	7			5		2		8		4
20-Apr	12,293	CARDIFF CITY	5-2	Sunderland	Hooper 2, Tapscott, McIntosh, M Charles		6		9		3		2	10	11	1		7				5			8		4
24-Apr	7,237	Luton Town	2-3	CARDIFF CITY	Hooper 3		6		9				2	10	11	1		7				5	3		8		4
27-Apr	19,702	Leeds United	3-0	CARDIFF CITY		10	6		9		3		2		11	1		7				5			8		4
01-May	9,673	CARDIFF CITY	2-1	Plymouth Argyle	Allchurch, Hole	8	6		9				2	10	11	1		7			3	5					4
04-May	10,538	Portsmouth	2-0	CARDIFF CITY		8	6		5				2	10	11	1		7			3				9		4
06-May	8,389	CARDIFF CITY	1-1	Preston North End	M Charles	10	6		9				2		11	1		7			3	5			8		4
11-May	9,628	Middlesbrough	3-2	CARDIFF CITY	McIntosh 2	10				8			2	6	11	1		7		5	3				9		4
18-May	8,774	CARDIFF CITY	3-0	Huddersfield Town	King 2, Tapscott	8	6						2		11	1	11	7			3	5			9		4
					Appearances	35	39	1	33	23	22	4	39	33	40	18	3	41	5	1	8	30	17	6	33	18	13
					Goals	12			11	6	1		1	5	22		3	9							10		

1 Ivor Allchurch
2 Colin Baker
3 Alistair Brack
4 Mel Charles
5 Alan Durban
6 Trevor Edwards
7 Gordon Fraser
8 Alan Harrington
9 Barry Hole
10 Peter Hooper
11 Dilwyn John
12 Peter King
13 Alan McIntosh
14 Alec Milne
15 Don Murray
16 Trevor Peck
17 Frank Rankmore
18 Ron Stitfall
19 Maurice Swan
20 Derek Tapscott
21 Graham Vearncombe
22 Gareth Williams

1963-64 15th in Division Two

Date	Att	Home	Score	Away	Scorers	1	2	3	4	5	6	7	8	9	10	11	12	13	14	15	16	17	18	19	20	21	22	23	24	25	26
24-Aug	21,977	CARDIFF CITY	3-1	Norwich City	King, J Charles, Allchurch	10		5	4		2				8		11			7					9	3			1		6
28-Aug	25,134	CARDIFF CITY	2-2	Manchester City	Allchurch, J Charles	10		5	8		2				6		11			7					9	3			1		4
30-Aug	8,366	Scunthorpe United	1-2	CARDIFF CITY	Williams, Tapscott	10					2				6	1	11			7		5			9	3	8				4
04-Sep	22,138	Manchester City	4-0	CARDIFF CITY		10			8		2				6	1	11			7		5			4	3					9
07-Sep	17,523	CARDIFF CITY	1-2	Portsmouth	J Charles	10		5	9		2				6	1	11			7					4	3	8				
11-Sep	15,855	CARDIFF CITY	2-1	Bury	Allchurch 2	10			9		2				6		11			7		5					8	3	1		4
13-Sep	11,568	Rotherham United	1-0	CARDIFF CITY		10			9		2				6		11					5			8		7	3	1		4
17-Sep	11,918	Bury	4-1	CARDIFF CITY	Allchurch	10		8	9		2				6					7		5					11	3	1		4
21-Sep	16,117	CARDIFF CITY	0-0	Leeds United		10		9			2				6	1	11			7		5					8	3			4
28-Sep	37,287	Sunderland	3-3	CARDIFF CITY	Allchurch 3	10		9			2				8	1	11			7		5		3	6						4
02-Oct	10,657	CARDIFF CITY	0-0	Grimsby Town		10	4		9		2					1	8		11	7		5		3	6						
05-Oct	10,178	CARDIFF CITY	1-0	Northampton Town	M Charles	10	4		9							1	8		11	7		5		3	6	2					
19-Oct	21,417	CARDIFF CITY	1-1	Swansea Town	Scott (p)	10	2	9						8	4	1	7		11			5			6	3					
26-Oct	26,534	Charlton Athletic	5-2	CARDIFF CITY	McIntosh, J Charles	10	4	5			2			9	8	1	7			11					6			3			
02-Nov	13,455	CARDIFF CITY	1-1	Middlesbrough	J Charles	10	4	9			2			8		1	7			11		5		3	6						
09-Nov	38,495	Newcastle United	0-4	CARDIFF CITY	King 2, Allchurch, J Charles	10	4	9			2			8		1	7			11		5		3	6						
16-Nov	14,398	CARDIFF CITY	2-1	Huddersfield Town	McIntosh, Baker	10	4	5			2			9			7			11				3	6		8		1		
23-Nov	11,852	Derby County	2-1	CARDIFF CITY	J Charles	10	4	9			2			8			7			11		5		3	6				1		
30-Nov	11,193	CARDIFF CITY	3-1	Plymouth Argyle	J Charles 2, Allchurch	10	4	9			2			8			7			11		5		3	6				1		
07-Dec	17,861	Southampton	3-2	CARDIFF CITY	Halliday, J Charles	10	4	9			2			8			7			11		5		3	6				1		
14-Dec	14,130	Norwich City	5-1	CARDIFF CITY	Halliday	10		9			7			8	4					11		5		3	6	2			1		
26-Dec	18,682	CARDIFF CITY	0-4	Preston North End		10		9			2				4		7			11		5		3			8		1		6
28-Dec	19,458	Preston North End	4-0	CARDIFF CITY			6	9			3			8	10	1				11	2	5					7				4
11-Jan	12,046	Portsmouth	5-0	CARDIFF CITY		11		9	5	10	7			8		1					2			3						6	4
17-Jan	8,773	CARDIFF CITY	2-1	Rotherham United	M Charles, Scott (p)	10		5	9		2						11	7			3				6		8		1		4
01-Feb	28,056	Leeds United	1-1	CARDIFF CITY	M Charles	10		5	9		2				11	1		7			3				6		8				4
08-Feb	15,600	CARDIFF CITY	0-2	Sunderland		10		5	9		2				11	1		7					3		6		8				4
15-Feb	11,871	Northampton Town	2-1	CARDIFF CITY	M Charles	10		5	9		2				8	1	11	7			3				6						4
22-Feb	8,690	CARDIFF CITY	2-1	Leyton Orient	Scott (p), M Charles	10		5	9		3				8	1		7					2		6		11				4
29 Feb	10,580	Huddersfield Town	2-1	CARDIFF CITY	Scott	10		5	9		3				6	1	7						2		8		11				4
07-Mar	8,066	CARDIFF CITY	1-1	Charlton Athletic	J Charles	10		5	9		3				6	1	7						2		8		11				4
20-Mar	9,096	CARDIFF CITY	2-2	Newcastle United	Allchurch, M Charles	10		5	9		3	7			6	1		11					2		8						3
27-Mar	22,318	Swindon Town	1-2	CARDIFF CITY	King, Lewis	10		5				7		9	6	1	8	11					2	3	4						
28-Mar	18,721	Swansea Town	3-0	CARDIFF CITY		10		5	9			11			6	1	8	7					2	3	4						
30-Mar	14,033	CARDIFF CITY	1-0	Swindon Town	M Charles	10		5	9			11			6	1	8	7					2	3	4						
04-Apr	8,238	CARDIFF CITY	2-1	Derby County	M Charles, King	10			9			11			6	1	8	7				5	2	3	4						
08-Apr	9,618	CARDIFF CITY	3-1	Scunthorpe United	Farrell 2, King	10		5	9			11			6	1	8	7					2	3	4						
11-Apr	14,993	Plymouth Argyle	1-1	CARDIFF CITY	King	10		5	9			11			6	1	8	7					2	3	4						
13-Apr	7,278	Leyton Orient	4-0	CARDIFF CITY		10		5	9			11				1	8	7					2	3	4						6
15-Apr	8,914	Grimsby Town	0-2	CARDIFF CITY	Scott (p), M Charles	19			9				4				11	7				5	2	3	6				1		8
18-Apr	10,727	CARDIFF CITY	2-4	Southampton	Williams, og	10		5					4		6		11	7					2	3	8				1		9
24-Apr	8,472	Middlesbrough	3-1	CARDIFF CITY	Allchurch	10	2		9						6	1	11	7					5	3	4						8
					Appearances	41	12	33	26	1	30	8	2	12	30	28	34	16	3	21	5	20	15	22	36	8	15	5	14	1	24
					Goals	12	1	11	9			2		2			7	11		2					5		1				2

1 Ivor Allchurch
2 Colin Baker
3 John Charles
4 Mel Charles
5 Graham Coldrick
6 Trevor Edwards
7 Greg Farrell
8 Steve Gammon
9 Tommy Halliday
10 Barry Hole
11 Dilwyn John
12 Peter King
13 Bernard Lewis
14 Richard Mallory
15 Alan McIntosh
16 Alec Milne
17 Don Murray
18 Trevor Peck
19 Peter Rodrigues
20 Dick Scott
21 Ron Stitfall
22 Derek Tapscott
23 Jim Upton
24 Graham Vearncombe
25 Phil Watkins
26 Gareth Williams

1964-65 13th in Division Two

Date	Att	Home	Score	Away	Scorers	1	2	3	4	5	6	7	8	9	10	11	12	13	14	15	16	17	18	19	20	21	22	23	24	25	26
22-Aug	16,911	CARDIFF CITY	0-0	Ipswich Town		10		5	9			7	4				6				8	11		3			2				1
26-Aug	15,805	CARDIFF CITY	3-3	Preston North End	Allchurch 2, Lewis	10		5	9				4				6			11	8	7		3			2				1
29-Aug	14,585	Plymouth Argyle	3-1	CARDIFF CITY	Hole (p)	10		5	9				4				6			11	8	7		3			2				1
31-Aug	23,303	Preston North End	1-1	CARDIFF CITY	Allchurch	10		5	8					9			6			11	7					3	2			4	1
05-Sep	13,501	CARDIFF CITY	1-3	Bolton Wanderers	Allchurch	10		5						9			6			11	7					3	2	8		4	1
12-Sep	22,770	Middlesbrough	0-0	CARDIFF CITY		10		5	8					9			6			11	7					3	2			4	1
16-Sep	9,392	CARDIFF CITY	1-1	Huddersfield Town	Hole (p)	10		5	8			11		9			6				7					3	2			4	1
19-Sep	11,826	CARDIFF CITY	1-1	Newcastle United	Allchurch	10		5		9		11					6				7		8			3	2			4	1
26-Sep	12,328	Northampton Town	1-0	CARDIFF CITY		10		5									6			11	7		8			3	2		9	4	1
29-Sep	5,640	Huddersfield Town	3-1	CARDIFF CITY	Allchurch	10		5			9						6				7	11				3	2		8	4	1
06-Oct	12,601	Rotherham United	3-1	CARDIFF CITY	Ellis	10			8		9						6				7	11			5	3	2			4	1
10-Oct	8,302	CARDIFF CITY	2-1	Derby County	P King, Tapscott	10					9						6				7	11			5	3	2		8	4	1
17-Oct	15,937	Swindon Town	3-3	CARDIFF CITY	M Charles 2, Hole (p)				10			7					6				8	11			5	3	2		9	4	1
24-Oct	8,696	CARDIFF CITY	1-0	Portsmouth	Tapscott						10	7					6				8	11			5	3	2		9	4	1
31-Oct	13,146	Manchester City	2-0	CARDIFF CITY							10	7					6				8	11			5	3	2		9	4	1
07-Nov	9,616	CARDIFF CITY	2-1	Charlton Athletic	Ellis 2						10	7			2		6				8	11			5		3		9	4	1
14-Nov	6,350	Leyton Orient	1-3	CARDIFF CITY	Ellis 2, Lewis						10	7			2		6				8	11			5		3		9	4	1
21-Nov	9,883	CARDIFF CITY	4-0	Bury	Tapscott 2, Ellis, Lewis						10	7			2		6				8	11			5		3		9	4	1
28-Nov	18,188	Crystal Palace	0-0	CARDIFF CITY							10	7			2		6				8	11			5		3		9	4	1
05-Dec	9,877	CARDIFF CITY	1-3	Norwich City	og						10	7			2		6				8	11			5		3		9	4	1
12-Dec	10,010	Ipswich Town	1-1	CARDIFF CITY	Ellis			4			9				2		6				10	11			5		3		7	8	1
19-Dec	9,555	CARDIFF CITY	4-0	Plymouth Argyle	Tapscott 2, Rodrigues, og						9	7			2		6	1			10	11			5		3		8	4	
26-Dec	17,875	Swansea Town	3-2	CARDIFF CITY	Ellis 2			4			9	7	8		2		6	1			10	11			5		3				
15-Jan	9,490	CARDIFF CITY	6-1	Middlesbrough	P King 3, Tapscott 2, Williams			4				7			2		6				10	11			5		3		9	8	1
23-Jan	37,291	Newcastle United	2-0	CARDIFF CITY							10	7			2		6				8	11			5		3		9	4	1
06-Feb	7,427	CARDIFF CITY	0-2	Northampton Town				9				7			2		6				8	11			5		3		10	4	1
13-Feb	14,740	Southampton	1-1	CARDIFF CITY	Allchurch	10		4			9	7					6				11				5	2	3			8	1
20-Feb	10,894	Derby County	1-0	CARDIFF CITY		10					9	7					6		11		8				5	2	3			4	1
27-Feb	9,197	CARDIFF CITY	2-0	Swindon Town	Ellis, Hole	10		4			9	7					6				11				5	2	3			8	1
06-Mar	18,036	Norwich City	2-1	CARDIFF CITY	Allchurch	10		4			9	7					6				11				5	2	3			8	1
12-Mar	9,094	CARDIFF CITY	2-2	Manchester City	Allchurch, P King	10		4			9	7					6				11				5	2	3			8	1
22-Mar	7,710	Charlton Athletic	2-2	CARDIFF CITY	Williams 2	10		4			9	7				3	6					11			5		2			8	1
24-Mar	9,642	CARDIFF CITY	2-2	Southampton	Williams, J Charles	10		4			9	7				3	6					11			5		2			8	1
27-Mar	7,627	CARDIFF CITY	0-2	Leyton Orient		10		4			9	7				3	6					11			5		2			8	1
03-Apr	4,292	Bury	1-2	CARDIFF CITY	P King, Hole	8		4								3	6		7		10	11			5		2			9	1
06-Apr	15,896	CARDIFF CITY	5-0	Swansea Town	Allchurch 3, J Charles 2	8		9								3	6		7		10	11			5		2			4	1
10-Apr	9,585	CARDIFF CITY	0-0	Crystal Palace		8	3	9									6		7		10	11			5		2			4	1
17-Apr	13,275	Portsmouth	1-0	CARDIFF CITY		8	3	9		5							6		7		10	11					2			4	1
19-Apr	11,228	CARDIFF CITY	3-1	Coventry City	Allchurch 2, P King	8	3	9									6		7		10	11			5		2			4	1
20-Apr	23,913	Coventry City	0-2	CARDIFF CITY	Lewis, Hole	8	3	9									6		7		10	11			5		2			4	1
24-Apr	9,794	CARDIFF CITY	3-2	Rotherham United	Allchurch, Rodrigues, P King	8	3	9									6		7		10	11			5		2			4	1
28-Apr	6,498	Bolton Wanderers	1-0	CARDIFF CITY			3			9		8					6		7		10	11			5	2				4	1
					Appearances	27	6	28	8	3	22	25	4	4	11	5	42	2	9	6	39	31	2	3	31	18	41	1	16	38	40
					Goals	15		3	2		9						6				8	4					2		9	4	

1 Ivor Allchurch
2 Colin Baker
3 John Charles
4 Mel Charles
5 Graham Coldrick
6 Kevin Ellis
7 Greg Farrell
8 Steve Gammon
9 Tommy Halliday
10 Alan Harrington
11 Gordon Harris
12 Barry Hole
13 Dilwyn John
14 George Johnston
15 Gerry King
16 Peter King
17 Bernard Lewis
18 Clive Lloyd
19 Alec Milne
20 Don Murray
21 Trevor Peck
22 Peter Rodrigues
23 Dick Scott
24 Derek Tapscott
25 Gareth Williams
26 Bob Wilson

1965-66 20th in Division Two

Date	Att	Home	Score	Away	Scorers	1	2	3	4	5	6	7	8	9	10	11	12	13	14	15	16	17	18	19	20	21	22	23	24
21-Aug	13,392	CARDIFF CITY	1-0	Bury	Charles		4*			9	5		7			3	6			10		11			2	12		8	1
25-Aug	15,260	CARDIFF CITY	2-1	Derby County	Charles, Harkin		3			9			7		10		6			8		11		5	2			4	1
28-Aug	13,437	Norwich City	3-2	CARDIFF CITY	Harkin, Johnston (p)		3			9			7		10		6			8		11		5	2			4	1
01-Sep	10,221	Derby County	1-5	CARDIFF CITY	Charles 2, Johnston 2(p), Harkin					9	2		7		10		6			8		11		5	3			4	1
04-Sep	19,827	CARDIFF CITY	1-4	Wolves	Johnston (p)					9	2		7		10		6			8		11		5	3			4	1
11-Sep	9,211	Rotherham United	6-4	CARDIFF CITY	Harkin 2, Johnston, Farrell					9			7		10	2	6			8		11		5	3			4	1
14-Sep	13,172	Charlton Athletic	5-2	CARDIFF CITY	Harkin, Johnston								7		10	2	6			8	9	11		5	3			4	1
18-Sep	11,365	CARDIFF CITY	4-3	Manchester City	Johnston 2, Harkin, Hole		3				4				9		6		1	7	10	11		5	2			8	
25-Sep	15,300	Bristol City	1-1	CARDIFF CITY	Lewis		3				4				10		6		1	7	8	11		5	2			9	
06-Oct	12,469	CARDIFF CITY	1-2	Coventry City	Williams		3				4*				10		6		1	7	8	11		5	2	12		9	
09-Oct	10,740	Plymouth Argyle	2-2	CARDIFF CITY	Farrell, Johnston								7		9	3	6		1	8	10	11		5	2			4	
16-Oct	11,781	CARDIFF CITY	1-2	Portsmouth	Johnston	9				5			7		10		6*			12	8	11		2	3	4			1
23-Oct	11,088	Bolton Wanderers	1-2	CARDIFF CITY	Andrews	9							7		12	2		6		8*	10	11		2	3	4			1
30-Oct	8,325	CARDIFF CITY	1-0	Ipswich Town	Farrell	9							7		10	2	4	6		8	11			5*	3	12			1
06-Nov	10,744	Birmingham City	4-2	CARDIFF CITY	Andrews 2	9					5		7		10	2	4	6		8	11				3				1
10-Nov	8,537	CARDIFF CITY	3-1	Charlton Athletic	Johnston 2(2p), Andrews	9					5		7		10	2	4	6		8	11				3				1
13-Nov	9,017	CARDIFF CITY	3-1	Leyton Orient	Johnston, Andrews, Toshack	9					5*		7			2	4	6		10	11				3		12	8	1
20-Nov	11,898	Middlesbrough	3-4	CARDIFF CITY	Toshack 2, Johnston (p), og	9	3						7			2	4	6		8	11						10	5	1
27-Nov	10,898	CARDIFF CITY	0-1	Huddersfield Town		9							7			2	4	6		8	11				3		10	5	1
04-Dec	11,527	Crystal Palace	0-0	CARDIFF CITY		9							7			2	4	6		8	11				3		10	5	1
11-Dec	10,754	CARDIFF CITY	1-3	Preston North End	Johnston	9							7			2	4	6		8	10	11			3			5	1
18-Dec	8,434	Portsmouth	3-1	CARDIFF CITY	Andrews	9							7			2	4	6		8	11			5	3			10	1
27-Dec	14,768	CARDIFF CITY	3-5	Southampton	Harkin, Andrews, og	9							7		10	2	6			8	11			5	3			4	1
01-Jan	8,890	CARDIFF CITY	5-1	Plymouth Argyle	Andrews 2, Harkin 2, Hole	9	12					1	7*	3	10	2	8	6			11			5				4	
08-Jan	5,516	Leyton Orient	1-1	CARDIFF CITY	Andrews	9						1	7	3	10	2*	6			8	11		12	5				4	
29-Jan	4,677	Bury	1-1	CARDIFF CITY	Johnston	9			2			1		3	10		6			8	11	7		5				4	
19-Feb	24,179	Wolves	1-2	CARDIFF CITY	Andrews	9		11	2			1		3			6			8	10	7		5				4	
26-Feb	9,184	CARDIFF CITY	0-0	Rotherham United		9		11	2			1		3			6			10	8	7		5				4	
05-Mar	8,951	CARDIFF CITY	1-1	Bolton Wanderers	Farrell	9			2			1	7	3			6			8	10	11		5				4	
12-Mar	29,642	Manchester City	2-2	CARDIFF CITY	Toshack, Johnston	8			2			1	7	3			6			10	11			5			9	4	
18-Mar	13,405	CARDIFF CITY	2-1	Bristol City	King, Toshack	8			2		6		7	3			5		1	10	11						9	4	
26-Mar	20,296	Coventry City	3-1	CARDIFF CITY	Andrews	9			2		5		7	3			6		1	11	8						10	4	
02-Apr	8,150	CARDIFF CITY	1-3	Birmingham City	Hole	9		11	2			1	7	3			6			8	10			5				4	
08-Apr	7,844	CARDIFF CITY	1-1	Carlisle United	Andrews	9		11	2			1	7	3			6			8	10			5				4	
09-Apr	10,392	Ipswich Town	2-1	CARDIFF CITY	Toshack	9			3		2	1	7				8	6			11			5			10	4	
12-Apr	11,252	Carlisle United	2-0	CARDIFF CITY		9		11	2			1	7	3*			6	12		8				5				4	
20-Apr	18,941	Southampton	3-2	CARDIFF CITY	King 2	9			3		2		7*				6	10	1	12	8	11		5				4	
23-Apr	19,138	Huddersfield Town	1-1	CARDIFF CITY	King	9			3		2		7				6	10	1		8	11		5				4	
30-Apr	9,420	CARDIFF CITY	1-0	Crystal Palace	King	9			3		2		7	12			6	8*	1		10	11		5				4	
03-May	12,935	CARDIFF CITY	5-3	Middlesbrough	Andrews 2, Hole, King, Farrell (p)	9			3		2		7	8			6		1		10	11		5				4	
07-May	10,018	Preston North End	9-0	CARDIFF CITY		8			2		4		7	3			10		1		9	11		5		6			
10-May	5,934	CARDIFF CITY	0-2	Norwich City		9			3		2		7					6	1	8	10	11		5		4			
					Appearances	31	8	5	17	7	18	11	36	15	20	17	40	17	12	36	35	24	1	32	22	7	8	35	19
					Goals	15				4			5		10		4			17	6	1					6	1	

1 George Andrews
2 Colin Baker
3 Ronnie Bird
4 Dave Carver
5 John Charles
6 Graham Coldrick
7 Lyn Davies
8 Greg Farrell
9 Bobby Ferguson
10 Terry Harkin
11 Alan Harrington
12 Barry Hole
13 David Houston
14 Dilwyn John
15 George Johnston
16 Peter King
17 Bernard Lewis
18 Pat Murphy
19 Don Murray
20 Peter Rodrigues
21 David Summerhayes
22 John Toshack
23 Gareth Williams
24 Bob Wilson

1966-67 20th in Division Two

Date	Att	Home	Score	Away	Scorers	1	2	3	4	5	6	7	8	9	10	11	12	13	14	15	16	17	18	19	20	21	22	23	24	25	26
20-Aug	7,628	CARDIFF CITY	0-2	Ipswich Town		9				2	6			7	3			1				8	11	5				10	4		
27-Aug	11,952	Bristol City	1-2	CARDIFF CITY	Toshack (p), Andrews	9				2	4			7	3			1				8	11	5				10	6		
31-Aug	14,208	CARDIFF CITY	0-3	Wolves		9				2	6			7	3			1				8	11	5				10	4		
03-Sep	6,902	CARDIFF CITY	4-2	Carlisle United	King 2, Andrews, Toshack	9				2	6			7	3			1				8	11	5				10	4		
07-Sep	10,344	CARDIFF CITY	1-1	Huddersfield Town	Andrews	9				2	6			7	3			1				8	11	5				10	4		
10-Sep	12,805	Blackburn Rovers	4-1	CARDIFF CITY	Toshack	9				2	6			7	3			1				8	11	5				10	4		
17-Sep	7,594	CARDIFF CITY	2-5	Bolton Wanderers	Andrews, Toshack (p)	9				2	6			7	3			1				8	11	5				10	4		
21-Sep	19,678	Wolves	7-1	CARDIFF CITY	Andrews	9	6			3	4	1		7	2							10	11*	5				12	8		
24-Sep	10,182	Charlton Athletic	5-0	CARDIFF CITY			11			2	6	1		7	3				8			9		5				10	4		
01-Oct	6,244	CARDIFF CITY	1-1	Derby County	og	9*	11			2	5	1					6		8		12	10	7			3			4		
08-Oct	9,407	CARDIFF CITY	2-4	Hull City	Lewis, Andrews	8			9	2	5	1							7			10	11			3	6		4		
15-Oct	14,404	Plymouth Argyle	7-1	CARDIFF CITY	Williams	8			9	2		1		7		6						10	11	5		3			4		
29-Oct	12,856	Millwall	1-0	CARDIFF CITY		8		11	9		2				3	6						10	7	5					4	1	
04-Nov	5,933	CARDIFF CITY	0-0	Rotherham United				11	9*		2			12	3	6			8			10	7	5					4	1	
12-Nov	11,283	Preston North End	4-0	CARDIFF CITY				11			2			8	3	6						7		5				9	4	1	10
19-Nov	5,910	CARDIFF CITY	3-0	Bury	Toshack 2, Brown			11	9		2			7	3	6			8					5				10	4	1	
26-Nov	19,682	Coventry City	3-2	CARDIFF CITY	Toshack 2			11	9		2			7	3	6			10					5				8	4	1	
03-Dec	5,540	CARDIFF CITY	2-0	Norwich City	Farrell, Coldrick			11	9		2			7	3	6						10		5				8	4	1	
10-Dec	17,046	Birmingham City	1-2	CARDIFF CITY	Coldrick, Brown			11	9		2			7	3	6						10		5				8	4	1	
14-Dec	7,954	CARDIFF CITY	4-2	Northampton Town	Coldrick 2, Williams 2			11	9		2			7*	3	6						10	12	5				8	4	1	
17-Dec	11,166	Ipswich Town	0-0	CARDIFF CITY				11	9		2				3	6						10	7*	5			12	8	4	1	
26-Dec	17,020	CARDIFF CITY	1-2	Crystal Palace	Williams			11	9		2			7	3	6						10		5				8	4	1	
27-Dec	13,553	Crystal Palace	3-1	CARDIFF CITY	Toshack			11	9		2			7	3	6						10		5				8	4	1	
31-Dec	12,306	CARDIFF CITY	5-1	Bristol City	Brown 2, Bird 2, og			11	9		2			7	3	6			8			10		5			12		4*	1	
07-Jan	10,295	Carlisle United	3-0	CARDIFF CITY				11	9		2			7	3	6			8			10		5			4			1	
14-Jan	11,322	CARDIFF CITY	1-1	Blackburn Rovers	Brown			11	9		2			7	3	6			8			10		5			4			1	
21-Jan	9,071	Bolton Wanderers	3-1	CARDIFF CITY	Johnston				9		2			11	3	6			8			10	7	5					4	1	
03-Feb	10,812	CARDIFF CITY	4-1	Charlton Athletic	Johnston 2, Bird, King			11	9		2				3	6			8	7		10		5					4	1	
11-Feb	14,573	Derby County	1-1	CARDIFF CITY	Brown			11	9		2			7	3	6			8			10		5					4	1	
25-Feb	23,629	Hull City	1-0	CARDIFF CITY					9		2				3	6			7			10		5				8	4	1	
04-Mar	10,845	CARDIFF CITY	1-1	Millwall	King			11		2				7	3	6			8			10		5				9	4	1	
18-Mar	11,787	Northampton Town	2-0	CARDIFF CITY				11	9	2			8		3	6				7		10		5					4	1	
22-Mar	11,727	CARDIFF CITY	0-0	Portsmouth				11	9		2		8		3	6				7		10		5					4	1	
25-Mar	11,696	CARDIFF CITY	4-1	Plymouth Argyle	Toshack, Dean, Jones, Brown				9	2	6		8		3					7		11		5				10	4	1	
27-Mar	16,363	Portsmouth	1-2	CARDIFF CITY	Williams, King			11	9	2	6		8		3					7		10		5					4	1	
01-Apr	8,585	Rotherham United	4-1	CARDIFF CITY	Jones			11	9	2	6		8		3					7		10		5					4	1	
08-Apr	9,630	CARDIFF CITY	4-0	Preston North End	Jones, King, Brown, og			11	9		2		10		3	6				7		8		5					4	1	
15-Apr	6,234	Bury	2-0	CARDIFF CITY				11	8		2		9		3	6				7		10		5					4	1	
22-Apr	19,739	CARDIFF CITY	1-1	Coventry City	Brown			11	8		2				3	6				7		10		5				9	4	1	
29-Apr	14,264	Norwich City	3-2	CARDIFF CITY	Williams, Dean			11*			2		9		3	6				7		10		5	12			8	4	1	
06-May	12,678	CARDIFF CITY	3-0	Birmingham City	Brown 2, Jones			11	8		2		9		3	6				7		10		5					4	1	
13-May	3,847	Huddersfield Town	3-1	CARDIFF CITY	Brown			11	8		2		9		3	6				7		10		5					4	1	
					Appearances	12	3	27	29	17	39	5	10	25	39	28	1	7	14	12	1	40	16	40	1	3	5	23	40	30	1
					Goals	6		3	14		2		2	1					3	4		6	1					10	6		

1 George Andrews
2 Gary Bell
3 Ronnie Bird
4 Bobby Brown
5 Dave Carver
6 Graham Coldrick
7 Lyn Davies
8 Norman Dean
9 Greg Farrell
10 Bobby Ferguson
11 Brian Harris
12 David Houston
13 Dilwyn John
14 George Johnston
15 Barrie Jones
16 Bryn Jones
17 Peter King
18 Bernard Lewis
19 Don Murray
20 Leighton Phillips
21 Derek Ryder
22 David Summerhayes
23 John Toshack
24 Gareth Williams
25 Bob Wilson
26 Jack Winspear

1967-68 13th in Division Two

Date	Att	Home	Score	Away	Scorers	1	2	3	4	5	6	7	8	9	10	11	12	13	14	15	16	17	18	19	20	21	22	23	24	25
19-Aug	17,169	CARDIFF CITY	1-1	Plymouth Argyle	Brown (p)	9			10	4			2				3	6	7		11				5				8	1
26-Aug	10,654	Bolton Wanderers	1-1	CARDIFF CITY	King			11	9	4			2				3	6	7		10				5				8	1
30-Aug	14,351	CARDIFF CITY	4-2	Crystal Palace	Jones, Brown, Bird, King			11	8				2		9		3	6	7		10				5				4	1
02-Sep	17,308	Portsmouth	3-1	CARDIFF CITY	Brown			11	8	2		12			9		3	6	7		10				5				4	1
05-Sep	8,523	Charlton Athletic	1-1	CARDIFF CITY	Brown			11	8	2		10					3	6	7		9				5				4	1
09-Sep	14,674	CARDIFF CITY	3-1	Norwich City	King, Brown (p), Jones			11	8				2				3	6	7		10				5			9	4	1
16-Sep	5,842	Rotherham United	3-2	CARDIFF CITY	King, Murray			11	8			10*	2				3	6	7		9				5			12	4	1
23-Sep	15,375	CARDIFF CITY	1-5	Derby County	Bird (p)	8*		11				12	2				3	6	7		10				5			9	4	1
27-Sep	20,424	Crystal Palace	2-1	CARDIFF CITY	Jones			11	8			10	2				3	6	7		9				5				4	1
30-Sep	13,735	Preston North End	3-0	CARDIFF CITY				11				8	2				3	6	7		10				5		12	9*	4	1
07-Oct	11,261	CARDIFF CITY	1-1	Ipswich Town	Toshack				8	3			2					6	7		10		11		5			9	4	1
14-Oct	15,609	Bristol City	1-1	CARDIFF CITY	Brown			11	10			4	2				3	6	7		8				5			9		1
24-Oct	10,441	CARDIFF CITY	3-0	Middlesbrough	Toshack 2, King			11	8			4	2				3	6	7		9				5			10		1
27-Oct	18,579	Hull City	1-2	CARDIFF CITY	Brown, Bird			11	8			4	2				3	6	7		9				5			10		1
11-Nov	11,324	Blackpool	3-1	CARDIFF CITY	Clarke			11	8	3		4	2					6	7		10				5			9		1
18-Nov	13,673	CARDIFF CITY	1-3	Birmingham City	Toshack			11	8			4				2	3	6	7		10				5			9		1
25-Nov	10,966	Carlisle United	1-3	CARDIFF CITY	Toshack 2, Bell		11		8			4				2	3	6	7		9				5			10		1
02-Dec	9,829	CARDIFF CITY	3-2	Blackburn Rovers	King 2, Clarke			11	8	3		4				2		6	7		10				5			9		1
05-Dec	11,993	CARDIFF CITY	2-2	Millwall	Toshack, Brown			11	8	3		4				2		6	7		9				5			10		1
09-Dec	8,552	Huddersfield Town	1-0	CARDIFF CITY					8	3		4			11	2		6	7		9				5			10		1
16-Dec	10,736	Plymouth Argyle	0-0	CARDIFF CITY			11		8	3		4	2					6	7		9				5			10		1
23-Dec	11,082	CARDIFF CITY	1-3	Bolton Wanderers	Brown				8	3		4	2					6	7		10	11			5			9		1
26-Dec	18,180	CARDIFF CITY	3-0	Aston Villa	Lea 2, Toshack		12		8	3		4	2*					6	7		9	11			5			10		1
30-Dec	17,667	Aston Villa	2-1	CARDIFF CITY	Dean							4			8	2	3	6	7		10	11			5			9		1
06-Jan	14,925	CARDIFF CITY	3-0	Portsmouth	Clarke, Bird, King			11				4		1		2	3	6	7		9	8			5			10		
20-Jan	8,748	CARDIFF CITY	2-2	Rotherham United	Bird, Phillips		3	11				4	2*	1		6			7		9	8			5	12		10		
03-Feb	18,096	Derby County	3-4	CARDIFF CITY	Clark 2, King 2		2				8	6		1		4	3		7		10	11			5	12		9		
10-Feb	12,897	CARDIFF CITY	2-0	Preston North End	Clark, Toshack						8	4		1		2	3	6	7		10	11			5			9		
24-Feb	15,580	Ipswich Town	4-2	CARDIFF CITY	Clark, Lea						8	4		1		2	3	6	7		9	11			5			10		
02-Mar	15,334	CARDIFF CITY	0-1	Bristol City							8	4		1		2	3	6	7		10	11			5			9		
09-Mar	15,582	Middlesbrough	2-3	CARDIFF CITY	Toshack, Clark, Jones			12			8	4		1		2	3	6*	7		10	11			5			9		
22-Mar	11,975	CARDIFF CITY	2-3	Hull City	Clark, King						8				4	2	3	6	7		9	11			5			10		1
30-Mar	7,904	Millwall	3-1	CARDIFF CITY	Lea						8	4	2	1		12	3	6	7		9	11			5			10		
06-Apr	14,416	CARDIFF CITY	1-3	Blackpool	King			11				4	2		8		3	6	7		10			5				9		1
12-Apr	23,043	Queen's Park Rangers	1-0	CARDIFF CITY							8	4	2*	1	12		3	6	7		9	11			5			10		
13-Apr	29,044	Birmingham City	0-0	CARDIFF CITY						2	8	10		1	4		3	6	7	12	9	11*			5					
16-Apr	20,021	CARDIFF CITY	1-0	Queen's Park Rangers	Toshack					2	8	4		1			3	6	7		9	11			5			10		
20-Apr	13,926	CARDIFF CITY	1-0	Carlisle United	Jones					2	8	4		1			3	6	7		10	11			5			9		
27-Apr	7,195	Blackburn Rovers	1-1	CARDIFF CITY	Jones (p)					2	8	4		1		6	3		7		10	11		5				9		
04-May	10,647	CARDIFF CITY	0-0	Huddersfield Town						2	8	4		1		2		6	7		10	11			5			9		
08-May	10,177	Norwich City	1-0	CARDIFF CITY						2		9		1	4		3	6	7		8	11			5			10		
11-May	8,396	CARDIFF CITY	0-0	Charlton Athletic						2	12	4		1	8		3	6	7		9	11			5			10		
					Appearances	2	5	20	21	19	14	36	20	16	10	17	32	39	42	1	42	20	1	2	40	2	1	35	11	26
					Goals		1	5	9		6	3			1				6		12	4			1	1		11		

1 Sandy Allan
2 Gary Bell
3 Ronnie Bird
4 Bobby Brown
5 Dave Carver
6 Brian Clark
7 Malcolm Clarke
8 Graham Coldrick
9 Fred Davies
10 Norman Dean
11 Steve Derrett
12 Bobby Ferguson
13 Brian Harris
14 Barrie Jones
15 Bryn Jones
16 Peter King
17 Leslie Lea
18 Bernard Lewis
19 Richie Morgan
20 Don Murray
21 Leighton Phillips
22 David Summerhayes
23 John Toshack
24 Gareth Williams
25 Bob Wilson

1968-69 5th in Division Two

Date	Att	Home	Score	Away	Scorers	1	2	3	4	5	6	7	8	9	10	11	12	13	14	15	16	17	18	19	20	21	22
10-Aug	16,373	CARDIFF CITY	0-4	Crystal Palace				11	2	8			1			3	6	7	9				5	4			10
14-Aug	11,979	CARDIFF CITY	0-1	Charlton Athletic				11	2	8			1			3	6	7	9				5			4	10
17-Aug	14,476	Norwich City	3-1	CARDIFF CITY	Bird			11	2	8	10	3	1	4			6	7	9				5				
21-Aug	7,214	Bury	3-3	CARDIFF CITY	Clark, Jones, Toshack		3	11		8	4	2	1				6	7	9				5				10
24-Aug	10,817	CARDIFF CITY	1-0	Preston North End	King		3	11		8	4	2	1				6	7	10				5				9
28-Aug	14,967	CARDIFF CITY	4-0	Birmingham City	Toshack 2, Bell, Clark		3	11*		8	4		1		2		6	7	9				5			12	10
31-Aug	21,871	Portsmouth	1-3	CARDIFF CITY	Clark, King, Toshack		3*			8	4	12	1		2		6	7	9				5			11	10
07-Sep	14,225	CARDIFF CITY	2-0	Middlesbrough	Clark, og		11			8	4	2	1		3		6	7	10				5				9
14-Sep	7,523	Huddersfield Town	3-0	CARDIFF CITY			3	11		8	4	2	1				6	7	9				5				10
21-Sep	10,809	CARDIFF CITY	2-1	Carlisle United	Clark, Jones		3*			8		12	1		2		6	7	9	11			5			4	10
28-Sep	20,632	Bristol City	0-3	CARDIFF CITY	King, Toshack, Jones		3			8			1		2		6*	7	10	11			5	12		4	9
05-Oct	17,113	CARDIFF CITY	1-1	Aston Villa	Toshack		3			8		2	1					7	9	11	6		5			4	10
08-Oct	28,238	Birmingham City	2-0	CARDIFF CITY			3	12		8	4	2	1					7		11*			5	9		6	10
12-Oct	13,893	Millwall	2-0	CARDIFF CITY			3			8		12	1		2		6*	7		11			5	9		4	10
19-Oct	12,026	CARDIFF CITY	0-2	Bolton Wanderers			3			8		2	1		6			7		11			5	10		4	9
26-Oct	17,027	Hull City	3-3	CARDIFF CITY	Toshack 2, Clark		3	11	2	8			1		6			7		9			5			4	10
02-Nov	11,672	CARDIFF CITY	2-1	Blackburn Rovers	Toshack, Bird		6	11	2	8			1		3			7		9*			5	12		4	10
09-Nov	12,085	Blackpool	1-2	CARDIFF CITY	Toshack 2		3	11	2	8			1		6			7		9			5			4	10
16-Nov	17,328	CARDIFF CITY	1-1	Derby County	Clark		3*	11	2	10			1		6			7		9			5	12		4	8
23-Nov	9,836	Oxford United	0-2	CARDIFF CITY	Clark, Toshack			11	2	8			1		6	3		7		9			5			4	10
30-Nov	14,255	CARDIFF CITY	4-1	Sheffield United	Bird 2(p), Clark, Jones		3	11	2	8			1		6			7		9			5			4	10
07-Dec	13,191	Fulham	1-5	CARDIFF CITY	Jones 2, Clark, Toshack, Lea		3	11	2	8			1		6			7		9			5			4	10
14-Dec	22,405	CARDIFF CITY	2-0	Millwall	Toshack, Clark		3	11	2	8			1		6			7		9			5			4	10
21-Dec	8,895	Bolton Wanderers	1-2	CARDIFF CITY	Bird, Jones		3	11	2	8			1		6			7		9			5			4	10
26-Dec	41,296	Aston Villa	2-0	CARDIFF CITY			3	11	2	8			1		6			7		9			5			4	10
28-Dec	24,815	CARDIFF CITY	3-0	Hull City	Clark, Bird, Toshack		3	11	2	8			1		6			7		9			5			4	10
11-Jan	12,100	Blackburn Rovers	1-0	CARDIFF CITY			3	11	2	8			1		6			7		9			5			4	10
25-Jan	26,210	CARDIFF CITY	3-0	Bristol City	Clark 2, King		3		2	8			1		6			7	11	9			5			4	10
01-Feb	34,589	Derby County	2-0	CARDIFF CITY			3		2	8			1		6			7	11	9			5			4	10
08-Feb	16,387	CARDIFF CITY	5-0	Oxford United	Clark 2, Toshack 2, Bird		3	11	2	8			1		6			7	9				5			4	10
12-Feb	24,206	CARDIFF CITY	1-0	Blackpool	Toshack		3	11	2	8*			1		6			7	10				5	12		4	9
01-Mar	19,663	Crystal Palace	3-1	CARDIFF CITY	Jones		3	12	2				1		6			7	9	8			5		11	4	10
07-Mar	21,389	CARDIFF CITY	3-1	Norwich City	Toshack, King, Bird		3	12	2	8			1		6			7	9				5		11*	4	10
11-Mar	14,508	Sheffield United	2-2	CARDIFF CITY	Clark, Jones		3*	11	2	8			1		6			7	9				5	12		4	10
15-Mar	10,752	Preston North End	0-1	CARDIFF CITY	Bird			11	2	8*		3	1		6			7	9				5	12		4	10
21-Mar	21,791	CARDIFF CITY	2-2	Portsmouth	Toshack 2		3		2	8			1		4		6	7	9				5		11		10
24-Mar	20,723	CARDIFF CITY	0-2	Fulham				12	2	8			1		3		6	7	9				5	4	11*		10
29-Mar	24,470	Middlesbrough	0-0	CARDIFF CITY				11	3	12			1		2		6	7	8				5	9*		4	10
04-Apr	21,832	Charlton Athletic	4-1	CARDIFF CITY	Murray		3*	11	2	8	4		1		6		12	7					5	9			10
07-Apr	13,232	CARDIFF CITY	2-0	Bury	Toshack, Allan	8		11	3				1		2		6	7	4	9			5				10
12-Apr	5,546	Carlisle United	1-0	CARDIFF CITY		8*		12	3				1		2			7	4	9		5	6		11		10
19-Apr	11,549	CARDIFF CITY	0-2	Huddersfield Town				11*	3	12	7		1		2			9	4	8	6		5				10
					Appearances	2	32	32	30	39	10	12	42	1	34	3	17	42	26	24	2	1	42	13	5	30	41
					Goals	1	1	9		17								9	5	1			1				22

1 Sandy Allan
2 Gary Bell
3 Ronnie Bird
4 Dave Carver
5 Brian Clark
6 Malcolm Clarke
7 Graham Coldrick
8 Fred Davies
9 Norman Dean
10 Steve Derrett
11 Bobby Ferguson
12 Brian Harris
13 Barrie Jones
14 Peter King
15 Leslie Lea
16 Terry Lewis
17 Richie Morgan
18 Don Murray
19 Leighton Phillips
20 Frank Sharp
21 Mel Sutton
22 John Toshack

1969-70 7th in Division Two

Date	Att	Home	Score	Away	Scorers	1	2	3	4	5	6	7	8	9	10	11	12	13	14	15	16	17	18	19	20
09-Aug	10,506	Carlisle United	2-3	CARDIFF CITY	Clark, Toshack, King		3		2	8		1			6	7	11	9		5			4	10	
13-Aug	27,932	CARDIFF CITY	2-2	Swindon Town	King 2		3		2	8		1			6	7	11	9		5			4	10	
16-Aug	19,745	CARDIFF CITY	0-0	Blackburn Rovers		12	3		2	8		1			6	7	11	9		5			4*	10	
19-Aug	21,849	Swindon Town	2-1	CARDIFF CITY	Clark		3	11	2	8		1			6	7	4	9		5				10	
23-Aug	23,237	Bristol City	0-2	CARDIFF CITY	Clark, Bird (p)		3	11	2	8		1			6	7	4	9		5				10	
27-Aug	21,623	CARDIFF CITY	1-0	Middlesbrough	Toshack		3		2	8		1			6	7	11	9		5			4	10	
30-Aug	21,048	CARDIFF CITY	2-1	Bolton Wanderers	Toshack, King		3		2	8		1			6	7	11	9		5	12		4*	10	
06-Sep	13,796	Charlton Athletic	0-0	CARDIFF CITY			3		2	8		1			6	7	11	9		5	4			10	
13-Sep	26,947	CARDIFF CITY	1-1	Leicester City	Toshack		3		2	8		1			6	7*	11	9		5	4		12	10	
20-Sep	17,196	Sheffield United	1-0	CARDIFF CITY				12	2	8	2	1			6	7*	11			5	9		4	10	
27-Sep	30,048	CARDIFF CITY	4-2	Queen's Park Rangers	Toshack 3, King		3		2	8	12	1				7	9		6	5		11*	4	10	
04-Oct	18,115	Blackpool	3-2	CARDIFF CITY	King 2		3		2	8		1			6	7*		9		5	12	11	4	10	
08-Oct	15,062	Blackburn Rovers	1-0	CARDIFF CITY			3		2	8		1			6		11	9		5	7		4	10	
11-Oct	25,871	CARDIFF CITY	4-0	Aston Villa	Toshack 2, Bird 2(p)		3	11	2	8		1			6		7	9		5			4	10	
18-Oct	23,596	CARDIFF CITY	0-1	Norwich City			3	11*	2	8	12	1			6		7	9		5			4	10	
25-Oct	28,287	Birmingham City	1-1	CARDIFF CITY	Clark	8	3		2	8		1			6		11	7		5			4	10	
01-Nov	20,419	CARDIFF CITY	6-0	Hull City	Clark 2, Tochack 2, Sutton, King (p)	9	3		2	8		1			6		11	7		5			4	10	
08-Nov	17,302	Portsmouth	3-0	CARDIFF CITY		9	3*		2	8		1	12		6		11	7		5			4	10	
15-Nov	11,092	Oxford United	1-1	CARDIFF CITY	Lea	11	3		2	8		1			6		7	9		5			4	10	
22-Nov	22,653	CARDIFF CITY	2-1	Preston North End	Clark, King		3		2	8		1			6		11	9		5			4	10	7
06-Dec	15,036	CARDIFF CITY	3-1	Watford	Clark 2, Bird		3	11	2	8		1			9		7			5			4	10	6
13-Dec	22,590	Leicester City	1-2	CARDIFF CITY	Clark, King		3	11	2	8		1			99		7			5			4	10	6
15-Dec	9,808	Millwall	1-2	CARDIFF CITY	King, Bird (p)		3	11	2	8		1			9		7			5			4	10	6
20-Dec	13,906	CARDIFF CITY	1-0	Charlton Athletic	Clark		3	11	2	8		1			9		7			5			4	10	6
29-Dec	18,479	CARDIFF CITY	1-0	Bristol City	Toshack		3	11	2	8		1			9		7			5			4	10	6
10-Jan	25,111	CARDIFF CITY	3-0	Sheffield United	Clark 2, Bird		3	11	2	8		1			9		7			5			4	10	6
17-Jan	22,033	Queen's Park Rangers	2-1	CARDIFF CITY	Toshack		3	12	2	8		1			6		7			5	11*		4	10	10
24-Jan	21,788	Huddersfield Town	1-0	CARDIFF CITY			3	11	2	8		1			9		7			5			4	10	6
31-Jan	24,586	CARDIFF CITY	2-2	Blackpool	Toshack 2		3	11	2	8		1			9		7*	12		5			4	10	6
07-Feb	27,024	Aston Villa	1-1	CARDIFF CITY	Clark		3	12	2	8		1			9		11	7*		5			4	10	6
14-Feb	20,120	CARDIFF CITY	1-1	Carlisle United	Woodruff		3	11	2	8		1			6		7	9		5				10	4
21-Feb	21,887	CARDIFF CITY	3-1	Birmingham City	Clark, King, Bird (p)		3	11	2	8		1			6		7	9		5				10	4
28-Feb	11,290	Norwich City	1-1	CARDIFF CITY	Clark		3	11	2	8		1			6		7	9		5				10	4
14-Mar	25,978	CARDIFF CITY	0-1	Huddersfield Town			3		2	8		1			9		7	11		5			4	10	6
18-Mar	10,434	Bolton Wanderers	0-1	CARDIFF CITY	Woodruff		3		2	10		1			6		7	8		5		11	4		9
21-Mar	17,152	Watford	2-1	CARDIFF CITY	Clark		3		2	8		1	12		6*		7	9		5		11	4		10
25-Mar	17,031	CARDIFF CITY	2-0	Portsmouth	Sutton, Woodruff		3		2	8				1	6			9		5		11	4	10	7
28-Mar	21,097	CARDIFF CITY	0-0	Oxford United			3		2	8				1	6			9		5		11	4	10	7
31-Mar	13,038	Hull City	1-1	CARDIFF CITY	Sharp		3		2	8		1			6		7	9		5		11	4	12	10*
04-Apr	13,859	Middlesbrough	2-1	CARDIFF CITY	Clark		3		2	8		1	12		6*		7	10		5		11	4	9	
15-Apr	8,423	CARDIFF CITY	0-0	Millwall			3		2	8		1					7	9		5	6	11	4	10	
20-Apr	8,012	Preston North End	1-2	CARDIFF CITY	Murray, Bird		3		2	8		1					7	9		5	6	12	4		10
					Appearances	5	41	19	42	42	3	40	3	2	39	12	39	32	1	42	9	10	36	39	21
					Goals			8		18							10	1		1		1	2	17	3

1 Sandy Allan
2 Gary Bell
3 Ronnie Bird
4 Dave Carver
5 Brian Clark
6 Graham Coldrick
7 Fred Davies
8 Steve Derrett
9 Jim Eadie
10 Brian Harris
11 Barrie Jones
12 Peter King
13 Leslie Lea
14 Terry Lewis
15 Don Murray
16 Leighton Phillips
17 Frank Sharp
18 Mel Sutton
19 John Toshack
20 Bobby Woodruff

1970-71 3rd in Division Two

Date	Att	Home	Score	Away	Scorers	1	2	3	4	5	6	7	8	9	10	11	12	13	14	15	16	17	18	19
15-Aug	27,578	Leicester City	0-1	CARDIFF CITY	Clark	3		2	7			8	6	11	5	1					4	10		9
22-Aug	25,283	CARDIFF CITY	2-2	Millwall	Toshack, King	3		2	7			8	6	11	5	1					4	10		9
26-Aug	16,896	Sheffield Wednesday	1-2	CARDIFF CITY	Clark, Sutton	3		2	7			8	6	11	5	1					4	10		9
29-Aug	24,969	Bristol City	1-0	CARDIFF CITY		3		2	7			8	6	11	5	1					4	10		9
02-Sep	21,421	CARDIFF CITY	1-1	Sheffield United	Clark	3	12	2	7*			8	6	11	5	1					4	10		9
05-Sep	21,690	CARDIFF CITY	2-0	Birmingham City	Toshack 2	3		2	8			7	6	11	5	1					4	10		9
12-Sep	11,086	Bolton Wanderers	0-2	CARDIFF CITY	Clark, Gibson	3		2	8			7	6	11	5	1					4	10		9
19-Sep	23,745	CARDIFF CITY	1-1	Norwich City	Clark	3		2	8			7	6	11	5	1					4	10		9
26-Sep	11,992	Orient	0-0	CARDIFF CITY		3		2	8			7	6	11	5	1					4	10		9
03-Oct	20,925	CARDIFF CITY	3-4	Middlesbrough	Clark, Woodruff, King	3		2	8			7	6	11	5	1					4	10		9
10-Oct	16,244	Watford	0-1	CARDIFF CITY	Clark	3		2	8		1	7	6	11	5						4	10		9
17-Oct	25,968	CARDIFF CITY	2-2	Leicester City	Gibson (p), Carver	3		2	8		1	7	6	11	5						4	10		9
24-Oct	10,955	Carlisle United	1-1	CARDIFF CITY	Toshack	3		2			1	7	6	11	5			9			4	10		8
28-Oct	18,510	CARDIFF CITY	1-0	Portsmouth	Toshack	3		2			1	7	6	11	5			9			4	10		8
31-Oct	21,837	CARDIFF CITY	5-1	Hull City	Toshack 3, Gibson, Phillips	3		2			1	7	6	11	5			9			4	8		10
07-Nov	14,268	Queen's Park Rangers	0-1	CARDIFF CITY	Phillips	3		2			1	7	6	11	5			9			4	8		10
14-Nov	17,213	CARDIFF CITY	4-1	Blackburn Rovers	Clark 2, Woodruff, King	3		2	8		1	7	6	11	5			9			4			10
21-Nov	10,788	Charlton Athletic	2-1	CARDIFF CITY	Woodruff	3	12	2	8		1	7	6	11*	5			9			4			10
28-Nov	26,666	CARDIFF CITY	0-0	Luton Town		3		2	8		1	7	6	11	5			9			4			10
05-Dec	12,286	Oxford United	1-0	CARDIFF CITY		3		2	8	6	1	7		11	5			12		10*	4			9
12-Dec	15,619	CARDIFF CITY	3-1	Sunderland	Gibson, Phillips, og	3		2	10	6	1	7		11	5			9			4			8
19-Dec	8,645	Millwall	2-1	CARDIFF CITY	Clark	3		2	10		1	7	6	11	5			9			4			8
26-Dec	24,800	CARDIFF CITY	1-1	Swindon Town	Sutton	3		2	8		1	7	6*	12	5			9			4		10	11
09-Jan	21,464	CARDIFF CITY	4-0	Sheffield Wednesday	Warboys 2, Bell, King	3		2			1	8	6	7	5			10	11		4		9	
16-Jan	24,747	Portsmouth	1-3	CARDIFF CITY	Warboys 2, Murray	3		2	12		1	8*	6	7	5			10	11		4		9	
06-Feb	14,853	CARDIFF CITY	1-0	Oxford United	Parsons	3		2	9		1	8	6	7	5		12	10	11		4*			
13-Feb	11,566	Sunderland	0-4	CARDIFF CITY	Clark, Gibson, Parsons, og	3		2	8		1	7		9	5		12	6	11				10	4
20-Feb	18,009	CARDIFF CITY	1-1	Charlton Athletic	Gibson (p)	3		2	10		1	7		9	5		8	6	11		4			
27-Feb	25,091	Hull City	1-1	CARDIFF CITY	Warboys	3		2	8*		1	7		9	5			6	11		4		10	12
06-Mar	22,371	CARDIFF CITY	4-0	Carlisle United	Warboys 4	3		2	12		1	8		7	5			6	11		4		9*	10
13-Mar	10,458	Blackburn Rovers	1-1	CARDIFF CITY	Clark	3		2	7		1			8	5			6	11		4		9	10
20-Mar	23,309	CARDIFF CITY	1-0	Queen's Park Rangers	Warboys	3	11	2			1	8		7	5			6			4		9	10
27-Mar	49,025	Birmingham City	2-0	CARDIFF CITY		3		2	12		1	8		7	5			6	11*		4		9	10
03-Apr	24,638	CARDIFF CITY	1-0	Bristol City	og	3	11	2			1	8*	12	7	5			6			4		9	10
07-Apr	21,282	CARDIFF CITY	1-0	Bolton Wanderers	Clark	3	11	2	8		1		12	7	5			6			4		10	9
10-Apr	21,393	Swindon Town	2-2	CARDIFF CITY	Warboys 2	3		2	8		1	7		11	5			6			4		10	9
13-Apr	19,559	Middlesbrough	1-1	CARDIFF CITY	King	3		2	8	12	1	7*		11	5			6			4		10	9
17-Apr	26,612	CARDIFF CITY	0-1	Watford		3		2	8		1	7		11	5			6			4		10	9
24-Apr	15,088	Norwich City	1-2	CARDIFF CITY	Warboys, Clark	3		2	8	6	1	7		11	5			9			4		10	
27-Apr	42,963	Sheffield United	5-1	CARDIFF CITY	Derrett	3		2	8	6	1	7		11	5			9*			4		10	12
01-May	15,750	CARDIFF CITY	1-0	Orient	Clark	3		2	8	6	1	7		11*	5			9			4		10	12
04-May	10,784	Luton Town	3-0	CARDIFF CITY		3		2	8	6	1	7		11	5			9			4		10	
					Appearances	42	5	42	35	7	32	40	26	42	42	10	3	30	9	1	41	16	18	36
					Goals	1			15	1		6						3			2	8	13	3

1 Gary Bell
2 Ronnie Bird
3 Dave Carver
4 Brian Clark
5 Steve Derrett
6 Jim Eadie
7 Ian Gibson
8 Brian Harris
9 Peter King
10 Don Murray
11 Frank Parsons
12 John Parsons
13 Leighton Phillips
14 Nigel Rees
15 Derek Showers
16 Mel Sutton
17 John Toshack
18 Alan Warboys
19 Bobby Woodruff

1971-72 19th in Division Two

Date	Att	Home	Score	Away	Scorers	1	2	3	4	5	6	7	8	9	10	11	12	13	14	15	16	17	18	19	20	21	22	23	24
14-Aug	23,004	CARDIFF CITY	2-2	Burnley	Clark 2	3	2	8			1	11	7							5				6		4		10	9
16-Aug	19,253	Blackpool	3-0	CARDIFF CITY		3	2	8		6	1	11*	7							5		12		4				10	9
21-Aug	7,824	Orient	4-1	CARDIFF CITY	og	3	2	10					7	6						5	1	8		11		4		9	
28-Aug	17,110	CARDIFF CITY	1-1	Hull City	Warboys	3	2	8			1	11	7	9						5				6		4		10	
31-Aug	23,525	Bristol C ity	2-0	CARDIFF CITY		3	2	8			1	11	7	9						5				6		4		10	
04-Sep	10,233	Watford	2-2	CARDIFF CITY	J Parsons, Clark	3	2*	8			1	11	7	4						5		12		6		9		10	
11-Sep	17,067	CARDIFF CITY	3-2	Sheffield Wednesday	Warboys 2, Clark	3		8			1	11*	7			2				5		12		6		4		10	9
18-Sep	18,288	Middlesbrough	1-0	CARDIFF CITY		3		8*			1		11			2		7		5				6	12	4		10	9
25-Sep	16,275	CARDIFF CITY	0-1	Swindon Town		3		8			1	12	7	11*		2				5				6		4		10	9
02-Oct	13,511	Preston North End	1-2	CARDIFF CITY	King, Clark	3		9			1	11*	8	4		2		7		5				6				12	10
09-Oct	17,931	CARDIFF CITY	1-2	Millwall	Clark	3		8					7	11	1	2				5				6		4		10	9
16-Oct	12,494	Burnley	3-0	CARDIFF CITY		3		8					11		1	2		7*		5		12		6		4		10	9
23-Oct	13,075	CARDIFF CITY	6-1	Charlton Athletic	Clark 2, J Parsons 2, Gibson (p), og	3	2	10					7		1					5		8		6	11	4			9
30-Oct	20,546	Norwich City	2-1	CARDIFF CITY	Clark	3	2	10				12	7		1					5		8		6	11*	4			9
06-Nov	16,892	CARDIFF CITY	0-0	Queen's Park Rangers		3	2	10					7		1					5		8*		6	11	4		12	9
13-Nov	10,700	Fulham	4-3	CARDIFF CITY	Clark 2, Warboys	3	2	8					11		1					5		12		6		4*	7	10	9
20-Nov	12,718	CARDIFF CITY	1-2	Sunderland	Gibson	3	2	8					11		1					5				6		4	7	10	9
27-Nov	6,845	Carlisle United	2-1	CARDIFF CITY	J Parsons	3	2	10	9				11		1				5			8		6			7		4
01-Dec	10,143	CARDIFF CITY	3-2	Portsmouth	Clark, Woodruff, Gibson (p)	3	2	8	9	6			11		1				5					4	12		7*		10
11-Dec	10,606	Luton Town	2-2	CARDIFF CITY	Phillips, Clark	3	2	8	9	6			11		1				5					4			7*	10	12
18-Dec	11,092	CARDIFF CITY	2-0	Watford	King, Warboys	3	2	8		6					1			7	5					4	11			10	9
27-Dec	40,793	Birmingham City	3-0	CARDIFF CITY		3	2	8		6			7		1				5					4	11	12		10	9*
01-Jan	12,758	CARDIFF CITY	1-0	Middlesbrough	Clark		2	8					7		1			9	6*	5				4	11	2		10	12
08-Jan	12,678	Hull City	0-0	CARDIFF CITY		3	2	8					7		1					5				6	11	4		10	9
22-Jan	11,039	Portsmouth	2-0	CARDIFF CITY		3	2	8				11	7		1			12		5				6		4*		10	9
29-Jan	11,197	CARDIFF CITY	3-4	Blackpool	Clark, Warboys, Gibson	3*	2	8				11	7		1			9		5		12		6				10	4
12-Feb	7,526	Charlton Athletic	2-2	CARDIFF CITY	Woodruff, Clark	3	2	8					7		1		4	9	5*					6	11			12	10
19-Feb	17,683	CARDIFF CITY	0-0	Norwich City		3	2	8					7		1		4	9		5				6			12	11*	10
04-Mar	13,122	CARDIFF CITY	1-0	Fulham	Clark	3	2	8					7		1		4	9		5				6	11			12	10*
11-Mar	13,702	Millwall	1-1	CARDIFF CITY	Warboys	3	2	8					7		1		9	11		5				6		4		10	
21-Mar	14,477	CARDIFF CITY	1-1	Oxford United	Clark		2	8					7		1		9	11		5			3	6		4		10	
25-Mar	12,511	Sheffield Wednesday	2-2	CARDIFF CITY	Warboys, Woodruff		2	8					7		1			11	6	5			3			4		10	9
29-Mar	13,241	CARDIFF CITY	5-2	Preston North End	Warboys 3, Clark, King		2	8					7		1			11		5			3	6		4		10	9
01-Apr	23,667	CARDIFF CITY	0-0	Birmingham City			2	8					7		1			11		5			3	6		4		10	9
04-Apr	15,641	Swindon Town	3-1	CARDIFF CITY	Clark		2	8					7*		1		12	11		5			3	6		4		10	9
08-Apr	15,224	Sunderland	1-1	CARDIFF CITY	Sutton		2	8					7		1			11		5			3	6		4		10	9
12-Apr	16,751	CARDIFF CITY	1-0	Orient	Woodruff		2	8				12	7		1			11		5			3	6		4		10	9
15-Apr	17,712	CARDIFF CITY	3-1	Carlisle United	King, Clark, Woodruff	,	2	8					7		1			11		5			3	6		4		10	9
22-Apr	9,092	Oxford United	1-0	CARDIFF CITY			2	8					7		1			11*		5			3	6	12	4		10	9
26-Apr	17,227	CARDIFF CITY	2-3	Bristol City	Warboys, Woodruff		2	8					7		1			11		5			3	6		4		10	9
29-Apr	12,570	CARDIFF CITY	1-1	Luton Town	Warboys		2	8					7		1			11		5			3	6		4		10	9
02-May	8,430	Queen's Park Rangers	3-0	CARDIFF CITY		3	2	8					12					9		5	1			6	11		7	10	4
					Appearances	30	36	42	3	5	9	12	41	7	31	6	6	23	8	36	2	11	11	41	13	31	7	38	36
					Goals			21					4					4				4		1		1		13	6

1 Gary Bell
2 Dave Carver
3 Brian Clark
4 Alan Couch
5 Steve Derrett
6 Jim Eadie
7 Alan Foggon
8 Ian Gibson
9 Roger Hoy
10 Bill Irwin
11 Ken Jones (2)
12 Billy Kellock
13 Peter King
14 Richie Morgan
15 Don Murray
16 Frank Parsons
17 John Parsons
18 Freddie Pethard
19 Leighton Phillips
20 Nigel Rees
21 Mel Sutton
22 Tony Villars
23 Alan Warboys
24 Bobby Woodruff

1972-73 20th in Division Two

Date	Att	Home	Score	Away	Scorers	1	2	3	4	5	6	7	8	9	10	11	12	13	14	15	16	17	18	19	20	21	22	23	24	25	26	27	28	29	30	31
12-Aug	16,345	CARDIFF CITY	2-1	Luton Town	Bell (p), Warboys		3	2	8			11*	7			1			6					5				4				10	12		9	
19-Aug	14,067	Portsmouth	3-1	CARDIFF CITY	Showers		3	2	8			4*	7			1			6					5				9				11			10	12
26-Aug	12,383	CARDIFF CITY	1-2	Blackpool	Bell (p)		3		8								4		6					5	1		2	9				11	12		10*	7
30-Aug	9,298	CARDIFF CITY	1-0	Millwall	Clark		3		8				7				4							5	1		2	6					11		10	9
02-Sep	8,300	Oxford United	2-1	CARDIFF CITY	Rees		3		8	12			7				4							5	1		2	6			11		10*			9
09-Sep	16,707	CARDIFF CITY	0-2	Aston Villa			3		8				7*				4						5		1		2	6			12	11			10	9
16-Sep	5,911	Carlisle United	4-0	CARDIFF CITY			3	2	8	12							4							5	1			6			10	11	7*			9
19-Sep	6,414	Nottingham Forest	2-1	CARDIFF CITY	Gibson		3	2	8	9			7			1	4							5				6			12	10*				11
23-Sep	14,102	CARDIFF CITY	1-3	Bristol City	Bell (p)		3	2	8				7			1	4							5				10	6	11						9
27-Sep	8,330	CARDIFF CITY	1-1	Brighton	Foggon		3	2	8			11	7			1								5				9	6	10						4
30-Sep	11,182	Queen's Park Rangers	3-0	CARDIFF CITY			3	2*	8			11	7			1	12							5				6	4	10						9
07-Oct	6,284	Orient	0-0	CARDIFF CITY			3				2	7				1	4							5				10	6	11		8				9
14-Oct	10,407	CARDIFF CITY	2-0	Middlesbrough	Vincent, Bell (p)		3				2					1	4							5		7		10	6	11		8		9		
21-Oct	13,442	Burnley	3-0	CARDIFF CITY			3				2					1	4							5				7	6	11*	12	10		8		9
28-Oct	12,087	CARDIFF CITY	3-0	Preston North End	Woodruff 2, McCulloch		3				2					1	4			9*				5				7	6	11		10		8		12
04-Nov	16,387	Brighton	2-2	CARDIFF CITY	Murray, Kellock		3				2					1	4		12			6		5				7				10	11	8		9
11-Nov	12,765	CARDIFF CITY	2-1	Nottingham Forest	McCulloch, Woodruff		3				2					1	4			10		6		5				7		11				8		9
18-Nov	5,886	Huddersfield Town	2-1	CARDIFF CITY	Reece		3				2					1	4			10		6		5				7		11				8		9
25-Nov	9,668	CARDIFF CITY	3-1	Fulham	McCulloch 2, Woodruff		3				2					1	4			10	12	6	5					7		11*				8		9
09-Dec	9,890	CARDIFF CITY	4-1	Sheffield Wednesday	Phillips 2, Woodruff 2		3				2					1	4			10		6	5					7					11	8		9
16-Dec	5,875	Hull City	1-1	CARDIFF CITY	Kellock		3*			12	2					1	7			8		6	5					4		11				10		9
26-Dec	20,490	Bristol City	1-0	CARDIFF CITY			3				2					1	7			8		6	5					4		11*		12		10		9
29-Dec	12,364	CARDIFF CITY	0-2	Portsmouth			3			12	2				6	1	7			8			5					4		11*				10		9
19-Jan	6,991	CARDIFF CITY	2-0	Oxford United	McCulloch 2		3				2			9		1	7			8				5				4	6	11				10		
27-Jan	28,856	Aston Villa	2-0	CARDIFF CITY			3				2			9		1	7			10				5				4	6	11				8*		12
10-Feb	7,800	CARDIFF CITY	1-0	Carlisle United	McCulloch		3				2					1	7		9	8		6		5				4				10		11		
17-Feb	10,422	Luton Town	1-1	CARDIFF CITY	Woodruff						2					1	7			8		6		5			3	4				10		11		9
27-Feb	10,015	Swindon Town	3-0	CARDIFF CITY		11	3				2					1		4		8				5				10	6			12		7		9
03-Mar	8,439	CARDIFF CITY	3-1	Orient	McCulloch 2, Bell (p)	11	3				2					1	9*			8				5				4	6			10		7		12
07-Mar	5,303	Blackpool	1-0	CARDIFF CITY		11	3				2					1				8	12			5				4	6			9		10		7*
10-Mar	7,686	Middlesbrough	2-0	CARDIFF CITY		11	3				2					1				9				5			7	6	4			10		8		
17-Mar	11,343	CARDIFF CITY	0-1	Burnley		11	3				2					1	8			9				5				4	6*	7		12		10		
24-Mar	6,889	Preston North End	0-0	CARDIFF CITY		11	3			10	2					1	7			8				5				4	6							9
31-Mar	6,262	Fulham	1-1	CARDIFF CITY	McCulloch	11	3			8	2					1	6			10				5				4	7							9
07-Apr	9,059	CARDIFF CITY	1-1	Swindon Town	McCulloch	11	3			4	2					1	7			8				5				6						10		9
14-Apr	10,912	Sheffield Wednesday	1-0	CARDIFF CITY		11	3				2			12		1			4	9		6		5				10		7				8*		
18-Apr	12,033	CARDIFF CITY	0-0	Queen's Park Rangers		11	3				2			12		1				8		6		5				4		7				10*		9
21-Apr	12,353	CARDIFF CITY	4-1	Huddersfield Town	McCulloch 2, Reece 2	11	3				2			10		1				8		6		5				4		7						9
23-Apr	27,551	Sunderland	2-1	CARDIFF CITY	Phillips	11	3				2			10		1				8		6		5				4		7						9
28-Apr	7,811	Millwall	1-1	CARDIFF CITY	McCulloch	11	3				2			10*		1				8		6		5				4		7			12			9
07-May	21,982	CARDIFF CITY	1-1	Sunderland	Woodruff	11	3				2			10		1				8*		6		5				4		7			12			9
09-May	6,235	CARDIFF CITY	0-2	Hull City		11	3				2			10		1						6		5				4		7				8		9
					Appearances	15	41	7	11	8	31	5	9	9	1	37	29	1	6	26	2	16	6	36	5	1	6	42	16	23	5	19	9	24	5	35
					Goals		5		1			1	1				2			14				1				3		3	1	1		1	1	8

1 Willie Anderson
2 Gary Bell
3 Dave Carver
4 Brian Clark
5 Alan Couch
6 Phil Dwyer
7 Alan Foggon
8 Ian Gibson
9 Roger Hoy
10 John Impey
11 Bill Irwin
12 Billy Kellock
13 Peter King
14 Albert Larmour
15 Andy McCulloch
16 Jimmy McInch
17 Peter Morgan
18 Richie Morgan
19 Don Murray
20 Frank Parsons
21 John Parsons
22 Freddie Pethard
23 Leighton Phillips
24 Dave Powell
25 Gil Reece
26 Nigel Rees
27 Derek Showers
28 Tony Villars
29 Johnny Vincent
30 Alan Warboys
31 Bobby Woodruff

1973-74 17th in Division Two

Date	Att	Home	Score	Away	Scorers	1	2	3	4	5	6	7	8	9	10	11	12	13	14	15	16	17	18	19	20	21	22	23	24	25	26	27
25-Aug	6,830	Carlisle United	1-1	CARDIFF CITY	Bell (p)	11	3			2					1						5		4		8		10	6	7			9
01-Sep	10,082	CARDIFF CITY	1-1	Portsmouth	McCulloch	11	3			2					1	12		8			5		6					4	7	10*		9
08-Sep	29,595	Sunderland	1-1	CARDIFF CITY	Vincent	11	3			2					1			8			5		6					4	7	10		9
12-Sep	8,529	CARDIFF CITY	5-0	Oxford United	McCulloch 3, Villars, og	11	3			2					1	12		8*			5		6					4	7	10		9
15-Sep	11,772	CARDIFF CITY	0-0	Fulham			3			2					1	11		8			5		6					4	7	10		9
22-Sep	18,290	Crystal Palace	3-3	CARDIFF CITY	Woodruff, Vincent, og		3			2					1			8			5		6				11	4	7	10		9
29-Sep	10,522	CARDIFF CITY	1-3	Hull City	Bell (p)		3			2					1			8			5		6				11	4	7	10		9
06-Oct	24,483	Aston Villa	5-0	CARDIFF CITY			3			2					1	11	4	10			5		6		7		9					8
13-Oct	8,050	CARDIFF CITY	1-0	Blackpool	Reece		3			2					1	12		8		5			6		7		9	4		11		10
20-Oct	7,745	CARDIFF CITY	0-1	Sheffield Wednesday			3			2					1	8		10			5		6		11		9		7			4
24 Oct	6,365	Oxford United	4-2	CARDIFF CITY	Anderson, Smith	11	3			2					1			8			5		6		7		12	4		10*		9
27-Oct	12,050	Preston North End	2-2	CARDIFF CITY	McCulloch, Reece	11	3			2					1			8			5		6		7			4		10		9
03-Nov	10,432	CARDIFF CITY	0-1	West Brom		11	3			2		1						8			5		6		7			4	12	10*		9
10-Nov	8,221	Millwall	2-0	CARDIFF CITY		11	3			2		1						10			5		6		7			4	8			9
14-Nov	5,999	CARDIFF CITY	0-0	Luton Town			3			2				4	1				8		5		6		11*		9		7	12		10
17-Nov	18,034	Middlesbrough	3-0	CARDIFF CITY			3			2				4*	1				8		5		6	7			10		11	12		9
24-Nov	9,584	CARDIFF CITY	1-0	Bolton Wanderers	Reece		3	4		2	7				1			8			5			6	10				11			9
01-Dec	9,564	Orient	1-2	CARDIFF CITY	Woodruff, McCulloch		3*	8		2	7				1			10			5			4	11			12	9			6
08-Dec	10,312	CARDIFF CITY	1-1	Nottingham Forest	Reece		3	8		2	7				1			10			5		12	4	9				11*			6
12-Dec	7,139	Luton Town	1-0	CARDIFF CITY			3	10*		2	7				1			8			5		11	4	9			12				6
15-Dec	9,368	CARDIFF CITY	0-1	Bristol City		12	3			2	7				1			8			5		10	6	11			4*				9
22-Dec	6,826	Hull City	1-1	CARDIFF CITY	Farrington	11	3	4*		2	7			12	1			8			5		10	6								9
26-Dec	10,056	CARDIFF CITY	2-1	Swindon Town	Farrington, Murray	11	3	10		2	7				1			8			5		9	4					6			
29-Dec	14,979	CARDIFF CITY	4-1	Sunderland	Farrington 3, Anderson	11	3	10		2	7				1			8			5		9	4					6			
01-Jan	20,062	Portsmouth	1-0	CARDIFF CITY		11	3	10		2	7			12	1			8			5		9	4*					6			
12-Jan	7,413	Fulham	0-1	CARDIFF CITY	McCulloch	11	3	10		2	7			4	1			8			5				9				6			
19-Jan	10,674	CARDIFF CITY	2-2	Carlisle United	McCulloch, Phillips	11	3	10		2	7			4	1			8			5		9*		12				6			
26-Jan	8,432	CARDIFF CITY	1-0	Notts County	Phillips	11*	3	10		2	7			4	1			8			5		9						6		12	
02-Feb	24,487	Bristol City	3-2	CARDIFF CITY	Phillips, McCulloch	11	3	10		2	7			4	1			8			5		9						6			
16-Feb	7,410	Blackpool	2-1	CARDIFF CITY	Farrington	11		10		2	7			4	1			8			5	3	6			12					9*	
23-Feb	12,184	CARDIFF CITY	0-1	Aston Villa		11		10		2	7			12	1			8			5	3		4	9				6			
02-Mar	5,319	Swindon Town	1-1	CARDIFF CITY	Powell	12				2	7			4	1			9			5	3	8	6	11						10	
09-Mar	7,099	CARDIFF CITY	2-0	Preston North End	Dwyer, Whitham	11				2	7				1			8			5	3	9	6					4		10	
16-Mar	13,723	Sheffield Wednesday	5-0	CARDIFF CITY		11				2	7				1			8			5	3	10	6			9*	4			12	
23-Mar	7,572	CARDIFF CITY	1-3	Millwall	McCulloch			11		2	7				1		4	8			5	3	9						6		10	
30-Mar	11,528	West Brom	2-2	CARDIFF CITY	Vincent 2(p)	11		8	6	2			1								5	3	4		9				7	10		
06-Apr	15,148	Bolton Wanderers	1-1	CARDIFF CITY	Reece	11		8	6	2			1							4		3	5		9				7	10		
13-Apr	12,861	CARDIFF CITY	3-2	Middlesbrough	Reece, Carlin, Vincent	11		8	4	2			1							5		3	6		9				7	10		
15-Apr	6,975	Notts County	1-1	CARDIFF CITY	Anderson, Smith	11		10	4	2			1							5		3	9		7				6	8		
20-Apr	11,138	Nottingham Forest	2-1	CARDIFF CITY	Vincent	11		8	4	2			1							6		3	5		9				7	10		
27-Apr	11,613	CARDIFF CITY	1-1	Orient	Reece	11		10	4	2			1							5		3	9		7				6	8		
30-Apr	27,139	CARDIFF CITY	1-1	Crystal Palace	Villars	11		10*	4	2			1							5		3	9		7		12		6	8		
					Appearances	29	29	22	7	42	19	2	7	11	33	6	2	32	2	7	35	13	38	14	25	1	11	16	32	19	6	22
					Goals	3	2	1		1	6							10			1		3	1	7			1	2	6	1	2

1 Willie Anderson
2 Gary Bell
3 Willie Carlin
4 Clive Charles
5 Phil Dwyer
6 John Farrington
7 Peter Grotier
8 Ron Healey
9 John Impey
10 Bill Irwin
11 Peter King
12 Albert Larmour
13 Andy McCulloch
14 Jimmy McInch
15 Richie Morgan
16 Don Murray
17 Freddie Pethard
18 Leighton Phillips
19 Dave Powell
20 Gil Reece
21 Peter Sayer
22 Derek Showers
23 George Smith
24 Tony Villars
25 Johnny Vincent
26 Jack Whitham
27 Bobby Woodruff

1974-75 21st in Division Two (Relegated)

Date	Att	Home	Score	Away	Scorers	1	2	3	4	5	6	7	8	9	10	11	12	13	14	15	16	17	18	19	20	21	22	23	24	25	26
17-Aug	10,006	CARDIFF CITY	1-1	Oxford United	Charles	11			3					1					8		5	2	4		9		10	6	7		
24-Aug	8,110	Fulham	4-0	CARDIFF CITY		11			3	2				1	6				8		5*		9		12			4	7	10	
27-Aug	6,321	York City	1-0	CARDIFF CITY		11			8*	2				1	12				10		5	3	6		9			4		7	
31-Aug	22,344	CARDIFF CITY	0-1	Manchester United		11			8*	2				1					7		5	3	6		9	12		4			10
07-Sep	9,983	Sheffield Wednesday	1-2	CARDIFF CITY	Anderson, Reece	11			8					1			2		7		5	3	6		10		9		4		
14-Sep	8,858	CARDIFF CITY	0-1	Bristol City		11	12		10					1			3		8		5	2	6		7*		9		4		
21-Sep	9,519	Portsmouth	2-2	CARDIFF CITY	Showers, Vincent				8		7			1	2				11*		5	3		6		12	9		4	10	
24-Sep	5,579	Blackpool	4-0	CARDIFF CITY					11*		7			1	2				10		5	3		6		12	9		4	8	
28-Sep	5,648	CARDIFF CITY	1-2	Hull City	Reece	11			12	2				1							5	3		6	10	8*	9	7	4		
05-Oct	10,312	Bristol Rovers	1-0	CARDIFF CITY		11				2	7					1				5		3		6			9	4	8	10	
12-Oct	6,737	CARDIFF CITY	0-2	West Brom		11				2	7					1				5		3		6	12		9	4	8*	10	
16-Oct	5,887	CARDIFF CITY	3-2	York City	Vincent 2(p), Reece	11		4		2		10				1				5		3		6*	7		9	8		12	
19-Oct	9,762	Bolton Wanderers	2-1	CARDIFF CITY	Buchanan	11		4		2		10				1				5		3			7		9	6		8	
26-Oct	6,727	CARDIFF CITY	3-1	Oldham Athletic	Vincent, Buchanan, Finnieston	11		4		2		10				1	12			5		3			7		9*	6		8	
02-Nov	9,856	CARDIFF CITY	2-0	Sunderland	Finnieston, Anderson (p)	11		4		2		10			12	1	6			5		3			7		9	8*			
09-Nov	6,772	Orient	1-1	CARDIFF CITY	Dwyer	11		4		2		10				1	6			5		3			7		9	8			
16-Nov	9,279	CARDIFF CITY	2-1	Nottingham Forest	Dwyer, Showers	11		4		2		10*			12	1	6			5		3			7		9	8			
29-Nov	10,640	CARDIFF CITY	2-2	Southampton	Whitham, Showers	11		4		2						1	6			5		3			7		9	8			10
07-Dec	17,337	Norwich City	1-1	CARDIFF CITY	Reece	11		4		2		10				1	6			5		3			7		9	8			
11-Dec	8,429	CARDIFF CITY	0-0	Fulham		11		4		2		10*				1	6			5		3			7		9	8		12	
14-Dec	8,218	Oxford United	1-0	CARDIFF CITY		11		4		2		10			12	1	6			5		3			7*		9	8			
21-Dec	6,646	CARDIFF CITY	0-0	Notts County		11		4		2						1	6	12		5		3					9	8		7*	10
26-Dec	12,484	Bristol City	0-0	CARDIFF CITY		11		4		2						1	6			5		3			7		9	8			10
28-Dec	11,060	CARDIFF CITY	3-1	Aston Villa	Showers, Buchanan, Whitham	11		4		2						1	6			5		3					9	8	7		10
11-Jan	10,951	CARDIFF CITY	2-1	Norwich City	Reece 2	11		4		2						1	6			5		3			10		9	8	7		
25-Jan	8,129	Millwall	5-1	CARDIFF CITY	Reece	11		4		2						1	6			5		3			9		10	8	7		
01-Feb	7,996	CARDIFF CITY	0-0	Orient		11		4		2						1	6			5		3			10		9	8	7		
08-Feb	29,315	Sunderland	3-1	CARDIFF CITY	Anderson	11		4		2						1	6			5		3			9*		10	7	12	8	
14-Feb	6,602	CARDIFF CITY	0-1	Millwall		11		4		2						1	6			5		3				12		8*	7	10	9
22-Feb	12,806	Nottingham Forest	0-0	CARDIFF CITY		11		4		2			8			1	6			5		3					9	7		10	
01-Mar	43,601	Manchester United	4-0	CARDIFF CITY		11		4		2			8			1	6			5		3			7		9			10	
08-Mar	7,830	CARDIFF CITY	1-1	Blackpool	Reece	11	2	4		10			8*			1	6			5		3			7		9			12	
15-Mar	5,248	Hull City	1-1	CARDIFF CITY	Showers	11	2	4	10	8						1	6			5*		3			9		12	7			
22-Mar	6,621	CARDIFF CITY	0-0	Sheffield Wednesday		11	2	4	10	5						1	6					3			9		8	7*		12	
29-Mar	8,105	Notts County	0-2	CARDIFF CITY	Dwyer, Charles	7	2	4	8	10						1	6			5		3				11	9				
02-Apr	9,624	CARDIFF CITY	1-0	Portsmouth	Sayer	7	2	4	8	10						1	6			5		3				11	9				
05-Apr	10,243	Oldham Athletic	4-0	CARDIFF CITY		7*	2	4	10	8						1	6			5		3				11	9			12	
09-Apr	32,748	Aston Villa	2-0	CARDIFF CITY			2	4	8	10					12	1	6			5*		3				11				7	9
12-Apr	13,896	CARDIFF CITY	2-2	Bristol Rovers	Dwyer, McClelland		2	7		4					6*	1	5	12	10			3			9	11				8	
19-Apr	10,071	West Brom	2-0	CARDIFF CITY			2		8*	4						1	6	10		5		3			7	11	9			12	
22-Apr	14,273	Southampton	2-0	CARDIFF CITY		11	2			4						1	6	12		5		3			9	7*		8		10	
26-Apr	6,376	CARDIFF CITY	1-2	Bolton Wanderers	Reece	11	2	4*		7			12			1	6			5		3			9					8	10
					Appearances	37	12	29	16	37	4	9	4	9	9	33	31	4	9	31	9	41	6	6	31	12	34	29	15	23	8
					Goals	3		3	2	4		2						1							9	1	5			4	2

1 Willie Anderson
2 Brian Attley
3 John Buchanan
4 Clive Charles
5 Phil Dwyer
6 John Farrington
7 Steve Finnieston
8 David Giles
9 Ron Healey
10 John Impey
11 Bill Irwin
12 Albert Larmour
13 John McClelland
14 Jimmy McInch
15 Richie Morgan
16 Don Murray
17 Freddie Pethard
18 Leighton Phillips
19 Dave Powell
20 Gil Reece
21 Peter Sayer
22 Derek Showers
23 George Smith
24 Tony Villars
25 Johnny Vincent
26 Jack Whitham

1975-76 2nd in Division Three (Promoted)

Date	Att	Home	Score	Away	Scorers	1	2	3	4	5	6	7	8	9	10	11	12	13	14	15	16	17	18	19	20	21	22
16-Aug	6,494	Grimsby Town	2-0	CARDIFF CITY				2	4		3	8	11	6				1		5			10	9			7
23-Aug	6,833	CARDIFF CITY	1-1	Bury	Villars			4			3	10	11*	2	5	12		1		6	7			9			8
30-Aug	11,406	Brighton	0-1	CARDIFF CITY	Villars			2			3	10		4	5	11		1		6	8					9	7
06-Sep	10,454	CARDIFF CITY	0-1	Crystal Palace				2			3	8		4	5*	11		1		6	10			12		9	7
13-Sep	6,684	Mansfield Town	1-4	CARDIFF CITY	Reece 2(p), Giles, Dwyer			2			3	10		4		11	8	1		6	7	5		9			
20-Sep	8,007	CARDIFF CITY	0-0	Halifax Town				2			3	10		4	5	11	8	1		6	7			9			
22-Sep	5,143	Port Vale	2-1	CARDIFF CITY	Attley			2			3	8		4	5	11		1		6	10			9			7
27-Sep	8,103	Preston North End	3-1	CARDIFF CITY	Evans			2*			3	10		4	5	11	12	1		6	8			9			7
04-Oct	7,730	CARDIFF CITY	3-0	Wrexham	Dwyer 2, Evans		11	2	8		3	9		4	5	10		1		6	7						
11-Oct	4,272	Rotherham United	1-0	CARDIFF CITY			11	2	8		3	9		4	5	10		1		6	7						
18-Oct	7,911	CARDIFF CITY	2-0	Sheffield Wednesday	Evans, og		11	2	8		3	12		4	5	10		1		6	7			9*			
22-Oct	3,687	Aldershot	2-1	CARDIFF CITY	Anderson		11	2	7*		3	8		4	5	9		1		6	10		12				
25-Oct	5,599	Chester	1-1	CARDIFF CITY	Evans		12	2	7*		3	8		4	5	11		1		6	10			9			
31-Oct	7,456	CARDIFF CITY	4-3	Chesterfield	Alston 2, Evans, Anderson	10	11	2			3			4	5	9		1		6	8						7
04-Nov	9,041	CARDIFF CITY	0-0	Walsall		10	11	12			3			4	5	9			1	6	8		2				7*
08-Nov	5,762	Gillingham	2-2	CARDIFF CITY	Anderson, Evans	9	11				3			4*	5	10	8		1	6	7		2	12			
15-Nov	7,045	CARDIFF CITY	2-0	Colchester United	Evans, Alston	9	11		12		3			2	5	10	8		1	6	4			7			
29-Nov	8,083	CARDIFF CITY	3-0	Shrewsbury Town	Evans, Alston, Anderson	9	11		4		3			2	5	10			1	6	8			7			
06-Dec	6,092	Millwall	1-3	CARDIFF CITY	Reece 2, Evans	9	11		4		3			2	5	10			1	6	8			7			
22-Dec	9,315	CARDIFF CITY	3-1	Southend United	Evans 2, Alston	10	11		7*		3			2	5	9	12		1	6	8			4			
26-Dec	10,202	Swindon Town	4-0	CARDIFF CITY		10	11				3			2	5	9	7		1	6	8			4			
27-Dec	16,073	CARDIFF CITY	5-2	Peterborough United	Dwyer 2, Evans 2, Anderson	10	11		7		3			2	5	9			1	6	8			4			
10-Jan	17,701	CARDIFF CITY	0-1	Brighton		9	11		8		3			2	5	10			1	6	7			4			
17-Jan	2,399	Halifax Town	1-1	CARDIFF CITY	England	10	11		4		3			2	5	9			1	6	8						7
20-Jan	9,737	CARDIFF CITY	1-0	Mansfield Town	Evans	10	11		7		3			2	5	9			1	6	8			4			
31-Jan	8,913	CARDIFF CITY	1-0	Aldershot	Alston	10	11		7		3			2	5	9			1	6	8			4			
04-Feb	12,962	Hereford United	4-1	CARDIFF CITY	Buchanan	10	11		7		3				5	9			1	6	8		2				4
07-Feb	7,109	Walsall	2-3	CARDIFF CITY	Alston 2, Dwyer	10	11		8		3			2		9		1		6	7	5	4				
14-Feb	10,912	CARDIFF CITY	4-1	Gillingham	Livermore, Buchanan, Evans, Alston	10			8		3			2		9		1		6	7	5	4		11		
21-Feb	3,248	Colchester United	3-2	CARDIFF CITY	Dwyer, Anderson (p)	10	11				3*			2		9	8	1		6	7	5	4		12		
25-Feb	9,109	CARDIFF CITY	1-1	Port Vale	Livermore	10	11		7*		3			2		9	12	1		6	8	5	4				
28-Feb	10,000	CARDIFF CITY	2-0	Chester	Alston, Buchanan	10	11*		4		3			2	5	9		1			8	6	12		7		
06-Mar	4,112	Chesterfield	1-1	CARDIFF CITY	Alston	10			4	7	3	11		2	5	9		1			8	6					
08-Mar	5,674	Wrexham	1-1	CARDIFF CITY	Evans	10			7	4	3	11		2	5	9		1		6	8						
13-Mar	11,698	CARDIFF CITY	1-1	Rotherham United	Alston	10			4	7	3	11		2	5	9		1			8	6					
17-Mar	9,013	Sheffield Wednesday	1-3	CARDIFF CITY	Evans, Charles, Clark	10			7	4	3	11		2	5	9		1			8	6					
20-Mar	7,573	Shrewsbury Town	3-1	CARDIFF CITY	Evans	10			7	4	3	11		2	5	9		1			8	6*	12				
27-Mar	12,185	CARDIFF CITY	0-0	Millwall		10				6	3	11		4	5	9	7*	1			8		2		12		
29-Mar	4,849	Southend United	0-2	CARDIFF CITY	Dwyer, Evans	10			7	4	3	11		6	5	9		1			8		2				
03-Apr	9,622	CARDIFF CITY	2-1	Grimsby Town	Evans, Buchanan	10	11		7	4				2	5	9		1		6	8		3				
07-Apr	12,408	CARDIFF CITY	1-0	Preston North End	Evans	10	11		7*	4				2	5	9		1		6	8		3		12		
10-Apr	25,863	Crystal Palace	0-1	CARDIFF CITY	Alston	10	11			4				2	5	9		1		6	8		3		7		
14-Apr	35,501	CARDIFF CITY	2-0	Hereford United	Livermore, Campbell	10	11			4				2	5	9		1		6	8		3	12	7*		
17-Apr	23,412	CARDIFF CITY	0-0	Swindon Town		10				4		12		2	5	9		1		6	7		3	11	8*		
19-Apr	6,846	Peterborough United	0-0	CARDIFF CITY		10	11			4				2	5	9	7	1		6	8		3				
04-May	7,133	Bury	0-1	CARDIFF CITY	Alston	10	11			4				2	5	9		1		6	8		3		7		
					Appearances	33	29	15	28	14	39	21	2	45	40	45	11	33	13	39	45	10	20	21	9	2	10
					Goals	14	6	1	4	1	1	1		8	1	21	1				3			4			2

1 Adrian Alston
2 Willie Anderson
3 Brian Attley
4 John Buchanan
5 Alan Campbell
6 Clive Charles
7 Brian Clark
8 Joe Durrell
9 Phil Dwyer
10 Mike England
11 Tony Evans
12 David Giles
13 Ron Healey
14 Bill Irwin
15 Albert Larmour
16 Doug Livermore
17 Richie Morgan
18 Freddie Pethard
19 Gil Reece
20 Peter Sayer
21 Derek Showers
22 Tony Villars

1976-77 18th in Division Two

Date	Att	Home	Score	Away	Scorers	1	2	3	4	5	6	7	8	9	10	11	12	13	14	15	16	17	18	19	20	21
21-Aug	9,762	Charlton Athletic	0-2	CARDIFF CITY	Showers 2	10	11			4	3							1	6	8		2	5	7	9	
25-Aug	12,665	CARDIFF CITY	1-2	Bristol Rovers	Charles (p)	10*	11		12	4	3							1	6	7		2	5	8	9	
28-Aug	11,845	CARDIFF CITY	2-1	Blackburn Rovers	Showers, Alston	12	11			4	3*		10					1	6	8		2	5	7	9	
04-Sep	8,511	Oldham Athletic	3-2	CARDIFF CITY	Evans, Livermore		11	3		4			10					1	6	7		2	5	8	9	
11-Sep	11,960	CARDIFF CITY	2-3	Notts County	Showers, Buchanan		11		12	4	3		10					1	6	7	5	2		8*	9	
18-Sep	5,743	Orient	3-0	CARDIFF CITY		9	11		8*	4	3		10					1	6	7	5	2		12		
24-Sep	10,325	CARDIFF CITY	0-0	Millwall		10			4		3	2	9					1	6	8	5*	12		7	11	
02-Oct	28,409	Chelsea	2-1	CARDIFF CITY	Charles (p)	10	11	2	4		3	5	9					1	6	8				7		
09-Oct	10,982	CARDIFF CITY	3-2	Bolton Wanderers	Alston (p), Buchanan, Evans	9	11		4		3	2	10					1	6	8				7		5
16-Oct	14,198	Plymouth Argyle	2-2	CARDIFF CITY	Evans, Dwyer	9	11		4		3*	2	10					1	6	8		12		7		5
23-Oct	12,148	CARDIFF CITY	2-2	Blackpool	Evans 2	9	11	12	4			2	10					1	6	7		3		8		5
30-Oct	12,031	CARDIFF CITY	0-2	Sheffield United		10	11		4		12	2	9					1	6	8		3*		7		5
06-Nov	12,366	Fulham	1-2	CARDIFF CITY	Buchanan, Evans	12	11		4			2	9				1		6	8		3		7	10*	5
10-Nov	15,160	CARDIFF CITY	1-0	Southampton	Dwyer		11		4			2	9				1		6	8		3		7	10	5
20-Nov	8,845	Luton Town	2-1	CARDIFF CITY	Evans	12	11		4			2	9				1		6	8		3*		7	10	5
27-Nov	12,741	CARDIFF CITY	0-3	Nottingham Forest		12	11*		4			2	9				1		6	8		3		7	10	5
04-Dec	8,967	Burnley	0-0	CARDIFF CITY		10*		2	4	7		5	9			11	1		6	8		3		12		
11-Dec	8,270	CARDIFF CITY	1-1	Hull City	Buchanan	10		2	4	7		5	9			11	1		6	8		3				
18-Dec	5,934	Carlisle United	4-3	CARDIFF CITY	Sayer, Buchanan, Evans			2	4	7		5	9			11	1		6	8		3*		12	10	
27-Dec	14,448	CARDIFF CITY	3-1	Hereford United	Evans 2, Giles			2	4		3	5	9		12	7	1		6	8				11	10	
01-Jan	20,243	CARDIFF CITY	3-0	Fulham	Friday 2, Buchanan				4		3	2	9	10		11	1		6	7				8		5
15-Jan	9,295	Bristol Rovers	1-1	CARDIFF CITY	Evans		12	3				2	9	10	4	7*	1		6	8				11		5
22-Jan	11,129	CARDIFF CITY	1-1	Charlton Athletic	Went			3				2	9	10	11	7	1		6	8				4		5
05-Feb	9,516	Blackburn Rovers	2-1	CARDIFF CITY	Sayer			3	4			2	9		10	11	1		6	7				8		5
12-Feb	12,689	CARDIFF CITY	3-1	Oldham Athletic	Friday, Evans, Sayer			3	4			2	10	9		11	1		6	7				8		5
19-Feb	9,401	Notts County	1-0	CARDIFF CITY				3	4			2	9	10		11	1		6	7				8		5
02-Mar	9,336	CARDIFF CITY	0-1	Orient				3*	12			2	9	10	11	7	1		6	8				4		5
05-Mar	9,479	Millwall	0-2	CARDIFF CITY	Evans 2				12		3	2	9	10	11	7*	1		6	8				4		5
08-Mar	12,907	Sheffield United	3-0	CARDIFF CITY					12		3	2	9	10*	11	7	1		6	8				4		5
12-Mar	20,168	CARDIFF CITY	1-3	Chelsea	Dwyer						3	2	9	10	11	7	1		6	8				4		5
26-Mar	9,567	CARDIFF CITY	0-1	Plymouth Argyle				3	11	4		2	9	10		7	1		6	8						5
02-Apr	7,356	Blackpool	1-0	CARDIFF CITY				3	8*	4		2	9	10		12	1			7		6		11		5
06-Apr	7,670	Hereford United	2-2	CARDIFF CITY	Sayer 2(p)			3	7	4		2		10		12	1			8		6		11	9*	5
09-Apr	15,422	CARDIFF CITY	2-2	Wolves	Sayer, Went			3	8	4		2	9	12		11	1			7*		6		10		5
11-Apr	22,674	Southampton	3-2	CARDIFF CITY	Friday, Evans			3	7	4		2	9	10		8	1					6		11		5
16-Apr	10,438	CARDIFF CITY	4-2	Luton Town	Friday 2, Sayer, Dwyer			2		7		4		10*	8	11	1		6	12		3		9		5
23-Apr	20,646	Nottingham Forest	0-1	CARDIFF CITY	Sayer			2		4		8			11	7	1			12		3	6	10	9*	5
26-Apr	21,324	Wolves	4-1	CARDIFF CITY	Sayer			2		4		8			11	7	1					3	6	9	10	5
30-Apr	11,247	CARDIFF CITY	0-1	Burnley				2		7		4		10	8	11*		1		12		3	6	9		5
07-May	3,511	Hull City	1-2	CARDIFF CITY	Buchanan 2(p)				8*	4		2	9	10		12	1		6	11		3		7		5
10-May	23,237	Bolton Wanderers	2-1	CARDIFF CITY	Buchanan (p)				11	4		3	9	10			1		6	7		2		8		5
14-May	15,775	CARDIFF CITY	1-1	Carlisle United	Campbell				8	4		2		10		11	1		6	7		3		9	12	5
					Appearances	15	16	22	32	21	15	36	34	19	12	25	29	13	35	40	3	28	7	40	16	30
					Goals	2			9	1	2	4	15	6	1					1				9	4	2

1 Adrian Alston
2 Willie Anderson
3 Brian Attley
4 John Buchanan
5 Alan Campbell
6 Clive Charles
7 Phil Dwyer
8 Tony Evans
9 Robin Friday
10 David Giles
11 Steve Grapes
12 Ron Healey
13 Bill Irwin
14 Albert Larmour
15 Doug Livermore
16 Richie Morgan
17 Freddie Pethard
18 Keith Pontin
19 Peter Sayer
20 Derek Showers
21 Paul Went

1977-78 19th in Division Two

Date	Att	Home	Score	Away	Scorers	1	2	3	4	5	6	7	8	9	10	11	12	13	14	15	16	17	18	19	20	21
20-Aug	7,581	CARDIFF CITY	1-1	Bristol Rovers	Went	3		4			2	9		11	7	1		6	8				10		5	
27-Aug	7,088	Blackburn Rovers	3-0	CARDIFF CITY		3	8		12	7	2			11			1	6*			4	9	10		5	
03-Sep	8,880	CARDIFF CITY	0-0	Tottenham Hotspur		3	12	8	7	44	2			11			1				6	9*	10		5	
10-Sep	7,330	Notts County	1-1	CARDIFF CITY	Dwyer	3		8	6	7	2			11			1				4	9	10		5	
17-Sep	6,843	CARDIFF CITY	1-1	Mansfield Town	Robson	8		4*	6	7	2	10		11	12		1				3	9			5	
24-Sep	8,789	CARDIFF CITY	3-1	Fulham	Robson, Evans 2	3		8	6	7	2	10		12			1				4	9*	11		5	
01-Oct	8,704	Blackpool	3-0	CARDIFF CITY		3*		8	7	4	2	10					1		12		6	9	11		5	
04-Oct	18,484	Sunderland	1-1	CARDIFF CITY	Livermore	3		11	7	4	2	9					1		8		6	10			5	
08-Oct	8,259	CARDIFF CITY	1-4	Luton Town	Dwyer	3		8	7	4	2	9					1				6	10	11		5	
15-Oct	5,444	Orient	2-1	CARDIFF CITY	Grapes	3		8		7	2				11		1			6	4	9	10		5	
22-Oct	6,892	CARDIFF CITY	1-0	Oldham Athletic	Went	3		8	12	7	4				11*		1			2	6	9	10		5	
29-Oct	22,740	Brighton	4-0	CARDIFF CITY		2		11		4			10	12	7*		1			3	6	9	8		5	
05-Nov	8,577	CARDIFF CITY	2-0	Stoke City	Dwyer, Sayer					4	8			11	7		1			3	6	9	10	2	5	
12-Nov	5,228	Hull City	4-1	CARDIFF CITY	Sayer (p)	12				4	8			7	11		1			3	6*	10	9	2	5	
19-Nov	7,069	CARDIFF CITY	2-1	Burnley	Dwyer, Sayer (p)	2		12		6	3			4	11*		1			10		9	7	5	8	
26-Nov	16,262	Crystal Palace	2-0	CARDIFF CITY		2		11	6	4	8			7			1			3		10	9		5	
03-Dec	6,395	CARDIFF CITY	1-6	Sheffield United	Buchanan	2		11		7	6			8			1			3		10	9	5	4	
10-Dec	18,072	Bolton Wanderers	6-3	CARDIFF CITY	Robson, Sayer, Bishop		12	11		4	2		9*	7			1			3	6	10	8		5	
17-Dec	5,663	CARDIFF CITY	0-0	Hull City			8	12		4	2			7	11		1	6		3		9*	10		5	
26-Dec	21,861	Southampton	3-1	CARDIFF CITY	Robson		10	12		4	2			7	11*		1	6		3		9	8		5	
28-Dec	8,253	CARDIFF CITY	4-1	Millwall	Buchanan 2, Bishop, Robson	11	10	8		4	2			7		1		6		3	5	9				
31-Dec	8,472	CARDIFF CITY	1-0	Charlton Athletic	og	11	10	8		4	2			7		1		6		3	5					9
02-Jan	11,957	Bristol Rovers	3-2	CARDIFF CITY	Giles, Pontin	11	10	8		4	2			7		1		6		3	5					9
14-Jan	7,025	CARDIFF CITY	1-1	Blackburn Rovers	Bishop	2	10			4	8			7	11	1		6		3	5	9*			12	
21-Jan	29,104	Tottenham Hotspur	2-1	CARDIFF CITY	Went		10	11*		4	2			8	7		1	6		3	5			12	9	
28-Jan	8,436	CARDIFF CITY	5-2	Sunderland	Buchanan 2(p), Went 2, Bishop		10	11*		4	2			8	7	1		6		3	5		12		9	
11-Feb	6,538	Mansfield Town	2-2	CARDIFF CITY	Bishop, Buchanan		8	11		4	2				7	1		6		3	5		10		9	
25-Feb	7,304	CARDIFF CITY	2-1	Blackpool	Went, Grapes		8	11		4	2			10	7	1		6		3	5				9	
04-Mar	6,029	Luton Town	3-1	CARDIFF CITY	Buchanan		10	11		4	2			8	7	1		6		3	5				9	
07-Mar	6,571	Fulham	1-0	CARDIFF CITY			10	11	7*	4	8				12	1		6		3	5			2	9	
18-Mar	7,581	Oldham Athletic	1-1	CARDIFF CITY	Went		8	11		4	7			10		1		6		3	5			2	9	
24-Mar	10,308	CARDIFF CITY	1-0	Brighton	Buchanan (p)		12	11		4		9*		8	7	1		6		3	5			2	10	
25-Mar	5,941	Millwall	1-1	CARDIFF CITY	Bishop		9	11*		4		12		8	7	1		6		3	5			2	10	
29-Mar	11,332	CARDIFF CITY	1-0	Southampton	Bishop		9	11		4	8				7	1		6		3	5			2	10	
01-Apr	14,804	Stoke City	2-0	CARDIFF CITY					12	4*	8			11	7	1		6		3	5			2	10	9
04-Apr	8,395	Charlton Athletic	0-0	CARDIFF CITY			9	11*		4	8			12	7	1		6		3	5			2	10	
08-Apr	9,314	CARDIFF CITY	2-2	Crystal Palace	Dwyer 2		9*	11		4	8	12			7	1		6		3	5			2	10	
15-Apr	11,610	Burnley	4-2	CARDIFF CITY	Buchanan, Evans		8	11*	12	4	7	9				1		6		3	5			2	10	
22-Apr	12,538	CARDIFF CITY	1-0	Bolton Wanderers	Bishop		12	11		4	8	9			7	1		6		3	5			2*	10	
29-Apr	13,687	Sheffield United	0-1	CARDIFF CITY	Evans		8	11		4	2	10			7	1		6		3	5				9	
03-May	9,506	CARDIFF CITY	2-1	Notts County	Buchanan, Went		8	11		4	2	9			7*	1		6		3	5			12	10	
09-May	8,238	CARDIFF CITY	0-1	Orient			8	11		4	2	9			7	1		6		3	5				10	
					Appearances	20	26	37	13	41	39	14	2	28	27	22	20	26	3	33	36	21	20	16	39	3
					Goals		8	10			6	4		1	2				1		1	5	4		8	

1 Brian Attley
2 Ray Bishop
3 John Buchanan
4 Gerry Byrne
5 Alan Campbell
6 Phil Dwyer
7 Tony Evans
8 Robin Friday
9 David Giles
10 Steve Grapes
11 Ron Healey
12 Bill Irwin
13 Albert Larmour
14 Doug Livermore
15 Freddie Pethard
16 Keith Pontin
17 Keith Robson
18 Peter Sayer
19 Rod Thomas
20 Paul Went
21 Chris Williams

1978-79 9th in Division Two

Date	Att	Home	Score	Away	Scorers	1	2	3	4	5	6	7	8	9	10	11	12	13	14	15	16	17	18	19	20	21	22	23	24	25	26	27
19-Aug	7,790	CARDIFF CITY	2-2	Preston North End	Went, Dwyer			10	11	7		4		9		8			1						3			6			2	5
23-Aug	16,007	Stoke City	2-0	CARDIFF CITY				10		7	11	4	1	9		8									3			6			2	5
26-Aug	6,907	CARDIFF CITY	1-3	Oldham Athletic	Buchanan	12			11	10		4	1	9		8*	7								3			6			2	5
02-Sep	6,815	Bristol Rovers	4-2	CARDIFF CITY	Roberts, Buchanan (p)				11	8		4	1	9			7	10							3		5	6			2	
09-Sep	6,141	CARDIFF CITY	1-0	Cambridge United	Buchanan		1	10*	11	8		4		9			7								3		5	6	12		2	
16-Sep	7,752	Luton Town	7-1	CARDIFF CITY	Bishop		1	12	9	8		7		11			6								5		3*	4	10		2	
23-Sep	6,234	CARDIFF CITY	2-0	Blackburn Rovers	Bishop, Stevens	12		10	11*			4		2			7		1		6	8			3		5		9			
30-Sep	11,766	Wrexham	1-2	CARDIFF CITY	Buchanan 2(p)			10	8			4*		2			7		1		6	11			3		5		9		12	
07-Oct	7,952	CARDIFF CITY	2-3	Notts County	Buchanan, Stevens			10	8			4		2			7		1		6	11			3		5		9			
14-Oct	6,063	Orient	2-2	CARDIFF CITY	Buchanan, Stevens				8			4*		2	10		7		1		6	11			12		5	3	9			
21-Oct	8,758	CARDIFF CITY	1-0	Leicester City	Stevens				8					3	10		7*		1		6	11			12		2	5	9		4	
28-Oct	23,477	Newcastle United	3-0	CARDIFF CITY					8		6*	7		2	10				1			11			12		5	3	9		4	
04-Nov	7,772	CARDIFF CITY	1-4	Charlton Athletic	Stevens			12	8			4		2	10		7*		1			11					5	3	9		6	
11-Nov	9,268	Preston North End	2-1	CARDIFF CITY	Evans			12	7*			4		2	10	8					6	11				1	5		9		3	
18-Nov	5,357	Oldham Athletic	2-1	CARDIFF CITY	Bishop	7		8				4		2	10						6	11				1	5		9		3	
25-Nov	8,723	CARDIFF CITY	2-2	Crystal Palace	Evans, Dwyer	8		11	7			4*		2	10						6	12				1	5		9		3	
02-Dec	5,551	Millwall	2-0	CARDIFF CITY		7		8	11			4		2	10*						6				12	1	5		9		3	
09-Dec	7,168	CARDIFF CITY	1-1	Sunderland	Evans (p)	11*		8	7			4		2	10				1		6				12		5		9		3	
16-Dec	11,913	Sheffield United	2-1	CARDIFF CITY	Evans (p)				7			4		2	10				1		6		11		8		5		9		3	
23-Dec	5,542	CARDIFF CITY	2-0	Fulham	Evans, Roberts	7			8*			4		9	10				1		6	11			3			5	12		2	
26-Dec	20,127	Brighton	5-0	CARDIFF CITY		7		12				4		10	9				1		6	11			3			5	8*		2	
30-Dec	9,821	Burnley	0-0	CARDIFF CITY		8		9				7		2	10				1		6	11			3		5				4	
13-Jan	5,344	Cambridge United	5-0	CARDIFF CITY		2		10	9					11	8		7		1		6				3		5	4				
24-Feb	8,239	CARDIFF CITY	1-0	Orient	Buchanan			12	9			4		5	10		7*		1	2				11			6		8	3		
28-Feb	7,158	Blackburn Rovers	1-4	CARDIFF CITY	Stevens, Grapes, Buchanan, Evans				11			4		6	10		7		1	2				9			5		8	3		
03-Mar	12,820	Leicester City	1-2	CARDIFF CITY	Dwyer, Stevens			8	11			6		5			7		1					9			4	2	10	3		
10-Mar	11,089	CARDIFF CITY	2-1	Newcastle United	Bishop, Stevens			8	11			6		5			7		1	2				9			4		10	3		
17-Mar	5,658	Charlton Athletic	1-1	CARDIFF CITY	Buchanan (p)			8*	11			4		6	12		7		1					9			5	2	10	3		
24-Mar	14,851	CARDIFF CITY	1-3	Stoke City	Buchanan (p)			8	11			4	1	5	10*		7					12		9			6	2		3		
27-Mar	8,211	Notts County	1-0	CARDIFF CITY				8	11			4		6	9		7		1					10			5	2		3		
31-Mar	18,511	Crystal Palace	2-0	CARDIFF CITY				8				4		6	9		7*		1			12		10			5	2	11	3		
07-Apr	7,695	CARDIFF CITY	2-1	Millwall	Stevens, og			8				4			9				1	2		7	12	10*				6	11	3	5	
11-Apr	6,067	Fulham	2-2	CARDIFF CITY	Dwyer, og			7	11			4		6	8				1	2				9			5		10	3		
14-Apr	12,686	CARDIFF CITY	3-1	Brighton	Stevens, Evans, Moore			8	7			4			9				1	2				10				6	11	3	5	
16-Apr	29,058	West Ham United	1-1	CARDIFF CITY	Bishop			7	11			4		6	8				1	2				9				5	10	3		
21-Apr	10,569	CARDIFF CITY	4-0	Sheffield United	Buchanan 3(p), Stevens			8	7			4		11	9				1	2								5	10	3	6	
25-Apr	10,522	CARDIFF CITY	2-1	Luton Town	Moore, Stevens			7	11			4*			8		12		1	2				9				5	10	3	6	
28-Apr	36,526	Sunderland	1-2	CARDIFF CITY	Moore, Bishop			8	7			4		6	9				1	2				10				5	11	3		
05-May	10,254	CARDIFF CITY	1-1	Burnley	Sullivan			8*	7			4		6	9		12		1	2				10				5	11	3		
07-May	10,363	CARDIFF CITY	2-0	Bristol Rovers	Stevens, Buchanan (p)				11			4		6	8		7		1	2				9				5	10	3		
11-May	13,124	CARDIFF CITY	0-0	West Ham United					11			4		6	8		7		1	2				9				5	10	3		
14-May	11,784	CARDIFF CITY	1-0	Wrexham	Buchanan				11			4		6	8		7		1	2				9				5	10	3		
					Appearances	10	2	31	36	6	2	40	4	39	31	4	24	1	32	14	15	16	2	18	19	4	27	28	34	19	23	3
					Goals			6	16					4	7		1							3				2	13	1		1

1 Brian Attley
2 Keith Barber
3 Ray Bishop
4 John Buchanan
5 Micky Burns
6 Gerry Byrne
7 Alan Campbell
8 John Davies
9 Phil Dwyer
10 Tony Evans
11 David Giles
12 Steve Grapes
13 Gary Harris
14 Ron Healey
15 Linden Jones
16 Albert Larmour
17 John Lewis
18 Tarki Micallef
19 Ronnie Moore
20 Freddie Pethard
21 Jim Platt
22 Keith Pontin
23 Dave Roberts
24 Gary Stevens
25 Colin Sullivan
26 Rod Thomas
27 Paul Went

1979-80 15th in Division Two

Date	Att	Home	Score	Away	Scorers	1	2	3	4	5	6	7	8	9	10	11	12	13	14	15	16	17	18	19	20	21	22	23
18-Aug	7,157	Notts County	4-1	CARDIFF CITY	Jones	8*	11	4			6					1		2		12		9		5	7	10	3	
22-Aug	11,577	CARDIFF CITY	1-0	Queen's Park Rangers	Stevens	7*	11	4			6					1		2			12	9		5	10	8	3	
25-Aug	11,465	CARDIFF CITY	1-2	Birmingham City	Stevens		11	4			6		7			1		2				9		5	10	8	3	
01-Sep	9,839	Wrexham	0-1	CARDIFF CITY	Stevens	7	11	4			6					1		2				9		5	10	8	3	
08-Sep	8,651	CARDIFF CITY	1-0	Shrewsbury Town	Stevens	7*	11	4				12				1		2				9		5	10	8	3	6
15-Sep	13,741	Watford	1-1	CARDIFF CITY	Stevens	7*	12	4			6	11				1		2				9	5		10	8	3	
22-Sep	8,519	CARDIFF CITY	0-0	Cambridge United			11	4			6	7				1		2				9	5		10	8	3	
29-Sep	8,974	Bristol Rovers	1-1	CARDIFF CITY	Pontin		11	4			6	7				1		2				9	5		10	8	3	
06-Oct	9,402	CARDIFF CITY	2-1	Luton Town	Bishop 2	7	12	4			6					1	11*	2				9	5		10	8	3	
09-Oct	12,225	Queen's Park Rangers	3-0	CARDIFF CITY		7		4			6					1	11	2				9	5		10	8	3	
13-Oct	6,450	Burnley	0-2	CARDIFF CITY	Bishop, Ronson	7	11	4			6					1		2				9	5		10	8	3	
20-Oct	15,992	CARDIFF CITY	1-2	Chelsea	Moore	7	11	4			6					1		2				9	5		10	8	3	
27-Oct	6,896	Charlton Athletic	3-2	CARDIFF CITY	Bishop, Hughes	7	11	4			6					1	12	2				9	5		10	8*	3	
03-Nov	8,316	CARDIFF CITY	3-2	Notts County	Bishop 2, Buchanan	7	8*	4			6					1			11			9	5		10	12	3	2
10-Nov	22,867	Newcastle United	1-0	CARDIFF CITY		7*	8	4			6					1			11			9	5		10	12	3	2
17-Nov	8,095	CARDIFF CITY	0-0	Orient			12	4					7			1		2	11			9	5		10	8	3	6
24-Nov	20,292	West Ham United	3-0	CARDIFF CITY		7		4	1		8							2*	11			9	5		10	12	3	6
01-Dec	7,048	CARDIFF CITY	1-0	Oldham Athletic	Bishop	8		4	1		2	7							11			9	5		10		3	6
08-Dec	25,370	Sunderland	2-1	CARDIFF CITY	Bishop	8		4	1		2	7							11*			9	5		10	12	3	6
15-Dec	6,711	CARDIFF CITY	0-2	Preston North End		7	12	4						1			11	2*				8	5		10	9	3	6
21-Dec	12,877	Leicester City	0-0	CARDIFF CITY		8		4			2			1			11*		7			12	5		10	9	3	6
26-Dec	8,105	CARDIFF CITY	1-0	Fulham	Pontin	8		4			2			1			11*		7			12	5		10	9	3	6
29-Dec	16,682	Birmingham City	2-1	CARDIFF CITY	Bishop	8		4						1				2	7			11	5		10	9	3	6
01-Jan	21,306	Swansea City	2-1	CARDIFF CITY	Lewis	8	11	4			2			1					7			9	5		10		3	6
12-Jan	10,803	CARDIFF CITY	1-0	Wrexham	Moore	8	11	4			2					1			7			9	5		10		3	6
19-Jan	6,870	Shrewsbury Town	1-2	CARDIFF CITY	Buchanan, Moore	8	11	4			2		10*			1			7			9	5			12	3	6
02-Feb	7,983	CARDIFF CITY	1-0	Watford	Lewis	8	11	4			2					1	3*		7			9	5		10	12		6
09-Feb	5,229	Cambridge United	2-0	CARDIFF CITY		8	11	4					2			1	3*		7			9	5		10	12		6
16-Feb	6,918	CARDIFF CITY	0-1	Bristol Rovers		8		4*		12			2			1			3		7	9	5		10	11		6
23-Feb	6,342	CARDIFF CITY	2-1	Burnley	Pontin, Stevens	8*		4			2		7			1			3		11	9	5		10	12		6
01-Mar	18,490	Chelsea	1-0	CARDIFF CITY				4			2		11			1			3		7	9	5		10	8		6
08-Mar	6,533	CARDIFF CITY	3-1	Charlton Athletic	Stevens 2, Buchanan	7*	12	4			2		11			1			3			9	5		10	8		6
14-Mar	9,246	Luton Town	1-2	CARDIFF CITY	Stevens, Buchanan		7	4			2		11			1			3			9	5		10	8		6
22-Mar	9,284	CARDIFF CITY	1-1	Newcastle United	Stevens		7	4			2		11*			1			3		12	9	5		10	8		6
29-Mar	4,081	Orient	1-1	CARDIFF CITY	Buchanan		7	4			2		11			1			3			9	5		10	8		6
07-Apr	14,634	CARDIFF CITY	1-0	Swansea City	Ronson		7	4			2		11			1			3			9	5		10	8		6
08-Apr	10,193	CARDIFF CITY	0-1	Leicester City			7	4			2		11			1			3			9*	5		10	8	12	6
12-Apr	6,339	Oldham Athletic	0-3	CARDIFF CITY	Buchanan, Stevens, Micallef	8*	7	4					2			1			11		12		5		10	9	3	6
15-Apr	5,161	Fulham	2-1	CARDIFF CITY	Bishop	9	7	4					11*			1			3		12		5		10	8	2	6
19-Apr	12,051	CARDIFF CITY	0-1	West Ham United		8*	10	4					2	1	11				3				5		7	9	12	6
26-Apr	7,493	Preston North End	2-0	CARDIFF CITY			7	4					2		11	1			3		8		5		10	9*		6
03-May	19,834	CARDIFF CITY	1-1	Sunderland	Bishop	8		4				7	2	1	11				3			9	5		10			6
					Appearances	31	31	42	3	1	32	7	18	7	3	32	8	17	28	1	8	38	37	5	41	38	30	30
					Goals	11	6										1	1	2		1	3	3		2	11		

1 Ray Bishop
2 John Buchanan
3 Alan Campbell
4 John Davies
5 Paul Davies
6 Phil Dwyer
7 Mark Elliott
8 Steve Grapes
9 Peter Grotier
10 Gary Harris
11 Ron Healey
12 Wayne Hughes
13 Linden Jones
14 John Lewis
15 Kevin J Lloyd
16 Tarki Micallef
17 Ronnie Moore
18 Keith Pontin
19 Dave Roberts
20 Billy Ronson
21 Gary Stevens
22 Colin Sullivan
23 Rod Thomas

1980-81 19th in Division Two

Date	Att	Home	Score	Away	Scorers	1	2	3	4	5	6	7	8	9	10	11	12	13	14	15	16	17	18	19	20	21	22
16-Aug	6,810	CARDIFF CITY	1-2	Blackburn Rovers	Stevens	7	11*	12		4			2	1					3		8	5		10	9		6
19-Aug	7,772	Wrexham	0-1	CARDIFF CITY	Bishop	7	8	4		3			2	1					11			5		10	9		6
23-Aug	5,690	Oldham Athletic	2-0	CARDIFF CITY		7	8*	4		3			2	1				12	11			5		10	9		6
30-Aug	5,671	CARDIFF CITY	4-2	Orient	Stevens 2, Dwyer, Buchanan	7	11	4		6			2	1				8	3			5		10	9		
06-Sep	15,787	Newcastle United	2-1	CARDIFF CITY	Kitchen	7	11	4		6			2	1				8	3			5		10	9		
13-Sep	6,532	CARDIFF CITY	1-1	Bolton Wanderers	Stevens	7	11	4		6			2	1				8	3			5		10	9		
20-Sep	6,117	CARDIFF CITY	2-1	Bristol Rovers	Ronson, Pontin	7	11	12		6*			2	1				8	3	4		5		10	9		
27-Sep	7,229	Notts County	4-2	CARDIFF CITY	Dwyer, Kitchen		11			6			2	1				8	3	4*	7	5		10	9		12
04-Oct	6,388	CARDIFF CITY	1-0	Watford	Micallef		11			6			2	1				8	3	4*	7	5	12	10	9		
07-Oct	20,402	West Ham United	1-0	CARDIFF CITY			11						2	1		4		8			7	5	6	10	9		3
11-Oct	15,606	Sheffield Wednesday	2-0	CARDIFF CITY		11*		4		12			2	1				8			7	5	6	10	9		3
17-Oct	4,140	CARDIFF CITY	1-2	Cambridge United	og			4		12			2	1			3	8	11*		7	5	6	10	9		
22-Oct	4,453	CARDIFF CITY	1-0	Queen's Park Rangers	Grapes	7	10			6			4*	1			2	8	3	11		5		8	12		
25-Oct	4,466	Shrewsbury Town	2-0	CARDIFF CITY		7	9			6			4	1			2	8	3	11*		5		10	12		
31-Oct	8,445	CARDIFF CITY	0-1	Chelsea		7	11			6			4*	1			2	8	3		12	5		10	9		
08-Nov	5,494	Preston North End	3-1	CARDIFF CITY	Kitchen	7	11			6				1		4	2	8	3			5		10	9		
12-Nov	4,780	CARDIFF CITY	1-0	Wrexham	Kitchen (p)		11			6			12		1	4	2	8	3		7*	5		10	9		
15-Nov	7,855	Blackburn Rovers	2-3	CARDIFF CITY	Kitchen 2, Buchanan		11			6		7			1	4	2	8				5		10	9		3
22-Nov	6,041	CARDIFF CITY	1-0	Luton Town	Buchanan		11*			6		7			1	4	2	8	12			5		10	9		3
29-Nov	15,581	Derby County	1-1	CARDIFF CITY	og		11			6		7			1	4	2	8				5		10	9		3
06-Dec	5,936	CARDIFF CITY	1-1	Grimsby Town	Kitchen (p)		11			6		7*			1	4	2	8	12			5		10	9		3
26-Dec	15,039	Bristol City	0-0	CARDIFF CITY			11			6					1	4	2	8	7			5	3	10	9		
27-Dec	21,198	CARDIFF CITY	3-3	Swansea City	Stevens, Kitchen, Buchanan	7	11			6*		12			1	4	2	8	3			5		10	9		
10-Jan	9,013	Luton Town	2-2	CARDIFF CITY	Kitchen, Giles		11*			6		7			1	4		8			12	5	2	10	9		3
17-Jan	3,838	Orient	2-2	CARDIFF CITY	Maddy 2		11					7			1	4		8		6		5	2	10	9		3
31-Jan	5,563	CARDIFF CITY	0-2	Oldham Athletic			11		9	4*		7			1	12	2	8		6		5		10			3
03-Feb	9,834	Queen's Park Rangers	2-0	CARDIFF CITY			11			6*		7			1	4	2	8		12	9	5		10			3
07-Feb	8,115	Bolton Wanderers	4-2	CARDIFF CITY	Buchanan 2		11					7			1		2	8			6	5	4	10	9		3
20-Feb	4,958	CARDIFF CITY	0-1	Notts County			11				3		4		1		2	8			7	5		10	9		6
25-Feb	4,226	CARDIFF CITY	1-0	Newcastle United	Kitchen		11				3		4	1			2	8	7			5		10	9		6
28-Feb	7,525	Bristol Rovers	0-1	CARDIFF CITY	Grapes		11				3		4	1			2	8	7			5		10	9		6
04-Mar	6,971	CARDIFF CITY	0-0	Sheffield Wednesday			11				3		4	1			2	8	7			5		10	9		6
07-Mar	10,114	Watford	4-2	CARDIFF CITY	Kitchen, Jones		11				3		4	1			2	8	7			5		10	9		6
21-Mar	3,719	Cambridge United	2-0	CARDIFF CITY			11			3				1		4	2	8	7			5		10	9		6
28-Mar	5,195	CARDIFF CITY	2-2	Shrewsbury Town	Lewis, Dwyer		11			3				1			2	8	7		4	5		10	9		6
04-Apr	11,569	Chelsea	0-1	CARDIFF CITY	Stevens		11			6			4		1		2	8	7			5		10	9	3	
11-Apr	4,987	CARDIFF CITY	1-3	Preston North End	Dwyer		11			6			4		1		2	8	7			5		10	9	3	
18-Apr	19,038	Swansea City	1-1	CARDIFF CITY	Kitchen					6		11*	4		1		2	8	7		12	5		10	9	3	
20-Apr	5,575	CARDIFF CITY	2-3	Bristol City	Grapes, Kitchen					6			4		1		2	8	7		11	5		10	9	3	
25-Apr	7,377	Grimsby Town	0-1	CARDIFF CITY	Stevens					6			4		1		2	8	7		11	5		10	9	3	
02-May	7,577	CARDIFF CITY	0-0	Derby County						6			4		1		2	8	7		11	5		10	9	3	
06-May	10,535	CARDIFF CITY	0-0	West Ham United						6			4*		1		2	8	7		11	5		10	9	3	12
					Appearances	13	35	9	1	34	5	11	28	22	20	14	29	40	32	8	18	42	8	42	40	7	23
					Goals	1	6			4		1	3				1	13	1	2	1	1		1	7		

1 Ray Bishop
2 John Buchanan
3 Alan Campbell
4 Paul Davies
5 Phil Dwyer
6 Tim Gilbert
7 Paul Giles
8 Steve Grapes
9 Peter Grotier
10 Ron Healey
11 Wayne Hughes
12 Linden Jones
13 Peter Kitchen
14 John Lewis
15 Paul Maddy
16 Tarki Micallef
17 Keith Pontin
18 Dave Roberts
19 Billy Ronson
20 Gary Stevens
21 Colin Sullivan
22 Rod Thomas

1981-82 20th in Division Two (Relegated)

Date	Att	Home	Score	Away	Scorers	1	2	3	4	5	6	7	8	9	10	11	12	13	14	15	16	17	18	19	20	21	22	23	24	25	26	27	28
29-Aug	4,374	Oldham Athletic	2-2	CARDIFF CITY	Stevens, Dwyer			11		6				4		1			2	8	7					5	10			9		3	
02-Sep	8,884	CARDIFF CITY	1-2	Chelsea	Kitchen			11		6				4*		1			2	8	7		12			5	10			9		3	
12-Sep	7,002	Rotherham United	1-0	CARDIFF CITY				11		6				4		1			2	8	7					5	10			9		3	
19-Sep	4,248	CARDIFF CITY	1-3	Blackburn Rovers	Ronson					6						1			2*	8	7	11	12			5	10		4	9		3	
22-Sep	9,015	Luton Town	2-3	CARDIFF CITY	Kitchen (p), Sayer, Stevens					6						1			2	8	7		11			5	10		4	9		3	
26-Sep	12,114	Barnsley	0-1	CARDIFF CITY	Stevens	7				6						1			2	8	11					5	10		4	9	8	3	
03-Oct	5,758	CARDIFF CITY	0-4	Newcastle United		7				6						1			2		11					5	10		4*	9	8	3	
10-Oct	15,839	Sheffield Wednesday	2-1	CARDIFF CITY	D Bennett	7				6		3*	12			1		10	2	12	11		8			5				9			4
17-Oct	3,874	CARDIFF CITY	2-1	Bolton Wanderers	Stevens, D Bennett	7				6		3			1			10	2*		11	4	8			5				9			12
24-Oct	4,353	CARDIFF CITY	1-1	Shrewsbury Town	Stevens	7				6		3		2	1			10			11	4*	8			5				9			12
31-Oct	4,041	Cambridge United	2-1	CARDIFF CITY	Micallef	7				6		3		2	1			10			11	4	8			5				9			
04-Nov	4,618	CARDIFF CITY	3-2	Wrexham	Micallef, Stevens, Lewis	7	5			6		3			1			10	2		11	4	8							9			
07-Nov	5,698	CARDIFF CITY	1-0	Norwich City	D Bennett	7	6					3			1			10	2		11	4	8							9			5
14-Nov	13,982	Watford	0-0	CARDIFF CITY		7	6					3			1			10	2		11	4	8			5				9			
21-Nov	6,656	CARDIFF CITY	3-1	Leicester City	Micallef, D Bennett, Stevens	7	6					3			1			10	2		11	4*	8			5				9	12		
24-Nov	3,625	Wrexham	3-1	CARDIFF CITY	Dwyer	7	6			12		3			1			10	2		11	4*	8			5				9			
28-Nov	10,225	Queen's Park Rangers	2-0	CARDIFF CITY		7*	6			4		3		2	1			10			11		8			5				9	12		
04-Dec	5,506	CARDIFF CITY	1-0	Derby County	Micallef	7	6					3		2		1		10			11	4	8			5				9			
28-Dec	7,879	CARDIFF CITY	0-1	Charlton Athletic		8	6			3				2		1		10			11	4*	7			5				9	12		
20-Jan	4,108	CARDIFF CITY	0-1	Oldham Athletic		7	6			10		3	11			1			2			4	8			5				9			
30-Jan	7,001	Blackburn Rovers	1-0	CARDIFF CITY		7	6			9		3	11			1			2	10		4	8			5							
06-Feb	3,818	CARDIFF CITY	1-2	Rotherham United	Kitchen	7	6			11	2	3	12			1				10		4	8			5				9*			
13-Feb	15,129	Newcastle United	2-1	CARDIFF CITY	Stevens	7	6*			11		3				1			2	10		4	8			5		12		9			
17-Feb	9,710	Chelsea	1-0	CARDIFF CITY		7	6			11		3				1			2	10		4	8			5				9			
20-Feb	4,500	CARDIFF CITY	0-0	Barnsley		7	6			4		3				1		11	2	10		12	8*			5				9			
27-Feb	5,767	CARDIFF CITY	0-2	Sheffield Wednesday		7	6			4*		3		12		1		11	2	10		8				5				9			
06-Mar	6,269	Bolton Wanderers	1-0	CARDIFF CITY		7					4	3	12	8		1		6	2	10*						5		11		9			
09-Mar	7,202	Crystal Palace	1-0	CARDIFF CITY		7					12	3	11	4		1		6	2	10		8				5				9*			
13-Mar	4,089	Shrewsbury Town	1-1	CARDIFF CITY	G Bennett	7	6					3		4		1		11	2	10		8*	12			5				9			
20-Mar	3,239	CARDIFF CITY	5-4	Cambridge United	Stevens 3, Kitchen 2	10	6					3		7*		1		5	2	9		12	8			4				11			
27-Mar	11,923	Norwich City	2-1	CARDIFF CITY	Gilbert	10						3		7		1	8	5*	2	9			12	6		4				11			
30-Mar	3,920	CARDIFF CITY	2-1	Grimsby Town	Stevens, og	10						3		7		1	8		2	9			5	6		4				11			
03-Apr	6,729	CARDIFF CITY	2-0	Watford	D Bennett, Micallef	10						3		7		1	8		2	9			5	6		4				11			
10-Apr	5,685	CARDIFF CITY	2-1	Orient	D Bennett, Kitchen	9*								7		1	3		2	11		12	8	5	6	4				10			
13-Apr	4,186	Charlton Athletic	2-2	CARDIFF CITY	Stevens, Mullen									7		1	8	12	2	9		10*	5	6	3	4				11			
17-Apr	13,650	Leicester City	3-1	CARDIFF CITY	Kitchen	12								7		1	8	10*	2	9			5	6	3	4				11			
24-Apr	5,974	CARDIFF CITY	1-2	Queen's Park Rangers	Micallef	10								7		1	8	12	2	9		11	5	6	3	4							
28-Apr	2,527	Orient	1-1	CARDIFF CITY	Maddy	10								7		1	8	5	2	9		11		6	3	4							
01-May	10,111	Derby County	0-0	CARDIFF CITY		10								7		1	8	5	2	9		11		6	3	4							
08-May	5,558	CARDIFF CITY	0-1	Crystal Palace		10			1			8		7					2	9*		12	5	6	3	4				11			
15-May	8,148	Grimsby Town	0-1	CARDIFF CITY	Micallef	11	9					8		7		1	3		2				5	6		4				10			
17-May	10,277	CARDIFF CITY	2-3	Luton Town	Kitchen, Micallef	11	9					8		7		1	3		2	12			5	6		4				10			
					Appearances	36	19	3	1	22	3	28	6	25	9	32	11	24	36	27	19	27	33	12	7	40	7	2	4	38	5	7	4
					Goals	6	1			2		1								8	1	1	8	1			1		1	13			

1 Dave Bennett
2 Gary Bennett
3 John Buchanan
4 Andy Dibble
5 Phil Dwyer
6 Peter Francombe
7 Tim Gilbert
8 Paul Giles
9 Steve Grapes
10 Peter Grotier
11 Ron Healey
12 Mick Henderson
13 Wayne Hughes
14 Linden Jones
15 Peter Kitchen
16 John Lewis
17 Paul Maddy
18 Tarki Micallef
19 Jimmy Mullen
20 Andy Polycarpou
21 Keith Pontin
22 Billy Ronson
23 Alan Sanders
24 Peter Sayer
25 Gary Stevens
26 Paul Sugrue
27 Colin Sullivan
28 Rod Thomas

1982-83 2nd in Division Three (Promoted)

Date	Att	Home	Score	Away	Scorers	1	2	3	4	5	6	7	8	9	10	11	12	13	14	15	16	17	18	19	20	21	22
28-Aug	5,018	CARDIFF CITY	1-2	Wrexham	DE Bennett	7	12	3			4*	9			10	1		2		11		6	5			8	
05-Sep	5,304	Millwall	0-4	CARDIFF CITY	D Bennett 2, Lewis, Gibbins	7	2	3			12	9			10				11*		4	6	5		1	8	
08-Sep	1,790	Orient	4-0	CARDIFF CITY		7	2	3				9			10			12		11	4	6	5		1	8*	
11-Sep	3,850	CARDIFF CITY	3-2	Wigan Athletic	Lewis, G Bennett, Woof	7	2	3				9						12	11		4	6	5*		1	8	10
18-Sep	3,161	Walsall	1-2	CARDIFF CITY	Hemmerman, Dwyer	7		3			5	9			10			2	11		4	6			1	8	
25-Sep	71,147	CARDIFF CITY	2-0	Sheffield United	D Bennett, Hemmerman	7		3			5	9			10		12	2	11*		4	6			1	8	
28-Sep	4,807	CARDIFF CITY	2-0	Exeter City	Hemmerman 2	7		3			5	9			10		12	2	11*		4	6			1	8	
02-Oct	6,205	Oxford United	2-2	CARDIFF CITY	Mullen, Gibbins	7*		3			5	9			10		12	2	11		4	6			1	8	
09-Oct	5,818	Bournemouth	3-1	CARDIFF CITY	Hemmerman	7	12	3			5	9			10		4	2*	11			6			1	8	
16-Oct	4,828	CARDIFF CITY	1-0	Gillingham	Ingram	7	6	3			5	9			10		4	2	11						1	8	
19-Oct	5,007	CARDIFF CITY	1-0	Bradford City	G Bennett	7*	6	3			5	9			10		4	2	11		12				1	8	
23-Oct	61,211	Huddersfield Town	4-0	CARDIFF CITY		7	6	3			5	9			10		4	2	11		12				1	8*	
30-Oct	7,082	CARDIFF CITY	1-0	Portsmouth	Hemmerman	7	6	3			5	9			10		8	2	11		4				1		
03-Nov	32,117	Reading	1-2	CARDIFF CITY	G Bennett, Dwyer	7	6	3			5	9			10		8*	2	11		4				1	12	
06-Nov	5,453	CARDIFF CITY	3-1	Preston North End	Hemmerman, D Bennett, Ingram	7	6	3			5	9			10		8	2	11		4				1		
13-Nov	6,585	Lincoln City	2-1	CARDIFF CITY	D Bennett	7		3*			5	9			10		12	2	11		4	6			1	8	
04-Dec	3,078	Doncaster Rovers	2-2	CARDIFF CITY	Micallef, Hemmerman			3		1	5	9	12	7	10			2	11		4*	6				8	
07-Dec	3,813	CARDIFF CITY	1-1	Chesterfield	Hatton	7		3		1	5	8		9	10			2	11			6				4	
17-Dec	3,743	Southend United	1-2	CARDIFF CITY	Hatton, Gibbins	7	3			1	5	8		9	10			2	11			6				4	
27-Dec	15,972	CARDIFF CITY	3-2	Newport County	Hemmerman 2, Hatton	7	6			1	5	8		9	10			2	11			3				4	
28-Dec	8,631	Plymouth Argyle	3-2	CARDIFF CITY	Hatton, G Bennett	7	6			1	5	8	10	9				2	11	12		3*				4	
01-Jan	11,050	CARDIFF CITY	3-1	Bristol Rovers	Hemmerman 2(p), G Bennett	7	6			1	5	8		9	10			2	11			3				4	
03-Jan	7,602	Brentford	1-3	CARDIFF CITY	Hemmerman 2, Gibbins		6	12		1	5	8	7*	9	10			2	11			3				4	
15-Jan	3,846	Wrexham	0-0	CARDIFF CITY		7	6			1	5	8		9	10			2	11			3				4	
22-Jan	6,115	CARDIFF CITY	3-1	Walsall	G Bennett, Hemmerman (p), D Bennett	7	6			1	5	8		9	10			2	11			3				4	
29-Jan	4,019	Exeter City	0-2	CARDIFF CITY	Hemmerman, Hatton	7	6	2		1	5	8		9	10				11			3				4	
01-Feb	5,643	CARDIFF CITY	3-0	Millwall	G Bennett, D Bennett, Hemmerman	7	6*	2		1	5	8		9	10			12	11			3				4	
05-Feb	11,641	Sheffield United	2-0	CARDIFF CITY		7	6	11		1	5	8		9	10			2*		12		3				4	
12-Feb	6,970	CARDIFF CITY	3-0	Oxford United	Hemmerman (p), D Bennett, Hatton	7		6*		1	5	8	12	9	10			2		11		3				4	
16-Feb	3,786	Bradford City	4-2	CARDIFF CITY	Dwyer, Gibbins			6		1	5*	8	12	9	10			2	11	7		3				4	
19-Feb	4,878	CARDIFF CITY	1-1	Bournemouth	Gibbins	7	6		1		5	8		9	10			2	11			3				4	
26-Feb	4,587	Gillingham	2-3	CARDIFF CITY	Hemmerman 2(p), Gibbins	7	6		1		5	8		9	10			2	11			3				4	
01-Mar	6,173	CARDIFF CITY	0-0	Reading		7	6*		1		5	8		9	10			2	11	12		3				4	
12-Mar	24,354	Portsmouth	0-0	CARDIFF CITY		7	6				5	8		9	10			2	11			3		1		4	
15-Mar	10,379	CARDIFF CITY	1-1	Huddersfield Town	Hatton	7	6	5				8		9	10			2	11			3		1		4	
19-Mar	4,611	Preston North End	2-1	CARDIFF CITY	Hemmerman	7	6				5	8		9	10			2			11	3		1		4	
26-Mar	80,211	CARDIFF CITY	1-0	Lincoln City	G Bennett	7	6				5	8		9	10			2			11	3		1		4	
02-Apr	7,146	CARDIFF CITY	0-0	Plymouth Argyle		7	6	12			5	8		9*	10			2			11	3		1		4	
04-Apr	16,052	Newport County	1-0	CARDIFF CITY			6				5	8	7*	12	10			2	9		11	3		1		4	
09-Apr	5,456	CARDIFF CITY	3-0	Doncaster Rovers	Tong 2, Gibbins		6	12			5	8		9	10			2	7*		11	3		1		4	
16-Apr	4,383	Wigan Athletic	0-0	CARDIFF CITY		12	6			1	5	8		9	10			2	7		11	3				4*	
23-Apr	6,141	CARDIFF CITY	4-1	Southend United	Lewis 2, Hatton, Hemmerman	7	6	5		1		8		9	10			2	11			3				4	
30-Apr	2,797	Chesterfield	0-1	CARDIFF CITY	D Bennett	7		5		1		6	8	9	10				2	11		3				4	
02-May	9,112	CARDIFF CITY	3-1	Brentford	Hatton, D Bennett, og	7	6	3		1	5	8		9	10			2	11							4	
07-May	11,758	CARDIFF CITY	2-0	Orient	Lewis, D Bennett	7	6			1	5	8		9	10			2	11			3				4	
14-May	10,731	Bristol Rovers	1-1	CARDIFF CITY	Gibbins	7	6	12		1	5	8		9	10			2	11			3				4	
					Appearances	41	36	31	3	20	41	46	7	30	44	1	11	43	39	8	20	39	4	7	15	44	1
					Goals	12	8				3	9		9	22		2		5		1	1				2	1

1 Dave Bennett
2 Gary Bennett
3 Paul Bodin
4 Jim Brown
5 Andy Dibble
6 Phil Dwyer
7 Roger Gibbins
8 Paul Giles
9 Bob Hatton
10 Jeff Hemmerman
11 Steve Humphries
12 Godfrey Ingram
13 Linden Jones
14 John Lewis
15 Paul Maddy
16 Tarki Micallef
17 Jimmy Mullen
18 Keith Pontin
19 Eric Steele
20 Martin Thomas
21 David Tong
22 Billy Woof

1983-84 15th in Division Two

Date	Att	Home	Score	Away	Scorers	1	2	3	4	5	6	7	8	9	10	11	12	13	14	15	16	17	18	19	20	21	22	23	24	25	26
27-Aug	4,590	Charlton Athletic	2-0	CARDIFF CITY			5	3		9	1	4			8				2		11	12		7		10*		6			
29-Aug	8,895	CARDIFF CITY	2-1	Manchester City	Boden 2		5	3		9	1	4			8				2		11			7		10		6			
03-Sep	5,315	CARDIFF CITY	3-1	Grimsby Town	Owen 2(p), Crawford		5	3*		9	1	4			8				2		11		12	7		10		6			
06-Sep	4,405	Shrewsbury Town	1-0	CARDIFF CITY			5	3		9	1	4			8				2		11		12	7		10*		6			
10-Sep	12,323	Leeds United	1-0	CARDIFF CITY			5	3		9	1	4			8				2		11	12	10	7*				6			
17-Sep	9,033	CARDIFF CITY	0-0	Portsmouth			5	3		9*	1	4			8				2		11	12	10	7				6			
01-Oct	6,378	CARDIFF CITY	0-3	Barnsley			11*	3			1	4	2		8							12	5	7				6		10	9
08-Oct	4,768	CARDIFF CITY	2-0	Carlisle United	Owen, Vaughan			3			1	4	2		8								5	7			11	6	12	10	9*
15-Oct	15,459	Chelsea	2-0	CARDIFF CITY				3			1	4	11		8							12	5	7			2	6	9*	10	
19-Oct	9,826	CARDIFF CITY	0-2	Newcastle United				3			1	4	11		8							12	5	7			2	6	9*	10	
31-Oct	5,940	Fulham	0-2	CARDIFF CITY	Bennett, Owen		9	3			1	4	11		8							12	5	7			2	6*		10	
05-Nov	7,686	Middlesbrough	2-0	CARDIFF CITY			9	3			1	4	11		8							12	5*	7			2	6		10	
08-Nov	5,330	Crystal Palace	1-0	CARDIFF CITY			9	3			1	5	11		8							4		7			2	6*	12	10	
12-Nov	4,730	CARDIFF CITY	5-0	Cambridge United	Gibbins 2, Vaughan, Owen, og		9	3			1	5	11		8							4		7			2	6	12	10	
19-Nov	3,587	Oldham Athletic	2-1	CARDIFF CITY	Dwyer	9	5	3			1	4	11		8							12		7			2*	6		10	
26-Nov	6,013	CARDIFF CITY	3-1	Huddersfield Town	Bodin, Owen, og	9	5	3			1	4	11*		8							12		7			2	6		10	
03-Dec	9,905	Brighton	3-1	CARDIFF CITY	Baird	9	5	3			1	4	11		8									7			2	6		10	
10-Dec	5,200	CARDIFF CITY	0-1	Blackburn Rovers		9	5	3				4		12	8							11*		7	1		2	6		10	
17-Dec	14,793	Sheffield Wednesday	5-2	CARDIFF CITY	Baird 2	9	5	3*	11		1	4		12	8									7			2	6		10	
26-Dec	14,580	CARDIFF CITY	3-2	Swansea City	Gibbins, Vaughan, Lee	9	5	3			1	4			8					11				7			2	6		10	
27-Dec	16,054	Derby County	2-3	CARDIFF CITY	Baird 2, Dwyer	9	5	3	7		1	4			8					11							2	6		10	
31-Dec	7,164	Grimsby Town	1-0	CARDIFF CITY		9	5	3	7*		1	4			8					11				12			2	6		10	
21-Jan	11,938	Portsmouth	1-1	CARDIFF CITY	Lee	9	5	3			1	4	2		8					11				7				6		10	
31-Jan	4,522	CARDIFF CITY	2-1	Charlton Athletic	Owen, Bennett	9	5				1	4	2		8					11				7			3	6		10	
04-Feb	7,107	Barnsley	2-3	CARDIFF CITY	Baird, Owen, og	9	5				1	4	2		8					11				7			3	6		10	
11-Feb	9,407	CARDIFF CITY	0-1	Leeds United			5				1	4	2		8	11		10						7			3	6		9	
19-Feb	7,149	CARDIFF CITY	0-4	Fulham		11*	5				1	4	2		8	12		10						7			3	6		9	
25-Feb	27,964	Newcastle United	3-1	CARDIFF CITY	Vaughan		5				1	4	2		8			10		11				7			3	6		9	
03-Mar	4,422	CARDIFF CITY	2-1	Middlesbrough	Elsey, Goldsmith		5*				1	4	10		8	12	3			11				7			2	6		9	
10-Mar	2,512	Cambridge United	0-2	CARDIFF CITY	Smith, Vaughan						1	4	2		8	11*	3	12		10				7			5	6		9	
17-Mar	3,870	CARDIFF CITY	2-0	Shrewsbury Town	Vaughan, Owen						1	4	2		8		3	10		11				7			5	6		9	
24-Mar	20,140	Manchester City	2-1	CARDIFF CITY	Owen						1	4	2		8		3	10		11				7			5	6		9	
31-Mar	11,060	CARDIFF CITY	3-3	Chelsea	Gibbins, Vaughan, Owen (p)						1	4	2		8	12	3*	10		11				7			5	6		9	
07-Apr	4,704	Carlisle United	1-1	CARDIFF CITY	Goldsmith						1	4	2		8	12	3*	10		11				7			5	6		9	
14-Apr	4,637	CARDIFF CITY	2-0	Oldham Athletic	Owen (p), Lee						1	4	2		8		3	10		11				7			5	6		9	
17-Apr	4,901	CARDIFF CITY	0-2	Crystal Palace							1	4	2		8	12	3	10		11				7			5*	6		9	
21-Apr	10,275	Swansea City	3-2	CARDIFF CITY	Smith, Owen		10				1	4	2		8	12	3*			11				7			5	6		9	
23-Apr	5,156	CARDIFF CITY	1-0	Derby County	Owen		3				1	4	2		8			10*		11			12	7			5	6		9	
28-Apr	5,599	Huddersfield Town	4-0	CARDIFF CITY			3	7*			1	4	2		8	10				11			12				5	6		9	
05-May	4,366	CARDIFF CITY	2-2	Brighton	Lee, Vaughan		5				1	4	10		8		3			11				7			2	6		9	
07-May	3,107	Blackburn Rovers	1-1	CARDIFF CITY	Lee		10	2			1	4			8		3			11		7					5	6		9	
12-May	14,176	CARDIFF CITY	0-2	Sheffield Wednesday			5	10			1	4			8		3			11				7			2	6		9	
					Appearances	12	32	26	3	6	41	42	29	2	42	9	12	11	6	21	6	14	12	39	1	4	34	40	5	36	2
					Goals	6	2	3		1		2	1		4	2				5				14			2			8	

1 Ian Baird
2 Gary Bennett
3 Paul Bodin
4 Marshall Burke
5 Andy Crawford
6 Andy Dibble
7 Phil Dwyer
8 Karl Elsey
9 Paul Evans
10 Roger Gibbins
11 Martin Goldsmith
12 David Grant
13 Jeff Hemmerman
14 Linden Jones
15 Trevor Lee
16 John Lewis
17 Wayne Matthews
18 Jimmy Mullen
19 Gordon Owen
20 Gary Plumley
21 Chris Rodon
22 Colin Smith
23 David Tong
24 Chris Townsend
25 Nigel Vaughan
26 Phil Walker

1984-85 21st in Division Two (Relegated)

Date	Att	Home	Score	Away	Scorers	1	2	3	4	5	6	7	8	9	10	11	12	13	14	15	16	17	18	19	20	21	22	23	24	25	26	27	28	29	30
25-Aug	5,020	CARDIFF CITY	0-3	Charlton Athletic			12	4	7					8	3*		2										10	1	5	11	6	9			
01-Sep	12,133	Sheffield United	2-1	CARDIFF CITY	Gibbins	12		4	7					8	3		2										10	1	5	11	6*	9			
08-Sep	4,634	CARDIFF CITY	2-4	Brighton	Elsey, Seasman (p)	6	11	4	3			7		8*											1		10		5		2	9		12	
12-Sep	6,802	CARDIFF CITY	2-1	Leeds United	Bodin, Dwyer	8	11	4	9			7		12	3		2*							1			10		5		6				
15-Sep	4,692	Barnsley	2-0	CARDIFF CITY		8	11	4	9			7		12	3		2*							1			10		5		6				
18-Sep	5,922	Blackburn Rovers	2-1	CARDIFF CITY	Summerfield		11	4	2			7		8	3									1			10		5	6		9			
22-Sep	6,089	CARDIFF CITY	0-3	Manchester City			11	4	9			7		8	3*		2							1			10		5	6		12			
29-Sep	4,259	Middlesbrough	3-2	CARDIFF CITY	Seasman, Vaughan		11*	4				7		8	3		2					12		1			10		5		6	9			
06-Oct	6,201	CARDIFF CITY	1-2	Portsmouth	Elsey			4	11			7*		8	3		2					12					10	1	5		6	9			
14-Oct	5,893	Notts County	2-0	CARDIFF CITY	Vaughan 2		10	4	11					8	3		2					7*					12	1	5		6	9			
20-Oct	5,363	Fulham	3-2	CARDIFF CITY	Elsey, C Smith		10*	4	11					8	3		2					7					12	1	5		6	9			
27-Oct	3,607	CARDIFF CITY	2-4	Grimsby Town	Jones, Vaughan		11	4	10					8	3*		2						12				7	1	5		6	9			
03-Nov	7,537	Wolves	3-0	CARDIFF CITY				4*	10					8	3		2					12	11					1	5	7	6	9			
10-Nov	3,429	CARDIFF CITY	2-2	Oldham Athletic	Vaughan 2			4	11		7			8	5							12	3					1	2	10	6*	9			
17-Nov	2,855	CARDIFF CITY	2-1	Carlisle United	Tong, Vaughan			4	11		7			8					5				3					1	2	10	6	9			
24-Nov	6,495	Huddersfield Town	2-1	CARDIFF CITY	Vaughan			4	11		7			8				2	5			10	3					1			6	9			
01-Dec	5,057	CARDIFF CITY	1-2	Birmingham City	Elsey		12	4	11	1	7			8				2	5				3							10	6	9*			
09-Dec	6,004	Crystal Palace	1-1	CARDIFF CITY	Gibbins			4	11	1	7			10				2	6		12		3							8	5	9*			
15-Dec	2,976	CARDIFF CITY	1-3	Wimbledon	Dwyer			4	11	1	7			6					5	12	8		3						2	10		9*			
22-Dec	3,429	CARDIFF CITY	1-3	Sheffield United	Withey			4	11	1	7			8				2	5			12	3								6*	9	10		
26-Dec	12,224	Oxford United	4-0	CARDIFF CITY				4	11*		7							2	5	12	8		3					1			6	9	10		
29-Dec	11,796	Leeds United	1-1	CARDIFF CITY	Withey			4	2		7		5	8							11	12	3					1			6*	9	10		
01-Jan	4,609	CARDIFF CITY	0-0	Shrewsbury Town				4	2		7		5	8							11		3					1			6	9	10		
02-Feb	2,564	CARDIFF CITY	2-1	Middlesbrough	Meacock 2			4	3		7			6				2		11	8		5	1								9	10		
09-Feb	7,354	Brighton	1-0	CARDIFF CITY				4	11		10*		5	9				2		7	8	12	3	1							6				
16-Feb	3,592	Oldham Athletic	0-1	CARDIFF CITY	Vaughan		12	4			7		5					2		11		8	3	1							6	9*	10		
23-Feb	4,694	CARDIFF CITY	0-0	Wolves				4			7		5	12				2*		11	8		3	1							6	9	10		
02-Mar	4,589	Grimsby Town	6-3	CARDIFF CITY	Gibbins, Mullen (p), Withey			4			7*		5	12				2		11	8		3	1							6	9	10		
05-Mar	3,930	Charlton Athletic	1-4	CARDIFF CITY	Withey 2, Dwyer, Mullen (p)			4	6		7		5	9				2		11	8		3	1									10		
09-Mar	4,293	CARDIFF CITY	0-2	Fulham				4*	6		7		5	9				2		11	8		3	1								12	10		
17-Mar	3,631	CARDIFF CITY	1-4	Notts County	Gibbins			4	6*		7		5	9				2		11	8		3	1								12	10		
23-Mar	13,620	Portsmouth	0-0	CARDIFF CITY			11						5	4				2		7*	8		3	1							6	9	10		12
30-Mar	20,047	Manchester City	2-2	CARDIFF CITY	Gibbins, Withey								5	4		11		2		7			3	1		8					6	9	10		
06-Apr	6,686	CARDIFF CITY	0-2	Oxford United									5	4		11		2		7	12			1		8					6	9	10		3
09-Apr	3,919	Shrewsbury Town	0-0	CARDIFF CITY							3		5	4		11		2		7	12			1		8*					6	9	10		
13-Apr	3,387	CARDIFF CITY	1-2	Blackburn Rovers	Vaughan		3*						5	4		11		2		7	8			1		12					6	9	10		
20-Apr	2,651	Carlisle United	0-1	CARDIFF CITY	Vaughan				3				5	4		11		2		7	8			1							6	9	10		
23-Apr	3,044	CARDIFF CITY	3-0	Barnsley	Vaughan 2, M Ford		7		3				5	4		11		2			8			1							6	9	10		
27-Apr	3,414	CARDIFF CITY	3-0	Huddersfield Town	Vaughan 2, Meacock		7				6		5	4		11		2			8		3	1								9	10		
04-May	15,868	Birmingham City	2-0	CARDIFF CITY			7				6		5	4		11		2			8		3	1								9	10		
06-May	5,207	CARDIFF CITY	0-3	Crystal Palace			7*						5	4		11		2		12	8		3	1							6	9	10		
11-May	3,252	Wimbledon	2-1	CARDIFF CITY	Micallef				7		2		5	4		11						8	3	1							6	10	9		
					Appearances	4	18	31	30	4	22	7	20	40	13	10	11	23	7	17	21	12	26	24	1	4	12	13	16	10	33	38	22	1	2
					Goals		1	3	4				1	5			1				3	1	2				2		1	1	1	15	6		

1 Paul Bannon
2 Paul Bodin
3 Phil Dwyer
4 Karl Elsey
5 Dave Felgate
6 Brian Flynn
7 Gerry Francis
8 Mike Ford
9 Roger Gibbins
10 David Grant
11 David Hamilton
12 Vaughan Jones
13 Jake King
14 Mick Martin
15 Paul McLoughlin
16 Kevin Meacock
17 Tarki Micallef
18 Jimmy Mullen
19 Gary Plumley
20 Mel Rees
21 Dean Saunders
22 John Seasman
23 Lee Smelt
24 Colin Smith
25 Kevin Summerfield
26 David Tong
27 Nigel Vaughan
28 Graham Withey
29 Jonathan Woods
30 Francis Ford

1985-86 22nd in Division Three (Relegated)

Date	Att	Home	Score	Away	Scorers	1	2	3	4	5	6	7	8	9	10	11	12	13	14	15	16	17	18	19	20	21	22	23	24	25	26	27	28	29	30	31	32
17-Aug	3,856	Notts County	1-4	CARDIFF CITY	McLoughlin, Farrington, Mullen (p), Vaughan		3				8	7		5	4			2			11			6					1					9	10		
24-Aug	3,386	CARDIFF CITY	0-2	Chesterfield			3				8	7		5	4			2			11			6					1					9	10		
26-Aug	5,027	Newport County	1-2	CARDIFF CITY	Mullen (p), Vaughan		3				8*	7		5	4			2			11		12	6					1					9	10		
31-Aug	3,539	CARDIFF CITY	1-3	Reading	McLoughlin		3				8	7		5	4						11		12	6					1				2	9*	10		
07-Sep	3,760	York City	1-1	CARDIFF CITY	Ford		3				8			5	4	11	7				2	10*	12	6				1							9		
14-Sep	4,412	CARDIFF CITY	1-3	Bristol City	Withey		3				8			5	4	11*	7				2		12	6				1							9		10
17-Sep	2,000	CARDIFF CITY	0-0	Bury			3				8	7		5	4						2	12	11*	6				1							9		10
21-Sep	3,783	Blackpool	3-0	CARDIFF CITY			3			12	8	7		5	4						2		11	6				1							9*		10
28-Sep	3,232	CARDIFF CITY	0-2	Derby County			3		5	12	8	7		11	4						2			6				1							9*	10	
01-Oct	2,906	Rotherham United	3-0	CARDIFF CITY			3		5	9	8	7*		11	4						2		12	6				1								10	
05-Oct	2,156	CARDIFF CITY	0-1	Bournemouth			3		5		8	7		4	2								12	6				1							10	11	9*
12-Oct	3,367	Gillingham	2-0	CARDIFF CITY					5		8*	7		4		11			3	10			12	6				1			2			9			
19-Oct	1,961	CARDIFF CITY	3-1	Wigan Athletic	Marustik, Turner, Vaughan		3		5					4		11				10	7	12		6			2*		1					9	8		
22-Oct	2,446	Darlington	4-1	CARDIFF CITY	McLoughlin		2*		5	12				4		7				10	3	11		6				1						9	8		
26-Oct	2,502	CARDIFF CITY	0-1	Bolton Wanderers				7			11			4				5		10	2			6					1			3		9	8		
02-Nov	3,934	Brentford	3-0	CARDIFF CITY				7						4		10		5			2		11	6					1			3		9	8		
05-Nov	3,282	Walsall	6-3	CARDIFF CITY	Mullen (p), Christie, Vaughan			7			10*			4				2	3	11	12			6					1			5		9	8		
08-Nov	1,894	CARDIFF CITY	0-1	Doncaster Rovers				7						4				2	3	11	10			6						1		5		9	8		
23-Nov	4,563	Bristol Rovers	2-1	CARDIFF CITY	Mullen (p)			7		2	12					3				4			11	6		10*				1		5			8		9
30-Nov	2,453	CARDIFF CITY	1-1	Wolves	Curtis			7*		11	12					3			2	4				6						1		5		9	8	10	
14-Dec	2,127	Lincoln City	0-4	CARDIFF CITY	Vaughan, Turner, Mullen (p), Farrington			7		2	12			11		3	4							6						1		5		9	8	10*	
20-Dec	1,773	Chesterfield	3-4	CARDIFF CITY	Turner, Christie, Vaughan, Farrington			7		2	12			10		3	4*						11	6						1		5		9	8		
26-Dec	8,375	CARDIFF CITY	1-0	Swansea City	Vaughan			7		2	10			4		3							11	6						1		5		9	8		
28-Dec	7,450	CARDIFF CITY	1-1	Newport County	Ford			7*		2	10			4		3							11	6						1		5		9	8	12	
01-Jan	8,520	Plymouth Argyle	4-4	CARDIFF CITY	Turner, Ford, Vaughan, Mullen (p)			7		2	10			4		3							11	6						1		5		9	8		
04-Jan	3,398	CARDIFF CITY	1-0	Brentford	Vaughan			7		2	12			4		3							11	6						1		5		9	8	10*	
11-Jan	7,004	Reading	1-1	CARDIFF CITY	Ford			7		2	12			4		3							11	6						1		5		9	8	10*	
18-Jan	2,410	CARDIFF CITY	1-3	Notts County	Mullen (p)			7		2	10*			5		3				4			11	6						1				9	8	12	
25-Jan	7,541	Bristol City	2-1	CARDIFF CITY	Wheeler			7*			10			4		3				2	12		11	6						1		5			8	9	
31-Jan	1,988	CARDIFF CITY	2-1	York City	Vaughan, Wheeler					2*	7			5		3				4	12		11	6						1				9	8	10	
04-Feb	2,222	CARDIFF CITY	0-1	Darlington						2*	7		5	11		3				4	12			6						1				9	8	10	
08-Feb	3,428	Wigan Athletic	2-0	CARDIFF CITY				12		2*	7		5	11		3				4				6						1				9	8	10	
22-Feb	2,430	CARDIFF CITY	1-0	Blackpool	Curtis			7		2			5	11		3				4				6						1				9	8	10	
01-Mar	11,014	Derby County	2-1	CARDIFF CITY	Vaughan			7*		2	12		5	11		3				4	6									1				9	8	10	
08-Mar	2,707	Bournemouth	1-1	CARDIFF CITY	Turner					2	10*			11		3				4	5		7	6						1				9	8	12	
15-Mar	2,579	CARDIFF CITY	1-1	Gillingham	Gummer					2			5	9		3	10			4	7			6		12				1					8	11*	
22-Mar	4,114	Bolton Wanderers	5-0	CARDIFF CITY		5				2	10		12	4		3					7			6						1				9	8	11*	
25-Mar	1,663	CARDIFF CITY	2-3	Rotherham United	McLoughlin, Mullen (p)	5				2			8	11		3				4*	7		10	6					1					9		12	
28-Mar	3,824	CARDIFF CITY	1-2	Plymouth Argyle	Nardiello	5							11	4		3				2	7		10*	6	9					1				12	8		
31-Mar	6,643	Swansea City	2-0	CARDIFF CITY		5				2				11		3				4	7		10*	6	8				1					9	12		
05-Apr	1,893	CARDIFF CITY	1-1	Walsall	Foley	5							9*	11		3				2	7		10	6	8				1					12	4		
08-Apr	1,720	Bury	3-0	CARDIFF CITY		5							9*	11		3				2	7		10	6	8					1				12	4		
12-Apr	2,051	Doncaster Rovers	0-2	CARDIFF CITY	Nardiello 2	5		7*		2				11		3				4	12		10		9		6			1					8		
19-Apr	2,735	CARDIFF CITY	2-0	Bristol Rovers	Vaughan, og	5				2				11		3				4	7		10	6	9					1					8		
26-Apr	3,353	Wolves	3-1	CARDIFF CITY	Nardiello	5							12	11		3				4	2			6	9				1					10	8	7*	
03-May	1,904	CARDIFF CITY	2-1	Lincoln City	Turner 2	5				2			9	11		3				4	12			6					1					10	8	7*	
					Appearances	10	13	19	6	27	31	10	12	44	11	34	5	7	4	26	32	4	28	44	7	2	2	9	13	24	1	14	1	34	43	21	5
					Goals			2		2	3		1	4			1			1	4			8	4									7	12	2	1

1 P Brignull
2 J Carver
3 D Christie
4 D Corner
5 W Curtis
6 M Farrington
7 B Flynn
8 W Foley
9 M Ford
10 R Gibbins
11 D Giles
12 J Gummer
13 J King
14 C Leonard
15 C Marustik
16 P McLoughlin
17 K Meacock
18 T Micallef
19 J Mullen
20 G Nardiello
21 T O'Connor
22 A Price
23 M Rees
24 C Sander
25 L Smelt
26 A Spring
27 N Stevenson
28 D Tong
29 R Turner
30 N Vaughan
31 P Wheeler
32 G Withey

1986-87 13th in Division Four

Date	Att	Home	Score	Away	Scorers	1	2	3	4	5	6	7	8	9	10	11	12	13	14	15	16	17	18	19	20	21	22	23	24
23-Aug	2,804	Hartlepool United	1-1	CARDIFF CITY	Turner		6	5			12	7*			2			1					11	3		8	10	9	4
30-Aug	3,546	CARDIFF CITY	0-0	Rochdale			6	5	10			7			2			1					11	3		8		9	4
06-Sep	5,740	Wolves	0-1	CARDIFF CITY	Wimbleton		6	5	10			7			2			1					11	3		8		9	4
13-Sep	2,868	CARDIFF CITY	0-2	Tranmere Rovers			6	5	10			7			2*			1					11	3		12	8	9	4
16-Sep	2,406	CARDIFF CITY	1-1	Lincoln City	Rogers		6	5	8			7			2			1					11	3		12	10	9	4*
20-Sep	3,066	Exeter City	0-0	CARDIFF CITY			6	5	8			7			2			1					11	3			10	9	4
27-Sep	3,353	CARDIFF CITY	4-1	Hereford United	Wheeler, Vaughan, Wimbleton (p), Curtis		6	5	8			7			2			1					11	3			10	9	4
01-Oct	2,858	Peterborough United	1-2	CARDIFF CITY	Vaughan, Wheeler		6	5	8			7			2			1			12		11	3			10	9	4*
04-Oct	3,571	CARDIFF CITY	1-1	Crewe Alexandra	Vaughan		6	5	8			7			2			1			12		11	3			10	9	4
11-Oct	2,926	Wrexham	5-1	CARDIFF CITY	Vaughan		6	5	8						2		7	1			12		11*	3			10	9	4
17-Oct	3,160	Colchester United	3-1	CARDIFF CITY	Wheeler		6	5	8						2		7				12	1	11	3			10	9	4*
25-Oct	2,145	CARDIFF CITY	1-1	Scunthorpe United	Boyle		6	5	8		3	7			2						12	1	11*				10	9	4
31-Oct	1,640	Halifax Town	1-1	CARDIFF CITY	Platnauer	12	6	5	8		3				2*		11				7	1					10	9	4
04-Nov	6,636	Preston North End	0-1	CARDIFF CITY	Ford		6	5	8		3				2		11				7	1					10	9	4
08-Nov	2,987	CARDIFF CITY	0-2	Southend United		12	6	5	8		3				2*		11				7	1					10	9	4
22-Nov	1,674	Stockport County	2-0	CARDIFF CITY		12	6	5		8	3				2		11				7	1					10	9	4
29-Nov	2,071	CARDIFF CITY	3-0	Cambridge United	Bartlett 2, Wimbleton (p)	8	6	5	7		3	2					11	1					9				10		4
13-Dec	2,443	CARDIFF CITY	2-0	Aldershot	Platnauer, Vaughan	8	6	5			3	2					11	1		9*	7						10	12	4
19-Dec	1,717	Burnley	1-3	CARDIFF CITY	Vaughan, Pike, Wimbleton	8	6	5			3	2					11	1		9	7						10		4
26-Dec	11,450	CARDIFF CITY	0-0	Swansea City		8	6	5	12		3	2					11	1		9	7*						10		4
28-Dec	11,138	Northampton Town	4-1	CARDIFF CITY	Pike	8	6	5	12		3				2		11	1		9	7						10		4*
03-Jan	3,038	CARDIFF CITY	1-1	Stockport County	Wheeler		6	5	8		3	2*					11	1			7		12				10	9	4
24-Jan	3,331	CARDIFF CITY	0-2	Wolves			6	5	10	12	3	2					11			9	7	1						8	4
07-Feb	1,954	Lincoln City	0-1	CARDIFF CITY	Wimbleton (p)	8	6	5	10		3				2		11	1		9	7								4
21-Feb	3,969	Hereford United	0-2	CARDIFF CITY	Horrix, og	12	6		10		3			9	5		2	1			7			8	11*				4
24-Feb	1,456	Tranmere Rovers	2-1	CARDIFF CITY	Simmons	12	6		10		3			9	5		2	1			7		8		11*				4
28-Feb	2,620	CARDIFF CITY	0-1	Peterborough United		12	6	5	7		3			9	2			1			10		11		8*				4
03-Mar	1,785	CARDIFF CITY	0-0	Halifax Town		12	6	5	7		3			9	2			1			10		11		8*				4
07-Mar	1,936	Scunthorpe United	1-3	CARDIFF CITY	Horrix 2, Kerr		6	5	10		3			9	2			1			7		11					8	4
10-Mar	1,386	Rochdale	0-0	CARDIFF CITY			6	5	10		3			9	2			1			7		11*		12			8	4
14-Mar	2,222	CARDIFF CITY	0-2	Colchester United			6	5	10		3		12	9	2*		11	1			7							8	4
17-Mar	2,411	Orient	2-0	CARDIFF CITY			6	5	10		3		11	9	2			1			7			12				8	4
21-Mar	1,556	CARDIFF CITY	0-0	Wrexham		12	6		10		3		11	9*	2						7	1		5				8	4
24-Mar	1,362	CARDIFF CITY	1-1	Orient	Platnauer	9	6		10		3		12		2						7	1		5			11	8	4*
28-Mar	1,762	Crewe Alexandra	1-2	CARDIFF CITY	Wheeler 2	9*	6		10		3		5		2	12					7	1					11	8	4
31-Mar	1,868	CARDIFF CITY	0-0	Exeter City		9*	6	5	10		3		11			12			2		7	1						8	4
03-Apr	3,917	Southend United	2-0	CARDIFF CITY			6	5	10		3		11*		2	9					7	1					12	8	4
11-Apr	2,528	CARDIFF CITY	1-1	Preston North End	Wimbleton	12	6	5*	10		3				2	9					7	1					11	8	4
18-Apr	1,840	CARDIFF CITY	3-1	Torquay United	Mardenborough, Curtis, Wheeler	12	6		10		3		5			9					7	1	11				2	8*	4
20-Apr	6,653	Swansea City	2-0	CARDIFF CITY			6	5	10		3		11*			9					7	1	12				2	8	4
25-Apr	2,003	CARDIFF CITY	1-0	Burnley	Wimbleton (p)		6		10		3		11			9					7	1	5				2	8	4
28-Apr	1,440	Torquay United	1-0	CARDIFF CITY		8	6		10		3		11*			9					7	1	5				2	12	4
01-May	1,368	Cambridge United	2-1	CARDIFF CITY	Gummer	8	6		10		3		11			9					7	1	5*				2	12	4
04-May	2,682	CARDIFF CITY	1-1	Northampton Town	Curtis		6		10		3		11			9					7	1	5				2	8	4
07-May	1,510	CARDIFF CITY	4-0	Hartlepool United	Curtis, Gummer, Bartlett, Wimbleton	12	6		10		3		11			9*					7	1	5				2	8	4
09-May	3,680	Aldershot	1-2	CARDIFF CITY	Gummer, Bartlett	9	6		10		3		11								7	1	5				2	8	4
					Appearances	23	46	34	42	2	36	16	15	9	31	11	17	25	1	6	38	21	27	15	5	5	32	37	46
					Goals	4	1		4		1		3	3	1	1				2	3		1		1	1	6	7	8

1 Kevin Bartlett
2 Terry Boyle
3 Phil Brignull
4 Alan Curtis
5 Gary Davies
6 Mike Ford
7 David Giles
8 Jason Gummer
9 Dean Horrix
10 Andy Kerr
11 Steve Mardenborough
12 Chris Marustik
13 Graham Moseley
14 Jason Perry
15 Chris Pike
16 Nicky Platnauer
17 Mel Rees
18 Alan Rogers
19 Steve Sherlock
20 Tony Simmons
21 Robbie Turner
22 Nigel Vaughan
23 Paul Wheeler
24 Paul Wimbleton

1987-88 2nd in Division Four (Promoted)

Date	Att	Home	Score	Away	Scorers	1	2	3	4	5	6	7	8	9	10	11	12	13	14	15	16	17	18	19	20	21	22	23
15-Aug	3,357	CARDIFF CITY	1-1	Leyton Orient	Gilligan				6	7		3	9	4*		11	12	10	1	2			8	5				
22-Aug	4,530	Bolton Wanderers	1-0	CARDIFF CITY			14		6	7		3	9			11*		10	1	2*	4		8	5		12		
29-Aug	5,790	CARDIFF CITY	1-0	Swansea City	Gilligan				6	7		3	9			11	2	10	1		4		8	5				
01-Sep	2,079	Cambridge United	0-0	CARDIFF CITY			12		6	7		3	9			11	2	10	1		4		8*	5				
05-Sep	2,258	CARDIFF CITY	3-2	Wolves	McDermott, Bartlett, Boyle		8		6	7		2	9*			11	4	10	1	5	3		12					
12-Sep	2,212	Wrexham	3-0	CARDIFF CITY		5	8	3	6	7*		2	9			11	14	10	1				12				4*	
15-Sep	2,138	CARDIFF CITY	3-1	Darlington	Bartlett 2, Abraham	5	8	3	6	7		2	9			11		10	1								4	
19-Sep	2,659	CARDIFF CITY	4-2	Carlisle United	Wimbleton, Ford, Boyle, Gilligan		8*	2	6	7		3	9			11		10	1		5		12				4	
25-Sep	2,543	Tranmere Rovers	0-1	CARDIFF CITY	Wimbleton		8*	2	6	7		3	9			11		10	1		5					12	4	
29-Sep	3,566	CARDIFF CITY	0-0	Halifax United			8		6	7		2	9			11*		10	1		3		12	5			4	
02-Oct	2,332	Stockport County	0-1	CARDIFF CITY	Bartlett		8*	2	6	7		3	9					10	1		11		12	5			4	
10-Oct	4,399	CARDIFF CITY	0-1	Hereford United			8	2	6	7		11	9			12		10*	1		3*		14	5			4	
17-Oct	3,473	Peterborough United	4-3	CARDIFF CITY	Ford 2, McDermott		14	2	6	7		11	9			5	8*	10*	1		3		12				4	
20-Oct	3,455	CARDIFF CITY	2-1	Torquay United	Ford, Gilligan			2	6	7		11	9	14	1	5	8*	10*			3					12	4	
24-Oct	2,872	Scunthorpe United	2-1	CARDIFF CITY	Sanderson			2	6			5	9		1	11	8*	10			3		14	12		7*	4	
31-Oct	3,046	CARDIFF CITY	1-0	Rochdale	Gilligan		12	2	6			4	9		1	11	8	10			3			5		7*		
04-Nov	2,599	Scarborough	1-1	CARDIFF CITY	Wimbleton			2	6	7		8	9		1	12		10			3		11	5*			4	
07-Nov	3,474	CARDIFF CITY	3-2	Exeter City	Gilligan 2, Boyle		12	2	6	7*		8	9		1	5	14	10			3		11*				4	
21-Nov	4,158	Newport County	1-2	CARDIFF CITY	Wimbleton, Platnauer		11*	2	6	7		8	9			5	12	10			3	1					4	
28-Nov	3,232	CARDIFF CITY	1-1	Hartlepool United	McDermott		10*	2	6	7		5	9		1	8*	12	11			3		14				4	
12-Dec	2,010	Crewe Alexandra	0-0	CARDIFF CITY				2	6			5	9		1		7	10			3			8		11	4	
19-Dec	3,401	CARDIFF CITY	2-1	Burnley	Gilligan 2		14	2	6			8	9		1	12	7*	10			3			5*		11	4	
26-Dec	5,233	CARDIFF CITY	3-0	Tranmere Rovers	Gilligan 2, Wimbleton			2	6	7	1	8	9			12		10*			3		14	5		11*	4	
28-Dec	2,599	Colchester United	2-1	CARDIFF CITY	Kelly			2	6	7*	1	8	9			11		10*			3		14	5		12	4	
01-Jan	9,560	Swansea City	2-2	CARDIFF CITY	Ford, Gilligan		14	2	6	7	1	8	9			12		10*			3			5		11*	4	
16-Jan	2,344	Carlisle United	0-0	CARDIFF CITY			11*	2	6	7	1	8	9					10			3		12	5			4	
30-Jan	3,940	CARDIFF CITY	4-0	Cambridge United	Wimbleton (p), Bartlett, McDermott, Boyle		11*	2	6	7		8	9				14	10			3*			5		12	4	1
02-Feb	2,332	Darlington	0-0	CARDIFF CITY			11*	2	6	7		8	9				12	10			3			5			4	1
06-Feb	10,077	Wolves	1-4	CARDIFF CITY	Gilligan 2, Wimbleton 2		11	2	6	7		8	9					10			3			5			4	1
13-Feb	5,458	CARDIFF CITY	1-0	Colchester United	Ford		11	2	6	7*		8	9				12	10			3			5			4	1
20-Feb	3,523	Leyton Orient	4-1	CARDIFF CITY	Bartlett		11	2	6	7*		8	9				12	10*			3			5	14		4	1
27-Feb	3,937	CARDIFF CITY	0-0	Stockport County				2	6	7		8	9			3		10*				1	12	5	11*	14	4	
01-Mar	1,128	Halifax Town	0-1	CARDIFF CITY	Bartlett		11	2	6			8	9			3		10				1	7	5			4	
04-Mar	4,172	CARDIFF CITY	0-0	Peterborough United			11*	2	6			8	9			3	12	10				1	7*	5		14	4	
13-Mar	3,210	Hereford United	1-2	CARDIFF CITY	Gilligan, Bartlett		11	2	6	7		8	9			3		10				1		5			4	
16-Mar	4,083	CARDIFF CITY	1-1	Wrexham	Gilligan		11*	2	6	7		8	9			3		10				1		5	12		4	
26-Mar	4,527	CARDIFF CITY	0-1	Scunthorpe United			11	2	6	7*		8	9			14		10*			3	1		5	12		4	
29-Mar	1,435	Rochdale	2-2	CARDIFF CITY	Bartlett, og		11*	2	6	7		8	9					10			3	1		5	12		4	
02-Apr	2,649	Exeter City	0-2	CARDIFF CITY	Bartlett 2		11*	2	6	7*		8	9			14		10			3			5	12		4	1
04-Apr	6,536	CARDIFF CITY	4-0	Newport County	Stevenson, Wimbleton, McDermott, Ford		11*	2	6	7		8	9				12	10			3			5			4	1
09-Apr	3,082	Torquay United	2-0	CARDIFF CITY			11	2	6	7		8	9*			14	12	10			3			5			4*	1
15-Apr	6,703	CARDIFF CITY	1-0	Bolton Wanderers	Gilligan		11	2	6	7		8	9			10					3			5			4	1
23-Apr	5,751	CARDIFF CITY	2-0	Scarborough	Curtis, McDermott (p)		11	2	6	7			9			10		8			3			5		12	4*	1
30-Apr	1,101	Hartlepool United	0-1	CARDIFF CITY	Gilligan		11	2	6	7		4	9			10		8			3			5				1
02-May	9,852	CARDIFF CITY	2-0	Crewe Alexandra	Bartlett, McDermott		11*	2	6	7		4	9			10		8			3			5		12		1
07-May	8,421	Burnley	1-2	CARDIFF CITY	Curtis, Gilligan		11*	2	6	7		4	9			10		8			3			5		12		1
					Appearances	2	37	40	46	40	4	45	46	2	8	36	21	45	13	3	38	8	21	36	6	16	37	13
					Goals	1	12		4	2		7	19			1		7			1		1	1			9	

1 Gareth Abraham
2 Kevin Bartlett
3 Phil Bater
4 Terry Boyle
5 Alan Curtis
6 Scott Endersby
7 Mike Ford
8 Jimmy Gilligan
9 Jason Gummer
10 Alan Judge
11 Mark Kelly
12 Steve Mardenborough
13 Brian McDermott
14 Graham Moseley
15 Jason Perry
16 Nicky Platnauer
17 Jon Roberts
18 Paul Sanderson
19 Nigel Stevenson
20 Ian Walsh
21 Paul Wheeler
22 Paul Wimbleton
23 George Wood

1988-89 16th in Division Three

Date	Att	Home	Score	Away	Scorers	1	2	3	4	5	6	7	8	9	10	11	12	13	14	15	16	17	18	19	20	21	22	23	24	25
27-Aug	6,084	CARDIFF CITY	1-2	Fulham	Walsh		12	2	6	7			9				11		4*	10		3		14	5		8*			1
03-Sep	48,311	Bolton Wanderers	4-0	CARDIFF CITY			12		6	7			9	10*			11		14			3*		2	5		8		4	1
10-Sep	3,891	CARDIFF CITY	3-0	Huddersfield Town	Walsh 2, Stevenson				6				9	10			11		7			3		2	5*	12	8		4	1
17-Sep	4,280	Port Vale	6-1	CARDIFF CITY	Gilligan			12	6*	7			9	10					11	8		3		2	5				4	1
23-Sep	3,225	Southend United	0-0	CARDIFF CITY				12	6	8			9	10*			11		7			3		2	5				4	1
01-Oct	5,023	CARDIFF CITY	2-2	Bristol Rovers	Gilligan, Bartlett		12	10*	6	8			9				11		7*	14		3		2	5				4	1
08-Oct	4,057	CARDIFF CITY	1-2	Reading	Curtis		8*	2	6	7			9				11			10	4	3			5			12		1
15-Oct	2,834	Chester City	0-0	CARDIFF CITY		4	8	2	6				9					10	11		3				5			7		1
22-Oct	3,566	Mansfield Town	2-2	CARDIFF CITY	Ketteridge, McDermott		8	2	6				9				4	10	11	7				3	5					1
29-Oct	3,849	Blackpool	1-0	CARDIFF CITY		6	8						9				4	10	11	12		2		3	5				7*	1
01-Nov	2,411	CARDIFF CITY	3-0	Bury	Gilligan, Bartlett, Ketteridge	6	12			7			9				10	8	11*			3		2	5				4	1
05-Nov	3,640	CARDIFF CITY	1-0	Gillingham	Bartlett	6	8			7			9				11	10				3		2	5				4	1
12-Nov	3,342	CARDIFF CITY	1-0	Northampton Town	Bartlett	6	8	12		7			9				11	10				3		2	5*				4	1
25-Nov	3,405	CARDIFF CITY	1-0	Brentford	Gilligan	5	8	12	6	7			9						11*			3		2		10			4	1
03-Dec	4,976	Preston North End	3-3	CARDIFF CITY	Bartlett 2, Gilligan	5	8	12	6	7			9						11			3		2		10*			4	1
17-Dec	7,493	Bristol City	2-0	CARDIFF CITY		5	8	12	6	7*			9	10					11			3		2				14	4	1
26-Dec	10,675	CARDIFF CITY	2-2	Swansea City	Gilligan 2	5	8		6	7			9	10*			12		11					2	3				4	1
30-Dec	4,621	CARDIFF CITY	2-2	Wigan Athletic	Bartlett, Curtis	5	8*		6	7			9				10		11					2	3			12	4	1
02-Jan	2,768	Aldershot	0-1	CARDIFF CITY	Curtis	5	8*		6	7			9				10		11					2	3			12	4	1
10-Jan	14,870	Wolves	2-0	CARDIFF CITY		5	8*	14	6	7*			9				10		11					2	3			12	4	1
14-Jan	4,212	CARDIFF CITY	1-0	Bolton Wanderers	Bartlett	5	8	6	14	7*			9				10*		11					2	3			12	4	1
21-Jan	4,869	Huddersfield Town	1-0	CARDIFF CITY		5*	8	6	14				9				10		11*			7		2	3			12	4	1
28-Jan	4,507	CARDIFF CITY	3-0	Port Vale	Gilligan 2, Bartlett		8	3	5				9				10*		11		12	7		2	6				4	1
04-Feb	5,815	Bristol Rovers	0-1	CARDIFF CITY	Gilligan		8*	3	5				9				10		11		14	7		2	6*			12	4	1
11-Feb	5,826	CARDIFF CITY	0-0	Sheffield United		7	8	6	5				9				10		11			3		2					4	1
18-Feb	4,359	Reading	3-1	CARDIFF CITY	Walsh	6		8*	5	7*			9				12		11			3		2			14	10	4	1
28-Feb	4,266	Notts County	2-0	CARDIFF CITY		6*		8	5	7			9						11			3		2			12	10	4	1
04-Mar	3,217	CARDIFF CITY	0-0	Mansfield Town		6		8	5	7			9				12		11			3		2			14	10*	4*	1
11-Mar	2,934	Gillingham	1-2	CARDIFF CITY	Boyle, Platnauer	6		14	5	7			9				8		11		12	3		2				10*	4*	1
18-Mar	4,261	Fulham	2-0	CARDIFF CITY		6		14	5	7			9				8*		11*		12	3		2				10	4	1
21-Mar	2,888	Chesterfield	4-0	CARDIFF CITY		6		11*	5	7			9				12		14		8*	3		2				10	4	1
25-Mar	3,251	CARDIFF CITY	3-2	Aldershot	Gilligan (p), Wheeler, Curtis			8	5	7			9			12			11*			3		2	6			10	4	1
27-Mar	9,201	Swansea City	1-1	CARDIFF CITY	Gilligan			8	5	7			9						11			3		2	6		12	10*	4	1
01-Apr	6,358	CARDIFF CITY	1-1	Bristol City	Platnauer			8	5				9				7		11		4	3		2	6		12	10*		1
04-Apr	7,219	CARDIFF CITY	1-1	Wolves	Platnauer				5	7		14	9						11		8*	3		2	6		12	10*	4	1
07-Apr	2,296	Wigan Athletic	1-0	CARDIFF CITY				8	5	7*		14	9						11			3		2	6		10*	12	4	1
11-Apr	11,618	Sheffield United	0-1	CARDIFF CITY	Abraham	5		8				7	9						11		4	3		2	6			10		1
15-Apr	2,124	Bury	1-0	CARDIFF CITY		5		8		12	14	7	9						11*		4	3		2	6			10*		1
18-Apr	3,073	CARDIFF CITY	0-1	Notts County		5		2		7	14	12	9				11*				4	3			6			10*	8	1
22-Apr	3,268	CARDIFF CITY	2-0	Southend United	Abraham, Gilligan	5		2		7	11*	10	9								4	3			6		12		8	1
29-Apr	3,194	Northampton Town	3-0	CARDIFF CITY		5		6		7	14	10	9				11*				4	3		2*	12				8	1
01-May	3,244	CARDIFF CITY	0-1	Chesterfield		5		8		7	11*	10	9	14							4	3		2	6*			12		1
05-May	3,196	CARDIFF CITY	0-0	Preston North End		5		8	6	7	11*	10	9	14							4	3		2*				12		1
09-May	2,962	CARDIFF CITY	2-0	Chester City	Boyle, Gilligan	5*		2	6	7	11*	10	9	8							4	3						12	14	1
13-May	4,865	Brentford	1-1	CARDIFF CITY	Gummer	5			6		11*	10	9	8	14						12	3	1			2		7*	4	
16-May	3,426	CARDIFF CITY	0-0	Blackpool		5		8*	6	7*	14	4	9	10					11		12	3		2						1
					Appearances	31	22	36	36	35	9	12	46	11	1	1	28	6	36	6	19	39	1	40	32	4	11	27	36	45
					Goals	2	9		2	4			14	1				2		1		3			1		4	1		

1 Gareth Abraham
2 Kevin Bartlett
3 Phil Bater
4 Terry Boyle
5 Alan Curtis
6 Chris Fry
7 Roger Gibbins
8 Jimmy Gilligan
9 Jason Gummer
10 Richard Haig
11 Matty Holmes
12 Mark Kelly
13 Steve Ketteridge
14 Steve Lynex
15 Brian McDermott
16 Jon Morgan
17 Nicky Platnauer
18 Jon Roberts
19 Ian Rodgerson
20 Nigel Stevenson
21 Steve Tupling
22 Ian Walsh
23 Paul Wheeler
24 Paul Wimbleton
25 George Wood

1989-90 21st in Division Three (Relegated)

Date	Att	Home	Score	Away	Scorers	1	2	3	4	5	6	7	8	9	10	11	12	13	14	15	16	17	18	19	20	21	22	23	24	25	26	27	28	29	30
19-Aug	4,681	CARDIFF CITY	0-2	Bolton Wanderers		5				7		12	4	9					10				3	8	6	11*		2						1	
26-Aug	5,268	Tranmere Rovers	3-0	CARDIFF CITY		5				7		12	4*	9		14			10				3	8	6	11*		2						1	
02-Sep	3,499	CARDIFF CITY	2-2	Brentford	Gilligan, Fry	5				7	3	12		9					10				4	8	6	11*		2						1	
09-Sep	2,767	Mansfield Town	1-0	CARDIFF CITY		5				7	3	12		9					10			11*	4	8*	6			2		14				1	
16-Sep	5,970	CARDIFF CITY	0-3	Bristol City		5				7	3	12		9					10				4*	8	6			2		11				1	
23-Sep	2,345	Wigan Athletic	1-1	CARDIFF CITY	Lynex	5				7	3	12		9					10			14	4*	8	6			2		11*				1	
26-Sep	2,801	CARDIFF CITY	2-3	Northampton Town	Pike, Lynex	5				7	3	12		9					10*				4	8	6	11		2						1	
30-Sep	5,013	Rotherham United	4-0	CARDIFF CITY		5				7	3	12	6						10	8			4			11		2		9*				1	
07-Oct	5,835	Huddersfield Town	2-3	CARDIFF CITY	Pike 2(p), Griffith	5	4				3	12			8*				10	9*			14	7	6	11		2					1		
13-Oct	3,675	CARDIFF CITY	1-1	Chester City	Barnard	5	4				3	11*			8			1	10	12	2		9	7	6										
17-Oct	6,377	CARDIFF CITY	1-1	Bristol Rovers	Kelly	5	4				3				8			1	10	9			7	12	6	11*		2							
21-Oct	3,502	Blackpool	1-0	CARDIFF CITY		5	4				3		6		8			1	10*	9	12		7*	11				2				14			
28-Oct	2,370	CARDIFF CITY	1-1	Leyton Orient	Griffith	5	4				3		6		8			1	10	9				7*		11		2	12						
31-Oct	7,468	Birmingham City	1-1	CARDIFF CITY	Morgan	5	4				3		6		8				10	9				7		11		2					1		
03-Nov	3,437	CARDIFF CITY	3-1	Bury	Pike 2, Barnard	5	4		11		3		6		8			1	10					7*		9	12	2							
11-Nov	4,030	Fulham	2-5	CARDIFF CITY	Pike 2, Griffith, Morgan, og	5	4		11		3	12	6		8*			1	10					7		9*		2	14						
25-Nov	3,307	CARDIFF CITY	3-0	Preston North End	Rodgerson, Pike, Griffith	5	4		11*		3	12	6		8			1	10					7		9*		2	14						
02-Dec	3,393	Crewe Alexandra	1-1	CARDIFF CITY	Morgan	5	4		11*		3	12	6		8			1	10				14	7		9*		2							
16-Dec	3,610	CARDIFF CITY	1-3	Notts County	Pike	5*	4		11		3		6		8				10				7*	12		9		2	14					1	
26-Dec	12,244	Swansea City	0-1	CARDIFF CITY	Barnard		4				3		6		8		14	1			10		11	7*	5	9*		2	12						
30-Dec	4,256	Walsall	0-2	CARDIFF CITY	Griffith, Pike		4				3		6		8			1			10		11	7	5	9		2							
13-Jan	4,300	CARDIFF CITY	0-0	Tranmere Rovers		5	4				3		6		8		12	1	11					7*	10	9		2							
20-Jan	7,017	Bolton Wanderers	3-1	CARDIFF CITY	Griffith	5*	4		7		3		6		8		12	1	11						10*	9		2							14
03-Feb	3,218	CARDIFF CITY	1-1	Wigan Athletic	Rodgerson	5	4		7		3	12	6		8*			1	11*		14				10	9		2							
10-Feb	11,982	Bristol City	1-0	CARDIFF CITY		5	4		12		3		6		8			1	11				14	7*	10*	9		2							
17-Feb	2,086	CARDIFF CITY	0-0	Crewe Alexandra		5	4		10		3		6		8			1	11				7			9		2							
21-Feb	5,174	Brentford	0-1	CARDIFF CITY	Abraham	5	4				3		6		8			1	10				11		7	9		2							
24-Feb	5,719	Preston North End	4-0	CARDIFF CITY		5*	4		14		3	12	6		8			1	10				11*		7	9		2							
02-Mar	2,751	CARDIFF CITY	0-1	Shrewsbury Town		14	4		11*		3	12	6		8			1	10					5*	7	9		2							
06-Mar	2,570	CARDIFF CITY	2-0	Rotherham United	Pike, Barnard	12	4		11		3		6		8			1	10*					5	7	9		2							
10-Mar	2,574	Northampton Town	1-1	CARDIFF CITY	Pike	10	4		11*		3	12*	6		8			1						5	7	9		2	14						
13-Mar	2,318	Shrewsbury Town	0-0	CARDIFF CITY		5	4				3		6		8		11*	1			12			7*	10	9		2			14				
17-Mar	2,628	CARDIFF CITY	1-5	Huddersfield Town	Pike	5					3	12	6		8			1	11		14			7*	10	9		2			4*				
20-Mar	1,874	Chester City	1-0	CARDIFF CITY		5	4		11		3*		6		8			1	7		12				10	9		2							
24-Mar	4,631	Bristol Rovers	2-1	CARDIFF CITY	Rodgerson	5	4	3	11*				6		8			1						7	10	9		2	12						
27-Mar	2,280	CARDIFF CITY	1-0	Mansfield Town	Barnard	12	4		11		3		6		8			1	5				7*		10	9		2							
31-Mar	2,850	CARDIFF CITY	2-2	Blackpool	Gibbins, Pike		4		11		3		6		8			1	5				7		10	9		2							
07-Apr	3,411	Leyton Orient	3-1	CARDIFF CITY	Pike	5	4		12		3		6		8			1	7						10	9		2	11*						
10-Apr	3,322	CARDIFF CITY	0-1	Birmingham City		5	4	12	11		3		6		8			1	7*						10	9		2							
14-Apr	3,198	Reading	0-1	CARDIFF CITY	Griffith	5*			11*		3	12	6		8			1	7				14	4	10	9		2							
16-Apr	8,356	CARDIFF CITY	0-2	Swansea City				12			3	11*	6		8			1	7				5	4*	10	9		2	14						
21-Apr	5,532	Notts County	2-1	CARDIFF CITY	Pike (p)		4				3	12	6		8			1	7				5	11*	10	9		2							
24-Apr	2,509	CARDIFF CITY	3-1	Walsall	Barnard, Pike, Griffith		4		5		3	12	6		8			1	7				11*		10	9		2							
28-Apr	3,666	CARDIFF CITY	3-3	Fulham	Daniel, Barnard, Rodgerson		4	12	5*		3	11*	6		8			1	7		14				10	9		2							
01-May	3,508	CARDIFF CITY	3-2	Reading	Barnard, Griffith, Pike (p)		4	5	11		3		6		8			1	7*		12				10	9		2							
05-May	4,224	Bury	2-0	CARDIFF CITY			4	5	11*		3		6		8			1	7		12			14	10	9		2							
					Appearances	37	35	6	24	8	43	23	38	7	38	1	4	35	41	7	11	2	26	32	36	41	1	45	9	4	2	1	2	9	1
					Goals	1	8				1	1	1	1	9				1				2	3		18		4							

1 Gareth Abraham
2 Leigh Barnard
3 Nathan Blake
4 Jeff Chandler
5 Alan Curtis
6 Ray C Daniel
7 Chris Fry
8 Roger Gibbins
9 Jimmy Gilligan
10 Cohen Griffith
11 Jason Gummer
12 Richard Haig
13 Roger Hansbury
14 Mark Kelly
15 David Kevan
16 Allan Lewis
17 Ian Love
18 Steve Lynex
19 Jon Morgan
20 Jason Perry
21 Chris Pike
22 Cliff Powell
23 Ian Rodgerson
24 Morrys Scott
25 Richard Sendall
26 Chris Thompson
27 Steve Tupling
28 Gavin Ward
29 George Wood
30 Eddie Youds

1990-91 13th in Division Four

Date	Att	Home	Score	Away	Scorers	1	2	3	4	5	6	7	8	9	10	11	12	13	14	15	16	17	18	19	20	21	22	23	24	25	26	27	28	29
25-Aug	3,819	CARDIFF CITY	0-0	Scarborough		5		4	12	14	3			9	8	1	11		7					6	10	2								
01-Sep	2,897	Hartlepool United	0-2	CARDIFF CITY	Griffith, Pike	5		4	12		3			9	8	1	11		7					6	10	2								
08-Sep	3,656	CARDIFF CITY	3-3	Torquay United	Pike 2(p), Griffith			4	5		3			9	8	1	11		7					6	10	2								
15-Sep	3,152	Lincoln City	0-0	CARDIFF CITY				4	5		3			9	8	1	11		7	14		12		6	10	2								
18-Sep	2,310	Aldershot	0-0	CARDIFF CITY				4	5		3			9	8	1	11		7			10		6		2								
22-Sep	3,374	CARDIFF CITY	3-3	Stockport County	Griffith, Pike, Gibbins			4	5		3			9	8	1	11					7		6	10	2								
29-Sep	2,573	Scunthorpe United	0-2	CARDIFF CITY	Pike 2(p)			4	12		3			9	8	1	11		7			5		6	10	2								
02-Oct	3,391	CARDIFF CITY	0-1	Rochdale				4	12		3			9	8	1	11		7	14		5		6	10	2								
05-Oct	3,452	CARDIFF CITY	1-0	Wrexham	Pike			4	1		3			9	8	1	11		7			5		6	10	2								
13-Oct	2,596	York City	1-2	CARDIFF CITY	Blake 2			4	10		3		14	9	8	1	11		7	5				6		2		12						
20-Oct	5,782	Hereford United	1-1	CARDIFF CITY	Jones			4	10		3			9	8	1	11		7	5				6	12	2								
23-Oct	3,891	CARDIFF CITY	0-2	Doncaster Rovers				4	10		3		12	9	8	1	11		7	5				6		2								
27-Oct	2,940	CARDIFF CITY	1-1	Peterborough United	Pike			4	9		3		12		8	1			7	5			14	6	10	2		11						
03-Nov	2,010	Maidstone United	3-0	CARDIFF CITY				4	12					9	8	1	11		7	5		2		6	10			3		14				
10-Nov	2,019	CARDIFF CITY	2-1	Chesterfield	Gibbins, Pike			4						9	8	1	11		7	2		5		6	10			3						
24-Nov	2,821	Gillingham	4-0	CARDIFF CITY			5						12		8	1	11		7	2			4	6		9		3	10	14				
01-Dec	6,353	Burnley	2-0	CARDIFF CITY								4		9	8	1	11		7	2		5	14	6	10			3	12					
15-Dec	2,017	CARDIFF CITY	0-2	Walsall					4			8	2	9		1	11			12		5		6	10			3			7			
21-Dec	3,033	Northampton Town	0-0	CARDIFF CITY					2			4	12	9	8	1	11					5		6	10			3			7			
26-Dec	2,281	CARDIFF CITY	3-1	Carlisle United	Taylor 2, Pike				4			6	2	9	8	1	11		12			5			10			3			7			
29-Dec	2,903	CARDIFF CITY	1-0	Halifax Town	Taylor				4			6	2	9	8	1	11		12	14		5			10			3			7			
01-Jan	3,151	Darlington	4-1	CARDIFF CITY	Griffith				4					9	8	1	11		2	12		5		6	10			3			7			
12-Jan	2,619	CARDIFF CITY	1-0	Hartlepool United	Griffith				4				10	9	8	1			2	11		5		6				3			7			
26-Jan	2,513	CARDIFF CITY	0-1	Lincoln City					4				12	9	8	1			6	11		2		5	10		7	3						
01-Feb	1,629	CARDIFF CITY	1-3	Aldershot	Gibbins			6	4				10	9	8	1				11		2		5	12		7	3						
15-Feb	2,170	CARDIFF CITY	2-0	Gillingham	Gibbins, Pike (p)			6	4					9	8	1	11					2	14	5	10		7	3						
19-Feb	1,192	Scarborough	1-2	CARDIFF CITY	Griffith 2			6	4				7	9	8	1	11			12		2		5	10			3						
23-Feb	3,065	Chesterfield	0-0	CARDIFF CITY				6	4				7	9	8	1	11					2		5	10			3	12					
26-Feb	3,376	Stockport County	1-1	CARDIFF CITY	Blake			6	4				7	9	8	1	11					2		5	10			3						
01-Mar	3,591	CARDIFF CITY	3-0	Burnley	Heard, Pike (p), Griffith			6	4				7	9	8	1	11					2		5	10			3						
09-Mar	3,950	Walsall	0-0	CARDIFF CITY				6	4				7	9	8	1	11					2		5	10			3						
12-Mar	1,569	Rochdale	0-0	CARDIFF CITY				6	4				7	9	8	1	11					2		5	10			3				12		
16-Mar	2,873	CARDIFF CITY	1-0	Scunthorpe United	Pike (p)			6	4				7	9	8	1	11			14		2		5	10			3				12		
19-Mar	2,620	CARDIFF CITY	2-1	York City	Heard, Barnard			6	4				7	9	8	1	11					2		5	10			3				12		
22-Mar	1,787	Wrexham	1-0	CARDIFF CITY				6	4				12	9	8	1	11			14		2		5	10			3				7		
30-Mar	2,263	Carlisle United	3-2	CARDIFF CITY	Matthews, Blake				4			6		9	8	1	11	7			10	2		5				3						
01-Apr	4,805	CARDIFF CITY	1-0	Northampton Town	og				4			6		9	8	1	11	7			10	2		5				3						
06-Apr	1,364	Halifax Town	1-2	CARDIFF CITY	Pike, Heard			12				4		9	8	1	11	7			6	2		5	10			3						
10-Apr	3,341	Torquay United	2-1	CARDIFF CITY	Gibbins			12				4		9	8	1	11	7		14	6	2		5	10			3						
13-Apr	4,544	CARDIFF CITY	0-1	Darlington								4		9	8	1	11	7		5	6	2			10			3						
17-Apr	4,813	Blackpool	3-0	CARDIFF CITY					8			4		9	12	1	11	7		14	6	2		5	10			3						
20-Apr	2,845	CARDIFF CITY	0-2	Hereford United					8			4		9	12	1	11	7		14	6	2		5	10			3						
27-Apr	2,227	Doncaster Rovers	1-1	CARDIFF CITY	Heath				12			4		9	8	1		7		11	6	2		5	10			3						
02-May	1,793	CARDIFF CITY	1-1	Blackpool	Griffith				11			4	12	9	8	1		7		6		2		5	10			3		14				
04-May	6,642	Peterborough United	3-0	CARDIFF CITY					11			4	12	9	8	1		7		6		2		5	10			3						
11-May	2,011	CARDIFF CITY	0-0	Maidstone United			2		11				9		8	1*		7	4	6				5	10			3					12	14
					Appearances	2	2	28	40	1	13	15	23	43	45	46	38	11	22	27	8	37	4	43	39	14	3	35	3	3	6	4	1	1
					Goals			1	4					5	9		3	1	1			1			14						3			

1 Gareth Abraham
2 Lee Baddeley
3 Leigh Barnard
4 Nathan Blake
5 Jeff Chandler
6 Ray C Daniel
7 Ken de Mange
8 Chris Fry
9 Roger Gibbins
10 Cohen Griffith
11 Roger Hansbury
12 Pat Heard
13 Phil Heath
14 Mark Jones
15 Allan Lewis
16 Kevin MacDonald
17 Neil Matthews
18 Jon Morgan
19 Jason Perry
20 Chris Pike
21 Ian Rodgerson
22 Kevin Russell
23 Damon Searle
24 Lee Stephens
25 Chris Summers
26 Mark Taylor
27 Cameron Toshack
28 Jamie Unsworth
29 Gavin Ward

1991-92 9th in Division Four

Date	Att	Home	Score	Away	Scorers	1	2	3	4	5	6	7	8	9	10	11	12	13	14	15	16	17	18	19	20	21	22	23	24	25	26	27	28
17-Aug	5,137	CARDIFF CITY	1-2	Lincoln City	Pike (p)	5*	12				4			9	1		11	2	6		8				10		3	7					
24-Aug	3,799	Crewe Alexandra	1-1	CARDIFF CITY	Dale	5				10	4			7*	1			2	14		8*	9		6	12	11	3						
31-Aug	4,096	CARDIFF CITY	1-0	Carlisle United	Jones (p)	5			12	10	4				1		8	2				9		6	7*	11	3						
04-Sep	1,019	Maidstone United	1-1	CARDIFF CITY	Dale	5			7*	10*	4			12	1		8	2				9		6	14	11	3						
07-Sep	4,029	CARDIFF CITY	1-2	Rochdale	Pike	5			7*	10	4			12	1		8	2				9		6	14	11	3						
14-Sep	3,931	Blackpool	1-1	CARDIFF CITY	og	5				10*	4			12				2	8			9		6	7	11	3					1	
17-Sep	1,041	Halifax Town	1-1	CARDIFF CITY	Dale	5				10	4			12			14	2	8			9		6	7*	11	3					1	
21-Sep	3,227	CARDIFF CITY	2-1	Scarborough	Heard, Dale					10	4			8			11*	2	5					6	9*	7	3		12	14		1	
28-Sep	4,000	Barnet	3-1	CARDIFF CITY	Dale		5		9	10	4			8			11	2	12					6		7*	3					1	
05-Oct	3,652	CARDIFF CITY	5-0	Wrexham	Pike 3, Dale, Blake		5		11	10*	4*			8				2		14	12			6	9	7	3					1	
19-Oct	3,180	Mansfield Town	3-0	CARDIFF CITY					11	10	4			8					5*		2	12		6	9	7*	3			14		1	
26-Oct	24,911	CARDIFF CITY	2-1	Doncaster Rovers	Pike 2 (2p)				11	10	4			8					5					6	9		3	7		2		1	
02-Nov	2,356	CARDIFF CITY	2-2	Scunthorpe United	Dale, Pike		5*		11	10	4			8	1			2	12					6	9	7	3						
05-Nov	2,467	Gillingham	0-0	CARDIFF CITY					11	10	4			12	1				5		2			6	9*	7	3	8					
23-Nov	2,922	CARDIFF CITY	3-2	Northampton Town	Dale 2, Gibbins		5		11	10	4			8	1				6		2	12			9*	7	3						
30-Nov	3,591	CARDIFF CITY	1-0	Rotherham United	Dale		5		11	10	4			8							2	12			9*	7	3	6				1	
14-Dec	1,904	York City	1-3	CARDIFF CITY	Dale 2, Pike		7			10	4		11	8							2			6	9*		3	12				1	5
26-Dec	3,162	Lincoln City	0-0	CARDIFF CITY			11*		12	10	4			8							2			6	9	7	3					1	5
28-Dec	3,080	Carlisle United	2-2	CARDIFF CITY	Pike (p), Ramsey				11	10	4			8							2			6	9	7	3					1	5
01-Jan	8,023	CARDIFF CITY	0-5	Maidstone United			12		11	10	4			8							2*			6	9	7	3					1	5
11-Jan	5,305	CARDIFF CITY	1-0	Hereford United	Dale	6*			11	10	4			8				2			12				9	7	3	14				1	5
18-Jan	3,654	Walsall	0-0	CARDIFF CITY			5		11	10	4		2	8			6								9	7	3					1	
25-Jan	5,131	CARDIFF CITY	4-0	Chesterfield	Pike 2, Dale, Blake		5		12	10	4		2	8		11*							6		9	7	3					1	
31-Jan	8,265	CARDIFF CITY	3-2	Mansfield Town	Pike (p), Blake, Newton		5*		11	10	4		2			8							6	12	9	7	3					1	
08-Feb	2,094	Doncaster Rovers	1-2	CARDIFF CITY	Dale, og				11	10	4		2	12		8*			14				6	5	9*	7	3					1	
11-Feb	3,827	Rotherham United	1-2	CARDIFF CITY	Newton, Blake	12			11	10	4		2			8							6	5	9*	7	3					1	
15-Feb	8,067	CARDIFF CITY	3-0	York City	Pike 2(p), Dale	5			11	10	4					8							6	2	9	7	3					1	
22-Feb	5,744	Hereford United	2-2	CARDIFF CITY	Ramsey, Harrison	5*			11	10	4		14	12		8							6	2	9*	7	3					1	
29 Feb	16,030	CARDIFF CITY	0-2	Burnley			5		11*	10	4		14	12		8*							6	2	9	7	3					1	
03-Mar	7,517	CARDIFF CITY	2-1	Walsall	Searle, Dale		5			10	4		12	11		8							6	2	9	7	3					1	
07-Mar	3,803	Chesterfield	2-2	CARDIFF CITY	Dale, Newton	12	5*			10	4			11		8							6	2	9	7	3					1	
10-Mar	8,521	CARDIFF CITY	2-3	Gillingham	Griffith, Dale	5*	12			10	4			11*		8					14		6	2	9	7	3					1	
14-Mar	2,766	Scunthorpe United	1-0	CARDIFF CITY			5			10	4	8	14	12	1						2		11	6	9*	7*	3						
28-Mar	2,678	Northampton Town	0-0	CARDIFF CITY				5		10	4	8		12	1								6	2	9	7	3				11*		
31-Mar	8,430	CARDIFF CITY	1-1	Blackpool	og			5	12	10	4	8*		111	1							14	6	2	9	7	3						
04-Apr	2,651	Rochdale	2-0	CARDIFF CITY				5	11	10	4			8	1							12	6	2	9	7	3*						
11-Apr	5,261	CARDIFF CITY	4-0	Halifax Town	Dale 2, Ramsey (p), Pike			5	11	10	4	14	2*		1							9*	8	6	12	7	3						
14-Apr	935	Scarborough	2-2	CARDIFF CITY	Pike 2			5	11	10	4	14		12	1			2*					8	6	9	7*	3						
20-Apr	7,720	CARDIFF CITY	3-1	Barnet	Pike (p), Dale, Newton		14	5	11	10	2*			8	1			12					4	6	9*	7	3						
22-Apr	12,400	Burnley	1-3	CARDIFF CITY	Pike (p), Newton, Blake			5	11	10				8	1						2	9	4	6		7	3						
25-Apr	4,002	Wrexham	0-3	CARDIFF CITY	Pike 2, Gill	6		5	11	10	4*	14		8	1							12		2	9	7*	3						
28-Apr	10,523	CARDIFF CITY	1-1	Crewe Alexandra	Blake	6		5	11	10	4			8	1							12		2	9*	7	3						
						15	18	9	31	41	41	6	11	37	18	10	8	14	12	1	15	15	18	36	40	39	42	6	1	3	1	24	5
									6	22	1	1		1		1	1	1					4		21	3	1						

1 Gareth Abraham
2 Lee Baddeley
3 Gary Bellamy
4 Nathan Blake
5 Carl Dale
6 Roger Gibbins
7 Gary Gill
8 Andy Gorman
9 Cohen Griffith
10 Roger Hansbury
11 Gerry Harrison
12 Pat Heard
13 Mark Jones
14 Allan Lewis
15 Paul Marriott
16 Neil M atthews
17 Paul Millar
18 Eddie Newton
19 Jason Perry
20 Chris Pike
21 Paul Ramsey
22 Damon Searle
23 Robin Semark
24 Cameron Toshack
25 Jamie Unsworth
26 Alan Walsh
27 Gavin Ward
28 W John Williams

1992-93 1st in (new) Division Three (Promoted)

Date	Att	Home	Score	Away	Scorers	1	2	3	4	5	6	7	8	9	10	11	12	13	14	15	16	17	18	19	20	21	22
15-Aug	8,399	CARDIFF CITY	0-0	Darlington				11	6	10			1	8	2			12	5	9	7		4*	3			
22-Aug	4,611	Walsall	2-3	CARDIFF CITY	Dale 2, Searle		12	11	6	10			1	8*	2			4	5	9	7			3			
29-Aug	7,692	CARDIFF CITY	1-2	Halifax Town	Dale, James			11	6	10			1	12	2			4	5	9*	7		8	3			
01-Sep	7,494	CARDIFF CITY	2-1	Northampton Town	Dale, Ramsey (p)			11	6	10			1	8	2			9	5	12	7		4*	3			
05-Sep	2,939	Torquay United	2-1	CARDIFF CITY	Pike			11	6*		12		1	8	2			10*	5	9	7		4	3			14
08-Sep	6,954	CARDIFF CITY	2-2	Carlisle United	Pike (p), Perry	5*		11*		10	12		1	8	2			4	6	9	7		14	3			
13-Sep	4,039	Hereford United	1-1	CARDIFF CITY	Blake		14	11	6	10	12		1	8*	2			7	5*	9			4	3			
19-Sep	6,356	CARDIFF CITY	3-1	Gillingham	Pike 2, Blake	5		11	6	10			1		2			8		9	7		4	3			
03-Oct	6,486	CARDIFF CITY	1-1	Rochdale	Pike	5		11	6	10			1	8	2			4*		9	7		12	3			
10-Oct	3,638	Crewe Alexandra	2-0	CARDIFF CITY		5		11		10	12			8	2			4	6	9*	7			3		1	
24-Oct	41,611	Shrewsbury Town	3-2	CARDIFF CITY	Dale, Pike (p)	5*		11	6	10			1	8	2			12	14	9	7		4*	3			
31-Oct	6,027	CARDIFF CITY	3-0	Scunthorpe United	Blake, Kelly, Ramsey (p)			9	6	10					2	8		11	5	12	7		4*	3		1	
03-Nov	2,590	Chesterfield	2-1	CARDIFF CITY	James			9	6	10					2	8	7	11	5	12			4*	3		1	
07-Nov	5,505	CARDIFF CITY	3-1	Colchester United	Dale, Blake, og			9	6	10	2				4	8	5	11			7			3		1	
22-Nov	4,181	Barnet	2-1	CARDIFF CITY	Dale			9	6	10	12				2	8*		11	5		7		4	3		1	
28-Nov	4,348	CARDIFF CITY	3-0	Bury	Blake, Griffith, og			9	6	10				14	2	8		11*	5	12	7		4*	3		1	
11-Dec	2,023	Doncaster Rovers	0-1	CARDIFF CITY	Millar			11	6	10					2			4	5		7		8	3	9	1	
18-Dec	6,832	CARDIFF CITY	1-2	Wrexham	Blake			11*	6	10*	12			14	2			4	5		7		8	3	9	1	
26-Dec	10,411	CARDIFF CITY	3-3	York City	Gorman, Stant, og	12	10*		6			11*		14	2			4	5		7		8	3	9	1	
28-Dec	4,359	Lincoln City	3-2	CARDIFF CITY	Ramsey, Millar	4	12		6					11*	2			10	5		7		8	3	9	1	
02-Jan	6,593	CARDIFF CITY	2-1	Hereford United	Stant, Richardson	5	10							11	6			4	5		7		8	3	9	1	
09-Jan	3,691	Carlisle United	1-2	CARDIFF CITY	Bird, Ratcliffe		10							11	2			47	5		7	6	8	3	9	1	
23-Jan	4,066	Gillingham	0-1	CARDIFF CITY	Griffith		12	10*						11	2		4	7	5			6	8	3	9	1	
26-Jan	1,339	Halifax Town	0-1	CARDIFF CITY	Stant			10						11	2		4	7	5			6	8	3	9	1	
30-Jan	9,012	CARDIFF CITY	2-1	Walsall	Stant, Griffith			10*						11	2		4	7	5	12		6	8	3	9	1	
06-Feb	1,775	Darlington	0-2	CARDIFF CITY	Pike 2(p)			10*	14					11	2		4	7	5	12		6	8*	3	9	1	
13-Feb	7,771	CARDIFF CITY	4-0	Torquay United	Stant 2, Millar, Blake			12						11	2		4*	7	5	10		6	8	3	9	1	
19-Feb	4,522	Northampton Town	1-2	CARDIFF CITY	Stant, Pike			12	4					11*	2			7	5	10		6	8	3	9	1	
27-Feb	10,012	CARDIFF CITY	1-1	Crewe Alexandra	Griffith			12	4					11	2			7	5	10*		6	8	3	9	1	
06-Mar	2,831	Rochdale	1-2	CARDIFF CITY	Griffith, Blake			9	4					11	2			7	5	10		6	8	3		1	
09-Mar	8,583	CARDIFF CITY	1-0	Scarborough	Stant		12	11	4						2*			7	5	10		6	8	3	9	1	
12-Mar	4,517	Colchester United	2-4	CARDIFF CITY	Pike 2, Richardson, Matthews				4					11	2		7		5	10		6	8	3	9	1	
20-Mar	6,756	CARDIFF CITY	2-1	Chesterfield	Dale, Richardson				4	10*					2		11		5	12	7	6	8	3	9	1	
23-Mar	3,574	Bury	1-0	CARDIFF CITY			12		4					10*	2		11		5		7	6	8	3	9	1	
27-Mar	16,073	CARDIFF CITY	1-1	Barnet	Griffith			11*	4					14	2		8*		5	10	7	6	12	3	9	1	
03-Apr	2,223	Scarborough	1-3	CARDIFF CITY	Pike (p), Richardson, Stant				4		12			11*	2		14		5	10	7	6*	8	3	9	1	
06-Apr	9,938	CARDIFF CITY	1-1	Doncaster Rovers	Perry			11*	4					12	2		6		5	10	7		8	3	9	1	
10-Apr	6,568	York City	3-1	CARDIFF CITY	Griffith			12	4					11	2		14		5	10*	7*	6	8	3	9	1	
12-Apr	11,257	CARDIFF CITY	3-1	Lincoln City	Stant, Blake, Ramsey (p)			10	4					11	2				5		7	6	8	3	9	1	
17-Apr	10,852	Wrexham	0-2	CARDIFF CITY	Griffith, Blake			10	4	12				11	2				5		7	6	8	3	9*	1	
01-May	17,253	CARDIFF CITY	2-1	Shrewsbury Town	Perry, Blake			9	4	10*				11	2				5	12	7	6*	8	3		1	
08-May	7,407	Scunthorpe United	0-3	CARDIFF CITY	Griffith 2, Stant			10	4					11	2				5		7		8	3	9	1	
					Appearances	8	9	34	34	20	8	1	10	34	42	5	14	33	39	28	30	19	39	42	24	32	1
					Goals		1	11		8		1		10	2	1	1	3	3	12	4	1	4	1	11		

1 Lee Baddeley
2 Tony Bird
3 Nathan Blake
4 Derek Brazil
5 Carl Dale
6 Roger Gibbins
7 Andy Gorman
8 Mark Grew
9 Cohen Griffith
10 Robbie James
11 Tony Kelly
12 Neil Matthews
13 Paul Millar
14 Jason Perry
15 Chris Pike
16 Paul Ramsey
17 Kevin Ratcliffe
18 Nick Richardson
19 Damon Searle
20 Phil Stant
21 Gavin Ward
22 Steve Williams

1993-94 19th in Division Two

Date	Att	Home	Score	Away	Scorers	1	2	3	4	5	6	7	8	9	10	11	12	13	14	15	16	17	18	19	20	21	22	23	24	25	26	27	28	29	30
14-Aug	9,920	CARDIFF CITY	2-0	Leyton Orient	Blake, Griffith				7	10	4								1*	11	2		12			5	6	8	3		9				
21-Aug	5,696	Fulham	1-3	CARDIFF CITY	Blake 2, Thompson			14	11	10	4		7*								2*		1		12	5	6	8	3		9				
28-Aug	7,687	CARDIFF CITY	2-2	Brighton	Blake, Cornwell			12	6*	10	4*		7							11	2		1			5		8	3		9		14		
31-Aug	3,049	Exeter City	2-2	CARDIFF CITY	Griffith, Cornwell					10	4		7							11	2		1		6	5		8	3		9				
04-Sep	8,140	Port Vale	2-2	CARDIFF CITY	Griffith, Blake			12		10			7							11	2		1		4*	5	6	8	3		9				
11-Sep	7,421	CARDIFF CITY	3-4	Hull City	Richardson 2(p), Thompson					10			4							7	2		1			5	6	8	3	9	11				
18-Sep	4,767	Blackpool	1-0	CARDIFF CITY				4	14											11	2	3*	1		7	5	6	8*	12	9	10				
25-Sep	6,362	CARDIFF CITY	2-3	Plymouth Argyle	Stant, Millar				7		8										2		1	5	11	4	6		3	9	10				
02-Oct	3,762	York City	5-0	CARDIFF CITY					8		6									11	2	3		5		4				9	10		7	1	
10-Oct	2,084	Barnet	0-0	CARDIFF CITY				6	7*	10	4									11			1	5	12	2			3	9*	8		14		
16-Oct	5,676	CARDIFF CITY	1-2	Bristol Rovers	Richardson (p)		6	14		10	4*									11			1	5*	7	2		8	3	12	9				
23-Oct	4,245	Wrexham	3-1	CARDIFF CITY	Bird		6	5	14	10	4									11			1		7	2		8	3*	12	9*				
30-Oct	3,710	CARDIFF CITY	2-2	Hartlepool United	Bird, Blake (p)		6	5	7	10	3									11			1		4*	2		8		9	12				
02-Nov	4,756	Brentford	1-1	CARDIFF CITY	Blake			5	7	10	2									11					4	6		8	3	9				1	
06-Nov	4,738	CARDIFF CITY	3-1	Stockport County	Blake 3(p)			5*	7	10	2									11					4	6		8	3	9*			12	1	14
19-Nov	3,076	Cambridge United	1-1	CARDIFF CITY	Bird		4	5	7	10	2								1	11						6		8	3	9					
27-Nov	4,213	CARDIFF CITY	1-1	Bradford City	Stant		4	5	7	10	2								1	11					12	6		8*	3	9					
11-Dec	5,120	CARDIFF CITY	1-0	Fulham	Blake		4	5	7	10	2*								1	11					12	6		8	3	9					
18-Dec	3,691	Leyton Orient	2-2	CARDIFF CITY	Stant, Thompson		4*	5	7		2								1	11					10	6		8	3	9	12				
22-Dec	9,815	CARDIFF CITY	1-0	Swansea City	Thompson		4*	5	14	10	2								1	11					12	6		8	3	9	7*				
01-Jan	10,257	CARDIFF CITY	3-0	Reading	Griffith, Aizlewood, Richardson		4	5			2								1	11					10	6		8	3	9	7				
03-Jan	3,405	Rotherham United	5-2	CARDIFF CITY	Millar 2(2p)		4	5	12		2									11					10	6		8	3	9	7*			1	
15-Jan	5,624	Bristol Rovers	2-1	CARDIFF CITY	Blake				12	10	2					4			1	11*					6	5		8	3	9	7*		14		
22-Jan	5,698	CARDIFF CITY	0-0	Barnet		14	4	12	11*	10	2								1	9					6*	5		8	3		7				
05-Feb	10,847	CARDIFF CITY	5-1	Wrexham	Blake 2, Adams, Richardson, Bird	9*	4	5	7	10	2*			14		12			1	11								8	3				6		
12-Feb	11,277	Burnley	2-0	CARDIFF CITY		9*		5	12	10	2			14					1	11					4	6		8	3		7*				
01-Mar	5,469	CARDIFF CITY	2-1	Burnley	Thompson, Stant			5	11*		2	4		12											10	6		8	3	9	7			1	
05-Mar	4,998	Hull City	1-0	CARDIFF CITY				5	11*		2	4		12						14					10	6		8	3	9	7*			1	
12-Mar	5,186	CARDIFF CITY	0-2	Blackpool				5			2*	4		12			10			11					14	6		8	3	9	7*			1	
15-Mar	2,385	Bournemouth	3-2	CARDIFF CITY	Dale, Griffith	12		5	9			4		10			2*			11					7	6		8	3					1	
19-Mar	9,587	Plymouth Argyle	1-2	CARDIFF CITY	Stant 2				7			4		10			2			11						6		8	3	9			5	1	
22-Mar	1,077	Hartlepool United	3-0	CARDIFF CITY		14		5	7*			4		10*			2			11						6		8	3	9			12	1	
26-Mar	4,806	CARDIFF CITY	0-0	York City			4	5	14			7		10*			2			11						6		8*	3	9			12	1	
29-Mar	3,583	CARDIFF CITY	1-0	Rotherham United	Bird		4	5	10		2	8					11*			7					12	6			3	9				1	
02-Apr	3,711	Swansea City	1-0	CARDIFF CITY			4	5	9*		2	8					11*			10					14	6		12	3				7	1	
04-Apr	5,525	CARDIFF CITY	2-2	Huddersfield Town	Brock, Perry	14	4	5*	10*		2	8					11			7					12	6			3	9				1	
09-Apr	7,129	Reading	1-1	CARDIFF CITY	og	10*	4				2	7					11			12			1		6	5*		8	3	9			14		
12-Apr	7,653	Brighton	3-5	CARDIFF CITY	Millar 3(2p), Stant, Fereday		4				2*	7					11			10			1		6	5		8	3	9			12		
16-Apr	5,268	CARDIFF CITY	1-1	Brentford	Brock	12						7*					2			11			1		6	5		8	3	9	10		4		
19-Apr	6,267	Huddersfield Town	2-0	CARDIFF CITY		7*			12					14			2			11*			1		6	5		8	3	9	10		4		
21-Apr	3,838	CARDIFF CITY	2-1	Bournemouth	Stant, Millar (p)	10*	4							14			2			11					6	5*		8	3	9	7		12	1	
23-Apr	5,455	Stockport County	2-2	CARDIFF CITY	Stant, og	4*			14					10			2			11					6			8*	3	9	7		12	1	5
26-Apr	4,631	CARDIFF CITY	2-0	Exeter City	Aizlewood, Dale	5	4		12			8*		10		2	3			11*					6					9	7			1	14
30-Apr	5,175	CARDIFF CITY	2-7	Cambridge United	Griffith, Dale	11	4		8*					10		2	3			12					6					9	7*		14	1	5
03-May	4,705	CARDIFF CITY	1-3	Port Vale	Stant		4*	5*						12			2			11			1		6			8	3	9	7		10		14
07-May	6,642	Bradford City	2-0	CARDIFF CITY		11			10						14	2		12					1		6*			8	3	9		7*	4		5
					Appearances	14	22	30	35	20	31	14	5	15	1	5	17	1	11	42	9	2	18	4	37	40	6	39	42	36	30	0	19	18	6
					Goals	1	2		5	14		2	2	3			1			6					7	1		5		10	5				

1 Darren Adams
2 Mark Aizlewood
3 Lee Baddeley
4 Tony Bird
5 Nathan Blake
6 Derek Brazil
7 Kevin Brock
8 John Cornwell
9 Carl Dale
10 Andy Evans
11 Terry Evans
12 Wayne Fereday
13 Ben Graham
14 Mark Grew
15 Cohen Griffith
16 Robbie James
17 Ian Jones
18 Phil Kite
19 Alan Knill
20 Paul Millar
21 Jason Perry
22 Kevin Ratcliffe
23 Nick Richardson
24 Damon Searle
25 Phil Stant
26 Gary Thompson
27 Lee Walker
28 Nathan Wigg
29 Steve Williams
30 Scott Young

1994-95 22nd in Division Two (Relegated)

Date	Att	Home	Score	Away	Scorers	1	2	3	4	5	6	7	8	9	10	11	12	13	14	15	16	17	18	19	20	21	22	23	24	25	26	27	28	29
13-Aug	5,139	Stockport County	4-1	CARDIFF CITY	Stant		4		10*	12	14		2	11	7*						6		5		8	3		9					1	
20-Aug	7,281	CARDIFF CITY	1-3	Oxford United	Stant	12	4*		10	3	14		2	11*				7			6		5		8			9				1		
27-Aug	2,861	York City	1-1	CARDIFF CITY	Millar				9*	5	10		2	11	7			12			6				8	3						1		4
30-Aug	4,903	CARDIFF CITY	0-0	Wrexham					12	5	10		2	11*	7			9			6				8	3						1		4
03-Sep	5,523	CARDIFF CITY	1-1	Swansea City	Richardson		4	14		5	10		2*		7			12			6				8	3	11*		9			1		
10-Sep	4,189	Blackpool	2-1	CARDIFF CITY	Richardson		4*			6	10		2		11*		5	12			7				8	3		9	14			1		
13-Sep	1,671	Chester City	0-2	CARDIFF CITY	Stant, Aizlewood		4		12	2	10				11		5				7		6		8	3		9*				1		
17-Sep	5,674	CARDIFF CITY	0-1	Plymouth Argyle			4	14	12	2	10				11		5*				7*		6		8	3			9			1		
24-Sep	3,177	Bournemouth	3-2	CARDIFF CITY	Scott, Griffith		4	5			10		2*		11			14			7		6		8	3			9*			1		12
01-Oct	4,225	CARDIFF CITY	1-2	Peterborough United	Fereday		4	5	14		10*			11	8			7*			6		2		12		3	9				1		
08-Oct	4,126	CARDIFF CITY	1-2	Crewe Alexandra	Stant	10	4			2		12		11*	7						6		5		8		3	9				1		
15-Oct	3,933	Bristol Rovers	2-2	CARDIFF CITY	Millar, Richardson	10*		5		2		12		11*	7			14			4		6		8		3	9				1		
22-Oct	3,580	CARDIFF CITY	3-1	Cambridge United	Stant 3			5		2	10			11	7			8			4		6			3		9				1		
30-Oct	5,937	Bradford City	2-3	CARDIFF CITY	Millar 2(p), Stant			5		2	10			11	7			8			4		6			3		9				1		
01-Nov	2,559	Leyton Orient	2-0	CARDIFF CITY				5		2	10			11	7			8			4		6			3		9				1		
05-Nov	5,004	CARDIFF CITY	3-0	Brighton	Stant 2, Baddeley			5	12	2				11	8*			10			4*		6	7		3		9			14	1		
19-Nov	5,391	Wycombe Wanderers	3-1	CARDIFF CITY	Stant		4	5							12			11			8		6	7			3	9	10*			1		2
25-Nov	4,226	CARDIFF CITY	0-2	Hull City			4*		14	5					12			11*			6			7	8		3	9	10			1		2
10-Dec	6,181	Oxford United	1-0	CARDIFF CITY				5		6	7			14	12			11*			4				8		3	9	10			1		2*
17-Dec	3,448	CARDIFF CITY	1-1	Stockport County	Dale		6*	5			8			11				12			4			7			3	9	10			1		2
26-Dec	4,933	Shrewsbury Town	0-1	CARDIFF CITY	Stant (p)			5			8	10		11	12		2				4		6	7			3	9				1		
28-Dec	7,420	CARDIFF CITY	0-1	Birmingham City				5			8	10		2	11*			12			4*		6	7			3	9				1		14
31-Dec	3,064	Rotherham United	2-0	CARDIFF CITY				5	14		8	10*		2	12			11			4*		6				3	9				1		7
02-Jan	5,253	CARDIFF CITY	2-3	Brentford	Stant, Bird			5	12		8			2*							4		6	7		11*	3	9	10			1		14
07-Jan	3,467	CARDIFF CITY	0-1	Blackpool				5			9	14		2*	11*					4	8		6	7			3		10			1		12
14-Jan	3,808	CARDIFF CITY	0-0	Huddersfield Town		9*		5	14		11			2				12		4	8*		6	7			3		10			1		
17-Jan	2,458	Cambridge United	2-0	CARDIFF CITY		9*		5	14		8				12			11			4		6	7			3		10*			1		2
04-Feb	3,903	Hull City	4-0	CARDIFF CITY			4	5			7			11		2				10*		9*		6	8		3		14			1		12
18-Feb	10,035	Huddersfield Town	5-1	CARDIFF CITY	Brazil		4	5		6	8			2		7*		12				9			10		3				11	1		
21-Feb	3,024	CARDIFF CITY	2-0	Wycombe Wanderers	Dale, Richardson		4*	5			8			11	12	2						9	6		10		3				7	1		
25-Feb	4,226	Peterborough United	2-1	CARDIFF CITY	Dale			5		4	8*	9		11		2							6		10		3				7	1		
04-Mar	3,008	CARDIFF CITY	1-1	Bournemouth	Dale		4	5		14		12		11		2						9	6		10		3				7	1		
07-Mar	3,942	Swansea City	4-1	CARDIFF CITY	Wigg		4	5		12				11	8*	2		14				9*	6		10		3				7	1		
11-Mar	2,689	CARDIFF CITY	1-2	York City	Griffith			5		12				3	4	2*		11		14		9	6		10*					8	7	1		
15-Mar	6,956	Brighton	0-0	CARDIFF CITY				5*						3	4	2		11		14		9	6		10					8*	7	1		12
18-Mar	3,106	Wrexham	0-3	CARDIFF CITY	Nicholls, Griffith, og										4	2		11		8		9	6		10		3				7	1		5
25-Mar	5,611	Plymouth Argyle	0-0	CARDIFF CITY				12		2*					4			11	14	8		9*	6		10		3				7	1		5
28-Mar	2,560	CARDIFF CITY	2-4	Bradford City	Perry, Millar										4	2		11	12	8		9	6		10		3				7*	1		5
01-Apr	4,405	CARDIFF CITY	2-1	Chester City	Dale, Millar			5	12	2	10				11			7		14		9*	6		8		3				4*	1		
04-Apr	4,324	CARDIFF CITY	2-1	Leyton Orient	Bird 2			5	12	2	10				11			7		14		9*	6*		8		3				4	1		
08-Apr	6,412	CARDIFF CITY	1-1	Rotherham United	Griffith			5	9	2	10	12			11			7*		14			6		8		3				4*	1		
15-Apr	17,455	Birmingham City	2-1	CARDIFF CITY	Millar			5	9	2	10				11			7					6*		8		3				4		1	12
17-Apr	4,677	CARDIFF CITY	1-2	Shrewsbury Town	Bird			5	9*	2	10	12			11			7		14					8		3				4		1	6*
22-Apr	8,268	Brentford	2-0	CARDIFF CITY		14		5	9*	2	10				11			7			12				8		3				4		1	6*
29-Apr	5,462	CARDIFF CITY	0-1	Bristol Rovers				5		2*	8	14			11			7	9*		12				10		3				4		1	6
06-May	4,382	Crewe Alexandra	0-0	CARDIFF CITY				5		2*	10	14			11			9*			12				8		3				4		1	7
					Appearances	6	17	36	19	30	35	12	7	27	38	10	4	35	3	12	30	12	34	11	33	13	32	19	13	2	19	40	6	22
					Goals		1	1	4	1	5			1	4			7		1			1		4	1		13			1			

1 Darren Adams
2 Mark Aizlewood
3 Lee Baddeley
4 Tony Bird
5 Derek Brazil
6 Carl Dale
7 Andy Evans
8 Terry Evans
9 Wayne Fereday
10 Cohen Griffith
11 Chris Honor
12 Ian McLean
13 Paul Millar
14 Paul Milsom
15 Ryan Nicholls
16 Charlie Oatway
17 John Pearson
18 Jason Perry
19 Paul Ramsey
20 Nick Richardson
21 Andy Scott
22 Damon Searle
23 Phil Stant
24 Garry Thompson
25 Lee Vick
26 Nathan Wigg
27 David Williams
28 Steve Williams
29 Scott Young

1995-96 22nd in Division Three

Date	Att	Home	Score	Away	Scorers	1	2	3	4	5	6	7	8	9	10	11	12	13	14	15	16	17	18	19	20	21	22	23	24	25	26	27	28	29	30	31	32	33	34	35
12-Aug	2,321	Rochdale	3-3	CARDIFF CITY	Bird 2, Dale		5	11		2	10								4										6		8			3	9		7	1		
19-Aug	7,772	CARDIFF CITY	0-2	Northampton Town			5*	11*		2	10								4		13								6		8			3	9		7	1		12
26-Aug	2,186	Doncaster Rovers	0-0	CARDIFF CITY			5	11*		2	10		12						4		13								6		8			3	9		7*	1		
29-Aug	4,444	CARDIFF CITY	0-1	Exeter City			5	11*		2	10		8						4						3				6		7				9		12	1		
02-Sep	1,895	Darlington	0-1	CARDIFF CITY	Dale (p)		5			2	10		8						4		12								6		7*			3	9*		11	1		13
09-Sep	4,318	CARDIFF CITY	0-0	Torquay United			5			2	10	11	8						4										6		7			3	9*		12	1		
12-Sep	2,390	CARDIFF CITY	2-1	Scarborough	Dale, og		5	11		2	10	7*							4		9								6					3			8	1		12
16-Sep	5,314	Gillingham	1-0	CARDIFF CITY		13	5	11		2*	10	7									9*								6		4			3			8	1		12
23-Sep	2,172	Hartlepool United	2-1	CARDIFF CITY	Dale (p)	7	5	11*			10								4		9	12							6		8			3				1		2
30-Sep	3,468	CARDIFF CITY	3-0	Mansfield Town	Dale 2(1p), Ingram		5				10							11	4		9	7							6		8			3				1		2
07 Oct	2,648	Cambridge United	4-2	CARDIFF CITY	Adams, Bird	13	5	10						9	12			11	4			7*							6		8*			3				1		2
14-Oct	3,342	CARDIFF CITY	1-1	Barnet	Dale	12	5	8			10			13	2			11	4		9*	7					9		6*									1		3
21-Oct	2,453	Lincoln City	0-1	CARDIFF CITY	Gardner	8*	5			2	10							11	4		13		12				9*							3			7*	1		6
28-Oct	3,207	CARDIFF CITY	1-2	Colchester United	Adams	8	5			2	10							11	4		13	12												3			7*	1		6
31-Oct	2,159	CARDIFF CITY	0-1	Scunthorpe United		8*		13	12	2*	10							11			9	7	5								4			3				1		6
04-Nov	7,434	Plymouth Argyle	0-0	CARDIFF CITY		8*		12		2							7	11			9		5								4			3			10	1		6
18-Nov	3,846	CARDIFF CITY	0-1	Bury		8				2*	9						7	11				13	5						12		4			3			10*	1		6
26-Nov	3,521	Hereford United	1-3	CARDIFF CITY	Dale 2, Adams	8	13	12			9						7*	11		10			5						2*		4			3				1		6
09-Dec	2,934	CARDIFF CITY	2-0	Hartlepool United	Dale 2						9						2	11	4	10			5							8	7			3				1		6
16-Dec	2,212	Mansfield Town	1-1	CARDIFF CITY	Searle	12					9						2	11	4	10			5							8	7*			3				1		6
19-Dec	2,284	Fulham	4-2	CARDIFF CITY	Dale, Rodgerson						9						2	11	4	10			5							8	7			3				1		6
26-Dec	6,521	CARDIFF CITY	0-0	Chester City		10					9						2	11	4		12		5							8*	7			3				1		6
01-Jan	8,346	Preston North End	5-0	CARDIFF CITY			13				9						2	11	4*	8		12*	5							10	7			3				1		6
06-Jan	2,873	CARDIFF CITY	0-0	Leyton Orient			13				9						2	11*	4*				5							10	7		8	3			12	1		6
13-Jan	4,454	Northampton Town	1-0	CARDIFF CITY			4			11	9					12	2*						5							10	13		8	3			7*	1		6
20-Jan	2,248	CARDIFF CITY	1-0	Rochdale	Gardner		7			12	9						2*	11	4				5							10			8	3				1		6
03-Feb	2,566	CARDIFF CITY	3-2	Doncaster Rovers	Dale 3		7				9*					12	2	11	4				5							10			8	3				1		6
10-Feb	3,564	Leyton Orient	4-1	CARDIFF CITY	Philliskirk					7	9					13	2	11*	4				5							10			8*	3			12	1		6
17-Feb	1,414	Scarborough	1-0	CARDIFF CITY			11				9							12	4				5					7		10	2		8*	3				1		6
20-Feb	2,225	CARDIFF CITY	0-2	Darlington			8				9						12	11*	4				5					7		10	2*		13	3				1		6
24-Feb	3,028	CARDIFF CITY	2-0	Gillingham	Dale, og		7				10						2	11	4				5							9			8	3				1		6
27-Feb	2,004	Torquay United	0-0	CARDIFF CITY			7				10						2*	11	4				5							9			8	3			12	1		6
02-Mar	2,308	Chester City	4-0	CARDIFF CITY						11	10						2	12	4				5							9			8	3			7*	1		6
05-Mar	1,611	CARDIFF CITY	3-0	Wigan Athletic	Gardner 2, Philliskirk		3			2	10							11	4				5					7		9	12		8*					1		6
09-Mar	3,489	CARDIFF CITY	1-4	Fulham	Dale		3			2	10							11	4*				5					7		9		13	8*				12	1		6
12-Mar	2,609	Exeter City	2-0	CARDIFF CITY			11			2*	10					13							5					4		9	8		7*	3			12	1		6
16-Mar	2,789	Wigan Athletic	3-1	CARDIFF CITY	Flack		2				10					11	8*	12	4				5					6		9	13		7*	3				1		
23-Mar	3,642	CARDIFF CITY	0-1	Preston North End			2				10					11*		7					5			8		6		9	12			3				1		4
30-Mar	2,440	CARDIFF CITY	1-1	Cambridge United	Dale (p)		5				10					9*		11	4*					13		8		12		7	2			3				1		6
02-Apr	21,107	Barnet	1-0	CARDIFF CITY							10							11*	4				5	12		8		7		9	2			3				1		6
06-Apr	3,349	Colchester United	1-0	CARDIFF CITY							10						12	11*	4				5	13		8		7		9	2*			3				1		6
08-Apr	2,788	CARDIFF CITY	1-1	Lincoln City	Dale						10							11	4				5	7		8		2		9				3				1		6
13-Apr	2,044	Scunthorpe United	1-1	CARDIFF CITY	Dale						10							11	4				5	12		8		7		9	2			3*					1	6
20-Apr	3,489	CARDIFF CITY	0-1	Plymouth Argyle							10					12	3	11*	4				5			8		7		9*	2					13			1	6
27-Apr	3,870	CARDIFF CITY	3-2	Hereford United	Philliskirk 2, Dale						10					8	2	11					5					7		9				3			4		1	6
04-May	5,658	Bury	3-0	CARDIFF CITY		14					10					8	2*	11*					5					7		9	12			3		13	4*		1	6
					Appearances	13	30	12	1	20	44	3	4	2	2	10	22	35	36	5	13	8	32	5	1	7	2	15	14	28	33	1	14	41	6	2	21	42	4	41
					Goals	3		3			21					1		4				1								4	1			1						

1 Darren Adams
2 Lee Baddeley
3 Tony Bird
4 Mirko Bolesan
5 Derek Brazil
6 Carl Dale
7 Gerald Dobbs
8 Keith Downing
9 Andy Evans
10 Terry Evans
11 Steve Flack
12 Hayden Fleming
13 Jimmy Gardner
14 Paul Harding
15 Alan Harper
16 Simon Haworth
17 Chris Ingram
18 Lee Jarman
19 Glenn Johnson
20 Ian Jones
21 Brian McGorry
22 Charlie Oatway
23 Russell Osman
24 Jason Perry
25 Tony Philliskirk
26 Ian Rodgerson
27 Andy Scott
28 Tony Scully
29 Damon Searle
30 Paul Shaw
31 Lee Vick
32 Nathan Wigg
33 David Williams
34 Steve Williams
35 Scott Young

1996-97 7th in Division Three

Date	Att	Home	Score	Away	Scorers	1	2	3	4	5	6	7	8	9	10	11	12	13	14	15	16	17	18	19	20	21	22	23	24	25	26	27	28	29	30	31	32
17-Aug	2,455	Scarborough	0-0	CARDIFF CITY			7			10			1			8			5	3							4		11	2					9		6
24-Aug	3,897	CARDIFF CITY	1-0	Brighton	Eckhardt		7					10*	1			8*	12		5	3							4		11	2		13			9		6
27-Aug	3,845	CARDIFF CITY	0-2	Wigan Athletic		12	7			10*		6	1			8	13			3							4		11*	2		5			9		
31-Aug	2,478	Cambridge United	0-2	CARDIFF CITY	White 2		7*		10			5	1			8*	12		13	3							4		11	2					9		6
07-Sep	3,659	CARDIFF CITY	2-1	Exeter City	White 2				8			10	1						5	3			7				4		11	2					9		6
10-Sep	2,041	Torquay United	2-0	CARDIFF CITY					8	12		4	1	10*			13		5	3			7						11*	2					9		6
14-Sep	2,121	Scunthorpe United	0-1	CARDIFF CITY	Middleton				8	10*		4	1				12		13	3			7				5		11*	2					9		6
21-Sep	4,124	CARDIFF CITY	2-2	Northampton Town	Middleton, Philliskirk		12		8	10		4	1							3			7				5		11*	2					9		6
28-Sep	2,925	Lincoln City	0-0	CARDIFF CITY		12	13		8*	10		4	1							3			7				5*		11	2					9		6
12-Oct	2,879	CARDIFF CITY	1-2	Barnet	Middleton		12			10		4	1			8*	3		11*	13			7				5			2					9		6
15-Oct	1,667	CARDIFF CITY	2-0	Darlington	Dale, White					10		4	1		2	8	3		11				7				5								9		6
19-Oct	4,972	Carlisle United	0-2	CARDIFF CITY	Dale, Fowler		12			10		4	1		2	8	3		11	14			7*				5*		13						9		6*
26-Oct	3,647	CARDIFF CITY	3-0	Leyton Orient	White (p), Gardner, Dale		13			10		4	1		2	8	3*		5	12			7						11*						9		6
29-Oct	2,775	Hull City	1-1	CARDIFF CITY	Middleton	12	13			10		4	1		2	8*			5*	3			7						11						9		6
02-Nov	3,213	Colchester United	1-1	CARDIFF CITY	White (p)	12	13			10		4	1		2	8*	3		5*				7						11						9		6
05-Nov	2,835	CARDIFF CITY	2-1	Rochdale	Bennett, Eckhardt	6	8			10*		4	1		2		3			12			7				5		11						9		
09-Nov	6,144	CARDIFF CITY	1-2	Fulham	White	6	12			10		4	1		2	8	3*						7				5		11						9		
23-Nov	3,904	CARDIFF CITY	2-0	Hereford United	White 2					10		4	1			6	11						8				2		3	7					9		5
26-Nov	1,540	Chester City	0-1	CARDIFF CITY	Young					10		4	1			6	11						8				2		3	7					9		5
30-Nov	4,512	Leyton Orient	3-0	CARDIFF CITY			12			10		4	1			6	11*						8		7		2		3						9		5
03-Dec	3,721	CARDIFF CITY	1-3	Swansea City	White					10		4	1			6	11	12					8*		7		2		3						9		5
21-Dec	2,238	CARDIFF CITY	1-2	Mansfield Town	Eckhardt							4				6	11*	12			5	13	8	1			2		10	7					9		3*
26-Dec	3,651	CARDIFF CITY	2-0	Torquay United	Burton 2			10				4				5	11		12				8	1	6		2		3*	7					9		
28-Dec	3,585	Exeter City	2-0	CARDIFF CITY				10				4			13	5	11	12					8	1	6		2		3*	7*					9		
01-Jan	4,416	Northampton Town	4-0	CARDIFF CITY		5		10				4			7		11	12	3				8*	1	6		2								9		
11-Jan	2,033	CARDIFF CITY	1-3	Lincoln City	Fowler			10		9		4			5*	7	11*		12				8	1	6		2		3						13		
18-Jan	1,704	Rochdale	1-0	CARDIFF CITY		5		10					1			7	11*	9		3			4		8		2			12					13		6*
25-Jan	2,328	CARDIFF CITY	2-0	Hull City	Haworth, Eckhardt	13						4	1			5*	11	10		3			7		8		2			12					9		6*
31-Jan	6,459	Fulham	1-4	CARDIFF CITY	White 2, Fowler, Haworth							4	1			5		10*	2	3			7*						14	12	13		8	11*	9		6
08-Feb	3,912	CARDIFF CITY	1-2	Colchester United	Haworth							4	1			5	13	10	2	3			7*							12			8	11	9		6*
11-Feb	1,120	Hartlepool United	2-3	CARDIFF CITY	Fowler, Eckhardt, Stoker							4	1			5		10	2	3			7					6	9				8	11			
16-Feb	5,137	Hereford United	1-1	CARDIFF CITY	Stoker							4	1			5*		10	2	3			7			13		6	9*	12			8	11			
22-Feb	2,971	CARDIFF CITY	2-0	Hartlepool United	Haworth, Davies					14	5*	4	1					10	2	3			7*			6		12	9*	13			8	11			
02-Mar	4,430	Swansea City	0-1	CARDIFF CITY	Haworth					12	5	4	1			6		10	2				7			8	3		11*		13				9*		
08-Mar	2,569	Mansfield Town	1-3	CARDIFF CITY	Haworth, Stoker, Dale					14	5	4*	1			6		10	12				7			8*	3		11		13		2		9*		
14-Mar	5,347	CARDIFF CITY	0-2	Doncaster Rovers						12	5		1			6		10	2	3			7			8*	4						11		9*		
18-Mar	2,823	CARDIFF CITY	1-1	Scarborough	Davies					9	5		1			6	12	10	2	3			7*			11	4						8				
22-Mar	9,683	Brighton	2-0	CARDIFF CITY						9	5		1			6	14	10					12			7	4		13		2		8*		11*		3*
31-Mar	4,634	Wigan Athletic	0-1	CARDIFF CITY	Haworth					9		4	1			6		10	2	3						7					11		8				5
05-Apr	3,410	CARDIFF CITY	0-0	Cambridge United						9			1			6	11*	10	2	3			4			7							8		12		5
08-Apr	1,989	Doncaster Rovers	3-3	CARDIFF CITY	Haworth 2, Fowler					9			1			6*		10	2	3			11			7	4				12		8				5
12-Apr	4,079	CARDIFF CITY	1-0	Chester City	Dale					9						6		10*	2	3			11			7	4				12		8			1	5
15-Apr	4,442	CARDIFF CITY	0-0	Scunthorpe United						9						6*		10	2	3			11			7*	4		13		12		8			1	5
19-Apr	2,497	Barnet	3-1	CARDIFF CITY	Dale					9							12	10	2	3*			11			7	4				6		8*		13	1	5
26-Apr	5,104	CARDIFF CITY	2-0	Caarlisle United	Dale (p), Lloyd					9						6*		10*	2	3*			11			7	4		12		13		8		14	1	5
03-May	3,686	Darlington	2-1	CARDIFF CITY	Dale					9		14				6*		10	2	3*			11			7*	4		12				8		13	1	5
					Appearances	9	14	5	6	33	6	35	36	1	10	37	28	24	32	31	1	1	41	5	8	15	35	3	33	21	10	2	17	5	38	5	32
					Goals		1	2		8	2	5				5	1	9		1			4						1				3		13		1

1 Lee Baddeley
2 Mickey Bennett
3 Deon Burton
4 Stacy Coldicott
5 Carl Dale
6 Gareth Davies
7 Jeff Eckhardt
8 Tony Elliott
9 Steve Flack
10 Hayden Fleming
11 Jason Fowler
12 Jimmy Gardner
13 Simon Haworth
14 Lee Jarman
15 Kevin Lloyd
16 Ray McStay
17 Jamie Michael
18 Craig Middleton
19 Pat Mountain
20 Keith O'Halloran
21 Scott Partridge
22 Jason Perry
23 Lee Phillips
24 Tony Philliskirk
25 Ian Rodgerson
26 Jimmy Rollo
27 Andy Scott
28 Gareth Stoker
29 Paul Ware
30 Steve White
31 Steve Williams
32 Scott Young

1997-98 21st in Division Three

Date	Att	Home	Score	Away	Scorers	1	2	3	4	5	6	7	8	9	10	11	12	13	14	15	16	17	18	19	20	21	22	23	24	25	26	27	28	29
09-Aug	5,455	Leyton Orient	0-1	CARDIFF CITY	Dale	3		11		10*				6		1	5		4		8			7							13	12	2	
23-Aug	2,743	Mansfield Town	2-1	CARDIFF CITY	Partridge, Greenacre	3		11						6	10	1	5		4		2		12	7		9*					8*	13		
30-Aug	6,191	CARDIFF CITY	1-1	Notts County	Young	3		11						6	9	1	5		12		2*		10	7							8*	13	4	
02-Sep	4,271	CARDIFF CITY	2-2	Shrewsbury Town	Partridge, O'Sullivan	3		11						6	9	1	5		2				10	7							8*	12	4	
09-Sep	4,843	Exeter City	1-1	CARDIFF CITY	Fowler	3						14		6*	9	1	5		2		12		7	11		8*					13	10*	4	
13-Sep	4,389	CARDIFF CITY	2-1	Rochdale	White Eckhardt	3						12		6	9*	1	5		2*				7	11				13			8	10	4	
16-Sep	3,949	CARDIFF CITY	0-2	Chester City		3		12				2		6	9	1	5						7	11*							8	10	4	
20-Sep	3,134	Lincoln City	1-0	CARDIFF CITY		3		10				2*		6	9	1	5		12		14		7	11*							8*	13	4	
27-Sep	2,730	Cambridge United	2-2	CARDIFF CITY	Greenacre, Eckhardt	3		11				2	12	6	9	1*	5				14		7	13							8*	10*	4	
04-Oct	3,941	CARDIFF CITY	1-1	Barnet	Eckhardt	3		11*				2		6	9*	1	5		10				7	12		8*					14	13	4	
18-Oct	3,189	Rotherham United	1-1	CARDIFF CITY	Penney (p)	3		11						6*	9	1	5		4		12		7			8			2			10		
21-Oct	2,278	Darlington	0-0	CARDIFF CITY		3		11						6	9	1	5				12		7			8	4		2			10*		
25-Oct	3,383	CARDIFF CITY	1-1	Hartlepool United	Crowe	3		11	9	12				6		1	5						7	10		8	4*		2					
02-Nov	6,459	CARDIFF CITY	0-1	Swansea City		3		11*	10					6		1	5				2*		7	14		8				9	12	13	4	
04-Nov	1,004	Doncaster Rovers	1-1	CARDIFF CITY	Saville	3		14	10*	13				6		1	5				2		7	12		8				9	11*		4*	
08-Nov	2,802	CARDIFF CITY	1-1	Torquay United	Stoker	3			10	12				6		1	5*				2		7		4	8				9	11			
11-Nov	2,340	CARDIFF CITY	0-0	Scunthorpe United		3		13	10	12				6*		1	5				2*		7		4	8				9	11			
18-Nov	2,509	CARDIFF CITY	2-1	Hull City	Saville, Penney	3		11	10*	12						1	5				2		7	6	4	8				9				
22-Nov	2,086	Brighton	0-1	CARDIFF CITY	og	3		11	10*	13			1				5						7	6	4	8				9*		12	2	
29-Nov	2,615	CARDIFF CITY	1-1	Scarborough	Dale	3		11	13	10			1				5*		12		2		7	6*	4	8				9				
13-Dec	3,488	CARDIFF CITY	0-0	Peterborough United		3		11		10						1	5				2		7	6		8				9			4	
20-Dec	2,403	Macclesfield Town	1-0	CARDIFF CITY		3		11		10*						1	5		12		2*		7	6*		8				9	13	14	4	
26-Dec	6,862	CARDIFF CITY	1-1	Exeter City	Dale	3		11		10				6		1	5				2		7			8				9			4	
28-Dec	3,238	Shrewsbury Town	3-2	CARDIFF CITY	Fowler, Young	3		11		10				6*		1	5				2*		7			8				9	12	13	4	
10-Jan	4,598	CARDIFF CITY	1-0	Leyton Orient	Penney (p)	3		11		10				6*		1	5				2	13	7			8				9*	12		4	
17-Jan	6,214	Notts County	3-1	CARDIFF CITY	Harris	3		11*		10		2*		6		1	5					13	7*			8			12	9		14	4	
20-Jan	1,924	Colchester United	2-1	CARDIFF CITY	Dale	3		11*		10		2*		6		1	5*		14			9	7	13		8				12			4	
27-Jan	1,757	Chester City	0-0	CARDIFF CITY		3		11				6				1	5				2		7	10*		8				9		12	4	
31-Jan	1,445	Rochdale	0-0	CARDIFF CITY		3		11*		10		6				1	5				2		7			8				9	4	12		
07-Feb	2,896	CARDIFF CITY	0-1	Lincoln City		3		11		10				6*		1	5		4		2*		7	13*					14	9	8	12		
14-Feb	2,406	Barnet	2-2	CARDIFF CITY	Saville, Fowler	3		11		10*		8		6		1	5				2		7*							9	12	13	4	
17-Feb	2,562	CARDIFF CITY	4-1	Mansfield Town	Saville (p), Fowler, Carss, Penney	3		11		13		5*		7		1	6				2		8			12				9		10*	4	
21-Feb	2,683	CARDIFF CITY	0-0	Cambridge United		3		11*		10*		5		7		1	6	8			2		13			14				9		12*	4	
24-Feb	2,731	CARDIFF CITY	2-2	Rotherham United	Saville, White	3		11				4		7*			5	8			2		12			6				9		10		1
28-Feb	2,135	Scunthorpe United	3-3	CARDIFF CITY	Saville 3	3		11				4		7		1	5	8			2					6				9		10		
03-Mar	3,358	Torquay United	1-0	CARDIFF CITY		3		11*				4		7		1		8			2			12		6				9		10	5	
08-Mar	5,621	Swansea City	1-1	CARDIFF CITY	Fowler	3						4		7		1		8	2				11			6		12		9		10*	5	
14-Mar	2,931	CARDIFF CITY	7-1	Doncaster Rovers	Saville 2, O'Sullivan, Roberts, Beech, Penney, Young	3*		12				4		7		1		8	2				11			6		10*		9		13	5	
21-Mar	3,408	Hull City	1-0	CARDIFF CITY	Roberts	3		7		12		4				1		8	2				11			6		10*		9			5	
28-Mar	3,519	CARDIFF CITY	0-0	Brighton		3		7		12	13	4		8		1			2				11*			6		10*		9			5	
03-Apr	2,905	Scarborough	3-1	CARDIFF CITY	Saville	3*	13	7		10*		4*		8		1			2		6		11				12	14		9			5	
11-Apr	2,809	CARDIFF CITY	0-2	Colchester United		3	13	7*		10*	12			8		1			2		6*		11				4*	14		9			5	
13-Apr	4,756	Peterborough United	2-0	CARDIFF CITY		3	13	7		10*	14					1			2		6		11				4	12		9			5*	
18-Apr	2,501	CARDIFF CITY	1-2	Macclesfield Town	Roberts	3	13	7*			14			8		1	5*		2	12			11			8	4	10*		9				
25-Apr	2,817	Hartlepool United	2-0	CARDIFF CITY		3		12			14			6		1	5*		2	13	7		11*			8	4*	10		9				
02-May	2,610	CARDIFF CITY	0-0	Darlington		3		12						6		1	5*		2		7		11			8	4	13		9		10*		
					Appearances	46	4	41	8	24	5	21	3	37	11	43	37	7	22	2	32	3	43	21	5	34	8	11	5	33	20	29	31	1
					Goals	1		1	1	4		3		5	2		1						2	2		5		3		11	1	2	3	

1 Chris Beech
2 Nathan Cadette
3 Tony Carss
4 Glen Crowe
5 Carl Dale
6 Rob Earnshaw
7 Jeff Eckhardt
8 Tony Elliott
9 Jason Fowler
10 Chris Greenacre
11 Jon Hallworth
12 Mark Harris
13 Danny Hill
14 Lee Jarman
15 Kevin Lloyd
16 Craig Middleton
17 Kevin Nugent
18 Wayne O'Sullivan
19 Scott Partridge
20 Scott Paterson
21 David Penney
22 Lee Phillips
23 Christian Roberts
24 Jimmy Rollo
25 Andy Saville
26 Gareth Stoker
27 Steve White
28 Scott Young
29 Peter Zois

1998-99 3rd in Division Three (Promoted)

Date	Att	Home	Score	Away	Scorers	1	2	3	4	5	6	7	8	9	10	11	12	13	14	15	16	17	18	19	20	21	22	23	24	25	26
08-Aug	2,591	Hartlepool United	1-1	CARDIFF CITY	Earnshaw		7			6	2	10*		3	11	1						4	12					9		8	5
15-Aug	5,629	CARDIFF CITY	1-3	Peterborough United	Saville		7			6*	2	13			11	1						4	10	12		3		9		8*	5
21-Aug	3,003	Shrewsbury Town	0-3	CARDIFF CITY	Eckhardt, Thomas, Nugent		7			6	2		3			1					12	4	11*	9	3*				10	13	5
29-Aug	5,356	CARDIFF CITY	0-1	Rotherham United			7		8	6*	2	14	3			1		12			13	4*		11					9	10*	5
31-Aug	3,925	Darlington	3-0	CARDIFF CITY			7		8	6	2	12	3			1						4*		11					9	10	5
05-Sep	3,939	CARDIFF CITY	1-0	Plymouth Argyle	og		7*		8	6*	2		3		12	1					13	4	10	11					9*	14	5
08-Sep	3,742	CARDIFF CITY	1-0	Barnet	O'Sullivan		7		8	6*	2		3		13	1					12	4	10	11					9*	14	5*
11-Sep	2,814	Halifax Town	1-2	CARDIFF CITY	Fowler, Thomas		7		8	6	2		3		13	1		5				4	10*	11*					9	12	
19-Sep	4,643	CARDIFF CITY	2-1	Rochdale	Brazier, Bonner		7		8	6	2*		3		12	1						4	10	11					9*	13	5
26-Sep	2,842	Chester City	2-2	CARDIFF CITY	Brazier, Jarman		7*		8	6	2		3*			1		12			13	4	10	11					9*	14	5
03-Oct	6,143	CARDIFF CITY	2-0	Brighton	Nugent, Williams		7*		8	6*	2				12	1		3			13	4	10	11					9*	14	5
09-Oct	8,594	Hull City	1-2	CARDIFF CITY	Thomas 2		7		8	6				3	2	1						4	10	11					9*	12	5
17-Oct	6,886	CARDIFF CITY	0-1	Cambridge United			7*		8	6				3	2	1					12	4	10	11					9*	13	5
20-Oct	5,001	CARDIFF CITY	0-0	Leyton Orient			7		8	6				3	2	1						4	10	11					9*	12	5
31-Oct	5,411	CARDIFF CITY	1-0	Exeter City	Middleton	8				6	2		3		7*	1					12	4	10	11*			13		9*	14	5
07-Nov	3,342	Torquay United	0-0	CARDIFF CITY		8				6	2		12	3*		1					7	4	10	11*			13		9*	14	5
10-Nov	4,422	CARDIFF CITY	1-0	Scarborough	Williams	8				6	2		12	3	7	1					11	4*	10							9	5
22-Nov	7,757	Swansea City	2-1	CARDIFF CITY	Williams	12				6	2			3	7	1	13				11*	4	10	8						9*	5
28-Nov	4,638	CARDIFF CITY	2-0	Southend United	Middleton, Nugent					6	2			3	7	1	13				11*	4	10	8			12			9*	5
01-Dec	2,700	Carlisle United	0-1	CARDIFF CITY	Nugent (p)					6	2			3	7	1	13				11*	4	10	8					12	9*	5
12-Dec	3,200	Scunthorpe United	0-2	CARDIFF CITY	Williams 2					6	2		13	3	7*	1	12				11	4	10	8*						9	5
19-Dec	9,013	CARDIFF CITY	4-2	Mansfield Town	Williams 2, Nugent 2					6	2			3		1	7*			12	11	4	10*	8					13	9	5
26-Dec	12,452	CARDIFF CITY	3-0	Shrewsbury Town	Williams, Nugent, Hill					6	2			3	11	1	7*			13	12	4	10*	8*					14	9	5
28-Dec	9,535	Brentford	1-0	CARDIFF CITY						6	2		12	3	11	1				13	7*	4	10	8						9	5*
09-Jan	7,766	CARDIFF CITY	4-1	Hartlepool United	O'Sullivan, Nugent, Eckhardt, Middleton					6	2		5	3		1	7*			12	11	4	10	8						9	
16-Jan	5,890	Peterborough United	2-1	CARDIFF CITY	Nugent					6	2		5	3	7	1	13			12	11*	4	10	8					9*		
23-Jan	5,803	CARDIFF CITY	3-2	Darlington	Carpenter, Williams, Middleton					6	2		5	3	7	1					11	4	10	8					12	9*	
30-Jan	11,509	CARDIFF CITY	4-1	Brentford	Williams, Eckhardt, Fowler, Nugent					6	2		5	3*	7*	1	13			12	11	4	10	8						9	
06-Feb	6,062	Plymouth Argyle	1-1	CARDIFF CITY	Legg			12		6			5		7	1	13			3	11*	4	10	8						9*	2
13-Feb	2,234	Barnet	1-0	CARDIFF CITY				13		6*		14	5		7	1	11	12		3		4				8*			10*	9	2
19-Feb	8,788	CARDIFF CITY	1-1	Halifax Town	Eckhardt			13		6	8		5		7	1	14			3	11*	4	10	12						9*	2
27-Feb	2,431	Rochdale	1-1	CARDIFF CITY	Legg					6	8		5		7	1	11*			3	13	4	10						12	9*	2
05-Mar	7,528	CARDIFF CITY	0-0	Chester City				13		6*	2		5		7	1	12			3	11*	4	10	14						9*	8
09-Mar	2,312	Brighton	0-2	CARDIFF CITY	Nugent, Young		13	9*		6			5		7	1	11*			3		4	10	2						12	8
13-Mar	6,956	CARDIFF CITY	2-2	Torquay United	Hill, Fowler			9		6			5		7	1	11*			3		4	10	2						12	8
16-Mar	3,663	Rotherham United	1-0	CARDIFF CITY			13	9		6			5		7	1	11*	12		3		4	10	2						14	8
20-Mar	3,653	Exeter City	0-2	CARDIFF CITY	Nugent 2		7	9*		6			5			1	11*			3	12	4	10	2*					14	13	8
27-Mar	7,094	CARDIFF CITY	2-1	Carlisle United	Nugent, Bowen		13	9		6			5		7	1	11*			3	12	4	10	2*							8
03-Apr	7,787	Cambridge United	0-0	CARDIFF CITY				9*		6			5	8	7	1	11*			3	13	4	10	2						12	
05-Apr	8,252	CARDIFF CITY	1-1	Hull City	Nugent (p)		11*	9		6			5	8*	7	1	13			3	12	4	10	2*						14	
10-Apr	5,238	Leyton Orient	1-1	CARDIFF CITY	Williams		14	9*		6			5	8	7*	1	11*			3	12	4		2					13	10	
13-Apr	3,923	Southend United	0-1	CARDIFF CITY	Williams		6	9					5	8	7				1	3	11	4		2						10	
18-Apr	10,809	CARDIFF CITY	0-0	Swansea City			6	13					5	8	7		12		1	3	11	4	10	2*						9*	
24-Apr	1,834	Scarborough	1-2	CARDIFF CITY	Eckhardt, Bowen		6	12		13			5	8			7*		1	3	11*	4	10	2						9	
11-May	12,455	CARDIFF CITY	0-0	Scunthorpe United			6	12					5	8	7		13		1	3	11*	4	10	2						9*	
08-May	4,032	Mansfield Town	3-0	CARDIFF CITY			6	9					5	8*	7*		2		1	3	11	4	10	12			14		13		
					Appearances	4	25	17	11	42	28	5	35	25	37	41	26	6	5	24	35	46	41	42	1	2	4	2	24	43	33
					Goals		1	2	2	1		1	5		3		2	1		2	4		15	2				1	4	12	1

1 Chris Allen
2 Mark Bonner
3 Jason Bowen
4 Matt Brazier
5 Richard Carpenter
6 Mark Delaney
7 Rob Earnshaw
8 Jeff Eckhardt
9 Mike Ford
10 Jason Fowler
11 Jon Hallworth
12 Danny Hill
13 Lee Jarman
14 Seamus Kelly
15 Andy Legg
16 Craig Middleton
17 Graham Mitchell
18 Kevin Nugent
19 Wayne O'Sullivan
20 David Penney
21 Lee Phillips
22 Christian Roberts
23 Andy Saville
24 Dai Thomas
25 John N Williams
26 Scott Young

1999-00 21st in Division Two (Relegated)

Date	Att	Home	Score	Away	Scorers	1	2	3	4	5	6	7	8	9	10	11	12	13	14	15	16	17	18	19	20	21	22	23	24	25	26	27	28	29	30
07-Aug	10,193	CARDIFF CITY	1-1	Millwall	Boland (p)	8	6	10		13				5	2		7	1	11*					3				12	4				9*		
14-Aug	6,423	Oxford United	2-3	CARDIFF CITY	Nugent 2, Faerber	8	6*	10		14		13		5	2	3	4*	1	11*			12		7				9							
20-Aug	11,168	CARDIFF CITY	1-1	Wrexham	Bowen	8*	6	10				12		5	2	3	4	1	11					7				9							
28-Aug	5,374	Luton Town	1-0	CARDIFF CITY				10		11	14	8*		5	2*	3	6*	1						7		13		9		12					4
30-Aug	8,006	CARDIFF CITY	1-1	Scunthorpe United	Hughes	12		10*		11	13	4		5	2*	3	6	1		14				7*		8		9							
11-Sep	4,982	Wycombe Wanderers	3-1	CARDIFF CITY	Bowen	8		10		11	6			5	2*	3		1						7				9			12				4
18-Sep	6,568	CARDIFF CITY	2-1	Notts County	Bowen, Eckhardt	8		10*			11*	14		5	2	12	6	1		13				7				9						3	4*
25-Sep	7,679	CARDIFF CITY	0-0	Wigan Athletic		8		10				11		5	2*		6*	1	13					7				9					12	3	4
28-Sep	5,247	Brentford	2-1	CARDIFF CITY	Cornforth	8		10				11		5	2	12	6*	1	13					7				9						3*	4
02-Oct	3,603	Bury	3-2	CARDIFF CITY	Nugent 2	8*		10				11*		5	2		6		13				1	7				9					12	3	4
09-Oct	7,363	Bristol Rovers	1-1	CARDIFF CITY	Hill	8*				14	12	6*		5	2	3		1	11*					7		13		9					10	4	
16-Oct	5,650	CARDIFF CITY	1-1	Oldham Athletic	Thomas	8*				13				5	2		6	1	11*					7		12		9	4				10	3	
19-Oct	6,146	CARDIFF CITY	1-2	Stoke City	Legg	8				12				5	2		6	1	11					7*				9	4				10	3	
23-Oct	5,728	Wigan Athletic	2-0	CARDIFF CITY		8				14		13		5	2		6*	1	11					7				9	4				10*	3	12
02-Nov	4,523	CARDIFF CITY	1-1	Blackpool	Nugent			10*		8	14			5	2	3	6	1	11*					7*	12			9			13			4	
06-Nov	4,471	Bournemouth	1-0	CARDIFF CITY		14		10		8	6			5	2*	3*		1	11*					7	12			9	13					4	
12-Nov	4,863	CARDIFF CITY	2-1	Chesterfield	Bowen 2	12		10		8	6			5	2			1	11*					7					4		9			3	
23-Nov	2,512	Colchester United	0-3	CARDIFF CITY	Humphreys 2, Brazier	12	8*	10*		11	6			5	2			1			9			7					4		13			3	
27-Nov	7,608	CARDIFF CITY	1-2	Gillingham	Legg		8*	10		11*	6			5	2	14		1	12		9*			7					4		13			3	
04-Dec	9,044	Millwall	2-0	CARDIFF CITY		12	8*	10*		11	6			5	2			1	13		9			7*					4		14			3	
18-Dec	9,888	Burnley	2-1	CARDIFF CITY	og	13	8*	10		12	11			5		3	6	1			9*			2*	7			14				4			
26-Dec	9,791	CARDIFF CITY	1-0	Reading	Nugent						11		12	5	2		3	1			10*				7	8		9	4			6			
28-Dec	4,250	Cambridge United	0-0	CARDIFF CITY			6				11			5	2		3*	1			10				7	8		9	4	12					
03-Jan	10,342	CARDIFF CITY	0-4	Preston North End			12	14		3	11			5	13		6	1			10				7*	8*		9	4			2*			
09-Jan	10,570	Bristol City	0-0	CARDIFF CITY			13	10			6			5			2	1	11*					3	7	8*		9	4		12				
15-Jan	6,914	CARDIFF CITY	1-1	Oxford United	Nugent	8	6	10			11			5		4		1						3	7			9				2			
22-Jan	4,350	Wrexham	2-1	CARDIFF CITY	Low	8	6*	10		12	11*			5		4		1	14		13			3*	7			9				2			
30-Jan	6,185	CARDIFF CITY	1-3	Luton Town	Bowen	8*	6	13			11			5*	12	3		1			10			2	7			9	4						
05-Feb	3,614	Scunthorpe United	0-0	CARDIFF CITY			6			8	11					3	10	1						2	7			9	4						5
12-Feb	5,478	CARDIFF CITY	1-1	Brentford	Fowler		6	12		8	11					3	10	1						2	7*			9	4						5
22-Feb	6,586	CARDIFF CITY	0-0	Bristol City			6	10		8	11		12			3	7*	1						2				9	4						5
26-Feb	5,334	Notts County	2-1	CARDIFF CITY	Carpenter	14	6	13		8	11*		10*	12		3	7*	1						2				9	4						5
02-Mar	5,011	CARDIFF CITY	2-2	Wycombe Wanderers	Nugent, Low		6	13		8*	11		10			3		1						2	12	7*		9	4						5
07-Mar	4,389	CARDIFF CITY	1-2	Bournemouth	Earnshaw	13	6	12		3			10	2			11*	1	14						7*	8*		9	4						5
11-Mar	5,015	Blackpool	2-2	CARDIFF CITY	Nugent (p), Bowen		6	12		8			10*	2			11	1						3	7			9	4						5
17-Mar	5,174	CARDIFF CITY	3-2	Colchester United	Bowen 2, Nugent		6	10	7*	8*	13					3	11*	1	14					2	12			9	4						5
21-Mar	2,348	Chesterfield	1-1	CARDIFF CITY	Perrett		6	10	9*	8	11			12		3	7	1	13					2					4		14				5*
25-Mar	10,044	Reading	0-1	CARDIFF CITY	Bowen		8	10			11			5	2	3	6	1						7			9		4						
01-Apr	6,457	CARDIFF CITY	1-2	Burnley	og		6	10	12		11			5*	2	3	6*	1						7	13		9		4						
08-Apr	13,794	Preston North End	0-0	CARDIFF CITY			6	10			11			5	2	3		1*					12	7			8	9	4						
15-Apr	6,592	CARDIFF CITY	0-4	Cambridge United			6	10	12		11			5	2*	3							1	7			8	9	4*						13
22-Apr	4,549	Oldham Athletic	1-2	CARDIFF CITY	Bowen, Brayson	8	6	10	7		11			5	2								1	3				9							4
24-Apr	6,781	CARDIFF CITY	0-2	Bury		8	6*	10	7*	13	11*			5	2				14				1	3			12	9							4
30-Apr	14,192	Stoke City	2-1	CARDIFF CITY	Young	8	6	10	7	11				5	2								1	3				9							4
02-May	9,176	Gillingham	4-1	CARDIFF CITY	Bowen	8	6*	10*	7*	13	11			5	2				12				1	3			14	9							4
06-May	6,655	CARDIFF CITY	1-0	Bristol Rovers	Young	8	6	10	7					5*	2				11				1	3				9		12					4
					Appearances	28	31	39	9	30	33	10	6	41	33	26	28	39	23	2	9	1	8	42	17	10	6	39	27	3	8	5	7	14	22
					Goals	1		12	1	1	1	1	1	1	1		1		1	1	2			2	2			10	1				1		2

1 Willie Boland
2 Mark Bonner
3 Jason Bowen
4 Paul Brayson
5 Matt Brazier
6 Richard Carpenter
7 John Cornforth
8 Rob Earnshaw
9 Jeff Eckhardt
10 Winston Faerber
11 Mike Ford
12 Jason Fowler
13 Jon Hallworth
14 Danny Hill
15 Jamie Hughes
16 Richie Humphreys
17 Lee Jarman
18 Seamus Kelly
19 Andy Legg
20 Josj Low
21 Craig Middleton
22 Kurt Nogan
23 Kevin Nugent
24 Russell Perrett
25 Lee Phillips
26 Christian Roberts
27 Jorn Schwinkendorf
28 Dai Thomas
29 Tony Vaughan
30 Scott Young

2000-01 2nd in Division Three (Promoted)

Date	Att	Home	Score	Away	Scorers	1	2	3	4	5	6	7	8	9	10	11	12	13	14	15	16	17	18	19	20	21	22	23	24	25	26	27	28	29	30	31	32
12-Aug	3,929	Exeter City	1-2	CARDIFF CITY	Brayson, Low	11	12	10	8	3						6*				5								7				9		2	1		4
19-Aug	11,019	CARDIFF CITY	1-1	Blackpool	Nugent	6	8		10	11							12			5						2		7				9		3*	1		4
26-Aug	2,266	Barnet	2-2	CARDIFF CITY	Low, Earnshaw	6*	8*		10	2		14				12	2			5		13				11*		7				9			1		4
28-Aug	7,628	CARDIFF CITY	2-2	Southend United	Nugent, Brayson		8		10*	2		14	12			6*	2*			5		12				11		7				9			1		4
02-Sep	2,824	Rochdale	1-1	CARDIFF CITY	Brayson		8		10*	2*				14		6	2			5		11*				7			12		13	9			1		4
09-Sep	6,741	CARDIFF CITY	1-1	Brighton	Hill		8*		10			12		13			2			5		11*		14		3		7*	6			9			1		4
12-Sep	5,087	CARDIFF CITY	4-2	Halifax Town	Young, Bowen, Earnshaw, Fortune-West		14	10*				8		7	13		2			5*		11		12		3			6*			9			1		4
16-Sep	3,263	Scunthorpe United	0-2	CARDIFF CITY	Nugent, Earnshaw			10*	12	3		8*		6	14		2			5		11				7*			13			9			1		4
23-Sep	8,003	CARDIFF CITY	0-0	Kidderminster Harriers			14	10*	12	3		8		6	13		2			5		11*				7						9*			1		4
30-Sep	5,503	Hull City	2-0	CARDIFF CITY			6	13	12	3		8*			9		2			5		11				7		10*							1		4
14-Oct	4,649	Leyton Orient	2-1	CARDIFF CITY	Fortune-West		8	10*	12	3		14	5		9		2					11*				7		13	6*						1		4
17-Oct	1,309	Carlisle United	2-2	CARDIFF CITY	Legg, Nugent		6	14	13	3		8		12	9		2									11*		7	5*			10*			1		4
21-Oct	4,625	CARDIFF CITY	2-0	Mansfield Town	Earnshaw, Brayson		11	10*	13			8	5	6	12		2									3		7				9*			1		4
24-Oct	5,440	CARDIFF CITY	2-0	Darlington	Earnshaw, Evans		11	10*	13			8	5	6	12		2									3		7				9*			1		4
28-Oct	5,378	Chesterfield	2-2	CARDIFF CITY	Evans, Bowen		11	10*				8	5	6	12		2									3		7	13			9*			1		4
04-Nov	61,011	CARDIFF CITY	4-0	York City	Bowen 2, Young, Earnshaw		11	10		13		8	5	6*	14		2								12	3		7*				9*			1		4
22-Nov	4,786	CARDIFF CITY	3-2	Lincoln City	Earnshaw, Brayson, og		11	10*	13			8		6	9		2*								5			7			12				1	3	4
25-Nov	6,251	CARDIFF CITY	3-2	Hartlepool United	Fortune-West, Bonner, Nogan		11	10*	14			8*		6	9		2								5			7	12		13				1	3*	4
02-Dec	2,427	Torquay United	1-4	CARDIFF CITY	Earnshaw 3, Brayson		11	10*	14		13	8*		6	9*		2											7	5		12				1	3	4
16-Dec	6,764	CARDIFF CITY	3-1	Cheltenham Town	Earnshaw, Brayson, Fortune-West		11	10*	14			8	13		9		2*									3		7	5*					12	1	6	4
23-Dec	8,088	CARDIFF CITY	2-0	Macclesfield Town	Young, Bowen		11*	10*	13			8*		14	9		2		12							3		7	5						1	6	4
26-Dec	8,543	Plymouth Argyle	2-1	CARDIFF CITY	Fortune-West	11*			10*			8*	5	6	9		2		12							3		7	14						1	13	4
01-Jan	9,038	CARDIFF CITY	6-1	Exeter City	Young, Gordon, Legg, Bowen, Brazier, Brayson			10	14	3		8					2		9*		7				12	11		13	5*						1	6	4*
13-Jan	4,601	Southend United	1-1	CARDIFF CITY	Fortune-West			10*		3		14		6*	9		2*		8		7					11		12	13						1	5	4
20-Jan	9,157	CARDIFF CITY	4-1	Plymouth Argyle	Earnshaw 2, Fortune-West, McCulloch	8*		10	13	3		12			9		2*				11					5		7	14						1	6	4*
27-Jan	2,376	Macclesfield Town	2-5	CARDIFF CITY	Earnshaw 2, Young 2, Bowen	11		10		3		8		7*	9		2								6*	5		12	14						1	13	4*
02-Feb	11,912	CARDIFF CITY	0-0	Rochdale		11		10*	8	3				6*	9*	14	2		13							5		7							1	12	4
10-Feb	6,922	Brighton	1-0	CARDIFF CITY		11		10*	8	3				12	9*		2		13							5		7			14				1	6*	4
13-Feb	4,301	Blackpool	1-0	CARDIFF CITY		8		12	10*	3				6*	13		2		9*				5			11		7			14				1		4
17-Feb	6,057	CARDIFF CITY	3-0	Scunthorpe United	Gabbidon 2, Brazier	11		10	8	13					9*		2*						5			3		7*	12		14				1	6	4
20-Feb	1,991	Halifax Town	1-2	CARDIFF CITY	Brayson 2	11		10	8						9*		2		12				5			3		7							1	6	4
25-Feb	4,317	Kidderminster Harriers	2-4	CARDIFF CITY	Young, Bowen, Gabbidon, Earnshaw	11		10*	8			13					2						5			3	9*	7			12				1	6	4
02-Mar	10,074	CARDIFF CITY	2-0	Hull City	Legg, og	11		10	8	3*		13*					2	12					5			7	9*				14				1	6	4
06-Mar	9,022	CARDIFF CITY	1-1	Leyton Orient	Earnshaw	11		10*	8	3*		14		7	9		2	12					5								13				1	6	4*
10-Mar	4,451	Lincoln City	2-0	CARDIFF CITY		11		13	10	3*		8*		7	9		2						5				12								1	6	4
13-Mar	3,847	Shrewsbury Town	0-4	CARDIFF CITY	Low, Fortune-West, Boland (p), Bowen	11		10	8	12				6*	9*		2						5*					7	13		14				1	3	4
17-Mar	7,130	CARDIFF CITY	4-1	Carlisle United	Brayson 2, Bowen 2	11		10	8						9*		2						5			3		7			12				1	6	4
01-Apr	5,139	Cheltenham Town	3-1	CARDIFF CITY	Young	11		10*	14		13	8			9*		2	12					5*			3		7							1	6	4
04-Apr	6,209	CARDIFF CITY	1-0	Barnet	Low	11		10				8		6	9*		2*	12	14				13			3		7		1						5	4*
07-Apr	8,210	CARDIFF CITY	2-1	Torquay United	Brayson, Fortune-West	11	13	10	8			12			14		2		9*				5*			3		7*		1						6	4
14-Apr	3,863	Darlington	2-0	CARDIFF CITY		11		10*	8		14	12		13	9		2	6*								3		7*		1						5	4
16-Apr	13,602	CARDIFF CITY	3-3	Chesterfield	Brayson 2(1p), Evans	11		10	8*	6		12		4	9		2									7				1				3		5	
21-Apr	3,881	York City	3-3	CARDIFF CITY	Fortune-West 3	11		10*	8	3		13		6*	9											7			12	1				2		5	4
24-Apr	2,304	Mansfield Town	2-1	CARDIFF CITY	Bowen	11	13	10*	8	3*		14		6*	9											7			12	1			5	2			4
28-Apr	12,188	CARDIFF CITY	3-1	Shrewsbury Town	Young 2, Earnshaw	11	12	10	8*			14		6	9*		2									7		13					5*		1	3	4
05-May	5,324	Hartlepool United	3-1	CARDIFF CITY	Earnshaw		13	12	10			8		6*	9		2									11		7*	5					14	1	3*	4
					Appearances	25	24	40	40	26	3	36	8	30	37	5	43	5	10	10	3	9	12	2	5	39	3	36	21	6	12	14	2	7	40	28	45
					Goals	1	1	12	15	2		19		3	12		3		1			1				3		4	1		1	4					10

1 W Boland
2 M Bonner
3 J Bowen
4 P Brayson
5 M Brazier
6 J Collins
7 R Earnshaw
8 J Eckhardt
9 K Evans
10 L Fortune-West
11 J Fowler
12 D Gabbidon
13 M Giles
14 G Gordon
15 D Greene
16 J Harper
17 D Hill
18 D Hughes
19 G Jones
20 A Jordan
21 A Legg
22 K Lightbourne
23 J Low
24 S McCulloch
25 C Muggleton
26 K Nogan
27 K Nugent
28 R Perrett
29 A Thompson
30 M Walton
31 R Weston
32 S Young

2001-02 4th in Division Two

Date	Att	Home	Score	Away	Scorers	1	2	3	4	5	6	7	8	9	10	11	12	13	14	15	16	17	18	19	20	21	22	23	24	25	26	27
11-Aug	17,403	CARDIFF CITY	1-0	Wycombe Wanderers	Gabbidon	1				14				10	13	6		9*	4	12			8	11	7*				3		2	5*
18-Aug	6,437	Peterborough United	1-1	CARDIFF CITY	Kavanagh	1	12			14				10	13	6		9*	4*	5			8	11	7*				3		2	
25-Aug	13,383	CARDIFF CITY	2-2	Bournemouth	Fortune-West, Earnshaw	1	7			13				10	9	6			4*				8	11	12			5	3*		2	
08-Sep	13,017	Reading	1-2	CARDIFF CITY	Fortune-West 2	1		11		7*				10*	9	6			4*				8	14	13	12		5	3		2	
15-Sep	3,454	Cambridge United	2-1	CARDIFF CITY	Legg	1		11		10					9*	6			4*		13		8	12		7*		5	3	14	2	
18-Sep	11,232	CARDIFF CITY	2-0	Northampton Town	Kavanagh, Brayson (p)	1	12	7*		10					13	6			4*				8	11				5	3	9	2	
22-Sep	12,280	CARDIFF CITY	1-2	Huddersfield Town	Thorne	1	4		12	7*					9	6							8	11				5	3	10	2	
25-Sep	11,667	Queen's Park Rangers	2-1	CARDIFF CITY	Kavanagh (p)	1	7			13					9	6			4*				8	11*	12			5	3	10	2	
29-Sep	12,022	CARDIFF CITY	1-1	Brighton	Brayson	1	11		14	9						6			4		13		8*	12	7*			5	3*	10	2	
09-Oct	13,804	Bristol City	1-1	CARDIFF CITY	Earnshaw (p)	1	4	13	11*	7				9		6			12				8					5	3	10	2*	
12-Oct	11,072	CARDIFF CITY	2-2	Wigan Athletic	Brayson, Thorne	1	4		11	7				9		6							8	13				5	3*	10	2	12
21-Oct	8,373	Swindon Town	0-3	CARDIFF CITY	Bowen, Kavanagh, Earnshaw	1	4		7	11*				9		6		14					8	12	13			5	3*	10*	2	
24-Oct	4,552	Port Vale	0-2	CARDIFF CITY	Earnshaw, Prior	1	4		7	11				9*	14	6		10*					8	3*	13			5			2	12
27-Oct	13,070	CARDIFF CITY	1-1	Tranmere Rovers	Bowen	1	4		7*	11*				9		6		10	12				8	3	13			5			2	
04-Nov	5,832	Wrexham	1-3	CARDIFF CITY	Kavanagh, G Gordon, Fortune-West	1	4		7	11				9	14	6		10*	13				8	3				5			2*	12
07-Nov	2,549	Bury	3-0	CARDIFF CITY		1	4*			11		14		10*	9*	6			7				8	3	12	13		5			2	
10-Nov	9,516	CARDIFF CITY	2-1	Chesterfield	Fortune-West, Earnshaw (p)	1	4	12		11*				10	9	2			7*				8*	3	13	14		5				6
20-Nov	8,013	CARDIFF CITY	1-1	Colchester United	Collins	1	4	13				11		10	9*	2			7				8*	3		12		5				6
24-Nov	6,313	Notts County	0-0	CARDIFF CITY		1	4	8*	7*			11		10	14	2	3							12		13	9*	5				6
01-Dec	10,004	CARDIFF CITY	3-1	Oldham Athletic	Kavanagh 2, Earnshaw	1	4	11	7*					10	13	2	3						8			12		5		9*		6
04-Dec	10,184	CARDIFF CITY	3-1	Brentford	Gabbidon, Earnshaw, Thorne	1	4	11	7					9*	13	2	3						8			12		5		10*		6
15-Dec	4,880	Blackpool	1-1	CARDIFF CITY	D Gordon	1	4	11	7*	12				10	13	2	3	9*					8					5				6
19-Dec	14,331	Stoke City	1-1	CARDIFF CITY	D Gordon	1	4	11*	7*	13				10	14	2	3	9					8					5			12	6*
26-Dec	16,708	CARDIFF CITY	2-2	Reading	Earnshaw 2	1	4	11	7*	14				9	13	2	3	10*					8*	12				5				6
29-Dec	16,149	CARDIFF CITY	1-3	Bristol City	Kavanagh	1	4	11*	7*	14				9	13	2	3*	10					8	12				5				6
12-Jan	11,301	CARDIFF CITY	0-2	Peterborough United		1	4*	11		7				9	14	2		10*					8	3	13			5*			12	6
19-Jan	7,165	Wycombe Wanderers	0-1	CARDIFF CITY	Kavanagh	1	7	11*	13	14				9*		4		10					8	3	2*	12					5	6
22-Jan	11,771	CARDIFF CITY	2-0	Stoke City	Legg, og	1		11	7	13				9*	14	6		10*	2*				8	3	12						4	5
31-Jan	6,117	Brighton	1-0	CARDIFF CITY		1	4	11*	10						9	6			12				8	3	13	7*					2	5
05-Feb	4,336	Bournemouth	1-3	CARDIFF CITY	Boland, Kavanagh, Earnshaw	1	4	11	10*	13				9*		6		14	7				8	3					12		2*	5
09-Feb	12,045	CARDIFF CITY	3-0	Swindon Town	Bowen 2, Earnshaw	1	11	7	10					9*		6		14*	2*				8	3				12		13	4	5
12-Feb	67,118	Brentford	2-1	CARDIFF CITY	Bowen	1	4	11	10	14					9*	6							8		7*	12			3*	13	2	5
16-Feb	5,487	Wigan Athletic	4-0	CARDIFF CITY		1	4	11	10	14		13				6*							8	3	7*			12		9*	2	5
19-Feb	8,273	CARDIFF CITY	1-0	Bury	Kavanagh (p)	1	4	11	10*	12					13	6							8	3	7					9*	2	5
23-Feb	10,182	CARDIFF CITY	2-0	Cambridge United	Kavanagh 2(1p)	1	9	7*	11							5							8	6	2	12				10	3	4
02-Mar	5,495	Northampton Town	1-2	CARDIFF CITY	Maxwell, Campbell	1	7			8*	11*				14	3*								5	9	6		12	13	10	2	4
05-Mar	13,425	CARDIFF CITY	1-1	Queen's Park Rangers	Young	1	8			6*	11				13	4								5	9	7		12		10	2*	3
09-Mar	11,629	CARDIFF CITY	2-2	Blackpool	Campbell 2	1	11*			13	10				14	5			12				8	6	2*	7		3		9*		4
16-Mar	6,786	Oldham Athletic	1-7	CARDIFF CITY	Campbell 3, Fortune-West 2, Young, Thorne	1	11				10*	12			9	6*						14	7*	3				4	13	8	2	5
22-Mar	15,702	CARDIFF CITY	3-2	Wrexham	Gabbidon, Young, Thorne	1	4			14	10	12			9	3							7	11				5	13	8*	2*	6
30-Mar	5,442	Chesterfield	0-2	CARDIFF CITY	Fortune-West, Campbell	1	4	13		14	10*		12		9	3							7	11*				5		8	2	6*
01-Apr	15,556	CARDIFF CITY	1-0	Port Vale	Thorne	1	4	11*		13	10*		12	14	9	3							7					5		8*	2	6
06-Apr	3,970	Colchester United	0-1	CARDIFF CITY	Prior	1	4	11			10*	12	3	13	9	6							7					5		8	2*	
09-Apr	11,660	Huddersfield Town	2-2	CARDIFF CITY	Thorne 2	1	4	11					12	10*	9	3*							7			13		5		8	2	6
13-Apr	17,105	CARDIFF CITY	2-1	Notts County	Young, Fortune-West	1	4	11					3	10	9								7					5		8	2	6
20-Apr	8,375	Tranmere Rovers	0-1	CARDIFF CITY	Croft	1	4	11*	14				3	10*	9								7			13		5		8	2	6*
					Appearances	46	42	29	25	34	8	8	6	30	36	44	7	15	19	2	2	1	43	35	22	17	1	37	17	26	37	33
					Goals		1		5	3	7	1	1	11	9	3	2	1					13	2		1		2		8		4

1 Neil Alexander
2 Willie Boland
3 Mark Bonner
4 Jason Bowen
5 Paul Brayson
6 Andy Campbell
7 James Collins
8 Gary Croft
9 Rob Earnshaw
10 Leo Fortune-West
11 Danny Gabbidon
12 Dean Gordon
13 Gavin Gordon
14 Des Hamilton
15 David Hughes
16 Leon Jeanne
17 Gethin Jones
18 Graham Kavanagh
19 Andy Legg
20 Josh Low
21 Layton Maxwell
22 Kevin Nugent
23 Spencer Prior
24 Mike Simpkins
25 Peter Thorne
26 Rhys Weston
27 Scott Young

2002-03 6th in Division Two

Date	Att	Home	Score	Away	Scorers	1	2	3	4	5	6	7	8	9	10	11	12	13	14	15	16	17	18	19	20	21	22	23	24	25	26
10-Aug	8,033	Oldham Athletic	1-2	CARDIFF CITY	Campbell, Earnshaw		1	5	7			11*	13	3	14	9	4				8	12					10*	2	6*		
13-Aug	13,296	CARDIFF CITY	3-1	Port Vale	Thorne, Fortune-West, Legg		1	5				7*		3	12	9	4				8	11			13		10	2	6*		
17-Aug	13,321	CARDIFF CITY	1-2	Northampton Town	Kavanagh		1	5*				7*		3	12	9	4				8	11			13	14	10	2	6*		
24-Aug	7,564	Swindon Town	0-1	CARDIFF CITY	Fortune-West		1	12				7*		3	14	9	4				8	11			13	5	10*	2*	6		
26-Aug	13,564	CARDIFF CITY	0-0	Luton Town			1		12			7*		3	13	9*	4				8*	11			14	5	10	2	6		
31-Aug	4,395	Cheltenham Town	1-1	CARDIFF CITY	Campbell		1		7			9*		3	13	12	4				8	11*				5	10	2	6		
14-Sep	11,546	CARDIFF CITY	2-1	Stockport County	Earnshaw, Kavanagh		1		7			12		3	9*		4				8	11			13	5	10	2	6*		
17-Sep	12,032	CARDIFF CITY	2-0	Brentford	Earnshaw, Legg		1		7			12		3	9*		4				8	11				5	10	2	6		
21-Sep	6,118	Notts County	0-1	CARDIFF CITY	Croft		1	13	7			12		3	9*		4				8	11*				5	10	2	6		
24-Sep	11,606	Plymouth Argyle	2-2	CARDIFF CITY	Earnshaw 2		1	13	7			12		3	9*		4				8	11*				5	10	2	6		
28-Sep	13,208	CARDIFF CITY	2-1	Crewe Alexandra	Earnshaw 2		1		7*			13		3	9	12	4				8	11*			14	5	10*	2	6		
05-Oct	8,047	Wigan Athletic	2-2	CARDIFF CITY	Earnshaw 2		1	12	7			13		3	11	9*	4				8*				14	5	10	2*	6		
12-Oct	13,130	CARDIFF CITY	1-0	Wycombe Wanderers	Kavanagh			12	7			13		3*	9		4				8	11		1		5	10	2	6*		
19-Oct	7,744	Blackpool	1-0	CARDIFF CITY			1		7*			13		3	9	12	4				8	11*			14	5	10*	2	6		
26-Oct	12,096	CARDIFF CITY	4-0	Tranmere Rovers	Thorne 2, Earnshaw (p), Weston		1	12	7			13		3	9*		4		14		8	11*			6*	5	10	2			
29-Oct	3,441	Mansfield Town	0-1	CARDIFF CITY	Thorne		1	6	7			12		3	9*		4		13		8				11*	5	10	2			
02-Nov	12,918	CARDIFF CITY	3-0	Peterborough United	Kavanagh, Earnshaw (p), Weston		1	12	7			13		3	9	14	4				8				11	5	10*	2*	6*		
09-Nov	10,894	Barnsley	3-2	CARDIFF CITY	Earnshaw 2		1	12	7					3	9	13	4*		14		8				11*	5	10	2	6*		
24-Nov	13,331	CARDIFF CITY	1-0	Chesterfield	Thorne		1	5	7			12		3	9*				13		8	11			6*	4	10	2			
29-Nov	14,345	Queen's Park Rangers	0-4	CARDIFF CITY	Earnshaw 3, Campbell		1	5	7			13		3	9*	12			6		8	11				4	10*	2			
14-Dec	15,239	CARDIFF CITY	0-2	Bristol City			1	3	7		14	12		2	9				6*		8	11			13*	4	10*				5
20-Dec	3,096	Colchester United	1-2	CARDIFF CITY	Earnshaw 2		1	3	6			7*		12	9*	13					8	11				5	10	2			4
26-Dec	7,805	Luton Town	2-0	CARDIFF CITY			1	3	4		13	7*			9	12					8	11				5	10	2			6*
29-Dec	13,703	CARDIFF CITY	4-0	Huddersfield Town	Bowen 2, Earnshaw 2		1	5	7		8			3	9	12						11			13	4*	10*	2		14	6*
01-Jan	13,062	CARDIFF CITY	1-1	Swindon Town	Earnshaw		1	5	8		7*	14		3*	9	13					12	11				4	10	2			6*
18-Jan	11,605	CARDIFF CITY	2-1	Cheltenham Town	Thorne, Earnshaw		1	3			7*	8*			9	12					6	11			13	4	10	2		5	
25-Jan	9,462	Huddersfield Town	1-0	CARDIFF CITY			1	3		8*		13		12	9	7*						11	14			4	10	2*		5	6
31-Jan	12,579	CARDIFF CITY	1-1	Oldham Athletic	Bowen		1	5	7		11			3	9*			13			8	12	4*				10	2		6	
04-Feb	4,553	Northampton Town	0-1	CARDIFF CITY	Earnshaw		1	5	7		11			3	9						8		6				10	2		4	
08-Feb	12,759	CARDIFF CITY	1-1	Barnsley	Gordon		1	5	7*	13	11*			3*	9			14			8	12	6				10	2		4	
21-Feb	14,006	CARDIFF CITY	1-1	Plymouth Argyle	Earnshaw		1	5	6	13	7*			3	9						8	11*				12	10	2		4	
25-Feb	3,831	Port Vale	0-2	CARDIFF CITY	Gordon, Thorne		1	5	7	6	12			3	9*			11			8						10	2		4	
01-Mar	5,385	Stockport County	1-1	CARDIFF CITY	Thorne		1	5	7	6				3	9			11*		2*	8		13				10			4	
04-Mar	5,727	Brentford	0-2	CARDIFF CITY	Young, Earnshaw		1	3	7	6			13	2	9	12					8		11*			5*	10			4	
08-Mar	11,389	CARDIFF CITY	0-2	Notts County			1	3	7	6*	13			2*	9			12			8		11			5	10			4	
14-Mar	9,637	Tranmere Rovers	3-3	CARDIFF CITY	Earnshaw 3		1	3	7	6				2	9						8		11			5	10			4	
18-Mar	11,788	CARDIFF CITY	2-1	Blackpool	Earnshaw, Mahon	7	1	5	11	13				3	9					2*	8	12	6*			4	10				
21-Mar	13,009	CARDIFF CITY	1-0	Mansfield Town	Earnshaw	7*	1	5	11	12				3	9					2	8		6			4	10				
05-Apr	15,245	CARDIFF CITY	1-2	Queen's Park Rangers	Thorne	7*	1	5	11					3*	9			13		2	8	12	6	1		4	10				
08-Apr	5,889	Wycombe Wanderers	0-4	CARDIFF CITY	Thorne 2, Mahon, Legg	7*		5	11	14				3	9		12				8	13	6*	1		4*	10	2			
13-Apr	4,398	Chesterfield	0-3	CARDIFF CITY	Thorne 2, Kavanagh	7*		5	11	14				3	9*		12	13			8		6	1		4*	10	2			
16-Apr	4,984	Peterborough United	2-0	CARDIFF CITY		7*		5	11					3*	9		4	13			8	12	6	1			10	2			
19-Apr	12,633	CARDIFF CITY	0-3	Colchester United		7*		5	11					12	9		4	14			8	3	6*	1			10	2*	13		
22-Apr	15,615	Bristol City	2-0	CARDIFF CITY		7	1	3	6*			13			9		5				8	11*				4	10	2	12		
26-Apr	14,702	CARDIFF CITY	0-0	Wigan Athletic		7*	1	3	6	14		13		12	9*		5*				8	11				4	10	2			
03-May	9,562	Crewe Alexandra	1-1	CARDIFF CITY	Earnshaw		1	5	7*	8		11*		3	13			9*			12	14				4	10	2	6		
					Appearances	9	40	40	41	14	11	28	2	43	46	19	24	10	6	4	44	35	15	6	16	37	46	38	19	12	6
					Goals						3	3		1	31	2		2			5	3	2				13	2		1	

1 Gareth Ainsworth
2 Neil Alexander
3 Chris Barker
4 Willie Boland
5 Mark Bonner
6 Jason Bowen
7 Andy Campbell
8 James Collins
9 Gary Croft
10 Rob Earnshaw
11 Leo Fortune-West
12 Danny Gabbidon
13 Gavin Gordon
14 Des Hamilton
15 Steve Jenkins
16 Graham Kavanagh
17 Andy Legg
18 Alan Mahon
19 Martyn Margetson
20 Layton Maxwell
21 Spencer Prior
22 Peter Thorne
23 Rhys Weston
24 Gareth Whalley
25 Scott Young
26 Fan Zhiyi

2003-04 13th in Division One

Date	Att	Home	Score	Away	Scorers	1	2	3	4	5	6	7	8	9	10	11	12	13	14	15	16	17	18	19	20	21	22	23	24	25	26
09-Aug	8,176	Rotherham United	0-0	CARDIFF CITY		1	3	4	7	13		10	12		9*		5			8				14			11*		6	2*	
16-Aug	16,421	CARDIFF CITY	0-2	Bradford City		1	3	7	12			13			9*		5			8*	14	10					11		4	2	6*
23-Aug	23,407	Nottingham Forest		CARDIFF CITY	Earnshaw, Kavanagh	1	3	4	12						9*		5			8	7	10					11*	13	6	2	
25-Aug	15,091	CARDIFF CITY		Derby County	Lee, Kavanagh (p), Earnshaw, Collins	1	3	4					5		9					8	7	10*					11*	13	6	2	12
30-Aug	8,974	Walsall		CARDIFF CITY	Whalley	1	3	4*					5		9					8	7	10					11*	12	6	2	13
13-Sep	15,057	CARDIFF CITY	5-0	Gillingham	Earnshaw 4(p), Thorne	1	3	4					5		9			12		8	7						11	10*	6	2	
16-Sep	15,810	Reading		CARDIFF CITY	Thorne	1	3	4		12			5		9					8	7						11*	10	6	2	
20-Sep	21,323	Sheffield United		CARDIFF CITY	Earnshaw 2, Langley	1	3	4	11*				5		9			12		8	7							10	6	2	
27-Sep	14,385	CARDIFF CITY	3-0	Crewe Alexandra	Thorne 2, Earnshaw	1	3	4*	11			12	13	14	9*		5			8	7							10*	6	2	
30-Sep	15,143	CARDIFF CITY	0-0	Wigan Athletic		1	3	4	11						9		5			8	7							10	6	2	
04-Oct	16,160	Crystal Palace		CARDIFF CITY	Kavanagh	1	3	4	11			12		13	9		5			8	7							10	6	2	
14-Oct	26,835	Sunderland	0-0	CARDIFF CITY		1	3	4	12			10		13	9		5		14	8	7						11		6	2	
18-Oct	11,767	Coventry City		CARDIFF CITY	Whalley, Gordon, Earnshaw (p)	1	3		8					2	9		5	10	12		7						11		6		4
25-Oct	19,202	CARDIFF CITY	0-0	West Ham United		1	3		4				12	2	9		5	10		8	7						11		6		
28-Oct	14,011	CARDIFF CITY	3-0	Watford	Earnshaw, Vidmar, Kavanagh	1	3		4				12	2	9	14	5	10	13	8	7						11		6		
01-Nov	10,886	Burnley		CARDIFF CITY	Earnshaw	1	3	4	7				12		9		5	10	13	8						2	11		6		
08-Nov	15,227	CARDIFF CITY		Stoke City	Earnshaw 2, Gabbidon	1	3	12	4					2	9		5	10	7	8	13						11		6		
22-Nov	5,056	Wimbledon	0-1	CARDIFF CITY	Croft	1	3	12	4					2	9		5	10	8		7						11		6		
25-Nov	17,678	CARDIFF CITY		West Brom	Earnshaw (p)	1	3	12	4					2	9		5	10	8		7						11	13	6		
29-Nov	17,833	CARDIFF CITY		Ipswich Town	Earnshaw (p), Thorne	1	3	12	4					2	9		5	13	8		7						11	10	6		
06-Dec	12,208	Stoke City		CARDIFF CITY	Thorne 3	1	3	4	14			13		2	9		5		8		7					12	11	10	6		
09-Dec	13,703	CARDIFF CITY		Preston North End	Thorne, Langley	1	3	8	4			13		2	9		5				7						11	10	6		12
13-Dec	18,428	Norwich City		CARDIFF CITY	Thorne	1	3	4				11		2	9		5				7	13						10	6	12	8
20-Dec	14,610	CARDIFF CITY		Millwall	Thorne	1	3	4	12			13			9		5			8	7							10	6	2	11
26-Dec	17,531	CARDIFF CITY	0-1	Walsall				11				12			9		5			8	7		1			3		10	6	2	4
28-Dec	15,512	Watford		CARDIFF CITY	Thorne		12	11	13			9			14		5			8	7		1			3		10	6	2	4
10-Jan	13,021	CARDIFF CITY		Rotherham United	Thorne, Kavanagh, Earnshaw			4						12	9		5			8	7		1		11	3		10	6	2	13
17-Jan	11,132	Bradford City	0-1	CARDIFF CITY	Langley		12	4						3	9		5			8	7	14	1		11			10	6	2	13
31-Jan	17,913	CARDIFF CITY	0-0	Nottingham Forest			3	4				12			9		5			8	7	14	1		11			10	6	2	13
07-Feb	20,958	Derby County		CARDIFF CITY	Earnshaw, Kavanagh		3	4				12			9		5			8	7	13	1		11			10	6	2	
14-Feb	25,196	West Brom		CARDIFF CITY	Lee		3	4				14			9		5			8	7	13	1		11		12	10	6	2	
21-Feb	17,337	CARDIFF CITY	4-0	Sunderland	Kavanagh, Langley, Gabbidon, Lee		3	4				12			9		5			8	7	14	1		11		13	10	6	2	
28-Feb	31,858	West Ham	1-0	Cardiff City			3	4				14			9		5			8	7	10	1		11	12	13		6	2	
02-Mar	14,376	CARDIFF CITY	0-1	Coventry City		15	3					13		2	9		5			8	12	10	1		7		11		6		4
13-Mar	16,317	CARDIFF CITY		Norwich City	Parry, Earnshaw		3	4						2	9		5	14			12	10	1		11	13	7		6		8
16-Mar	14,051	CARDIFF CITY		Reading	Earnshaw, Bullock		3	4			12			2	9		5				7	10	1				11		6		8
20-Mar	6,650	Crewe Alexandra	0-1	CARDIFF CITY	og		12				8		3	2	9		5	13			7	10	1				11		6		4
27-Mar	13,666	CARDIFF CITY		Sheffield United	Langley, Robinson		12	4			14	13	3	2	9		5				7	10	1				11		6		8
03-Apr	7,852	Gillingham		CARDIFF CITY	Earnshaw, Bullock		12				14	13	2	3	9		5				7	10	1		8		11		6		4
07-Apr	9,584	Millwall	0-0	CARDIFF CITY							14	12	2	3	9		5	13			7	10	1		8		11		6		4
10-Apr	16,656	CARDIFF CITY	0-2	Crystal Palace							14	12	2	3	9		5	13			7	10	1		8		11		6		4
13-Apr	8,052	Wigan Athletic	3-0	CARDIFF CITY							13	12	2	3	9		5				7	10	1		8		11		6		4
17-Apr	13,525	CARDIFF CITY	2-0	Burnley	Langley (p), Campbell			8			14	12	2	3	9		5				7	10	1		13		11		6		4
24-Apr	11,972	Preston North End		CARDIFF CITY	Campbell, Gabbidon		3	4			8	9	6		12		5				7	10	1		13		11			2	
01-May	15,337	CARDIFF CITY		Wimbledon	Robinson			4			7	10	2	3	9	13	5	14			12		1		8		11		6		
09-May	28,703	Ipswich Town		CARDIFF CITY	Bullock		12	4			8		2	3	9		5*				7	10	1		13		11*		6		
					Appearances	25	39	37	20	2	11	25	20	27	46	2	41	15	9	27	44	23	22	1	17	7	34	23	45	23	22
					Goals						3	2	1	1	21		3	1		7	6	3			1		2	13	1		2

1 Neil Alexander
2 Chris Barker
3 Willie Boland
4 Mark Bonner
5 Jason Bowen
6 Lee Bullock
7 Andy Campbell
8 James Collins
9 Gary Croft
10 Rob Earnshaw
11 Stuart Fleetwood
12 Danny Gabbidon
13 Gavin Gordon
14 Julian Gray
15 Graham Kavanagh
16 Richard Langley
17 Alan Lee
18 Martyn Margetson
19 Leyton Maxwell
20 Paul Parry
21 Spencer Prior
22 John Robinson
23 Peter Thorne
24 Tony Vidmar
25 Rhys Weston
26 Gareth Whalley

2004-05 16th in Championship

Date	Att	Home	Score	Away	Scorers	1	2	3	4	5	6	7	8	9	10	11	12	13	14	15	16	17	18	19	20	21	22	23	24	25	26	27	28	29	30	31	32
07-Aug	7,339	Crewe Alexandra	2-2	CARDIFF CITY	Robinson, Lee						8	13	14	12	9*		5				4		7		10	1			6		11*			3		2*	
10-Aug	14,031	CARDIFF CITY	2-1	Coventry City	Earnshaw, Bullock						8	12			9*		5				4		7		10	1			6		11			3		2	
13-Aug	12,697	CARDIFF CITY	0-1	Plymouth Argyle							8*	13	12		9		5				4		7*		10	1			6	14	11			3		2*	
21-Aug	21,828	Ipswich Town	3-1	CARDIFF CITY	Lee							13	5		9*		2*				4		7		10		8*		6	14	11			3	1	12	
28-Aug	12,929	CARDIFF CITY	0-1	Stoke City					7*		12	9	3				5				4				10		8		6	13	11*				1	2	
30-Aug	9,004	Wigan Athletic	2-1	CARDIFF CITY	Lee (p)				7*		12	9					5				4				10		8		6	13	11*			3	1	2	
11-Sep	21,607	Notts Forest	0-0	CARDIFF CITY					7			9*					5				4				10	15	8		6	12	11*		13	3	1*	2	
14-Sep	10,606	CARDIFF CITY	0-3	Watford				12	7*			9*					5				4				10		8		6	13	11		14	3	1	2	
18-Sep	12,008	CARDIFF CITY	0-2	Derby County				3			8	13				9*	5				4				12		7			11*			10	6	1	2	
25-Sep	27,896	Wolves	2-3	CARDIFF CITY	Parry, Thorne, Kavanagh			3	7		12						5				4				9*		8*	13		11			10	6	1		2
28-Sep	7,200	Burnley	1-0	CARDIFF CITY				3			12						5				4				9*		7	8		11			10	6	1		2
02-Oct	17,006	CARDIFF CITY	0-0	Leeds United				3				9*					5			12							8	4		11			10	6	1		2
16-Oct	11,004	CARDIFF CITY	2-0	Rotherham United	Thorne 2			3									5				4			12	9		7	8		11			10	6	1		2
19-Oct	6,112	Brighton	1-1	CARDIFF CITY	Bullock			3			12	13					5				4			11*	9*		7	8					10	6	1		2
23-Oct	10,476	Millwall	2-2	CARDIFF CITY	O'Neil, Lee			3									5				4			11	9		7	8					10	6	1		2
30-Oct	13,759	CARDIFF CITY	0-0	Leicester City				3			12		6				5			13	4			10	9*		7	8		11*					1		2
02-Nov	14,222	CARDIFF CITY	4-1	West Ham United	Lee, Ledley, Parry, McAnuff			3	12				6				5			13	4			11	9		7	8*		10*					1		2
06-Nov	5,093	Rotherham United	2-2	CARDIFF CITY	Ledley, Parry			3	12				6				5			13	4			11	9		7*	8		10*					1		2
13-Nov	16,107	Reading	2-1	CARDIFF CITY	Jerome			3	8		12		6			13	5			14	4			11	9*		7*			10*					1		2
19-Nov	10,950	CARDIFF CITY	0-1	Preston North End				3*	4*		8		6				5			13				11	9		7			10		14			1	12	2*
27-Nov	15,146	Queen's Park Rangers	1-0	CARDIFF CITY				3	4		8		6				5			13				11*	9*		7			10			12		1		2
04-Dec	10,623	CARDIFF CITY	3-1	Gillingham	Thorne 2(1p), Jerome			3	4				6				5	12		9*				11			7			10			8		1		2
11-Dec	12,528	CARDIFF CITY	0-2	Sunderland				3	8*				5					13		9	4			11			7*			12			10	6	1		2
18-Dec	18,240	Sheffield United	2-1	CARDIFF CITY	Harris			3	8				6				5	9		11*	4			7*			13			12			10		1		2
26-Dec	16,699	CARDIFF CITY	1-1	Wolves	Jerome			3	8				6			13	5		14	9*			12	11*			7*						10	4	1	2	
28-Dec	13,409	Watford	0-0	CARDIFF CITY				3	4		13		6*				5		8*	9*					14		7		12				10	11	1	2	
01-Jan	22,800	Derby County	0-1	CARDIFF CITY	Thorne			3					6				5		8	9*	4		11		12		7*			13			10		1	2	
03-Jan	13,545	CARDIFF CITY	3-0	Notts Forest	Thorne 2(1p), Kavanagh			3					6				5		8*	9*	4		11		12		7			13*			10	14	1	2	
15-Jan	29,548	Leeds United	1-1	CARDIFF CITY	Thorne (p)			3					6				5		8*	9*	4		11	13	12		7						10		1	2	
22-Jan	11,562	CARDIFF CITY	2-0	Burnley	Langley, Kavanagh	1		3				10*	6				5		8		4		11	13	9		7							12		2	
06-Feb	23,716	West Ham United	1-0	CARDIFF CITY		1		3					6				5		8*		4		11	13	9		7						10	12		2*	
12-Feb	11,435	CARDIFF CITY	2-0	Brighton	Thorne (p), Collins	1		3			12		6				5		8*		4		11	13	9*		7						10			2	
22-Feb	11,424	CARDIFF CITY	0-1	Millwall		1		3			12		6				5		8	14	4		11*	13	9*		7						10			2*	
26-Feb	32,788	Sunderland	2-1	CARDIFF CITY	Vidmar	1		3									5		8*	9*	4		11	13	12		7						10	6		2*	14
05-Mar	12,250	CARDIFF CITY	1-0	Sheffield United	Ledley	1		3			12		6			13	5		4	9*			11	8			7						10*			2	
12-Mar	17,059	Coventry City	1-1	CARDIFF CITY	Bullock	1		3			10		6			12	5		4	9*			11	8			7									2*	13
15-Mar	11,768	CARDIFF CITY	0-1	Ipswich Town		1		3			10		6			12	5		4*	9		13	11*	8			7									2	
19-Mar	10,007	CARDIFF CITY	1-1	Crewe Alexandra	Gabbidon	1		3			12		6				5		4*	10		13	11	8	9*		7									2	
02-Apr	18,045	Plymouth Argyle	1-1	CARDIFF CITY	Langley	1	7	3		14			6				5			9*			8	4	13		11						10*	12		2*	
05-Apr	12,785	Stoke City	1-3	CARDIFF CITY	Jerome 2, Thorne (p)	1	7	3		13			6				5			9*			8	4	12		11						10*	2			
09-Apr	16,858	CARDIFF CITY	0-2	Wigan Athletic		1	7	3		13			6				5			9			8	4	12		11*						10*	2			
16-Apr	15,141	Preston North End	3-0	CARDIFF CITY		1	7	3	13	14			6				5			9*			8	4	12		11*						10*	2			
19-Apr	21,336	Leicester City	1-1	CARDIFF CITY	Ardley	1	7*	3	4				6				5			9*			8	13	12		11						10	2			
23-Apr	14,821	CARDIFF CITY	2-0	Reading	Thorne, Jerome	1	7	3	4				6				5			9*			8		12		11						10	2*			13
30-Apr	10,810	Gillingham	1-1	CARDIFF CITY	Parry	1	7	3	4		14		6				5			9*			8		12		11*			13			10				2*
08-May	15,722	CARDIFF CITY	1-0	Queen's Park Rangers	McAnuff	1	7	3	4				6				5			9*			8		14		11			13			10*	12			2
					Appearances	17	8	39	21	4	21	12	34	1	4	6	45	3	14	29	28	2	25	28	38	4	43	9	9	24	8	1	31	28	26	25	20
					Goals		1				3		1		1		1	1		6	3		2	3	5		2	1		4	1		12	1			

1 N Alexander
2 N Ardley
3 C Barker
4 W Boland
5 M Boulding
6 L Bullock
7 A Campbell
8 J Collins
9 G Croft
10 R Earnshaw
11 S Fleetwood
12 D Gabbidon
13 N Harris
14 J Inamoto
15 C Jerome
16 G Kavanagh
17 T Koskela
18 R Langley
19 J Ledley
20 A Lee
21 M Margetson
22 J McAnuff
23 G O'Neil
24 R Page
25 P Parry
26 J Robinson
27 D Thomas
28 P Thorne
29 T Vidmar
30 T Warner
31 R Weston
32 D Williams

2005-06 11th in Championship

Date	Att	Home	Score	Away	Scorers	1	2	3	4	5	6	7	8	9	10	11	12	13	14	15	16	17	18	19	20	21	22	23	24	25
06-Aug	24,292	Ipswich Town	1-0	CARDIFF CITY		1	7	3		4*	11	6	2			9			13			12		10*	5					8
09-Aug	15,231	CARDIFF CITY	2-1	Leeds United	Koumas, Purse (p)	1	7	3		4*	11*	6	2			9	12		14			13		10*	5					8
12-Aug	9,256	CARDIFF CITY	1-3	Watford	Jerome	1	7	3			11	6*	2			9	12		13	14		4*		10*	5					8
20-Aug	23,153	Derby County	2-1	CARDIFF CITY	Jerome	1	7	3		12	11*	6	2			9	4		13					10*	5					8
27-Aug	11,502	CARDIFF CITY	2-2	Wolves	Jerome 2	1	12			4	3*			13		9	7	11	10*	6					5				2	8
10-Sep	10,431	Burnley	3-3	CARDIFF CITY	Jerome, Loovens, Purse (p)	1		3			11*					9	7	8	13	4				12	5	10*			6	2
13-Sep	9,196	CARDIFF CITY	1-0	Leicester City	Ricketts	1	12	3			11*					9	7*	4	14	6				13	5	10*			2	8
17-Sep	11,647	CARDIFF CITY	1-0	Crystal Palace	Ricketts	1		3			11*					9	7	4		6				12	5	10			2	8
24-Sep	9,254	Millwall	0-0	CARDIFF CITY		1		3			11					9	7	4	12	6					5	10*			2	8
27-Sep	12,240	Stoke City	0-3	CARDIFF CITY	Jerome 2, Purse	1		3			11*					9	7	4	13	6				12	5	10*			2	8
01-Oct	14,657	CARDIFF CITY	1-2	Luton Town	Ricketts	1	7	3			11*					9	8*	4	14	6		13		12	5	10			2*	
15-Oct	6,485	Brighton	1-2	CARDIFF CITY	Koumas, Lee	1		3			11*					9	7	4	13	6				12	5	10*			2	8
18-Oct	9,574	CARDIFF CITY	2-2	Preston North End	Ledley, Koumas	1		3			11*					9*	7	4	12	6				13	5	10			2	8
22-Oct	10,815	CARDIFF CITY	6-1	Crewe Alexandra	Ricketts, Ledley, Cooper, Purse (p), Jerome, Kc	1		3			11*	12				9	7	4	14	6*				13	5	10*			2	8
29-Oct	25,311	Sheffield United	0-0	CARDIFF CITY		1		3			11					9	7	4	12	6					5	10*			2	8
01-Nov	23,838	Norwich City	1-0	CARDIFF CITY		1	12	3			11*					9	7	4	14	6				13	5	10*			2*	8
06-Nov	11,424	CARDIFF CITY	0-0	Coventry City		1		3			11*			13		9	7	4	10*	6				12	5				2	8
09-Nov	20,324	Sheffield Wednesday	1-3	CARDIFF CITY	Jerome 2, Koumas	1	12	3			11*					9	7	4	10*	6				13	5				2	8
19-Nov	13,904	Preston North End	2-1	CARDIFF CITY	Loovens	1	7	3		12							11	4	10	6				13	5	9*			2*	8
22-Nov	9,595	CARDIFF CITY	1-1	Brighton	Lee	1	13	3				12				9	7	4	10	6*				11	3				2*	8
28-Nov	8,724	CARDIFF CITY	2-1	Ipswich Town	Ricketts, Koumas	1		3				5				9	7	4	12	6				11		10*			2	8
03-Dec	18,364	Hull City	2-0	CARDIFF CITY		1		3*				12				9	7	4	13	6				11*	5	10			2	8
10-Dec	20,597	Leeds United	0-1	CARDIFF CITY	Koumas	1	12	3		7	11*	5				9	10	4		6									2	8
17-Dec	12,500	CARDIFF CITY	0-0	Derby County		1		3			11					9	7	4		6					5	10			2	8
26-Dec	16,403	CARDIFF CITY	0-2	Plymouth Argyle		1		3*			11*	14				9*	7	4	13	6				12	5	10			2	8
28-Dec	12,329	Queen's Park Rangers	1-0	CARDIFF CITY		1	2	3		4	11*	5				9	7	10	13	6				12						8*
31-Dec	13,377	CARDIFF CITY	2-1	Southampton	Ledley, Jerome	1	2	3				5				9	7	4	12	6				11		10*				8
02-Jan	22,061	Reading	5-1	CARDIFF CITY	Jerome	1	13	3			11*		12			9	7	4	10	6					5				2*	8
14-Jan	10,872	CARDIFF CITY	3-0	Burnley	Thompson 2, Koumas	1	7	3		8	12	6				9	11*	4					13		5*		14	10*	2	
21-Jan	20,140	Leicester City	1-2	CARDIFF CITY	Jerome, Koumas	1	7	3		12	13	6				9*	11	4					14		5		8	10*	2*	
31-Jan	12,378	CARDIFF CITY	1-1	Millwall	Jerome	1	7	3			12	6				9	11	4					13		5		8	10*	2*	
04-Feb	17,962	Crystal Palace	1-0	CARDIFF CITY		1	7	3*		4*	11	6	12			9	8	10					13		5		2			
11-Feb	10,780	CARDIFF CITY	3-0	Stoke City	Cox 2, Cooper	1	2	3		4	11	6				9		8					10		5		7			
14-Feb	7,826	Luton Town	3-3	CARDIFF CITY	Koumas 2, Scimeca	1	2	3			11*	6		12		9	8	4					10*		5		7			13
18-Feb	11,047	CARDIFF CITY	1-0	Hull City	Jerome	1	2	3				6				9*	11	4							5		7	10	12	8
25-Feb	17,419	Watford	2-1	CARDIFF CITY	Whitley	1	2	3				6				9	11	4							5		7	10	12	8*
04-Mar	11,851	CARDIFF CITY	1-0	Sheffield Wednesday	Jerome	1	2	3				6				9	11	4					12		5		7	10*		8
11-Mar	23,996	Wolves	2-0	CARDIFF CITY		1	2*	3			13	6				9	11	4					14		5		7	10*	12	8*
18-Mar	13,494	Plymouth Argyle	0-1	CARDIFF CITY	Thompson	1	2	3			11					9*	8	4		6			12		5		7	10		
25-Mar	14,271	CARDIFF CITY	0-0	Queen's Park Rangers		1	2	3			11*					9	8	4		6					5		7	10	12	
01-Apr	22,388	Southampton	3-2	CARDIFF CITY	Jerome, Purse	1	2	3		12	11*	13		14		9	8	4		6*			10*		5		7			
08-Apr	11,866	CARDIFF CITY	2-5	Reading	Jerome, Parry	1	2			8	11*					9	7	4		6				12	5		3	10		
14-Apr	11,006	CARDIFF CITY	0-1	Sheffield United		1				8*	11*	12				9	7	4		6				13	5*		3	10	2	14
17-Apr	5,865	Crewe Alexandra	1-1	CARDIFF CITY	Koumas	1			12			5	2			9	7	4		6				11			3	10		8*
22-Apr	11,590	CARDIFF CITY	0-1	Norwich City		1		3*			12	5	2		13	9*	8	4		6				11			7	10		
30-Apr	22,536	Coventry City	3-1	CARDIFF CITY	Thompson	1	12			8		5	2*				7	4		6	13		9*	11			3	10		
					Appearances	46	30	41	1	15	36	27	9	4	1	44	44	42	25	33	1	4	11	27	39	17	18	14	30	34
					Goals						2	2				18	12	3	2	2				1	5	5	1	4		1

1 Neil Alexander
2 Neil Ardley
3 Chris Barker
4 Darcy Blake
5 Willie Boland
6 Kevin Cooper
7 Neil Cox
8 Jermaine Darlington
9 Andrea Ferretti
10 Joe Jacobson
11 Cameron Jerome
12 Jason Koumas
13 Joe Ledley
14 Alan Lee
15 Glenn Loovens
16 Curtis McDonald
17 Phil Mulryne
18 Guylain N'Dumbu Nsungu
19 Paul Parry
20 Darren Purse
21 Michael Ricketts
22 Riccy Scimeca
23 Steve Thompson
24 Rhys Weston
25 Jeff Whitley

2006-07 13th in Championship

Date	Att	Home	Score	Away	Scorers	1	2	3	4	5	6	7	8	9	10	11	12	13	14	15	16	17	18	19	20	21	22	23	24	25	26	27	28	29	30
05-Aug	12,082	Barnsley	1-2	CARDIFF CITY	Ledley, Thompson	1			13		10*				14		2				12		11	6	3	8	7	5*			4	9*			
08-Aug	18,506	CARDIFF CITY	1-1	West Brom	Scimeca	1			13		10				12		2				5		11	6	3	8	7*				4	9*			
12-Aug	13,965	CARDIFF CITY	1-0	Coventry City	Chopra	1			14		10*				12		2*	13					11	6	3	8	7	5			4	9*			
19-Aug	18,246	Leeds United	0-1	CARDIFF CITY	Flood	1	14				10*				13						12	7*	3	6	2*	8	11	5			4	9			
26-Aug	20,109	CARDIFF CITY	2-0	Birmingham City	Ledley, Parry	1			12		10						2				5		11	6	3	8	7				4	9*			
09-Sep	12,435	Preston North End	2-1	CARDIFF CITY	Chopra	1					10				12		2				5	13	11	6	3	8*	7*				4	9			
12-Sep	11,655	Plymouth Argyle	3-3	CARDIFF CITY	Chopra 2, Thompson	1			13		10				12		2				6		11		3	8	7*	5			4	9*			
16-Sep	14,108	CARDIFF CITY	4-1	Luton Town	Chopra 2, Parry, Purse (p)	1					10				12		2	13				14	11	6	3*	8	7*	5			4	9*			
24-Sep	7,901	Southend United	0-3	CARDIFF CITY	Purse, Scimeca, og	1			12		10*				13		2					14	11*	6	3	8	7*	5			4	9			
30-Sep	19,915	CARDIFF CITY	4-0	Wolves	Scimeca, Kamara, Parry, og	1			12		10				13		2					14	11	6	3*	8	7*	5			4	9*			
14-Oct	18,876	Crystal Palace	1-2	CARDIFF CITY	Chopra, Scimeca	1			12	3	10						2					13	11*	6		8	7	5			4	9*			
17-Oct	19,345	CARDIFF CITY	1-0	Southampton	Thompson	1				3	10						2						11	6		8	7	5			4	9			
21-Oct	25,014	Norwich City	1-0	CARDIFF CITY		1			12	3					13		2	10*				14	11*	6		8	7	5			4	9*			
28-Oct	17,371	CARDIFF CITY	2-2	Derby County	Loovens, Chopra	1				3	10										12		11	6*	2	8	7	5			4	9			
31-Oct	25,014	Sunderland	1-2	CARDIFF CITY	Chopra 2	1			12	3	10											13	11	6	2*	8	7	5			4	9*			
04-Nov	5,393	Colchester United	3-1	CARDIFF CITY	Chopra	1			9	3	10				12						14	13	11*	6*	2	8	7*	5			4				
11-Nov	15,744	CARDIFF CITY	1-0	Burnley	Scimeca	1			9*	3	10				12						13		11	6	2	8	7*	5			4				
17-Nov	13,250	CARDIFF CITY	0-1	Queen's Park Rangers		1					10									2		12	11	6	3	8	7*	5			4	9			
25-Nov	23,935	Sheffield Wednesday	0-0	CARDIFF CITY		1			13		10										6	12	11		3	8	7*	5			4	9*			2
28-Nov	16,039	Stoke City	3-0	CARDIFF CITY		1			12		10										6	13	11*		2	8	7	5			4	9*			3
02-Dec	13,512	CARDIFF CITY	0-0	Colchester United		1			12		10	13									6	8*	11		3		7	5			4	9*			2
09-Dec	16,015	CARDIFF CITY	2-2	Ipswich Town	Purse 2(1p)	1			9*		10	14						13		3	6	8*	11		2			5			4	12			7*
16-Dec	23,089	Hull City	4-1	CARDIFF CITY	Chopra	1					10			14	8*			13		3		12*	11	6	2		7	5			4	9			
23-Dec	22,274	Leicester City	0-0	CARDIFF CITY		1	12				10						2*						11	6	3	8	7	5			4*	9			13
26-Dec	17,299	CARDIFF CITY	2-2	Plymouth Argyle	Thompson 2	1	13				10				12						6		11		2	8	7*	5			4	9			3*
30-Dec	13,704	CARDIFF CITY	0-0	Crystal Palace		1	13		12		10	14			7*		2						11	6	3*	8		5			4	9*			
01-Jan	8,004	Luton Town	0-0	CARDIFF CITY		1	13				10	12			7*		2*			14			11*	6		8		5			4	9			3
13-Jan	13,822	CARDIFF CITY	0-1	Southend United		1			9*		10				7*		2	12					11	6	3*	8		5			4			13	
20-Jan	16,772	Wolves	1-2	CARDIFF CITY	Chopra, Byrne	1		14			10				12						13		11	6	2	8	7	5*			4	9*		3*	
27-Jan	12,057	CARDIFF CITY	3-2	Leicester City	Chopra 3	1		14			10				13		2				5		11	6	12	8	7				4*	9*		3*	
02-Feb	11,549	CARDIFF CITY	2-0	Barnsley	Whittingham, Chopra	1		14			10				13		2				5		11*	6	12*	8	7					9*	4	3	
10-Feb	17,107	Coventry City	2-2	CARDIFF CITY	Chopra (p), Whittingham	1					10				13		2*				5		11	6	12	8	7			14		9*	4	3*	
17-Feb	16,664	CARDIFF CITY	1-0	Leeds United	Chopra	1		13			10						2*			12	5		11		3	8	7					9*	4	6	
20-Feb	18,802	West Brom	1-0	CARDIFF CITY		1	4	10*	13						12					2	5		11		3	8	7*			14		9*		6	
23-Feb	12,889	CARDIFF CITY	4-1	Preston North End	Chopra 2(1p), Whittingham, Johnson			12			10*					1			13		5		11	6	2	8	7				4	9*		3	
04-Mar	28,223	Birmingham C ity	1-0	CARDIFF CITY		1					10						12		13		5		11	6	2*	8	7				4	9*		3	
10-Mar	13,276	CARDIFF CITY	1-0	Norwich City	Parry	1		13			10									12	5		11	6	2	8	7*				4	9*		3	
13-Mar	20,383	Southampton	2-2	CARDIFF CITY	Thompson, Whittingham	1		9*			10									12	5		11	6*	2	8	7				4	13		3	
17-Mar	27,689	Derby County	3-1	CARDIFF CITY	Parry	1		12			10*								13	2	5		11		3	8	7					9	4	6	
31-Mar	19,353	CARDIFF CITY	0-1	Sunderland		1		12			10*		14							2	5		11		3	8	7*				4*	9	13	6	
07-Apr	13,621	CARDIFF CITY	1-2	Sheffield Wednesday	Johnson						10		9*			1			13		6		11		2	8	7	5				12	4	3*	
09-Apr	11,347	Burnley	2-0	CARDIFF CITY			13				10		9*			1			14	2	6		11		3	8	7*	5				12		4*	
14-Apr	11,664	CARDIFF CITY	1-1	Stoke City	Chopra						10				13	1	12			2	6		11		3	8	7*	5*				9		4	
21-Apr	12,710	Queen's Park Rangers	1-0	CARDIFF CITY			13				10		14		7*	1	2*			5	6		11		3	8	12					9*		4	
28-Apr	12,421	CARDIFF CITY	0-1	Hull City			2						10		12	1				13	6		11		3*	8	7*	5	14			9		4*	
05-May	26,488	Ipswich Town	3-1	CARDIFF CITY	Parry		4						10*			1	12		14	13	6		11		2	8*	7*	5				9		3	
					Appearances	39	10	10	19	7	42	4	6	1	25	7	24	6	6	15	32	15	46	30	42	43	42	31	1	2	35	43	6	19	7
					Goals			1			22				1						2	1	2	1			6	4			5	6		4	

1 N Alexander
2 D Blake
3 J Byrne
4 K Campbell
5 J Chambers
6 M Chopra
7 K Cooper
8 W Feeney
9 A Ferretti
10 W Flood
11 D Forde
12 K Gilbert
13 L Glombard
14 M Green
15 C Gunter
16 R Johnson
17 M Kamara
18 J Ledley
19 G Loovens
20 K McNaughton
21 S McPhail
22 P Parry
23 D Purse
24 A Ramsey
25 I Redan
26 R Scimeca
27 SThompson
28 S Walton
29 P Whittingham
30 A Wright

2007-08 12th in Championship

Date	Att	Home	Score	Away	Scorers	1	2	3	4	5	6	7	8	9	10	11	12	13	14	15	16	17	18	19	20	21	22	23	24	25
11-Aug	18,840	CARDIFF CITY	0-1	Stoke City				3		10*				5	7	6	9	2	8*		13		4				11		1	12
18-Aug	12,596	Queen's Park Rangers	0-2	CARDIFF CITY	MacLean, Parry			3*		12		14		5	7	6	9*	2*	8		10		4				11		1	13
25-Aug	16,407	CARDIFF CITY	0-1	Coventry City				3		12		2*		5	7*	6	9*		8		10	14	4				11		1	13
01-Sep	24,292	Norwich City	1-2	CARDIFF CITY	Whittingham, Johnson	14		3			10*	2*	9	5	7*	6			8		12		4				11		1	13
15-Sep	11,591	Plymouth Argyle	2-2	CARDIFF CITY	Rae, Thompson			3			14	2*	9*	5	12			6	8		11		4				7	13	1	10*
19-Sep	13,169	CARDIFF CITY	1-2	Watford	Hasselbaink			3			10*	2*	9	5				6	8		11		4				7	13	1	12
22-Sep	11,772	CARDIFF CITY	2-2	Preston North End	Fowler 2			3			10*	12	9	5	2			6	8	1	11*		4				7*	14		13
29-Sep	10,709	Barnsley	1-1	CARDIFF CITY	Hasselbaink			3			10		9	5	7	6		2	8	1	12		4				11*			
02-Oct	26,186	Sheffield United	3-3	CARDIFF CITY	Ledley, Fowler (p), Rae			3			10		9	5	7	6		2	8	1	11		4							
06-Oct	12,914	CARDIFF CITY	2-1	Burnley	Ledley, Parry			3			10*		9*	5	7	6*		2		1	11	12	4	14				13		8
21-Oct	20,796	Southampton	1-0	CARDIFF CITY				3			10		9	5	7*	6	14	2*	8	1	11*		4				13			12
24-Oct	15,000	CARDIFF CITY	2-3	Wolves	Fowler (p), Hasselbaink			3			10*		9*		7*	6	12	2	8	1	11	5	4				13	14		
27-Oct	11,850	CARDIFF CITY	1-1	Scunthorpe United	McPhail			3			10*		9	6	7			2*	8		12	5	4		1		11	13		
06-Nov	11,781	CARDIFF CITY	1-1	Crystal Palace	Purse			3			10*		9	6	7			2	8		11*	5	4		1		12	13		
10-Nov	22,866	Charlton Athletic	3-0	CARDIFF CITY				3			13		9*	5	7			2	8		11*	6	4		1			10		12
24-Nov	15,173	CARDIFF CITY	1-0	Ipswich Town	Parry			3				2	9	12	7*	6			8		11	5	4		1			10*		13
26-Nov	27,246	Leicester City	0-0	CARDIFF CITY				3				2	9*		7	6	12		8		11*	5	4		1			10		13
01-Dec	16,269	Hull City	2-2	CARDIFF CITY	Thompson, Johnson			3*				2	12	6	7		9		8		11	5	4*		1			10		13
04-Dec	11,874	CARDIFF CITY	0-2	Charlton Athletic				3*				2	12		7	6	9*		8		11	5	4		1			10		13
08-Dec	11,006	CARDIFF CITY	4-1	Colchester United	Thompson, Whittingham, Hasselbaink, og			12				2	9*	5	7	6	14	3*	8*		11		13		1			10		4
11-Dec	7,214	Blackpool	0-1	CARDIFF CITY	Thompson			3				2	9*	5	7	6*	13	3	8		11	14	12		1			10		4*
15-Dec	15,753	Bristol City	1-0	CARDIFF CITY				3			14	2	9*	5	7	6	13	3*	8		11		12		1			10		4*
22-Dec	12,869	CARDIFF CITY	1-0	Sheffield United	Parry			3					9*	5	7	6	12	2	8		11	13	4		1					10*
26-Dec	17,014	Watford	2-2	CARDIFF CITY	Johnson, Whittingham			3						5	7	6	9*	2	8		11	12	4		1					10
29-Dec	12,046	Preston North End	1-2	CARDIFF CITY	Johnson, Ledley			3					9*	5	7	6	12	2	8		11		4		1					10
01-Jan	14,965	CARDIFF CITY	1-0	Plymouth Argyle	Ledley			3					9*	5	7	6	12	2	8		11		4		1			13		10*
12-Jan	14,015	CARDIFF CITY	1-0	Sheffield Wednesday	Hasselbaink			3					9*	5	7	6		2	8	1	11		4					12		10
19-Jan	22,325	West Brom	3-3	CARDIFF CITY	Parry 2, Ledley	13		3					9*	5	7	6		2*	8	1	11		4					12		10
29-Jan	13,602	CARDIFF CITY	3-1	Queen's Park Rangers	Ledley 2, Parry	13		3	15				9*	5	7	6		2		1*	11		4	8				12		10*
02-Feb	15,045	Stoke City	2-1	CARDIFF CITY	Hasselbaink			3					9*	5	7	6		2	8	1	11		4					12		10
09-Feb	11,937	CARDIFF CITY	1-2	Norwich City	Rae			3					9*	5	7	6		2	8	1	11		4					12		10
12-Feb	15,260	Coventry City	0-0	CARDIFF CITY			14	3	1				9*	5	7*	6		2	12		11		4	8				13		10*
23-Feb	18,539	Sheffield Wednesday	1-0	CARDIFF CITY				3	1				9	5				2	8*		11	6	4	7				12		10
01-Mar	13,355	CARDIFF CITY	0-1	Leicester City				3	1				9	5				2	8*		11	6	4	7		13		12		10*
04-Mar	13,446	Crystal Palace	0-0	CARDIFF CITY				3	1					5		6		2	8		11		12	13		4*	7*	9		10
12-Mar	17,555	CARDIFF CITY	1-0	Hull City	McPhail			3	1	14				5	13	6		2*	8		11*		12			4*	7	9		10
15-Mar	4,699	Colchester United	1-1	CARDIFF CITY	Parry	2		3	1				9*	5	7*	6					11		4	8*		14	13	12		10*
22-Mar	16,458	CARDIFF CITY	2-1	Bristol City	Johnson, Whittingham	2		3	1					5	7	6			8		11		4	12				9		10*
29-Mar	12,955	CARDIFF CITY	1-0	Southampton	Parry			3	1					5	7	6			8		11		4	2		13	12	9*		10*
01-Apr	13,915	CARDIFF CITY	0-0	West Brom				3	1	12*				5	7	6		2	8		11*		4			13	10	9*		14
09-Apr	20,311	Ipswich Town	1-1	CARDIFF CITY	Rae	2		3*	1				14	5	7*	6			8				4	11		10*	12	9		13
12-Apr	14,715	CARDIFF CITY	3-1	Blackpool	McPhail, Sinclair, Whittingham		12	3	1					5				2	8			6	4	7			11	9		10
19-Apr	4,727	Scunthorpe United	3-2	CARDIFF CITY	Hasselbaink, Ledley			3	1				9*	5	7	6		2*	8				4	11			13	10		12
22-Apr	20,862	Wolves	3-0	CARDIFF CITY		12		3	1				9*	5	7	6		2	8				4	11*		13		14		10*
26-Apr	10,694	Burnley	3-3	CARDIFF CITY	Ledley (p), Ramsey, Thompson	2		3	1				9*		12	6			8*			5		7		4	11	10		13
04-May	14,469	CARDIFF CITY	3-0	Barnsley	Parry, McNaughton, Ledley			3*	1				9	5	7	6*		2	8		11*	13	4	14				12		10
					Appearances	8	2	44	16	5	13	13	36	42	41	36	15	35	43	11	41	18	45	15	14	9	21	36	6	41
					Goals						4		7	5	10		1	1	3		10	1		1			1	5		5

1 Darcy Blake
2 Jon Brown
3 Tony Capaldi
4 Peter Enckelman
5 Warren Feeney
6 Robbie Fowler
7 Chris Gunter
8 Jimmy Floyd Hasselbaink
9 Roger Johnson
10 Joe Ledley
11 Glenn Loovens
12 Steve MacLean
13 Kevin McNaughton
14 Stephen McPhail
15 Michael Oakes
16 Paul Parry
17 Darren Purse
18 Gavin Rae
19 Aaron Ramsey
20 Kasper Schmeichel
21 Riccy Scimeca
22 Trevor Sinclair
23 Steve Thompson
24 Ross Turnbull
25 Peter Whittingham

2008-09 7th in Championship

Date	Att	Home	Score	Away	Scorers	1	2	3	4	5	6	7	8	9	10	11	12	13	14	15	16	17	18	19	20	21	22	23	24	25	26	27
09-Aug	19,749	CARDIFF CITY	2-1	Southampton	Thompson, Johnson		13							1		4	5		9	3	11	2	8		12		7				10*	6*
16-Aug	11,873	Doncaster Rovers	1-1	CARDIFF CITY	McCormack		13				12			1		4	5		9		10	2*	7		11	3			8*		14	6*
23-Aug	18,032	CARDIFF CITY	2-2	Norwich City	McCormack 2(1p)	2	10*				12			1		4	5*		9		11*		8		6	3			7		14	13
30-Aug	29,226	Sheffield United	0-0	CARDIFF CITY			10*				5			1	12	4			7		11*	2	8		9	3					13	6
13-Sep	19,312	CARDIFF CITY	0-0	Bristol City			11				5			1		4			9		12	2	8		10*	3	7					6
16-Sep	11,282	Barnsley	0-1	CARDIFF CITY	Whittingham		12				5			1		4			9		10*	2	8		11	3	7					6
20-Sep	28,007	Derby County	1-1	CARDIFF CITY	McCormack (p)		12				5			1	13	4			9		11*	2	7		10	3	8					6*
27-Sep	18,304	CARDIFF CITY	1-2	Birmingham City	McCormack		10				5*			1	13	4	12		7		11	2			9*	3	8					6
30-Sep	16,312	CARDIFF CITY	2-1	Coventry City	Bothroyd, McCormack (p)		10							1		4	5		9		11	2	8			3	7					6
04-Oct	7,328	Blackpool	1-1	CARDIFF CITY	Parry		10				12			1	13	4	5		9*		11	2	7*		14	3	8					6
18-Oct	17,310	CARDIFF CITY	2-0	Charlton Athletic	McCormack 2		10*				12			1	13	4	5				11	2	8		9*	3	7					6
21-Oct	13,461	Watford	2-2	CARDIFF CITY	Bothroyd 2		10				12			1	13	4	5				11	2*	7		6	3	8					9*
25-Oct	19,468	Notts Forest	0-1	CARDIFF CITY	McCormack (p)		10				13		12	1		4	5*		9*		11	2	7		6	3*	8					14
28-Oct	17,570	CARDIFF CITY	2-0	Blackpool	Whittingham, McCormack		10				5*			1	13	4			9		11	2	8		6*	3	7					12
01-Nov	17,734	CARDIFF CITY	1-2	Wolves	McCormack		10*				12			1	13	4			5		11*	2	8		9	3	7					6
08-Nov	13,347	Queen's Park Rangers	1-0	CARDIFF CITY						11	5		12	1	10*	4			9*			2	8		13	3	7					6
15-Nov	17,478	CARDIFF CITY	2-1	Crystal Palace	Chopra (p), Ledley	12				11				1	10	4	5		9			2	8		13	3	7*					6*
22-Nov	11,438	Plymouth Argyle	2-1	CARDIFF CITY	Chopra	13				11	14	12		1*	10	4	5					2*	8		9*	3	7	6				
25-Nov	17,154	CARDIFF CITY	2-2	Reading	Routledge, McCormack (p)	12	10			11	2	1	3		13	4	5*				9		8				7	6				
30-Nov	18,053	Swansea City	2-2	CARDIFF CITY	Ledley, McCormack (p)		10			11		1	3			4	5		8*		9	2	7		13		14	6	12			
06-Dec	16,560	CARDIFF CITY	2-0	Preston North End	Johnson, Chopra (p)		10*			14	12	1	3			4	5*		7		11*	2			9		8	6	13			
09-Dec	11,230	Burnley	2-2	CARDIFF CITY	Bothroyd, Routledge		10*			11	12	1	3		13	4	5		7			2			9*		8	6				
13-Dec	19,665	Ipswich Town	1-2	CARDIFF CITY	Bothroyd, Gyepes		10			11*		1	3		13	4	5		8			2	14		9		7	6				
20-Dec	17,600	CARDIFF CITY	2-0	Sheffield Wednesday	Johnson, Chopra (p)		10			11*	12	1	3		13	4	5		8			2*			9		7	6				
26-Dec	22,770	Reading	1-1	CARDIFF CITY	Chopra		10			11		1	3			4	5		8			2			9*		7	6				12
28-Dec	19,145	CARDIFF CITY	1-0	Plymouth Argyle	Bothroyd		10			11		1	3			4	5		8			2			6*		7	9				12
17-Jan	19,853	Birmingham City	1-1	CARDIFF CITY	Ledley		10*	12				1	3		14	4	5		7		11	2	13		6*		8					9*
28-Jan	14,922	Coventry City	0-2	CARDIFF CITY	Bothroyd, McCormack		10	6			12	1	3			4	5		8*		11	2*	13		9		7					
31-Jan	18,779	CARDIFF CITY	2-0	Nottingham Forest	Parry, Bothroyd		10	6			13	1	3*		14	4	5		7		11*	2			9	12	8					
22-Feb	22,093	Wolves	2-2	CARDIFF CITY	Chopra, Johnson		10*	14		11	12		3			4	5	1	8		6*	2*			9		7					13
25-Feb	17,340	CARDIFF CITY	0-0	Queen's Park Rangers				9		10*	12					4	5	1	7		11	2*		14	6	3	8					13
28-Feb	18,526	Southampton	1-0	CARDIFF CITY				6			2*		3		12	4	5	1	8		10			13	11		7					9*
03-Mar	15,902	CARDIFF CITY	3-1	Barnsley	Ledley, Chopra, Whittingham	2				10*			3		11	4	5	1	8		13			12	6*		7					9
07-Mar	17,821	CARDIFF CITY	3-0	Doncaster Rovers	Chopra, Bothroyd, E Johnson	2	10*			11*	12		3		13	4	5*	1	7		14				6		8					9
10-Mar	23,706	Norwich City	2-0	CARDIFF CITY		2		14	5*	11			3		10	4		1	8		13			12	9		7					6*
15-Mar	17,487	Bristol City	1-1	CARDIFF CITY	McCormack		10*	12	5	11			3		14	4			7		13	2	8		9*					1		6*
18-Mar	17,899	CARDIFF CITY	2-1	Watford	Bothroyd, McCormack (p)		10	9*	5	13			3			4			8		11	2	7		6*					1		12
22-Mar	17,942	CARDIFF CITY	0-3	Sheffield United			10*	6*		11*	13		3		14	4	5		8		9	2	12				7			1		
05-Apr	20,156	CARDIFF CITY	2-2	Swansea City	Chopra, McCormack (p)		10			11					12	4	5*		7		9	2	8		6*	3	14			1		13
08-Apr	18,403	CARDIFF CITY	4-1	Derby County	Johnson, Rae, Bothroyd, E Johnson		10*	12		11			3		14	4	5				9*	2	8		13		6			1		7*
11-Apr	14,814	Crystal Palace	0-2	CARDIFF CITY	McCormack 2(1p)		10*			11*	12		3		14	4	5		9		6	2	8		13		7			1		
13-Apr	19,379	CARDIFF CITY	3-1	Burnley	Bothroyd, McCormack 2		10*			11*			4		12		5		6		9	2	7			3	8			1		13
18-Apr	13,692	Preston North End	6-0	CARDIFF CITY			10*			13	12		3		14	4	5*		9		11	2	8				7			1		6*
21-Apr	19,390	Charlton Athletic	2-2	CARDIFF CITY	Burke, Gyepes		10	12		11*	2		3	1	13	4*	5		9		8				6*	14	7					
25-Apr	19,129	CARDIFF CITY	0-3	Ipswich Town			10	9		14			3	1	12	4	5		7		11*	2	13		6*		8*					
03-May	30,658	Sheffield Wednesday	1-0	CARDIFF CITY			10	9*		11*	12			1		4	5*				13	2	7	14		3	8					6
					Appearances	7	39	14	3	27	30	12	27	21	30	45	36	6	40	1	38	39	32	5	40	23	41	9	4	8	4	33
					Goals		12	1		9			2		2	5			4		21				2		1	2			1	3

1 Darcy Blake
2 Jay Bothroyd
3 Chris Burke
4 Tony Capaldi
5 Michael Chopra
6 Miguel Comminges
7 Peter Enckelman
8 Gabor Gyepes
9 Tom Heaton
10 Eddie Johnson
11 Roger Johnson
12 Mark Kennedy
13 Dimi Konstantopoulos
14 Joe Ledley
15 Glenn Loovens
16 Ross McCormack
17 Kevin McNaughton
18 Stephen McPhail
19 Quincy Owusu-Abeyie
20 Paul Parry
21 Darren Purse
22 Gavin Rae
23 Wayne Routledge
24 Riccy Scimeca
25 Stuart Taylor
26 Steve Thompson
27 Peter Whittingham

2009-10 4th in Championship

Date	Att	Home	Score	Away	Scorers	1	2	3	4	5	6	7	8	9	10	11	12	13	14	15	16	17	18	19	20	21	22	23	24	25	26	27
08-Aug	22,264	CARDIFF CITY	4-0	Scunthorpe United	Chopra 2, Bothroyd, Whittingham (p)		11*	13		10*					4		3	5	7*	1	14		9		8	2	12			6		
15-Aug	7,698	Blackpool	1-1	CARDIFF CITY	Chopra		11	12	5	10					4		3		7	1		14	9*		8*	2*	13			6		
18-Aug	11,918	Plymouth Argyle	3-1	CARDIFF CITY	Chopra 3(1p)		11*	8	5	10*	12				4		3		8	1	13	2					7			6		
23-Aug	20,853	CARDIFF CITY	3-0	Bristol City	Chopra, Rae, og		11*	6		10*			12		4		3		8	1	13	2				5	7			9		
29-Aug	9,742	Doncaster Rovers	2-0	CARDIFF CITY			11*	6*	5	10			12		4		3		7	1	13	2					8		14	9*		
13-Sep	25,630	CARDIFF CITY	0-1	Newcastle United			11	9	5	10			12		4		3		8	1						2	6			7*		
16-Sep	16,687	Reading	0-1	CARDIFF CITY	Burke		11	9		10*					4		3	5	8*	1		2*			7	13	14		12	6		
19-Sep	20,121	CARDIFF CITY	0-2	Queen's Park Rangers			11*	9		10					4		3	5	7	1	12					2	13	14	8*	6*		
26-Sep	18,959	Sheffield Wednesday	3-1	CARDIFF CITY	Whittingham (p)		11	6*	12	10					4		3	5*	7	1	13	2					8			9		
29-Sep	18,640	CARDIFF CITY	6-1	Derby County	Chopra 4, Burke, Whittingham		11	6		10*					4		3	5		1	14	2			8*		7*	13	12	9		
03-Oct	13,895	Watford	0-4	CARDIFF CITY	Whittingham 2(1p), Bothroyd, Matthews		11	6		10*					4		3	5*	13	1		2	14		8	12	7*			9		
17-Oct	21,457	CARDIFF CITY	1-1	Crystal Palace	Whittingham		11*	6*		10				13	4		3	5	8	1		2	12				7			9		
20-Oct	19,038	CARDIFF CITY	2-0	Coventry City	Gerrard, Whittingham (p)		11	6		10					4		3	5	7	1		2			8					9		
24-Oct	25,021	Sheffield United	3-4	CARDIFF CITY	Whittingham 3(1p), Bothroyd		11	6*		10					4		3	5	7	1		2	13		8*		12			9		
01-Nov	20,413	CARDIFF CITY	1-1	Nottingham Forest	Bothroyd		11	6		10					4		3	5	7	1		2			8*		12			9		
07-Nov	18,209	Swansea City	3-2	CARDIFF CITY	Hudson, Bothroyd		10	6	9*						4		3	5	8	1		2	11				7		12			
21-Nov	11,903	Barnsley	1-0	CARDIFF CITY				6		10				13		4	3	5	7	1			11*	2*		12	8			9		
29-Nov	19,463	CARDIFF CITY	1-2	Ipswich Town	Whittingham		11	6*		10		12	13			4	3	5	7	1*		2	14				8*			9		
05-Dec	18,735	CARDIFF CITY	1-0	Preston North End	Burke		11	6		10*					4*		3	12	7*	1			13	2		5	14	8		9		
08-Dec	20,742	West Brom	0-2	CARDIFF CITY	Burke, Whittingham			6		11			10*		4		3	12		1			14	5*		2	8	7*		9	13	
13-Dec	17,232	Middlesbrough	0-1	CARDIFF CITY	Burke		11	6		10			12*		4		3		7	1		13	14	5*		2	8			9*		
26-Dec	24,010	CARDIFF CITY	0-1	Plymouth Argyle			11	6*		10*			12		4		3		8	1		12	14	5		2*	7			9		
28-Dec	9,786	Peterborough United	4-4	CARDIFF CITY	Ledley 2, Whittingham, Bothroyd		11*	8		14			13		4		3		7	1		2	10*	5*		12	6			9		
09-Jan	19,147	CARDIFF CITY	1-1	Blackpool	Hudson			6*		13				14	4		3		7	1	10*	12	11*	5		2	8			9		
16-Jan	5,032	Scunthorpe United	1-1	CARDIFF CITY	Whittingham		11	6*		10					4		3		7	1		2*	12	5		13				9	8	
26-Jan	13,875	Bristol City	0-6	CARDIFF CITY	Chopra 2, McCormack 2, Whittingham, og	12	11*	14		10				13	4	3		5	8	1		2	9				7*			6*		
30-Jan	19,730	CARDIFF CITY	2-1	Doncaster Rovers	Chopra, Bothroyd	12	11	6*		10					4	3		5*		1		2	9	14			8*		13	7		
05-Feb	44,028	Newcastle United	5-1	CARDIFF CITY	Wildig	8	11*	12		10					4	3		13		1		2*	9	5	7*					6	14	
09-Feb	17,686	CARDIFF CITY	2-0	Peterborough United	Burke, Gerrard	7*	11*	6		10				13	4	3		5		1				2	8*				13	9	12	
16-Feb	20,758	CARDIFF CITY	1-1	West Brom	Whittingham (p)	13	11	9		10					4	3		5		1			12	2			7			6*	8*	
20-Feb	19,753	CARDIFF CITY	0-2	Barnsley			11	6		10		1			4*	3		5				13	12	2			7			9	8*	
27-Feb	11,777	Preston North End	3-0	CARDIFF CITY			11	9		10		1			4	3*		12				13	8	5		2*	7			6		
06-Mar	19,803	CARDIFF CITY	1-0	Middlesbrough	Bothroyd	7	11*	6	12	10					4	3				1		2	9	5			8					
09-Mar	19,997	Ipswich Town	2-0	CARDIFF CITY		7	11	6	12	10					4	3				1		2*	9	5			8					
13-Mar	22,767	Leicester City	1-0	CARDIFF CITY		7	11	6							4			5		1		2*	10	3	8		12			9		
16-Mar	16,038	Coventry City	1-2	CARDIFF CITY	Burke, Whittingham (p)	8	11	6							4			5		1		2*	10	3*	7	13	12			9		
21-Mar	20,130	CARDIFF CITY	3-1	Watford	McCormack, Whittingham, Burke	4	11	6	12	14				13		3		5*		1			10*		7	2	8			9		
24-Mar	18,715	CARDIFF CITY	1-1	Sheffield United	Bothroyd	4	11*	6	5	12						3				1			11*		8	2	7			9		
27-Mar	13,464	Crystal Palace	1-2	CARDIFF CITY	Gyepes, Burke	4	10	6	5*	11*			10*	14		3		12		1			13		8	2	7			9		
30-Mar	20,438	CARDIFF CITY	2-1	Leicester City	McCormack, Whittingham	4*		6	13				10*	14		3		5*		1		12	11		8	2	7			9		
03-Apr	25,130	CARDIFF CITY	2-1	Swansea City	Chopra 2	4	11		5	10			13		3				12	1		2	9*		8*		7*			6	14	
05-Apr	22,185	Notts Forest	0-0	CARDIFF CITY		4	11			10			6*		3			5	8	1		2	9		7						12	
10-Apr	21,248	Reading	0-0	CARDIFF CITY		4	11	14		10*			6*		3			5	7*	1			12	2	8					9	13	
17-Apr	12,832	Queen's Park Rangers	0-1	CARDIFF CITY	Ledley	4	11	6*		13			12		3			5	7	1			10*	2	8					9		
24-Apr	23,304	CARDIFF CITY	3-2	Sheffield Wednesday	Bothroyd 2, Whittingham	4*	11	13	5	10			6*		3		12		8	1				2	7*					9	14	
02-May	31,102	Derby County	2-0	CARDIFF CITY				6	5			1	9*	10*		4	3				13	14	11			2			7*		8	12
					Appearances	18	40	44	15	41	1	4	16	9	39	16	27	30	29	43	9	32	34	21	21	22	37	4	8	41	11	1
					Goals		11	9		16	1				2	1	2		3			1	4				1			20	1	

1 Darcy Blake
2 Jay Bothroyd
3 Chris Burke
4 Tony Capaldi
5 Michael Chopra
6 Miguel Comminges
7 Peter Enckelman
8 Kelvin Etuhu
9 Warren Feeney
10 Anthony Gerrard
11 Gabor Gyepes
12 Mark Hudson
13 Mark Kennedy
14 Joe Ledley
15 David Marshall
16 Josh Magennis
17 Adam Matthews
18 Ross McCormack
19 Kevin McNaughton
20 Stephen McPhail
21 Paul Quinn
22 Gavin Rae
23 Riccy Scimeca
24 Solomon Taiwo
25 Peter Whittingham
26 Aaron Wildig
27 Aaron Morris

Appendix 2. Ninian Park and Cardiff City Stadium Players

Complete Cardiff City records for the players that appeared for the Bluebirds in the last season at Ninian Park and the first at the Cardiff City Stadium. Play-off appearances and goals are included in the cup sections.

Name	Date of Birth	Born	First Season	Last Season	From	To	Appearances League	Appearances Cup	Goals League	Goals Cup
Blake, Darcy	13.12.88	New Tredegar	2005		YTS		44	13	0	0
Bothroyd, Jay	05.05.82	Islington	2008		Wolves		79	13	23	2
Burke, Chris	02.12.83	Glasgow	2008		Rangers		58	10	10	1
Capaldi, Tony	12.08.81	Porgrunn	2007	2009	Plymouth		56	15	0	0
Chopra, Michael	23.12.83	Newcastle	2006		Newcastle		106	12	47	5
Comminges, Miguel	16.03.82	Les Abymes	2008		Swindon		31	4	0	0
Enckelman, Peter	10.03.77	Turku	2007	2009	Blackburn	St Johnstone	32	10	0	0
Etuhu, Kelvin	30.05.88	Kano	2009	loan	Man City		16	4	0	0
Feeney, Warren	17.01.81	Belfast	2007	2009	Luton	Oldham	20	2	0	0
Gerrard, Anthony	06.02.86	Liverpool	2009		Walsall		39	8	2	0
Gyepes, Gabor	26.06.81	Budapest	2008		Northampton		43	6	3	0
Heaton, Tom	15.04.86	Chester	2008		Man Utd		21	3	0	0
Hudson, Mark	30.03.82	Guildford	2009		Charlton		27	6	2	0
Johnson, Eddie	31.03.84	Florida	2008	loan	Fulham		30	3	2	0
Johnson, Roger	28.04.83	Ashford	2006	2008	Wycombe	Birmingham	119	17	12	2
Kennedy, Mark	15.05.76	Clonsilla	2008	2009	C Palace	Ipswich	66	10	0	0
Konstantopoulos, D	29.11.78	Thessaloniki	2008	loan	Coventry		6	0	0	0
Ledley, Joe	21.01.87	Cardiff	2004	2009	YTS	Celtic	226	30	26	4
Loovens, Glenn	22.10.83	Doetinchem	2005	2008	Feyenoord	Celtic	100	13	3	0
Magennis, Josh	15.08.90	Bangor NI	2009	2009	YTS	Aberdeen	9	1	0	1
Marshall, David	05.05.85	Glasgow	2009		Norwich		43	7	0	0
Matthews, Adam	13.01.92	Swansea	2009		YTS		32	3	1	0
McCormack, Ross	18.08.86	Glasgow	2008		Motherwell	Leeds	72	13	25	3
McNaughton, Kevin	28.08.82	Dundee	2006		Aberdeen		137	20	1	1
McPhail, Stephen	09.12.79	Westminster	2006		Barnsley		139	20	3	0
Morris, Aaron	30.12.89	Cardiff	2009	2009	YTS		1	1	0	0
Owuse-Abeyie Q	15.04.86	Amsterdam	2008	loan	S Moscow		5	0	0	0
Parry, Paul	19.08.80	Newport	2003	2008	Hereford	Preston	191	23	24	3
Purse, Darren	14.02.77	Stepney	2005	2008	West Brom	Sheff Wed	111	12	10	2
Quinn, Paul	21.07.85	Wishaw	2009		Motherwell		25	5	0	0
Rae, Gavin	28.11.77	Aberdeen	2007		Rangers		123	20	6	1
Routledge, Wayne	07.01.85	Sidcup	2008	loan	Aston Villa		9	5	2	0
Scimeca, Riccy	13.06.75	Leamington	2005	2009	West Brom	retired	70	7	6	0
Taiwo, Solomon	29.04.85	Lagos	2009		Dagenham		8	2	0	0
Taylor, Stuart	28.11.80	Romford	2008	loan	Aston Villa		8	0	0	0
Thompson, Steve	14.10.78	Paisley	2005	2008	Rangers	Burnley	97	9	16	1
Whittingham, Peter	08.09.84	Nuneaton	2006		Aston Villa		134	25	32	10
Wildig, Aaron	15.04.92	Hereford	2009		YTS		11	6	0	1